ETHICAL & LEGAL ISSUES

IN SCHOOL COUNSELING

2ND

EDITION

Theodore P. Remley, Jr., J.D., Ph.D
Mary A. Hermann, J.D., Ph.D
Wayne C. Huey, Ph.D.
Editors

AMERICAN
SCHOOL
COUNSELOR
ASSOCIATION

CITATION GUIDELINES

When citing materials in the introduction to the book or in the introductions to the chapters, please cite as follows:

Remley, T. P., Jr., Hermann, M. A., & Huey, W. C. (Eds.). (2003). *Ethical & legal issues in school counseling* (2nd ed.). Alexandria, VA: American School Counselor Association.

When citing materials within articles in this book, cite as follows (example is from the final article in the book):

Herlihy, B., Gray, N., & McCollum, V. (2003). Legal and ethical issues in school counselor supervision. In T. P. Remley, Jr., M. A. Hermann, & W. C. Huey (Eds.), *Ethical & legal issues in school counseling* (2nd ed., pp. 445–455). Alexandria, VA: American School Counselor Association.

Copyright © 2003 by the American School Counselor Association.

All rights reserved.

Minor edits have been made for grammar, punctuation, and spelling.

American School Counselor Association
801 N. Fairfax St., Suite 310
Alexandria, VA 22314-1757

Library of Congress Cataloging-in-Publication Data

Ethical and legal issues in school counseling.

1. Personnel service in education–United States.
2. Student counselors—Professional ethics—United States.
3. Personnel service in education—Law and legislation—United States.

I. Theodore P. Remley, Jr.
II. Mary A. Hermann, and
III. Wayne C. Huey

ISBN 1-929289-03-0

Printed in the United States of America.

CONTENTS

Appendix H
American School Counselor Association
Position Statements

REFERENCES FOR ARTICLES IN THIS BOOK

in the Order of Appearance

CHAPTER 1
Ethical Decision Making and Legal Issues

Remley, T. P., Jr., & Huey, W. C. (2002). An ethics quiz for school counselors. *Professional School Counseling, 6*, 3–11.

Cottone, R. R. (2001). A social constructivism model of ethical decision making in counseling. *Journal of Counseling and Development, 79,* 39–45.

Davis, J. L., & Mickelson, D. J. (1994). School counselors: Are you aware of ethical and legal aspects of counseling? *The School Counselor, 42,* 5–13.

Hermann, M. A. (2002). A study of legal issues encountered by school counselors and their perceptions of their preparedness to respond to legal challenges. *Professional School Counseling, 6,* 12–19.

CHAPTER 2
Students at Risk for Suicide

Capuzzi, D. (2002). Legal and ethical challenges in counseling suicidal students. *Professional School Counseling, 6,* 36–45.

Remley, T. P., Jr., & Sparkman, L. B. (1993). Student suicides: The counselor's limited legal liability. *The School Counselor, 40,* 164–169.

CHAPTER 3
Students at Risk for Violence

Hermann, M. A., & Finn, A. (2002). An ethical and legal perspective on the rule of school counselors in preventing violence in schools. *Professional School Counseling, 6,* 46–54.

Isaacs, M. L. (1997). The duty to warn and protect: Tarasoff and the elementary school counselor. *Elementary School Guidance & Counseling, 31,* 326–342.

Bailey, K. A. (2001). Legal implications of profiling students for violence. *Psychology in the Schools, 38,* 141–155.

Daniels, J. A. (2002). Assessing threats of school violence: Implications for counselors. *Journal of Counseling & Development, 80,* 215–218.

CHAPTER 4
Confidentiality and Privileged Communication

Glosoff, H. L., & Pate, R. H., Jr. (2002). Privacy and confidentiality in school counseling. *Professional School Counseling, 6,* 20–27.

Isaacs, M. L., & Stone, C. (1999). School counselors and confidentiality: Factors affecting professional choices. *Professional School Counseling, 2,* 258–266.

Davis, T., & Ritchie, M. (1993). Confidentiality and the school counselor: A challenge for the 1990s. *The School Counselor, 41,* 23–30.

Sealander, K. A., Schwiebert, V. L., & Weekley, J. L. (1999). Confidentiality and the law. *Professional School Counseling, 3,* 122–127.

Eades, R. W. (1986). The school counselor or psychologist and problems of defamation. *Journal of Law and Education, 15,* 117–120.

CHAPTER 5
Records

Cameron, S., & turtle-song, i. (2002). Learning to write case notes using the SOAP format. *Journal of Counseling and Development, 80,* 286–292.

Stenger, R. L. (1986). The school counselor and the law: New developments. *Journal of Law and Education, 15,* 105–116.

CHAPTER 11
Sexual Harassment

Stone, C. B. (2000). Advocacy for sexual harassment victims: Legal support and ethical aspects. *Professional School Counseling, 4,* 23–30.

CHAPTER 12
Special Education

Milsom, A. S. (2002). Students with disabilities: School counselor involvement and preparation. *Professional School Counseling, 5,* 331–338.

Schacht, T. E., & Hanson, G. (1999). Evolving legal climate for school mental health services under the Individuals with Disabilities Education Act. *Psychology in the Schools, 36,* 415–426.

Havey, J. M. (1998). Inclusion, the law, and placement decisions: Implications for school psychologists. *Psychology in the Schools, 35,* 145–152.

Erk, R. R. (1999). Attention deficit hyperactivity disorder: Counselors, laws, and implications for practice. *Professional School Counseling, 2,* 318–326.

CHAPTER 13
Supervision

Herlihy, B., Gray, N., & McCollum, V. (2002). Legal and ethical issues in school counselor supervision. *Professional School Counseling, 6,* 55–60.

Biological information for authors is reprinted from the original article and may have changed.

ABOUT THE EDITORS

Theodore P. Remley, Jr., J.D., Ph.D., is a professor of counseling and department chair at the University of New Orleans, New Orleans, Louisiana (tremley@uno.edu);

Mary A. Hermann, J.D., Ph.D., is an assistant professor of counseling at Mississippi State University in Starkville, Mississippi (mhermann@colled.msstate.edu); and

Wayne C. Huey, Ph.D., retired, is former director of counseling at Lakeside High School, Decatur, Georgia (whuey@mindspring.com).

This book is
dedicated to the memory of

Mary Gehrke McAllister
Past ASCA President

Leader, Colleague, and Friend

INTRODUCTION

School counselors contend with some of the most challenging ethical and legal dilemmas facing any counselor today. This comes as no surprise to those of us in the industry. First, school counselors have many distinct roles that can lead to conflicting priorities. Second, the primary clients of school counselors are minors, whose legal rights belong to their parents or guardians. And, finally, school counselors deal with some of society's most perplexing and difficult issues, such as violence and drug use, on a daily basis. Because of these challenges, which change daily, it's essential that school counselors keep current with the professional literature to better themselves, the school counseling profession, and, equally important, the lives of children.

For example, on a particular day, a school counselor may provide a child with mental health counseling, step into the role of administrator for a principal who is off-site, care for a child in the absence of a parent, teach a classroom guidance lesson, and consult with an educator on a classroom behavior issue. Thus, it is easy to see why multiple roles are common and how juggling them increases the chances of role confusion and conflict. Oftentimes, when a conflict does occur, a school counselor must first determine the role he or she is in to ensure an appropriate response.

Additionally, the fact that nearly all school students are minors poses a challenge for school counselors. Counselors have ethical obligations to their minor clients that are specifically articulated in codes of conduct published by the American School Counselor Association (ASCA, Appendix A) and the American Counseling Association (ACA, Appendix B). Yet, school counselors also have legal obligations to the parents or guardians of their minor student clients. As you might predict, when the interests of students and their parents or guardians collide, school counselors can find themselves in a bind—with ethical obligations to the minor and conflicting legal obligations to the parents or guardians.

A primary reason the resolution of such challenges is more difficult for school counselors in comparison to counselors in other settings is because of the nature of the situations that arise. Contemporary schools must cope with some of society's most pressing problems, and school counselors must then be prepared to provide counseling in all of the following difficult situations: suspected child abuse; child custody disputes; student suicide; sexual activities of minors; drug use; and students who may be at risk for harming others. Solving each of these problems individually is difficult, and school counselors are called upon to deal with all of them regularly.

This informative book includes a total of 29 articles in 13 topic areas related to ethics and law in school counseling. We have prefaced each topic area with an insightful, updated introductory section, and each of the introductory sections includes an "at a glance" summary of the topics addressed.

The chapters begin with a review of the ethical standards of ASCA and ACA, with other associations' guidelines also referenced. In addition, the text also reviews ethical decision making models and summarizes a study of legal issues faced by practicing school counselors.

The next chapters address the ethical and legal problems related to identifying and managing students who may be at risk for suicide or violence, while later chapters are devoted to other recurring student problems, such as substance abuse, sexual identity issues, sexual harassment and, within Chapter 9, abortion and academic decision making. A chapter addresses how to best handle court appearances and even offers advice on averting them, while another summarizes the nature of appellate court decisions and how they affect the practice of school counselors.

In the later chapters, we review the more delicate issues of confidentiality, privileged communication and counseling records, as well as parents' rights. Special education, an area that encompasses much federal and state legislation and a multitude of appellate court decisions, is also examined. The book then closes with a review of the ethical and legal issues related to supervision, addressing the roles of both supervisor and supervisee.

Primary sources for this book include professional journal articles, most of which were specifically written for school counselors within the last decade. Because two other important areas have only been more recently addressed—multicultural counseling and Internet counseling—there are no articles included, but other resources have been provided to bring perspective to these key topics.

The counseling profession has recognized that, since diversity issues abound in counseling relationships, multicultural counseling must be infused throughout all of the industry's preparation programs. As such, a competent school counselor must understand diversity and be equipped to provide high-quality counseling services to all clients, including those who have diverse backgrounds. Practicing school counselors are encouraged to seek continuing education in multicultural counseling and to read literature addressing this topic. With that understanding, we strongly recommend the *Journal of Multicultural Counseling*. As an additional aid, ASCA's position statement, *The Professional School Counselor and Cross/Multicultural Counseling*, is included in Appendix H–10 of this book. We encourage scholars to write more articles about the ethical and legal duties of school counselors to be multiculturally competent.

Because counseling via the Internet is a relatively new phenomenon, articles have yet to be written that explore the ethical and legal issues of Internet counseling for school counselors. However, ASCA has produced a position statement titled *The Professional School Counselor and Student Safety on the Internet*, which is included in Appendix H–22. In addition, three appendices in this book include guidelines for Internet counseling. Although not specifically written for school counselors, this information should be useful for any counselor who uses the Internet to deliver services. The Internet guideline documents include: *Online Counseling Guidelines* published by the National Board of Certified Counseling (Appendix E); *The Practice of Internet Counseling* published by the American Counseling Association (Appendix F); and *Guidelines for the Use of the Internet for Provision of Career Information and Planning Services* published by the National Career Development Association (Appendix G).

Because we encourage school counselors to perform at the highest ethical and legal levels and because we know this can be overwhelming, our hope is that this book provides not only insight but also concrete guidelines for practice.

First and foremost, however, it is imperative that school counselors focus on providing quality counseling services to their clients and not on protecting themselves from complaints or lawsuits. If a school counseling program spends more time completing forms for self-protection than counseling clients, something is wrong with the program. School counselors will always be vulnerable to individuals accusing them of wrongdoing, and there is no way to guarantee complaints won't arise. With this in mind, our goal is to reduce the likelihood of complaints and to help school counselors prevail should they occur.

Know that information and help is out there if you need it. We leave you with the following risk management guidelines:

- Always try to do what is best for your clients; keep their welfare in mind.

- Know the ethical standards of ASCA and ACA and consult those documents when dilemmas arise.
- Consult with other school counselor colleagues when making difficult practice decisions that might be considered ethical in nature.
- Request legal advice from administrators when dealing with problems or issues that have legal dimensions.
- Purchase and maintain your own personal professional liability insurance policy that covers your activities as a school counselor.

Chapter 1:
Ethical Decision
Making and Legal
Issues

INTRODUCTION

Although there is a common belief that ethical and legal issues pose separate and distinct dilemmas for school counselors, our experience has shown that ethical and legal principles are often based on the same societal values. This understood, however, differences remain; and, although these variations are subtle, they are important.

Professionals develop ethical standards to guide the practices and activities of other professionals. Codes of ethics provide an idealized standard of practice to which counselors should aspire. Legal standards, on the other hand, are developed by legislators (and interpreted by judges)

I

to set the minimum professional standards as tolerated by society. The test to determine whether or not a counselor has behaved legally is to ask, "What would a similarly educated, reasonable school counselor in this locality have done in a similar situation?"

As a result of the way standards are developed, ethical standards are idealistic, whereas legal standards are realistic and minimal. So, if a school counselor is practicing ethically, usually he or she also will be practicing legally. On the contrary, although a counselor might be within legal standards, he or she simultaneously may not be meeting the higher ethical standards.

For school counselors who have a high tolerance for ambiguity, ethical decision making is an interesting and invigorating process. But, for those who want to ensure they are doing the right thing, ethical decision making can be terrifying and distressing. Thus, accepting that there seldom are absolute answers to ethical and legal questions is an important step for school counselors wishing to reduce stress related to resolving these dilemmas.

So, how should school counselors go about making ethical decisions? First, we recommend reading and understanding the provisions of the *Ethical Standards of School Counselors* created by the American School Counselor Association (ASCA, 1998, Appendix A) and the *Code of Ethics and Standards of Practice* published by the American Counseling Association (ACA, 1995, Appendix B). The ACA document is for all counselors, while the ASCA standards are more specific for counselors within in a school setting.

If and when an ethical dilemma arises, we suggest rereading the ASCA and ACA ethical documents to determine whether or not you have enough information to resolve the situation. If codes do not provide specific-enough guidelines, the school counselor may be required to interpret the situation, analyze facts, and make a professional judgment. After careful thinking, it is wise to consult with two or more colleagues to determine a consensus of opinions as to the best course of action. Note that this type of consultation would be evidence of having met the legal test stated above: "What would a similarly educated, reasonable school counselor in this locality have done in a similar situation?" Of course, to meet the legal test, school counselors would then have to follow the advice of their colleagues. Thus, it is important to document in case notes when consultations occurred and the exchange that took place between the counselor and his or her advisors.

After this consultation, school counselors must then decide how to proceed and be prepared to defend their decisions if later questioned. All ethical dilemmas are fascinating in that there is no right or wrong way to proceed in most circumstances. A final decision depends on the particular facts of a situation.

Remley and Huey (2002) have provided a test in this chapter so that school counselors can assess their knowledge of the ASCA and ACA ethical standards. Before taking this quiz, school counselors or graduate students are encouraged to read and reflect upon the ASCA and ACA codes of ethics (Appendices A & B). Supervisors, counselor educators, and trainers of school counselors are encouraged to use this quiz as a tool to assist aspiring and practicing school counselors in developing a deeper understanding of the provisions of these documents.

Because the process for making ethical decisions outlined above is rather linear (and perhaps even boring), school counselors who prefer a more modern or constructivist approach to ethical decision making should carefully review the thought-provoking article by Cottone (2001). His view of ethical decision making takes social influences into account.

Davis and Mickelson (1994) surveyed school counselors in Wisconsin to determine their ability to make appropriate ethical and legal decisions in their work. The authors found that, although school counselors scored high and reacted appropriately to scenarios depicting ethical dilemmas, many school counselors did not have a basic understanding of ethical and legal requirements.

Hermann (2002) later investigated the fact that, though many school counselors seem concerned about resolving legal issues on a day-to-day basis, no data had been collected that chronicled the actual legal challenges they faced. As a result of these findings, she asked school counselors nationwide to further explain the legal issues they have struggled with in their practices.

Hermann (2002) uncovered valuable information. Among her findings: that school counselors are often faced with assessing whether or not a student is suicidal; determining whether or not to report cases of suspected child abuse; or ascertaining whether or not a student is a danger to others. In addition, she found that school counselors often were pressured to verbally reveal information they considered confidential. They were also frequently dealing with clients who expressed dissatisfaction with their counseling services.

The school counselors in Hermann's (2001) study reported feeling well prepared to determine whether or not to report suspected child abuse and particularly ill prepared to respond if they received a subpoena to appear as a witness in a legal proceeding. Study respondents who had participated in continuing education in the area of legal issues reported feeling significantly more prepared to deal with them than those school counselors who had not been involved in continuing education activities.

Therefore, because it is difficult for school counselors to interpret laws and understand complex legal concepts, it is vital that school counselors request legal advice from their supervisors or principals when legal issues arise that they cannot resolve alone. Supervisors and principals have a duty to provide legal advice to school counselors upon request.

When resolving ethical dilemmas, school counselors have resources beyond the ethical codes published by ASCA and ACA. When seeking career or group counseling data, counselors can reference documents such as the *Ethical Standards* published by the National Career Development Association (1991, Appendix C) or the *Best Practice Guidelines* promulgated by the Association for Specialists in Group Work (1998, Appendix D). Other associations have similar specialty guidelines for ethical practice.

Ethical and legal dilemmas in school counseling are constant and unpredictable. To be prepared to effectively deal with such challenges, school counselors must know the ASCA and ACA codes of ethics, must be deliberate in the process of decision making, and must continually update their knowledge.

An Ethics Quiz for School Counselors

Theodore P. Remley, Jr.
Wayne C. Huey

All practicing counselors, including those in schools, are encouraged to review the contents of the professional codes of ethics that apply to them and to consult ethical standards documents when ethical dilemmas arise (Corey, Corey, & Callanan, 1998; Cottone & Tarvydas, 1998; Gladding, Remley, & Huber, 2001; Herlihy & Corey, 1996; Huey & Remley, 1988; Madden, 1998; Remley & Herlihy, 2001). School counselors who know their codes of ethics are in a much better position to conduct themselves in an ethical manner.

The language in codes of ethics is aspirational in nature and quite often is broad in order to cover many possible situations. However, the words, phrases, and sentences in ethical standards documents can be helpful to counselors and are an excellent beginning point of reference when a school counselor is trying to decide a course of action in a difficult situation. The law of malpractice requires a school counselor to act as a reasonable counselor would in a similar situation (Remley & Herlihy, 2001). Legal standards represent the minimum behavior society will tolerate of a professional. On the other hand, best practice in school counseling would include a purposeful adherence to professional ethical standards. As a result, school counselors who practice ethically seldom lose a counseling malpractice lawsuit and are able to defend any of their actions that might be questioned.

School counselors could possibly have a number of ethics documents with which they have agreed to comply. For example, a school counselor who is a member of the American School Counselor Association (ASCA) and the American Counseling Association (ACA), who is certified by the National Board of Certified Counselors (NBCC), and who is licensed by his or her state counseling licensure board has agreed to abide by four separate sets of ethical standards. Fortunately, there are few conflicts among the many codes of ethics that have been promulgated by counseling groups, and most codes cover the same basic, counseling-related issues. However, there are some variations in the different counseling ethical standards documents as the quiz in this article demonstrates.

It is impossible to review all codes of ethics to which school counselors might subscribe. As a result, we have chosen to apply the *Ethical Standards of School Counselors* (American School Counselor Association, 1998) and the *Code of Ethics* (American Counseling Association, 1995) to situations often faced by school counselors. The ACA code was created to cover counseling that takes place in all settings. Therefore, the ACA standards do not address in a detailed manner some of the issues important to school counselors such as counseling minors; consulting with parents, guardians, teachers, and administrators; and working within a school environment. The ASCA standards were developed by school counselors for school counselors to help them address issues that may be unique to the school setting. Both standards would most likely be referenced in the event a school counselor was accused of wrong doing, so it is important for school counselors to be knowledgeable of both the ASCA and ACA ethical documents.

This quiz is intended to stimulate school counselors to evaluate their own knowledge of codes of ethics to which they should adhere and to test their ability to apply the codes' sections to actual practice. Counselor educators who prepare school counselors and those who instruct practicing school counselors in the area of ethics are invited to use the quiz in this article as a teaching tool.

For this quiz, we chose real situations that are experienced by school counselors on a daily basis, many of which have been explored in recent counseling literature. Counselors who wish to explore the situations presented in more depth may wish to read the recent articles and books referenced that explore each of the difficult issues in detail. The situations in this quiz address the following familiar challenges faced by school counselors:

- Providing confidentiality for minor student clients (Davis & Garrett, 1998; Isaacs & Stone, 1999; Jackson & White, 2000)
- Assessing student clients who are possibly suicidal (King, Price, Telljohann, & Wahl, 2000; Paulson & Worth, 2002; Popenhagen & Qualley, 1998)

- Counseling in a rural school (Morrissette, 2000)
- Counseling students who may be violent (Hazler & Carney, 2000; Riley & McDaniel, 2000)
- Properly using test results (Walsh & Betz, 1995)
- Using the Internet for counseling (Wilson, Jencius, & Duncan, 1997)
- Managing child custody issues when parents separate or divorce (Richardson & Rosén, 1999; Wilcoxon & Magnuson, 1999)
- Counseling students to enhance their self-esteem (Miller & Neese, 1997)
- Coordinating with mental health professionals outside the school setting (Osborne & Collison, 1998; Ponec, Poggi, & Dickel, 1998)
- Coping with school policies that hinder the counseling process (Daniels, 2001)
- Being culturally sensitive (Constantine & Yeh, 2001; Fontes, 2002; Lee, 2001; Yeh, 2001)
- Opening a private practice while still a school counselor (Richards, 1990)
- Dealing with the behavior of a colleague who is perceived to be unethical (Herlihy & Corey, 1997)
- Supervising graduate student counseling interns (Agnew, Vaught, Getz, & Fortune, 2000; Crutchfield et al., 1997; Kahn, 2000; Nelson & Johnson, 1999; Page, Pietrzak, & Sutton, 2001; Peace & Sprinthall, 1998).

Twenty situations that have ethical components are presented and readers are asked to decide whether they agree or disagree with the counselor's action in each case. Relevant code sections that relate to each situation presented from both the ASCA and ACA ethics documents are cited. Our answers to the quiz and our positions on the dilemmas are revealed in the short discussion of each situation that follows the quiz. For most ethical dilemmas, there is rarely a right or wrong answer. Ethical principles must be applied, and all situations are different from one another. The cases described do not have substantial detail, so it is possible that there may be valid arguments in opposition to our answers to the 20 quiz items.

Before you begin the quiz, please take note of the following wording issues: (1) the designations of the ethics documents, *code of ethics* and *ethical standards*, are used interchangeably. The ASCA document is titled, "ethical standards," while the ACA document is titled a "code of ethics;" and (2) the words *counselee*, which is used in the ASCA document; *client*, which is used in the ACA document; and *student* are used to refer to student clients of school counselors.

ETHICS QUIZ

Directions: Mark each situation with an "A" if you agree with the school counselor's action, or with a "D" if you disagree with the school counselor's action.

_____ 1. A counselor in a new high school was trying to decide how she should inform all students of the meaning of confidentiality in counseling situations and give them information regarding the limits of confidentiality. She considered informing the students by including a section on the topic in the student handbook given to all students as they enrolled in the school. However, she decided that putting the information in the handbook was not a good idea because few students would actually read it, and that making an announcement at an assembly at the beginning of each academic year would be the best approach.

_____ 2. An elementary counselor received a subpoena to appear at a child custody hearing related to a child in his school that he had been counseling. The counselor conferred with his principal who arranged for the counselor to meet with the school board attorney. The attorney advised the counselor that because one of the child's parents had caused the subpoena to be issued, the parent had waived any privacy rights related to the counseling and that the counselor had a legal obligation to attend the hearing and to answer any factual questions posed to him regarding his counseling sessions with the student. The attorney further cautioned the counselor not to answer any questions related to his opinion regarding the competency of either parent or regarding which parent should be awarded custody. The counselor told the attorney that he would not attend the hearing and would not answer any questions because the *Ethical Standards for School Counselors* (American School Counselor Association, 1998) required him to keep all counseling sessions confidential.

_____ 3. A school counselor is counseling a client who has exhibited some indicators associated with individuals who may be suicidal. However, the counselor is unsure of whether the student's behavior rises to the point that the student should be considered potentially at risk for suicide and whether to inform the student's parents. The counselor decides to confer with another counselor at her school, one of her former university counselor educators, and the school district's guidance director regarding the situation. Her plan is to follow the consensus of her peers regarding how she should handle the situation, if they all agree, even if she still has doubts herself.

_____ 4. A school counselor is on the witness stand at a trial. An attorney asks the counselor to repeat statements made to the counselor by a student in a confidential counseling session. The school counselor is not licensed by the state as a "professional counselor" and there is no statute in the state granting privilege to communications between student clients and school counselors. The counselor replies to the attorney that he does not believe he should reveal the information because it was communicated in a counseling session in which the student expected that he would have privacy and believed that the counselor would keep the information confidential. After the attorneys argue with each other regarding whether the counselor should be required to reveal the information as a matter of law, the judge explains to the counselor that he must answer the questions. In an effort to get the judge to change his mind, the counselor then asks the judge if he could explain the importance of keeping counseling sessions confidential.

_____ 5. A high school counselor in a small rural school is the only counselor in the building. The counselor's nephew is a sophomore in the school and is experiencing emotional distress because he has been the victim of some recent bullying incidents. The principal asks the counselor to counsel the student on a weekly basis. Although the counselor recognizes the problems inherent in counseling a close relative, she decides to counsel her nephew because she is convinced he needs help, she suspects he will not receive counseling if she does not provide it, and she believes she can assist him in an objective manner. She informs her nephew's parents that she will be counseling him, consults with a counselor in another school on a monthly basis regarding her work with her nephew, and documents in her case notes the content of the sessions.

_____ 6. A high school English teacher gives a counselor a paper written by a student in which the student says that he has thought about "ending it all and taking my tormenters with me." The counselor talks to the student and decides that he could be at risk for committing violent acts. Through consultations, the counselor's decision is affirmed by two of her counselor colleagues in the school. The counselor informs the principal of the details of the situation immediately and waits for the principal to take action directly with the student and his parents.

_____ 7. A high school offers a senior calculus class that cannot accommodate all the students who wish to take it. A counselor observes the teacher of the class reviewing the records of all students who are juniors who have expressed an interest in taking the class the next academic year. When the counselor asks the teacher what he is doing, the teacher explains that he selects the students who will be allowed to take the class based on their math scores on an aptitude test all students take at the beginning of their junior year. He explains that in the past he had also tried to consider grades, motivation, diversity, and other factors in selecting students, but that the process has become too time consuming, so now he selects students based only on their math aptitude scores. He insists that he gets the best students in the class through using the test scores as the only criterion for admission. The counselor explains that the Educational Testing Service has taken a strong stand that aptitude scores should not the be the sole criterion for entry into academic programs, but the teacher insists he does not have time to review other factors. The counselor wonders whether the matter should be brought to the attention of the principal, but decides that she does not want to upset the math teacher, so she decides that oversight of the math teacher's selection process is not her responsibility.

___ 8. A high school counselor secures permission from his principal to conduct group counseling sessions one night a week in an Internet chat room for students whose parents are going through a divorce. The principal asks the counselor to provide her with professional guidelines for counseling in this manner and to demonstrate how the procedures the counselor has developed comply with the professional standards. The counselor replies that since Internet counseling is so new, standards have not yet been adopted, but he assures the principal he will conduct the group sessions in a professional manner.

___ 9. The mother of an enrolling elementary school student tells the counselor that if the child's father requests information from the counselor regarding their daughter, the counselor must not give him any information because the mother has custody of the child. The counselor explains that, unless the father's legal rights have been terminated (which is more than a custody order), the school has a policy of providing the same information to noncustodial parents as is given to custodial parents. When the mother offers a copy of the custody order to the counselor as proof that the father is not entitled to any information, the counselor asks the mother to see the principal regarding the matter.

___ 10. A school counselor places the following statement in a parent handbook given to all parents as they enroll their child in the school: "If you are interested in any counseling relationship I might have with your child, please contact me. I respect the rights of parents, encourage parental involvement in their child's life, and am always willing to provide you with information."

___ 11. A middle school counselor receives a call from the mother of a student the counselor has been seeing recently related to the student's reluctance to participate in group activities. The student has been talking to the counselor about his shyness, anxiety around peers, negative self-concept, and interest in developing more self-confidence. The mother tells the counselor that her son has told her he is seeing the counselor. The mother thanks the counselor for talking to her son, asks what her son has been talking about in the counseling sessions, and inquires as to whether there is any way in which she can be helpful. The counselor thanks the mother for her call and explains that the counseling relationship is confidential and that she cannot disclose what the student has been talking to her about. She tells the mother she will contact her if there is anything she needs to know.

_____ 12. A middle school counselor is seeing a sixth-grader regularly because her parents are going through a contentious divorce and the process is very upsetting to the student. The student's English teacher approaches the counselor and asks whether anything is wrong with the student because she appears distracted in class, her grades have declined, and she is quieter than usual. The counselor explains that counseling relationships with students are confidential and that the counselor cannot disclose private information regarding the student.

_____ 13. A high school counselor has been seeing a student who is a senior on a regular basis after the student was referred for counseling after being disciplined several times for fighting with other students. At the third counseling session, the student informs the counselor that she sees a licensed professional counselor (LPC) in private practice weekly and has been in counseling with the LPC for about 6 months. The counselor asks the student if the counselor may contact the LPC and discuss the student's situation with her and the student agrees. The counselor has the student sign a form giving permission for the exchange of information and asks the student to have her mother or father sign the form as well. After the form has been signed by the student and a parent, the counselor calls the LPC, summarizes her counseling interventions with the student, and asks the LPC to consult with her regarding their work with the student. The LPC and the counselor agree regarding goals for the student and interventions they will use in the future.

_____ 14. A high school student tells a counselor that she has heard students talking about parties they have attended at which alcohol is served that are being held at a history teacher's home, and the teacher is identified. The student says she has never participated in the parties, but believes the other students' stories. The counselor questions the student about details and is satisfied that the parties may be occurring. The student gives the counselor the names of four students who have said they have attended the parties, but insists that the counselor not tell anyone that she told the counselor. The counselor agrees to keep the identity of the student confidential, if possible, and informs the student he will report the information, the history teacher's name, and the four students' names to the principal. The counselor gives the principal the information and the principal asks which student gave the details to the counselor. The counselor tells the principal that she would rather not identify the student unless it becomes necessary.

___ 15. An elementary school counselor is frustrated because his principal insists that the counselor obtain written permission from a student's parent or guardian before having a counseling session with the student. In his school, the counselor has found that the students who need counseling the most have parents or guardians who do not return permission forms that are sent home. Even after obtaining oral permission on the telephone from parents or guardians, the counselor has found that they fail to follow up by signing and returning the permission form. The school board attorney has advised all principals that written permission from parents is not legally required because parents know that counseling services are offered in the schools and would expect that their children would be counseled from time to time. Despite the attorney's position on the matter, the principal states that she "does not want any parents to ever be upset" by discovering that their child is being counseled. After several attempts by the counselor to convince the principal to change her mind and stop requiring written permission from parents, the counselor asks the principal if she would be willing to discuss this matter with the counselor and the school system's guidance coordinator (who the counselor knows is also opposed to requiring written permission from parents).

___ 16. An African-American counselor accepts a position in a middle school that includes a majority of Asian-American students, many of whom are recent immigrants. The counselor finds it difficult to accept in career development classroom guidance sessions the insistence of her students that their parents will make their choices for them regarding their career futures. In an effort to better understand the situation, the counselor invites three sets of parents to come to the school to talk to her about their perspectives on the career choices of their children.

___ 17. A high school counselor has recently become licensed as a professional counselor by her state and has decided to open a part-time private counseling practice. Very few counselors in her community have the background to counsel adolescent clients, and she believes there is a market for her services. She talks with the school district guidance coordinator, and they both agree that the high school counselors in her district do no personal counseling because their days are filled with administrative duties, testing, scheduling students, and classroom career development activities. The counselor and the guidance director agree that it would be appropriate for the counselor to accept students as clients in her private practice from the school where the counselor works because she would not be able to provide them with personal counseling at the school and some of them need personal counseling.

___ 18. A school counselor (counselor #1) is consulted by a counselor (counselor #2) at a different school regarding the activities of a third counselor (counselor #3) in their school district. Counselor #2 says that counselor #3 is a single parent and regularly hires female students in his high school who are assigned to him for counseling to baby-sit for him (sometimes overnight at his home), and even takes the student baby sitters on vacation with him and his children on some occasions. Counselor #1 agrees that counselor #3's behavior is inappropriate, and perhaps even unethical. Counselor #1 advises counselor #2 to confront counselor #3 with her concerns and urge him to discontinue his practices. Counselor #2 says that she is anxious about talking to counselor #3 about the issue because she is afraid he will react negatively and will be angry at her. Counselor #2 says that she would rather just tell his principal or file an ethics complaint with ASCA. Counselor #1 insists that counselor #2 talk with counselor #3 and try to convince him to change his behavior before taking any other action regarding the situation.

_____ 19. A male counselor in a high school accepted an intern from a local university, and she began her internship under his supervision at the beginning of the academic year. The intern was about the same age as the counselor (early 30s), neither had ever been married, and they discovered that they had many mutual interests. The counselor asked the intern to attend some evening and weekend social activities with him. The counselor asked his principal whether it would be acceptable for him to date his intern, and the principal told the counselor that since they were both adults, she saw no problem with them dating. The principal pointed out that several members of the faculty dated and some were married to each other.

_____ 20. A intern from a local university has begun his internship in a middle school under the supervision of the counselor. From the first day of the internship, and continuing for 3 weeks, the intern has been resistant to following the directions of the counselor, challenges many of the school policies and procedures, has had disagreements with two or three of the teachers regarding his counseling relationships with the teachers' students, and continues to wear clothing to school that the counselor believes is too casual for a professional. The intern appears to have good counseling skills, but in some instances has seemed to be too friendly or informal with his student clients. The counselor has had three formal meetings with the intern during the 3-week period, has pointed out specific behaviors of the intern that the counselor considers inappropriate, and has insisted that the intern improve his behavior. At the end of the third week, the counselor informs the intern that she will be asking the university to find another internship site for him and will be giving him an unsatisfactory evaluation for the time he has been under her supervision.

QUIZ ANSWERS AND DISCUSSION

1. **Disagree.** ASCA §A.2.a.; ACA §A.3. The *Ethical Standards* for School Counselors (ASCA, 1998) require that the "meaning and limits of confidentiality" be communicated to clients "through a written and shared disclosure statement." This is one of the few instances in which the ASCA and ACA codes differ. The *Code of Ethics* (ACA, 1995) requires that counselors inform clients that they have a right to expect confidentiality and that there are limitations, but it is not required that clients be informed in writing. Although the counselor may be correct in her perception of the lack of effectiveness of the handbook, it probably is best practice to inform clients in writing of the meaning and exceptions to confidentiality. The counselor may wish to refer to the confidentiality section of the handbook in an assembly announcement for emphasis.

2. **Disagree.** ASCA §A.2.b.; ACA §B.1.c. The ASCA standards and the ACA code clearly specify that when a counselor is legally obligated to reveal information the counselor might consider confidential, the counselor should reveal it. This position is taken so that counselors will not find themselves penalized by the legal system for attempting to practice in an ethical manner.

3. **Agree.** ASCA §A.2.b.; ACA §B.1.c. Both the ASCA and ACA codes direct counselors to consult with other professionals when in doubt as to the validity of an exception to confidentiality. Consulting helps to protect counselors from accusations of wrongdoing if their clinical judgment later is proven to have been faulty. In such situations, the legal test of what a counselor should have done is whether or not he or she did what a reasonable counselor would have done under similar circumstances. By consulting with peers and by following their consensus of opinion, a counselor would be doing what reasonable peers would have done.

4. **Agree.** ASCA §A.2.d.; ACA § B.1.e. The ASCA standards and the ACA code require counselors to request that they not be required to disclose confidential information if they are ordered to do so by a court. These standards are meant to avoid situations in which counselors simply comply with court orders without attempting to explain why confidentiality is important and without asking that the order be withdrawn.

5. **Agree.** ASCA §A.4.; ACA §A.6.a. The ASCA and ACA standards both require that counselors avoid dual relationships when possible. However, when they cannot be avoided in a reasonable fashion, the codes allow dual relationships and advise counselors to take precautions such as obtaining informed consent, seeking consultation or supervision regarding the case, and documenting their activities.

6. **Disagree.** ASCA §A.7.; ACA §B.1.f. The ASCA standards require

that in such situations, counselors inform the student of actions that might be taken to minimize the student's confusion and to clarify expectations. The ACA code requires that, to the extent possible, clients are informed before confidential information is disclosed. In this situation, in an effort to be respectful of the student, the counselor might have informed the student of her decision before informing the principal (if she did not fear an immediate violent response on the part of the student), or might have met with the student and the principal when the principal confronted the student regarding the situation.

7. **Disagree.** ASCA §A.9.c.; ACA § E.4.a. Both standards require that counselors do not misuse assessment results and "take reasonable steps" to prevent others from misusing test results. Although it might be argued that the counselor had fulfilled her ethical obligation by bringing the problem to the teacher's attention, because students might be treated unfairly as a result of the teacher's process for selecting students to be in his class, it would seem necessary for the counselor to go further in an effort to prevent the teacher from misusing the test results.

8. **Disagree.** ASCA §A.10.b.; ACA §A.12. The ASCA standards require specifically that school counselors who communicate with clients on the Internet should follow the requirements in *The Practice of Internet Counseling* (National Board for Certified Counselors, 2001). The ACA code offers only general guidelines for the use of computers in counseling. However, ACA has also developed a separate document (that must be used in conjunction with the ACA ethics code) for Internet counseling, *Ethical Standards for Internet Online Counseling* (American Counseling Association, 1999).

9. **Agree.** ASCA §B.1.c.; ACA §B.3. ASCA standards require that school counselors recognize that all parents, both custodial and noncustodial, have rights and responsibilities for the welfare of their children and have legal rights. The ACA standards do not address the issue of noncustodial parents specifically, but only have a general standard related to including parents in the counseling process as appropriate. When legal issues arise with a parent or guardian, school counselors should either refer the parent or guardian to the principal or should ask the principal for legal advice to resolve the problem.

10. **Disagree.** ASCA §B.2.a.; ACA §B.3. Although the ASCA standards do acknowledge parental rights and responsibilities for their children, the standards specifically require that a school counselor inform parents of the role of the counselor "with emphasis on the confidential nature of the counseling relationship between the counselor and counselee." The ACA code requires that in counseling relationships with minors, counselors "take measures to safeguard confidentiality." This counselor's statement seems to disregard the privacy of student clients and infers that par-

ents will be given any information they seek regarding counseling sessions with their child.

11. Disagree. ASCA §B.2.b.; ACA §B.3. The ASCA standards require that school counselors provide parents with "accurate, comprehensive, and relevant information in an objective and caring manner." The standards also require that ethical responsibilities to the student be considered. The ACA code allows counselors to include parents or guardians in the counseling process "as appropriate." In this situation, the counselor should have found a way to fulfill her ethical obligations to the mother and to the student. Possible options for the counselor might have included asking the student to give more information to his mother regarding their counseling sessions, scheduling a joint session with the mother and student, or providing the mother with general information regarding her son's concerns.

12. Disagree. ASCA §C.2.b.; ACA §B.1.i. A school counselor should, according to the ASCA standards, provide other school personnel with information that is necessary to assist a student who is being counseled. The ACA standards do not address this school-based issue, but the standards do acknowledge that "treatment teams" exist in which professionals share information. The ACA standards require that counselors inform clients when private information is being shared among professionals. In this situation, the teacher had a need to know the student's personal situation because it was affecting the student's academic performance. Best practice would require the counselor to inform the student that the information needed to be shared and encourage the student to tell the teacher herself. If the student declined to disclose the cause of her distress to the teacher, the counselor should give the teacher some information about the student's situation and emphasize to the teacher its confidential nature.

13. Agree. ASCA §C.2.c.; ACA §A.4. Both ASCA and ACA standards require that counselors who provide counseling services to clients who are being served by another professional, with the client's consent, inform the other professional and "develop clear agreements to avoid confusion and conflict" for the client. The counselor in this situation followed the guidelines of the ethical standards.

14. Agree. ASCA §D.1.b. The ASCA standards require that school counselors inform "appropriate officials of conditions that may be potentially disruptive or damaging to the school's mission, personnel, and property while honoring the confidentiality between the counselee and counselor." The ACA code has no provisions that address such school-based situations. In this situation the counselor appropriately reserved the right to disclose the informant's name at a later time, if necessary, but was attempting to address the problem without revealing the informing student's name. This is an example of how the ASCA standards address specific issues that occur in schools that are not specifically addressed in the ACA code.

15. Agree. ASCA §§D.1.c. & G.; ACA §D.1.c. Both the ASCA and ACA codes advise counselors that they should notify their employers or appropriate officials of working conditions that might limit their effectiveness as professionals. In this situation, the counselor is taking a risk that the principal might be irritated because of his request to include an administrator at the school district level in their discussions of a policy that is under the control of the principal, but the ethical standards requires that practices that have a negative effect on a counselor's practice be addressed.

16. Agree. ASCA §E.2.; ACA §§A.1.d. & A.2.b. According to both the ASCA and ACA standards, counselors should be active in seeking understanding of cultural differences. Both codes suggest that counselors learn how their own "cultural/ethnic/racial identity" affects their values and beliefs about counseling. This counselor is taking action in an effort to better understand the cultural differences of the population she serves.

17. Disagree. ASCA §F.1.f.; ACA §D.3.a. Counselors do not recruit or obtain clients for their private practices through their professional positions, according to both the ASCA and ACA standards. In this situation, even though the counselor may not be providing what she considers "personal counseling" to her students, her position at the school and in the private practice is that of counselor. Therefore, she should not accept clients from her own school.

18. Agree. ASCA §G.2.; ACA §H.2.d. Both sets of standards suggest that counselors who suspect other counselors of unethical actions attempt to get the counselor to change his or her behavior before filing an ethics complaint, if at all possible. In this situation, the counselor being consulted was correct in insisting that the counselor who was concerned confront the counselor whom she believed to be engaging in unethical activities.

19. Disagree. ACA §F.1.b. The ASCA standards do not include guidelines for supervisor/supervisee relationships. However, the ACA code requires specifically that supervisors clearly define their relationships with supervisees and maintain social relationship boundaries. The reason given for this standard is that a differential in power exists between supervisors and supervisees, and supervisees may not be aware of the power differential. Problems could arise between the counselor and the intern professionally if their personal relationship did not remain positive. There often is some level of social interaction between school counselors and their interns, but the ACA code requires that boundaries be maintained. The principal in this situation would not be expected to know the counselor's code of ethics, but the counselor would be held to it. The ACA Code of Ethics §F.1.c. also requires that counselors not engage in sexual relationships with their supervisees.

20. **Agree.** ACA §§F.1.g., F.1.h., & F.3.a. The ASCA standards do not have any provisions related to counselors and counseling interns. The ACA code specifies that counselors are responsible for insuring that supervisees provide quality professional services to clients, do not endorse the work of an unqualified supervisee, and dismiss supervisees who are unable to perform adequately in a professional environment. The counselor in this situation gave the intern an opportunity to remediate his negative behavior. When he did not improve, the counselor had an ethical obligation to end his internship.

RECOMMENDATIONS

Hopefully, school counselors will find that they are able to apply the ASCA and ACA ethical standards to challenges found in schools on a routine basis and will have high scores on this quiz. If school counselors score less on this ethics quiz than they would have liked, it is suggested that they read the ASCA and ACA ethics documents carefully and reflect upon how items are related to their practice as counselors within a school. There are a number of books (Corey et al., 1998; Cottone & Tarvydas, 1998; Huey & Remley, 1988; Madden, 1998; Remley & Herlihy, 2001) and continuing education opportunities in ethics available to school counselors as well, and they are encouraged to take advantage of those.

This ethics quiz for school counselors might be used by workshop leaders or counselor educators as a stimulus for discussion before ASCA and ACA codes are reviewed in detail. Allowing workshop participants or graduate students to discuss the situations in small groups before providing them with the quiz answers might heighten their interest in ethical issues and increase their understanding of the ethical responsibilities of school counselors.

Theodore P. Remley, Jr., J.D., Ph.D., *is professor and chair, Department of Educational Leadership, Counseling, and Foundations at the University of New Orleans, LA. E-mail: tremley@uno.edu.* **Wayne C. Huey, Ph.D.,** *retired, is former director of Counseling at Lakeside High School, Decatur, GA.*

REFERENCES

Agnew, T., Vaught, C. C., Getz, H. G., & Fortune, J. (2000). Peer group clinical supervision program fosters confidence and professionalism. *Professional School Counseling, 4,* 6–12.

American Counseling Association. (1995). *Code of ethics.* Alexandria, VA: Author.

American Counseling Association. (1999). *Ethical standards for Internet online counseling.* Alexandria, VA: Author.

American School Counselor Association. (1998). *Ethical standards for school counselors.* Alexandria, VA: Author.

Constantine, M. G., & Yeh, C. J. (2001). Multicultural training, self-construals, and multicultural competence of school counselors. *Professional School Counseling, 4,* 202–207.

Corey, G., Corey, M. S., & Callanan, P. (1998). *Issues and ethics in the helping professions.* Pacific Grove, CA: Brooks/Cole.

Cottone, R. R., & Tarvydas, V. M. (1998). *Ethical and professional issues in counseling.* Upper Saddle River, NJ: Prentice Hall.

Crutchfield, L. B., Price, C. B., McGarity, D., Pennington, D., Richardson, J., & Tsolis, A. (1997). Challenge and support: Group supervision for school counselors. *Professional School Counseling, 1*(1), 43–46.

Daniels, J. A. (2001). Managed care, ethics, and counseling. *Journal of Counseling and Development, 79,* 119–122.

Davis, K. M., & Garrett, M. T. (1998). Bridging the gap between school counselors and teachers: A proactive approach. *Professional School Counseling, 1*(5), 54–55.

Fontes, L. A. (2002). Child discipline and physical abuse in immigrant Latino families: Reducing violence and misunderstandings. *Journal of Counseling and Development, 80,* 31–40.

Gladding, S. T., Remley, T. P., Jr., & Huber, C. H. (2001). *Ethical, legal, and professional issues in the practice of marriage and family therapy* (3rd ed.). Upper Saddle River, NJ: Prentice Hall.

Hazler, R. J., & Carney, J. V. (2000). When victims turn aggressors: Factors in the development of deadly school violence. *Professional School Counseling, 4,* 105–112.

Herlihy, B., & Corey, G. (1996). *ACA ethical standards casebook* (5th ed.). Alexandria, VA: American Counseling Association.

Herlihy, B., & Corey, G. (1997). Codes of ethics as catalysts for improving practice. In *Ethics in therapy* (pp. 37–56). New York: Hatherleigh.

Huey, W. C., & Remley, T. P., Jr. (Eds.). (1988). *Ethical and legal issues in school counseling.* Alexandria, VA: American School Counselor Association.

Isaacs, M. L., & Stone, C. (1999). School counselors and confidentiality: Factors affecting professional choices. *Professional School Counseling, 2,* 258–266.

Jackson, S. A., & White. J. (2000). Referrals to the school counselor: A qualitative study. *Professional School Counseling, 3,* 277–286.

Kahn, B. B. (2000). Priorities and practices in field supervision of school counseling students. *Professional School Counseling, 3,* 128–136.

King, K. A., Price, J. H., Telljohann, S. K., & Wahl, J. (2000). Preventing adolescent suicide: Do high school counselors know the risk factors? *Professional School Counseling, 3,* 255–263.

Lee, C. C. (2001). Culturally responsive school counselors and programs: Addressing the needs of all students. *Professional School Counseling, 4,* 257–261.

Madden, R. G. (1998). *Legal issues in social work, counseling, and mental health.* Thousand Oaks, CA: Sage.

Miller, G. M., & Neese, L. A. (1997). Self-esteem and reaching out: Implications for service learning. *Professional School Counseling, 1*(2), 29–32.

Morrissette, P. J. (2000). The experiences of the rural school counselor. *Professional School Counseling, 3,* 197–207.

National Board for Certified Counselors. (2001). *The practice of Internet counseling.* Greensboro, NC: Author.

Nelson, M. D., & Johnson, P. (1999). School counselors as supervisors: An integrated approach for supervision school counseling interns. *Counselor Education and Supervision, 39,* 89–100.

Osborne, J. L., & Collison, B. B. (1998). School counselors and external providers: Conflict or complement. *Professional School Counseling, 1*(4), 7–11.

Page, B. J., Pietrzak, D. R., & Sutton, J. M., Jr. (2001). National survey of school counselor supervision. *Counselor Education and Supervision, 41,* 142–150.

Paulson, B. L., & Worth, M. (2002). Counseling for suicide: Client perspectives. *Journal of Counseling and Development, 80,* 86-93.

Peace, S. D., & Sprinthall, N. A. (1998). Training school counselors to supervise beginning counselors: Theory, research, and practice. *Professional School Counseling, 1*(5), 2–8.

Ponec, D. L., Poggi, J. A., & Dickel, C. T. (1998). Unity: Developing relationships between school and community counselors. *Professional School Counseling, 2,* 95–102.

Popenhagen, M. P., & Qualley, R. M. (1998). Adolescent suicide: Detection, intervention, and prevention. *Professional School Counseling, 1*(4), 30–36.

Remley, T. P., Jr., & Herlihy, B. (2001). *Ethical, legal, and professional issues in counseling.* Upper Saddle River, NJ: Prentice Hall.

Richards, D. L. (1990). *Building and managing your private practice.* Alexandria, VA: American Counseling Association.

Richardson, C. D., & Rosén, L. A. (1999). School-based interventions for children of divorce. *Professional School Counseling, 3,* 21–16.

Riley, P. L., & McDaniel, J. (2000). School violence prevention, intervention, and crisis response. *Professional School Counseling, 4,* 120–125.

Walsh, W. B., & Betz, N. E. (1995). *Tests and assessment* (3rd ed.). Upper Saddle River, NJ: Prentice Hall.

Wilcoxon, S. A., & Magnuson, S. (1999). Considerations for school counselors serving noncustodial parents: Premises and suggestions. *Professional School Counseling, 2,* 275–279.

Wilson, F. R., Jencius, M., & Duncan, D. (1997). Introduction to the Internet: Opportunities and dilemmas. *Counseling and Human Development* 29(6), 1–16.

Yeh, C. J. (2001). An exploratory study of school counselors' experiences with and perceptions of Asian-American students. *Professional School Counseling, 4,* 349–356.

A Social Constructivism Model of Ethical Decision Making in Counseling

R. Rocco Cottone

Social constructivism is defined as an intellectual movement in the mental health field that directs a social consensual interpretation of reality. A social constructivism approach redefines the ethical decision-making process as an interactive rather than an individual or intrapsychic process. The process involves negotiating, consensualizing, and when necessary, arbitrating. Counselors are guided by social and cultural factors in defining what is acceptable ethical practice.

In a recent review of the literature on ethical decision-making models in counseling and psychology, Cottone and Claus (2000) found few models that were theoretically grounded (e.g., Betan, 1997; Kitchener, 1984; Rest, 1984) and many models that seemed to frame the decision-making process as an individual or intrapsychic process (e.g., Kitchener, 1984; Rest, 1984). Several models seemed to mix both individual and social factors that affect decisions (e.g., Tarvydas, 1998). Only recent publications have begun to conceptualize the process of ethical decision making in broader and more purely social terms. For instance, Hill, Glaser, and Harden (1995) developed a model of ethical decision making based on a theory of feminism. Betan (1997) proposed a "hermeneutic" approach, meaning that there is an interaction of ethical principles and the subjectivity of human relations. Cottone, Tarvydas, and House (1994) addressed the social (or systemic) influences on counselor ethical decision making in a preliminary empirical study assessing the influence of number and types of relationships on counseling student decisions. Aside from these works, there was an absence of works focusing primarily on social aspects of decision making in counseling.

Given the expanding literature on social systems theory and social constructivism (or constructionism) as applied to mental health services, it is surprising that there are no social constructivism models of ethical decision making. The term *social constructivism* is used here to represent an intellectual movement in the mental health field that crosses both the psychological and systemic-relational paradigms of mental health services (see the related discussions in Lyddon, 1995, and Cottone, 1992). Generally, social constructivism implies that what is real is not objective fact; rather, what is real evolves through interpersonal interaction and agreement as to what is "fact" (Ginter et al., 1996). The radical constructivist position, deriving from the works of von Foerster (1984), von Glasersfeld (1984), and specifically Maturana (Maturana, 1978, 1988; Maturana & Varela, 1980), has been embraced by theorists in the field of marriage and family therapy as an offshoot of social systems theory. It is unique in that it is a biologically grounded theory (the biology of cognition) and ultimately allows for a biosocial interpretation of what is "real." In essence, biologically based social constructivism argues that all that is known is known through biological and social relationships. Even the biological bases of knowledge are best interpreted as deriving from complex physiological *relations* whereby observing organisms interact to construct a reality.

Maturana's (Maturana, 1978, 1988; Maturana & Varela, 1980) work is used as a foundation to argue that the biological system is not a static system that creates language; rather it is a "plastic" system that is ever-changing through the influence of social interaction (which is the context for language creation). In contrast, the social constructionist movement in psychology (e.g., Geren, 1985) is more rooted in the social psychology literature and avoids in-depth theorizing about biological bases. Gergen (1985, 1991, 1994) has thrown down a broad theoretical gauntlet arguing for a social relational interpretation of human understanding. Gergen (1991) state the following: "The reality of the individual is giving way to the relational reality" (p. 160). The term *social constructivism*, therefore, is used here to represent the biologically rooted but radical constructivism deriving primarily from the works of Maturana, while acknowledging the seminal works of Gergen, which are grounded in social psychology.

The need for a social constructivism model of ethical decision making is threefold. First, it may provide a distinct view of the decision–making process. It would be distinct in that it would be based purely on a relational view of reality. Other models tend to portray the decision maker as a psychological "entity" making the decision alone or within some social context. For example, Kitchener, in her frequently cited 1984 work, described ethical decisions as involving the decision maker's "intuitive" and "critical evaluative" reasoning. In contrast, the social constructivism perspective places the decision in the social context itself, not in the head of the decision maker; decision making becomes an interpersonal process of "negotiating," "consensualizing," and "arbitrating" (three terms defined later in this article). A second rationale for developing a social constructivism model is that it may lead to empirical testing of social versus psychologically based ethical decision-making models. Because a constructivism approach is so unique theoretically, it provides a competitive perspective to more psychologically based models. Critical paradigm experiments (Cottone, 1989a, 1989b) may be designed to test the social perspective against the more traditional psychological perspective. Such experiments will help researchers and practitioners weigh the relative merits of one approach against another, providing an empirical foundation that is sorely needed in this area of study. Third, a social constructivism model may appeal to practitioners as an alternative perspective for framing ethical decisions. Although there is a plethora of ethical decision-making models, those practitioners who are more aligned with a systemic or relational worldview will have an alternative to psychologically based or hybrid models. Furthermore, because the model is parsimonious and does not involve complex steps or stages, it may be easier for counselors to implement during the stressful times that accompany an ethical challenge.

UNDERSTANDING THE APPLICATION OF SOCIAL CONSTRUCTIVISM TO ETHICAL DECISION MAKING

"Objectivity in Parentheses"

What social constructivism means to ethical decision making is that decisions can no longer be viewed as occurring internally. As described earlier, many other decision-making models portray the decision as the responsibility of the individual decision maker. As examples, an individual is asked to decide on a best course of action (Corey, Corey, & Callanan, 1998), to select an action by weighing competing values in a given context (Tarvydas, 1998), to make the decision (Keith-Spiegel & Koocher, 1985), or to deliberate and to decide (Welfel, 1998). From a constructivism perspective, decisions are moved out of the intrapsychic process and into the interpersonal realm. Gergen (1985) wrote,

> From this perspective, knowledge is not something people possess somewhere in their heads, but rather, something people do

together. Languages are essentially shared activities. Indeed, until the sounds or markings come to be shared within a community, it is inappropriate to speak of language at all. In effect, we may cease inquiry into the psychological basis of language (which account would inevitably form but a subtext or miniature language) and focus on the performative use of language in human affairs. (p. 270)

Furthermore, Gergen (1985) said, "The mind becomes a form of social myth; the self-concept is removed from the head and placed within the sphere of social discourse" (p. 271). From this vantage point, all that is done, all activity, and all to which language is applied, is a reflection of what has been shared previously in the community. Language is not generated spontaneously; it is socially transmitted. All that is done (in language or otherwise) is bound to heritage. Decisions, therefore, cannot be located "in" the individual. Rather, they are in the social matrix.

The social constructivism position is contrary to the positions taken by ethicists in counseling that seem to be bound predominantly to psychological theorizing about how decisions are made. Decision-making models tend to lay out steps for ethical choice (see Cottone & Claus, 2000), but almost across the board they fail to describe adequately how that choice occurs; it somehow disappears into the head (or mind) of the individual making the decision either intuitively or based on utilitarian values (cf. Hare, 1991). For example, how are values weighed by the individual? Few models actually answer that question (see, for example, Gutheil, Bursztajn, Brodsky, & Alexander, 1991, who grounded their decision model in probability theory and weighing probabilities). With most models, how a decision is made is a psychological mystery.

The social constructivism approach to ethical decision making places the ethical decision out in the open—in the interaction between individuals as they operate in what Maturana (1978) identified as the "consensual domain" (p. 47). A decision is never made in a social vacuum. A decision is always made in interaction with at least one other individual.

The interactive aspects of a decision are undeniable. In professional ethics, a decision to enter into a dual relationship with a client is a decision made in interaction with the client. Likewise, a decision to breach a client's confidentiality is a decision made in relation to a third party. Decisions are not compelled internally; rather, they are socially compelled. This is the social constructivism position.

Some decisions may be viewed as "good" within a social context, whereas others may be viewed as "bad" within a social context. But that is not to say that decisions are "relative." What differentiates the social constructivism approach from purely relative models of right or wrong (in which right and wrong are relative truths) is that the social constructivism approach defies the view within a social consensual domain as *absolutely true* within that social context. As Maturana (1988) described it, "objectivity" is "in parentheses," where the parentheses are the boundaries of human interaction. In other words, reality is viewed as socially constructed, and within the social context it is an absolutist's view. To demonstrate this point, consider that there can be competitive social consensualities, competitive absolute truths, so to speak. Understanding that there can be competitive absolute truths (a logical contradiction) helps to clarify the distinction between social constructivism and objectivism (in which there is one absolute truth) and relativism (in which truth is relative to each individual). Social constructivism stands apart from objectivism and relativism in the primacy of relationships. In effect, there are pockets of objectivities, and each pocket is demarcated by the group that acts according to what is believed to be true. For example, according to social constructivism, there can be several competitive truths, even competitive "gods." Each of a number of competitive gods represents absolute truth within a social consensual domain represented by the religion's adherents. In addition, each god effectively competes for what is absolutely true against other gods (other socially consensually constructed realities). Ironically, some people literally war over some religions, however, there is no irony from a social constructivism perspective because, in those cases, the warring individuals believe absolutely in the "truths" represented by their god and will fight to the death to preserve such principles. Just as people war over religion, so too can mental health professionals war over what is considered ethical practice. Past court cases have frequently represented the battlefield. The classic and well-known Tarasoff legal decision (see VandeCreek & Knapp, 1993) is a good example. In that case, a therapist working for the University of California took what he believed were acceptable actions to warn authorities of a dangerous client. The therapist took actions that were, up to that moment, directed by the professional consensus as to obligations of counselors in that circumstance. The surprise was that the courts ruled in favor of a different view—siding with the family of the murdered individual targeted by the student—and the courts assessed liability. VandeCreek and Knapp (1993) explained,

> The decision was based, to a large extent, on the affirmative duty to act which arises out of the "special relationship" between a psychotherapist and a patient. According to the common law, an individual usually has no duty to control the behavior of another in order to protect a third party. Nevertheless, once a "special relationship" has been established, the law may require affirma-

tive obligations. These socially recognized relationships, such as parent to child or possessor of land to renter, imply a legal duty to attempt to protect others from harm, or to warn them of potential harm. (p. 5)

The professionals involved were essentially trying to protect the confidentiality of the client consistent with ethical standards to that date; however, in interaction with the legal system, the actions and the defense did not hold weight. Accordingly, a serious implication for professional ethics in counseling is derived from a social constructivism perspective, because there is no one socially constructed ethical stance that can be considered inherently better than another—predominance only derives from negotiation, consensus building, arbitration, or combinations of the three. As with the Tarasoff decision, the involved parties were acting according to what was socially directed by the consensus of their communities. The fact that there was an unresolved clash of consensualities led to arbitration.

Conflicting Consensualities

Professionals must identify the levels of consensus that operate around an action of a dilemma. The fact that there is a dilemma means there is a possible disagreement, a conflict of consensualities, between groups of people with which the professional has interacted.

The ethical codes of the American Counseling Association (ACA, 1995) and the American Psychological Association (APA, 1992) reflect consensualities as to what is acceptable practice, and membership in either the APA or the ACA indicates interaction with the consensualizing process the association represents. Counselors also interact with clients and client families, lawyers, judges, physicians, and other mental health professionals. Each interaction may represent the coming together of two systems of thought, and each may represent a distinct consensus on an issue. When there is a disagreement over an ethically sensitive issue that is resistant to easy negotiation, there is a conflict of consensualities. For example, one of the most salient cases of a breach of ethical standards is sexual intimacies with a client. The counselor who enters a sexual relationship with a client acts in a way that represents rejection of the professional standard banning sexual intimacies while acting in a way that represents acceptance of the risks of the social-sexual relationship. The sexual relationship may also represent linkage to a system that may not fit well within the constraints of a secret, professionally banned relationship. For example, the client may have family, friends, or an attorney who advises that such a relationship is "wrong." When a disagreement arises between the professional and the client's system, a clash of consensualities may result (a disagreement over the nature or course of the relationship) with potential legal and professional threat to the counselor. The action to enter into such a relationship is an act of vulnerability for the professional: The counselor's livelihood is at stake. Nothing professionally damaging may occur, but there is a possibility that the couple's initial consensus that the relationship exists (or may be acceptable at some level) may deteriorate under the strain of other relationships and competing consensualities that come to bear on their interaction. Of course, there is a consensus established in the professional literature that sexual intimacies with clients are unethical (ACA, 1995; APA, 1992) and harmful (e.g., Bouhoutsos, Holroyd, Lerman, Forer, & Greenberg, 1983), so a counselor would be well served to avoid such dual relationships. There will be little support for an offending professional given current ethical and professional standards.

A decision to breach an ethical standard (as with an offending counselor) or the decision to challenge a professional's ethics (as with the educated client) is a decision that derives from past and present interactions. There are no psychological determinants but only biological and social forces affecting interactions one way or another. In other words, the actions of the client and the counselor can be completely conceptualized as resulting from physical and social forces, not psychological needs. In addition, the action to mount an ethical challenge to the counselor also derives from physical and social factors impinging the client. What seems to be an ethical (or unethical) decision is simply an action take in concert with the emerging social consensus of the moment.

Social constructivism ethical decision making means that the professional must avoid linkages of vulnerability and cultivate linkages of professional responsibility. Relationships should be chosen wisely and in accord with the larger socio-legal consensus that pervades professional practice. In other words, ethical decision making occurs well before a crisis of consensualities arises. It is implicit in the professional culture. It means a rich professional network is established and that actions are taken to prevent and to avoid contact with social networks in which challenges of "right" and "wrong" must be answered.

Therefore, social constructivism ethical decision making is not classic psychological decision making at all. It is linkage to professional culture. One either does or does not fully enter into a professional culture. Those interactions that help to engage a professional fully in the ethical professional climate are actions of ethical choice. Such activity happens most basically in educational institutions where counselors are introduced by seasoned clinicians to professional culture and to the rules that guide acceptable practice. At that level, it is the responsibility of the profession to convey the importance of linkage to professional culture so that communicating on ethical issues becomes an ongoing activity of the student professional.

The Interpersonal Processes of Negotiating, Consensualizing, and Arbitrating

Counseling practice is complex, and ethical dilemmas arise as new challenges confront practitioners. Even a counselor who is closely aligned with an ethically sensitive professional community may face an ethical challenge. Should there be accusations of unethical practice, counselors must act to protect their own and their clients' interests. In such cases, the social constructivism alternative to psychologically based ethical decision making must occur. It does not occur in the decision maker's "head." Instead, social constructivism ethical decision making is a process of negotiating (when necessary), consensualizing, and arbitrating (when necessary) that occurs in the interpersonal process of relations that come to bear at critical moments of professional practice.

Negotiating is the process of discussing and debating an issue in which at least two individuals indicate some degree of disagreement. For example, if a client's attorney were to contact a counselor about testifying at a worker's compensation or disability hearing, the counselor should first request permission from the client to release confidential information (to talk to the attorney). Afterward, the counselor should consult with the attorney and determine whether the counselor's testimony would be crucial to the client's case. Should there be a formal request to testify, a waiver of privileged communication might be necessary, depending on laws in the jurisdiction. Should there be a disagreement as to the nature of the testimony or its potential effects, the counselor might refuse to testify, recognizing that a subpoena might result. Negotiation, therefore, is a process of discussing and debating a position taken by the counselor; negotiation requires operation in language and some level or expressed disagreement.

Consensualizing is a process whereby at least two individuals act in agreement and in coordination on an issue. Consensus is viewed as an ongoing interactive process, not a final outcome or "thing." Cottone (1992) stated, "The idea of consensus must not be viewed solely as a formal language-based activity. In fact, consensus is probably best understood by the actions of individuals as they relate mutually, verbally and non-verbally, within certain interpersonal contexts" (p. 269). Where there is language, social interaction, and co-operation, there is an evolving consensuality. (Notice that the word "co-operation" is hyphenated; the hyphen is purposeful and indicates that individuals operate—act—in a coordinated fashion.) Maturana (1970) described this as the "consensual domain" (p.50). The individuals who consensualize may have been involved in negotiation, but it is not necessary to negotiate in order to consensualize. Negotiation requires that there is some degree of disagreement, whereas consensualizing may or may not involve disagreement. For example, if an attorney requests that a counselor testify, the counselor may agree (with minimal discussion or no debate) and may just show up at the scheduled hearing ready to testify. In this case, the attorney and counselor have consensualized by coordinated action as to the request to testify. Consensualizing is the process of socially constructing a reality. If there is disagreement or discordant action (where consensualizing is not evident), then arbitrating may be necessary.

Arbitrating is a process in which a negotiator or negotiators seek the judgment of consensually accepted individuals (alone or in groups) who are socially approved as representatives of socio-legal consensus—arbitrators. Arbitrators make judgments in interaction with each other, complainants, defendants, the authority of agreed-on rules or law, and past judgments (e.g., case law). In most cases, the arbitrator has a final say, unless of course there is an appeal to higher consensually accepted arbitrator (e.g., a court of appeals). Arbitrating is the social process whereby a socially constructed reality is imposed.

RESPONSE TO A CHALLENGE

When accused of or questioned about ethical misconduct, a professional may respond in a way that acknowledges, disputes, or further questions the alleged or questionable behavior. The response of the counselor probably derives as much from the nature of the relationship to the accuser or enquirer as it does from the nature of the alleged misconduct. To deny an accusation to a "nemesis" may prevent meaningful negotiation even in the case of acceptable conduct, setting up an adversarial circumstance and a clash of consensualities to be settled by consensually agreed-on higher authorities (e.g., the courts). Denial to a friendly colleague, on the other hand, may bring about negotiation as to whether a breach has occurred (against some agreed-on standard, such as an ethics code). The moment of accusation or enquiry is a critical moment, and social forces influence what may seem to outsiders as a "decision."

THE SOCIAL CONSTRUCTIVISM PROCESS
OF ETHICAL DECISION MAKING

At critical moments, such as when a concern arises or when there has been an accusation or enquiry, the ethically sensitive professional operating from a social constructivism mode would take several steps: (a) obtain information from those involved, (b) assess the nature of the relationships operating at that moment in time, (c) consult valued colleagues and professional expert opinion (including ethics codes and literature), (d) negotiate when there is a disagreement, and (e) respond in a way that allows for a reasonable consensus as to what should happen or what really occurred. Every relationship involved must be examined for potential linkage to another (possibly adversarial) system of thought. In addition, every involved relationship must be assessed for a potential conflict of opinion over what should or did happen. If consensus is not possible, further negotiation, interactive reflection, or arbitration may be necessary.

As Figure 1 shows, after information is obtained, the nature of relationships is assessed, and valued colleagues and experts are consulted, the interactive process of socially constructing an outcome to an ethical dilemma involves negotiating (if necessary), consensualizing, and arbitrating (if necessary). The ultimate goal is to establish consensus among involved parties about what should or did happen in questionable circumstance. When consensualizing fails, then parties may partake in *interactive reflection*, a process of conversation with trusted individuals

FIGURE 1 **The Interactive Process of Socially Constructing an Outcome to an Ethical Dilemma**

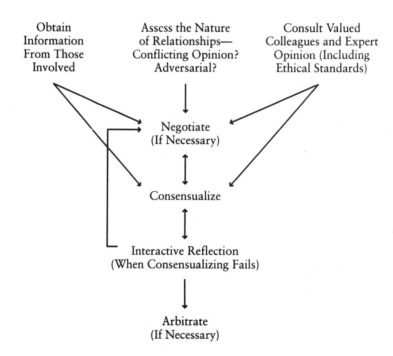

to come to agreement as to whether arbitration should be sought or whether a position needs to be modified to reenter negotiation. If consensualizing fails after interactive reflection, then arbitration is necessary.

"A TRUTH" VERSUS "THE TRUTH"

It is hoped that what happens between people can be accounted for by discussion or reasonable negotiation of what should happen (or what actually occurred). Unfortunately, "the truth" may be a matter of dispute. If counselors, in fact, plan to break the rules (or have broken the rules), then it would be hoped that they would accept the consequences of their actions imposed by the socio-legal consensus in the profession and in the courts. Otherwise, they might act to protect their own professional interests, possibly at the expense of clients, by denying a wrongdoing.

It may be that only a client and a professional know the actions that have occurred, and where there is a difference of opinion about an act, a conflict of consensualities, arbitration may be the only answer. In such cases, "the truth" may never be known, even though a judgment may occur. Aside from arbitration, when there is a dispute (i.e., there are competing truths), it is only in cases of repeated offenses that "a truth" can be established. When there are repeated offenses, such "a truth" is established around the victims, whose stories combine to constitute a systemic imperative for legal or professional action. Some professionals may "come clean" in such a circumstance. Other professionals may resist acceptance of professional or legal mores (or may possibly be the victims or a conspiracy, however unlikely). Whatever the professional's action, it reflects the physical and social forces affecting the counselor at that moment in time.

Once an ethical course of action has been chosen, it is wise for counselors to take additional steps in line with the recommendation of Tarvydas (1998) to engage in "a period of reflection and active processing of what the counselor intends to do" (p. 153). Reflection, however, from a social constructivism position is not a process of mind—rather it is a continued reappraisal of actions in context and in consultation with others that can provide a perspective representative of their linkage to the professional community. It is a continued process of seeking alternative opinions or perspectives. Should different perspectives emerge that allow for different views and a negotiated settlement (before an arbitrated decision), then it is not too late to reappraise the circumstance. In the constructivism model, such reflection takes the form of "interactive reflection."

CASE EXAMPLE

The following case scenario, based on a actual case discussed in a graduate course on ethical issues in counseling, is offered to demonstrate the interactive processes involved in decision making. Terms associated with the social process of ethical decision making are bracketed as related to the flow chart in Figure 1. Applicable sections of ACA's *Code of Ethics and Standards of Practice* (ACA, 1995) are also referenced in parentheses.

A 12-year-old girl living with her grandmother enters counseling through a family counseling agency funded by both private and government funds. The grandmother signs the consent for treatment as the child's legal guardian (A.3.b.,c.; B.3.). After several counseling sessions, the grandmother demands to know what the child reported. The child, in counseling, reports to the counselor that the grandmother is not her legal guardian, which is substantiated [assessment of the nature of relationships]. Her mother is identified as legal guardian [assessment of the nature of relationships]. The mother lives 60 miles from the counseling center and has not been involved with the child for some time. The counselor is faced with a dilemma—technically there has been no informed consent (A.3.b.,c.), because the grandmother fraudulently signed the consent form as the legal guardian. However, the counselor has an ethical "responsibility" to the child according to ethical standards (A.1.a.). The counselor consults the executive director of the agency (who is not a counselor) who informs her that counseling cannot continue without informed consent or procedures would be breached, threatening the service contract [consultation of colleagues]. The clinical service supervisor is consulted and informs the counselor that, aside from informed consent, she still has an obligation to the child [consultation of colleagues] (A.1.a.). The counselor attempts to seek the mother's permission but fails on several phone attempts (obtaining information from involved parties). She even arranges through certified mail to meet the mother, drives 60 miles, and is disappointed when the mother does not show for the scheduled meeting at the arranged site [attempt to negotiate]. The counselor then seeks the joint counsel of her clinical supervisor and the executive director [consultation with colleagues]. The executive director takes a firm legal stance and directs her not to work with the child without legally executed informed consent by the responsible adult. An agreement is reached among the professionals to request the grandmother's assistance in procuring the informed consent of the mother [consensualizing] but faced with the non-cooperation of the mother [non-consensus], the grandmother obtains legal custody of the child only after threatening the mother with charges of child neglect [threat of arbitration leading to coordinated action between the mother and the grandmother].

Counseling is reinitiated with the consent of the grandmother as the legal guardian (A.3.b.,c.). The child is informed that the grandmother has legally been given access to information provided in counseling (B.1.g.).

As this scenario demonstrates, the outcome of an ethical dilemma is highly social and can be clearly conceptualized as an interactive, not intrapsychic, process.

CONCLUSION

Gergen (1991) stated, "When individuals declare right and wrong in a given situation they are only acting as local representatives for larger relationships in which they are enmeshed. Their relationships speak through them" (pp. 168-169). The social constructivism approach to ethical decision making is a purely social interpretation of the decision-making process. The social constructivism decision–making approach is a process of negotiating and consensualizing. All acts occur in a social context. From the constructivism perspective, decisions always occur in interaction. Professionals are less vulnerable to ethical challenges if they are linked to a rich professional culture, which is not supportive of a breach of ethical standards. When concerns arise a critical moments of professional practice, the social constructivist obtains information from those involved, assesses the nature of relationships operating at the moment, consults valued colleagues and professional expert opinion (including ethical codes), negotiates when necessary, and responds in a way that allows for a reasonable consensus. In cases in which negotiation must occur—when there is a conflict of consensualities—the counselor may accept or challenge an opposing position, knowing that an adversarial relationship may be established and judgment may occur in consensually agreed on "courts" of arbitration.

R. Rocco Cottone *is a professor of counseling and family therapy in the Division of Counseling at the University of Missouri–St. Louis. Special thanks go to M. J. Gepilano Crawford, Ronald E. Claus, Patricia McCallister, and Constance Fournier. Correspondence regarding this article should be sent to R. Rocco Cottone, University of Missouri–St. Louis (469 MH), 8001 Natural Bridge Rd., St. Louis, MO 63121-4499 (e-mail: cottone@umsl.edu).*

REFERENCES

American Counseling Association. (1995). *Code of ethics and standards of practice.* Alexandria, VA: Author.

American Psychological Association. (1992). *Ethical principles of psychologists and code of conduct.* Washington, DC: Author

Betan, E. J. (1997). Toward a hermeneutic model of ethical decision making in clinical practice. *Ethics and Behavior, 7,* 347–365.

Bouhoutsos, J., Holroyd, J., Lerman, H., Forer, B. R., & Greenberg, M. (1983). Sexual intimacy between psychotherapists and patients. *Professional Psychology: Research and Practice, 14,* 185–196.

Corey, G., Corey, M. S., & Callanan, P. (1998). *Issues and ethics in the helping professions* (5th ed.). Pacific Grove, CA: Brooks/Cole.

Cottone, R. R. (1989a). Defining the psychomedical and systemic paradigms in marital and family therapy. *Journal of Marital and Family Therapy, 15,* 225–235.

Cottone, R. R. (1989b). On ethical and contextual research in marital and family therapy: A reply to Tagart. *Journal of Marital and Family Therapy, 15,* 243–248

Cottone, R. R. (1992). *Theories and paradigms of counseling and psychotherapy.* Needham Heights, MA: Allyn & Bacon.

Cottone, R. R., & Claus, R. E. (2000). Ethical decision-making models: A review of the literature. *Journal of Counseling & Development, 87,* 275–283

Cottone, R. R., Tarvydas, V., & House, G. (1994). The effect of numbers and type of consulted relationship on the ethical decision making of graduate students in counseling. *Counseling and Values, 39,* 56–68.

Foerster, H. von (1984). On constructing a reality. In P. Watzlawick (Ed.), *The invented reality* (p. 41–61). New York: Norton.

Gergen, K. J. (1985). The social constructionist movement in modern psychology. *American Psychologist, 40,* 266–275.

Gergen, K. J. (1991). *The saturated self.* New York: Basic Books.

Gergen, K. J. (1994). *Toward transformation in social knowledge* (2nd ed.). London: Sage.

Ginter, E. J. (Chair), Ellis, A. Guterman, J. T. Ivey, A. E., Lock, D. C. & Rigazio-Digilio, S. A. (1996, April). *Ethical issues in the postmodern era.* Panel discussion conducted at the 1996 world conference of the American Counseling Association, Pittsburgh, PA.

Glasersfeld, E. von (1984). An introduction to radical constructivism. In P. Watzalick (Ed.), *The invented reality* (p. 17–40). New York: Norton.

Gutheil, T. G., Bursztajn, H. J., Brodsky, A., & Alexander, V. (1991). *Decision making in psychiatry and the law.* Baltimore, MD: Williams & Wilkins

Hare, R. (1991). The philosophical basis of psychiatric ethics. In S. Block & P. Chodoff (Eds.), *Psychiatric ethics: Second edition* (pp. 33–46). Oxford, England: Oxford University Press.

Hill, M., Glaser, K., & Harden, J. (1995). A feminist model for ethical decision making. In E. J. Rave & C. C. Larsen (Eds.), Ethical decision making in therapy: *Feminist perspectives* (pp. 18–37). New York: Guilford.

Keith-Spiegel, P., & Koocher, G. P. (1985). *Ethics in psychology.* New York: Random House.

Kitchener, K. S. (1984). Intuition, critical evaluation, and ethical principles: The foundation for ethical decision in counseling psychology. *Counseling Psychologist, 12,* 43–55.

Lyddon, W. J. (1995). Forms and facets of constructivist psychology. In R. A. Neimery & M. J. Mahoney (Eds.), *Constructivism in psychotherapy* (pp. 69–92). Washington, DC: American Psychological Association.

Maturana, H. R. (1970). Biology of cognition. In H. R. Maturana & F. J. Varela (1980), *Autopoiesis and cognition: The realization of the living* (pp. 5–58). Boston: Reidel.

Maturana, H. R. (1978). Biology of language: The epistemology of reality. In G. A. Miller & E. Lenneberg (Eds.), *Psychology and biology of language and thought* (pp. 27–63). New York: Academic Press.

Maturana, H. R. (1988). Reality: The search for objectivity or the quest for a compelling argument. *Irish Journal of Psychology, 9*(1), 25–82.

Maturana, H. R., & Varela, F. J. (1980). *Autopoiesis and cognition: The realization of the living.* Boston: Reidel.

Rest, J. R. (1984). Research on moral development: Implications for training counseling psychologist. *Counseling Psychologist, 12,* 19–29.

Tarvydas, V. M. (1998). Ethical decision-making process. In R. R. Cottone & V.M. Tarvydas (Authors and Eds.), *Ethical and professional issues in counseling* (pp. 144–155). Columbus, OH: Merrill/Prentice-Hall.

VandeCreek, L., & Knapp, S. (1993). *Tarasoff and beyond: Legal and clinical considerations in the treatment of life-endangering patients.* Sarasota, FL: Professional Resource Press.

Velfel, E. R. (1998). *Ethics in counseling and psychotherapy: Standards, research, and emerging issues.* Pacific Grove, CA: Brooks/Cole.

School Counselors: Are You Aware of Ethical and Legal Aspects of Counseling?

Jerry L. Davis
Douglas J. Mickelson

School counselors, in the process of helping students, make decisions each day that require an understanding of professional ethics and state statutes. Applying ethical codes and state laws to the numerous situations that arise is challenging because it involves values, knowledge, and professional judgment. The application of ethical standards and state statuettes can be confusing at times, because what the lay requires and what the codes stipulate may be in conflict. This is particularly true in cases involving confidentiality. A growing national trend is that state legislatures are limiting the boundaries of confidentiality through the passage of mandatory reporting laws (Corey, 1990). In addition, because the majority of students with whom counselors work are minors, school counselors face an additional burden. Parents' right to know can often conflict with a fundamental tenet of counseling: the opportunity for clients to have a confidential relationship. The net result is that school counselors are making decisions based on legal and ethical standards that are not always clear and precise in pointing to the correct decision.

Because codes and laws are not always precise and ethical codes tend to reflect what most professional can agree on rather than ideal counseling practices (Kitchener, 1984), counselors need to learn to engage in ethical decision making. A further complicating factor is that in some situations no one behavior seems entirely ethical (Post, 1989).

Several recent studies have systematically investigated the application of ethics to counseling situations (Gibson & Pope, 1993; Robinson & Gross, 1989; Stadler 1989; Strein & Hershenson, 1991). None of these studies, however, focused specifically on the ethical concerns of school counselors. An exception was a study conducted by Wagner (1981), that examined counselors' attitudes and practices toward confidentiality with such topics as written records, release of information, and allegiance to the parents' right to know in spite of what the students requested. Zingaro (1983) noted that Wagner's results were particularly disturbing because some counselors tented to disclose information to the parents or guardians based on the counselors' general perceptions of what they believed parents and other adults ought to know rather than on the students' wishes. Also, counselors tend to make decisions concerning the release of information based on what they thought would be the effects of the release of information on the students rather than using ethical guidelines. The problem, of course, is that the risk may be greater for the client than for the counselor when unanticipated consequences occur. The counselor is not the one who would have to deal with those consequences.

Since Wagner's study in 1981, the ethical and legal issues confronting counselors have intensified. Issues like physical abuse, alcohol and other drug use, divorce, poverty, violence, and the Acquired Immune Deficiency Syndrome (AIDS) epidemic have posed significant dilemmas for the school counselor and have intensified the need for school counselors to develop decision-making skills using ethical and legal principles in responding to such dilemmas.

A dilemma can be defined as a situation in which a counselor experiences conflict in deciding on an appropriate decision. The counselor usually feels pulled in several directions, and at times, is confronted with a situation that seems to place professional ethics in direct opposition to the expressed desires of others or with the legal system that requires that certain activities be reported to the police or to social services units. The counselor may also be faced with determining an appropriate standard of conduct while considering obligations to two or more constituencies (e.g., the student, parent, teacher, professional ethical standards, and the law). Many school counselors face these issues and confront difficult decisions daily. At some point during their work, all school counselors face substantial challenges in deciding what is the best course of action for them and their clients.

School counselors, in particular, often have difficulty in applying the ethical standard of confidentiality to their work because the majority of their clients are under the age of 18. All states have laws that stipulate that individuals under the age of 18 are not adults and are not able to make informed decisions. Confidentiality is based on the premise that clients have the ability to make informed decisions regarding who shall have access to the information they share during a counseling session. For students under 18, the law stipulates that students do not have that ability. This places the school counselor in direct conflict with being able to offer confidential counseling services and parents' right to know regarding the information their sons and daughters share with their counselors. As Shah (1969) remarked, counselors must constantly walk the tightrope between being a counselor or an informer. This dilemma is further heightened by the national trend among state legislatures to restrict confidentiality.

Current data on the types of ethical and legal dilemmas faced by practicing school counselors are urgently needed to assist our profession. Research findings would assist counselor educators in identifying concerns confronting practicing counselors and, thus, enable them to address these issues in counselor training. The results would also be beneficial to counseling supervisors in preparing in-service training programs for school counselors. Research would help identify those dilemmas that are particularly difficult for school counselors. Finally, the findings might help practicing school counselors to become more competent in applying ethical codes and legal statutes to dilemmas they face in their schools. This study was conducted, therefore, to address the need for more data on ethical and legal issues confronting school counselors and to answer the following questions:

1. How congruent are the decisions of school counselors with ethical and legal principles?
2. Which ethical and legal issues cause the most difficulty for school counselors?
3. How familiar are school counselors with ACA/ASCA codes of ethics and Wisconsin State Statutes and Federal Laws governing counseling practice?

METHOD

Participants

The participants in this study were selected from the population of certified, practicing school counselors in Wisconsin. A list of all 1,778 certified and employed elementary, middle, and secondary school counselors was obtained from the Wisconsin Department of Public Instruction. To ensure a representative sample of the population, sample size procedures recommended by Krejcie and Morgan (1970) were followed that yielded a sample of 300 for a population of over 1,700 subjects.

Although 165 school counselors (55% of the sample) returned completed questionnaires, the characteristics of the participants closely resembled the profile of Wisconsin school counselors. Of the 165 participants included in the study, 45% (N=75) were male and 55% (N=90) were female. The counselors ranged in age from 27 to 68 years with the average age being 44; the mode was 37 years. The participants had an average of 12 years experience as school counselors. A little ore than 5% (N=8) of the counselors were minority. More than 96% possessed master's degrees, with only two counselors holding bachelor's degrees and one counselor holding a doctorate. Of the participants, 28% (N=46) were employed as elementary counselors, 23% (N=38) as middle school counselors, 38% (N=62) as secondary school counselors, and 11% (N=19) held an administrative position such as director guidance, director of special services, or director of pupil personnel.

Instrumentation

The Ethical and Legal Issues Questionnaire was developed specifically for this study and contained a total of 35 items of which 31 are ethical or legal dilemmas. All but two of the dilemmas are based on actual events presented to school counselors. The dilemmas were collected by the investigators during the previous 3 years as we supervised school counselor graduate students, consulted with practicing school counselors, and conducted in-service training sessions for pupil services staff. Ethical codes and state statutes were also examined to create potential dilemmas. This process yielded two additional dilemmas that were added to the questionnaire. Of the 31 dilemmas selected for the study, 16 were ethical dilemmas and 15 were legal dilemmas. Based on the American Association for Counseling and Development (AACD, now American Counseling Association [ACA]) *Ethical Standards* (1988) and Wisconsin and Federal Statutes, the investigators identified the preferred ethical response or the correct legal response for each item.

The last four items of the 35-item questionnaire asked participants to indicate their perceived knowledge and understanding of ethical codes and state statutes and their efforts to stay current with ethical and legal developments. For each item, participants were asked to indicate whether they: Strongly Agree (SA), Mildly Agree (MA), Mildly Disagree (MD), or Strongly Disagree (SD) with the counselor's action.

The initial draft of the questionnaire was administered to 28 advanced graduate students in counseling to determine the clarity of the items and to assess the approximate time required to complete the instrument. Also, two faculty members in counselor education reviewed the questionnaire. As a result of this process, two items were modified to be more concise and a number of editorial changes were made to ensure a precise and clear set of dilemmas.

Procedures

The Ethical and Legal Issues Questionnaire, along with a cover letter describing the nature of the research, was mailed to each of the randomly selected 300 school counselors. Within the first 5 weeks, 131 (44%) school counselors returned completed questionnaires. At that time, a follow-up mailing was made to the 169 participants who failed to respond to the first request. As a result of the follow-up, 34 more questionnaires were returned for a total of 165 (55%) completed and useable questionnaires.

RESULTS

For each of 31 dilemmas, the investigators identified the preferred ethical or the correct legal response based on AACD *Ethical Standards* (1988) and appropriate state and federal statutes. A summary of the participants' responses to each of the dilemmas was conducted. For 24 of the dilemmas, 65% or more of the participants' responses were in agreement with the preferred ethical responses or the correct legal responses. This high percentage of agreement was determined by the investigators to mean that the participants were knowledgeable and informed regarding many of the ethical and legal issues. The participants demonstrated an understanding of their professional ethical codes when responding to the ethical dilemmas that focused on the following: use of test scores, consultation with professional colleagues, consultation with teachers and parents, and incidents suggesting clear and imminent danger to clients or others. The legal aspects of counseling that posed no problems for the participants involved mandated reporting of suspected sexual abuse or physical abuse or both. For the remaining seven dilemmas that were difficult for the participants, defined as less than 50% agreement with the preferred ethical or correct legal choices, five were legal issues and two were ethical issues involving issues of privacy, confidentiality and parents' right to be informed, and testing.

The seven dilemmas that were identified as being difficult are presented as follows:

Dilemma 1 presents the counselor with the issue of parental notification when referring a student who is experiencing problems resulting from the use of alcohol or other drugs to an appropriate community agency. The appropriate counselor response to this dilemma is guided by Wisconsin statute §118.126. As originally enacted, certain school professionals were authorized to make such referrals without parental consent or notification. The Governor vetoed that section of the bill, however, because he believed that the family unit should not be circumvented by the school or social service agencies. No school employee shall make such

DILEMMA 1 Counselor Response by Level

You have been assigned the role of school alcohol and drug liaison with the local community agencies. One of your 15-year-old students has come to you seeking help and treatment for what she describes as a serious drinking problem. She wants you to help her because you have established a reputation as someone who is trustful and understanding. She does not want you to tell her parents because they will kick her out of the house. It is clear she needs treatment so you honor her request and refer her to one of the local treatment facilities.

	SA	MA	MD	SD
Elementary	19%	47%	19%	16%
Middle	31%	18%	38%	13%
Secondary	38%	29%	14%	19%
Administrative	30%	24%	6%	42%

Note. SA=Strongly Agree; MA=Mildly Agree; MD=Mildly Disagree; SD=Strongly Disagree.

DILEMMA 2 Counselor Response by Level

The vice president of a nearby college has asked you for a list of the seniors' names, addresses, and phone numbers so that information on available scholarships from their college can be made known to all the seniors. You deny the request because it violates the students' right to privacy.

	SA	MA	MD	SD
Elementary	42%	27%	24%	6%
Middle	46%	18%	23%	13%
Secondary	65%	13%	11%	11%
Administrative	53%	18%	18%	12%

Note. SA=Strongly Agree; MA=Mildly Agree; MD=Mildly Disagree; SD=Strongly Disagree.

referrals without parental notification (Clark, 1987). Counselors may be more inclined to follow the ethical standard regarding confidentiality because they are less aware of parental rights.

Dilemma 2 concerns third-party access to selected student information. The type of information requested by the college was directory data, as defined by the Family Educational Rights and Privacy Act (FERPA; PL 93-380). School districts are allowed to release such information without parental consent. The assumption is that parents who wish to have their children excluded from the directory have done so and they would not be included in the directory data. Thus, the students' right to privacy would not be violated by the release of such data.

DILEMMA 3 Counselor Response by Level

The district administrator asks to administer an intelligence test to a fifth grade student for placement purposes. You realize that you do not have any training in administering this test. You are, however, the only person in your school who understands general testing principles. You read the test manual and administer the intelligence test to the student.

	SA	MA	MD	SD
Elementary	3%	38%	23%	36%
Middle	13%	38%	26%	23%
Secondary	15%	38%	24%	23%
Administrative	11%	33%	6%	50%

Note. SA=Strongly Agree; MA=Mildly Agree; MD=Mildly Disagree; SD=Strongly Disagree.

It was somewhat surprising that there was such strong agreement with the counselor's decision to withhold the data when there is legislation permitting such release. Districts may refuse to release directory data or provide public notice of the conditions under which such release would occur. Although the dilemma may not contain all the necessary preconditions regarding release the strength of support for the counselor's refusal was surprising. Again, the participants may have been guided ore by the ethical concept of confidentiality than the legal concept of privacy.

Dilemma 3 relates to the AACD *Ethical Standards* (Section C[4]) (1988) regarding measurement and evaluation in which members "...must recognize the limits of their competence and perform only those functions for which they are prepared." The fact that nearly half of all the participants agreed with the unethical action of the counselor, as reported in Dilemma 3, is disturbing. Although the strength of the agreement was not strong, the participants seem to believe that in certain situations pragmatism and their interpretation of student need may take precedence.

Dilemma 4 is a test of the participants' knowledge of the rights of parental access to student records. In this instance, the participants did not seem to be aware of parental rights. FERPA (PL 93-380) ensures parental access to the educational records of their children if the children are under the age of 18. If the child is 18 years or older, the parents generally would not have access unless permission were obtained in writing from the student. A highly relevant exception to this is that there is not need to secure the consent of a student 18 or older to release educational records to his or her parents, if the student is still a dependent parents, if the student is

DILEMMA 4 Counselor Response by Level

An 18-year-old senior has requested that you restrict her parent's right of access to her progress records. She does not want anyone to have access to her records without her permission. You know she is still living at home and that the basis for the request is her strong belief that since she is now 18, her records belong to her. You honor her request.

	SA	MA	MD	SD
Elementary	6%	32%	50%	12%
Middle	36%	36%	21%	8%
Secondary	29%	29%	24%	18%
Administrative	33%	22%	22%	22%

Note. SA=Strongly Agree; MA=Mildly Agree; MD=Mildly Disagree; SD=Strongly Disagree.

still a dependent of the parent under the federal tax laws (Fischer & Sorenson, 1991). In this dilemma, the student is clearly a dependent.

With the increasing incidence of alcohol, dugs, and weapons in the schools, locker searches have been initiated by school officials in efforts to reduce the presence of these disruptive factors. In Dilemma 5, the counselor may refuse, but not because it was illegal. Although some courts have cause the student has given implicit consent in advance, there should be reasonable cause that something dangerous or illegal has been concealed in a particular place before conducting the search. In this dilemma, there is reasonable cause for such a search; however, nearly half of the participants believed it was illegal.

Dilemma 6 presents an ethical issue to the participants concerning working with a client who already is receiving counseling. According to the AACD *Ethical Standards* (1988), Section B(3), members are not to enter into a counseling relationship with a person who already is in counseling, without first contacting and receiving the approval of the other professional. It is rather startling that many counselors agreed to not contact the other professional when the ethical standard is so specific.

School counselors are constantly faced with balancing the rights of parents to be informed about their children's behavior and the need to maintain confidentiality to work effectively with students. In Dilemma 7, the participants were confronted with this issue. The ethical standards do allow counselors the opportunity to break confidence in certain situations. Although there are no precise guidelines that define these situations, the participation that define these situations, the participation of a 13-year-old in the described sexual activities would be one of the incidents in which parents have a right to be informed and, in Wisconsin,

DILEMMA 5 Counselor Response by Level

School administration and many members of the community have become concerned about suspected drug use in the schools. Many students have expressed concern to you about the growing use of drugs in school. The administration had decided to conduct an unannounced locker search and asked you to participate. You refuse because such a search is illegal.

	SA	MA	MD	SD
Elementary	27%	23%	26%	24%
Middle	31%	15%	39%	15%
Secondary	19%	27%	20%	34%
Administrative	44%	17%	22%	17%

Note. SA=Strongly Agree; MA=Mildly Agree; MD=Mildly Disagree; SD=Strongly Disagree.

DILEMMA 6 Counselors Response by Level

An 11-year-old student informs you during a counseling session that she is seeing a psychiatrist once a week about her low self-esteem. She asks you not to consult with her psychiatrist because she trusts you more. You have been successful in helping other students to overcome their feelings of low self-esteem and consider yourself to be proficient in that area. You agree not to consult with the psychiatrist.

	SA	MA	MD	SD
Elementary	18%	35%	27%	21%
Middle	15%	15%	50%	20%
Secondary	26%	25%	22%	28%
Administrative	22%	17%	22%	39%

Note. SA=Strongly Agree; MA=Mildly Agree; MD=Mildly Disagree; SD=Strongly Disagree.

counselors are mandated to report such incidents to social services or to the police department.

The last four items of the 35-item questionnaire sought the participants' perceived knowledge of ethical codes and state statutes and their reported efforts to stay current. The firs two items focused on the participants' perceived familiarity with the AACD *Ethical Standards* (1988) and American School Counselor Association (ASCA) *Ethical Standards for School Counselors* (1992). Approximately 63% reported that they were familiar with the AACD code of ethics and approximately 69% reported that they were familiar with the ASCA code of ethics. A third item asked the participants to report their degree of familiarity with state

DILEMMA 7 Counselor Response by Level

Jean is an emotionally immature 13-year-old. She has been talking to you about her interest in sex and that she has had sex with more than one boy. You are concerned about her immaturity and ability to make such decisions by herself. You tell her that you must tell her parents. She objects strenuously, is very angry with you, and feels betrayed. In spite of her protests, you inform her parents.

	SA	MA	MD	SD
Elementary	24%	32%	8%	37%
Middle	23%	33%	26%	37%
Secondary	13%	24%	26%	37%
Administrative	29%	18%	35%	18%

Note. SA=Strongly Agree; MA=Mildly Agree; MD=Mildly Disagree; SD=Strongly Disagree.

and federal laws governing counselor records, privacy, confidentiality, and counseling practice. Approximately 80% of the school counselors indicated that they were quite familiar with the appropriate laws. The final item asked the participants to indicate their efforts to stay current and informed about legal and ethical issues in counseling by attending workshops, reading professional journals or newsletters, like *Education Week* and *School Lay News*. About 84% of the school counselors reported that they mad efforts to stay current and informed.

DISCUSSION

The counselors' responses to the dilemmas indicate considerably more awareness of their professional codes of ethics as compared to their knowledge of state and federal statutes. This conclusion is based on the finding that five of the dilemmas found to be difficult for counselors focused on legal aspects of counseling, whereas only two involved ethical issues in counseling. This is contrary to their self-reports as counselors indicated a good understanding of both legal and ethical aspects of their profession. In our own clinical experiences with practicing school counselors, we have found that counselors express confidence in their ability to make correct legal decisions. When pushed to cite relevant statutes to support their decisions, however, they are often at a loss. This may be because districts often establish policies that may be contrary to students' rights (e.g., locker searches) but are supported by parents. Because no one challenges the policies, counselors assume their legality.

The legal aspects of counseling that seem to be most confusing to counselors focus primarily on parents' and students' right to privacy and the release of certain types of student information. Definitions, directives, and procedures regarding privacy are covered in the Family Educational Rights and Privacy Act (PL 93-380). Our data suggests that counselors need to better understand those parts of legislation affecting their practices. Some of the misinformation may be because counselors are often not the designated custodian of the records. This should not excuse counselors, however, from being knowledgeable about pertinent aspects of the law. Caution must be used in generalizing the results focusing on legal aspects of counseling because an understanding of Wisconsin law was necessary to respond to two dilemmas. Future research needs to be conducted to determine counselors' understanding of laws governing counseling in other states.

One ethical aspect that counselors need to address more carefully centers on dual relationships. When a counselor determines that a student is currently seeing a therapist outside of school, the counselor is obligated to consult with the therapist. The other ethical concern found in this study focuses on the use of tests in the counseling process. More than 50% of the counselors indicated they would administer a test that they were not trained to use. The ethical codes clearly indicated that a counselor should not use tests without being fully trained in all aspects of the test.

Although it is gratifying, on the one hand, to learn that approximately two thirds of the participants reported that they are familiar with ethical and legal aspects of counseling, it is alarming that one third would indicate a lack of knowledge of these essential aspects of their profession. This clearly suggests the need to provide more focus on ethical and legal aspects of counseling in counselor training and to promote systematic in-service training for counselors with the expressed purpose of helping counselors to keep current with ethical and legal aspects of counseling.

Furthermore, it is certainly encouraging to find that 84% of the participants indicated they are engaging in a variety of professional activities to stay current with their profession. We must also acknowledge, however, that 16% suggested they do not read about their profession not do they attend professional conferences or workshops. Counselor educators, counseling supervisors, and professional school counselors must engage in a concentrated effort to ensure that all counselors make a professional commitment to keep current regarding ethical and legal aspects of their work as counselors.

Jerry L. Davis *is a professor and* **Douglas J. Mickelson** *is an associate professor, both in the Department of Educational Psychology, 757 Enderis Hall, University of Wisconsin–Milwaukee, Milwaukee, WI 53201.*

REFERENCES

American Association for Counseling and Development. (1988). *Ethical Standards.* (rev. ed.). Alexandria, VA: Author.

American School Counselor Association (1992). *Ethical Standards for School Counselor.* Alexandria, VA: Author.

Clark, J. F. (1987, July). Privileged Communications: Copying with student use of alcohol, drugs. *Wisconsin School News*, pp. 27–29.

Corey, G. (1990). *Theory and practice of group counseling.* Pacific Grove, CA: Brooks/Cole.

Fischer, L., & Sorenson, G. P. (1991). *School law for counselors, psychologists, and social workers* (2nd ed). White Plains, NY: Longman.

Gibson, W. T., & Pope, K. S. (1993). The ethics of counseling: A national survey of certified counselors. *Journal of Counseling & Development, 71*, 330–336.

Kitchener, K. S. (1984). Intuition, critical evaluation and ethical principles: The foundation for ethical decisions in counseling psychology. *The Counseling Psychologist, 12*, 43–55

Krejcie, R. V., & Morgan, D. W. (1970, June). Determining sample size for research activities. *Educational and Psychological Measurement, 30*(4), 607–610.

Post, P. (1989). The use of the ethical judgment scale in counselor education. *Counselor Education and Supervision, 28*, 229–233.

Robinson, S. E. & Gross, D. R. (1989). Applied ethics and mental health counselor. *Journal of Mental Health Counseling, 11*, 289–299.

Shah, S. (1969). Privileged communications, confidentiality, and privacy. *Professional Psychology, 1*(1), 56–59.

Stadler, H. A. (1989). Balancing ethical responsibilities: Reporting child abuse and neglect. *The Counseling Psychologist, 17*(1), 102–110.

Strein, W., & Hershenson, D. B. (1991). Confidentiality in non-dyadic counseling situations, *Journal of Counseling & Development, 69*, 312–316.

Wagner, C. A. (1981). Confidentiality and the school counselor. *Personnel and Guidance Journal, 59*, 305–310.

Zingaro, J. C. (1983). Confidentiality: To tell or not to tell. *Elementary School Guidance & Counseling, 17*, 261–267.

A Study of Legal Issues Encountered by School Counselors and Perceptions of Their Preparedness to Respond to Legal Challenges

Mary A. Hermann

School counselors are encountering many legal issues (Corey, Corey, & Callanan, 1998; Fernandez, 1992), and various authors have discussed the areas of school counselors' legal vulnerability. Lawrence and Kurpius (2000), Remley and Herlihy (2001), and White and Flynt (2000) explained that failing to report suspected child abuse can result in civil and criminal liability. Lawrence and Kurpius noted that confidentiality can be a difficult legal issue, especially when counseling minors. Remley and Herlihy posited that counselors can be subpoenaed to produce records and appear at court proceedings. Failure to effectively manage a client's threats of violence and acting negligently when counseling suicidal clients can result in malpractice lawsuits as well (Ahia & Martin, 1993; Corey et al.; Glosoff, Herlihy, & Spence, 2000; Remley & Herlihy; Remley & Sparkman, 1993).

Researchers have identified laws of particular relevance to school counselors and assessed school counselors' knowledge of these laws (Davis & Mickelson, 1994; Herndon, 1990; Rawls, 1997). Herndon reviewed laws that may have an impact on school counseling. Rawls studied school counselors' knowledge of school law, and Davis and Mickelson studied school counselors' knowledge of their legal and ethical responsibilities. According to these studies, school counselors face legal dilemmas in the areas of student privacy, reporting suspected child abuse, counseling students who pose a danger to others, and ensuring the safety of students.

Variables potentially related to counselors' knowledge of legal and ethical issues have also been identified. Rawls (1997) studied the possibility of a relationship between school counselors' knowledge of school law and demographic variables including the type of education in school law, recency of school law education, years of experience as a counselor, memberships in professional organizations, and highest degree obtained. Gibson (1992) explored the relationship between counselors' knowledge of and confidence in ethics beliefs and credentials, membership in professional organizations, year of graduation, highest degree obtained, and amount of instruction in ethics.

Though the literature contains references to potential legal issues facing school counselors and school counselors' knowledge of these issues, no studies to date considered which legal issues were most prevalent. The current study assessed the types and frequency of legal issues being encountered by school counselors. This study also examined school counselors' perceptions of their ability to respond to prevalent legal issues. Whether participants' perceptions of their ability to respond to these issues were related to having completed a course in ethics or legal issues, having completed continuing education in ethics or legal issues, degree held, years of experience, whether licensed by their state, and whether certified by the National Board for Certified Counselors (NBCC) was also considered. The results of this study are intended to help determine whether school counselors need more exposure to legal issues as part of their graduate program and through continuing education in order to practice in a legally sound manner and thus avoid unnecessary litigation.

METHOD

Participants

Five hundred members of the American School Counselor Association (ASCA) and 500 members of the American Mental Health Counselors Association (AMHCA) were selected to participate in this research project. The respondents included 273 school counselors. The data provided by the 273 school counselors were analyzed for this article.

The sample of school counselors consisted of 23.1% males and 75.8% females. The participants were African American (6.6%), Native American (.7%), Hispanic American (1.1%); European American (87.9%), and Asian American (1.1%). Although 88% of the respondents

TABLE 1 **Percentage of Participants Who
Encountered Legal Issues in Past 12 Months**

Legal Issue	Encountered Issue	Encountered Issue Two or More Times
Determining Whether to Report Suspected Child Abuse	89%	74%
Being Pressured to Verbally Reveal Confidential Information	51%	34%
Being Asked to Turn Over Confidential Records	19%	10%
Determining Whether a Client Posed a Danger to Others	73%	51%
Determining Whether a Client Was Suicidal	90%	76%
Being Subpoenaed to Appear as a Witness in a Legal Proceeding	18%	4%
Clients Expressing Dissatisfaction with Participants' Counseling Services	42%	19%

held master's degrees, 8% of the respondents also held specialist degrees, and 4% of the respondents had earned doctoral degrees in counseling. Counselors from every state except Montana, Oklahoma, West Virginia, and Wyoming participated in the study. One school counselor from the District of Columbia and one school counselor from outside of the United States also participated.

Two percent of the participants reported that they worked in elementary schools, 28% indicated that they worked in middle schools or junior high schools, and 60% reported that they worked in a high school setting. Three percent of the participants indicated that they worked in a school for both elementary and middle school students. Furthermore, 4% of the respondents reported that they worked in a school for both middle and high school students and 3% of the participants reported that they worked in a school for elementary, middle school, and high school students.

The respondents' years of experience as school counselors ranged from one to 35 with a mean of 11.83 (SD = 9.84). Thirty-six percent of the participants had less than 5 years of experience and 64% of the participants had 5 or more years of experience as school counselors.

Almost three fourths (73.6%) of the school counselor participants indicated that they had completed a course in ethics or legal issues in counseling. More than one half (56.8%) of the respondents had recently completed continuing education in ethics or legal issues. Approximately one half (49.8%) of the participants were licensed professional counselors. A total of 23.8% were certified by NBCC.

Survey

No studies that addressed the particular legal concerns of school counselors, the prevalence of the legal issues actually faced by school counselors, or school counselors' perceptions of their ability to effectively address legal issues were found in the literature. Thus, a survey was constructed to gather this information. This survey was titled the Legal Issues in Counseling Survey.

Section 1 of the survey was created to assess the legal issues being encountered by counselors and the prevalence of these issues. The prominent legal issues addressed in the literature (e.g., Davis & Mickelson, 1994; Herndon, 1990; Rawls, 1997) and reflected in the survey included:

- Determining whether to report suspected child abuse
- Counselor/student confidentiality
- Determining whether a student poses a danger to others
- Determining whether a student is suicidal
- Responding to a subpoena

Participants were provided with an opportunity to add other legal issues they had encountered in the past year. In addition, participants were asked to indicate how many times each of the legal issues had been encountered in the past year.

Section 2 of the survey presented the same legal issues and asked respondents to indicate how prepared they felt to effectively manage the legal issues. A Likert-type scale from one, "not prepared," to five, "very prepared," was presented to respondents. The final section of the survey was created to gather information on the independent variables in this study. These variables were determined based on previous research on similar topics (e.g., Gibson, 1992; Rawls, 1997) and included having completed a course in ethics or legal issues, having completed continuing education in ethics or legal issues, degree held, years of experience, whether licensed by their state, and whether certified by NBCC.

The face validity of the survey was tested before the surveys were sent to the participants. The survey was sent to five experts in legal issues in the counseling field. These experts were asked for feedback about the survey, including whether the experts believed the major legal issues in the counseling field had been identified in the survey. Additionally, 12 counselors who had worked or currently worked in school or community mental health settings were asked to complete a draft of the survey and

TABLE 2 **Participants' Perceptions of Their Preparedness to Respond to Legal Issues**

Legal Issue	Not Prepared	Well Prepared	M	SD
Determining Whether to Report Suspected Child Abuse	2%	91%	4.43	.72
Being Pressured to Verbally Reveal Confidential Information	14%	57%	3.66	1.06
Being Asked to Turn Over Confidential Records	22%	52%	3.47	1.17
Determining Whether a Client Posed a Danger to Others	13%	63%	3.72	.97
Determining Whether a Client Was Suicidal	6%	72%	3.95	.90
Being Subpoenaed to Appear as a Witness in a Legal Proceeding	54%	23%	2.50	1.31
Clients Expressing Dissatisfaction with Participants' Counseling Services	20%	48%	3.36	1.16

Note: "Not Prepared" represents responses of one and two of this survey. "Well Prepared" represents responses of four and five.

answer questions regarding their ability to understand what was being asked of them. Information about the survey's clarity, the problems experienced when completing the survey, and the amount of time required to complete the survey was requested. Feedack about the survey was used to enhance the survey's clarity.

Procedure

A cover letter and survey were mailed to the prospective participants. A self-addressed stamped envelope was included in the packet to encourage response and to protect anonymity. Two weeks after mailing the packets, a postcard was mailed to each potential participant which reminded them that they had recently received the survey and requested that they complete and return it if they had not already done so.

RESULTS

Legal Issues Encountered by School Counselors

Participants were asked to indicate the approximate number of times in the past year they had encountered the legal issues listed on the survey. School counselor participants' responses are summarized in Table 1. According to these results, having to determine whether a client was suicidal and having to determine whether to report suspected child abuse were the most prevalent issues faced by school counselors. Another prevalent issue for school counselors was having to determine whether a client posed a danger to others. The legal issues encountered least often were being asked to turn over records that the school counselor considered to be confidential and being subpoenaed to appear as a witness in a legal proceeding.

The participants indicated that they had dealt with some legal issues that were not included on the survey. Three participants reported they had counseled students who had been sexually harassed by other students, one participant had encountered a case of statutory rape, and another participant added minors' abortion rights to the legal issues presented on the survey. Three participants indicated they were asked to play a role in child custody proceedings. Furthermore, one participant reported that legal issues related to the Family Educational Rights and Privacy Act of 1974 (FERPA) were being encountered. Seven participants indicated legal issues related to special education laws were encountered. Additionally, two participants reported they were threatened with lawsuits related to professional services and one participant had been named as a defendant in a lawsuit for educational malpractice.

School Counselors' Perceived Level of Preparedness to Respond to Legal Issues

Participants were asked to indicate the degree to which they felt prepared to respond to the legal issues listed on the survey. The survey presented a continuum from one to five, one indicating that the school counselor did not feel prepared to deal with the issue and five indicating that the school counselor felt very prepared to deal with the issue. The results of these data are summarized in Table 2.

School counselors felt better prepared to respond to certain legal issues. Over 90% of the school counselor respondents felt well prepared to determine whether to report suspected child abuse. The participants felt more prepared to respond to this legal issue than any other issue presented on the survey. Additionally, almost three fourths (72%) of the school counselor respondents felt well prepared to determine whether a client was suicidal. School counselors felt least prepared to respond to being subpoenaed to appear as a witness in a legal proceeding. Less than one fourth (23%) of the participants felt that they were well prepared to deal with this issue.

Relationship of Variables to Perceived Degree of Preparedness to Respond to Legal Issues

This study sought to determine whether certain variables were related to the perceived degree of preparedness of school counselors to respond to legal issues. These variables included taking a course in ethics or legal issues in counseling, recently completing continuing education in

TABLE 3   Results of t-tests Between Participants Completing an Ethical/Legal Course and Those Who Did Not

Legal Issue	Completed Course		No Course			
	M	SD	M	SD	t	df
Determining Whether to Report Suspected Child Abuse	4.45	.72	4.38	.71	.76	268
Being Pressured to Verbally Reveal Confidential Information	3.73	1.07	3.45	1.02	1.90	267
Being Asked to Turn Over Confidential Records	3.56	1.14	3.20	1.27	2.17	266
Determining Whether a Client Posed a Danger to Others	3.82	.89	3.41	1.14	2.70	96
Determining Whether a Client Was Suicidal	3.98	.88	3.83	.97	1.20	109
Being Subpoenaed to Appear as a Witness in a Legal Proceeding	2.64	1.30	2.13	1.28	2.80*	264
Clients Expressing Dissatisfaction with Participants' Counseling Services	3.39	1.20	3.26	1.07	.78	262

$p < .01$

TABLE 4   Results of t-tests Between Participants Completing Ethical/Legal Continuing Education and Those Who Did Not

Legal Issue	Continuing Education		No Continuing Education			
	M	SD	M	SD	t	df
Determining Whether to Report Suspected Child Abuse	4.55	.63	4.27	.79	3.16*	215
Being Pressured to Verbally Reveal Confidential Information	3.82	1.04	3.44	1.05	2.92*	269
Being Asked to Turn Over Confidential Records	3.60	1.19	3.29	1.13	2.12	268
Determining Whether a Client Posed a Danger to Others	3.91	.92	3.47	.97	3.83*	269
Determining Whether a Client Was Suicidal	4.14	.79	3.69	.98	4.08*	215
Being Subpoenaed to Appear as a Witness in a Legal Proceeding	2.65	1.37	2.30	1.20	2.22	260
Clients Expressing Dissatisfaction with Participants' Counseling Services	3.48	1.18	3.19	1.12	2.00	264

$p < .01$

TABLE 5 **Results of t-tests Between Participants Licensed as Professional Counselor and Those Who Were Not**

Legal Issue	Licensed		Not Licensed		t	df
	M	SD	M	SD		
Determining Whether to Report Suspected Child Abuse	4.49	.73	4.38	.70	1.19	270
Being Pressured to Verbally Reveal Confidential Information	3.84	1.01	3.47	1.08	2.87*	269
Being Asked to Turn Over Confidential Records	3.64	1.14	3.30	1.18	2.40	268
Determining Whether a Client Posed a Danger to Others	3.90	.93	3.53	.97	3.21*	269
Determining Whether a Client Was Suicidal	4.08	.84	3.81	.94	2.46	268
Being Subpoenaed to Appear as a Witness in a Legal Proceeding	2.59	1.35	2.42	1.27	1.03	266
Clients Expressing Dissatisfaction with Participants' Counseling Services	3.49	1.10	3.22	1.22	1.88	264

*$p < .01$

TABLE 6 **Results of t-tests Between NBCC and non-NBCC Participants**

Legal Issue	Certified		Not Certified		t	df
	M	SD	M	SD		
Determining Whether to Report Suspected Child Abuse	4.43	.73	4.43	.71	.02	268
Being Pressured to Verbally Reveal Confidential Information	3.81	.96	3.60	1.09	1.47	118
Being Asked to Turn Over Confidential Records	3.67	1.22	3.39	1.15	1.67	266
Determining Whether a Client Posed a Danger to Others	4.02	.91	3.63	.97	2.91*	114
Determining Whether a Client Was Suicidal	4.22	.74	3.87	.93	2.72	266
Being Subpoenaed to Appear as a Witness in a Legal Proceeding	2.75	1.43	2.41	1.26	1.81	264
Clients Expressing Dissatisfaction with Participants' Counseling Services	3.32	1.19	3.36	1.16	.27	262

*$p < .01$

ethics or legal issues, level of education (master's degree, specialist degree, or Ph.D.), years of experience as a school counselor, licensure as a professional counselor, and certification by NBCC. Independent t-tests were used to determine if significant differences existed in the participants' perceived degree of preparedness to respond to each legal issue based on these variables. Differences were considered significant at the .01 level. The results of these analyses are presented in Tables 3 through 6.

According to this study, school counselors who recently participated in continuing education on ethics or legal issues felt better prepared to determine whether to report suspected child abuse, respond to pressure to reveal confidential information, and to determine whether a student was a danger to self or others. This study also found that participants who took a course in ethics or legal issues felt better prepared to respond to being subpoenaed to appear as a witness in a legal proceeding. Participants who obtained state licensure as professional counselors indicated that they felt better prepared to respond to pressure to reveal confidential information and to determine if a student is a danger to others. Participants who were certified by the NBCC felt better prepared to determine if a student was a danger to others. Level of education and years of experience had no significant relationship to school counselors' perceptions of preparedness to manage legal issues.

DISCUSSION

Determining whether students are suicidal is the legal issue that participants reported encountering most frequently. This finding supports the research of King, Price, Telljohann, and Wahl (1999) who reported that 74% of the respondents in their study indicated that at least one student had attempted suicide at the high school where the counselor was employed while the counselor was working there.

The school counselors surveyed in this study felt most prepared to determine whether to report suspected child abuse and to determine whether a client was suicidal. Counselors felt least prepared to respond to a subpoena to appear as a witness in a legal proceeding. It is noteworthy that participants encountered the issues of determining whether a client was suicidal and reporting suspected child abuse most frequently, and they encountered having to respond to a subpoena to appear as a witness in a legal proceeding least frequently. These results seem to indicate that school counselors feel better prepared to deal with legal issues that they encounter on a regular basis.

The finding that the participants felt more prepared to determine whether to report suspected child abuse than any other issue on the survey also supports the findings of Davis and Mickelson (1994) who reported that school counselors responded in a legally appropriate manner to survey items related to mandatory child abuse reporting. Conversely, the finding that 72% of the school counselors in this study reported that they felt prepared to determine whether students are suicidal does not support the work of Rawls (1997) and King et al. (1999). Rawls noted that school counselors experienced difficulty with legal issues such as counseling suicidal students. King et al. found that only 38% of high school counselors felt that they could determine if a student was at risk for suicide. This discrepancy merits additional investigation.

One of the most important findings of this research study was that school counselors who recently participated in continuing education related to ethics or legal issues in counseling felt better prepared than their colleagues who had not recently participated in this type of continuing education to respond to the legal issues encountered most frequently by the participants. For the legal issue reporting suspected child abuse, participation in continuing ethical or legal education was the only variable that had a relationship to the participants' perceptions of their preparedness to respond. Considering these findings, it is notable that almost one half of the participants did not participate in continuing education in legal and ethical issues.

School counselors' perceived level of preparedness to respond to legal issues did not differ significantly considering the school counselors' years of experience or level of education. King et al. (1999) also found that counselors' confidence in their ability to identify students at risk for suicide did not differ significantly based on years of experience as a high school counselor or the education level of the counselors. Conversely, Gibson (1992) found a positive relationship between counselors' confidence in ethics beliefs and counselors' highest degree obtained, and Rawls (1997) found significant differences in counselors' knowledge of legal issues considering counselors' level of education. Once again, these conflicting results are worthy of future study.

In many states, school counselors are not required to be licensed as professional counselors, yet 49.8% of the school counselors in this study were licensed professional counselors. Furthermore, this study found that school counselors who were licensed felt better prepared to respond to being asked to reveal confidential information. This finding could relate to the laws in many states requiring a counselor to be licensed before a counselor can protect a client's right to confidentiality in a court of law. Thus, school counselors who are licensed may feel more comfortable in dealing with issues of client privacy.

Remley and Herlihy (2001) noted that malpractice lawsuits against mental health practitioners have increased dramatically in the past 10 years. However, they explained that the total number of lawsuits against mental health practitioners is still relatively small. In this study, the two legal issues which are likely to be indicative of involvement in litigation, being asked to turn over confidential records and being subpoenaed to appear as a witness in a legal proceeding, were encountered by participants least often. Furthermore, when asked to specify other legal issues encountered in the past year, only three of the 273 participants indicated that they had been threatened with a lawsuit or sued. Accordingly, the results of this study seem to support the premise that though counselors are dealing with legal issues more often, the amount of litigation involving counselors is still very low.

LIMITATIONS

One limitation of this study is that the sample consisted of school counselors who were members of ASCA. Not all school counselors are members of ASCA. Members of professional organizations may have more access than nonmembers to professional literature and professional development activities. Thus, the school counselors in this study may have been more knowledgeable about legal issues.

Another limitation of the study related to state counselor licensure laws. Some states do not provide licensure for counselors. Consequently, some of the participants did not have the opportunity to be licensed. Thus, the statistics based on the licensure variable may have been affected by state licensure opportunities.

Some universities do not teach ethics as a course, but include discussions of legal and ethical issues in the courses they do offer. Accordingly, the school counselors in this study may have had course work in legal and ethical issues in counseling, even though they did not take a specific course in legal and ethical issues. This limitation may have affected the statistics related to the course work completed by the respondents.

The study was further limited by the data-gathering potential of the survey, the self-report nature of the data, and the statistical procedures employed. For example, the use of the Likert-type scale to assess the degree to which counselors felt prepared to effectively manage legal issues limits the range of answers to the questions. Moreover, malpractice is a sensitive issue. Thus, participants may have indicated they encountered fewer legal issues than they actually have encountered and that they are better prepared to manage legal issues than they actually are.

IMPLICATIONS FOR SCHOOL COUNSELORS

This study's identification of the legal issues currently being encountered by school counselors can help school counselors become aware of specific areas of legal vulnerability. The study found that the most prevalent legal issue being encountered by school counselors is determining whether a student is suicidal. Accordingly, school counselors need to be cognizant of the warning signs of suicidal behavior and should have the skills necessary to assess a client's risk for suicide (Capuzzi & Gross, 2000). Furthermore, school counselors need to know what steps to take once they determine a student is at risk for suicide (Remley & Herlihy, 2001).

School counselors are also having to determine whether to report suspected child abuse and whether students pose a danger to others. The legal mandates related to these legal issues vary by state. Thus, school counselors need to be knowledgeable about relevant state statutes and case law.

School counselors who participated in continuing education in ethics or legal issues felt better prepared to respond to the legal issues encountered most frequently by the school counselors in this study. Yet, almost one-half of the respondents did not take part in continuing education in ethics or legal issues in counseling. Continuing legal education is particularly valuable to school counselors considering that laws related to education are constantly changing as new legal precedents and statutory law emerge. Hopefully, these findings will encourage school counselors to participate in continuing education on legal and ethical issues in counseling.

The results of this study indicate that school counselors are encountering many legal issues. Thus, school counselors are legally vulnerable. Being aware of the prevalent legal issues in the school counseling community and obtaining the education necessary to respond to these issues can help school counselors provide appropriate services for students and minimize the risk of unnecessary litigation.

Mary A. Hermann, J.D., Ph.D., *is an assistant professor, Counselor Education and Educational Psychology, Mississippi State University, Mississippi State, MS.*

REFERENCES

Ahia, C. E., & Martin, D. (1993). *The danger-to-self-or-others exception to confidentiality.* Alexandria, VA: American Counseling Association.

Capuzzi, D., & Gross, D. R. (Eds.). (2000). *Youth at risk: A prevention resource for counselors, teachers, and parents* (3rd ed.). Alexandria, VA: American Counseling Association.

Corey, G., Corey, M. S., & Callanan, P. (1998). *Issues and ethics in the helping professions* (5th ed.). Pacific Grove, CA: Brooks/Cole.

Davis, J. L., & Mickelson, D. J. (1994). School counselors: Are you aware of ethical and legal aspects of counseling. *The School Counselor, 42,* 5–13.

Fernandez, S. M. (1992). School counselor liability: A growing juggernaut (Educational Specialist Thesis, Central Missouri State University, 1992). *Dissertation Abstracts International, 31–02,* 524.

Gibson, W. T. (1992). Ethics beliefs of National Certified Counselors (Doctoral dissertation, University of Wyoming, 1992). *Dissertation Abstracts International, 53–09A,* 3108.

Glosoff, H. L., Herlihy, B., & Spence, E. B. (2000). Privileged communication in the counselor-client relationship. *Journal of Counseling and Development, 78,* 454–462.

Herndon, E. H. (1990). Legal aspects of the role of the public school counselor in North Carolina (Doctoral dissertation, University of North Carolina, Greensboro, 1990). *Dissertation Abstracts International, 51–09A,* 2985.

King, K. A., Price, J. H., Telljohann, S. K., & Wahl, J. (1999). How confident do high school counselors feel in recognizing students at risk for suicide? *American Journal of Health Behavior, 23,* 457–467.

Lawrence, G., & Kurpius, S. E. (2000). Legal and ethical issues involved when counseling minors in nonschool settings. *Journal of Counseling and Development, 78,* 130–136.

Rawls, R. K. (1997). Virginia high school counselors and school law (Doctoral dissertation, Virginia Polytechnic Institute and State University, 1997). *Dissertation Abstracts International, 58–08A,* 3024.

Remley, T. P., Jr., & Herlihy, B. (2001). *Ethical, legal, and professional issues in counseling.* Upper Saddle River, NJ: Prentice Hall.

Remley, T. P., Jr., & Sparkman, L. B. (1993). Student suicides: The counselor's limited legal liability. *The School Counselor, 40,* 164–169.

White, J., & Flynt, M. (2000). The school counselor's role in prevention and remediation of child abuse. In J. Wittmer (Ed.), *Managing your school counseling program: K–12 developmental strategies* (pp. 149–160). Minneapolis, MN: Educational Media.

Chapter 2: Students at Risk for Suicide

INTRODUCTION

Unfortunately, one of the most common dilemmas faced by school counselors today is one that poses some of the most complex challenges – students at risk for suicide. According to the American School Counselor Association (ASCA), school counselors are expected to fully respect each student's right to privacy (see ASCA position statement, *The Professional School Counselor and Confidentiality*, Appendix H–6). When students threaten to harm themselves or others, however, school counselors can no longer guarantee this confidentiality.

This exception to confidentiality is documented in the ASCA *Ethical Standards for School Counselors* (1998, §A.7.). The ASCA standards advise school counselors to consult with other professionals when working with a student who may pose a danger to him or herself (ASCA, §A.7.). Furthermore, when a counselor decides what needs to be done to protect the student, the standards dictate that school counselors inform the student of the actions to be taken (ASCA, §A.7.).

Courts have found that school personnel can be held legally liable for failing to exercise reasonable care to prevent a student's suicide (*Eisel v. Board of Education*, 1991). Courts have defined "reasonable care" as taking every threat of suicide seriously, taking precautions to protect the child, and notifying the student's parents that their child is at risk for suicide (*Grant v. Board of Trustees of Valley View School District No. 365-U*, 1997). Even so, courts have only held school counselors and other school personnel liable when they have been grossly negligent.

Though it is imperative that school counselors seriously evaluate all threats of suicide, Remley and Sparkman (1993) warned of the dangers of overreacting to such threats. Terms like "I could just shoot myself" and "I'd rather die" are often simply expressions of speech and do not indicate a serious intent to do self-harm. Thus, Remley and Sparkman not only advised school counselors to take all threats seriously but to also exercise professional judgment in determining if the student is actually at risk. Taking steps to prevent a suicide before determining that these steps are warranted is unethical, and such action could result in psychological harm to students and their families. Furthermore, if a school counselor considers the threats serious, Remley and Sparkman advised taking the least intrusive steps to keep students safe from harm.

Remley and Sparkman (1993) stated that the suicide prevention and intervention skills school counselors need to possess include the ability to recognize behaviors indicative of potential suicidal behaviors and the interpersonal skills necessary to effectively intervene when a student threatens to commit suicide. According to ASCA, the objective is to identify and intervene before students engage in self-destructive behavior (see ASCA position statement, *The Professional School Counselor and Students-at-Risk*, Appendix H–21). ASCA takes the position that school counselors should identify suicidal students, counsel them, and refer them to appropriate outside resources (see ASCA position statement, *The Professional School Counselor and Students-at-Risk*, Appendix H–21). School counselors should also to be able to provide referral sources to students and parents who need them.

The ASCA position statements highlight consultation with other school personnel as a means to identify at-risk youth (see ASCA position statement, *The Professional School Counselor and Students-at-Risk*,

Appendix H–21). Courts have also addressed the need for training all school employees in suicide prevention (*Wyke v. Polk County School Board*, 1997). School counselors can provide in-service support presentations to staff on risk factors and indicators of suicidal ideation.

To limit legal liability, schools need to create a protocol to follow should an at-risk student be identified. All school personnel, including food service staff, custodians, and bus drivers, need to be aware of this code of conduct. Capuzzi (2002) has reiterated that school personnel who are not mental health professionals must be cognizant that their role is not providing personal counseling but recognizing behaviors consistent with suicidal ideation and referring students exhibiting these behaviors to school counselors.

In this chapter, Capuzzi (2002) and Remley and Sparkman (1993) have addressed the legal and ethical issues related to counseling students at risk for suicide. Capuzzi has provided valuable information about identifying at-risk students, and planning and implementing suicide prevention programs, postvention activities, and crisis management. Additionally, he has discussed the ethical obligations of school counselors when a student has been identified as potentially suicidal, shared how to provide these at-risk youth with the services they need, and explored the legal ramifications of students attempting or completing suicide.

Likewise, Remley and Sparkman focused on why school counselors need not be overly concerned about lawsuits related to student suicide if they practice in an ethical manner and act as other school counselors would in similar circumstances.

Legal and Ethical Challenges in Counseling Suicidal Students

David Capuzzi

Suicide rates for adolescents have risen more than 300% since the 1950s, yet the rates for the population in general have remained relatively stable (King, 2001). In 1997, the suicide rate among 15- to 24-year-olds was 11.4 per 100,000 (King, 1997). Almost 86% of all suicides by youths under the age of 20 occur in 15- to 19-year-olds (National Center for Health Statistics, 1996) and estimates of completed youth suicides range from 7,000 to 9,000 a year. Even more alarming is the fact that, for every youth suicide, there are between 100 to 200 youth suicide attempts in this country (National Center for Health Statistics, 1992). Since a teacher in a typical U.S. high school classroom can expect to have at least one young man and two young women who attempted suicide in the last year (King, 2000), many states are requiring that schools include guidelines for suicide prevention, crisis management, and postvention in their written tragedy-response plans. In addition, a number of states require that all school faculty, administration, and staff participate in workshops that address the parameters of youth suicide and provide school personnel with information about risk factors and signs and symptoms as well as direction for the protocol to be followed when youth are identified as being at risk of self-harm.

Typically, school counselors are an integral part of school-based suicide prevention, crisis management, and postvention efforts, and the increased involvement with this segment of a school's population presents a number of legal and ethical challenges to counselors as well as other school faculty, administration, and staff. What are the ethical obligations of school counselors and other school personnel once a youth has been identified as potentially suicidal or has attempted or completed suicide? What are the roles of faculty, staff, and administrators and how do their roles differ from those of the school counselor and crisis team member? How do schools work with parents and guardians of minors to ensure that an appropriate constellation of services is provided for a suicidal youth? Can the school or school district be sued by families after an attempted or completed youth suicide?

The purpose of this article is to answer these questions by addressing "best practices" in the process of providing suicide prevention programs in schools. Best practices are the aspirational standards an ethical and well-informed school counselor should strive to attain in the process of planning and implementing school-based prevention, crisis management, and postvention efforts. They can be distinguished from minimally acceptable practices which, though meeting most legal standards, may not provide maximum protection to students and their families.

Since best practices, both legal and ethical, are always informed by awareness of the guidelines that theory and research provide, a brief overview of some of the literature available to school counselors on the topics of ethnic and gender differences, methods, risk factors, precipitants of acts of self-harm, myths, and the profile of a potentially suicidal adolescent is provided. This is followed by a description of best practices for creating and implementing prevention, crisis management, and postvention programs. The article concludes by highlighting the most important legal implications for school counselors' roles.

BACKGROUND

The information needed by counselors prior to planning and implementing a suicide prevention, crisis management, and postvention program for a school or school district is extensive. Such information is available to counselors through a variety of resources. Ethnic and gender differences, methods, risk factors, precipitants of attempts and completions, myths, and the possible "profile" of a suicidal youth are the topics that must be studied by school counselors interested in reaching out to this at-risk population. These topics are briefly reviewed for the purpose of providing school counselors with the background needed to meet the legal and ethical challenges they will encounter when counseling potentially suicidal students. Counselors may use the articles and books cited in this section for further study.

Ethnic and Gender Differences

Some studies on youth suicide report that the suicide rate is higher among adolescent males than among females (although adolescent women attempt three to four times as often as adolescent men). Caucasian, adolescent males complete suicide more often than any other ethnic group (Canetto & Sakinofsky, 1998; Metha, Weber, & Webb, 1998; Popenhagen & Qualley, 1998). Although a number of explanations have been proposed to account for the differences in rates among genders and races, no clear answers have been found. Some models used to explain racial differences in suicide have suggested that the extreme stress and discrimination that African Americans in the United States confront helps to create protective factors such as extended networks of social support, that lower the risk and keep the suicide rates for African American adolescents lower than those of Caucasian adolescents (Bush, 1976; Gibbs, 1988). Despite the overall pattern suggested by the data, during the period between 1980 and 2000, the suicide rates for African American adolescent males showed an increase of over 300% in the 10–14 age group and an increase of approximately 200% in the 15–19 age group (Metha et al.; Speaker & Petersen, 2000).

The literature on youth suicide continues to document the fact that Native Americans also have high adolescent suicide rates in the United States. There is considerable variability across tribes. The Navajos, for example, have suicide rates close to the national average of 11 to 13 per 100,000 of the population; some Apache groups have rates as high as 43 per 100,000 (Berlin, 1987). The high suicide rates in the Native American population have been associated with factors such as alcoholism and substance abuse, unemployment, availability of firearms, and child abuse and neglect (Berman & Jobes, 1991). In general, less traditional tribes have higher rates of suicide than do more traditional tribes (Wyche, Obolensky, & Glood, 1990). Suicide rates for both Asian-American and Hispanic-American adolescents continue to be lower than those for African-American and Native-American youth even though the 1980–1994 time period bore witness to much higher rates than previously recorded (Metha et al, 1998).

Methods

The use of firearms outranks all other methods of completed suicides; firearms are used by both genders. Studies in the United States show that availability of guns increases the risk of adolescent suicide (Brent et al., 1993; King, 2000). The second most common method is hanging and the third most common is gassing. Males use firearms and hanging more often than do females, but females use gassing and ingestion more often than do males for completed suicides (Berman & Jobes,

1991). The most common method used by suicide attempters is ingestion or overdose of medicine.

Risk Factors

As noted by Garland and Zigler (1993) and Shaffer and Craft (1999), the search for the etiology of suicide spans many areas of study. Studies of counselor awareness of risk factors continue to take place (King, 2000). Examples of risk factors that have been studied include neurotransmitter imbalances and genetic predictors, psychiatric disorders, poor self-efficacy and problem-solving skills, sexual or physical abuse, concerns over sexual identity or orientation, availability of firearms, substance abuse, violent rock music, divorce in families, unemployment and labor strikes, loss, disability, giftedness, and, interestingly, phases of the moon. It is important for school counselors to note that almost all adolescent suicide victims have experienced some form of psychiatric illness. The most prevalent psychiatric disorders among adolescents who have completed suicide appear to be affective disorders, conduct disorders or antisocial personality disorders, and substance abuse disorders (Shaffer, 1988: Shaffer & Craft). Among affective disorders, particular attention should be paid to bipolar illness and depressive disorder with comorbidity such as attention deficit disorder, conduct disorder, or substance abuse disorders (Rohde, Lewinsohn, & Seeley, 1991).

The suicide of a family member or a close friend of the family can also be a risk factor for youth suicide. Prior attempts also escalate risk and are still the best single predictors (Shaffer, Garland, Gould, Fisher, & Trautman, 1988). An adolescent experiencing a physical illness that is chronic or terminal can also be at higher risk (Capuzzi, 1994). Many researchers have studied cognitive and coping-style factors (e.g., generalized feelings of hopelessness and poor interpersonal problem-solving skills) as risk factors for youth suicide (Garland & Zigler, 1993). High neuroticism and low extraversion, high impulsiveness, low self-esteem, giftedness, disability, and an external locus of control have also been studied and can be used to predict risk (Beautrais, Joyce, & Mulder, 1999).

Precipitants

Often, attempted or completed suicide is precipitated by what, to the adolescent, is interpreted as a shameful or humiliating experience (e.g., failure at school or work, or interpersonal conflict with a romantic partner or parent). Mounting evidence indicates that adolescents who do not cope well with major and minor life events and who do not have family and peer support are more likely to have suicidal ideation (Mazza & Reynolds, 1998). The humiliation and frustration experienced by some adolescents struggling with conflicts connected with their sexual orientation may precipitate suicidal behavior (Harry, 1989; McFarland, 1998), although being gay or lesbian in and of itself may not be a risk factor for suicide (Blumenthal, 1991). Hoberman and Garfinkel (1988) found the most common precipitant of suicide in a sample of 229 youth suicides to be an argument with a boyfriend, a girlfriend, or a parent (19%), followed by school problems (14%). Other humiliating experiences such as corporal punishment and abuse also serve as precipitants; the experience of sexual or physical assault seems to be a particularly significant risk factor for adolescent women (Hoberman & Garfinkel).

Myths

One of the biggest problems connected with youth suicide is the fact that parents, teachers, mental health professionals, and the adolescent population itself are not made aware of a variety of myths and misconceptions associated with this topic. Since subsequent discussion of best practices for prevention, crisis management, and postvention in this article is based on prior awareness of this topic, the reader is referred to Capuzzi and Gross (2000) for a more complete discussion of the following myths:

- Suicide is hereditary
- Suicide happens with no warning
- Adolescents from affluent families attempt or complete suicide more often than adolescents from poor families
- Once an adolescent is suicidal, he or she is suicidal forever
- If an adolescent attempts suicide and survives, he or she will never make an additional attempt
- Adolescents who attempt or complete suicide always leave notes
- Most adolescent suicides happen late at night or during the predawn hours
- Never use the word suicide when talking to adolescents because using the word gives some adolescents the idea
- Every adolescent who attempts suicide is depressed.

THE PROFILE

The suicidal profile has been analyzed from the perspectives of both the practicing counselor or mental health practitioner and that of the empirically based researcher. Although no constellation of traits and characteristics has been identified as predictive of suicidal attempts, a number of experts (Beautrais et al., 1999; Capuzzi, 1994; Capuzzi & Golden, 1988; Capuzzi & Gross, 2000; Curran, 1987; Davis, 1983; Hafen & Frandsen, 1986; Hussain & Vandiver, 1984; Johnson & Maile, 1987;

Mazza & Reynolds, 1998) believe that about 90% of the adolescents who complete suicide (and lethal first attempts can result in completions) give cues to those around them in advance. Whether these cues are limited or numerous will depend on the adolescent, since each adolescent has a unique familial and social history. It is important for school counselors and other school personnel to recognize the signs and symptoms to facilitate prevention efforts. One of the essential components of the best practices discussed in a subsequent section of this article is teaching the profile of the suicidal or potentially suicidal youth so that referral and intervention can take place. Behavioral, verbal, and cognitive cues and personality traits are the four areas around which counselors can make observations to base their assessments of the extent of suicidal ideation and risk. They are presented below in abridged form. The reader is referred to Capuzzi and Gross (2000) for more extensive description and discussion.

Behaviors

A number of common behaviors can be noted by counselors and other practitioners as possible cues: lack of concern about personal welfare; changes in social patterns; a decline in school achievement; altered patterns of sleeping and eating; attempts to put personal affairs in order or to make amends; use or abuse of alcohol or drugs; unusual interest in how others are feeling; preoccupation with death and violence themes; sudden improvement after a period of depression; and sudden or increased promiscuity.

Verbal Cues

As noted by Schneidman, Farbverow, and Litman (1976), verbal statements can provide cues to self-destructive intentions. Such statements should be assessed and considered in relation to factors such as behavioral signs, changes in thinking patterns, motivations, and personality traits. There is no "universal" language or "style" for communicating suicidal intention. Some adolescents will openly and directly say something like "I am going to commit suicide" or "I am thinking of taking my life." Others will be far less direct and make statements such as "I'm going home," "I wonder what death is like," "I'm tired," "She'll be sorry for how she has treated me," or "Someday I'll show everyone just how serious I am about some of the things I've said."

Thinking Patterns and Motivations

In addition to behavioral and verbal cues, thinking patterns and motivations of suicidal adolescents can also be assessed and evaluated. For such an assessment to occur, it is necessary to encourage self-disclosure to learn about changes in an adolescent's cognitive set and distortions of logic and problem-solving ability. As noted by Velkoff and Huberty (1988), the motivations of suicidal adolescents can be understood more readily when suicide is viewed as fulfilling one of three primary functions: (a) an avoidance function that protects the individual from the pain perceived to be associated with a relationship or set of circumstances; (b) a control function that enables an adolescent to believe he or she has gained control of someone or something thought to be out of control, hopeless or disastrous; and (c) a communication function that lets others know that something is wrong or that too much pain or too many injuries have been accumulated.

Personality Traits

As previously noted, it would be ideal if the research on the profile of the suicidal youth provided practitioners with such a succinct profile of personality traits that youth at risk for suicide could be identified far in advance of any suicidal risk. Adolescents who fit the profile could then be assisted through individual and group counseling or other means. Although no consensus has yet been reached on the "usual," "typical," or "average" constellation of personality traits of the suicidal adolescent, researchers have agreed on a number of characteristics that seem to be common to many suicidal youth. Among these are low self-esteem, hopelessness/helplessness, isolation, high stress, need to act out, need to achieve, poor communication skills, other directedness, guilt, depression, and poor problem-solving skills.

BEST PRACTICES

At the end of the introduction to this article, four questions were posed that relate to the legal and ethical challenges in counseling suicidal students. The first three of these questions ("What are the ethical obligations of school counselors and other school personnel once a youth has been identified as potentially suicidal or attempted or completed suicide?", "What are the roles of faculty, staff, and administrators, and how do their roles differ from those of the school counselor or crisis team member?", and "How do schools work with parents and guardians to ensure that an appropriate constellation of services is provided for a suicidal youth?") are addressed through brief descriptions of school preparedness for prevention, crisis management, and postvention.

Prevention

Since a growing number of legal opinions have indicated that unanticipated acts of violence in schools (and suicide is an act of violence) can be predicted (Hermann & Remley, 2000), courts, in the future, probably will expect schools to have prevention programs in place. If they do not, courts may hold the schools accountable for suicides. A number of steps must be taken to facilitate a successful school-community prevention effort. Communication with administrators, faculty/staff in-service, preparation of crisis teams, providing for individual and group counseling options, parent education, and classroom presentations are necessary to fulfill ethical obligations and to delineate roles.

Communication with administrators. There is a compelling need for prevention, crisis management, and postvention programs for the adolescent suicide problem to be implemented in elementary, middle, and high schools throughout the country (Metha et al., 1998; Zenere & Lazarus, 1997). One of the biggest mistakes made by counselors, educators, and coordinators of counseling/student services is to initiate suicide prevention programs without first obtaining the commitment and support of administrators and others in supervisory positions. Building principals and superintendents must be supportive; otherwise efforts may not be effective.

In addition to the groundwork that must be done on the building level, it is also important to effect advance communication and planning on the district level. The superintendent, assistant superintendent, curriculum director, staff development director, student services coordinator, research and program evaluation specialist, must all commit their support to intervention efforts.

Faculty/staff in-service. Since teachers and other faculty and staff usually learn of a student's suicidal preoccupation prior to the situation being brought to the attention of the school counselor or another member of the crisis team (assuming such a team exists), all faculty and staff (e.g., teachers, aides, secretaries, administrators, custodians, bus drivers, food service personnel, librarians, school social workers) must be included in building or district level in-service on the topic of youth suicide. All should be taught the background information previously delineated so that they can make referrals to the school counselor. It is imperative that all adults in schools be educated about both youth suicide and building and district policies and protocols for prevention, crisis management, and postvention. They must be cautioned against attempting to provide personal counseling; their roles are to recognize risk and facilitate referrals. A growing number of publications provide excellent guidelines for elements of prevention programming focused on school faculty and staff (Davidson & Range, 1999; Metha et al., 1998; Zenere & Lazarus, 1997).

Preparation of crisis teams. Most schools have crisis teams composed of faculty, staff, and parents connected with a particular building. These teams often exist in conjunction with a program for the prevention and intervention efforts necessary to cope with the drug problem among young people in today's schools. With education beyond that which is provided during faculty/staff in-service programs discussed previously as well as additional supervision and evaluation of clinical skills, a crisis team can be taught how to facilitate prevention efforts in a school as well as how to respond to a student already experiencing a suicidal crisis or in need of postvention efforts.

Individual and group counseling options. Prior to providing students with any information about suicide and suicide prevention efforts in a school, arrangements must be made for the individual and group counseling services that will be needed by those who seek assistance for themselves or their friends. School counselors rarely have the opportunity to provide the counseling needed by students identified as potentially suicidal because of other responsibilities as well as very high student-to-counselor ratios. Unless such counseling options are available, any effort at prevention, crisis management, or postvention will be doomed to failure.

If the school district cannot make a commitment to providing counseling, then arrangements for referral to community agencies and private practitioners must be made. It is important to provide adolescents and their families with a variety of referral possibilities along with information on fee schedules. There may be some question about whether the school district will be liable for the cost of such counseling if the referral is made by the school. (This issue should be explored by whatever legal counsel is retained by the district.) The dilemma, of course, is that unless counseling takes place when a suicidal adolescent has been identified, the probability is high that an attempt or a completion will take place. If the school is aware of a teenager's suicidal preoccupation and does not act in the best interests of such a teenager, families may later bring suit against the district.

Parent education. Parents of students in a school in which a suicide prevention program is to be initiated should be involved in the school's efforts to educate, identify, and assist young people in this respect. Parents have a right to understand why the school is taking such steps and what the components of a school-wide effort will be. Evening or late afternoon parent education efforts can be constructive and engender additional support for a school or school district. Parents have the same information needs as faculty and staff with respect to the topic of adolescent suicide.

Classroom presentations. Debate continues surrounding the safety of adolescent suicide prevention programs that contain an educational component presented to adolescents. This debate is similar to the one that emerged years ago when schools initiated staff development and classroom presentations on the topic of physical and sexual abuse. In conjunction with this debate, a number of advocates of education and discussion efforts are focused on students in a school-wide suicide prevention effort (Capuzzi, 1988, 1994; Capuzzi & Golden, 1988; Curran, 1987; Ross, 1980; Sudak, Ford, & Rushforth, 1984; Zenere & Lazarus, 1997). These advocates recommend providing an appropriate forum in which adolescents can receive accurate information, ask questions, and learn about how to obtain help for themselves and their friends. They believe that doing so does not precipitate suicidal preoccupation or attempts (Capuzzi; Capuzzi & Gross, 2000).

A carefully prepared and well-presented classroom presentation made by a counselor or member of the school's crisis team is essential. Such a presentation should include both information on causes, myths, and symptoms as well as information about how to obtain help through the school. Under no circumstances should media be used in which adolescents are shown a suicide plan.

On the elementary level, school faculty should not present programs on the topic of suicide prevention. Their efforts are better focused on developmental counseling and classroom presentations directed at helping children develop resiliency and overcome traits (e.g., low self-esteem or poor communication skills) that may put them at risk for suicidal behavior at a later time. Although these efforts should be continued through secondary education, middle and high school students are better served through presentations that address adolescent suicide directly.

Crisis Management

School counselors often receive student referrals from other adults in the building when the student is thought to be experiencing a suicidal crisis. The principles delineated below are shared for the purpose of providing succinct guidelines for a suicide-risk assessment so that steps can be taken to prevent a possible attempt. Any assessment, phone call, or step taken in this context should be documented in case notes.

Remember the meaning of the term *crisis management*. When thinking of crisis management, it is important to understand the meaning of the word *crisis* as well as the word *management*. The word *crisis* means that the situation is not usual, normal, or average; circumstances are such that a suicidal adolescent is highly stressed and in considerable emotional discomfort. The word *management* means that the professional involved must be prepared to apply skills that are different than those required for preventive or postvention counseling. An adolescent in crisis must be assessed, directed, monitored, and guided for the purpose of preventing an act of self-destruction.

Be calm and supportive. A calm, supportive manner on the part of the intervener conveys respect for the perceptions and internal pain of an adolescent preoccupied with suicidal thoughts. Remember that such an adolescent usually feels hopeless and highly stressed. The demeanor and attitude of the helping person are pivotal in the process of offering assistance.

Be nonjudgmental. Statements such as "You can't be thinking of suicide, it is against the teachings of your church," or "I had a similar problem when I was your age and I didn't consider suicide" are totally inappropriate during a crisis situation. An adolescent's perception of a situation is, at least temporarily, reality and that reality must be respected.

Encourage self-disclosure. The very act of talking about painful emotions and difficult circumstances is the first step in what can become a long-term healing process. A professional helper may be the first person with whom such a suicidal adolescent has shared and trusted in months or even years, and it may be difficult for the adolescent to confide simply because of lack of experience with communicating thoughts and feelings. It is important to support and encourage self-disclosure so that an assessment of lethality can be made early in the intervention process.

Acknowledge the reality of suicide as a choice but do not "normalize" suicide as a choice. It is important for professionals to let adolescents know that they are not alone and isolated with respect to suicidal preoccupation. It is also important to communicate the idea that suicide is a choice, a problem-solving option, not a good choice, and that there are better choices and options.

Actively listen and positively reinforce. It is important, during the initial stages of the crisis management process, to let the adolescent who is potentially at risk for suicide know you are listening carefully and really understanding how difficult life has been. Being listened to, heard, and respected are powerful and empowering experiences for anyone who is feeling at a loss for how to cope.

Do not attempt in-depth counseling. Although it is very important for a suicidal adolescent to begin to overcome feelings of despair and to develop a sense of control as soon as possible, the emotional turmoil and stress experienced during a crisis usually makes in-depth counseling impossible. Developing a plan to begin lessening the sense of crisis an adolescent may be experiencing is extremely important, however, and should be accomplished as soon as possible. Crisis management necessitates the development of a plan to lessen the crisis; this plan should be shared with the adolescent so that it is clear that circumstances will improve. In-depth counseling cannot really take place during the height of a suicidal crisis.

Do not do an assessment alone. It is a good idea to enlist the assistance of another professional, with expertise in crisis management, when an adolescent thought to be at risk for suicide is brought to a school counselor's attention. School counselors should ask a colleague to come into the office and assist with assessment. It is always a good idea to have the support of a colleague who understands the dynamics of a suicidal crisis; in addition, the observations made by two professionals are more likely to be more comprehensive. Since suicidal adolescents may present a situation that, if misjudged or mismanaged, could result in a subsequent attempt or completion, it is in the best interests of both the professional and the client for professionals to work collaboratively whenever possible. It should also be noted that liability questions are less likely to become issues and professional judgment is less likely to be questioned if assessment of the severity of a suicidal crisis and associated recommendations for crisis management have been made on a collaborative basis.

Ask questions to assess lethality. A number of dimensions must be explored to assess lethality. This assessment can be accomplished through an interview format (a crisis situation is not conducive to the administration of a written appraisal instrument). Readers are referred to Capuzzi and Gross (2000) for a complete description of the assessment process and a list and explanation of the questions. It is important to understand that the role of the school counselor and crisis team is to determine if a student is potentially suicidal. Once this determination has been made, the student should be reassessed by the agency identified by the school district to make the final decision about the degree of risk for a suicide attempt or completion.

Make crisis management decisions. If, as a result of an assessment made by at least two professionals, the adolescent is thought to be potentially suicidal, the student should be seen by an outside agency. Under no circumstances should the student be left alone or asked to return home or meet with a mental health counselor without being accompanied by a parent or guardian.

Notify parents. Parents of minors must be notified and asked for assistance when an adolescent is determined to be at risk for a suicide attempt. Often, adolescents may attempt to elicit a promise of confidentiality from a school counselor who learns about suicidal intent. Such confidentiality is not possible or required (Remley & Herlihy, 2001); the welfare of the adolescent is the most important consideration.

Sometimes parents do not believe that their child is suicidal. At times, parents may be adamant in their demands that the school or mental health professional withdraw their involvement. Although some professionals worry about liability issues in such circumstances, liability is higher if such an adolescent is allowed to leave unmonitored with no provision for follow-up assistance. Schools should confer with legal counsel to understand liability issues and to make sure that the best practices are followed in such circumstances. It may be necessary to refer the student to protective services for children and families when parents or guardians refuse to cooperate.

Consider hospitalization. Hospitalization can be the option of choice during a suicidal crisis, if the parents are not cooperating, when the risk is high. An adolescent who has not been sleeping or eating, for example, may be totally exhausted or highly agitated. The care and safety that can be offered in a psychiatric unit of a hospital is often needed until the adolescent can experience a lowered level of stress, obtain food and rest, and realize that others consider the circumstances painful and worthy of attention. The protocol in the school and school district's written tragedy response plan should be followed in such circumstances. School counselors and crisis team members should not take it upon themselves to transport a student to the psychiatric unit of a local hospital; this should be facilitated by the staff of the agency the school collaborates with when such circumstances arise.

Refuse to allow the youth to return to school without an assessment by a mental health counselor, psychologist, psychiatrist, or other qualified professional. An increasing number of school districts are adopting this policy. Although it could be argued that preventing a suicidal youth from returning to school might exacerbate suicidal ideation and intent, this policy increases the probability that the youth will receive mental health counseling and provides the school with support in the process of preventing the youth from engaging in self harm. Acquiring a release from a third party for a student's return also provides an element of protection in the event that an attempt or completion takes place at a later time and the family files a lawsuit.

Postvention

When an adolescent has attempted or completed a suicide, it is imperative, particularly in a school setting, for the counselors to be aware of the impact of such an event on the "system." Usually, within just a few hours, the fact that an adolescent has attempted or completed suicide has been chronicled through the peer group. This could present a problem to the faculty and staff in a given school building since not answering questions raised by students can engender the sharing of misinformation or rumors. The following guidelines should prove helpful to school counselors in the process of planning and implementing postvention efforts:

- The principal of the building in which a student has attempted or completed suicide (even though such an incident most likely occurred off the school campus) should organize a telephone network to notify all faculty and staff that a mandatory meeting will take place prior to school the next morning. The principal should share information and answer questions about what happened during such a meeting. In the case of a suicide completion, it is recommended that the principal provide all faculty and staff with an announcement that can be read in each class rather than over a public address system, so that everyone in the school receives the same information. The announcement should confirm the loss and emphasize the services the school and community will be providing during the day and subsequent days. Details about the circumstances or the family of the deceased should not be given so that confidentiality is maintained in that regard.

- Faculty and staff should be instructed to answer student questions that spontaneously arise.
- Faculty and staff should be told to excuse students from class if they are upset and need to spend time in the office of the building counselor or another member of the crisis team.
- Parents who are upset by the suicidal incident should be directed to a designated individual to have questions answered. Parents should also be provided with options for counseling, whether this counseling is provided by school personnel or referred to members of the mental health community.
- At times, newspaper and television journalists contact the school for information about both the attempt or the completion and the school's response to the "aftermath." It is important to direct all such inquiries to a designated individual to avoid the problems created by inconsistency or sharing inaccurate information.
- Be alert to delayed or enhanced grief responses on the part of students prior to the anniversary of a suicide completion. Often students will need opportunity to participate in a support group with peers or individual counseling prior to and, perhaps, beyond the anniversary date.
- Do not conduct a memorial service on the school campus after a suicide because doing so may provide reinforcement to other students preoccupied with suicidal ideation. This means that it is unwise to conduct an on-campus memorial service after a death for any reason—it is difficult to explain why a student who has suicided is not being remembered when another student, faculty or staff has been memorialized previously. Excuse students to attend the off-campus memorial or funeral. Do the same thing for deaths for other reasons.
- Early in the sequence of events, one or two individuals from the school should contact the family and ask if there is any support it might need that the school can provide. It is a good idea to offer such assistance periodically, since so many families are left alone with their grief once the memorial or funeral has taken place.

ADDITIONAL CONSIDERATIONS

The fourth question posed in the beginning of this article is "Can the school or school district be sued by families after an attempted or completed suicide?" In a pertinent review of the results of school violence litigation against educators, Hermann and Remley (2000) noted that, even though school personnel are expected to exert reasonable care to prevent harm to students, courts have been reluctant to hold educators liable for injuries related to violence or self-harm. Usually state law claims fail because so much of today's school violence (and suicide attempts and completions are components of school violence) results from what can be termed spontaneous acts of violence. This statement should not, however, lull school personnel into a false sense of security, since a growing number of legal opinions have indicated that an unanticipated act of violence can be predictable and thus actionable under state law. Counselors, teachers, administrators, and other members of school staffs can protect themselves by writing and implementing prevention, crisis-management, and postvention policies and procedures for protecting youth from self-harm.

These policy and procedural documents should mandate in-service for school personnel so that all adults in the school environment recognize risk factors, myths, and possible behavioral, verbal, cognitive, and personality indicators as well as role responsibilities and limitations. Best practices are more likely to be followed if schools take a proactive rather than a reactive stance to this growing epidemic in our nation's schools.

CONCLUDING COMMENTS

Because of the legal and ethical considerations delineated in this article, counselors and other school personnel who are interested in learning how to identify potentially suicidal youth must obtain more extensive information than that provided here. In addition, since school counselors may need to provide follow-up supportive counseling once a suicidal youth returns to school, school counselors should obtain supervision from professionals who are experienced in working with suicidal youth after a suicidal crisis or a suicide attempt. Generally, prevention, crisis management, and postvention activities should not be attempted by anyone who has not completed a 2-year CACREP accredited or CACREP equivalent graduate program. Membership in the American Association of Suicidology or the American Foundation of Suicidology, participation in workshops and conferences focused on the topic of youth suicide, and consistent reading of the *Journal of Suicide and Life-Threatening Behavior* and other books and journals is imperative so that best practices are followed in a way that ensures that legal and ethical standards are integrated into the prevention, crisis management, and postvention efforts of school counselors.

A youth who becomes suicidal is communicating the fact that he or she is experiencing difficulty with issues such as problem-solving, managing stress, and expressing feelings. It is important for school counselors to respond in constructive, safe, informed ways, because the future of their communities is dependent upon individuals who are positive, functional, and able to cope with the complex demands of life.

David Capuzzi, Ph.D., LPC, *is a professor and coordinator, Counselor Education, Graduate School of Education, Portland State University, OR.*

REFERENCES

Beautrais, A. L., Joyce, P. R., & Mulder, R. T. (1999). Personality traits and cognitive styles as risk factors for serious suicide attempts among young people. *Suicide and Life-Threatening Behavior, 29,* 37–47.

Berlin, I. N. (1987). Suicide among American Indian adolescents: An overview. *Suicide and Life Threatening Behavior, 17,* 218–232.

Berman, A. L., & Jobes, D. A. (1991). *Adolescent suicide: Assessment and intervention.* Washington, DC: American Psychological Association.

Blumenthal, S. J. (1991). Letter to the editor. *Journal of the American Medical Association, 265,* 2806–2807.

Brent, D. A., Perper, J. A., Moritz, G., Baugher, M., Schweers, J., & Roth, C. (1993). Firearms and adolescent suicide: A community case-control study. *American Journal of Diseases in Children, 147,* 1066–1071.

Bush, J. A. (1976). Suicide and Blacks. *Suicide and Life-Threatening Behavior, 6,* 216–222.

Canetto, S. S., & Sakinofsky, I. (1998). The gender paradox in suicide. *Suicide and Life-Threatening Behavior, 28,* 1–23.

Capuzzi, D. (1988). *Counseling and intervention strategies for adolescent suicide prevention.* (Contract No. 400-86-0014). Ann Arbor, MI: ERIC Counseling and Personnel Services Clearinghouse.

Capuzzi, D. (1994). *Suicide prevention in the schools: Guidelines for middle and high school settings.* Alexandria, VA: American Counseling Association.

Capuzzi, D., & Golden, L. (Eds.). (l988). *Preventing adolescent suicide.* Muncie, IN: Accelerated Development.

Capuzzi, D., & Gross, D. (2000). "I don't want to live": The adolescent at risk for suicidal behavior. In D. Capuzzi & D. Gross (Eds.), *Youth at risk: A prevention resource for counselors, teachers and parents* (3rd ed., pp. 319–352). Alexandria, VA: American Counseling Association.

Curran, D. F. (l987). *Adolescent suicidal behavior.* Washington, DC: Hemisphere.

Davidson, M. W., & Range, L. M. (1999). Are teachers of children and young adolescents responsive to suicide prevention training modules? Yes. *Death Studies, 23,* 61–71.

Davis, P. A. (l983). *Suicidal adolescents.* Springfield, IL: Charles C. Thomas.

Garland, A. F., & Zigler, E. (1993). Adolescent suicide prevention: Current research and social policy implications. *American Psychologist, 43,* 169–182.

Gibbs, J. T. (1988). Conceptual, methodological, and sociocultural issues in Black youth suicide: Implications for assessment and early intervention. *Suicide and Life-Threatening Behavior, 18*, 73–79.

Hafen, B. Q., & Frandsen, K. J. (1986). *Youth suicide: Depression and loneliness.* Provo, UT: Behavioral Health Associates.

Harry, J. (1989). Sexual identity issues. *Report of the Secretary's Task Force on Youth Suicide: Vol. 2. Risk factors for youth suicide* (DHHS Publication No. ADM 89-1622). Washington, DC: Government Printing Office.

Hermann, M. A., & Remley, T. P., Jr. (2000). Guns, violence, and schools: The results of school violence—litigation against educators and students: Shedding more constitutional rights at the school house gate. *Loyola Law Review, 46*, 389–439.

Hoberman, H. M., & Garfinkel, B. D. (1988). Completed suicide in children and adolescents. *Journal of the American Academy of Child and Adolescent Psychiatry, 27*, 688–695.

Hussain, S. A., & Vandiver, K. T. (1984). *Suicide in children and adolescents.* New York: SP Medical and Scientific Books.

Johnson, S. W., & Maile, L. J. (1987). *Suicide and the schools: A handbook for prevention, intervention, and rehabilitation.* Springfield, IL: Charles C. Thomas.

King, K. A. (1997). Suicidal behavior in adolescence. In R. W. Maris, M. M. Silverman, & S. S. Canetto (Eds.), *Review of suicidology* (pp. 61–95). New York: Guilford.

King, K. A. (2000). Preventing adolescent suicide: Do high school counselors know the risk factors? *Professional School Counseling, 3*, 255–263.

King, K. A. (2001). Tri-level suicide prevention covers it all. *Education Digest, 67*, 55–61.

Mazza, J. J., & Reynolds, W. M. (1998). A longitudinal investigation of depression, hopelessness, social support, and major and minor life events and their relation to suicidal ideation in adolescents. *Journal of Suicide and Life-Threatening Behavior, 28*, 358–374.

McFarland, W. P. (1998). Gay, lesbian, and bisexual student suicide. *Professional School Counseling, 1*(1), 26–29.

Metha, A., Weber, B., & Webb, L. D. (1998). Youth suicide prevention: A survey and analysis of policies and efforts in the 50 states. *Suicide and Life-Threatening Behavior, 28*, 150–164.

National Center for Health Statistics. (1992). Advance report of final mortality statistics. *NCHS Monthly Vital Statistics Report, 40*(6). Hyattsville, MD: Author.

National Center for Health Statistics. (1996). Advance report of final mortality statistics, 1994. *NCHS Monthly Vital Statistics Report, 45* (Suppl. 3). Hyattsville, MD: Author.

Popenhagen, M. P., & Qualley, R. M. (1998). Adolescent suicide: Detection, intervention, and prevention. *Professional School Counseling, 1*(1), 30–35.

Remley, T. P., Jr., & Herlihy, B. (2001). *Ethical, legal, and professional issues in counseling.* Upper Saddle River, NJ: Merrill/Prentice Hall.

Rohde, P., Lewinsohn, P., & Seeley, J. R. (1991). Comorbidity of unipolar depression: Comorbidity with other mental disorders in adolescents and adults. *Journal of Abnormal Psychology, 100*, 214–222.

Ross, C. (1980). Mobilizing schools for suicide prevention. *Suicide and Life-Threatening Behavior, 10*, 239–243.

Schneidman, E., Farbverow, N., & Litman, R. (1976). *The psychology of suicide.* New York: Jason Aronson.

Shaffer, D. (1988). The epidemiology of teen suicide: An examination of risk factors. *Journal of Clinical Psychiatry, 49*, 36–41.

Shaffer, D., & Craft, L. (1999). Methods of adolescent suicide prevention. *Journal of Clinical Psychiatry, 60,* 70–74.

Shaffer, D., Garland, A., Gould, M., Fisher, P., & Trautman, P. (1988). Preventing teenage suicide: A critical review. *Journal of the American Academy of Child and Adolescent Psychiatry, 27,* 675–687.

Speaker, K. M., & Petersen, G. J. (2000). School violence and adolescent suicide: Strategies for effective intervention. *Educational Review, 52,* 65–73.

Sudak, H., Ford, A., & Rushforth, N. (1984). Adolescent suicide: An overview. *American Journal of Psychotherapy, 38,* 350–369.

Velkoff, P., & Huberty, T. J. (1988). Thinking patterns and motivation. In D. Capuzzi & L. Golden (Eds.), *Preventing adolescent suicide* (pp. 111–147). Muncie, IN: Accelerated Development.

Wyche, K., Obolensky, N., & Glood, E. (1990). American Indian, Black American, and Hispanic American youth. In M. J. Rotheram-Borus, J. Bradley, & N. Obolensky (Eds.), *Planning to live: Evaluating and treating suicidal teens in community settings* (pp. 355–389). Tulsa: University of Oklahoma.

Zenere, F. J., III, & Lazarus, P. J. (1997). The decline of youth suicidal behavior in an urban, multicultural public school system following the introduction of a suicide prevention and intervention program. *Suicide and Life-Threatening Behavior, 27,* 387–403.

Student Suicides: The Counselor's Limited Legal Liability

Theodore P. Remley, Jr.
Lavinia B. Sparkman

Skilled school counselors who practice in an ethical manner should not be overly concerned about the possibility of lawsuits related to student suicides being brought against them. Because there are few available options that will ensure the safety of a suicidal client (short of hospitalization), Furrow (1980) concluded that counselors will seldom be held responsible for the failure to prevent a suicide.

Lawsuits may always be filed in our system of justice, but only counselors who lack appropriate skills or who are negligent in their care of students will be held accountable by courts for suicide attempts or deaths of their students. The suicide prevention skills a school counselor should possess include the ability to recognize behaviors of students who have a potential for committing suicide; the interpersonal skills necessary to help students, their families, and other affected individuals when a suicide attempt is threatened; and the knowledge of referral resources that are necessary in crisis situations. Practicing in an ethical manner includes keeping private information confidential; informing others after it has been determined that a student is at risk; consulting with colleagues and experts when uncertainty exists regarding the potential for suicide attempts; and staying informed of current information in the area of student suicides.

DIFFICULTY IN PREDICTION

As in other areas of human behavior that involve future behavior such as dangerousness, substance abuse, or criminal activity, it is impossible to predict future suicide attempts of individuals (Dawidoff, 1973). Whether a particular student will attempt suicide can never be known for sure. There is a body of knowledge regarding the warning signs of suicide that school counselors have the responsibility of knowing (Dempsey, 1986; Herring, 1990; Kalafat, 1990; Martin & Dixon, 1986; Matter & Matter, 1984; McBrien, 1983; Peach & Reddick, 1991; Perrone, 1987; Wellman, 1984). Even if counselors possess this information, however, they still must exercise their professional judgment when a potential suicide situation arises with a particular student (Huey & Remley, 1988). All professionals are required to exercise their judgment from time to time, and courts do not hold professionals responsible for errors in judgment unless the judgment was clearly substandard to what the public has a right to expect from professionals with similar backgrounds, education, and experience (Prosser, 1971). Negligence must be proven in malpractice cases (Simon, 1987).

A primary factor that distinguishes professionals from their non-professional counterparts is that professionals possess specialized knowledge and skills. In professional fields, differences of opinion exist regarding proper procedures, and professionals are expected to exercise their best judgment with no guarantees their decisions will achieve desired results. If professional judgment were not required in anticipating student suicides, nonprofessionals could assess and prevent such unfortunate acts. Because predicting future human behavior will always be limited to educated guesses, however, the care of suicidal students will continue to be the responsibility of school counselors and other mental health professionals.

Overreactions

Most school counselors worry that they will either fail to recognize a potentially suicidal student or will do too little to prevent an attempt once a suicidal student has been identified. Such a concern is, of course, justified, because human life is at risk; however, some school counselors who are uninformed regarding their professional responsibilities overreact when they have the slightest suspicion that a student may be suicidal. Although suicidal ideation cannot be ignored (Stefanowski-Harding, 1990), inappropriate reactions may include hysterical calls to parents, attempts to physically restrain students, or calls to emergency squads. Such unwarranted responses are detrimental to students and to the credibility of school counseling programs.

Although it is true that every mention of suicidal ideation by students should be taken seriously, school counselors still have the responsibility of exercising their professional judgment, and could, in some circumstances, determine that students who mention the possibility of suicide are not currently at risk. This responsibility for the exercise of professional judgment is always present for school counselors. Automatically taking extreme steps to prevent a potential suicide without first determining that such steps are warranted is unethical and unprofessional and could cause serious psychological injury to students and their families.

Consider the following scenario: An eighth-grade student is discussing with his school counselor the recent separation of his parents and the pain the event has caused him. In the past, he has been a well-adjusted student. Near the end of the counseling session, the student says that he would rather be dead than go through this experience. The counselor makes a reassuring response and ends the session. When the student leaves, the counselor immediately calls both parents and tells them that he fears their child might commit suicide because of their impending divorce and recommends that immediate steps be taken to prevent their son from committing suicide.

It is not difficult to imagine the negative results of this counselor's precipitous action. The student will feel betrayed that the counseling relationship he considered confidential has been disclosed. He might be reluctant to seek help for emotional problems in the future because of this incident. The student's parents will be alarmed and most likely will overreact themselves, and their marital problems could be intensified because of this counselor's inappropriate actions.

Although such suits are seldom filed because the harm is so difficult to prove, the parents could sue this counselor for malpractice, claiming that the counselor should have known better than to react in the manner in which he did. The parents could claim that the stress they and their son experienced as a result of this counselor's inappropriate action was severe enough to warrant that they be compensated for damages. The likelihood of such suits is slim, but this scenario was presented to demonstrate that counselors have not only an ethical, but also a legal responsibility to exercise sound judgment and to avoid overreacting to suicidal ideation. The duty of care owed to clients by professional counselors includes the avoidance of actions that add to their problems.

In the situation described earlier, the school counselor should have questioned the student further regarding his statement that he would rather be dead. Had the counselor found no further evidence through such questioning that the student might be suicidal, an appropriate response for the counselor might have been to schedule another appointment with the student in the near future, deciding that the remark was simply an exaggerated statement of the student's feelings. If the counselor determined that the student was suicidal, he should have been taken the least intrusive steps available to ensure the student's safety (such as informing his parents in an appropriate manner) and should have included the student in the planning and the process.

CONFIDENTIALITY

School counselors have a general ethical and legal responsibility to keep secret any confidential information related to them by students, parents, teachers, and other school officials. Nonetheless, there are some clear exceptions to this confidentiality obligation (VandeCreek & Knapp, 1984). Exceptions include situations in which (a) the other party gives permission or requests that the counselor relate the information to a third person, (b) the counselor is ordered by a court to disclose information and there is no privileged communication statute in the state protecting such information; and (c) the other party is a danger to self or others. The danger to self or others is an exception to the ethical confidentiality obligation that must be used quite often by counselors who provide services for minors, because children are assumed not to be capable of making many important decisions for themselves.

The ethical concept of confidentiality and the legal concept of privileged communication have been implemented by our society to encourage clients to give accurate, complete information to professionals who have the responsibility of helping them. If clients did not feel sure that their secrets would be kept confidential by professionals, they might not seek help or might only disclose partial information. Despite the importance of privacy in counseling relationships, certain considerations outweigh the general goal of confidentiality. Society values human life above all other considerations. Therefore, when clients present a danger to themselves, school counselors must set aside their concern for confidentiality and take whatever steps are necessary to prevent students from taking their own lives. Stadler (1990) has commented, however, that this exception to the general rules of confidentiality is easier to articulate than it is to implement. It is very stressful for counselors to make decisions when working with suicidal clients.

PREVENTION PROGRAMS

School counselors may determine that an active student suicide prevention program is necessary in their particular school. Such a professional decision might be made because of the particular population served, the number of at-risk students in the school, or the unfortunate fact that suicide attempts or suicides have occurred in the school (Coder, Nelson, & Aylward, 1991; Martin, Martin, Barrett-Kruse, & Waterstreet, 1988; Siehl, 1990).

Prevention programs are offered because school counselors feel their students need such interventions. Counselors have an ethical obligation to provide students with the counseling services they need. On the other hand, there does not appear to be a legal requirement that prevention programs be made available to students under any circumstances. It would seem impossible to prove that a school counselor's failure to provide a suicide prevention program was the direct or primary cause of a student's attempting suicide or committing suicide. Therefore, fear of being held legally accountable for not providing a suicide prevention program should not be the motivation for offering such a service. Instead, school counselors should only provide suicide prevention programs when they have made a professional determination that such a program would benefit their students.

School counselors who do not offer a suicide prevention program have a responsibility to be knowledgeable about the subject matter and to deliver their services in an ethical and professional manner.

Some discussion in the profession has suggested that school suicide prevention programs might actually precipitate, rather than prevent, student suicides. There is always the possibility that suicide attempts or suicides may occur in a school after a suicide prevention program has been delivered. Therefore, school counselors who decide to offer such programs should be convinced themselves that more of a danger exists in not offering such a program than there would be in offering it. In addition, counselors should be ready to defend their professional decision to offer a suicide prevention program if it is ever questioned. They should be able to cite the professional literature that favors such programs and counter any arguments that they are more harmful than helpful.

All school counseling programs involve some degree of risk that students may react in a manner that is harmful to them as a result of the intervention. School counselors must not, however, become so fearful of being held accountable for their interactions with students that they stop providing services needed by their students. Professionals must be willing to assume some risks if they are to be effective. School counselors who spend a great deal of energy protecting themselves from legal liability probably have little time or creativity left for serving the needs of their students.

INVOLVING ADULTS

Unfortunately, school counselors who inform school administrators or parents that a student is at risk find that some adults are reluctant to become involved. Although most react appropriately with care and concern, occasionally other adults accuse the school counselor of overreacting and deny that this particular student, who seems so well-adjusted, could be in danger of committing suicide (Wellman, 1984).

The school counselor's legal liability ends when school authorities or parents have been notified that a student is at risk and appropriate preventative actions have been recommended. Nonetheless, if students are not helped at that point by other responsible and significant adults, the counseling needs of the student certainly have not been met.

If the warning and advice of school counselors regarding an at-risk student are ignored or discounted, one possible response is for counselors to become more directly involved with suicidal students. Scheduling frequent visits with such students, requesting promises from the students that they will not harm themselves, and giving the students hot-line telephone numbers may be appropriate. School counselors have an ethical responsibility to do all they can to prevent student suicides, even when school authorities or parents of students refuse to involve themselves in the problem. Of course, school counselors who are forced to assume the responsibility alone for preventing suicides of students do assume more risk for liability if students do attempt to end their lives, but sometimes there are no other alternatives and assumption of additional legal liability may be the only way to discharge an ethical obligation.

Further exploration of this problem is needed, and strategies must be developed to assist school counselors in enlisting the help of administrators and parents with suicidal students when they are reluctant to become involved (Nelson & Crawford, 1990).

RECOMMENDATIONS

Student suicide is a problem that concerns many school counselors. Although counselors are most interested in protecting the safety and preserving the lives of their students, they also may be fearful of their legal liability regarding the identification of suicidal students.

School counselors are advised that they are responsible for taking action to prevent students from harming themselves if it is determined that a student is at risk. Determinations are difficult to make, but counselors must become familiar with the warning signs. The approach that is ethically sound and protects them legally when they are unsure whether a student is at risk is for counselors to consult with colleagues and experts (Sheeley & Herlihy, 1989). Because there is no certainty in predicting future student behavior, a consensus of professional opinions is the most a court of law could expect.

School counselors are responsible for identification of student problems and referral, if necessary. The counselor's role and responsibilities in the school environment do not allow for the rendering of extended or intensive counseling services needed by some students. Counselors must refer and then consult with and support the work of counselors outside the school, but they are not responsible for providing continuing counseling services for students who have been identified as suicidal.

School counselors are encouraged to provide their students with the counseling services needed. A counselor's only legal obligation is to practice in a competent manner.

Theodore P. Remley, Jr., *is the executive director of the American Counseling Association in Alexandria, Virginia.* **Lavinia B. Sparkman** *is a counselor in continuing education, Mississippi State University, Starkville.*

REFERENCES

Coder, T. L., Nelson, R. E., & Aylward, L. K. (1991). Suicide among secondary students. *The School Counselor, 38*, 358–361.

Dawidoff, D. J. (1973). *The malpractice of psychiatrists.* Springfield, IL: Thomas.

Dempsey, R. A. (1986). *The trauma of adolescent suicide: A time for special leadership by principals.* Reston, VA: National Association of Secondary School Principals.

Furrow, B. R. (1980). *Malpractice in psychotherapy.* Lexington, MA: Heath and Company.

Herring, R. (1990). Suicide in the middle school: Who said kids will not? *Elementary School Guidance & Counseling, 25,*129–137.

Huey, W. C., & Remley, T. P., Jr. (Eds.). (1988). *Ethical and legal issues in school counseling.* Alexandria, VA: American School Counselor Association.

Kalafat, J. (1990). Adolescent suicide and the implications for school response programs. *The School Counselor, 37,* 359–369.

Martin, M., Martin, D., Barrett-Kruse, C., & Waterstreet, D. (1988). A community response to an adolescent suicide. *The School Counselor, 35,* 204–209.

Martin, N. K., & Dixon, P. N. (1986). Adolescent suicide: Myths, recognition, and evaluation. *The School Counselor, 33,* 265–271.

Matter, D. E., & Matter, R. M. (1984). Suicide among elementary school children: A serious concern for counselors. *Elementary School Guidance & Counseling, 13,* 260–267.

McBrien, R. J. (1983). Are you thinking of killing yourself? Confronting students' suicidal thoughts. *The School Counselor, 30,* 75–82.

Nelson, R. E., & Crawford, B. (1990). Suicide among elementary school-aged children. *Elementary School Guidance & Counseling, 25,* 123–128.

Peach, L., & Reddick, T. L. (1991). Counselors can make a difference in preventing adolescent suicide. *The School Counselor, 39,*107–110.

Perrone, P. A. (1987). Counselor response to adolescent suicide. *The School Counselor, 35,* 51–57.

Prosser, W. L. (1971). *Handbook of the law of torts* (4th ed.). St. Paul, MN: West.

Sheeley, V. L., & Herlihy, B. (1989). Counseling suicidal teens: A duty to warn and protect. *The School Counselor, 37*, 89–97.

Siehl, P. M. (1990). Suicide prevention: A new disaster plan—What a school should do when faced with a suicide. *The School Counselor, 38*, 52–57.

Simon, R. I. (1987). *Clinical psychiatry and the law.* Washington, DC: American Psychiatric Press.

Stadler, H. A. (1990). Confidentiality. In B. Herlihy & L. B. Golden (Eds.), *Ethical standards casebook* (pp. 102–110). Alexandria, VA: American Association for Counseling and Development.

Stefanowski-Harding, S. (1990). Child suicide: A review of the literature and implications for school counselors. *The School Counselor, 37*, 328–336.

VandeCreek, L., & Knapp, S. (1984). Counselors, confidentiality, and life-endangering clients. *Counselor Education and Supervision, 24*, 51–57.

Wellman, M. M. (1984). The school counselor's role in the communication of suicidal ideation by adolescents. *The School Counselor, 32*, 104–109.

Chapter 3: Students at Risk for Violence

INTRODUCTION

School violence remains a key legal and ethical issue for the school counselor. Because prevention and awareness can go a long way in reducing this growing threat, it is important we dedicate a chapter to understanding the whole picture so we can tackle the dilemmas surrounding it.

Most in the profession know school counselors are ethically and legally obligated to make reasonable efforts to prevent school violence. The *Ethical Standards for School Counselors* (American School Counselor Association, ASCA, 1998) provide that, when a student's behavior is indicative of clear and imminent danger to others, school counselors also must inform the appropriate authorities (ASCA, § A.7.). The ethical standards also recommend that school counselors consult with other professionals when working with students who may pose a danger to others (ASCA, § A.7.).

Likewise, legal standards also dictate school counselors take reasonable action when a student poses a danger to others (Bailey, 2001).

Courts have found that schools have a duty to prevent potential violence in the school setting (*Lavine v. Blaine School District*, 2001). In fact, current case law reveals all indicators of potential violence be taken seriously (Hermann & Finn, 2002). Furthermore, courts have held that school personnel acted reasonably by removing students from school when they have threatened harm or exhibited homicidal imagery in schoolwork (Hermann & Finn). Courts also have supported school personnel who removed students from school until a psychiatrist's evaluation determined the student did not pose a danger to others—even if the at-risk behavior exhibited was minimal and no other evidence indicating a serious threat of harm existed (Hermann & Finn).

Though school officials have a legal duty to provide a safe environment for children to learn, courts recognize it is scientifically impossible for professionals to accurately predict all violent acts. Yet, faced with increasing school violence, school personnel have struggled to find methods for identifying at-risk students. One trend in predicting violence has been student profiling, in which students are identified as being at risk for violence because they exhibit certain traits. There is, however, no accurate profile of students at risk for violence. Furthermore, profiling students is poor policy because students exhibiting these "potentially violent" behavior patterns can unwillingly become stigmatized and, as such, may compromise their constitutional privacy rights.

Though student profiling has serious legal implications, students who commit acts of violence often do reveal indicators of impending violent behavior, and school counselors can use these indicators to help identify potentially violent students and intervene before violent acts occur (Daniels, 2002). Still, although knowledge of youth violence characteristics is important, Daniels has advised school counselors to remain flexible and open to a variety of risk assessment strategies until more empirical information on school violence is available. Daniels also stressed the importance of school counselors in seeking training in threat assessment and crisis response. Daniels also has suggested that school counselors use their knowledge and skills to help schools design and implement violence prevention programs and crisis response plans.

ASCA also has provided school counselors with guidelines to identify and manage school violence, with a position that one of the school counselor's roles is to help identify at-risk students (see ASCA position statement, *The Professional School Counselor and Students-at-Risk*, Appendix H–21). Since the school counselor's role also includes supporting programs related to violence prevention and intervention (see ASCA position statement, *The Professional School Counselor and the Promotion of Safe Schools*, Appendix H–16), ASCA also recommends that school counselors implement comprehensive, developmental counseling programs and work with other school personnel and community resources to provide early identification and intervention for at-risk students. Programming should emphasize teaching nonviolent alternatives to dispute resolution, communication skills, and diversity acceptance. School counselors also should be prepared to become school leaders when emergencies arise (see ASCA position statement, *The Professional School Counselor and Critical Incident Response in the Schools*, Appendix H–9).

Also in this chapter, Hermann and Finn (2002) have presented a legal and ethical perspective on the role of school counselors in preventing school violence with an article that examines the legal and ethical duties of counselors, characteristics of at-risk students and strategies for prevention. Equally important, Isaacs (1997) discussed the *Tarasoff* case and the implications of this case for school counselors, and Bailey (2001) reviewed the legal implications of identifying potentially violent students through the use of profiling. Finally, Daniels (2002) described risk assessment approaches for students' violent threats.

School counselors can play a vital role in reducing school violence. To effectively do so, they need to sharpen their skills and become aware of the resources available to them. First, they should learn the risk factors and warning signs of at-risk students. Next, they should understand how to intervene appropriately in the lives of at-risk students. And third, school counselors should help prevent school violence by initiating violence prevention programs and a referral system for school personnel and students seeking additional resources. It is our hope these articles show the whole picture and help school counselors keep current about effective prevention, risk assessment, and intervention.

An Ethical and Legal Perspective on the Role of School Counselors in Preventing Violence in Schools

Mary A. Hermann
Abbé Finn

Recent, highly publicized school shootings have had a tremendous impact on the public's perception of school safety (Vossekuil, Reddy, Fein, Borum, & Modzeleski, 2000). These events have prompted school officials to consider prevention strategies for targeted violence in schools. School officials are increasingly turning to school counselors for help in identifying and providing interventions for students who may pose a danger to others (Riley & McDaniel, 2000). School counselors are meeting this challenge by providing violence prevention activities, assessing students' risk of engaging in violent behavior, and providing appropriate interventions when the potential for violence exists. This article offers school counselors an overview of their ethical obligations related to school violence and an explanation of their legal duty to protect students from harm. In order to adhere to ethical and legal dictates concerning school violence, it is necessary to be familiar with the characteristics of students who may be at risk for violent behavior and strategies for preventing school violence; thus, these topics are also discussed. This article concludes with specific recommendations for school counselors to follow as they attempt to keep violence from occurring in schools.

ETHICAL DUTY TO PROTECT STUDENTS FROM VIOLENCE IN SCHOOL

There are two ethics documents that inform the practice of school counselors: the *Ethical Standards for School Counselors* (American School Counselor Association [ASCA], 1998) and the Code of Ethics (American Counseling Association [ACA], 1995). Ethical standards require school counselors to inform appropriate authorities when a student's behavior is indicative of clear and imminent danger to others (ACA, § B.1.c.; ASCA, § A.7.). Yet, the best means of accurately determining whether a student is potentially violent has been the subject of much scholarly debate (Bailey, 2001; Reddy et al., 2001; Vossekuil et al., 2000). Accordingly, the ethical standards recommend that school counselors consult with colleagues when working with students who may be at risk for violence (ACA, § B.1.c.; ASCA, § A.7.).

Though school counselors are ethically obligated to respond to and work to prevent imminent school violence, they are also required to consider the welfare of potentially violent students. When school counselors decide to take action to prevent potential violence, the ethical standards direct school counselors to inform students of the actions to be taken in order to clarify expectations and minimize confusion (ASCA, 1998, § A.7.). Furthermore, school counselors have an ethical duty to keep informed about laws related to the rights of their students and ensure that their students' rights are protected (ASCA, § A.1.d.).

LEGAL DUTY TO PROTECT STUDENTS FROM VIOLENCE IN SCHOOL

School officials, including school counselors, have a legal obligation to take action when students pose a danger to other students (Bailey, 2001). In 1999, the U.S. Supreme Court commented on school authorities' duty to address school violence (*Davis v. Monroe County Bd. of Educ.*, 1999). The Court explained that school personnel are on notice that they can be held responsible for failing to protect students from student-on-student violence.

Though the legal duty of school personnel to protect students from harm is clear, courts have been reluctant to find school authorities liable in school violence cases (Hermann & Remley, 2000). This trend is evident in courts' recent decisions about the culpability of school personnel in cases related to multiple homicides perpetrated by students in school settings. For example, in August 2000, a federal court in Kentucky dismissed the claims filed against school personnel in the West Paducah, Kentucky, school shooting (Glaberson, 2000). The court found that the perpetrator was the only responsible party for the shootings in spite of evidence that the student assailant showed students his guns when he brought them to school and wrote of homicidal and suicidal thoughts in school papers.

In late November 2001, a federal district court in Denver dismissed the lawsuits of families of victims alleging that school officials, including school counselors, failed to recognize warning signs from the student assailants (Kass, 2001). These warning signs included a violent Web site and a videotape made for a video production class portraying Harris and Klebold enacting a scenario in which they shot students with the motive of revenge (McPhee, 2000). Additionally, in both psychology classes and creative writing classes, Harris and Klebold expressed their anger, hatred, and intent to kill, and wrote that they possessed firearms. According to the pleadings in the case, these communications demonstrated a serious threat of harm to students at Columbine High School and school administrators, counselors, and teachers were negligent in their failure to respond (Able, 2000). However, the judge ruled that the warning signs were not enough to predict the impending violence. Victims' families report that they will appeal the court's decision to dismiss their case (Kass).

Though school counselors have yet to be held legally accountable for school violence, school counselors still find themselves legally vulnerable because of their role in determining whether students pose a risk of harm to others and deciding on appropriate interventions with these students. Thus, school counselors are wise to keep up-to-date on current court decisions related to school personnel and school violence.

School officials, including school counselors, have been held liable for failing to protect students from foreseeable harm (e.g., *Eisel v. Bd. of Educ.*, 1991; *Maynard v. Bd. of Educ.*, 1997). Courts have consistently found that school personnel have a duty to exercise reasonable care to protect students from foreseeable harm (Hermann & Remley, 2000). Courts have explained that students' violent acts were foreseeable if students threatened to do harm, especially if students have engaged in violent activities in the past (Hermann & Remley). Current case law also indicates that any indicator of potential violence needs to be taken seriously. Accordingly, courts are supporting the temporary removal from the school setting of students who exhibit indicators of potentially violent behavior.

In *Brian A. v. Stroudsburg Area School District* (2001), a federal district court considered the case of a 15-year-old student who was expelled because he wrote a note stating, "There's a Bomb in this School bang bang!!" (p. 505). The incident took place only a few weeks after the Columbine school shooting. The student claimed that he wrote the note as a joke and forgot to throw it away. In making their decision to expel the student, school officials considered the fact that the student was on probation because of an incident that involved blowing up a shed on the property of another school. The court held that school officials' act of expelling the student was a reasonable response to a bomb threat, especially considering the student's previous delinquent acts.

In addition to evidence of the student's intent to do harm and the student's prior violent history, courts have taken into consideration recent school violence when determining if school officials have acted reasonably when faced with a student's threats of violence. In *Lovell v. Poway Unified School District* (1996), a federal appeals court considered the appropriateness of a 15-year-old student's suspension after she allegedly threatened to shoot her school counselor because she was dissatisfied with her schedule. The student defended her actions by stating that she "merely uttered a 'figure of speech'" (pp. 368–369) and immediately apologized for her inappropriate behavior. The student did not act in a physically threatening manner toward the counselor, and yet the counselor reported that she felt threatened by the student because the counselor had witnessed the student's volatile nature and lack of impulse control on other occasions. The court commented, "in light of the violence prevalent in schools today, school officials are justified in taking very seriously student threats against faculty or other students" (p. 372). The court upheld the student's suspension.

Other courts have considered students' constitutional rights and focused on whether threats of violence made in school settings were believable (Hermann & Remley, 2000). Though threats that present a "clear and present danger" have never been afforded first amendment protections, some courts are still finding that for a threat to be punishable, the threat must meet the objective "true threat" test (e.g., *Lovell v. Poway Unified Sch. Dist.*, 1996). According to these courts, a "true threat" is a threat that a reasonable person in the same circumstances would find to be a serious and unambiguous expression of intent to do harm based on the language and context of the threat.

The application of the "true threat" doctrine is illustrated in *D. G. v. Independent School District No. 11, Tulsa County Oklahoma* (2000). In this case, the court considered the suspension of an 11th grade student for writing a poem about killing a specific teacher. The student explained that she was upset with the teacher at the time and she wrote the poem to express her frustration. The student did not intend for the teacher to see the poem. Neither the teacher nor the school administrator considered the threat to be a "true threat" because the student had never been engaged in or threatened to engage in violent conduct at school. But, the school had a "zero tolerance" policy for student threats. The court held that the student's suspension was appropriate while the threat was being investigated; however, the court added that once a psychologist determined that the threat was not a "true threat," the school was violating the student's constitutional rights by not allowing the student to return to school.

Similarly, in *Lavine v. Blaine School District* (2001), a student sued school officials, including his school counselors, after being expelled because of a poem he wrote. The poem contained suicidal and homicidal imagery including a passage depicting a school shooting, 28 people dying, the shooter feeling no remorse, and the perpetrator shooting himself. The English teacher who read the poem was concerned and notified the school counselor. The school shooting in nearby Springfield, Oregon had just occurred. In a previous school year, the student admitted to the school counselor that he had thought about committing suicide. Suicidal ideation is highly correlated with violent behavior (Vossekuil et al., 2000). The school counselor was also aware of recent, serious problems the student was having at home and that the student was reportedly stalking the girl with whom he had just broken up. The student had a discipline record which included a fight and an incident of insubordination to a teacher. Based on these facts, the principal expelled the student.

After the student's removal from school, the student was evaluated by a psychiatrist who found that the student could safely return to school. Though the student returned to school, the student's father sued school officials claiming that his son's expulsion had violated his son's constitutional rights. Addressing this claim, the court stated that recent school shootings have "put our nation on edge and have focused attention on what school officials, law enforcement and others can do or could have done to prevent these kinds of tragedies" (*Lavine v. Blaine Sch. Dist.*, 2001, p. 987). The court continued by stating that "the school had a duty to prevent any potential violence on campus" (p. 989). Considering the facts of the case and the recent school shootings, the court held that school personnel acted reasonably by removing the student from the school environment until a psychiatrist evaluated the student and determined that the student was not a danger to himself or others.

Case law related to student suicide also has legal implications for school counselors as they engage in violence prevention and intervention activities. As in school violence cases, in student suicide cases educators' liability emanates from their responsibility to keep students safe from harm (Hermann & Remley, 2000). Thus, the reasoning of courts addressing student suicide could be applied by analogy to school violence cases (Hermann & Remley).

In student suicide cases, courts have found that school personnel need to take seriously every threat indicating suicidal ideation. School counselors have a duty to use reasonable care to attempt to prevent a student's suicide when they are on notice of a student's suicidal intent (*Eisel v. Bd.*

of Educ., 1991). Courts have found that students' writing assignments, such as disturbing entries in students' journals, could make a student's suicide reasonably foreseeable (*Brooks v. Logan*, 1995). Courts addressing school violence could also find that a student's disturbing writing assignments were evidence of premeditated violence. In student suicide cases, courts have also addressed the need for educating school personnel in suicide prevention, noting that without such education, school personnel are likely to underestimate the lethality of suicidal behaviors (*Wyke v. Polk County Sch. Bd.*, 1997). Just as courts are beginning to expect school personnel to be educated in suicide prevention, courts could find that there is an expectation that school personnel be knowledgeable about violence prevention as well (Hermann & Remley, 2000).

According to current school violence and student suicide jurisprudence, school counselors are justified in taking every threat of violence or suicide seriously. Yet, some courts have recognized that not all threats are serious threats to do harm. School counselors play a vital role in assessing these threats and working with administrators as they determine whether to remove a student from school because of a violent threat. According to legal dictates, threat assessment includes determining whether the language and context of the threat indicate a serious intent to do harm. A school counselor's previous interactions with the student are relevant in this determination, especially if the counselor has noted volatile behavior or the student has indicated suicidal ideation. Finally, school counselors need to consider other corroborating evidence such as the student's history of violent behavior.

It is important to note that judges do not expect school counselors be perfect in their prediction of school violence. Assessment of risk is not an exact science (Dwyer, Osher, & Warger, 1998). School officials are also not expected to anticipate random acts of violence (Remley & Hermann, 2000). Consequently, school counselors are only expected to act reasonably to prevent foreseeable school violence (*Lavine v. Blaine Sch. Dist.*, 2001). In determining what actions are considered reasonable, courts have found that school counselors are expected to exercise the degree of care that would be exercised by other school counselors with similar education and experience (*Wyke v. Polk County Sch. Bd.*, 1997). School counselors are only exposed to legal liability if they fail to exercise reasonable care in preventing foreseeable school violence (Remley & Hermann, 2000).

Legal Issues Related to Addressing School Violence Through the Use of Student Profiles

Although school counselors have a legal duty to exercise reasonable care to protect students from foreseeable harm, school counselors also have an ethical duty to ensure that students' legal rights are protected. The use of criminal profiling as a means to identify students at risk for violence could be violative of students' constitutional rights. Reddy et al. (2001) described criminal profiling as a technique to assess individuals who have exhibited disturbing behaviors and communications based on characteristics of previous perpetrators. In the context of school violence, the use of this technique has been severely criticized.

Researchers studying school violence have consistently found that there is no accurate profile of students at risk for violence (Bailey, 2001; Reddy et al., 2001; Vossekuil et al., 2000). Most notably, in October 2000, the U.S. Secret Service released their preliminary findings based on a comprehensive research project which analyzed information related to the behavior and thinking of students involved in 37 school shootings between 1974 and 2000 (Vossekuil et al.). The goal of the project was to provide this information to school and law enforcement personnel responsible for preventing school violence. In the school shooting incidents studied, the attackers ranged from excellent to failing in academic performance, from socially isolated to popular, and from no behavioral problems to multiple behavioral difficulties in school. The assailants came from a variety of ethnic backgrounds. Less than one third of the perpetrators abused drugs or alcohol. Few perpetrators showed any significant change in academic performance, friendship patterns, or disciplinary problems at school prior to the incident. The only demographic variable that was consistent was that young men committed all of the school shootings studied. However, the consistency of this demographic variable changed after the preliminary report was issued. In March, 2001, an eighth grade girl shot a classmate at the Catholic school both girls attended (Morse, 2001).

Vossekuil et al. (2000) concluded that an accurate profile of a school shooter does not exist. They explained that the vast majority of students who fit any given profile actually do not pose a risk of school violence, and some students who do pose a risk of violence do not fit any given profile. Violent student profiles have been characterized as over-inclusive, biased, stigmatizing, and potentially violative of students' constitutional rights (Bailey, 2001; Reddy et al., 2001; Vossekuil et al.).

Bailey (2001) discussed the constitutional law issues involved in using profiles to prevent school violence. He explained that assigning students to alternative education programs based on a student's likeness to a profile could be seen as a deprivation of the right to equal educational opportunities and thus could pose serious constitutional questions. Bailey reasoned that for an individual to be singled out and receive special treatment based on the individual's resemblance to a profile, the profile must be reliable and used in an objective manner. He found that there is no violent student profile supported by comprehensive research and generally accepted by the scientific community. Bailey concluded that interventions based on using such profiles as a predictor of violence could be violative of students' constitutional rights.

Bailey (2001) noted the difference in using profiles to assign students to alternative educational programs and using profiles to direct students to violence prevention or mental health services. He explained that the latter could have constitutional implications, but courts would likely see the allocation of mental health services to students potentially in need of these services as an additional opportunity for students as opposed to a deprivation of rights. However, school counselors can avoid the possibility of litigation related to the use of student profiles by presenting all students with the opportunity for violence prevention activities and using means other than profiles to assess whether students are potentially violent.

CHARACTERISTICS OF STUDENTS WHO MAY BE IN NEED OF VIOLENCE PREVENTION INTERVENTION

Though interventions based on the use of a mythical violent student profile could be violative of students' constitutional rights, school counselors still have a legal and ethical duty to act reasonably to prevent school violence. Assessing a student's potential risk of violence is implicit in this duty. Consideration of certain risk factors related to violent behavior can help school counselors make this assessment. In *Youth Violence: A Report of the Surgeon General* (U.S. Department of Health and Human Services, 2001), a risk factor was described as any factor that increases the likelihood that a person will suffer harm. Risk factors differ from violent student profiles because they encompass a broad range of indicators as opposed to one rigid, stereotypical profile. Though no risk factor or set of risk factors can accurately predict that a student will become violent, a risk factor increases the possibility that a student will become violent. The presence of multiple risk factors further increases the possibility that a student may become violent.

The research on risk factors and the prediction of violence has relied upon retrospective studies of students who have already become violent. This was accomplished by conducting psychological postmortems after violent incidents to discover common characteristics related to behavior, development, and psychosocial history (Borduin & Schaeffer, 1998; Dwyer et al., 1998; Hamburg, 1998; Hardwick & Rowton-Lee, 1996; Kashani, Jones, Bumby, & Thomas, 1999; Poland & McCormick, 1999; Vossekuil et al., 2000). For example, Vossekuil et al. studied 37 school shootings and found that most students do not impulsively go on shooting rampages. Over three fourths of the school shootings studied were planned and more than one half of the shootings were planned at least 2 days prior to the shooting. Furthermore, over one half of the attackers developed the idea to harm others at least 2 weeks prior to the event.

Vossekuil et al. (2000) found that in almost every case, the perpetrator engaged in behavior that caused others to express concern about the student. In over three fourths of the cases, an adult expressed concern because the student was engaging in behaviors such as attempting to gain access to weapons and writing suicidal or homicidal thoughts in school work. Vossekuil et al. reported that in over 75% of the incidents, perpetrators told at least one person what they were planning to do before carrying out the plan. Stevens, Lynm, and Glass (2001) also found that in over half of the violent school attacks, students wrote a note, made a journal entry, or advertised their plan in some other manner.

Students' threats to do harm are a powerful indicator of future violence (Dwyer et al., 1998; Fitzgerald, 2001). A student's threat may be obscure or it may be given in great detail. The threat may have been for homicide, suicide, or both. Vossekuil et al. (2000) found a high correlation between suicidal and homicidal behaviors. In almost three fourths of the school shootings Vossekuil and his colleagues studied, the students had threatened or attempted to commit suicide prior to perpetrating the school shootings.

Students' motivation for committing violent acts at school has included alienation, disaffection, powerlessness, and revenge (Dwyer et al., 1998; Glasser, 2000; Sandhu, 2000). Vossekuil et al. (2000) noted that in over three fourths of the school shootings they studied, the perpetrators were having difficulty coping with a major relationship change or another loss. Some students who have been violent in school were alienated from the mainstream of the student body (Dwyer et al.; Sandhu). The motivation for some student violence has been rejection by peers. In the Jonesboro, Arkansas; and Pearl, Mississippi, school shootings, the perpetrators had been rejected by their romantic interests. The assailants specifically targeted these girls in their violent attacks.

Vossekuil et al. (2000) found that in over two thirds of the incidents, the perpetrators had been bullied, threatened, or attacked prior to the shooting, and more than one half of the attackers were motivated by revenge. The students believed that their violence was justified (Ross, 1996). Some violent students even pictured themselves as heroic figures serving as avenging angels righting past wrongs (Gibbs & Roche, 1999). The shooters at Columbine High School targeted athletes who they believed had been their bullies and tormentors. Yet, in over 75% of the school shooting incidents that Vossekuil and his colleagues studied, the attackers did not alert the targeted victim or victims of their plans.

A history of childhood sexual, physical, or emotional abuse can also increase the risk for violent behavior (James & Gilliland, 2001). Other risk factors include having access to identified victims, the ability to acquire weapons, increased environmental stress, disconnection and alienation from mainstream culture, high levels of anger and frustration, and use of drugs and alcohol (Dwyer et al., 1998; Glasser, 2000; James & Gilliland; Ross, 1996). In addition, many of the students who have committed acts of violence had psychiatric diagnoses. They were either in treatment in which the severity of their problems was not addressed or they were noncompliant with their medications (James & Gilliland). Some of the perpetrators intentionally went off of their medications in order to increase their level of anger and violent behavior. Because the students were emotionally unstable, they were further alienated from emotionally healthy friends who could have discouraged the violent behavior or alerted authorities about the students' cataclysmic plans. (Borduin & Schaeffer, 1998; Kashani et al., 1999).

Harm to small animals is another indicator of possible risk of school violence. For example, the perpetrator of the Pearl, Mississippi, school shootings tortured and killed his family dog (Bagley, 1999). He beat the dog and then set it on fire while it was still alive. He wrote about this incident in his school journal, but this information was not relayed to his mother or the authorities.

Other warning signs of violent behavior include an unusual interest in violence (Dwyer et al., 1998). The perpetrators in Columbine, Colorado; Moses Lake, Washington; Jonesboro, Arkansas; and Pearl, Mississippi, all expressed a fascination with weapons and violent films and video games. The Trench Coat Mafia of Columbine and the perpetrator in Moses Lake dressed like their favorite characters in violent movies.

Finally, the school environment itself can contribute to school violence. The risk of school violence increases when adult supervision is insufficient, bullying and teasing are tolerated, special privileges are afforded to identifiable populations such as athletes or honor students, the faculty is disconnected from the students and community, students in need of care have little access to intervention, and violent threats are ignored (Fagan & Wilkinson, 1998; Futrell, 1996; Mayer, 1999; Ross, 1996; Stevens et al., 2001; Trump, 1997; Weinhold, 2001). Remaining alert to environmental and individual risk factors associated with school violence is vital to school counselors as they work to prevent school violence.

STRATEGIES FOR PREVENTING SCHOOL VIOLENCE

School counselors are ethically and legally obligated to work toward preventing school violence. Many strategies have been suggested to combat violence in and around schools. They range from implementing high security at schools (Friday, 1996; Mercy & Rosenberg, 1998; Trump, 1997), to promoting kinder, gentler school environments in which every student feels nurtured and their emotional as well as educational needs are met (Farrell, Meyer, & White, 2001; Glasser, 2000; U. S. Department of Health and Human Services, 2001). There is little consensus regarding the most appropriate interventions. Most experts do agree that the problem of violence in the schools is complex, with multiple etiologies requiring multidimensional prevention and intervention plans (Dwyer et al., 1998; Futrell, 1996; Samples & Aber, 1998; Stevens et al., 2001).

Based on a comprehensive review of violence prevention activities, the U.S. Department of Health and Human Services (2001) noted that there are numerous effective intervention programs aimed at reducing and preventing youth violence. The most effective youth violence prevention and intervention programs addressed environmental conditions as well as individual student's risk factors. It was reported that a program's effectiveness depended on the quality of implementation as much as the intervention.

It is important to note that though many violence prevention strategies have been effective, the U.S. Department of Health and Human Services (2001) found that almost one half of the violence prevention strategies they studied were ineffective. A few of the strategies were even harmful. The U.S. Department of Health and Human Services highlighted effective and ineffective strategies that have been used to reduce youth violence. Effective strategies included skills training, behavior monitoring and reinforcement, cooperative learning, bullying prevention programs, and parent education programs. Ineffective strategies included peer counseling and peer mediation. Programs like Drug Abuse Resistance Education (DARE) were criticized for being developmentally inappropriate. However, newer versions of DARE, in which these criticisms were addressed, have yet to be evaluated. Clearly, continued evaluation of violence prevention programs is critical. And, school counselors need to stay up-to-date on which programs are effective in preventing youth violence and which programs are not.

In order to prevent violence, Poland and McCormick (1999) suggested educating school personnel, parents, and students to recognize the warning signs of homicide and suicide. Part of this instruction with students should focus on breaking the code of silence students maintain with each other. This is important because after a violent incident it is usually discovered that several students knew of the plans and knew that a student was armed that day at school. Students must learn that some secrets are too dangerous to keep (James & Gilliland, 2001). The faculty should also be encouraged to take the warnings seriously because denial can have fatal consequences (Hardwick & Rowton-Lee, 1996). School personnel, students, and parents must be united in their determination to act in order to prevent violence. When students are identified as needing intervention, quick efforts are important because there may be a narrow window of opportunity to prevent the violence (Poland & McCormick).

Glasser (2000) and Dwyer et al. (1998) concluded early identification and intervention with students are the best means of violence prevention. Therefore, school counselors' focus in the assessment process should be on identification of students in need of intervention, and efforts should be made to link specific interventions with the individual needs of the student as well as the severity of the situation. Glasser found that if this is done effectively, the risk of violence will be reduced.

Reddy et al. (2001) considered several approaches being utilized in an effort to prevent school violence. Finding that profiles and other inductive methods of addressing this issue are ineffective, they advocated for focusing on the facts of each case through threat assessment techniques. Waldo and Malley (1992) explained that when a student has threatened violence, it is advisable to obtain the necessary information to make a determination about the student's dangerousness. Pietrofesa, Pietrofesa, and Pietrofesa (1990) and Costa and Altekruse (1994) suggested that school counselors assess dangerousness according to the student's plan for implementing the violent act and the student's ability to carry out the act. Reddy and her colleagues advised examining a student's ideas and behaviors and the progression of these ideas and behaviors from multiple sources over time. When there is even a small amount of evidence indicative of potential violent behavior, early intervention would be appropriate.

According to Reddy et al. (2001), determining whether an alarming behavior or communicated threat could be indicative of violent action involves assessing the student's motivation for making the threat or engaging in the behavior, the student's other communications and behaviors, consistency between the student's communications and behaviors, any unusual interest in violence, evidence of planning violent behavior, the student's mental condition, the student's cognitive ability to formulate and execute a violent act, the student's recent losses or perceived failures, others' perception of the individuals potential for violence, and other relevant factors in the student's circumstances. Corroboration from teachers, peers, family members, and school records is important in determining a student's potential for violent behaviors. Waldo and Malley (1992) recommended that school counselors consult with other mental health professionals for clinical advice in these situations.

When students are identified as at risk for violence, there should be protocols for obtaining help for students. Referrals to resources within the school and community should be provided. The school's resources should include staff prepared to provide ongoing individual counseling and group intervention (Gottfredson, Gottfredson, & Skroban, 1998) and could include violence prevention activities.

Loeber, Farrington, Rumsey, and Allen-Hagen (1998) found that modifying the school climate is one of the most effective strategies for preventing school violence. School counselors can help establish an environment in which students know that school personnel care about their well-being. Students also need to know that they will be held accountable for their actions. Without trust and accountability, students do not feel safe in reporting their concerns about their classmates (James & Gilliland, 2001). In this more compassionate school environment, all students are equally valued and differences are acknowledged and respected. Furthermore, all forms of violence, including hazing and bullying, are not tolerated.

School counselors can help create or update school policies related to violence prevention, including specific steps to ensure student safety. School personnel must be apprized of the policies and the importance of following the policies. Courts have found that school personnel were negligent when they failed to follow a policy implemented to keep students safe and a student was injured as a result of the failure to follow the policy (*Garcia v. City of New York*, 1996). Thus, once a school policy for violence prevention has been created, it is imperative that the policy be followed.

RECOMMENDATIONS FOR SCHOOL COUNSELORS

In the context of school violence, school counselors have an ethical and legal duty to prevent clear and imminent danger to others. Though courts have upheld taking every threat of violence in school settings seriously, to date courts have refused to hold school counselors legally accountable for school violence. Courts have found that even blatant warning signs were not enough to predict impending violence. Yet, school counselors are still legally vulnerable. Courts have consistently found that school officials have a duty to exercise reasonable care in order to prevent potential school violence. Implementing violence prevention programming, assessing students' risk for violence, and providing appropriate interventions are reasonable activities related to addressing school violence.

The practice of school counselors is guided by the *Ethical Standards for School Counselors* (ASCA, 1998) and the *Code of Ethics* (ACA, 1995). In addition, the activities of school counselors are informed by the court cases cited in this article. The following recommendations are offered to school counselors to assist them in addressing the difficult issue of school violence in a manner that is ethically sound and legally appropriate:

1. Keep up-to-date on effective violence prevention activities, risk assessment techniques, and interventions when the potential for violence exists.
2. Avoid providing interventions based solely on a student's resemblance to a profile.
3. Help create or update school policies related to violence prevention, including specific steps to ensure student safety.
4. Provide violence prevention programming for school personnel and students.
5. Create an effective referral system for teachers and staff to notify school counselors of potential violent behavior.
6. Take every threat of violence seriously.
7. Assess each threat by considering the language and context of the threat, student's previous violent activities and suicidal ideation, and other corroborating evidence.
8. Consult with other mental health professionals.
9. If you determine that a student may pose a danger to others, alert appropriate authorities and inform the student of the actions to be taken.
10. Obtain, and keep readily available, information on community resources for students at risk for violence.
11. Keep current on relevant legal and ethical mandates related to school violence.
12. Consult legal counsel, especially regarding state laws related to school violence.
13. Document actions taken to prevent school violence.
14. Maintain professional liability insurance.

Mary A. Hermann, J.D., Ph.D., *is an assistant professor, Counselor Education and Educational Psychology, Mississippi State University, Mississippi State, MS. E-mail: mhermann@colled.msstate.edu.* **Abbé Finn, Ph.D.,** *is an assistant professor, Department of Leadership and Counselor Education, School of Education, University of Mississippi, University, MS. E-mail: afinn@olemiss.edu.*

REFERENCES

Able, C. (2000, July 19). Suits name Columbine officials, families amend complaint, finding fault with principal, two dozen others. *Denver Rocky Mountain News*, p. 5A.

American Counseling Association. (1995). *Code of ethics and standards of practice.* Alexandria, VA: Author.

American School Counselor Association. (1998). *Ethical standards for school counselors.* Alexandria, VA: Author.

Bagley, S. (1999). Why young kill. In K. Freiberg (Ed.), *Human development* (29th ed., pp. 141–143). Guilford, CT: McGraw-Hill/ Dushkin.

Bailey, K. A. (2001). Legal implications of profiling students for violence. *Psychology in the Schools, 38,* 141–155.

Borduin, C. M., & Schaeffer, C. M. (1998). Violent offending in adolescence: Epidemiology, correlates, outcomes, and treatment. In T. P. Guillotta, G. R. Adams, & R. Montemayor (Eds.), *Delinquent violent youth: Theory and interventions* (pp. 144–174). Newberry Park, CA: Sage.

Brian A. v. Stroudsburg Area Sch. Dist., 141 F. Supp. 2d 502 (M.D. Pa. 2001).

Brooks v. Logan, 903 P.2d 73 (Idaho, 1995).

Costa, L., & Altekruse, M. (1994). Duty-to-warn guidelines for mental health counselors. *Journal of Counseling and Development, 72,* 346–350.

Davis v. Monroe County Bd. of Educ., 119 S. Ct. 1661 (1999).

D. G. vs. Indep. Sch. Dist. No. 11 of Tulsa County Oklahoma, 2000 U.S. Dist. LEXIS 12197, (N.D. Okla. 2000).

Dwyer, K., Osher, D., & Warger, C. (1998). *Early warning, timely response: A guide to safe schools.* Washington, DC: U.S. Department of Education.

Eisel v. Bd. of Educ., 597 A.2d 447 (Md. 1991).

Fagan, J., & Wilkinson, D. (1998). Social contexts and functions of adolescent violence. In D. Elliott, B. Hamburg, & K. Williams (Eds.), *Violence in American schools* (pp. 55–93). New York: Cambridge University.

Farrell, A., Meyer, A., & White, K. (2001). Evaluation of responding in peaceful and positive Ways (RIPP): A school-based prevention program for reducing violence among urban adolescents. *Journal of Clinical Child Psychology, 30,* 451–463.

Fitzgerald, S. (2001, December 4). Violent students give warning signs that are often overlooked, study shows. *The Philadelphia Inquirer,* p. A6.

Friday, J. (1996). Weapon-carrying in schools. In A. Hoffman (Ed.), *Schools, violence, and society* (pp. 21–31). Westport, CT: Praeger.

Futrell, M. (1996). Violence in the classroom: A teacher's perspective. In A. Hoffman (Ed.), *Schools, violence, and society* (pp. 3–19). Westport, CT: Praeger.

Garcia v. City of New York, 646 N.Y.S. 2d 508 (App. Div. 1996).

Gibbs, N., & Roche, T. (1999, December 20). The Columbine tapes. *Time,* 40–60.

Glaberson, W. (2000, August 4). Judges dismiss civil suits in school killings. *The Times-Picayune,* p. A-4.

Glasser, W. (2000). School violence from the perspective of William Glasser. *Professional School Counseling, 4,* 77–80.

Gottfredson, D. C., Gottfredson, G. D., & Skroban, S. (1998). Can prevention work where it is needed most? *Evaluation Review, 22,* 315–340.

Hamburg, M. (1998). Youth violence as a public health issue. In D. Elliott, B. Hamburg, & K. Williams (Eds.), *Violence in American schools* (pp. 31–54). New York: Cambridge University.

Hardwick, P. J., & Rowton-Lee, M. A. (1996). Adolescent homicide: Towards assessment of risk. *Journal of Adolescence, 19,* 263–276.

Hermann, M. A., & Remley, T. P., Jr. (2000). Guns, violence, and schools: The results of school violence—litigation against educators and students shedding more constitutional rights at the school house gate. *Loyola Law Review, 46,* 389–439.

James, R., & Gilliland, B. (2001). *Crisis intervention strategies* (4th ed.). Belmont, CA: Brooks/Cole.

Kashani, J., Jones, M., Bumby, K., & Thomas, L. (1999). Youth violence: Psychosocial risk factors, treatment, prevention, and recommendations. *Journal of Emotional and Behavioral Disorders, 7,* 200–211.

Kass, J. (2001, November 29). Columbine seeks closure—out of court. *The Christian Science Monitor,* p. 2.

Lavine v. Blaine Sch. Dist., 257 F.3d 981 (9th Cir. 2001).

Loeber, R., Farrington, D. P., Rumsey, C. A., & Allen-Hagen, B. (1998). Serious and violent juvenile offenders. *Juvenile Justice Bulletin.* Washington, DC: U.S. Department of Justice.

Lovell v. Poway Unified Sch. Dist., 90 F.3d 367 (9th Cir. 1996).

Mayer, G. R. (1999). Constructive discipline for school personnel. *Education and Treatment of Children, 22*(1), 36–55.

Maynard v. Bd. of Educ., 663 N.Y.S.2d 717 (App. Div. 1997)

McPhee, M. (2000, October 3). Lawsuits criticize teachers DeAngelis, others cited in new papers. *The Denver Post,* p. A-06.

Mercy, J., & Rosenberg, M. (1998). Preventing firearm violence in and around schools. In D. Elliott, B. Hamburg, & K. Williams (Eds.), *Violence in American schools* (pp. 159–187). New York: Cambridge University.

Morse, J. (2001, March 19). Girlhood Interrupted. *Time, 157*(11), 28.

Pietrofesa, J. J., Pietrofesa, C. F., & Pietrofesa, J. D. (1990). The mental health counselor and the "duty to warn." *Journal of Mental Health Counseling, 12,* 129–137.

Poland, S., & McCormick, J. (1999). *Coping with crisis: Lessons learned.* Longmont, CO: Sopris West.

Reddy, M., Borum, R., Berglund, J., Vossekuil, B., Fein, R., & Modzeleski, W. (2001). Evaluating risk for targeted violence in schools: Comparing risk assessment, threat assessment, and other approaches. *Psychology in the Schools, 38,* 157–173.

Remley, T. P., Jr., & Hermann, M. A. (2000). Legal and ethical issues in school counseling. In J. Wittmer (Ed.), *Managing your school counseling program: K–12 developmental strategies* (pp. 314–329). Minneapolis, MN: Educational Media.

Riley, P. L., & McDaniel, J. (2000). School violence prevention, intervention, and crisis response. *Professional School Counseling, 4,* 120–125.

Ross, D. (1996). *Childhood bullying and teasing: What school personnel, other professionals, and parents can do.* Alexandria, VA: American Counseling Association.

Samples, F., & Aber, L. (1998). Evaluations of school-based violence prevention programs. In D. Elliott, B. Hamburg, & K. Williams (Eds.), *Violence in American schools* (pp. 217–252). New York: Cambridge University.

Sandhu, D. S. (2000). Alienated students: Counseling strategies to curb school violence. *Professional School Counseling, 4,* 81–86.

Stevens, L., Lynm, C., & Glass, R. (2001). Youth violence in schools. *Journal of the American Medical Association, 286,* 2695–2702.

Trump, K. (1997). Security policy, personnel, and operations. In A. Goldstein & J. Conoley (Eds.), School violence intervention: A practical handbook (pp. 265–289). New York: Guilford.

U.S. Department of Health and Human Services. (2001). *Youth violence: A report of the Surgeon General.* Rockville, MD: U.S. Department of Health and Human Services, Centers for Disease Control and Prevention, National Center for Injury Prevention and Control; Substance Abuse and Mental Health Services Administration, Center for Mental Health Services; and National Institutes of Health, National Institute of Mental Health.

Vossekuil, B., Reddy, M., Fein, R., Borum, R., & Modzeleski, W. (2000). *U.S.S.S. Safe School Initiative: An interim report on the prevention of targeted violence in schools.* Washington, DC: U.S. Secret Service, National Threat Assessment Center.

Waldo, S. L., & Malley, P. (1992). Tarasoff and its progeny: Implications for the school counselor. *The School Counselor, 40,* 46–54.

Weinhold, B. (2001). Bullying and school violence: The tip of the iceberg. In D. Rea & R. Warkentin (Eds.), *Ensuring safe schools building a nonviolent society* (pp. 3–11). New York: McGraw-Hill Primis.

Wyke v. Polk County Sch. Bd., 129 F.3d. 560 (11th Cir. 1997).

The Duty To Warn And Protect: Tarasoff And The Elementary School Teacher

Madelyn L. Isaacs

Today's school counselors find their young clients more frequently exposed to violence, more willing to commit violent acts, and more likely to threaten to commit suicide than in years past. The full range of adult psychological problems seems to be more pervasive in younger children. Recent cases of young children coming to elementary schools with guns and other weapons, elementary students who have sought to poison a teacher's drink, or even those who have threatened to harm themselves by suicide suggest that elementary school counselors have been increasingly faced with duty to warn decisions, as have their secondary school and mental health counterparts. Increases in consultation activities with teacher and families have made elementary counselors more privy to adult information obtained in ill-defined counseling or consulting relationships. Moreover, school counselors who deal with sensitive issues may be in unclear territory if their job descriptions and contracts specify educationally related counseling only.

With the initial decision in 1974 and the full appeal decision in 1976, the California *Tarasoff* case (*Tarasoff v. Regents of the University of California*, 1974/1976) generated dual duties to warn and to protect third parties of potentially dangerous client behavior. These duties concern how counselors work with dangerous clients or those clients who may pose a danger to others or to themselves. With the legal precedent set in California, counselors began to worry about balancing absolute confidentiality, the hallmark of the trusting therapeutic relationship, with duties to clients and to the potential victims of possibly dangerous clients. These difficult issues had to be balanced while avoiding legal liability for malpractice (Hopkins & Anderson, 1990).

For years, elementary school counselors were practically removed from the implications of *Tarasoff* since their clients were usually too young to present danger to themselves or to others. However, Baker (1996) recently identified *Tarasoff* and its effects on school counselors as an unclear area. Furthermore, several societal factors have evolved which have raised duty to warn issues more frequently for elementary school counselors. Huey and Remley (1989) noted that in the 1990s, school counselors would be dealing with more sensitive issues and thus be more vulnerable to legal action. Others (for example, Herlihy & Sheeley, 1988) have noted that our society is increasingly litigious and school counselors cannot consider themselves immune from this trend.

The *Tarasoff* decision has had far reaching effects in all mental health professions. Although not case or statutory law in many states, the principles of protection of third parties vying against confidentiality have been argued and legislated in many jurisdictions with different outcomes. For school counselors, especially those working with younger children, the duty to warn and protect may be governed by a combination of state statute, ethics, case law, or school board policy (Fischer & Sorenson, 1996). Regardless of what governs its disposition, school counselors are faced with breaching confidentiality in cases where there is an imminent risk of a particular person or persons being in harm's way.

The American School Counselor Association (ASCA, 1974, 1986) established its commitment to confidentiality in school counseling relationships in a 1974 position paper that was reestablished and revised in 1986. In the position paper, ASCA established confidentiality as an ethical privacy right and privilege as a legal privacy requirement accorded to counselors and students differentially in different legal jurisdictions. Confidentiality was to be protected and could only be breached with student permission in counseling and consulting situations.

The practical dimensions of client management are commingled with the more philosophical dimensions of the ethical dilemma posed by dangerous clients. A school counselor's primary ethical obligation is to protect student rights and promote student welfare. However, counselors are also ethically obligated to consider the best interests and safety of society. Since obligations to potentially dangerous clients often seem to conflict with obligations to others, the counselor who is faced with a potentially violent client is involved in an ethical dilemma. A dilemma, according to Kitchner (1984), is "a situation in which there are two good reasons to take different courses of action" (p. 52).

The original *Tarasoff* case involved a psychologist and many subsequent cases have involved psychologists and psychiatrists. However, most court cases deal with factual issues and thus do not state which or if all related professionals are covered (Rosenhan, Teitelbaum, Teitelbaum, & Davidson, 1993). The common term "therapist" has often been presumed to apply to all mental health practitioners and may include school counselors since work sites are usually not designated in case decisions. However, mental health professionals in general and professional counselors specifically are not treated equally before the law within and among states. Therefore, whether school guidance counselors are bound by duty to protect under common law is unclear in contrast to the obligations incurred under ethical codes. It is important to note that ethical obligations may not be legally enforceable when an injured parent, client, or students brings suit to seek legal remedy. Breaches of ethical codes can result in professional discipline.

Tarasoff is a confusing legal precedent because it is a California case with local jurisdiction that has been inconsistently applied in other states. Furthermore, the legal concept of the duty to warn or otherwise protect is not a static concept even within individual jurisdictions. Recent cases in Florida and Virginia have demonstrated a distinct move away from *Tarasoff* as a measure of professional responsibility or negligent liability by finding against plaintiffs who brought suits based on *Tarasoff*-like conditions or duties to warn or protect. However, statutes and case law in other states have recognized the legitimacy of *Tarasoff* as a legal doctrine. These states concurrently recognize through statute, however, that *Tarasoff* and the duty to warn and protect may be in the best interest of the client or public. The concept of the duty to protect is further complicated for school counselors when coping with AIDS, child abuse, domestic violence, teen pregnancy, and group or family confidentiality and confidential relationships with minors (see for examples, Gray & Harding, 1988; Herlihy & Golden, 1990; Huber, 1994; Pietrofesa, Pietrofesa & Pietrofesa, 1990; Standard & Hazler, 1995). Each of these issues falls under duty to protect and confidentiality premises, yet may have specific legal reporting requirements that differ from *Tarasoff*.

Thus, counselors struggle to understand varying legal applications in different jurisdictions of a principle that has limiting effects on professional judgment, specific ethical directives, and varying local policy, state law and case law. They struggle to understand the *Tarasoff* principle in the rapidly changing environment of statutory law and emerging case law precedent. This struggle is concurrent with the assessment and disposition of dangerous clients. Few school counselors are really trained to understand the process of legal precedent and differential application; especially when confronted with urgent care decisions. Many school counselors were certified before program and certification changes required the study of law and ethics. Therefore, they may have little formal training to understand and follow their legal obligations. An informal survey (Isaacs, 1995) of more than 41 school counselors, 32 of whom had been certified more than 10 years ago, indicated that most (84% or 83%) had never heard of *Tarasoff* and were only vaguely familiar with duty to warn and protect principles. This may be due to the limited precedent of the California case for other states or because legal and ethical issues have been added to most curricula relatively recently. Yet these counselors had some familiarity with some current requirements about breaching confidentiality. Their preprofessional counseling training would not have ordinarily led to an understanding that statutory law is legislatively defined and court interpreted and that case law continues to evolve and alter the course of legal precedent.

School counselors are not alone in their confusion about *Tarasoff* and its implications for professional practice. In *Hopewell v. Adebimpe* (1978), a psychiatrist believed he was obligated to breach confidentiality after misinterpreting *Tarasoff* as law in his state. His patient sued for malpractice and won based on breach of that state's law which preserved confidentiality. Misinterpreting out of state legal precedents not keeping up to date with current laws in one's own state can be a costly mistake.

The purpose of this article is to help elementary school counselors identify whether if or how *Tarasoff* affects them and their students, students' families, or others who may reveal dangerous possibilities through counseling and consulting relationships. Changes in ACA's Code of Ethics are reviewed and compared to ASCA's Code of Ethics to identify a consistent professional framework in which to make responsible professional decisions. Suggestions concerning prudent professional practice are made.

TARASOFF

In the first, and subsequently vacated *Tarasoff* decision (1974), the California Supreme Court imposed a duty on psychotherapists to warn potential third party victims threatened by their patients. The court's second opinion (*Tarasoff v. Regents of the University of California*, 1976), now the "official" *Tarasoff* decision, broadened the duty of care to take reasonable steps necessary to protect third parties threatened by patients. The now famous case involved a graduate student client at the University of California, Berkeley's counseling center who had threatened to kill his girlfriend during a therapy session and subsequently carried out the threat. The court held that "When a therapist determines, or pursuant to the standards of his profession should determine, that his patient presents a serious danger of violence to another, he incurs an obligation to use reasonable care to protect the intended victim against such danger" (p 346).

The *Tarasoff* case, and other duty to protect cases that followed, departed from common law, which held "one was not duty bound to control the behavior of another nor to warn those endangered by such conduct" (Fischer & Sorenson, 1996, p. 19). Fischer and Sorenson (1996) suggested that courts have based the departure from common law on the special relationship between the counselor and the client. That relationship places the counselor in a position to exercise reasonable care and skill to foresee danger to third persons and to avoid the danger by warning others or by controlling the client's conduct. According to the *Tarasoff* principle, a special relationship coupled with foreseeability of harm creates an obligation to act to protect potential victims (VandeCreek & Knapp, 1993).

Prior to the *Tarasoff* decision in California, a counselor's duty to third parties had been a discretionary professional duty based on professional ethics and established standards of practice (Givelber, Bowers, & Blitch, 1984). Ethical codes allowed threats to the welfare of others to suspend confidentiality; however, the decision to warn or to use other interventions to deal with potentially violent clients remains a matter of professional judgment. With the *Tarasoff* ruling, these historically professional concerns became subject to scrutiny by the courts in California or in those states where cases with similar principles were brought.

Tarasoff: The Reach Beyond California and Its Uneven Application

During the 20 odd years since *Tarasoff*, courts in most states have heard cases based on failure to warn or failure to protect. Many courts have examined the *Tarasoff* principle with some expanding the legal doctrine and most others restricting or clarifying its application (Greenberg, 1992). According to Greenberg (1992), 22 state jurisdictions, in addition to California, have adopted a duty to protect law "or other related affirmative duty" (p. 262). Thus, while clearly not a national or universal standard, it has clearly affected case and statutory law in many states. Consequently, the *Tarasoff* decision has been accepted as potential law throughout the United States, and psychotherapists nationwide incorrectly believe that they are legally bound by the ruling (Beck, 1982; Givelbar et al., 1984; *Hopewell v. Adebimpe*, 1978; Rosenhan, Teitelbaum, Teitelbaum, & Davidson, 1998). Similar studies of school counselors' beliefs about *Tarasoff* however, have not been reported.

The *Tarasoff* case has been prolific in spawning other decisions that have broadened the legal responsibilities of mental health professionals. Corey, Corey and Callahan (1993) cite a number of court rulings have expanded the *Tarasoff* duty and extended liability to situations factually unlike the circumstances in the *Tarasoff* case (such as *Brady Center v. Wessner*, 1982; *Hedlund v. Superior Court*, 1983) in which duty to protect was extended to committing dangerous patients. These courts also extended protection to those in close proximity to the intended victim who might also be in danger. Fulero (1988) cites a Vermont case (*Peck v. Counseling Service of Addison County*, 1985), in which counselors were held liable for property damage under *Tarasoff* principles of foreseeability and identifiability of a victim. Kermani and Drob (1987) noted two cases that broadened the *Tarasoff* doctrine to include the potential victims of clients who have not threatened a violent act or identified a specific victim (see *Lipari v. Sears, Roebuck & Co.*, 1980, and *McIntosh v. Milano*, 1979). Fischer and Sorenson (1996) also report a case in which the duty to protect a student who threatens suicide (*Eisel v. Board of Education*, 1991) may invoke a duty to harm. When deciding this case, which may serve as legal precedent for other cases, the court took into account such issues as in *loco parentis*, foreseeability, closeness of connection between conduct and injury, moral blame, and recognition of the nationwide problem with high school suicide (*Eisel v. Board of Educ.*, 1991). Certainly such precedent will be considered as cases involving elementary school student suicide and threats come forward thereafter.

The expansion of *Tarasoff* has been counterbalanced by decisions that limit its scope, particularly based on the foreseeability of harm. In *Thompson v. County of Alameda* (1980), a counselor had no duty to warn when a juvenile offender made vague threats (cited in Fulero, 1988). Other similar cases where the victim was not identified include *Brady v. Hopper* (1983), *Mavroudis v. Superior Court for County of San Mateo* (1983), and *Leedy v. Hartnett* (1981) (cited in Fulero, 1988). Finally, Fisher and Sorenson (1996) reported that suicide threats made to non-counseling professionals were not considered requirements similar to *Tarasoff*'s.

For almost two decades then, courts have alternated between limiting and expanding *Tarasoff*'s application. As a result, counselors are often uncertain about the parameters of their legal duty to protect (Kaufman, 1991). In response to the confusion and expansion of liability under many duty to protect decisions, state legislatures have attempted to define the legal doctrine and place limits on the liability of counselors for the acts of their patients (Geske, 1989; Kaufman, 1991; Rudegeair & Appelbaum, 1992; VandeCreek & Knapp, 1993). Kagle and Kopels (1994) identified 17 states that have enacted statutes that limit liability when warning under *Tarasoff* principles of identifiability of victim and risk of imminent danger. In general, these statutes clarify the circumstances under which a duty to warn and protect will be imposed (Geske, 1989). The statutes vary in terms of which professionals are subject to the duty, the types of threats that trigger the duty, the required identifiability of the victim, and the required methods of discharging the duty (Geske, 1989). Most of the statutes grant immunity to mental health professionals who are required to breach confidentiality in order to discharge the duty to warn. However, school counselors and their minor clients are not clearly included in these immunity laws.

School Counselors Versus Other Mental Health Professionals

The contrast between a duty to warn type statute and one that limits liability when warning a third party of impending harm is exemplified by the Florida statute (Fla. Stat. Ann. § 455.2415). It does not require warning but merely permits disclosure of communications of violent intentions without liability for breach of confidentiality (Fla. Stat. Ann. § 455.2415). However, this immunity law only specifies professionals who are regulated under the state's Medical Quality Assurance Board (e.g., mental health counselors). School counselors are certified as teaching professionals under the regulation of the Florida's Department of Education. Their immunity under this rule has not been tested in the courts. This distinction, between counselors based on the legal regulation of different parts of the profession by different governing bodies and rules, may not be clear in all states nor among all counselors or mental health professionals. It is critical that school counselors who find that their state has an immunity law for breaching confidentiality, make sure that school counselors are covered by it.

Training and practice then becomes complex in states which distinguish between counselors in such ways. For example, counselors have general professional ethics (American Counseling Association, 1995), and specific professional ethics (American Counseling Association, 1992) which promote similar principles regarding confidentiality. Counselors' ethics training would be parallel in terms of developing and making professional judgments, but practice as governed by law is necessarily different.

There are other implications of the differences between school counselors and other counselors governed by state regulation. The first, involuntary commitment, is a reasonable clinical response in some cases, to be used by some mental health professionals. It is not available to school counselors. A second premise that may not pertain to school counselors is controllability. Controllability is when counselors can detain or commit clients, which school counselors cannot do. Foreseeability, yet a third premise, is the degree to which a counselor can reasonably predict or foresee harm to a third party or to the client. Foreseeability may be impossible with a population who may not be able to developmentally or legally distinguish real threats from others, or carry out dangerous threats themselves. The counselor's job under such a premise would be to act on those threats determined to be legitimate. Under these circumstances of differences with other mental health professionals, courts may find that school counselors do not have "special relationships" with their student clients and thus may not have a duty to warn and protect.

School counselors may also encounter confidentiality and duty to protect issues arising from consultations with families. While consultation is an accepted and encouraged school counselor practice since the 1970s (Baker, 1996) and consultation is expected to be a confidential activity, immunity or duties to protect arising from consulting relationships are not specified in statutory or case law. Thus, the obligation to adult role as consultee who may reveal information or who may be dangerous is less clear. Counselors would have to identify whether or not a consulting relationship was established and to what extent confidentiality is owed based on that relationship. Informed consent procedures which clearly communicate an understanding of the limits and nature of the consulting relationship are critical. In fact, Ferris and Linville (1988) specifically question whether a client's right to privacy is compromised in any consulting relationship by its very nature of third party communication.

Children, Confidentiality and Competence

The application of *Tarasoff* is based partially on a client's rights to confidentiality and competence to manage such rights. However, all states do not all treat the confidentiality of children's communications to counselors in a uniform way. Elementary school-aged children are not always accorded the competence or capacity to make and maintain confidential relationships because they are not always seen as able to participate fully in informed consent or to understand the implications of confidentiality or its breach. Furthermore, there are differing opinions concerning who owns a child's confidential information (parent or child). As of 1987, Sheeley and Herlihy reported that only 20 jurisdictions specifically protect students with privileged communication, while Fischer and Sorenson (1996) only identified 18 state jurisdictions which protect counselor communication, 16 of which directly grant privilege to teacher and counselors.

The distinction between real and idle threats also hinges on a child's competence to make and carry out real threats, or distinguish between what is real or imagined themselves. There are a few statutes that allow professionals to distinguish between real and idle threats, (e.g., Colorado, Montana, and Louisiana) (Kaufman, 1991). However, if children are not accorded confidentiality or competence, then such distinctions for purposes of breaching confidentiality may be a moot point. Therefore, school counselors cannot consistently apply legal principles of confidentiality or use professional judgment of seriousness of threats or danger with their young clients when the ownership of confidentiality is in question.

Moving Away From the Legal Duty to Protect

Recently, some courts have rejected the premise of imposing a legal duty to protect through warning. For example, a Florida District Court of Appeal (*Boynton v. Burglass*, 1991) and the Virginia Supreme Court have directly rejected the *Tarasoff* doctrine and the premises of special relationship and controllability upon which the duties to warn and protect have been based. In the Florida case, Blaylock, a psychiatric outpatient of Dr. Milton Burglass, shot and killed Boynton after having communicated his intention and the means to seriously harm him. Boynton's parents sued, but both the trial and appeal courts dismissed the complaint (*Boynton v. Burglass*, 1991). The dismissal was based on a lack of a Florida common or statutory law to mandate a duty to warn, on the ethical and statutory duty of confidentiality, and on the near impossibility of accurately predicting dangerousness (McIntosh & Cartaya, 1992). The court cited the Restatement (Second) of Torts stating that "under the common law, a person had no duty to control the conduct of another or to warn those placed in danger by such conduct; however, an exception to that general rule can arise when there is a special relationship between the defendant and the person whose behavior needs to be controlled" (*Boynton v. Burglass*, 1991, p. 449). The *Boynton* majority, finding the *Tarasoff* decision unpersuasive, concluded that "the relationship between a psychiatrist and an outpatient [is] not such a special relationship" (Greenberg, 1992, p. 245). One could speculate that the relationship between a school counselor and an elementary student would similarly not be considered a special relationship either in Florida. However, the *Boynton* court conceded that the duty to warn may arise from social obligations and ethical responsibilities in the absence of a special relationship and a duty to control (*Boynton v. Burglass*, 1991). This is consistent with both ACA and ASCA ethical codes. The *Boynton* court concluded that the duty to warn is unreasonable because it requires the breach of confidentiality that it asserted would destroy or at least hamper the trust and confidence of the relationship (*Boynton v. Burglass*, 1991). Thus, in at least one state, predicting dangerousness, controlling the behavior of another person, and counseling as a special relationship were all rejected in favor of the duty of confidentiality and the necessity of trust in a counseling relationship.

Two other Florida cases that are based on the notion that mental health professionals cannot control client behavior illustrate the trend of not imposing an affirmative duty to protect. In both cases, the issue of controlling a voluntary patient or mandating involuntary commitment to protect a third party was directly addressed and generally rejected

(*Paddock v. Chacko*, 1988 & *Santa Cruz v. Northwest Dade Community Health Center*, 1991). The importance of these cases relates to their reliance on the principle that counselors are unable to control clients rather than counselors' ability to foresee harm to identifiable victims. Both of these factors may have particular bearing for school counselors. It is likely that school counselors could not control a child's behavior, especially off-premises, even if they could foresee the possibilities of dangerous behavior. Changes in the reasons courts give for making their decisions, then, make predicting court decisions in future cases even more difficult. The school counselor is put in the unenviable position of trying to identify current and possible future changes in judicial considerations before taking action.

ETHICAL CODES

Ethical codes and standards, which are guidelines for professional behavior and responsibility, serve as a framework by which professional judgments are made, and also serve as a vehicle for professional identity (Mabe & Rollin, 1985). Ethical codes are not meant to be applied in a mechanical manner and final authority in determining a specific course of action rests with the professional (Corey et al., 1993). In some respects, codes of ethics and law each represent the consensus of a society; ethic and ethical obligations can be distinguished from law and legal duties (Corey et al., 1993). Haas (1990) noted that law develops from political processes and focuses primarily on the avoidance of harm to society through punishment. Ethics develop from rational processes and focuses on achieving higher ideals of human behavior. Even though most codes of ethics and standards of practice recognize the law as superceding the professional behavior defined by the codes (see for example, ACA, 1995), codes can add the force of professional standards of practice and aspirational conduct, as well as a sense of right and good. The force of codes of ethics and standards of practice, however, is in professional discipline and not in legal enforcement. As noted by Givelber et al. (1984), many counselors already see the duty to warn and protect as a matter of personal ethics and responsibility. Radest (1989), and Tennyson & Strom (1985) discuss how ethics are internalized and how a sense of professional responsibility is defined and developed. They discuss ethics as internally motivated, proactive decisions which may be a sharp contrast to action based in law that focuses on avoidance of unpleasant consequences.

The Nature of Ethical Dilemmas

According to many moral philosophers, ethics are distinguished by three features: "it is [sic] based on principles; the principles are universalizable; and proper behavior may be deduced from the principles by reasoning" (Haas, 1990, p. 636). Thus, ethics "involve adherence to a consistent set of principles assumed to be relevant for all actors in similar situations, which result (deductively) in obligations to take particular actions" (Haas, 1990, p. 636). Kitchner (1984) identified the principles of autonomy, beneficence, nonmalificence, justice, and fidelity as critical in evaluation of ethical dilemmas in the helping professions. According to Kitchner (1984), these ethical principles are more fundamental than rules or codes, which may be too narrow in some situations and too broad in others, and therefore provide a more consistent framework for resolving a variety of dilemmas. Ethical principles are not absolute but they are always relevant and can only be superceded when there are stronger ethical obligations (Kitchner, 1984).

A primary ethical justification for a duty to protect or to warn is the principle of beneficence. Beneficence, as defined by Kitchner (1984), is to do good or promote good for others. Confidentiality of client communications falls under the competing principles of fidelity or faithfulness to an implied contract and nonmalificence or do no harm. The ethical obligation to act beneficently applies to both the client and the community at large (Mills, Sullivan & Eth, 1987). Mental health professionals generally accept their dual responsibilities and, according to Quinn (1984), recognition of obligations to third parties has long been reflected in professional codes of ethics as exceptions to the rule of confidentiality. Slovenko (1975) questioned the significance of the _Tarasoff_ decision and asserted that it was accepted practice to warn appropriate persons when a client presented a serious threat of violence. Slovenko expressed that "trust—not absolute confidentiality—is the cornerstone of psychotherapy ... imposing control where self control breaks down is not a breach of trust when it's not deceptive" (p. 139).

The foregoing discussion of ethical dilemma and their resolution creates the impression of a ready resolution to a difficult problem by application of a standard process. However, the addition of varying legal requirements, permissions and prohibitions makes resolution of this dilemma using ethical decision-making extremely difficult. These have created competing principles for decision-making between the client's best interests (confidentiality), society's best interests (safety and protection), and the practitioner's best personal and professional interests (avoidance of litigation and malpractice). Neukrug, Lovell and Parker (1996) assert that ethical decision-making is confounded by level of moral development. Those whose moral development is on a rule or legalistic oriented level may well find this dilemma differently solved than those whose development is oriented more toward principled decisions and behavior.

The Overlap Between Legal Issues and Ethical Codes

The American Counseling Association (ACA) recently revised their Ethical Standards (1955). *Tarasoff* is clearly reflected in Standard B.1.c as an exception to a client's right to privacy as required "to prevent clear and imminent danger to the client or others" (p. 5) or when legal requirements take precedence. Section B.1.g obligates counselors to inform clients of possible limits to confidentiality and situations in which it would be breached (with the implication that such information is governed by the counselor's state laws.) In the new 1995 *Codes of Ethics and Standards of Practice* appended to the ACA Ethical Standards, Standard of Practice SP-9 refers to confidentiality as not absolute when "disclosure is in the best interest of clients, is required for the welfare of others, or is required by law" (p. 39). These standards continue the premise of the earlier 1988 Ethical Standards (ACA, 1988) in Section B.4., Counseling Relationship, in which it is stated that "when the client's condition indicates there is a clear and imminent danger to the client or others, the member must take reasonable personal action or inform responsible authorities" (p. 2). The 1988 version also specified confidentiality and client welfare issues in sections B.1. and B.2.

The ACA *Codes of Ethics and Standards of Practice* remains consistent in its intent with the earlier ASCA (1992) Code of Ethics. The ASCA code states clearly in section A.8 and A.9 that counselors are obligated both to protect confidentiality and to inform authorities in cases of clear and imminent danger after careful deliberation and consultation with others. However, like the ACA Code of Ethics, ASCA's code defers to state law which is enforceable in court.

Both groups have responded specifically to *Tarasoff* and have continued a tradition of responsibility for clients and broader society, as well as to variations in local regulations and case law. By including these criteria in their codes, counselors have recognized the higher or aspirational obligations to clients and to the community. However, by adding disclaimers that identify law as taking precedence over the code, more confusion about how to resolve conflicts may be created since law is unclear in its application to school counselors and since each jurisdiction regards these principles differently. Still, counselors who are not required by statute or case law to pay attention to the *Tarasoff* principle are obliged more generally by their personal and professional ethics to promote the welfare of clients and to protect others from harm.

Accordingly, many counselors look to ethical principles and good practice standards to inform professional judgment. However, as previously noted, these can sometimes lead to a double bind situation. An example involving child abuse reporting illustrates this dilemma. Surveys of therapists legally required to report child abuse indicate that therapists do not consistently follow mandatory reporting laws because reporting necessitates a breach of confidentiality, reporting is punitively oriented rather than therapeutically oriented, and reporting threatens the therapeutic relationship (Butz, 1985). The results of that survey indicate that when reporting abuse or other legal interventions conflict with the welfare of clients and families, professional decisions are based on personal, ethical, and therapeutic priorities rather than on a desire to comply with the law (Crenshaw, Lichtenberg, & Bartell, 1993). This contrasts with the notion that counselors' primary motivation for professional decisions will be the avoidance of litigation. Since both motivations may exist between or within counselors, the application of ethical standards and decision-making may be uneven.

Current Guidelines for Counselors and Dangerous Clients in Light of *Tarasoff*

It may be a safe assumption that, like other mental health professionals, counselors are increasingly aware of their responsibilities for dangerous clients and protecting third parties when faced with a threatening client. Counselors may wish to warn because it is a decisive action. Those who know about *Tarasoff* may mistakenly think that warning is their only option or obligation. For school counselors, many of the recommended practices to manage dangerous clients remain ill-defined.

Recent articles by Pietrofesa et al. (1990), and Costa and Altekruse (1994) offer guidelines for assessing dangerousness and implementing warnings to third parties. Such paradigms concern assessing clients' specific intentions and/or plans to commit violence, ability to carry out a plan, understanding of actions and their consequences, and capability to collaborate to control behavior if necessary (Costa & Altekruse, 1994; Pietrofesa et al., 1990). The goals of such behavior are determining client needs and determining if warnings or other actions designed to protect clients or third parties are advised. However, each prescription may present unique situations for the elementary school counselor in assessing client capacity and competence to meet these criteria.

Other sections of these guidelines (Costa & Altekruse, 1994; Pietrofesa et al., 1990) suggest procedures that are consistent with codes of ethics and with the practice of making professional judgments. For example, these authors noted that counselors should choose their clients carefully based on knowledge of their own competence. If the therapist has any doubt about their ability to deal with a potentially violent client, an appropriate referral should be made. School counselors cannot follow the first advice of choosing their clients carefully since all students in the school may potentially be a client, at least until information is revealed which may make referral necessary. However, once the information is revealed to the school counselor and a referral is made, the student may no longer be a client but remains in the school environment. In addition, if information is revealed prior to referral, referral may not obviate the decision to breach confidentiality.

Depending upon age of the child and the jurisdiction, other steps may not be available to school counselors. Informing clients of the limits of confidentiality and obtaining informed consent at the outset of treatment may not be consistently required in each state due to variations in notions of capacity. Taking a detailed history in assessing potential dangerousness and maintaining detailed records of the progress of counseling, including any indications of potential danger, to self or others, may also not be practical with younger children due to their more recent entry to school and therefore unavailability of prior records, or younger children's lack of reliable information about their own history. If a client's history indicates a duty to protect or to warn others, Costa & Altekruse (1994) and Pietrofesa et al. (1990) recommend courses of action the school counselor can follow including consulting with supervisors or peers; notifying the intended victim(s) with due care; and obtaining the client's cooperation and involvement in the process.

Informed consent becomes more complex when addressing consultation. Counselors are encouraged to develop strong confidentiality guidelines that cover the tripartite consultation relationship and to delineate consultee rights using ongoing informed consent procedures (American Counseling Association, 1995; Dogherty, 1995). However, since school counselors often consult in less formal arrangements while working with parents and teachers, full informed consent may not be practical. Moreover, less formal or short-term consultation raises issues about whether a "special relationship" as defined by *Tarasoff*, or a counseling relationship as defined by ACA's or ASCA's Code of Ethics, would exist and invoke duty to protect or confidentiality rights.

School counselors may develop contingency plans for such situations. These plans can include the identification of other school counselors, school administrators, mental health practitioners, and attorneys who can be consulted. School counselors can also develop clear procedures they will follow in the event of dangerous clients or crises. Since it is accepted that most threats or discussions of hostility do not lead to action, counselors are urged not to routinely reveal confidential communication unless serious intent can be identified (Corey et al., 1998). School counselors should also make sure that they have adequate coverage for legal representation and liability through private policies, professional association or union membership, or through school administrative policies.

Guidelines for treating dangerous clients and for conducting violence or suicide assessments are routinely included in training programs and textbooks of various kinds and periodic suicides among school-aged children have raised awareness of suicide prevention, assessment, and response among school counselors. A suggestion that is increasingly included in professional codes and training programs for a variety of dilemmas is increased consultation, which constitutes a different kind of breach of confidentiality to another professional under controlled and anonymous circumstances. It should be noted, however, that training and professional preparation standards tend to focus on clinical management that is based on more singular principles of client welfare and clinical management issues than the complicating factor of a legal duty to warn and protect. The best advice often given to school counselors is not always practical given everyday time limits and a lack of training to interpret law (Hopkins & Anderson, 1990; VandeCreek & Knapp, 1993, 1994). Additionally, even with good suggestions for managing dangerous clients and making duty to warn decisions, the potential for liability remains (Costa & Altekruse, 1994; Pietrofesa et al., 1990).

While legal and mental health professionals agree that society deserves protection from violence, there is little consensus regarding the best way to protect third parties from dangerous clients (Mills et al., 1987). Mills et al. suggests that under the *Tarasoff* principle, mental health practitioners can protect themselves from legal liability by warning potential victims, but warnings do not necessarily protect third parties or help clients. Warning a potentially violent client's intended victim or others may be the appropriate response; such ethical dilemmas cannot be adequately resolved by strict adherence to a prescribed behavior. According to Kitchner (1984), following a principle without exception and without regard to the circumstances may lead to an unethical act. Therefore, acceptance of the idea that society deserves protection from dangerous persons does not absolve the counselor from thoughtful decision making.

CONCLUSION

Tarasoff has influenced mental health practitioner behavior for more than 20 years and it will more than likely continue to do so through ethics and through law. The literature is replete with commentary on the *Tarasoff* doctrine and its effects on the mental health professions. Cases where elementary students and their counselors are faced with duty to protect decisions are more frequent. Models of ethical decision making are complicated when the counselor's own protection is pit against those of the client and third parties. Furthermore, jurisdiction variations make standard principles for response difficult to develop and follow.

The variations in specific statutes, local or school district policy, case law, and school counselor job descriptions or contracts create confusion when they vary within and between jurisdictions. It arises particularly in jurisdictions where mental health professionals are lumped together or specifically names, and the counselor must ferret out how school counseling is or may be affected, or how minor clients are treated for purposes of confidentiality and informed consent. Whether legally required, legally permissible or not, the principles of *Tarasoff* are embedded in ethical codes and ingrained into the ways of thinking, judging and practicing counselors (American Counseling Association, 1995; American School Counseling Association, 1992). This principle is broadly and incorrectly incorporated into training and professional preparation as if it were universal.

It is also clear that counselors have been confused by the commingling of a California case, case law in other jurisdictions, statutory requirements for other mental health practitioners and ethical guidelines. As the practice of law and laws evolve, mental health practitioners will need to continue to develop ethically consistent ways to practice, and personal methods for making professional judgments in difficult situations. As noted by Standard and Hazler (1995), counselors must have an ethical theory or framework to rely on, because rules and codes only provide guidelines that sometimes conflict and that do not cover all potential dilemmas.

Counselors can also develop a *priori* protocols that enable them to respond to dangerous clients with consistent principles and confidence and according to the ethical theory or framework Standard and Hazler (1995) propose. These protocols can include:

- keeping abreast of current standards of care, practicing the highest standards of care and professional behavior allowable by the school district policy or specific job description
- developing a list of treatment alternatives for dangerous patients that may not involve warning (breaching confidentiality)
- including full informed consent in all counseling and consulting interactions and including students in decisions about dangerousness and steps toward warning and protecting
- keeping abreast of law changes; especially after degrees or certifications have been earned
- developing an understanding of consulting relationships with parents or other adults whose revelations may invoke a duty to warn others
- routinely consulting with others and developing a consultation network for when more urgent situations occur
- keeping abreast of local case law changes through one's local or state counseling or school counseling association

- consulting school attorneys to determine how recent statutory, case law or certification changes affect school counselors
- encouraging development of school policy that helps school counselors manage potentially dangerous elementary school clients or information and allows them to honor ethical commitments to confidentiality
- understanding if the state has a local immunity law and how or if it affects school counselors
- understanding the responsibility that testifying in a case may bring with regard to impacting current case law
- urging local school districts to update counselors on current case law and statute as it affects them through newsletters or periodic in-service training activities
- using internet interest groups to keep abreast of issues and for informal consultation about broader issues of professional conduct.

The above will not foreclose urgent care decisions or replace careful consideration of the ethical principles involved. They will prepare school counselors to readily identify the issues, know their options, and identify needed information when urgent decisions must be made.

Madelyn L. Isaacs *is an assistant professor in the Counselor Education department at University of South Florida–Fort Myers. Correspondence regarding this article should be sent to Madelyn L. Isaacs, 8111 College Parkway, University of Southern Florida at Fort Myers, Fort Myers, Florida 33919.*

REFERENCES

American Counseling Association. (1988). *Ethical Standards* (rev ed.). Alexandria, VA: Author.

American Counseling Association. (1995). *Code of Ethics and Standards of Practice,* Alexandria VA: Author.

American School Counseling Association. (1974). *The school counselor and confidentiality.* Alexandria VA: Author

American School Counseling Association. (1986). *The school counselor and confidentiality.* Alexandria VA: Author

American School Counseling Association. (1992). *Code of Ethics.* Alexandria VA: Author

Baker, S. (1996). *School counseling for the twenty-first century.* Englewood Cliffs, NJ: Merrill.

Beck, J. C. (1982). When the patient threatens violence: An empirical study of clinical practice after *Tarasoff. Bulletin of the American Academy of Psychiatry and Law, 10,* 189-202.

Boynton v. Burglass, 590 So. 2d 446 (Fla. App. 3rd Dist. 1991).

Butz, R. A. (1985). Reporting child abuse and confidentiality in counseling. Social Case Work: *The Journal of Contemporary Social Work, 66*, 83-90.

Corey, G., Corey, M. S., & Callanan, P. (1993). *Issues and ethics in the helping professions*. Pacific Grove, CA: Brooks/Cole.

Costa. L., & Altekruse, M. (1994). Duty-to-warn guidelines for mental health counselors. *Journal of Counseling and Development, 72*, 346-350.

Crenshaw, W. B., Lichtenberg, J. W., & Bartell, P. A. (1993). Mental health providers and child abuse: A multivariate analysis of the decision to report. *Journal of Child Sexual Abuse, 2*, 19-42.

Dougherty, M. (1995). *Consultation: Practice and perspectives in school and community settings*. (2nd ed.). Pacific Grove, CA:Brooks/Cole.

Eisel v. Board of Educ., 59i A2d 447 (Md Ct. App. 1991)

Ferris, P. & Linville, M. (1988). *The child's rights: Whose responsibility?* In W. Huey & T. Remley, Jr., Ethical issues in school counseling (pp. 20-80). Alexandria, VA:American Counselor Association.

Fischer, L., & Sorenson, G. P. (1996). *School law for counselors, psychologists and social workers* (3rd ed.). New York: Longman.

Fla. Stat. Ann., 455.2415 (West Supp. 1995).

Fulco, S. M. (1988). *Tarasoff, 10 years later. Professional Psychology, 19*, 184-190.

Geske, M. R. (1989). Statutes limiting mental health professional's liability for the violent acts of their patients. *Indiana Law Journal, 64*, 891-422.

Givelber, D. J., Bowers, W. J., & Blitch, C. L. (1984). *Tarasoff, myth and reality: An empirical study of private law in action. Wisconsin Law Review, 2*, 443-497.

Gray, L., & Harding, A. (1988). Confidentiality limits with clients who have the AIDS virus. *Journal of Counseling and Development, 65*, 219-226.

Greenberg, A. C. (1992). Florida rejects a *Tarasoff* duty to protect. *Stetson Law Review, 22*, 239-282.

Haas, L. J. (1990). Professional ethics and the psychologists' code of ethics: An introduction and overview for the private practitioner. In E.A. Margenau (Ed.), *The encyclopedia handbook of private practice* (pp. 634-650). New York: Gardner.

Herlihy, B., & Golden, L. B. (Eds., (1990). *Ethical standards casebook*. Alexandria, VA: American Counseling Association.

Herlihy, B. & Sheeley V. L. (1988). Counselor liability and the duty to warn: selected cases, statutory trends, and implications for practice. *Counselor Education and Supervision, 27*, 203-215.

Hopewell v. Adebimpe, (1978) Court of Common Pleas of Allegheney County, Pennsylvania Civil Case No. G.D. 78-28756.

Hopkins, E. R. & Anderson, B. S. (1990). *The counselor and the law*. Alexandria, VA: American Counseling Association.

Huber, C. H. (1994). *Ethical legal and professional issues in the practice of marriage and family therapy* (2nd ed.). Columbus, OH: Merrill.

Huey, W. C. & Remley, T. P., Jr. (Eds.). (1989). *Ethical and legal issues in school counseling*. Alexandria, VA: American Counseling Association.

Isaacs, M. (1995). *Survey of practicing counselors about knowledge of* Tarasoff. Unpublished raw data.

Kagle, J. D., & Kopels, S. (1994). Confidentiality after *Tarasoff. Health and Social Work, 19*, 217-222.

Kaufman, M. (1991). Post-*Tarasoff* legal developments and the mental health literature. *Bulletin of the Menninger Clinic, 55*, 308-322.

Kermani, E. J., & Drob, S. L. (1987). *Tarasoff* decision: A decade later dilemma still faces psychotherapists. *American Journal of Psychotherapy, 41*, 271-285.

Kitchner, K. (1984). Intuition, critical evaluation and ethical principles: The foundation for ethical decisions in counseling psychology. *The Counseling Psychologist, 12*(3), 43-55.

Mabe, A. R., & Rollin, S. A. (1985). The role of a code of ethical standards in counseling. *Journal of Counseling and Development, 64,* 294-297.

McIntosh, D. M., & Cartaya, C. Y. (1992). Psychotherapist as clairvoyant: Failing to predict and warn. *Defense Counsel Journal, 59,* 569-573.

Mills, M. J., Sullivan, G., & Eth, S. (1987). Protecting third parties: A decade after *Tarasoff. American Journal of Psychiatry, 144,* 68-74.

Neukrug, E., Lovell, C. & Parker, R. J. (1966). Employing ethical codes and decision-making models: A developmental process. *Counseling and Values, 40,* 98-106.

Paddock v. Chacko, 522 So. 2d. 410 (Fla. App. 5th Dist. 1988).

Pietrofesa, J. J., Pietrofesa, C. F., & Pietrofesa, J. D. (1990). The mental health counselor and "duty to warn." *Journal of Mental Health Counseling, 12,* 129-137.

Quinn, K. M. (1984). The impact of *Tarasoff* on clinical practice. *Behavioral Sciences and the Law, 2,* 319-330.

Radest, H. B. (1989). *Can we teach ethics?* New York: Praeger.

Rosenhan, D. L., Teitelbaum, T. W., Teitelbaum, K. W., & Davidson, M. (1993). Warning third parties: The ripple effects of *Tarasoff. Pacific Law Journal, 24,* 1165-1232.

Rudegeair, T. J., & Appelbaum, P. S. (1992). On the duty to protect: An evolutionary perspective. *Bulletin of the American Academy of Psychiatry and Law, 20,* 419-426.

Santa Cruz v. Northwest Dade Community Health Center, 590 So. 2d 444 (Fla. App. 3rd Dist. 1991).

Sheeley, V. L. & Herlihy, B. (1987). Privileged communication and the school counseling: a status update. *The School Counselor, 34,* 268-272.

Slovenko, R. (1975). Psychotherapy and confidentiality. *Cleveland State Law Review, 24,* 375-391.

Standard, R., & Hazler, R. (1995). Legal and ethical implications of HIV and duty to warn for counselors: Does *Tarasoff* apply? *Journal of Counseling & Development, 73,* 397-400.

Tarasoff v. Regents of the University of California, 118 Cal. Rptr. 129, 529 P 2d 533 (1974).

Tarasoff v. Regents of the University of California, 17 Cal 3d 425, 551 P 2d 334 (1976).

Tennyson, W. W., & Strom, S. M. (1985). Beyond professional standards: Developing responsibleness. *Journal of Counseling and Development, 64,* 298-302.

VandeCreek, L. & Knapp, S. (1993). Tarasoff *and beyond: Legal and clinical considerations in the treatment of life-endangering patients.* Sarasota, FL: Professional Resource Press.

VandeCreek, L. & Knapp, S. (1994). Ethical and legal issues. In F. M. Datillo & A. Freeman, (Eds.). *Cognitive-behavioral strategies in crisis intervention.* New York: Guilford.

Legal Implications of Profiling Students for Violence

Kirk A. Bailey

Predicting violent activity with a youth violence profile in schools raises a host of legal concerns focusing on the validity and use of profiles as social science evidence: the impact of potential discrimination, search and seizure, and the implications for privacy. Schools differ from airports or other settings where profiles are used. Profiles are useful if they properly establish reasonable suspicion to stop an individual. They raise more problematic constitutional issue when they support referring a student to alternative educational services. Where a profile identifies students based on race, gender, or proxies for these characteristics, it is invalid. It can also be invalid if it is not a reasonable method of achieving the government's interest in safe schools. In addition, profiles present significant problems for confidentiality. These issues rest on fundamental concerns about the general validity of profiles as scientific tools: their objectivity, accuracy, sensitivity, over-inclusiveness, and general scientific acceptance. Consequently, the use of profiles in a school setting is highly problematic and controversial.

INTRODUCTION

In April 2000, the Secretary of the Department of Education, Richard W. Riley, announced his opposition to the use of behavioral profiling systems to identify potentially violent students in schools, in a speech to school counselors in Chicago (Cooper, 2000). Secretary Riley went on to state "[w]e simply cannot put student behaviors into a formula to come up with an appropriate response. The Secretary's comments are some of the latest in a long-standing debate over the use of violence-prediction tools to identify potentially violent students before they unleash their carnage on an unsuspecting school or community.

On the other side of the issue, parent groups, students, and law enforcement who see the daily press reports of school violence, teen shootings, and similar tragedies throughout America are calling for effective ways to prevent school violence. (For a full discussion of school violence trends see Coggeshall & Kingery, 2001, in this special issue.) In light of the level of violence affecting America's youth, it only seems natural that as each new school shooting grips the public's attention, parents, teachers, school officials, and policy-makers would demand a profile of school shooters to identify the source of potential violence before it erupts. Typically, a profile identifies a person likely to commit an act (usually criminal) of a certain type. These types of profiles are developed from extensive research and analysis of the crimes and behaviors of actual perpetrators: terrorists, drug couriers, and assassins, for example. The assembled information is compiled to identify the key characteristics of each type of crime and the corresponding characteristics of the type of person most likely to commit that type of crime. Accordingly, they are used to assess all persons in a given location or under a particular set of circumstance to determine if they match the profile and represent a potential threat to the safety of others.

A youth violence profile would most closely resemble the dangerous passenger profile used by the Federal Aviation Administration to identify possible drug couriers and terrorists in the airport setting. First, both are based on the methodology just described. Second, both are utilized in specific, highly insular environments—namely, an airport or a school. Third, they identify potentially violent individuals from a large population of highly similar individuals, most of whom are engaged in innocent behavior. Finally, the assessment based on the profile is done under significant time constraints: time is of the essence in deciding on a profile match before a person boards a plane or enters a school.

Predicting violent activity in the school context raises a host of legal and ethical concerns. These concerns center on the validity (meaning the profile's ability to measure what it purports to measure and conformance to accepted scientific standards), and use of profiles as social science evidence, the impact of potential discrimination, search and seizure, and implications for privacy and the use of student records. The use of profiles as social science evidence will be addressed in the initial section of this article regarding "General Validity," while the search-and-seizure aspects of profile usage are addressed under the second section, "Profiles as Grounds for Search and Seizure." The third section, "Constitutional Issues: Access to Education Services Based on Profiles," addresses constitutional issues involving referral of students to alternative education based on profile matches. The implications for student privacy are discussed in the fourth section on "Privacy and Educational Records." This article attempts to outline the breadth of these issues without suggesting concrete answers. The development of the law and ethics in this area is too new to allow for statements of definitive guidelines, and true to form—a legal article is long on problems and short on solutions. In truth, this is less a testament to the limitations of legal analysis than it is a recognition of the need to engage in the thoroughly democratic process of assembling potential rules of conduct and guidelines for profiles in a comprehensive and collaborative fashion involving all the disciplines of science, medicine, health, and law. Hopefully, this special issue will contribute to the creation of just such a shared understanding.

GENERAL VALIDITY: OBJECTIVITY, OVER-INCLUSIVENESS, EVIDENTIARY ISSUES

The general validity of a profile depends on the circumstances of its use. There is no governing legal rule or case involving a youth violence profile or the use of a profile in a school setting. As discussed in the Introduction, however, profiles have been used in a number of other settings and their validity assessed by the Supreme Court and a number of lower federal courts. The courts have avoided ruling on broad cases involving profiling instead focusing on the specific facts of individual cases. Based on this body of law, it may be said that where a profile is used as an investigation tool to assist the determination of the need to stop and search a suspect, it is generally regarded as a valid practice (*U.S. v. Lopez*, 1971). In the case of *U.S. v. Riggs*, the court upheld stopping a suspect for identification and inquiry purposes because the Federal Aviation Administration's "behavioral profile" gave security "reasonable and objectively articulable grounds to suspect Riggs of both trafficking in narcotics and also posing a threat to aircraft security" (*U.S. v. Riggs*, 1972). The contours of the use of profiles as an investigation approach are explored more deeply in the next section on search and seizure, but it is important to consider the court's reference to objectivity before leaving the matter for later discussion.

Profile Objectivity

Typically, the Supreme Court requires that an "[e]ffective profile is one that may be 'objectively employed by the ticket seller [teacher] without requiring any subjective interpolation'" (*U.S. v. Bell*, 1972). In *U.S. v. Lopez*, despite upholding the general use of a profile in an airport-search context, a lower federal court suppressed the use of the profile because its objectivity and neutrality had been compromised. The court was concerned with the elimination of fundamental terrorist characteristics established by research, the addition of "an ethnic element for which there [was] no experimental basis" and the requirement of "an act of individual judgment on the part of airline employees" (*U.S. v. Lopez*, 1971). The court went on to state "[t]he approved system survives constitutional scrutiny only by its careful adherence to absolute objectivity and neutrality. When elements of discretion and prejudice are interjected it becomes constitutionally impermissible" (*U.S. v. Lopez*, 1971). The court suggested that the appropriate remedy for this oversight lies in the continuous supervision and control of personnel who have the power and authority to use the profile (*U.S. v. Lopez*, 1971).

Clearly, the court is concerned that profiles be free from issues of race and prejudice and supported by a thorough analysis of the factors involved in the profile. The concept of neutrality implies that the implementation of a profile will be free of any bias based on impermissible factors, such as race, religion, gender, or a host of other classifications, which our society deems an inappropriate base for judging individuals. Presumably, this also includes the absence of bias based on prior association of the parties involved, meaning that there should be no significant or compelling personal history between teachers and students that suggests unfairness, animosity, rancor or the like. Moreover, it seems reasonable to suggest that the limits of this neutrality stretch to prohibit even the appearance of bias in the implementation of a profile. Even the suggestion of unfairness or inappropriate application of a profile threatens to undermine its validity and acceptance by the general public and the affected population namely, youth, teachers, school officials, and parents.

Issues of individual discretion are somewhat cloudier, however. The law is concerned primarily with an individual employee's discretion regarding the factors included in the profile in the first instance rather than the exercise of judgment in applying those factors. This concern is particularly compelling in the case of a youth violence profile where numerous and differing risk factor lists exist that might be used as profiles. Our brief foray into this area revealed different formulations compiled by the Centers of Disease Control, the American Psychological Association, the U.S. Department of Justice, and the U.S. Department of Education. With so many, the risk of individual decisions at the classroom or school levels seems greatly heightened.

Yet it may be impossible to ensure that the required objectivity and neutrality is present because simply and fundamentally, schools and airports are too different. In an airport, strangers come together for a brief time for a utilitarian purpose (travel), while schools, in contrast, are places where people form long-term, intimate, personal relationships focusing on social and cooperative goals. It may well be that in the context of an airport or other public place that a profile will be implemented in a fashion that allows for its objective use. Usually in such a highly public setting, the passengers, travel agents, airline personnel, security officers, and others are largely unknown to each other. This anonymity promotes a greater level of tolerance for the unavoidable diversity one is likely to encounter during travel. In this scenario, security officials are more likely to utilize a profile in an objective manner—all they have to go on is the factors listed in the profile, and they are actively seeking those individuals who meet several of the criteria and disregarding at a moment's reflection those who do not. Under such circumstances, the security officers to not have time or inclination to consider subjective factors such as concerns about past actions of individuals, beliefs about political or social issues, personal habits or hobbies, or relationships with other members of the traveling community.

The situation is exactly the opposite in the school setting. In most cases, the students, teacher and administrators in any given school will be relatively well known to each other, at least in the immediate group of association. Teachers will be reasonably familiar with the lives, interests, problems, hopes, dreams, and fears of many of their students. In fact, as a society we hope that teachers will concern themselves with such matters. Consequently, teachers will be aware of those students who excel or are "problem" students. Under such circumstances, the probability that a profile might be applied subjectively and selectively increases dramatically. An integral part of the growth and learning process involves exploration of the bounds of social acceptance through a process of rebellion and antipathy to authority. While some of this behavior may rise to the level of violence or criminality, much of it remains relatively harmless and free of violence. Students exhibiting such behavior tend to generate more attention, however, and will certainly be well known to their teachers and the school administration. Moreover, these same students are likely to score high on the factors associated with any profile, if for no other reason than they are more highly visible among the student population, or consume the greater part of a teacher's time. For these reasons, it is not altogether clear that a profiling tool could be described accurately as "objective."

In any case, what is clear is that the use of a profile requires an objective and neutral application of its elements and that employees should not be allowed to freedom to include or omit factors based on their subjective perspectives.

Profiles as Evidence: Over-Inclusiveness

In contrast to the investigation context, profile evidence is not admissible, generally, in a court proceeding to establish guilt, on the rationale that profile evidence would be "too sweeping and over-inclusive, and hence potentially misleading to juries and unfairly prejudicial to defendants" (Kirkpatrick, 1998).

Typically, a profile includes a number of factors that taken individually would result in the selection of almost any individual in a given circumstance or locale as a potential match to the profile, and most of these individuals will be innocent of any wrongdoing whatsoever. This is especially true in the case of a youth violence profile in light of the relative infancy of the predictive tools and the imprecision of existing measures.

The social science research in this area concerns itself with several factors including the level of positive prediction (accuracy), the sensitivity of the profile, and interrelationship of these two factors. The odd dynamic is that as the level of accuracy increases, the level of sensitivity decreases, and vice versa (Derzon, 2000). In other words, as prediction (accuracy) improves, the effort becomes less precise in solving the problem of violence because a significant number of violent youth will not be identified by the profile. On the other hand, as sensitivity is improved, the effect is to identify more persons who do not belong in the prediction. This relationship is described more fully by Derzon (2001, in this special issue).

In any case, the sensitive dynamic is the over-inclusiveness problem commonly associated with profiles. These profiles are based on samples of compiled data regarding the known characteristics of known shooters. As such, they focus on the characteristics of a known population, heighten the impact of those characteristics on selection and improve the level of sensitivity. In doing so, however, they cast their net too wide and include youth who will not exhibit violence but who may possess one or more of the identified risk factors. This over-inclusiveness problem severely diminishes the general validity of a profile and presents serious constitutional issues discussed in a separate section below.

The dynamic between profile accuracy and sensitivity does suggest some policy implications worth a moment's reflection, however. If sensitivity is society's concern, namely to account for all the violent youth, then the intervention program used in response should be positive, educational and nurturing rather than punishing and retributive. This is so because we are likely to identify youth who may be at risk but will never commit a crime or exhibit any violent tendencies. Inflicting a penal-type solution on these youth would exacerbate their problems, while a strong educational and social skills approach promises great returns in terms of their employment prospects, social development, contribution to society, and savings to the criminal justice system. However, if programs and interventions aimed at the potential outcome, youth violence, are harsh, punitive and penal in nature, then greater predictive strength (accuracy) will be needed and should be desired. This argues for placing as much emphasis on accuracy as possible because society will want to guarantee that those who are subjected to limitations on their educational opportunity and civil rights are a true threat.

Clearly, however, this latter approach is fraught with difficulty, so much so that it proves unworkable. The greatest legal objection is that it somehow implies that youth may be deprived certain rights or opportunities based on their potential for violent or criminal acts, rather than an act or wrongdoing itself. Our legal tradition abhors this approach. The *U. S. v. Lopez* court remarked disapprovingly on this very subject in stating:

> Undoubtedly there are persons with objectively observable characteristics who provide a higher statistical probability of danger than the population as a whole. But our criminal law is based on the theory that we do not condemn people because they are potentially dangerous. We only prosecute illegal acts. Putting a group of potential violators in custody on the ground that this group contained all or nearly all of the people who would commit crimes in the future would raise the most serious constitutional issues. (*U.S. v. Lopez*, citing Williams, Bonkalo, Woods).

For these reasons, profile evidence is generally avoided as a basis for the potential deprivation of liberty or rights, especially as evidence to be used in a formal trial or hearing. As a matter of policy however, it is worthwhile to consider how such evidence would be treated if the general prohibition did not exist.

The most appropriate legal standards that might establish the validity of profile use as evidence may be drawn from the Supreme Court's rulings on the admissibility of scientific syndrome evidence, notably the *Daubert v. Merrell Dow Pharmaceuticals* (1993) case. Syndrome evidence relates to descriptions of "pattern[s] of behavior or psychological reactions typical of a particular type of offender or crime victim..." an area closely related to the focus of profiles (Kirkpatrick, 1998). The Daubert case relies on a two-part test that is based on federal evidence rules for admitting scientific expert testimony (*Daubert v. Merrell Dow Pharmaceuticals*, 1993). This test requires a determination by a trial judge, that an expert will testify to (a) scientific knowledge that (b) will assist a jury in understanding key facts of the case.

The latter factor is generally viewed as a relevancy requirement, namely that information must be relevant to an issue in the case and provide the jury some information otherwise not available to it. Generally, all information related to a case is considered relevant. It seems clear that profile information indicates something about the person and/or the crime or wrongdoing that would be informative and persuasive for a jury or hearer of fact. Undoubtedly, a determination regarding a referral to mental health counseling services or the presence of mitigating factors in a suspension/expulsion hearing would be aided by the availability of information regarding a student's match with profile characteristics.

The former requirement presents the more difficult case because it is generally viewed by creating an evidentiary reliability standard that information be based on scientific inquiry that has been subjected to appropriate validation (Ingram, 1998). Several factors provide guidance on appropriate validation:

1. Whether the conclusion can be tested.
2. Whether the procedure and basis of conclusion has been subjected to peer review and publication.
3. The test's known or potential rate of error.
4. Standards of control for the technique's operation.
5. The level of general acceptance in the scientific community (Ingram, 1998).

Whether profiles based on social science research and particularly those involving youth violence meet these requirements seems an entirely open question. Arguably youth violence profiles ultimately will be constructed according to standard methods of scientific inquiry such as surveys of school shooters and the compilation of statistics and risk factors for youth to identify trends. Yet, it is not clear that these profiles have been assembled to date according to standard and accepted lines of scientific inquiry, which is not to suggest that the social science identifying particular risk factors for violence among youth is invalid, but only that it cannot fairly be said to have been developed with the purpose of serving as a law enforcement tool in mind. At a more fundamental level, the social science methods that assemble these risk factor analyses often represent aggregated information regarding the risk that a given population will be involved in a specific behavior. This aggregation provides useful information about the group at risk for violence but may not have significant predictive ability when focused on individuals. In this light, a profile might be useful in identifying a "hot spot," a community, neighborhood, or school, more at-risk than others that needs additional prevention and intervention effort.

In addition, few could argue that social scientists, educators, or policy makers have had sufficient time to evaluate the effectiveness of these profiles as predictive tools. To bolster this argument, there clearly has not been sufficient time to subject these profiles to independent testing and verification or for them to gain general acceptance in the scientific community. Moreover, to improve the predictive strength of these profile models as applied in individual cases, a more complete understanding of the correlation between a profile and the outcome it addresses is needed. Therefore, more empirical data are necessary. A significant problem, however, is that referencing back from school shootings to assemble a profile is probably mathematically flawed in that it over-samples those individuals who are clearly positive for the violence outcome (Derzon & Wilson, 2000). This over-sample contributes to the over-inclusiveness of profiles when they are applied to a general population, as previously discussed.

In sum, these considerations indicate that a legitimate profile will be one based on objective and neutral factors, established by comprehensive research and replication, and accepted generally by the scientific community. Lacking these assurances, schools, education leaders, and the general public would be justified in treating profiles with significant skepticism. The presence of these conditions, however, will improve the use of profiles by practitioners and enhance their treatment in areas of the law considered in the remainder of this article. We now turn to those additional issues.

Profiles as Grounds for Search or Seizure

In some circumstances, a list of risk factors for youth violence or a profile of a potentially dangerous student may be used as grounds to stop a student for questioning or to search his or her possessions or person. There is no Supreme Court case addressing the use of risk factor lists or profiles in the school setting. Consequently, we must turn to the Court's leading decisions on search and seizure in the school setting in combination with its jurisprudence on the use of passenger profiles used in airports for guidance regarding the issues implicated by the use of a profile in a school.

Generally, school officials may search a student "if a search is justified at its inception and is conducted in a manner reasonably related in scope to the circumstances" (*New Jersey v. T.L.O.*, 1985). The reasonableness standard is intended "to ensure student's rights [will] be invaded no more than necessary to maintain order in schools, not to authorize all searches conceivable to school officials" (*New Jersey v. T.L.O.*, 1985).

A search will be justified where there are reasonable grounds for suspecting a search will reveal contraband or evidence that a student is violating school rules (Rapp, 1999). The scope of the search is permissible when the measures used are reasonably related to the objective of the search and not excessively intrusive given the age and sex of the student and nature of the infraction (Rapp, 1999). Accordingly, school officials may inspect a student's bag (purse, backpack, duffel) and clothing for hidden weapons, cigarettes, and drugs when they have reason to do so: e.g., a tip, observation of material associated with drug use, bulges characteristic of weapons, the student lacks the proper school pass and acts excited or aggressive when confronted by school officials (Rapp, 1999). Security officers may stop and frisk a student and proceed on reasonable suspicion resulting from the stop (Rapp, 1999).

In addition, the court has expressly approved the use of "probabilistic" profiles in the airport setting to identify potential drug couriers or terrorists (*U.S. v. Sokolow,* 1989). The basis for this conclusion rests on the notion that while "[a]ny one of [the] factors is not by itself proof of any illegal conduct and is quite consistent with innocent [activity]...taken together they amount to reasonable suspicion" (*U.S. v. Sokolow,* 1989). In these circumstances, the fact that lists of factors giving rise to reasonable suspicion are also part of a profile "does not somehow detract from their evidentiary significance..." (*U.S. v. Sokolow,* 1989). Numerous other cases have allowed the search of individuals, particularly in the airport setting, based on their identifications through the use of a profile and noted that under the circumstances the officers possessed reasonable suspicion to stop a suspect (*U.S. v. Riggs,* 1972).

In short, profiles contribute to the formation of reasonable suspicion authorizing school officials to stop and search students for suspected wrongdoing. So long as they are used in an investigatory manner, consistent with the requirement for reasonable suspicion to stop an individual, they are probably a valid tool. Caution must be exercised however, to ensure that the scope of the search does not exceed the original justification for the search, namely that the search is consistent with the profile factors. However, the appropriateness of profile use in the school setting may be questioned at a fundamental level.

Critical Zones

The difference between the use of a profile in an airport setting and a school setting involves a fundamental question about the similarity of the settings in the first instance: Are they really the same or are there significant differences between them that impact whether it is reasonable to use a profile?

Airports are recognized as a "critical zone," where more intensive and intrusive searches are reasonable in light of the extreme risk to life and property represented by weapons in a plane (Smith, 1998). The notion that airports are a critical zone rests on the extreme vulnerability of the individuals utilizing the air-travel system. As stated by the Fifth

Circuit Court of Appeals, the need for heightened security in airports as an "exceptional and exigent situation" is based on a variety of factors:

> At the core of this problem is the hijacker himself. In some cases, he is a deeply disturbed and highly unpredictable individual—a paranoid, suicidal schizophrenic with extreme tendencies towards violence. Although the crime of air piracy exceeds all others in terms of the potential for great and immediate harm to others, its undesirable consequences are not limited to that fact. Among other things, it has been used as an avenue of escape for criminals, a means of extorting huge sums of money and as a device for carrying out numerous acts of political violence and terrorism. Perhaps most disturbing of all is the fact that aerial hijacking appears to be escalating in frequency (*U.S. v. Moreno*, 1973).

For these reasons, it is reasonable to implement the most effective and comprehensive prophylactic measures possible to ensure the safety of an airport, airplanes, and the traveling public. Consequently, few question the need for metal detectors, multiple check points, video surveillance, or the use of profiles to identify potential terrorist in the airport setting.

In contrast, it is not altogether clear that a school is a "critical zone," as it is understood in the airport setting. Strong arguments exist on both sides. First, individuals at a school (students, teachers, administrators, staff) may readily escape a situation rapidly escalating toward violence. They can leave a room, jump out a window, or desert the campus location altogether if they feel their safety is threatened. Their choice to do so does not necessarily present them with the threat of imminent death represented by escaping an airplane flying at 30,000 feet.

In addition, the potential for harm is somewhat lesser in a school setting. A terrorist can destroy an entire plane with a bomb or well-placed gunshot, killing hundreds of people with a single, brief act. However, the school shootings that have occurred to date, while horrible, have not claimed hundreds of lives, and the average incident of violence involves person-on-person violence harming single individuals or small groups. It is harder in the school or community setting for a perpetrator to harm a great number of individuals than it is in an airport setting. No judgment of the relative importance of airport or school violence in human, emotional, or personal terms is intended by these comments, only recognition of the difference in scale involved in each circumstance.

Finally, and perhaps foremost, the perpetrator in a school setting, whether a highly motivated gang member, homicidal teen or garden-variety bully, is generally not the crazed fanatic associated with acts of international terrorism. It seems unfair, and at least an overstatement, to describe these youth as "paranoid, suicidal schizophrenics with extreme tendencies to violence," the concern so eloquently stated by the Fifth Circuit (Moreno). While it is true, that school shooters may be extremely disturbed and highly motivated, as was the case with the Columbine High shooters, it is probably not true in the case of the young boy from Mt. Morris, Michigan, who killed Kayla Rolland, a fellow first-grader, in February 2000. In fact, his crime was based on anger, confusion, and misunderstanding and he lacks the capacity to be charged in Michigan due to his age. Claiming he was a paranoid schizophrenic would hardly capture the circumstances of his life that involved heavy drug use by guardians, poor living conditions, and ready access to guns. A fair comparison would not place a terrorist and a potential school-shooter necessarily in the same category. For these reasons, it is hard to see a school as a critical zone.

On the other hand, strong arguments support viewing schools as "critical zones." Perhaps the most persuasive argument rests on the American belief in the fundamental value of children and our concern for preserving the safety and innocence of young people. As a society we place a high premium on protecting our children often couched in terms of fulfilling the promise of our most precious resource and preserving a legacy to our future.

In addition, schools are a critical zone in light of their salience as a target for domestic terrorism in its many possible forms. Clearly, the use of a school as an intended target would afford significant leverage in forcing compliance by the political action, or bargain for release of fellow gang members.

Consequently, the use of profiles to identify potentially violent individuals is probably justified as an investigation technique to the extent schools are viewed as "critical zones" deserving heightened levels of security. Significant legal hurdles remain, however, before a profiling too may be used for other purposes in the school environment.

CONSTITUTIONAL ISSUES: ACCESS TO EDUCATION SERVICES BASED ON PROFILES

Beyond the investigation context, the use of a profile in the school setting may implicate constitutional protections in a variety of ways. Primarily, we must be concerned with the due process and equal-protection concerns of using the profile to assign the student to specific service or educational environments. This section seeks to explore the scope of the former issue. Before services that must be afforded all students equally. Accordingly, this discussion does not reach the use of profiles as a diagnostic tool to direct students to medical, mental health, or violence prevention services because those services exceed the minimum level of service required of schools and are based on need. The Constitution is concerned with deprivations of rights not the allocation of important health services.

Generally, constitutional law requires that all individuals be afforded equal enjoyment of fundamental rights (*Neil Broadly et al. v. Meriden Board of Education et al.*, 1992, citing *Campbell v. Board of Education*, 1984). The protection of equal enjoyment grows out of equal protection law, which requires that individuals affected by a governmental action or statute be treated uniformly; in other words, that the rights, privileges, or responsibilities imposed on an identified segment of the population apply equally to all members of that group (*Franklin v. Berger*, 1989 citing *Reynolds v. Sims*, 1964, and *Cleburne v. Cleburne Living Center*, 1985). This does not mean pure or absolute equality; rather it requires that government classifications stand on reasonable grounds (*Franklin v. Berger*, 1989).

What constitutes reasonable grounds will depend on whether the classification or government action affects a fundamental right or an "inherently suspect" group. Where state action infringes on a fundamental right or impacts an "inherently suspect group, strict scrutiny will apply, requiring that the state action be narrowly tailored to achieve a compelling state interest" (*Reynolds v. Sims*, 1964, and *Cleburne v. Cleburne Living Center*, 1985).

Accordingly, when a youth violence profile is utilized as a matter of school policy to identify and refer students to an alternative education program, to the extent the profile selects students based on race, ethnic background, or gender, it will clearly have constitutional problems. An "inherently suspect" group has traditionally been defined as a "discrete and insular minority" subject to "invidious discrimination" and is commonly understood to include racial minorities and ethnic groups (*Cleburne v. Cleburne Living Center*, 1985). There are almost no circumstances under which such a classification can be argued to be a narrowly tailored attempt at achieving a compelling government interest. Of course, the presence of such factors in a profile is unlikely for exactly this reason, and notably the factors identified in most risk factor lists that could be utilized as profiles do not include any of the prohibited factors.

The fact of selection according to a profile probably does not create a "discrete and insular" group deserving of protection under constitutional standards. Several courts have ruled that special education students or exceptional students are not considered a "discrete and insular minority" deserving of heightened judicial protection (*Neil Broadly et al. v. Meriden Board of Education et al*, 1992). Accordingly, a class of violators of school rules, or potential violators of school rules does not seem discrete and insular or deserving of exceptional judicial protection. The more difficult case involves possible proxies for the prohibited factors, namely, characteristics that appear benign as an initial matter, but when utilized in a profile have the effect of selecting individuals who are disproportionately members of a protected class. Characteristics included in the youth profile that might work as proxies in this way include poverty, school achievement or skills, weapons possession, or history of suspension. Minorities, particularly Blacks, are disproportionately represented in these characteristics, raising the question, if not the conclusion, of invidious discrimination. A study in Michigan, for example, established that African American students were suspended and expelled from school at a rate 350% greater than white students (Andrejevic, 1995). While the question of invidious discrimination in profile implementation is untested in any case law to date, it is easy to see the extreme problems created by utilizing a profile that may work in this way so over identify racial minorities, the learning disabled, or other protected classes.

In contrast, where neither a fundamental right nor a "discrete and insular minority" is involved, the state action is valid provided it rests on some rational basis, meaning that it is reasonably related to achieving a legitimate state purpose (*Reynolds v. Sims,* 1964, and *Cleburne v. Cleburne Living Center,* 1985). In this case, it is not necessary for the state to utilize the best possible methods to achieve its goals; rather all that is required is that the methods actually used be reasonable (*Tyler v. Vickery,* 1976).

It has been longstanding belief that the government has a compelling interest in ensuring a strong system of education, necessarily implying it is free of violence. In *Brown v. Board of Education* (1954), the Supreme Court observed:

> Education is perhaps the most important function of state and local governments. ...It is a principal instrument in awakening the child to cultural values, in preparing him for later professional training, and in helping him to adjust normally to his environment....It is doubtful that any child may reasonably be expected to succeed in life if he is denied the opportunity of an education (*Brown v. Board of Education,* 1954).

For this reason, school officials have a strong obligation, both moral and legal, to take action in dealing with undisciplined youths, who may potentially threaten the welfare and safety of the other children in attendance. School safety is probably not a compelling enough interest to select youth for attention by prevention or intervention programs based on race, however. Race-based classifications are upheld only in situations designed to remediate past discrimination, such as in college admissions (and even this purpose is under serious question). Maintaining school security is critically important to the well-being of young people, but probably not so important as to justify race-based classifications from all manner of education practice. To insert such considerations back into the educational environment would play to the worst instincts and base assumptions about violence in America.

Even if the state has a sufficient interest in using a profile under some circumstances, it may find difficulty in arguing that the profile is reasonable, much less "narrowly tailored," in achieving its goal due to concerns about objectivity and over-inclusiveness discussed earlier. The issue of objectivity questions whether a youth violence profile can be described as such when the basic elements of the profile may not yet be established with any general scientific agreement and when the application of a profile in the school setting may be tainted by subjective concerns, teacher-student relationships, and other appearances of bias. Requiring that a profile be objective does not require that it be the best possible method of achieving the government's interest. It simply means that it must bear indications of validity, fairness, and reliability that society as a whole would be prepared to recognize as proper. The absence of agreed-upon profile factors makes it difficult to describe a profile as reasonable, for if it were so, general agreement would seem a relatively easy matter. More important, a reasonable approach by the government surely would not allow for the potential of bias and tainted application by those charged with implementing the profile. A reasonable method would encourage fairness and protect both teacher and student alike from the possibility or temptation of misuse prejudice, or animosity. A reasonable formulation of a youth violence profile would make allowances for the close and familiar circumstances of a school setting to ensure it accurately identified those most at risk

A more compelling concern regarding the reasonableness of profiles stems from the tendency of such tools to be over-inclusive in their scope. As previously discussed, these profiles, which are keyed to be highly sensitive to select all youth who may be violent, tend to identify individuals engaged in perfectly innocent and normal activity. Reducing this likelihood entails improving the accuracy of the profile but the corresponding effect is to reduce the sensitivity of the tool, meaning that fewer potentially violent youth are identified. So, if the very construction of the profile oscillates between better accuracy and better sensitivity, can the profiling tool be accurately described as reasonable? We miss more potentially violent youth than we actually identify and include too many innocent youth with these methods, making the existing technology in this field too speculative to be reasonable in the eyes of the constitutional law.

For these reasons, it seems unwarranted to consider profiling a reasonable attempt at achieving the government's interest in preserving safe schools and a strong educational system. Logic dictates that to the extent that a profile is not reasonable in achieving the government's stated objectives, it cannot be narrowly tailored to achieving those ends. Consequently, serious doubt exists regarding the constitutionality of profiles as a selection mechanism for many school programs aimed at at-risk youth.

PRIVACY AND EDUCATIONAL RECORDS

The development of passenger profiles enjoyed extensive cooperative efforts between a variety of law enforcement agencies, including the Federal Bureau of Investigations (FBI), Department of Justice, Customs Service, Secret Service (Department of Treasury), Federal Aviation Administration, and the Central Intelligence Agency. The frightening prospect of the intersection of profiling and database interconnectivity was anticipated by the Lopez court when it observed "employing a combination of psychological, sociological, and physical sciences to screen, inspect and categorize unsuspecting citizens raises visions of abuse in our increasingly technological society" (*U.S. v. Lopez*, 1971, see also Smith, 1998). Other commentators have pointed out that marketing and insurance companies have collected personal information on databases, while the government has gathered information as well for Social Security purposes, public school operations, commercial regulation, and national defense. In particular, they have observed that "[a]irport security officials have longed for the day when they would have access to these databases for the purpose of singling out potential terrorists" (Smith, 1998).

So, the natural question concerns the next step in the development of youth violence profiles: Will school safety efforts involve data sharing across education, health and human service, and juvenile justice resources to personalize profiles (Smith, 1998)? If so, what information will be included and who will have access to it? The leading federal statute on the use of school-based information regarding students, the Family Educational and Privacy Rights Act (FERPA), ensures that students and their parents will have access to students' records, be able to correct erroneous facts, and be notified when that information is shared with other schools, organizations, or entities. This parental access and control of student records extends to profile-match information.

Family Educational and Privacy Rights Act (FERPA)

The important student records issue rests on the classification of a profile, or more specifically, the profile match regarding a particular student, as an educational (medical) record or a disciplinary record. Generally, FERPA requires that schools obtain prior written permission from a parent before releasing the educational records of a student to an individual, agency, or organization. Federal funding may be denied if a school maintains a policy or practice that does not require this prior parental permission. Educational records are defined in the statue as "those records, files, documents, and other materials which (a) contain information directly related to a student; and (b) are maintained by an educational agency or institution or by a person acting for such agency or institution." (FERPA, 1999).

Accordingly, educational records may include attendance records, academic information, general administrative records, and records of extracurricular activity to name only a few examples. In addition, educational records may include a variety of medical records such as psychological evaluations and the results of Rorschach tests used for diagnostic purposes (Theumann, 1993). Based on this definition, it seems clear that information relating to a student's match with a profile would be considered an educational record under FERPA. Further, if the profile were utilized as a screening device to direct at-risk students to counseling, health or alternative education programs, it would also be a medical record, which is expressly viewed as an educational record by the statute and corresponding case law.

On the other hand, the statute exempts certain information from the definition of educational records, only one of which is important for our discussion; namely, "records maintained by a law enforcement unit of the educational agency or institution that were created by that law enforcement unit for the purpose of law enforcement" are not considered education records (FERPA, 1999). Despite this exemption, schools may include information concerning disciplinary action taken against a student for conduct that "poses a significant risk to the safety or well-being of that student, other students or other members of the school community" in the educational records of a student (FERPA). Thus, to the extent a profile is utilized by school security to promote law-enforcement purposes, profile match information may be a disciplinary record, exempt from consideration and treatment as an educational record.

Consequently, when the profile match is viewed as a medical or psychological record, it qualifies as an educational record. In contrast, if it is a security or law-enforcement record it will be a disciplinary record and may be treated as exempt from a student's educational records or may be included in educational record. In the latter situation, notice to the student's parents and permission prior to release is not required. Consequently. Parents may not necessarily be informed of the existence of such information on their child or be afforded an opportunity to review and correct the information if necessary.

Sharing Educational Records

The confidentiality of juvenile records (educational and medical) has long been regarded as a compelling state interest, requiring trial courts, state agencies, and school districts to take reasonable steps to ensure that privacy is maintained. So, for example, juvenile educational and medical records may be sealed in court proceedings despite a presumption that such proceedings are open to the public and media (*State ex rel Garden State Newspapers v. Hoke,*1999).

Reporting information collected by a school to an outside agency or another school is a delicate matter, but one squarely addressed by FERPA provisions. Generally, a school that discloses an educational record must take three steps:

1. Make a reasonable attempt to notify the parent (or student of age of majority).
2. Provide a copy of the record that was released.
3. Provide a hearing if requested (34 Code of Federal Regulations 99.34).

A school may disclose information to another school or institution that the student is attending if the student is enrolled or receives services from the other institution and the preceding conditions are met. In addition, student disciplinary records may be shared between schools attended by the student in question, provided that the teachers or school officials have a "legitimate educational interest in the behavior of the student" (FERPA, 1999). Consequently, sharing a profile match on a student with another school will probably be permissible regardless of the classification of the information as a disciplinary record or an educational record. Schools generating such information will simply need to ensure that the recipient school has a legitimate educational interest in the child, a relatively easy obstacle to overcome.

Sharing student records with law-enforcement personnel is also specifically provided for in FERPA, which allows disclosure of even personally identifiable information from educational records without the consent of student or parents to state or local juvenile justice officials of in health and safety emergencies (FERPA, 1999; sea also Rapp, 1999). Exceptions of this type are sufficiently broad to even allow possession of a criminal defendant's school records by a prosecutor when the records had no apparent relation to the case being prosecuted (Theumann, 1993).

In the case of profile match information, it seems clear that this information, regardless of its classification as an educational record or not, can be shared with law-enforcement agencies in keeping with the provisions of FERPA. If personally identifiable information may be shared with law-enforcement and juvenile-justice authorities, then profile information undoubtedly is also available for their use. Once again, schools generating profile information should ensure that recipient agencies have a legitimate interest in the information and the child as a matter of policy. It may be useful to note that the Gun-Free Schools Act requires state laws on reporting weapons in schools and serious violence to law enforcement, thereby providing at least one legitimate interest required by FERPA (Gun-Free Schools Act of 1994).

The area of difficulty rests in the release of educational records to non-law-enforcement or school agencies such as the media, social service agencies, or private companies. At least one court has held that newspapers may be entitled to receive and publish criminal investigation and incident reports compiled by school security, where such reports do not contain information required for enrollment or attendance, or academic data, because these reports are not exempt from disclosure under state public records law nor protected as "educational records" under FERPA (*Bauer v. Kincaid*, 1991). So, we return full circle to the record-classification issue. If profile-match information is regarded as a disciplinary record, its release to media organizations may be permissible. Moreover, the release of that information may or may not require notice to the parents. In contrast, if it is considered an educational record, the possibility that the information may be withheld from the media is greater and the protections afforded parents and student through notification and a hearing must be maintained.

CONCLUSION

Clearly then, the use of profiling techniques present truly formidable concerns when focused on youth violence issues and used in an educational setting. The rush to stop the violence in our schools is understandable in light of the school shootings in the last three years and the chronic levels of violence among youth. The expansion in, and arguably effective, use of profiling in other areas such as law enforcement, drug interdiction, and terrorism prevention, promotes the notion that such techniques will bring the same results for schools.

Schools are different places, however, with different rules, norms and customs than airports or any other places where profiles are commonly used. In a school, how a problem is addressed is often more important that the purported message of any given lesson. Consequently, administrators, teachers, and school safety officers walk a very delicate balance between ensuring a safe environment through the use of all the methods potentially available to them, and creating a sense of fear, paranoia, infringement of personal rights, and violation of constitutional guarantees through the use of those same methods. As we have seen, in the investigation context, profiles are generally useful tools so long as they lead to proper assessment of reasonable suspicion to stop an individual. Profiles present more problematic constitutional issues where they are used as tools for referring a student to alternative education or counseling services. Even if it doesn't implicate these issues, it may be an invalid tool because it may not be a reasonable method of achieving the government's interest in safe schools. In addition, profiles present significant school record-keeping and right to privacy problems depending on whether they are educational records or disciplinary records. All of these issues rest on fundamental concerns about the general validity of profiles as scientific tools: their objectivity, accuracy, sensitivity, tendency to be over-inclusive, and general acceptance in the scientific community. For these reasons, the use of profiles involving youth in a school setting is highly problematic and controversial.

Kirk A. Bailey *is from The Hamilton Fish Institute on School and Community Violence.*

The author wishes to thank Laird Kirkpatrick, U.S. Department of Justice, and many members of the staff of the Hamilton Fish Institute, including Paul Kingery, James Derzon, Nancy Budd, Aaron Alford, and Janet Humphrey; for their contributions and suggestions for this article. The strength of this article is the result of their clarifying arguments, concise editorial comments, and significant intellectual curiosity; while any deficiencies remain those of the author.

The Hamilton Fish Institute is administered by The George Washington University Institute for Education Policy Studies, Graduate School of Education and Human Development. Prepared under a grant from the Office of Juvenile Justice and Delinquency Prevention, Office of Justice Programs, U.S. Department of Justice (97-MU-FX-K012), points of view or opinions in this document are those of the Institute and do not necessarily represent the official position or policies of the U.S. Department of Justice.

Correspondence to: Kirk A. Bailey, The Hamilton Fish Institute, 2121 K Street, NW, Suite 200, Washington, DC 20037-1830.

REFERENCES

34 Code of Federal Regulations 99.34.

Andrejevic, M. (1995, March 27). Expelled students in limbo, *Lansing State Journal*, p. 1A, cited in Bogos, P. M. (1997). Expelled. No excuses. No exceptions. University of Detroit Mercy Law, *Review, 74*, 357.

Bauer v. Kincaid, 759 F. Supp. 575 (W.D. Mo. 1991).

Broadly et al. v. Meriden Board of Education et al., 1992 Conn. Super. LEXIS 2444, No. 27 35 07. THIS DECISION IS UNREPORTED AND MAY BE SUBJECT TO FURTHER APPELLATE REVIEW. COUNSEL IS CAUTIONED TO MAKE AN INDEPENDENT DETERMINATION OF THE STATUS OF THIS CASE (status confirmed – no adverse appellate review); *citing Horton v. Meskill*, 486, A.2d 1099 (1985)(Horton III); *Horton v. Meskill*, 376 A.2d 359 (1977)(Horton I); See also, *Bennett v. School District*, 114 A.D. 2d 58 (1985), Driscoll, 82 F.3d 383, *Arundar v. DeKalb City Sch. District*, 620 F.2d 493 (5th Cir. 1980), *O'Connor v. Board of Educ. Of School Dist.* No.23, 645 F.2d 578 (7th Cir.) cert. denied 454 U.S. 1084 (1981); *Johnson v. Ann Arbor Public Schools*, 569 F. Supp. 1502 (E.D. Mich. 1983); *Davis v. Maine Endwell Cent. School Dist.* 542 F. Supp. 1247 (N.D.N.Y. 1982); *Johnpoll v. Elias*, 513 F. Supp. 420 (E.D.N.Y. 1980).

Brown v. Board of Education, 347 U.S. 483 (1954).

Campbell v. Board of Education, 475 A.2d 289 (1984).

Cleburn v. Cleburn Living Center, Inc., 473 U.S. 432 (1985).

Cooper, K. J. (2000, April 29). Riley rejects schools' profiling of potentially violent students, *The Washington Post*, p. A11.

Daubert v. Merrell Dow Pharmaceuticals, 509 U.S. 579 (1993).

Derzon, J. H. (2001, this issue). Antisocial predictors of violence: A meta-analysis. *Psychology in the schools, 38*, 93–106

Derzon, J. H. (2000, June). *The homogeneous continuity of violence and other anti-social behaviors: Evidence from meta-analysis.* Paper presented at the Society for Prevention Research, Montreal, Canada.

Derzon, J. H., & Wilson, D. B. (2000). *Too much of a good thing: Correcting upward bias in retrospective sampling frames.* Manuscript in preparation.

Family Education and Privacy Rights Act, 20 USCS § 1232(g) (4)(A), (4)(B)(ii), (4)(h)(2); §1232 (h)(1) (1999).

Franklin v. Berger, 560 A.2d 444 (1989).

Gun-Free Schools Act of 1994 (GFSA), 20 USCA § 8921 (1994).

Ingram, S. (1998). If the profile fits: Admitting criminal psychological profiles into evidence in criminal trials, *Washington University Journal of Urban & Contemporary Law, 54*, 239.

Kirkpatrick, L. C. (1998). Profile and syndrome evidence: Its use and admissibility in criminal prosecutions. *Security Journal, 11*, 225–258.

New Jersey v. T. L. O., 469 U.S. 325 (1985).

Rapp, James A. (1999). Education Law, 9.04[1][c]. [11][d]; 13.04[8][b].

Reynolds v. Sims, 377 U.S. 533 (1964).

Smith, D. (1998). Passenger profiling: A greater terror than terrorism itself? *John Marshall Law Review, 32*, 167.

State ex rel. Garden State Newspapers, Inc. v. Hoke, 205 W. Va. 611, 520 S. E. 2d 186 (1999).

Theumann, J. (1993). *Annotation: Validity, construction and application of the Family Educational and Privacy Rights Act of 1974*, 112 A.L.R. Fed. 1, at 22.

Tyler v. Vickery, 517 F.2d 1089 (5th Cir. 1975), cert. denied, 426 U. S. 940 (1976).

U. S. v. Bell, 363 F.2d 667 (2nd Cir. N.Y. 1972).

U. S. v. Lopez, 328 F. Supp. 1077 (1971); Also citing, *Cf.* Williams. Neural factors related to habitual aggression: Consideration of differences between those habitual aggressives and others who have committed crimes of violence, (1969). *Brain: A Journal of Neurology, 92,* 503; Bonkalo, (1967). Electroencephalography in criminology. *Canadian Psychiatric Association Journal, 12,* 281; Woods. (1961). Adolescent violence and homicide. *Archives of General Psychiatry, 5*(6), 38. See also, Tribe, (1970). An ounce of detention: Preventive justice in the world of John Mitchell, *Virginia Law Review, 56,* 371, 379–380, 394–396. But. Cf. Korematsu v. United States, 323 U.S. 214 (1944); Also citing. Roszak, T. (1969). *The making of a counter culture: Reflections on the technocratic society and its youthful opposition.* Garden City, NJ: Anchor Books.

U. S. v. Moreno, 475 F.2d 44 (5th Cir. 1973)

U. S. v. Riggs, 374 F. Supp. 1098(E.D.N.Y. 1972). *aff'd,* 474 F.2d 699 (2d Cir. N. Y. 1973), *cert denied.* 414 U. S. 820, 38 L. Ed. 2d 53, 94 S. Ct. 115, 1973 U. S. Lexis 311 (1973).

U. S. v. Sokolow, 490 U. S. 1 (1989)

Assessing Threats of School Violence: Implications for Counselors

Jeffrey A. Daniels

The author describes important considerations when assessing students' threats made at schools. In a recent article, M. Reddy et al. (2001) presented four approaches to assessing the risk of school violence. They submitted important issues and problems with three commonly used approaches and suggested a fourth approach as an alternative. Implications for school counselors are explored.

Although school violence has been impressed on the consciousness of the American public in recent years, there is evidence to suggest that violence among adolescents is on the decline (Koplan, Autry, & Hyman, 2001). However, recent school shootings across the nation in such places as Pearl, Mississippi; West Paducah, Kentucky; Jonesboro, Arkansas; Littleton, Colorado; and Santee, California have created widespread concern about school safety. Various agencies have been working to develop intervention strategies and to identify warning signs of school violence. Among them are the U.S. Department of Education (Dwyer, Osher, & Warger, 1998), the Federal Bureau of Investigation (O'Toole, 2000), and the U.S. Surgeon General (Kaplan, et al.). In their book *Psychology in the Schools*, Reddy et al. (2001) recently presented an overview and critique of three approaches to threat assessment and offered a fourth approach for consideration. The purpose of this article is to review the Reddy et al. article and then to examine implications for counselors.

ASSESSMENT APPROACHES

Reddy et al. (2001) made a distinction between *general aggression* and *targeted school violence.* Targeted school violence entails the intentional harm or murder of a specific individual or individuals. Although general violence is much more common among adolescents than targeted violence, the focus of the Reddy et al. article is on identifying risk factors associated with targeted violence. The three current assessment approaches to targeted violence include behavioral profiling, guided professional judgment and structured clinical assessment, and automated decision making. Finally, the authors describe an alternative method, the threat assessment approach.

Behavioral Profiling

Historically, profiling has entailed carefully investigating a crime scene "to generate a set of hypotheses about the characteristics—physical, demographic, personality, and others—of the person most likely to have committed the crime" (Reddy et al., 2001, p.161). However, profiling has also been used to identify potential perpetuators of violence. This method attempts to identify characteristics of an individual and predict the likelihood that he or she will commit a crime in the future. Prospective profiling has some problems associated with it. For example, there is substantial risk of false positives, of identifying a student, based on his or her profile, who will not become violent. Moreover, "the accuracy of school shooter profiles is questionable" (Reddy et al., 2001, p.162). Because incidents of targeted school violence are so uncommon, it is unsound practice to make generalizations to previously nonviolent students. Moreover, there is no empirical support for the validity of prospective profiling. Finally, prospective profiling may label and stigmatize students as dangerous and may violate their civil liberties.

Guided Professional Judgment

Guided professional judgment, also known as structured clinical assessment, commonly involves a professional interviewing a student and using instruments or checklists to help make a decision about the student's potential to be violent. One problem with this method again relates to the low incidence of targeted school violence and one's ability to evaluate risk from a dubious base rate. Second, because no empirical research has been done to identify risk factors for targeted school violence, professionals may not know what information to gather. Related to this issue is the questionable practice of using existing research on general violence as a basis to assess the risk of targeted school violence. Finally, Reddy et al. (2001) pointed out that standard psychological measures have not been validated as predictors of targeted school violence.

Automated Decision Making

The third risk assessment approach is termed automated decision making. This includes use of actuarial formulas and expert systems and artificial intelligence systems. With automated decision making, the data leads to a decision about risk, rather than the professional making this decision. The most obvious problem with this approach is that "appropriate actuarial equations do not yet exist to determine risk of targeted violence, particularly school-based targeted violence" (Reddy et al., 2001, p. 166). Second, experts have not yet agreed on issues related to evaluating targeted school violence, use of these methods may "fail to gather information on the student or situation that may be relevant to appraising risk and thus produce a flawed assessment" (Reddy et al., 2001, p. 167).

Threat Assessment Approach

Unlike the inductive methods previously described, the threat assessment approach is deductive. This method uses the facts presented in a given case to guide inferences about potential for violence. The guiding principles of the threat assessment method are the following:

1. There is no single "type" of person perpetuating targeted violence. Instead, the violence is viewed within its context, in which such factors as the perpetrator, the victim(s), the situation, and the setting are considered in toto.
2. "There is a distinction between making a threat (expressing, to the target or others, an intent to harm a target) and posing a threat (engaging in behaviors that further a plan to harm a target)" (Reddy et al., 2001, p. 168).
3. Targeted violence is not a random act, nor do people commit targeted acts of violence because they just "snap." Therefore, many incidents of targeted violence can be prevented.

Threat assessment entails the professional gathering of information to determine the extent to which an individual is at risk for violent behavior. Reddy et al. (2001) listed 10 questions that the evaluator must consider:

1. motivation for the behavior that brought the person being evaluated to official attention;
2. communication about ideas and intentions;
3. unusual interest in targeted violence;

4. evidence of attack-related behaviors and planning;
5. mental condition;
6. level of cognitive sophistication and organization to formulate and execute an attack plan;
7. recent losses (including losses of status);
8. consistency between communications and behaviors;
9. concern by others about the individual's potential for harm; and
10. factors in the individual's life and/or environment or situation that might increase or decrease the likelihood of attack. (p. 169)

Answers to the above questions can help the school administration decide on the extent to which an individual is moving toward an act of targeted violence. If it is determined that the student is at risk for targeted violence, professionals can intervene.

IMPLICATIONS FOR COUNSELORS

Although the majority of the counselors who will first come into contact with issues of targeted school violence are school counselors, some school districts are contracting with mental health agencies to provide more intensive mental health services to troubled students. Moreover, mental health counselors may come in contact with victims, friends, and family members, and the perpetrators after an incident of school violence. Thus, the implications for counselors that are addressed herein potentially apply to all counselors. The remainder of this article explores issues related to the assessment of possible targeted school violence and for intervention considerations for potentially violent youth and others after a violent incident in a school.

Assessment Issues

Students who engage in targeted violence are not likely to attack "out of the blue." Instead, there are early warning signs that may be present in subtle forms. School counselors are in a good position to assess troubled youth in an effort to identify and intervene before an act of violence occurs. What, specifically, can counselors do to assess students for risk of possible violent behavior?

First, it is important to remember that targeted school violence is an uncommon event, so there are few data available to guide counselors. Thus, any recommendations concerning assessment or treatment are either based on a limited data set or extrapolated from similar groups of violent offenders. Until we have more empirical information about targeted school violence, the counselor must remain flexible and open to alternative strategies.

Threat assessment. Assessment of risk for targeted school violence is in its infancy. However, Reddy et al. (2001) argued for the utility of a threat assessment approach. This approach is also recommended by a special task force headed by the critical Incident Response group and the National Center for the Analysis of Violent Crime, both within the FBI (O'Toole, 2000). Using the threat assessment approach, the counselor makes a determination of the level of risk based on information available from teachers and staff, other students, parents, and the youth making the threat. Not all threats are equal, so it is the counselor's job to assess the severity of the threat. O'Toole pointed out that there are three levels of threat severity. At the *lowest level*, the threat is vague and indirect, the threat itself is implausible or unrealistic and may lack detail, and the content suggests that the individual is not likely to carry it out. A *medium level* of threat is one that could be carried out by the individual, but it does not seem to be very realistic. Such a threat is more direct, the wording suggests that the person has given some thought to how it will be carried out, and there may be a general suggestion of a possible place and time. Moreover, it is apparent that the person has taken some preparatory steps to carry out the threat, although these are likely to be vague or veiled. A *high level* of threat "appears to pose an imminent and serious danger to the safety of others" (O'Toole, 2000, p. 9). This level of threat is specific, direct, and plausible. Within the threat, it is apparent that the individual has taken specific steps to carry it out. An example of a high level of threat is "At eight o'clock tomorrow morning, I intend to shoot the principal. That's when he is in the office by himself. I have a 9mm. Believe me, I know what I am doing. I am sick and tired of the way he runs this school" (O'Toole, 2000, p. 9).

Warning signs. In addition to assessing the seriousness of a threat, the counselor also is in a position to look for warning signs in troubled youth. Please be aware, however, that just because a student exhibits some of the following warning signs it does not mean that he or she will become violent (Dwyer et al., 1998). The counselor needs to be involved with the students and earn their trust. It is helpful to make oneself visible to students, such as walking down the halls visiting with students between classes whenever possible or eating in the cafeteria with the students on occasion. As a result of getting to know the students, those who are heading down the path toward violence may come to the attention of the school counselor.

The National School Safety Center (NSSC; 1998) has developed a list of 20 characteristics of youth who have killed at school. These characteristics may be used as warning signs for the counselor to consider (see Appendix).

Using the threat assessment approach, the counselor is able to assess the severity of a threat that has been made and to identify those students who may be at risk for future violence. As in any counseling situation, assessment is only the initial step in the helping process. What can the counselor do once a student has been identified as potentially violent or in the aftermath of an incident of targeted school violence?

Interventions

Helping potentially violent students. Once a student has been identified as being at risk for violence, it is imperative that professionals intervene immediately. Interventions will focus on building a caring relationship that is characterized by trust and respect. Studer (1996) suggested that interventions with potentially violent students include anger control strategies in which the student learns to identify triggers to his or her anger, reducing the physical responses to anger, and learning self-assessment techniques. In addition to anger control, students must be taught assertiveness skills. These youth may not know the differences between assertiveness, aggressiveness, or passiveness. Counselors are also encouraged to work with violent youth on problem-solving strategies and conflict mediation skills (Studer, 1996). A multidisciplinary approach to working with at-risk youth will be most effective. Teachers and other school personnel, parents, and other community contacts should be included to reinforce the skills being taught and monitor the student's progress.

Helping people after the violence. There are two considerations when working with survivors of school-based violence. Juhnke (1997) described a critical incident stress debriefing model for working with students and parents immediately after an act of violence. As a follow-up, Brown (1996) presented counseling strategies for working with the victims who develop symptoms of posttraumatic stress disorder (PTSD).

Critical incident stress debriefing includes discussing and describing reactions one has had to a traumatic event. This takes place in a small group format, and participants are encouraged to process their reactions with the others and to describe the symptoms of PTSD they are experiencing. Through a combination of processing and psychoeducation, students come to an understanding of PTSD and develop a sense of closure regarding the event (Juhnke, 1997). Juhnke described seven stages to his adapted critical incident stress debriefing process. In the *introduction stage*, participants are introduced, and ground rules are described. Issues of confidentiality are also addressed. The second stage, the *fact-gathering stage*, entails participants' descriptions of what they were doing when the event occurred. At this time, participants are requested to present only the facts and not discuss their feelings yet. The third stage is the *thought stage*. It is in this stage that participants begin moving from the cognitive to the affective domains. Students are asked to describe their thoughts during the incident. The *reaction stage* focuses on the students' reactions to the incident and tends to be laden with emotion. The next stage of the adapted critical incident stress debriefing model is the *symptom stage*. At this time, the counselor will help bring the students back to the cognitive level, with an emphasis on symptoms the students are experiencing. After the symptom stage, the group moves on to the *teaching stage*. This is when the counselor normalizes the symptoms students are reporting and educates them about future symptoms that may develop. Finally, the group enters the *reentry stage* in which students start to experience closure to the incident.

Brown (1996) described having some success treating students experiencing PTSD as a result of violence. He indicated that counselors should pursue three goals with students experiencing PTSD. These are, first, to help children control intrusive thoughts and images. Second, the counselor should help students develop strategies to control the symptoms that coincide with intrusive thoughts. Third, counselors can help students develop a sense of safety once again. Interventions center on restructuring thoughts associated with the incident and helping students develop coping responses to their thoughts.

The counselor should not forget to consider the impact of the incident on her- or himself, parents, teachers, and administrators. Referrals to mental health professionals may be needed. Nims (2000) indicated that "teachers who have witnessed violence...can suffer from fatigue, headaches, stomach pains, and hypertension" (p. 4).

CONCLUSION

Although the incidence of school-related targeted violence is a major social issue in the United States, the fields of education, law enforcement, and counseling are beginning to better understand the dynamics associated with the school shooter. We are also developing appropriate assessment and intervention strategies for school counselors. This article reviewed assessment methods and considerations for interventions before and after an incident of school violence. Counselors are urged to seek training in the areas of threat assessment and crisis response and to use their knowledge and skills to help their school districts develop and implement crisis response and prevention programs. Counselors are also encouraged to develop the trust and respect of students in their schools. As Ronald Stevens (2000), the executive director of the NSSC stated, "the single most effective strategy for keeping schools safe continues to be the physical presence of responsible and caring adults" (p. ix). May counselors ever work to be such responsible and caring adults in the lives of our youth.

Jeffrey A. Daniels *is an associate professor in the Psychology Department at Central Washington University in Ellensburg. Correspondence regarding this article should be sent to Jeffrey A. Daniels, Central Washington University, Department of Psychology, 400 E. Eighth Ave., Ellensburg, WA 98926-7575 (e-mail: danielsj@cwu.edu).*

REFERENCES

Brown, D. (1996). Counseling the victims of violence who develop posttraumatic stress disorder. *Elementary School Guidance & Counseling, 30,* 218–227.

Dwyer, K., Osher, D., & Warger, C. (1998). *Early warning, timely response: A guide to safe schools.* Washington, DC: U. S. Department of Education.

Juhnke, G. A. (1997). After school violence: An adapted critical incident stress debriefing model for student survivors and their parents. *Elementary School Guidance & Counseling, 31,* 163–170.

Koplan, J. P., Autry, J. H., & Hyman, S. E. (2001). *Surgeon General's report on youth violence.* Pittsburgh, PA: U. S. Government Printing Office.

National School Safety Center. (1998). Checklist of characteristics of youth who have caused school-associated violent deaths. In-School associated violent deaths report. Westlake Village, CA: Author. Retrieved May 9, 2001, from *http://www.nssc.org/*reporter/checklist.htm.

Nims, D. R (2000). Violence in our schools: A national crisis. In D. S. Sandhu & C. B. Aspy (eds.), *Violence in American Schools: A practical guide for counselors* (pp. 3–20). Alexandria, VA: American Counseling Association.

O'Toole, M. E. (2000). *The school shooter: A threat assessment perspective:* Quantico, VA: Federal Bureau of Investigation.

Reddy, M., Borum, R., Berglund, J., Vossekuil, B., Fein, R., & Modzeles, W. (2001). Evaluating risk for targeted violence in schools: Comparing risk assessment, threat assessment, and other approaches. *Psychology in the Schools, 38,* 157–172.

Stevens, R. D. (2000). Forward. In D. S. Sandhu & C. B. Aspy (Eds) *Violence in American Schools: A practical guide for counselors* (pp. i–xi). Alexandria, VA: American Counseling Association.

Studer, J. (1996). Understanding and preventing aggressive responses in youth. *Elementary School Guidance & Counseling, 30,* 194–203.

APPENDIX

Checklist of Characteristics of Youth Who Have Caused School-Associated Violent Deaths

1. Has a history of tantrums and uncontrollable angry outbursts.
2. Characteristically resorts to name calling, cursing, or abusive language.
3. Habitually makes violent threats when angry.
4. Has previously brought a weapon to school.
5. Has a background of serious disciplinary problems at school and in the community.

6. Has a background of drug, alcohol, or other substance abuse or dependency.
7. Is on the fringe of his/her peer group with a few or no close friends.
8. Is preoccupied with weapons, explosives, or other incendiary devices.
9. Has previously been truant, suspended, or expelled from school.
10. Displays cruelty to animals.
11. Has little or no supervision and support from parents or a caring adult.
12. Has witnessed or been a victim of abuse or neglect in the home.
13. Has been bullied and/or bullies or intimidates peers or younger children.
14. Tends to blame others for difficulties and problems she/he causes her/himself.
15. Consistently prefers TV shows, movies, or music expressing violent themes and acts.
16. Prefers reading materials dealing with violent themes, rituals and abuse.
17. Reflects anger, frustration, and the dark side of life in school essays or writing projects.
18. Is involved with a gang or an antisocial group on the fringe of peer acceptance.
19. Is often depressed and/or has significant mood swings.
20. Has threatened or attempted suicide.

Chapter 4:
Confidentiality and
Privileged
Communication

INTRODUCTION

Because confidentiality is so critical to the success of the counseling relationship (Isaacs & Stone, 1999), it is important that all school counselors understand the legal and ethical issues, concerns, and questions surrounding it.

The American School Counselor Association (ASCA) takes the position that it is the responsibility of school counselors to respect students' right to privacy (see ASCA position statement, *The Professional School Counselor and Confidentiality*, Appendix H–6). Yet, confidentiality is not absolute, and exceptions exist under the law and codes of ethics. For example, the *Ethical Standards for School Counselors* (ASCA, 1998) state that disclosure of confidential information may be required to pre-

vent clear and imminent danger to a counselee or others (§A.2.b.).
Furthermore, the ethical standards explain that, in a group setting, the
school counselor is expected to stress the importance of confidentiality
but must clearly state that confidentiality cannot be guaranteed (ASCA,
§A.2.f.).

Legally, minors do not have the same right to confidentiality as
adults. If parents request information, counselors may be legally
required to give it. Yet, ethically, students do have a right to confidentiality. To help navigate these opposing requirements, Glosoff and Pate
(2002) have provided guidance on handling confidentiality with parents.
For instance, although students do have an ethical right to confidentiality, ethical dictates also provide that school counselors should respect
the rights of parents and attempt to establish a collaborative relationship
with them (ASCA, §B.1.a.). An approach that elicits cooperation
among counselors, students, and parents can help minimize conflicting
ethical and legal difficulties.

Though certain tensions exist between ethical and legal dictates, ethical standards acknowledge that legal requirements could result in the
disclosure of confidential information (ASCA, §A.2.b.). Reporting suspected child abuse is an example of a legal requirement involving
breaching confidentiality. Davis and Ritchie (1993) have noted that all
states have laws requiring school personnel to report suspected child
abuse. These laws protect school personnel from legal liability if they
make the report based on an honest belief that some form of child abuse
may be occurring. School counselors need to be aware that the definition of child abuse varies according to state law and can include physical, emotional, or sexual abuse, as well as parental neglect. Therefore, it
is essential for counselors to know the exact language of their state child
abuse reporting statute. The statute will provide information such as
who makes the report, whether or not to report suspected past abuse,
and whether or not a written report is necessary. Furthermore, Davis
and Ritchie have suggested that school counselors speak with authorities from local child protective services to further clarify what constitutes
child abuse according to state law.

School counselors can be served with subpoenas requesting that they
produce records or appear in a court proceeding. Failure to respond to a
subpoena can result in being held in contempt of court and fined or
jailed. Yet, school counselors can be accused of violating a student's right
to privacy if they comply with an invalid subpoena. Thus, school counselors must seek legal counsel before responding to a subpoena to ascertain its validity and how to best respond. If the school counselor is
required to participate in court proceedings, ethical standards direct
school counselors to inform the court that releasing confidential infor-

mation about a counselee may harm the counselee, and counselors should request that they not be required to disclose such information (ASCA, §A.2.d.).

There is an exception to the general rule that requires permission to release confidential information of which all school counselors should take note. When a court is ordering disclosure of confidential information, the school counselor is not required to obtain written permission from the student's parents. Although disclosure of confidential information to a third party usually requires the written consent of the client or, if the client is a minor, the client's parent or guardian, this does not apply for court-ordered disclosures. It does, however, apply in other situations. For instance, school counselors often encounter this situation when working with a student who is also being seen by another mental health professional, such as a psychiatrist. Before the school counselor consults with the psychiatrist, the school counselor should obtain written permission to do so from the student's parent or guardian.

Privileged communication is a legal term that relates to the admissibility of information gained in a counseling session as evidence in a court proceeding. Under privileged communication laws, clients can prevent counselors from disclosing information obtained in a counseling relationship. Privileged communication is granted through state statute. Forty-five states and the District of Columbia extend privileged communication protection to client-counselor communication (Glosoff & Pate, 2002), though many of these statutes require a counselor to be licensed before privileged communication can be asserted. This limitation is detrimental to many school counselors who are not also licensed professional counselors. Even so, Glosoff and Pate have noted that some states do extend privilege to relationships with school counselors. Furthermore, they suggest that, even if communications between a student and school counselor are not considered privileged communication, a school counselor can request that the judge grant privilege. If a judge still requires the school counselor to testify, school counselors should limit their disclosures in court by providing only information that is relevant to the proceedings.

In addition to becoming aware of school district policies on student confidentiality, it's important that school counselors stay current on ethical and legal issues related to confidentiality and privileged communication. With this in mind, school counselors are wise to consult with attorneys regarding legal issues related to confidentiality and privileged communication.

Privacy and Confidentiality in School Counseling

Harriet L. Glosoff
Robert H. Pate, Jr.

Trust is an essential component in the development of helping relationships. Counselors regard the promise of confidentiality to be essential for the development of client trust. Most individuals seeking counseling services assume that what they divulge in counseling will be kept in confidence by their counselor, with limited exceptions (Glosoff, Herlihy, & Spence, 2000). This is most likely true for children and adolescents as well as adults. Managing confidentiality when counseling minors, however, is more complex than when counseling adults. School counselors must balance their ethical and legal responsibilities to their clients, clients' parents, and school systems. This complex balancing act is one reason that the topic of maintaining the confidences of student clients is raised in virtually every discussion of ethical and legal issues in school counseling. In attempting to weigh their legal and ethical obligations, it is helpful for school counselors to clearly identify those they consider to be "clients." School counselors are part of an educational community. As such, they consult with teachers, administrators, and parents. It is important for school counselors to clarify that their consultation is on behalf of students and that only the students are their clients (except if school counselors offer counseling to students' families).

The *Code of Ethics and Standards of Practice* of the American Counseling Association (ACA, 1995) and the *Ethical Standards for School Counselors* of the American School Counselor Association (ASCA, 1998) are two resources available to help school counselors manage privacy and confidentiality in their counseling relationships. School counselors can also look to moral principles or "shared beliefs or agreed-upon assumptions that guide the ethical reasoning of helping profession-als" (Remley & Herlihy, 2001, p. 3) upon which the codes of ethics are based. The moral principles most often cited in relation to ethical prac-tices of counselors include the following:

- Veracity or telling the truth
- Justice or fairness
- Nonmaleficence or doing no harm
- Beneficence or doing good
- Autonomy or respecting free choice
- Fidelity or keeping promises

The moral principle of *beneficence* refers to the responsibility to help clients gain something positive from engaging in counseling. It also includes counselors' duty to "help society in general and people who are potential clients" (Welfel, 2002, p. 34). *Autonomy* refers to respecting the freedom of clients to choose their own directions and make their own choices within the counseling relationship. Respecting a clients' autono-my does not mean that counselors encourage clients to make decisions independent of significant others (e.g., parents) in their lives or regardless of community and cultural implications. It does mean that "counselors refrain from imposing goals, avoid being judgmental, and are accepting of different values" (Herlihy & Corey, 1996, p. 4).

Applying moral principles to situations involved in respecting the rights of minor clients served in school settings is not always easy. To be effective advocates for their clients' rights, school counselors must have a good grasp of issues related to the following concepts: the legal status of minors and the legality and ethics of privacy, confidentiality, privileged communication, and informed consent. Each of these are reviewed along with relevant ethical standards and factors that complicate school coun-selors' ability to maintain a relationship based on students' confidence that they can speak freely and without fear of disclosure. Finally, impli-cations for the practice of school counselors is presented.

THE LEGAL STATUS OF MINORS

The ACA (1995) *Code of Ethics and Standards of Practice* specifically references the term minor twice, both in relation to matters of consent. The *Ethical Standards for School Counselors* (ASCA, 1998) include stan-dards specific to counseling minors throughout the entire document. Neither set of ethical guidelines, however, defines the term minor. Typically, 18 is considered the legal age of majority, unless otherwise des-ignated. Minors, therefore, can legally be defined as those persons under the age of 18. Amendment XXVI (1971) to the U.S. Constitution established the right of 18-year-old citizens to vote and by extension has influenced the generally accepted age at which minors are extended other adult rights. For example, 18 is cited in the Family Educational Rights and Privacy Act (FERPA) as the age at which the transfer of rights from parents to students occurs (FERPA, 1974). School counselors, therefore are faced with 18 as the age at which their clients are legally assumed to be mature, to have full ownership and control of their privacy rights.

The legal concept of the age of majority has implications for minor clients' rights to make choices about entering into counseling as well as their rights to privacy and confidentiality. Overall, although minor clients have "an ethical right to privacy and confidentiality in the counseling relationship ... [the] privacy rights of minors legally belong to their parents or guardians" (Remley & Herlihy, 2001, p. 184). Isaacs and Stone (1999) noted that the Supreme Court has upheld parents' legal right to make critical decisions about their children. (The term parents refers to all who function in the parental role and have the legal rights of parents.) Many people consider the decision to enter into counseling to be an example of a critical decision. Further, because counseling is considered to be a contractual relationship, "minors cannot legally agree to be counseled on their own" (Remley & Herlihy, p. 179). There are some exceptions to this. For example, many states have enacted laws allowing for individuals younger than 18 to receive counseling or medical services without parental consent. Additionally, most states have laws that allow minors to be declared "legally emancipated" from their parents and a few states allow for minors to be deemed a mature minor and capable of understanding the ramifications of counseling.

Legal Status and Informed Consent

Informed consent is both a legal and ethical principle requiring school counselors to adequately disclose to clients potential risks, benefits, and alternatives to proposed counseling. Minor clients, however, cannot legally give informed consent, only their parents can. Although the majority of clients served by school counselors cannot legally give informed consent, they can assent to counseling without parental consent. Some school districts or school principals have policies that require counselors to obtain parents' permission before beginning counseling students, and others require counselors to seek permission if they see students for more than a specified number of counseling sessions (e.g., two or three). Unless there is school policy or a state or federal law to the contrary, Remley and Herlihy (2001) asserted that school counselors do not need parental permission before they provide counseling to students. According to Welfel (2002), many ethical scholars suggest that counselors obtain both the assent of minor clients and the informed consent of their parents, especially if they anticipate that there will be several counseling sessions. School counselors' obligations to uphold parental rights and attend to clients' ethical rights is discussed below in further detail in relation to confidentiality and informed consent.

PRIVACY AND CONFIDENTIALITY

The concepts of privacy and confidentiality are integrally related, especially in regard to the counseling relationship, privacy being broader in nature. Beauchamp and Childress (2001), in a widely acknowledged work on biomedical ethics, noted the importance of allowing those clients professionals attempt to help to limit and control access to information about themselves. They defined privacy as allowing individuals to limit access to information about themselves while defining confidentiality as allowing individuals to control access to information they have shared.

The Beauchamp and Childress (2001) definition of privacy includes decisions about sharing or withholding information about one's body or mind, one's thoughts, beliefs, feelings, and fantasies. Clients must share private information to form the trusting therapeutic relationship that is necessary for counseling to be successful. When individuals begin counseling they make decisions about the extent to which they are willing to share personal information with their counselors in order to gain the assistance they want. In part, they make these decisions based on their desire to be helped by their counselors and, in part, by their understanding of who might have access to the information they choose to share.

The issue of students' privacy rights is discussed so much and so often because there are no easy answers to the questions typically raised by school counselors who are concerned about students' ethical rights and the legal rights of parents. In fact, the topic is one often cited to demonstrate that conflicting legal and ethical obligations can create dilemmas for school counselors. Birdsall and Hubert (2000), writing about ethical issues in school counseling, observed that school counselors often inquire about issues they think are ethical when they are clearly linked to legal obligations. The source of the dilemma is easy to describe; however, a satisfactory resolution is elusive. Although ethically, minor clients have the same right to confidentiality as adults, they legally have no right to keep secrets from their parents. Further, the parents of minors have a legal right, except for limited exceptions, to control the professional services provided their children and to be involved in planning those services. As noted previously, the ethics of all counseling-related professions recognize that clients have, again absent some limited exceptions, a right to privacy. Most counselors consider both of these rights, unless there is a conflict between them, to be reasonable. The fundamental conflict is between the privacy rights of minors and the right (some might add obligation) of parents to be actively involved in a counseling process that affects their children. This conflict most often arises in matters of confidentiality.

Confidentiality

Confidentiality is a professional's promise or contract to respect clients' privacy by not disclosing anything revealed during counseling except under agreed upon conditions. The moral principles of fidelity, nonmaleficence, and beneficence apply to clients' rights to confidentiality. In applying the moral principle of fidelity, school counselors make explicit and implicit promises to clients that they will actively work against disclosing clients' secrets, except under agreed upon conditions. Without this assurance, most students would be hesitant to seek the help they need to improve their mental health. Clients' trust in their counselors may be violated when information is communicated without their knowledge and permission, and when information, including details beyond what is minimally required, is communicated to third parties.

School counselors are expected to adhere to the moral principle of nonmaleficence when trying to make decisions about communicating confidential information. If counselors break their promise of confidentiality or disclose information without clients' consent, clients may feel betrayed. As a result, they may lose trust in their counselors and hold back other personal information or they may prematurely terminate the counseling relationship. These actions could cause harm to clients. The moral principle of beneficence raises interesting issues for school counselors. If students who would benefit from counseling learn that the school counselor shared information without client consent, they may not seek the very services they need. Likewise, community support for the school and school counseling may be diminished if parents believe school counselors withhold information vital to proper exercise of their parental duties.

School counselors do not give up their ethical obligation to apply the basic moral principles when counseling children and adolescents. However, they must apply these principles in developmentally appropriate ways and attempt to honor the rights of children and adolescents to make decisions while appropriately including their parents and school personnel. Relying simply on chronological age as the basis of making decisions about when it is necessary to breach confidentiality does not make sense from a developmental perspective. For example, are clients, on the day they become 18, suddenly more capable then they were the day before to make decisions about their privacy? Based on developmental theories (e.g., Piaget), most counselors would assume that there is a stage at which the developing young person could understand the concept of secrets and could be involved in making informed decisions about confidentiality. Likewise, at some point in their development, most would view young people as, or almost as, mature as they will be at 18. A developmental approach, while more complex than a chronological approach, could be based on characteristics and abilities of the clients involved and the nature of their discussion with their counselors. "Generally, the more mature the minor, the greater the measure of confidentiality that young person is given in counseling" (Welfel, 2002, p. 102).

Research indicates that counselors implicitly endorse such a developmentally based approach to confidentiality rather than making decisions about sharing information with third parties based only on clients' chronological ages. For example, Isaacs and Stone (1999) received surveys from 627 school counselors in which they identified under what conditions they would divulge confidential information. Their research results indicate that elementary and middle school counselors would breach confidentiality more frequently than secondary school counselors. These results fit well with developmental theories that indicate younger children tend to be both less capable of making informed choices as well as less concerned about confidentiality than preadolescents and adolescents.

Limitations to Confidentiality

Regardless of clients' ages, there are times when school counselors may or must breach confidentiality. The *Ethical Standards for School Counselors* (ASCA, 1998) and the *Code of Ethics and Standards of Practice* (ACA, 1995) both specify that counselors are ethically required to take appropriate action if clients engage in behavior that presents clear and imminent danger to themselves or others. The idea that danger to self or others supersedes clients' rights to privacy and confidentiality is accepted in both the ethical standards and legal concepts that govern counseling practice. The concept is difficult to apply to adults when the ethical principles of autonomy and beneficence collide, but the complexity multiplies when counselors attempt to be faithful to promises to parents. What is a "danger"? As demonstrated by the Isaacs and Stone (1999) study, most counselors would agree parents need to be informed of drug experimentation by an 8-year-old. Many however, would disagree about whether to tell parents that a 16-year-old client reported "occasional" experimentation with marijuana. In making decisions about whether to disclose this information to parents, it is important for school counselors to recognize how their own values and beliefs may influence how dangerous they perceive students' behaviors to be. In addition, school counselors should assess the client's developmental capabilities as well as patterns of the behavior before deciding if something is dangerous. For example, in trying to determine the degree of danger to the 16-year-old client who has experimented with marijuana, it seems important to ascertain what the client means by "experimental" and "occasional use" along with the client's intent to continue using marijuana. School counselors may be less likely to perceive the client who has tried marijuana twice, did not drive under the influence, and has decided that she dislikes it as being at risk as compared to the client who defines occasional as meaning she has been smoking marijuana at parties most weekends for the past 3 months and then driving home. The examples could continue but the only universal answer is that, in making decisions about whether the level of danger exhibited warrants sharing confidential information, school counselors need to know their state laws and the policies in the school jurisdiction. Finally, before making final decisions, school counselors are advised to consult with supervisors and colleagues.

In addition to danger to self or others, counselors must disclose confidential information if they suspect child abuse or neglect. Ethical standards and legal obligations coincide on this issue. Another typical exception to confidentiality is when school counselors receive a court order to testify or produce records in legal proceedings. In addition, ASCA (1998) directs counselors to respect parents' "rights and responsibilities ... for their children" (p. 2) and advises a counselor to make "reasonable efforts to honor the wishes of parents and guardians concerning information that he/she may share regarding the counselee" (p. 2). ASCA's *Ethical Standards for School Counselors* also include references to counselors' responsibilities to other school professionals such as faculty, staff, and administrators. For example Standard D. 1 specifies that the school counselor "informs appropriate officials of conditions that may be potentially disruptive or damaging to the school's mission, personnel, and property while honoring the confidentiality between the counselee and counselor" (ASCA, p. 3). Simply because student clients are in school situations, however, does not mean that all teachers and other school personnel have a legal basis to ask counselors to violate students' requests for confidentiality.

When required to disclose confidential information without a client's permission, school counselors are to reveal only "essential" information (ACA, 1995). For example, even during an individualized educational program meeting at which all participants have a general idea of a student's counseling goals and how these relate to other academic goals, counselors will be expected to present information related to the student's progress in meeting these goals but should not disclose specific details of their counseling sessions. Two good questions for counselors to ask themselves before sharing information about what a client divulged in counseling or about how they conceptualize a client's issue are, "Do team members need to know this?" and "How will knowing this help the team make decisions that will facilitate the student's educational progress?"

PRIVILEGED COMMUNICATION

Counselors' ethical obligation to maintain confidentiality does not allow them to disobey a court order to disclose information relevant to legal proceedings. In order to legally maintain the confidentiality of clients' communications or counseling records in judicial proceedings, the communications or records must be protected by a legal privilege (Glosoff et al., 2000). Privileged communication allows clients to ask counselors to keep their communications and records of those communications confidential. Privilege belongs to the counselee and the counselor acts for the counselee in asserting privilege. Unless privilege exists or is granted, counselors can be compelled to disclose counseling notes and information given to them by clients or face contempt or court penalties. There are three common bases for privilege as it relates to professional counseling communications: (a) English Common Law as is the case for attorneys; (b) the constitution as is the case for those who decline to speak under oath for fear of self-incrimination; and (c) state statute as is the case for many licensed professional counselors.

The concept of privileged communication is contrary to the philosophy of rules of evidence in court proceedings. The legal requirement to reveal information in a court unless a privilege has been granted is grounded in evidentiary law established to allow courts to seek the truth. The traditional standard for privilege is that the communication originated in confidence, confidentiality was essential to the relationship, society wants to foster the relationship, and the harm caused by breaking the trust would not be offset by the gain for justice (Wigmore, 1961). Professional groups such as physicians, attorneys, clergy, professional counselors, psychologists, and social workers have claimed that their relationships with their clients deserve privilege because they meet these criteria.

As of 2001, 45 states and the District of Columbia had professional counselor licensure or certification laws regulating the profession of counseling or the titles practicing counselors may and may not use in a jurisdiction. Glosoff et al. (2000) reported that 45 of the 46 jurisdictions also had statutes that granted privileged communication to the counselor-client relationship. School counselors should note the trend for state credentials that allow professionals that work in public schools to be called licenses rather than certificates. School counselors should avoid confusing the license to work in school with a license to practice outside of school settings. This distinction is important in those states that have statutes that specifically limit privilege to interactions between clients and licensed professional counselors. In some states, communications between clients and other categories of counselors such as substance abuse and school counselors are also privileged. Fischer and Sorenson (1996) noted that only 16 states grant statutory privilege directly to counselors who are certified or licensed by state boards of education to practice as school counselors. Given the variations in state privileged-communication statutes, it is important for school counselors to determine if the statutes in their state afford privilege to their clients.

The already complex issue of privileged communication for school counselors is made even more complex by the question of who has the privilege. Parents of minors rather than minor counselees are assumed to control the privilege if one exists. Counselors are sometimes subpoenaed for court appearances when the parents do not agree on whether the counselor's testimony is desired and when a parental dispute over custody may be the heart of the legal proceeding. The resolution of such disputes between parents is the responsibility of the court. ACA and ASCA ethical standards recognize that school counselors may have limits to their ability to protect counselee confidences. The *Ethical Standards for School Counselors* specify "the professional school counselor respects the inherent rights and responsibilities of parents for their children ..." (ASCA, 1998, B.1.a.). In addition, the *Ethical Standards* refer to counselors' obligations to follow both state laws and local guidelines (e.g., school board policies).

The Family Education Rights and Privacy Act (FERPA) clearly establishes that parents control the privacy rights of students under the age of 18. School counselors are sometimes confused by a FERPA provision that allows confidential notes or memory aids to be protected from FERPA's requirement that official school records be disclosed to parents. However, unless there is a specific privilege granted by statute or by a court, any material, including counselors' "confidential" case notes, can be subpoenaed. Counselors have no legal reason to refuse to testify or produce records if their counselee or the parents of a minor counselee request disclosure or waive their right to privilege.

Even in cases where communications between clients and counselors are not protected by statutory privilege or precedent, school counselors can appeal to the presiding judge to grant privilege. A statutory provision of privilege that must be overturned by the judge is a stronger position but a school counselor without statutory privilege could appeal to the judge on the basis of Wigmore's (1961) conditions. This means that the communication should have originated in confidence. Clients, or counselors on their behalf, cannot request privilege if a third person was present in the session. The logic and force of the 1966 Supreme Court *Jaffee v. Redmond* ruling can be an important part of a school counselor's request to a court for privilege (Remley, Herlihy, & Herlihy, 1997). The ruling supports the second Wigmore condition, that confidentiality is necessary for the counseling relationship. School counselors can also argue that society has sanctioned the counseling relationship through credentials for counselors and publicly supported counselor education programs. Finally, the Jaffee decision lends credence to the idea that the potential threat to justice posed by counselors' disclosure of confidential information does not outweigh the potential harm to the counseling relationship. Even if judges deny school counselors' request for privilege, counselors know they have done everything possible short of contempt of court to protect their counselee's confidences.

INFORMED CONSENT

With so many stipulations and exceptions to confidentiality and privilege, it is critical that school counselors engage in effective informed consent practices with their clients and significant adults. Informed consent, as an ethical principle, rests primarily on the moral principles of autonomy and fidelity, as described earlier. The principle of autonomy is consistent with counseling principles that require counselors to respect their clients as capable individuals who have the right to make choices regarding entering into counseling and being actively involved in the counseling process. Fidelity, in addition to the traditional definition of keeping promises, means that counselors create "a trusting and therapeutic climate in which people can search for their own solutions, and taking care not to deceive or exploit clients" (Herlihy & Corey, 1996, pp. 4-5).

Adherence to the moral principles of autonomy and fidelity fit well with the idea that clients have the right to actively participate in setting their goals for counseling and to make informed choices about the direction of their treatment. As noted previously, however, minor clients cannot legally give informed consent and, depending on their developmental functioning, may or may not be capable of understanding the risks and benefits of counseling or the limitations of confidentiality. Both ASCA and ACA indicate the importance of recognizing parents as stakeholders in their children's counseling. It is critical for school counselors to be clear about the roles and functions of parents and other stakeholders such as teachers in the counseling process and how these roles influence the bounds of confidentiality. After all, how can clients make informed decisions about what information to reveal to a counselor if they do not understand the limits of their counselor's ability to maintain their secrets?

But how can a student be encouraged to talk freely to a counselor if the session begins with a series of exceptions to confidentiality that may be perceived by the student as a warning rather than invitation?

One way to effectively approach the ethics of informed consent is to view it as an ongoing process rather than trying to cover every possible consideration in the first session. In addition, tailoring informed consent practices to the developmental level of the clients is critical. For example, a simple statement such as, "Whatever you tell me will be just between us unless I am worried about your health or safety. Do you have any questions about that?" may be sufficient during the first session with a 7-year-old client. If counseling a 15-year-old, however, it is probably more important to expand on this by discussing examples of conditions under which the counselor may need to disclose confidential information to the client's parents or to school personnel.

IMPLICATIONS FOR SCHOOL COUNSELORS

As stated earlier, the issue of confidentiality in school counseling is complex. School counselors have the ethical obligation to respect the privacy of minor clients and maintain confidentiality. This obligation is often in conflict with laws related to minors because parents have the right to know about most treatments and to decide what is in the best interest of their children. Counselors must also take into consideration codes of ethics, applicable statutes, and policies of their local education agencies and their individual schools. Given this type of balancing act, it is not surprising that school counselors often face ethical dilemmas related to maintaining the confidentiality of client information.

Prevention

The adage, "an ounce of prevention is worth a pound of cure," is helpful to keep in mind in relation to prevention of ethical problems. School counselors' anticipation of times when they may be faced with a possible need to breach clients' confidentiality may actually prevent the breach from occurring. Even if counselors do need to breach confidentiality, if well prepared, a sense of anticipation along with strong informed consent practices may prevent or lessen negative consequences to the clients or trauma to the counseling relationship. Preparation can take many forms. For example, school counselors have a responsibility to stay up-to-date on their state laws and their local school district policies related to clients' privacy. They can do this by attending professional development activities, requesting and reading policy manuals, and discussing these policies with their principals. If school policies conflict with the ACA (1995) or ASCA (1998) ethical standards, school counselors should discuss these with their principals and attempt to reconcile the policies with the ethical standards.

Counselors can also request that their school districts provide professional development workshops on current local and state policies and laws regarding confidentiality and their duty to protect students from danger (Isaacs & Stone, 1999). These professional development sessions should also include information on procedures to be followed when confidentiality must be breached. Isaacs and Stone noted that it is important for counselors to be aware of their own values regarding dangerous behaviors and how they believe age influences clients' right to self-responsibility. They also maintained that it is helpful for counselors to have a network of peers with whom they can consult when difficult situations arise. When possible, counselors can broaden their own perspectives by including colleagues in their network who work at other school levels as well as those who work in nonschool settings.

Educating and Aligning with Stakeholders as a Form of Prevention

In trying to balance ethical and legal obligations to clients and parents, we believe it is helpful for school counselors to approach parents as allies or partners in the counseling process. There may be times when the best interests of minor clients are served by including parents rather than trying to withhold information from them. The same holds true for dealing with other stakeholders such as other family members and school personnel. We are not, however, implying that counselors should automatically share confidential information with these stakeholders. Rather, we are suggesting that counselors acknowledge the likelihood that certain people will want information about student clients and to deal with this in a preventive manner by engaging in strong informed consent practices. Informed consent is an ongoing process that can begin before counseling ever does.

We recommend that school counselors routinely start the year by sending information to parents, teachers, and administrators about the role of the school counselor, the possible benefits of counseling, and the nature of both guidance and counseling activities. In addition to written materials, we suggest that counselors conduct in-service sessions with school personnel and present at PTA meetings so that stakeholders have an opportunity to ask questions and have concerns addressed. Educating stakeholders about the parameters of confidentiality when it is not related to any one specific child is a first step. It is also important to educate students through presentations in classrooms and assemblies. Of course, this should be followed by discussing relevant information with individual student clients and their parents once counseling begins. At that time, it is important for counselors, parents, and clients to come to an agree-

ment about the parameters of confidentiality (e. g., the types of information that the counselor will and will not share with the parents).

When Conflicts Arise

Even when counselors are extremely diligent and effective in communicating information with all relevant parties about the parameters of
confidentiality, there will be times when counselors perceive there is a
conflict between their obligations to clients and obligations to parents or
other stakeholders. For example, a parent requests information about the
progress her son is making in counseling and asks for specific examples
of things he has said in sessions. Rather than automatically assuming that
the client does not want the parent to have this information, it is important for the counselor to talk with the student to determine what, if any,
information he is willing to disclose or whether he is willing to give the
counselor permission to disclose information to his parent. If a student
client gives permission to share information with her or his parent, there
is no conflict. What becomes problematic is when parents ask for information and counselors believe that it is not in the clients' best interest to
disclose such information, or when clients express that they do not want
information disclosed. In these cases, we suggest that counselors attempt
to educate parents about the counseling process and how disclosing
against the child's wishes may result in negative consequences.

In educating parents, it is also important for school counselors to
assure parents that they will be informed if the counselor believes their
child to be in harm's way. The determination of what is potential harm is
not easy as the example of the marijuana smoking student presented earlier demonstrates. Once again, unless counselors have reasons to believe
otherwise, we suggest they assume parents are asking for the information
out of love and concern and to try to form alliances with parents. In our
experiences, parents who are convinced that neither their interests nor
those of their child will be well served by disclosure of specific information are often satisfied with a more general assessment or report (e.g., "I
believe your son is working hard in our counseling sessions to make
progress in the agreed upon goals. I wonder if you've noticed any
improvement at home?").

If parents still want counselors to disclose information, we suggest
that counselors schedule a session to meet with the parent(s) and client to
facilitate a discussion between them. If clients are not willing to share
information through this process and parents still insist, it may be necessary for counselors to tell their clients that, although it is against their
wishes, the counselors will need to disclose information to the parents. To
maintain the integrity of the counseling relationship, we suggest counselors do this before disclosing the information to the parents and then

adhere to the standard of minimal disclosure by sharing only what is essential.

SUMMARY OF SUGGESTIONS FOR SAFEGUARDING CLIENTS' PRIVACY AND CONFIDENTIALITY

We wish we could give easy answers, but we can only suggest that school counselors be vigilant and use the following measures to safeguard the privacy of their student clients:

1. Know the applicable ethical codes.
2. Know the applicable law in the jurisdiction.
3. Know the school system and building policies and procedures.
4. Refresh knowledge through professional reading and workshops.
5. Practice prevention through education and involvement of stakeholders.
6. Work diligently and specifically to make parents partners in the counseling process.
7. Remember the Three Cs: CONSULT – CONSULT – CONSULT.

Harriet L. Glosoff, Ph.D., *is an associate professor of Counselor Education, and* **Robert H. Pate, Jr., Ph.D.**, *is a professor of Counselor Education. Both are with the University of Virginia, Charlottesville. E-mail: hglosoff@virginia.edu.*

REFERENCES

American Counseling Association. (1995). *Code of ethics and standards of practice.* Alexandria, VA: Author.

American School Counselor Association. (1998). *Ethical standards for school counselors.* Alexandria, VA: Author.

Beauchamp, T. L., & Childress, J. F. (2001). *Principles of biomedical ethics* (5th ed). New York: Oxford University.

Birdsall, B., & Hubert, M. (2000, October). Ethical issues in school counseling. Retrieved January 19, 2002, from http://www.counseling.org/members/ctoline/ct1000/ethical.cfm.

Family Educational Rights and Privacy Act. (1974). 20 U.S.C.A. §1232.112 ALR Fed 1.

Fischer, L., & Sorenson, G. P. (1996). *School law for counselors, psychologists, and social workers* (3rd ed.). New York: Longman.

Glosoff, H. L., Herlihy, B., & Spence, B. (2000). Privileged communication in the counselor-client relationship: An analysis of state laws and implications for practice. *Journal of Counseling and Development, 78,* 454–462.

Herlihy, B., & Corey, G. (1996). *ACA ethical standards casebook* (5th ed.). Alexandria, VA: American Counseling Association.

Isaacs, M. L., & Stone, C. (1999). School counselors and confidentiality: Factors affecting professional choices. *Professional School Counseling, 2,* 258–266.

Jaffee v. Redmond et al., 1996 WL 3148411 (U.S. June 13, 1996).

Remley, T. P., Jr., & Herlihy, B. (2001). *Ethical, legal, and professional issues in counseling.* Upper Saddle River, NJ: Merrill Prentice Hall.

Remley, T. P., Jr., Herlihy, B., & Herlihy, S. B. (1997). The U. S. Supreme Court decision in *Jaffee v. Redmond*: Implications for counselors. *Journal of Counseling and Development, 75,* 213–218.

Welfel, E. R. (2002). *Ethics in counseling and psychotherapy. Standards, research, and emerging issues.* Pacific Grove, CA: Brooks/Cole.

Wigmore, J. H. (1961). *Evidence in trials at common law* (Vol. 8). Boston: Little-Brown.

School Counselors and Confidentiality: Factors Affecting Professional Choices

Madelyn L. Isaacs
Carolyn Stone

Confidentiality has long been held as critical to gaining a client's trust. Children have the right to expect that the adult protection includes protection of their privacy rights (Huey & Remley, 198Sa). Zingaro (1983) believes that a child's right to privacy, regardless of the child's age, should only be compromised in very extreme circumstances, however, extreme circumstances can be variously interpreted. It is widely believed that without the assurance of confidentiality, many students would not seek help or would not be entirely forthcoming (Ford, Millstein, Halpern-Felsher, & Irwin, 1997).

School counselors are frequently confronted with the challenge of balancing the rights of minor clients for confidentiality with the legitimate rights and concerns of others and a counselor's responsibility to act in a minor child's best interest. In a 1983 unsuccessful suit *Roman v. Appleby*, brought by parents against school counselor, a U. S. federal district court noted that in schools the constitutional rights of children, parents, administrators, and teachers all compete (American Counseling Association, 1993). Managing confidentiality is often the most difficult ethical issue facing school counselors.

COUNSELOR CODES AND CONFIDENTIALITY FOR MINORS

The primacy of confidentiality is clear in the codes of ethics and standards of practice for the American Counseling Association (ACA) and the American School Counselors Association (ASCA), which devote considerable attention to confidentiality. ACA (1995) defines a counselor's obligations to all clients and to minor clients in particular, "Counselors act in the best interests of clients and take measures to safeguard confidentiality (p 3). The American School Counselor Association (1992) makes its position clear: "Each person has the right to privacy and thereby the right to expect the counselor-client relationship to comply with all laws, policies and ethical standards pertaining to confidentiality" (P.1). Concurrently, both ACA and ASCA suggests collaboration with parents and families in situations that involve minor clients and their confidentiality," A school counselor respects the inherent rights and responsibilities of the parents for their children and endeavors to establish a cooperative relationship of the counselee" (ASCA, 1992, p.2).

COMPLICATING FACTORS

Inconsistent Rules and Confidentiality with Minors

ASCA (1992; 1986) repeatedly refers to counselors' obligations to law and local guidelines. Yet these guidelines often vary considerably between states and/or local jurisdictions and may vary within school districts or by level of school (Baker, 1996). Courts have dealt both with parental rights and the establishment of a mature-minor concept in terms of an adolescent owning their privacy as well as other rights (Fischer & Sorenson, 1996). Schmidt (1996) suggests that some states have specifically granted confidentiality (in the form of privilege) to students while other states are mute. School board policies and community standards may necessitate breaking confidentiality. One Florida school board has established specific procedures for school personnel when dealing with issues of contraceptives and abortion (Clay County Public School Board, 1996).

Even when the administrative policies or rules are clear, some counselors express ambivalence about following them. In Davis and Mickelson's (1994) survey of school counselors, ethical dilemmas that involved issues of student client privacy, confidentiality and parental rights received less than 50% agreement regarding the preferred ethical or correct legal choices. Research with helping professionals, for example, suggests that knowledge of the rules of abuse reporting does not always predict compliance (Butz, 1985; Crenshaw, Lichtenberg & Bartell, 1993).

Parental Rights

ASCA (1992; 1986) recognizes that school counselors have multiple obligations that extend beyond their student client, including families, teachers, administrators, and other students. Consistent with professional codes, judicial decisions have historically protected parental rights. The

Supreme Court of the United States continues to assert parents' legal ability to raise their children and to provide guidance in the values and decisions governing their children. In deciding a case involving the Utah statute requiring physician notification of parents or guardians of a minor upon whom an abortion is to be performed, the Supreme Court stated, "We have recognized that parents have an important guiding role to play in the upbringing of their children which presumptively includes counseling them on important decisions" (H.L. Etc., *Appellant v. Scott Matheson*, 1981). Furthermore, courts generally have vested the rights of minors in their parents. In 1979 the United States Supreme Court declared:

> We have recognized three reasons justifying the conclusion that the constitutional rights of children cannot be equated with those of adults; the peculiar vulnerability of children; their inability to make critical decisions in an informed, mature manner, and the importance of the parental role in child rearing (*Bellotti v. Baird*, 1979).

If parents request disclosure of information their child reveals in a counseling session, they probably have a legal right to access this. Huey and Remley (1988b) believe that this premise is the logical extension of privacy rights that belong to the parent, even in cases when the child or adolescent expressly requests confidentiality. In contrast, Fischer and Sorenson (1996) believe that school counselors do not have to disclose the content or substance of their counseling sessions unless expressly written in school board policy.

Responsibility to Educators

Counselors are in a precarious position because they are charged with being consultants to other educators, who may not have the same obligations to a student's privacy that the counselor does. While minimal disclosure might be recommended, it is not always possible to do so. Teachers need to be informed regarding the special needs and circumstances of children, as they are often in the best position to impact positively on a child's life during and beyond the school day. Additionally, administrators or other student services personnel sometimes request information about counseling sessions for appropriate reasons.

Age and Informed Consent

The younger the client, the more control parents have over decisions governing their children. Furthermore, the less competent children are to provide full informed consent on their own behalf, the more dependent they are on adults to protect their privacy and rights. Legally, there has been precedent established concerning children's rights varying with age (ACA, 1993; Fischer & Sorenson, 1996). For example, teenagers (especially after the age of 14 or when considered a mature minor) are routinely given medical rights regarding abortion and the treatment of sexually transmitted diseases and the right to influence custody decisions (ACA, 1993).

For school counselors it is difficult to determine when a client is mature enough to discern dangerous situations and handle them independently of their parents' guidance. High school counselors have to navigate the tricky waters between confidentiality that teenagers demand and parents' rights to govern their children with full knowledge of important issues their children are facing. For example, in Florida teenagers may receive an abortion without parental consent. It is unclear, however, whether counselors who were told of impending abortion plans might see such an act as constituting a danger to self and therefore have justification for informing the parents. To further complicate matters, the law makes distinctions based on a single age, whereas counselors often view age as a range of maturation levels. Thus, the law may allow the 14-year-old and the 17-year-old to have equal self-referred access to abortion while school counselors may perceive these two children differently and therefore have different responses in terms of obligations to parents.

INVOKING DUTY TO WARN OR DUTY TO PROTECT

When counselors believe that a student's behavior may lead to harm to self or others, they may attempt to warn someone else by breaching confidentiality or may be required by state or local law to breach confidentiality (Schmidt, 1996). Isaacs (1997) had noted that there are no clear standards for duty to warn among states, nor clear guidelines for school counselors who work with minor clients. Duty to protect is closely related concept to duty to warn that is well established in the ethical codes. Clearly younger dependent children are seen as requiring protection from the behavior of others and their own immature judgment.

There is considerable variation in counselors' interpretations of the kind of circumstances worthy of breaching confidentiality to warn or protect. Vernon (1993) suggests that counselors consider student client age and capability, the possible impact of disclosures on therapeutic progress, and the ethical standards and legal requirements of the state, agency, or district in which one works. However, what constitutes extreme circumstances may vary directly with a counselor's religious or personal values. Is satanic worship, cigarette smoking, or body piercing different than extreme drug use or abortion? Counselors may take different courses of action in protecting a client's rights, protecting a client from harm, and seeking parental involvement when mixing highly charged issues like abortion with personal and professional values. Many school counselors with knowledge that an 11-year-old client is smoking will evoke duty to warn and will report this to the parents. Other school counselors view such a report to parents as a serious breach of confidentiality.

COUNSELOR ROLES AT DIFFERENT LEVELS

Few studies have been conducted to verily how counselors at different levels function (Carroll, 1993; Hardesty & Dillard, 1994). However, Hardesty and Dillard found that consultation with teachers concerning problem students was a more prevalent role for elementary counselors as compared to secondary counselors. Nugent (1990) noted that elementary counselors have much more contact with families and teachers than school counselors at other levels. This might suggest that school counselors at different levels have varying direct interaction with families. Counselors who have more contact with families may be more sensitive to family involvement in counseling about difficult student issues.

Wagner (1981) explored ethics and elementary, middle, and high school counselor roles and noted that elementary school counselors are less stringent in practice with confidentiality of students' confidences (Wagner, 1981). Elementary counselors were also more likely to give information to parents. Additionally, Wagner's (1981) study found parents of elementary school students were more likely to inquire about what was discussed in a counseling session and that elementary counselors were more likely to perceive confidentiality as a commodity that does not necessarily apply to students in elementary schools.

How counselors handle confidentiality, the hallmark of a counseling relationship, is often seen as critical to the success of the helping relationship. In schools where the rights of minor clients compete with parent's and school officials' rights and legitimate needs to know, decisions concerning maintaining confidentiality can be critical. Both chronological age and developmental age are often factors in legal and ethical considerations of child's rights. One question addressed in the present study was: Under what conditions will counselors consider breaching a student's confidentiality? We also explored the influence of such demographic variables as student's age and level of school counselor employment on counselor's ethical decision making.

METHOD

Questionnaires were mailed to district guidance supervisors in eight Florida school districts. Each distributed and collected them from counselors at the appropriate level in their district. Questionnaires were completed anonymously and then returned as a group. Districts from all over the state and of different sizes were included in the sample based on the student services director's agreement to participate or large numbers of school counselors attending workshops completed the questionnaires as a group.

A total of 627 counselors responded representing 145 high school counselors (23%), 71 middle school counselors (11%), and 411 elementary school counselors (66%). A greater proportion of elementary school counselors responded than were initially sampled. Questionnaires were distributed through single individuals (district supervisors), who then collected data from larger groups of counselors, and all surveyed districts responded. It is therefore estimated that more than 90% of available counselors in each district responded.

Questionnaire

The Confidentiality and Minors Questionnaire was designed by the authors based on information from current court decisions and legislative mandates about managing student's confidential information. For example, the Maryland high court in *Eisel v. Board of Education* (1991) ruled that school counselors had a duty to share with parents' information regarding the student's intention to commit suicide. Each questionnaire asked for demographic information, including the setting of employment (rural, small town, suburban, and urban), years of experience as a counselor, the number of situations encountered during the past 2 years (ranging from zero to more than 15).

Parallel forms of the questionnaire were developed in which ages of students were manipulated. For example, elementary counselors were asked if they would breach confidentiality when "A fifth grader tells you she will be seeking an abortion the next day." Middle school counselors were asked the same question separately about 12- and 14-year-olds and high school counselors were asked about 14- and 17-year-olds.

Twenty two scenarios (or 23 depending upon the student age level and level represented in the survey) were described, and school counselors were asked to consider if the counselor would break confidentiality by choosing "Yes, it is very likely that I would break confidentiality," "No it is unlikely that I would break confidentiality," or "I am not certain what I would do in this situation." Issues which were commonly assessed included smoking cigarettes, marijuana or crack cocaine; sneaking out of the house and having sexual intercourse with a boyfriend (or multiple partners), seeking an abortion, crime (including shoplifting, armed robbery), depression/suicide, and victimization by another student.

For each level, a second set of 13 or 14 personal action statements that were to be judged True or False followed. These statements followed the words "I would..." under the presented condition. Issues covered in this section included contraceptive advice or referral, revealing session contents to parents or teachers upon request, knowledge of the whereabouts of a runaway, sharing information about a family with community agencies, sharing information in a letter of recommendation, conditions and timing of explanations of confidentiality limits, and the degree of responsibility to a student or parents.

Data Analysis

Frequency analysis was completed on counselors as a whole and based on their primary employment setting. A Chi Square analysis was used to compare frequency of responses for each question among elementary, middle, and high school counselors. Alpha at .001 was identified as a threshold of significance to account for the number of items in the questionnaire.

RESULTS

Tables 1 and 2 present results for all counselors, separated for each of the three levels of counselors surveyed for sections 1 and 2 of the questionnaire respectively. Additionally, each question for which Chi-Square analysis was significant at the $p < .001$ is identified. Results were also obtained for years of experience and setting of work (rural or urban), though no significant differences were noted and are therefore not reported. Table 3 lists comparative results for questions in which absolute age can be compared across level. Chi Square analysis is indicated for those items where significant differences were found at $p < .001$.

The majority of counselors report that they would breach confidentiality for the following issues (in descending order of the percentage who would likely breach confidentiality): impending suicide or suicide pact; retaliation for victimization; use of crack cocaine; sexual intercourse with multiple partners when HIV positive; armed robbery; indications of depression; abortion; and marijuana use. As well, the majority of counselors (in descending order of percentage who agree) would not drive a student to an abortion appointment; inform students of confidentiality limits *at some point* during counseling; would not reveal counseling session contents to parents or teachers; would share information with counselors at another school about former students of theirs; would inform students of confidentiality limits *at the outset* of counseling; would refer students for contraceptive information; do not feel confident dealing with many issues of concern in small groups; or would protect whereabouts of students who had run away from dysfunctional families. While these results were found for all counselors who responded, there are differences in counselor responses based on level of employment.

TABLE 1 Overall Percentage Responses for Counselors and for Each Level of Employment in Percentages for Likeliness to Breach Confidentiality

The counselor (respondent) would breach confidentiality in the following scenario:	All Counselors Surveyed			Elementary School (n=411)			Middle School (n=71)			High School (n=145)		
	Likely	Unlikely	Uncertain	Likely	Unlikely	Uncertain	Likely	Unlikely	Uncertain	Likely	Unlikely	Uncertain
An older student will be seeking an abortion the next day.*	69.1	20.3	10.6 (n=627)	83.3	9.8	6.9	56.9	22.2	20.8	34.7	49.3	16.0
A younger student will be seeking an abortion the next day.	53.7	27.8	18.4 (n=216)				61.3	21.0	17.7	50.0	31.3	18.8
A student tells you he/she has committed armed robbery.*	77.1	14.0	8.9 (n=627)	82.3	9.3	8.4	69.4	23.6	6.9	66.2	22.8	11.0
Fourth grader regularly beaten up by older brother.				87.6	7.1	5.4						
Student plans to destroy bulldozer in environmental protest.	56.8	22.6	20.6 (n=216)				56.3	23.9	19.7	57.2	21.4	21.4
An older student confides is using crack cocaine.*	83.7	9.2	7.1 (n=216)	92.7	2.9	4.4	71.4	17.1	11.4	54.4	23.3	12.3
A younger student confides is using crack cocaine.	75.8	16.4	7.8 (n=216)				77.8	15.3	6.9	74.7	17.1	8.2
Student says is depressed and life is sometimes too tough for living.	76.9	8.9	9.6 (n=627)	77.1	14.3	8.6	61.1	25.0	13.9	76.0	16.4	7.5
Student has access to a gun and plans to shoot self.	97.6	1.1	1.7 (n=627)	97.6	1.0	1.5	100.0			96.6	1.4	2.0

Scenario													n
Fourteen-year-old is HIV positive and having sexual intercourse with multiple partners.	80.7	9.3	10.0				80.6	6.9	12.5	80.7	10.3	9.0	(n=216)
Student confides is smoking marijuana.*	68.7	23.0	8.3	82.2	11.7	6.1	41.7	45.8	12.5	43.8	43.8	12.5	(n=627)
Student having sexual intercourse with multiple partners.				79.8	10.2	10.0							
Student says mother doesn't love him now that has a new husband.				20.3	76.4	3.3							
Student says has been paying other student to do homework.				37.9	52.5	9.7							
Student tells of plans to rob convenience store that night.	79.5	10.7	9.8				72.2	18.1	9.7	83.2	7.0	9.8	(n=216)
Student says is having sexual intercourse with her boyfriend.				71.0	15.6	13.4							
Student says has been shoplifting.*	41.4	45.3	13.3	47.9	37.3	14.7	33.3	58.3	8.3	25.5	61.4	13.1	(n=627)
An older student in the level of school tells has been smoking cigarettes.*	38.3	3.7	8.0	55.5	34.3	10.2	8.5	87.3	4.2	4.3	92.1	3.6	(n=627)
A younger student in the level of school tells has been smoking cigarettes.*	54.1	40.1	5.8	74.7	18.7	6.6	14.3	80.0	5.7	15.3	81.3	3.5	(n=627)
An older student in the level of school tells has been sneaking out to see boyfriend.*	53.4	35.0	11.6	68.7	19.7	11.6	39.4	43.7	16.9	17.1	74.3	8.6	(v627)

The counselor (respondent) would breach confidentiality in the following scenario:	All Counselors Surveyed			Elementary School (n=411)			Middle School (n=71)			High School (n=145)		
	Likely	Unlikely	Uncertain	Likely	Unlikely	Uncertain	Likely	Unlikely	Uncertain	Likely	Unlikely	Uncertain
A younger student in the level of school tells has been sneaking out to see boyfriend.	43.5	25.1	31.4 (n=216)				40.8	45.1	14.1	44.8	15.2	67.1
Student says has been stealing money from mother's purse.				47.7	36.9	15.5						
Student confides hates stepmother.				7.6	89.5	2.9						
Learn from a classmate that there is suicide pact but one of the two members denies it when asked.	88.0	4.9	7.1 (n=627)	91.2	2.9	5.9	81.9	11.1	6.9	82.2	7.5	10.3
Student says teacher is nice to everyone in class but him.				15.9	79.0	5.1						
Student reveals is having unprotected sexual intercourse with multiple partners.	50.9	33.2	15.9 (n=216)				54.9	28.2	16.9	49.0	35.7	15.4
Student tired of being victimized by another student plans to end harassment by shooting the perpetrator.	94.2	3.6	2.2 (n=627)	93.2	4.1	2.7	98.6	1.4		95.2	2.7	2.0

Note: Blank cells exist where comparable questions were not asked of counselors at that level of employment.
*Chi Square contingency statistics $p > .000$.

TABLE 2 Overall Percentages of Responses to Scenarios

Counselors were asked how they would respond to the following situations:	All Counselors (N=627)		Elementary School (n=411)		Middle School (n=71)		High School (n=145)	
	True	False	True	False	True	False	True	False
If student has exhausted all other avenues for help (but her parents), I would drive her to her appointment for an abortion at her request.	2.1	97.9	1.9	98.1	2.8	97.2	2.1	97.9
I would refer a student to an outside agency for help on contraceptive information.*	19.7	20.3	12.6	87.4	25.7	74.3	37.1	62.9
I would offer advice on contraceptives to a student who asked me for help.*	53.0	47.0		74.9	44.3	55.7	57.3	42.7
I would refer a student to an outside agency for help on contraceptive information if asked.*	71.4	28.6		63.9	58.6	41.4	77.8	22.2
I inform students of limits of confidentiality only at time when begin discussion which may require that I break confidentiality.*	36.8	63.2		68.3	35.8	64.2	50.0	50.0
I inform my students of limits of confidentiality during the first session.*	76.6	23.4	83.1	16.9	62.5	37.5	65.0	35.0
Former student moves to new school and is a behavior problem. Guidance counselor of new school has student record but seeks more information. Calls and asks for information on student and family. Have been working with student and family for 2 years. Would share information.	80.1	19.9	82.0	18.0	81.8	18.2	74.6	25.4

Counselors were asked how they would respond to the following situations:	All Counselors (N=627)		Elementary School (n=411)		Middle School (n=71)		High School (n=145)	
	True	False	True	False	True	False	True	False
I can deal with any issue of concern to students in small group, e.g., being victim of incest, as long as explain to students in group the need for confidentiality.*	38.4	61.6	34.0	66.0	32.9	67.1	53.5	46.5
I do not inform students about limits of confidentiality.*	5.7	94.3	4.4	95.6	22.2	77.8	1.4	98.6
I would comply with parent request to reveal content of counseling session with their child.*	14.5	85.5	18.5	81.5	3.0	97.0	9.1	90.9
I can state in a letter of recommendation that student's poor grades were due to death of parent.							76.9	23.1
With regards to confidentiality, I have a greater responsibility to parents of students than to student.	12.1	87.9	13.9	86.1	10.1	89.9	7.9	92.1
Can reveal to agency counselor (elementary) or in letter of recommendation (high school) that student's poor grades were due to being rape victim.*			24.1	75.9			9.8	90.2
I would reveal whereabouts (safe with a good family) of a student who had run away from a dysfunctional, emotionally abusive home when the student's parents ask.	41.1	58.9	43.0	57.0	45.6	54.4	33.8	66.2

| I would comply with teacher request to reveal contents of counseling session with their student.* | 9.4 | 90.6 | 12.4 | 87.6 | 7.5 | 92.5 | 2.1 | 97.9 |

Note: Blank cells exist where comparable questions were not asked of counselors at that level of employment.
*Chi Square and contingency statistics *p* <.000.

TABLE 3 Absolute Comparisons Between Ages of Students and Likeliness to Breach Confidentiality

Issue	Elementary School			Middle School			High School		
	Likely	Unlikely	Uncertain	Likely	Unlikely	Uncertain	Likely	Unlikely	Uncertain
14-year-old smoking marijuana				42.9	42.9	12.9	41.1	45.2	12.3
14-year-old (middle and high); 12-year-old (elementary) smoking cigarettes*	53.3	33.7	9.8	8.2	84.9	4.1	15.0	79.6	4.1
14-year-old smoking crack				68.5	16.4	11.0	74.1	17.0	8.2
12-year-old smoking crack*	91.2	3.2	4.5	76.7	15.1	6.8			
14-year-old sneaking out of house				38.4	42.5	16.4	39.5	44.2	15.0
12-year-old sneaking out of house*	65.8	20.4	11.4	39.7	43.8	13.7			
14-year-old having an abortion*				56.2	21.9	20.5	49.0	30.6	18.4
12-year-old having an abortion*	81.4	10.1	6.9	63.0	19.2	15.1			

Note: Blank cells exist where comparable questions were not asked of counselors at that level of employment.
*Chi Square and contingency statistics *p* <.000.

Impact of Demographic Variables

Years of experience as a counselor had no relationship to responses to questionnaire items. No differences from setting (rural, small town, suburban and urban) were detected. However, sample sizes placing the majority of respondents (more than 75%) in suburban and urban settings may have confounded the ability of this study to draw conclusions about these relationships.

There were differences across grade levels in counselor prediction/certainty of future behavior to breach confidentiality as indicated in Tables 1 and 2. Issues on which counselors at different levels differed significantly included older students seeking abortions; involvement in armed robbery; older students using crack cocaine; smoking marijuana; shoplifting; sneaking out to see a boyfriend; and smoking cigarettes. In all cases, counselors at the elementary level were more willing to breach confidentiality.

High school counselors were more willing to refer students for contraceptive information in general and respond with contraceptive information when asked for it directly. Additionally, high school counselors were willing to deal with a group concerning an incest victim with confidentiality explained, and inform students of the limits of confidentiality. Elementary school counselors were most likely to inform their clients of the limits of confidentiality during the first session, conform with parents' requests to reveal counseling session contents, and reveal to an outside agency that a student's poor grades were due to a rape.

Working in an elementary, middle, or high school had no effect on counselor willingness to breach confidentiality for serious issues of younger students seeking an abortion, younger students using crack cocaine, student depression and suicidal expressions, student plans for shooting self, HIV-positive student having sex with multiple partners, student revelation about impending robbery, younger student sneaking out to see her boyfriend, learning about a suicide pact, a student having unprotected sex with multiple partners, and a student shooting a victimizer. It also did not affect whether counselors would drive a student to have an abortion, would share family information with a counselor at a new school about a family's problems, would reveal whereabouts of runaway student from a dysfunctional home, or whether counselors feel greater responsibility to parents of students than students.

Findings noted in Table 3 help identify areas in which counselors dealing with the same aged child and the same situation varied by level of employment. In several cases, situations for 12-years-olds (who would be oldest in elementary school and youngest in middle school) and 14-year-olds (who would be oldest in middle school and youngest in high school) are reported as significantly different between groups in areas of smoking cigarettes, smoking crack, sneaking out of the house, and having an abortion. In all cases, the higher the level of school, the less likelihood of breach of confidentiality.

DISCUSSION

Counselors who work with children regularly face ethical dilemmas of confidentiality for which there are few definitive answers. Ethical guidelines such as those of ACA and ASCA provide practical suggestions when counselors continue to deal with issues of confidentiality with children. It is ultimately the responsibility of school counselors to negotiate the rights and privileges of their clients with regard to issues of duty to warn and the legal rights of families and other educators. These decisions are made against the background of counselor personal and professional values, which may impact their judgment of what constitutes danger to self or others.

It would appear that counselor judgment of when to breach confidentiality is determined in part by the degree of dangerousness of the perceived behavior (e.g., smoking crack cocaine is seen as more dangerous than smoking cigarettes). School counselors generally express certainty in predicting their behavior although ambivalence grows as students get older. Judgment to breach confidentiality is also significantly impacted by level of employment and by age of student within level of employment. Counselors tend to see serious drug use, abortion, use of crack cocaine, suicide intent, robbery, and sex with multiple partners as areas which are serious enough to warrant a breach of confidentiality, though less so at the high school level. Apparently, most counselors perceive these behaviors as constituting danger to self or others for younger children more than for older children. Counselors were more likely to provide contraceptive information to high school students or make referrals to outside agencies and to tell students of confidentiality limits if the session appeared to cover content requiring a breach of confidentiality. They were more confident of ensuring confidentiality in a group with an incest victim. Elementary school counselors were most assiduous about informing students about the limits of confidentiality in the first session and in revealing counseling session contents to parents and teachers (though far fewer would tell teachers than tell parents). The survey results suggest that counselors see younger students as more dependent, needing more protection, and having less right to confidentiality than their older counterparts.

On the other hand, for issues concerning smoking cigarettes, sneaking out of the house, and abortions, counselors tended to vary based on level even when the absolute age was held constant. This indicated that counselors see students in terms of their relative ages to other students in the school and not absolute developmental or chronological age under certain circumstances.

The finding that high school counselors would breach confidentiality less often than elementary or middle school counselors is consistent with the legal concept of informed consent and ability to make mature decisions as a student gets older and closer to being considered a mature minor. The finding that elementary counselors advocate breaching confidentiality more often may reflect the multiple role responsibilities elementary school counselor have and their more frequent contact with parents and teachers. As well, elementary counselors' willingness to breach confidentiality most frequently about most issues confirms earlier research by Wagner (1981).

Our findings suggest that school counselors protect younger students to a greater degree by warning others or including families in children's issues. Middle and secondary school counselors seem to be considering the privacy rights of older students more frequently. Thus, school counselors believe that regardless of professional ethics and rules, the age of the child is the most significant variable in dealing with dilemmas related to confidentiality. As a result of such thinking, interested adults (teachers and parents) may be privy to more information.

One interesting finding concerns relative age within school level versus absolute age of a student. School counselors seem to become encapsulated by the level of their work, almost to the exclusion of developmentally appropriate practices based on age of a child. That is, 12- or 14-year-olds are seen as having different privacy rights and different decision-making abilities depending upon whether they are in elementary, middle or high school,

School counselors may increasingly face situations in which students or others warrant protection. They must consider a number of issues when faced with dilemmas about breaching confidentiality as a way of protecting students and others from potentially dangerous situations. They should prepare themselves and their clients and stakeholders (students, families, school personnel, and agency personnel) for situations when breach of confidentiality may be appropriate or required. This can be done by counselors doing the following:

- Ensure periodic update on current laws as well as district policies pertaining to breaching confidentiality. These may change in response to recent outbreaks of violence or suicide.
- Examine their own values and experiences to identify biases about dangerous behavior and about the age and behavior that signals increasing self-responsibility.
- Establish in advance the kinds of behaviors and issues that might warrant breach of confidentiality.

Couple these with strategies to help children reveal information to others.

- Establish a network of peers who can be routinely and confidentially consulted when situations arise. Include counselors who work at other school levels and who work in nonschool settings with children to get broad perspectives.
- Ascertain alternative actions to breaching confidentiality to protect students or others. These may include working with larger groups of students in more general ways, instituting policies or procedures for all, which may serve to also protect a few known students.
- Continually engage in professional development activities through local, regional, and national professional organizations. Advocate for discussion and policy or procedure development if issues are unclear.
- Request periodic in-service presentations that update local and state policies and procedures concerning confidentiality and protecting students from danger.
- Purchase liability insurance through professional organizations or affiliations and consult with resources to determine appropriate courses of action.
- Educate all stakeholders concerning the rationale for confidentiality in counseling and for the conditions or limits placed on confidentiality with minor students. Develop and use a consistent informed-consent protocol.

Continued research is needed to explore counselor attitudes and behavioral dispositions in nonschool settings (agencies and private practices). Other areas that warrant further exploration are the effects on ethical behavior and knowledge of different training models, of in-service training on ethics, and of school counselors' knowledge of school district, and state policies and laws. Researchers would also do well to replicate this work with larger samples of secondary school counselors in middle and high school settings. Such studies have significant implications with regard to training as well as standards for appropriate professional behavior.

Madelyn L. Isaacs, Ph.D., *is an associate professor of Counselor Education and assistant director of the School of Education, Florida Gulf Coast University, Ft. Myers.* **Carolyn Stone, Ph.D.,** *is an assistant professor of Counselor Education, University of North Florida, Jacksonville, FL.*

REFERENCES

American Counseling Association. (1995). *Code of ethics and standards of practice.* Alexandria, VA: Author.

American Counseling Association (1993). *Counseling minor clients.* Alexandria, VA: Author

American School Counselor Association. (1992). *Ethical standards for school counselors.* Alexandria, VA: Author

American School Counselor Association (1986). *The school counselor and confidentiality.* Alexandria, VA: Author

Baker, S. B. (1996). *School counseling for the twenty-first century.* Engelwood Cliffs, NJ: Merrill.

Bellotti v. Baird, 443 U.S. 622 (1979).

Butz, R. A. (1985). Reporting child abuse and confidentiality in counseling. *Social Case Work: The Journal of Contemporary Social Work, 66,* 83–90.

Carroll, B. W. (1993). Perceived roles and preparation experiences of elementary counselors: Suggestions for change. *Elementary School Guidance and Counseling, 27,* 216–226.

Clay County Public School Board. (1996). *Clay County public schools policies and procedures.* Green Cove Springs, FL: Author

Crenshaw, W. B., Lichtenberg, J. W. & Bartell, P. A. (1993). Mental health providers and child abuse: A multivariate analysis of the decision to report. *Journal of Child Sexual Abuse, 2,* 19–42.

Davis, J. I., & Mickelson, D. J. (1994) School counselors: Are you aware of ethical and legal aspects of counseling? *The School Counselor, 42,* 5–12.

Eisel v. Board of Education of Montgomery County, 597 A.2. 2d 447 (Md. 1991)

Fischer, P. P., & Sorenson, L. (1996). *School law for counselors, psychologists and social workers* (3rd ed.). White Plains, NY: Longman.

Ford, C., Millstein, S., Halpern–Felsher, S., & Irwin, C. E. (1997). Influence of physician confidentiality assurances on adolescents' willingness to disclose information and seek future health care. A randomized controlled trial. *The Journal of the American Medical Association, 278,* 1029–1034.

Hardesty, P. H., & Dillard, J. M. (1994). The role of elementary school counselors compared with their middle and secondary school counterparts. *Elementary School Guidance and Counseling, 29,* 83–91.

H. L. Etc., Appellant b. Scott M. Matheson, 101 S. Ct. 2727 (1981).

Huey, W. C., & Remley, T. P., Jr. (1988a). Confidentiality and the school counselor: A challenge for the 1990's. *School Counselor, 41,* 23–30.

Huey, W. C., & Remley, T. P., Jr. (1988b). *Ethical and legal issues in school counseling.* Alexandria, VA: American School Counselor Association.

Isaacs, M. L. (1997). The duty to warn and protect: Tarasoff and the elementary school counselor. *Elementary School Guidance and Counseling, 31*(4), 326–342.

Nugent, F. A. (1990). *An introduction to the profession of counseling.* New York: Merrill.

Schmidt, J. J. (1996). *Counseling in schools: Essential services and comprehensive programs.* Needham Heights, MA: Allyn & Bacon.

Vernon, A. (1993). *Counseling children and adolescents.* Denver, CO: Love

Wagner, C. A. (1981). Confidentiality and the school counselor. *Personnel and Guidance Journal, 59*(5), 305–310.

Zingaro. (1983). Confidentiality: To tell or not to tell. *Elementary School Guidance and Counseling, 17,* 261–267.

Confidentiality and the School Counselor: A Challenge for the 1990s

Tom Davis
Martin Ritchie

School counselors traditionally have been trained in the sanctity of the relationship between themselves and their clients. Confidentiality is considered an essential ingredient in establishing trusting relationships with students. According to the American Association for Counseling and Development's ethical standards (AACD, 1988) "The counseling relationship and information resulting there from must be kept confidential, consistent with the obligations of the member as a professional person" (Section B.2). Similarly, the American School Counselor Association's ethical standards (1992) state, "Each person has the right to privacy and thereby the right to expect the counselor-client relationship to comply with all laws, policies and ethical standards pertaining to confidentiality"(Preamble).

All of this may lead some counselors into a false sense of security about the confidential nature of their relationships with students when, in reality, the issue of confidentiality is quite complex. During the 1980s, counselors, along with other mental health providers, were being held more accountable for their actions, and more responsible for the actions of their clients (Huey & Remley, 1989). Because school counselors are expected to deal with sensitive issues such as pregnancy, drug abuse, and suicide, it is likely they will become more vulnerable to legal action. Herlihy and Sheeley (1988) pointed out that we now live in a litigious society with an ever growing attitude that if someone is injured, someone must pay. With this in mind, school counselors must take every precaution to protect not only their clients but also themselves by being aware of the ethical and legal ramifications of their actions.

The purpose of this article is to critically analyze the ethical and legal aspects of confidentiality and privileged communication as they relate to school counselors. Suggestions are made for establishing confidentiality in a school setting while taking into account scope of practice issues and obligations of informed consent. Guidelines are presented for when and how to break confidentiality in situations in which the duty to warn or the duty to testify may outweigh the duty to withhold information. Finally, suggestions are made for keeping parents and teachers informed of the progress of clients without jeopardizing the confidential relationship.

SCOPE OF PRACTICE

School counselors who agree to provide treatment in situations for which they are not qualified are open to lawsuits. Prescribing treatment the therapist is not qualified to provide may constitute malpractice (Keith-Spiegel & Koocher, 1985). Providing treatment that is ineffective or harmful may also constitute malpractice (*Nally v. Grace Community Church of the Valley*, 1984). School counselors are exposed to every psychological problem that exists in school-age populations. When a student is referred or seeks the help of a counselor, that counselor feels a strong obligation to do whatever he or she can to help that student. Nevertheless, school counselors must be cognizant of the limits of their training and abilities and know when to refer students to more capable helpers. Failure to do so may result in legal culpability.

School counselors should review the kinds of problems they are qualified to treat and the kinds of treatment they are competent to provide. These qualifications and competencies should be written and displayed in the form of a statement of competencies or scope of practice. This information should be shared with school personnel, students, and parents. Of course, establishing a scope of practice does not mean that school counselors turn away students who have nowhere else to go. Empathic listening may be the only treatment available in some cases.

PRIVILEGED COMMUNICATION

The concepts of confidentiality and privileged communication are two similar topics that counselors must understand. *Confidentiality* is an ethical concept and one of the bases for counseling effectiveness. The assurance that what is said between a counselor and the client is confidential is crucial to the helping relationship. Privileged communication, on the other hand, is a legal right of clients as a result of a statute that protects the client's confidential communications from being disclosed in a court of law. Sheeley and Herlihy (1989) reported that 20 states currently have privileged communication statutes that extend full or partial protection of communication between school counselors and the students that they serve. School counselors must enter a court of law with caution regarding what they will testify to, and for or against whom they will testify. Counselors have me obligation to know both ethical (confidentiality) and legal (privileged communication) standards that guide their need to break the confidence of a client.

HOW TO ESTABLISH CONFIDENTIALITY

Obligations and limitations to the confidentiality of the relationship between the school counselor and student are partially determined by how the counselor establishes confidentiality in the first place. Before establishing confidentiality, the school counselor must become familiar with local policies. Promises of confidentiality in situations in which it cannot be honored may constitute unethical behavior. Failure to break confidentiality in some situations, such as child abuse, constitutes illegal behavior.

Become Familiar With Local Policies

Local policies include ethical standards of the profession, licensure and legal standards, school policies, and community standards. Obligations of confidentiality under the ACA codes have already been mentioned. Some 20 states extend confidentiality to the school counselor-client relationship through statute, but all states mandate the reporting of suspected child abuse (Camblin & Prout, 1989). This may necessitate breaking confidentiality. In addition, school policy (and some statutes) may mandate the reporting of certain behaviors, such as suspected drug use, to the principal or another official. School counselors should review school policy to determine if there are rules or regulations that might interfere with their effectiveness. For instance, if the school counselor is required to report all cases of suspected sexual activity to the principal it is likely that few students would seek the counselor's help on relationship issues. If the school counselor believes certain rules may interfere with the ability to perform his or her duties, the counselor should attempt to negotiate for changes with the administration. If no concessions can be made and the rules clearly violate professional ethical standards the counselor has an ethical obligation not to work in that institution (AACD, 1988).

The school counselor should become familiar with accepted community standards, that is, what behaviors the community does or does not tolerate from students and from school counselors. For instance, providing birth control information to minors may not be acceptable in some communities. Counselors should not base decisions solely on prevailing community attitudes; however, if a counselor is called to justify his or her actions in a court of law, adherence to or deviance from accepted standards of practice may be used by a judge in determining the case.

Informed Consent

Once the school counselor has decided that he or she is competent and capable of providing treatment, the next legal obligation involves securing informed consent. The AACD ethical standards (1988) state that, "a member must inform the client of the purpose, goals, techniques, rules of procedures, and limitations that may affect the relationship at or before the time that the counseling relationship is entered"(Section B.8). School counselors must explain, in language understood by the client, what will occur in the counseling process, along with expected outcomes.

The ASCA ethical standards (1992) address the issue of informed consent in two sections. Section A.3 states that the school counselor "informs the counselee of the purpose, goals, techniques and rules of procedure under which he/she may receive counseling assistance at or before the time when the counseling relationship is entered. Prior notice includes confidentiality issues such as the possible necessity for consulting with other professionals, privileged communication, and legal or authoritative restraints." When working with children under the age of consent the counselor has a responsibility to their parents or guardians. Section B.1 of the ASCA standards states that the school counselor "respects the inherent rights and responsibilities of the parents for their children and endeavors to establish a cooperative relationship with parents to facilitate the maximum development of the counselee." Section B.2 states that the school counselor "informs the parent of the counselor's role with emphasis on the confidential nature of the counseling relationship between the counselor and counselee."

School counselors are wise to secure written consent when dealing with sensitive issues or before engaging a client in long-term counseling. Many school counselors' contracts deal with educational or career concerns and require between one and three sessions. In these situations, neither written nor oral consent may be necessary. When the counselor wishes to engage the client in counseling involving personal or social issues not clearly related to the curriculum, it would be advisable to secure written consent from the client, of if the client is a minor, from the parent or guardian. In a recent survey of 218 school counselors in Ohio, fewer than 10% reported securing written consent from parents of children they were counseling on a regular basis (Ritchie & Partin, 1990).

Clients' Right to Know. Regardless of how innocent a counseling encounter may seem, clients should always have the right to know what they are about to experience. They should have the right to say no. The principle vehicle in achieving this is the consent process (Grundner, 1986). There are three primary elements that can aid the school counselor in determining adequate informed consent. The first deals with the capability of the client to make a reasonable decision about engaging in counseling: Can the client understand what is expected of him or her, and what is expected of the counselor? Second, there must be assurances that the client is entering the counseling relationship voluntarily. The third element relates to the fact that the client understands what he or she is consenting to (Bray, Shepherd, & Hays, 1985). If the client is a minor, the informed consent must come from the parent or legal guardian.

Client's Right to Obtain Counseling. In some cases school counselors see clients without the permission of the parent or legal guardian. Is this illegal? Probably not, if the counseling is considered part of the school's curriculum. According to Van Hoose and Kottler (1978) as long as school counselors are treated under the law as teachers, and as long as the service they provide (e.g., counseling, testing) is deemed part of their normal duties, they have the right to provide these services with or without permission of the parent (cf. *Abington Township v. Schempp*, 1963; *Cornwell v. State Board of Education*, 1970; Schmidt, 1987). On the other hand, if the school counselor performs duties not deemed part of the school's curriculum (e.g., arranging for an abortion), he or she may not have the same protection.

WHEN BREAKING CONFIDENTIALITY MAY BE NECESSARY

Situations may arise in which the school counselor finds it necessary to break confidentiality to protect the client or other persons, for instance, when there is clear and imminent danger to the client or others, in cases of suspected child abuse, or when ordered to testify by a judge. In these situations the duty to warn or testify may override the obligation of confidentiality.

Child Abuse

All states have some kind of provision requiring teachers and counselors to report suspected cases of child abuse. The counselor or teacher is protected against legal action that could be brought by the parents, and there are sanctions against the teacher or counselor for failing to report suspected child abuse (Camblin & Prout, 1989). Although the exact procedure varies by state, typically the school counselor would call the local child protective services authority to report suspected abuse. What constitutes suspected abuse is not so clear and may vary among states. It is a good idea for school counselors to spend time speaking with members of their child protective services authority to become familiar with exactly what constitutes child abuse and what signs to look for. Once a case is reported, a social worker or children's service specialist will call on the home to interview the child and the parents. Depending on the severity of the case, the child may be removed from the home. Once a school counselor is familiar with what to look for, any case of suspected child abuse must be reported regardless of any confidentiality agreement with the client.

Duty to Warn

Clear and Imminent Danger. Other situations that may warrant a breach of confidentiality occur when, in the professional judgment of the counselor, the client or other identifiable person is in clear or imminent danger. This perceived danger may be in the form of a threat to harm another, a threat to harm oneself, or in threats or warnings which come from other students. For instance, if a student informs the school counselor that another student told her that he plans to commit suicide, the counselor is obliged to investigate. The counselor may call the other student into the office to ascertain the seriousness of the threat, and if the threat is real, would not want to let the child out of his or her sight until safely in the custody of parents or other responsible guardians. Counselors have been found liable for the action of their clients, and in cases when there is clear and imminent danger to the client or others, the counselor has a responsibility to protect the threatened persons by notifying them or notifying others who are in a capacity to protect them from harm (Herlihy & Sheeley, 1988; Pate, 1992). Interestingly, it seems that notifying police is not sufficient action to protect the counselor from a lawsuit if the client's threat is carried out (*Tarasoff v. Regents of the University of California*, 1976).

Possible Danger to Self or Others. In cases in which the client threatens suicide or threatens bodily harm to another, establishing clear and imminent danger may be clear and a duty to warn may be obvious. In some cases, however, the danger is less clear and the duty to warn less obvious. What if a child threatens to run away because his parents do not understand him? Does the counselor have an obligation to notify the parents about the wishes of the child? What if the counselor honors the child's request, does not notify the parents, and the child subsequently runs away and is seriously injured? Can the school counselor be held accountable for not preventing the runaway and subsequent harm? What if the school counselor is told, in confidence, of an unsupervised party on the weekend involving alcohol? And what if some of the students are injured or killed in an auto accident leaving the party? Can the school counselor be held accountable for not intervening to prevent the party? The law is less clear in these hypothetical cases. Putting yourself in the place of the parent of one of these children may help you appreciate how counselors' knowledge of possible danger may put them in particularly vulnerable positions of responsibility. Breaking confidentiality in these cases could jeopardize the counselor's relationship with the students; failing to break confidentiality might jeopardize their lives.

Balancing Confidentiality and Duty to Warn. When counselors learn of situations in which there may be danger, they must weigh the importance of the confidential relationship against the possible danger and use their own judgment in deciding what to do. It might be useful to imagine taking each possible course of action and then having to defend that action if the worst scenario occurs. Although there have not been enough cases involving school counselors to establish clear precedents, there is evidence that counselors can defend their actions based on professional judgment and professional codes of conduct (Liberty, 1987). In other words, adhering to the ethical standards, or your professional interpretation of the standards, could be used as a defense. In situations in which danger may or may not be present, taking no action would seem to be the most difficult decision to defend if someone is harmed. Consulting other school counselors is also advisable.

There are other situations in which the counselor may have to decide between confidentiality or a duty to warn: for instance, suspected substance abuse of students or parents, suspected criminal activity, pregnancy, or sexual promiscuity. Some of these situations are particularly controversial, and weighing the best interests of the student may result in different courses of action depending on the student, the counselor, and the community. If the client waives his or her right to confidentiality, then informing others entails no legal violations. If privileged communication between the counselor and the client is recognized by law, then disclosing information without the consent of the client is illegal, unless there is clear and imminent danger (Hopkins, 1989).

How to Break Confidentiality

Once the decision has been made that it is in the best interest of the client (or others) to break confidentiality, the school counselor must decide whom to inform. If the counselor is compelled to inform authorities of confidential information, does the counselor first inform the student that he or she must break confidentiality? Does the counselor inform the parents or the school principal? Obviously the answers to these questions will depend on the nature of the situation. In a case of suspected child abuse, the school counselor may choose not to inform the parents before informing the authorities, but may inform the child. If the school counselor believes the child might run away, he or she may decide to inform the parents without informing the child. Each case must be considered on its own merits and decisions about whom to inform and when to inform them will vary from one situation to another. It is best when the school counselor can explain to the client the necessity of breaking confidentiality. Often this can be done without eroding the counseling relationship, and in some cases, the client will waive the privileged communication upon hearing the counselor's reasons for informing others.

Informing Parents. Usually parents will be informed when confidentiality must be broken. In most cases, whatever action the counselor takes will become known to the parents eventually. It is usually better for the counselor to explain to the parents what is being reported, and to whom, than for them to learn from another source. For instance, "Mrs. Jones, I am the school counselor. Your son has informed me that he and several other boys have been selling drugs in the school. I have explained to Danny that I am compelled by school policy (or by law) to report this to the police but I wanted to call you first to give you an opportunity to be here with Danny." Unpleasant situations like this can be opportunities to secure parental involvement with their child's problem. Failing to inform parents may send them the message that their help and support are not wanted or needed.

Informing Others. Often school counselors will want to keep their principal or supervisor informed of any actions that could have legal repercussions for the school. This does not mean that counselors should routinely break confidentiality by discussing clients with teachers and principals; however, when a situation arises in which the counselor needs to break confidentiality, he or she typically would consult the principal or supervisor and keep them apprised of their actions. It is difficult for a principal to defend the action of his or her counselor if the principal was unaware of the situation to begin with.

Written Informed Consent to Disclose Information

It is advisable for the counselor to secure an informed consent to disclose written information such as records provided the client understands the informed consent form and that securing the consent will not jeopardize the safety of the client or others (Bray, Shepherd, & Hays, 1985). When the client is a minor, the informed consent should be signed by the parent or legal guardian. Informed consent to disclose information is a written document and should include (a) the name of the counselor, the client, and the school; (b) the name of the person or organization to whom the disclosure will be made; (c) the reason or purpose of the disclosure; (d) the exact information to be disclosed; and (e) dates and signatures of counselor, client, or legal guardian (Piazza & Yeager, 1990). It is also advisable to state a date after which the consent to disclose will expire. School counselors should have copies of these forms readily available. If they do not exist they should be devised in consultation with the principal, supervisor, and legal representative.

Court Orders and Subpoenas

There will be times when the school counselor is called on to provide testimony in a court of law. School counselors are increasingly being subpoenaed to testify in custody hearings. Subpoenas may order the counselor to appear and testify or appear and bring any documents such as case notes and files relevant to the case (KeithSpiegel & Koocher, 1985). Subpoenas do not authorize or compel the counselor to disclose confidential information if the relationship is recognized as privileged by law. "Even in the presence of a subpoena, the client's written consent is still required to release confidential information" (Piazza & Yeager, 1990, p. 125). In most states, however, the school counselor-client relationship is not recognized as privileged.

If a judge determines that the school counselor possesses information relevant to the case, he or she may issue a court order for the release of that information. A court order permits, but does not compel, the counselor to release confidential information. If the school counselor receives both a subpoena and a court order, he or she is compelled to release the information with or without the consent of the client. Failure to do so may result in a charge of contempt of court (Piazza & Yeager, 1990). Any time a school counselor is served with a subpoena or court order, he or she should contact an attorney (Remley, 1991).

Keeping Parents and Teachers Informed Without Breaking Confidentiality

With the complex, and sometimes conflicting, ethical and legal obligations faced by the school counselor, it is easy to forget that it is usually possible to keep parents and teachers apprised of clients' progress without breaking confidentiality. When a school counselor engages a student in a confidential relationship, it may be beneficial to the student's progress to involve parents, teachers, or others. In these circumstances, the school counselor should follow the guidelines for informed consent to release information; that is, he or she should explain why information should be shared and make it clear to the student what is to be shared and with whom. If the student refuses permission to share information, then this should be honored. In most cases the student will have no objections to keeping parents or teachers informed of their general progress and how the parents or teachers can assist in the treatment plan. Also, involving parents and teachers multiplies the effectiveness of the counselor.

CONCLUSION

As school counselors are faced with more psychosocial issues, they will also find themselves making legal and ethical decisions of major significance to both their students and themselves. Understanding the boundaries of confidentiality as well as knowing the rights of privilege of one's client are critical. The ability of a school counselor to make sound decisions in this area could potentially be the difference between making the appropriate legal or ethical decision or facing legal action.

Tom Davis *is an associate professor in the counselor education program, College of Education, Ohio University, Athens.* **Martin Ritchie** *is a professor in the Department of Counselor and Human Services Education, College of Education and Allied Professions at The University of Toledo, Toledo, Ohio.*

REFERENCES

Abington Township v. Schempp, 374 U.S. 300 (1963).

American Association for Counseling and Development. (1988). *Ethical standards of the American Association for Counseling and Development.* Alexandria, VA: Author.

American School Counselor Association. (1992). *Ethical standards for school counselors.* Alexandria, VA: Author.

Bray, J. H., Shepherd, J. N., & Hays, J. R. (1985). Legal and ethical issues in informed consent to psychotherapy. *American Journal of Family Therapy, 12*, 50–60.

Camblin, L. D., Jr., & Prout, H. T. (1989). School counselors and the reporting of child abuse: A survey of state laws and practices. In W. C. Hucy & T. P. Remley, Jr. (Eds.), *Ethical and legal issues in school counseling* (pp. 16–172). Alexandria, VA American Counseling Association.

Cornwell v. State Board of Education, 400 U.S. 942 (1970).

Grundner, T. M. (1986). *Informed consent: A tutorial.* Owings Mills, MD: National Health Publishing.

Herlihy, B., & Sheeley, V. L. (1988). Counselor liability and the duty to warn: Selected cases, statutory trends, and implications for practice. *Counselor Education and Supervision, 27*, 203–215.

Hopkins, B: R. (1989, February 2). Counselors and the law. *Guidepost, 13*, 15.

Huey, W. C., & Remley, T. P., Jr. (Eds.). (1989). *Ethical and legal issues in school counseling.* Alexandria, VA: American Counseling Association.

Keith-Spiegel, P., & Koocher, G. P. (1985). *Ethics in psychology: Professional standards and cases.* New York: Random House.

Liberty, L. H. (1987). *Selected litigated court cases involving counseling professionals.* Jamaica, NY: St. John's University. (ERIC Document No. ED285054)

Nally v. Grace Community Church of the Valley, 204 Cal, Rptr., 303 Cal. App., (1984).

Pate, R. H., Jr. (1992). Are you liable? *American Counselor, 1*(3), 15–19.

Piazza, N. J., & Yeager, R. D. (1990). Federal confidentiality regulations for substance abuse treatment facilities: A case of applied ethics. *Journal of Mental Health Counseling, 12*, 120–128.

Remley, T. P. (1991). *ACA Legal Series: Vol. 1. Preparing for court appearances.* Alexandria, VA: American Counseling Association.

Ritchie, M. H., & Partin, R. L. (1990). *Ohio school counselor's involvement with parents.* Unpublished manuscript.

Schmidt, J. J. (1987). Parental objections to counseling services: An analysis. *The School Counselor, 34*, 387–391.

Sheeley, V. L., & Herlihy, B. (1989). Privileged communication in school counseling: Status update. In W. C. Huey & T. P. Remley, Jr. (Eds.), *Ethical and legal issues in school counseling* (pp. 85–91). Alexandria, VA: American Counseling Association.

Tarasoff v. Regents of the University of California et al., 13 Cal. 3d 177, 529 P.2d 553 (1974), vacated, 17 Cal. 3d 425, 551 P.2d 334 (1976).

Van Hoose, W. H., & Kottler, J. A. (1978). *Ethical issues in counseling and psychotherapy.* San Francisco, CA: Jossey-Bass.

Confidentiality and the Law

Karen A. Sealander
Valerie L. Schwiebert
Thomas A. Oren
Jean L. Weekley

In an increasingly complex society, parents have concerns that personal information about their children in school records is accurate and that access is restricted to those individuals with a justifiable purpose for their use of that information. At the same time, teachers, counselors, and school administrators must be aware of the rights afforded students and their parents regarding school records. Hence, the notions of confidentiality in the schools and protection of student privacy have recently received much attention. The aim of this paper is to introduce readers to the laws that govern and protect students, teachers, and school counselors, and the issues surrounding confidentiality in the schools.

The laws safeguarding the confidentiality of student information are established in four main congressional acts.

- The Family Educational Rights and Privacy Act (FERPA, 1974), also known as the Buckley Amendment, is the major legislation that sets parameters on accessibility and disclosure of student records.
- The Grassley Amendment (1994) to the Goals 2000: Educate America Act of 1994 details privacy of student participation in surveys, analysis, and evaluation.
- Drug and alcohol treatment records of students kept by any institution receiving federal assistance are protected under Drug Abuse Office and Treatment Act (1976).
- Records of students in special education are affected by the above laws plus the Individuals with Disabilities Education Act (IDEA, 1997).

These four acts provide a structure for laws concerning confidentiality and its application as a safeguard for students and professionals. These laws specify certain requirements and obligations of participating agencies, including local educational agencies (LEA), in the control and disbursement of records, and provide parents and students rights to access these records. The four acts will be discussed in the sections that follow along with their implications for school counselors.

FERPA

The Family Educational Rights and Privacy Act of 1974, also known as the Buckley Amendment, is a four-part act that gives parents and students who have reached the age of majority the right to review and inspect school records. Part one of the Buckley Amendment states that school districts receiving federal funds must comply with FERPA or risk losing their funding. Part two states that schools must receive parental consent before evaluating or admitting students in school programs that would change their values or behavior. Part three addresses federal funding and denies such funds to schools that do not restrict unauthorized access to student information and protect the privacy of their records. Finally, part four protects children who are being used to gather data for federal surveys (FERPA, 1974).

FERPA applies to all educational records that are defined as any personally identifiable record collected, maintained, or used by a school that the student has attended. Personal logs, treatment records, and directory information, however, are exceptions to the above act. The above mentioned are excluded for the following reasons: Personal logs are records of instructional, supervisory, administrative, and associated educational personnel that are the sole possession of the individual and have not been shared with any other peer or professional. Treatment records are records of a physician, psychiatrist, psychologist, or other recognized professional acting in his or her role as a professional and used only in connection with the treatment of the student. Directory information are records that include the student's demographic information, grade or field of study, participation in extracurricular activities, physical descriptions, and dates of attendance (FERPA, 1974; Underwood & Mead, 1995).

School records may not be released without the consent of the parents and written consent must be obtained for special education students. Schools must inform the parents before a disclosure of student information. (See table, Consent Exceptions.) Additionally, Parents have the right to challenge the information contained in the records if they believe it to be inaccurate or misleading. The school must provide an opportunity for a hearing if they disagree or refuse to alter the record.

Consent Exceptions

Informed Consent is not necessary when:

1. Disclosing information to school officials, including teachers, who are determined to have legitimate educational interest in the record

2. Complying with a judicial order or subpoena

3. Authorized federal, state, or local officials, in connection with the audit and evaluation of a federally or state-supported program, request student information

4. An emergency requires information to protect the safety of the student or others

5. Parents of an adult pupil who is dependent on the parent for federal income tax purposes request information

6. The officials of other schools in which the student seeks to enroll request information, provided the opportunity for a hearing is allowed

7. The student applies for financial aid

8. Organizations conduct educationally related studies, ensure the confidentiality of the information, and the data is destroyed in a timely manner (FERPA, 1974; Underwood & Mead, 1995).

Amendments to the FERPA regulations (1974) were made in response to the passage of the Improving America's School Act (1994). The following is a summary of these changes. First, the new changes give educational agencies greater flexibility by removing a previous regulatory provision requiring schools to adopt a formal, written, student-records policy. Instead, the school may include additional information in the annual notification of rights. A model notification is included in the appendix of the regulations. Second, state educational agencies must afford parents and eligible students access to education records that they maintain. Third, the amendments clarify that an educational agency or institution initiating legal action against a parent or eligible student must make a reasonable effort to notify, in advance, the parent or student of its intent to disclose the information from education records to a court of law. Fourth, FERPA was amended so that a school is not required to notify a parent or eligible student before complying with certain subpoenas if the court has ordered notification not be made. Fifth, FERPA was amended to allow disclosures of education records, without prior consent, to certain state and local officials, pursuant to a State statute that allows the disclosure in connection with a juvenile justice system. Sixth, the amendments clarify that an educational agency may include information in a student's education records concerning disciplinary action taken against a student for conduct that posed a significant risk to that student or other members of the school community. Seventh, in connection with the previous amendment, clarification was made that an educational agency may disclose information without prior consent to those who have legitimate educational interests in the behavior of the student. Eighth, if a third party discloses information in violation of FERPA, that agency is prohibited from accessing education records for a period of not less than 5 years. Finally, the amendments clarify that a person filling a complaint under FERPA must have legal standing, that is must be a parent of an eligible student affected by the violation (AACRAO Government Relations, 1999).

GRASSLEY AMENDMENT

The Grassley Amendment (1994) replaced and modified the Hatch Amendment to the General Education Provisions Act. The Hatch Amendment speaks to the protection of pupil rights in conjunction with any survey, analysis, or evaluation of any applicable program within the school setting. This amendment applies to all programs where federal money is involved in the implementation or maintenance of the program. The Grassley Amendment expanded language to cover all surveys, analysis, or evaluation projects. It also grants individuals the right to inspect materials (e.g. manuals, tapes, films) used in connection with any survey, analysis, or evaluation. Written consent of parents or eligible students by school districts must be secured for the above activities before information is collected that reveals:

- Political affiliations
- Mental or psychological problems
- Sexual behavior or attitudes
- Illegal, anti-social, self-incriminating, and demeaning behavior
- Critical appraisals of other individuals with whom the students have a close family relationship
- Legally recognized privileged or analogous relationships, such as those of physicians, lawyers, or ministers
- Income, except for that information required to determine eligibility for financial assistance

The statute does not apply to information gathering that is entirely voluntary.

Difficulties exist as a result of the Grassley Amendment (FERPA, 1974). First, although it requires written consent from parents, the words *informed consent* do not appear in the law. This may create difficulties as parents may give consent without being truly informed and thus fully understanding the consent they are providing to the school or researcher. Additionally, on June 6, 1991, the U.S. Department of Education revised federal regulations concerning research with human beings, experimental procedures used in public schools to develop new instructional methods. Curricula or classroom management techniques are now exempt from the regulations. No institutional review board (IRB) review is necessary for experiments in public schools and therefore, no protections gained from IRB review are afforded to students. No explanation of potential risks is necessary. No permission is necessary. Protection has been essentially stripped away from children. U.S. children can legally be forced to take part in experiments to develop new instructional methods and curricula (psychological and otherwise) despite the objections of their parents. New ideas can legally be tested in individual public school classrooms with no accountability if something goes wrong. The revised regulations appear in the *Federal Register*, volume 56, §117, dated June 18, 1991, on page 28012.

DRUG ABUSE OFFICE AND TREATMENT ACT

Confidentiality of records of persons receiving drug or alcohol abuse treatment are protected under federal law (Drug Abuse Office and Treatment Act, 1976). This statute applies to any program assisted in any way by the federal government. These requirements apply to all records relating to the identity, diagnosis, prognosis, or treatment of any student involved in any federally assisted substance abuse program. All records must be maintained in a locked and secure area. Since these regulations are generally more strict, they should be maintained separately from other educational records. Records, generally, may not be disclosed without written consent of the student. Under applicable state law, minor clients with legal capacity must give consent for any release of information, including to the minor's parents. If state law requires parental consent to obtain treatment, then both parent and student must give consent before disclosure of information. Three disclosures may be made without consent:

- To medical personnel in the case of a bona fide medical emergency
- To qualified personnel conducting scientific research or audits without individual identities disclosed
- To any person with an appropriate court order

Treatment records can not be used to conduct a criminal investigation or substantiate criminal charges against a person (Yeager, 1994).

IDEA

The Individuals with Disabilities Education Act (1997) requires procedures to provide a free and appropriate public education (FAPE) for all children with disabilities. Inherent within FAPE are safeguards prohibiting the disclosure of any personally identifiable information.

Clear guidelines have been set forth for public schools when collecting, storing, releasing, or destroying personally identifiable information on students. These guidelines are set forth in federal legislation and state educational plans and include any participating agency that collects, maintains, or uses personally identifiable information.

Under laws governing confidentiality, participating agencies must have written procedures, in the primary language of the parents, that notify parents of their right to inspect records, and how information is stored, disclosed, retained, and destroyed. In addition, annual notice must be given to parents on their right to file a complaint or amend their child's records.

PARENTAL RIGHTS

Participating agencies, including local educational agencies (LEA), have specific responsibilities to parents in regards to confidential information. Most importantly, each LEA must have a "written authorization for release of information" form that designates that the school district will not release any personally identifiable information regarding a child except with written permission by the parents, specifying the records to be released, reasons for such release, and to whom the records would be released. This information may not be distributed to any other party without the written consent from the parents and may only be used for the purpose for which the disclosure was made. The LEA must have an established procedure to be followed in the event a parent refuses to give consent (Underwood & Mead, 1995).

One individual (e.g., a school administrator) in each participating agency is designated to provide oversight in all matters relating to confidentiality issues. Parents must be given the name of this individual and to whom they may address their requests to examine their child's records. All persons who participate in the collection or use of confidential information must receive training in the policies and procedures for handling confidential data. Each school district or participating agency must maintain for public inspection a current listing of employees by name and position who may have access to the personally identifiable data. The agency must obtain parental consent before disclosing student information to anyone other than those officials of educational agencies using the records for educational purposes. Anyone, other than personnel specified in the current listing of persons having access to student information, must receive parental permission and sign a record of disclosure. A record of disclosure must be kept on each request permitting access to confidential information. The disclosure must show the name of the party, the date access was given, and the purpose for which the party is authorized to view the records (Underwood & Mead, 1995).

LEAs may presume that either parent of the student has the authority to inspect records of the student unless the LEA has been provided evidence that there is a legally binding instrument, state law, or court order governing such matters as divorce, separation, or custody, which provides to the contrary. Authorized representatives of the parents have the right to inspect and review records, with written parental consent. There are instances when written parental consent is not necessary. These have been referred to above in the discussion of FERPA.

Additionally, LEAs must permit a parent of a student or eligible student who is, or has been, in attendance in the district to inspect and review the educational records of the student. States may grant students access to records prior to age 18 (Underwood & Mead, 1995). Such requests for student records shall be complied with within a reasonable time and in no event longer than 45 days after the request has been made. The right to inspect and review educational records by parents includes reasonable requests for explanations and interpretations of the records and the right to obtain copies of the records. A fee for copies may be charged, although not for retrieval of information, unless the fee would prevent a parent from having access to the records.

Parents also have the right to have their child's records amended. If a parent believes that records on file are inaccurate, misleading, or violate the privacy or other rights of the student, the parent may request that the agency amend the records. The agency shall decide whether to amend the record in a timely manner. If the school district, or agency, decides to refuse to amend the records, it shall so inform the individual and at the same time advise the parent(s) of the right to a hearing. Parent(s) or eligible students have the right to place a statement in the record setting forth the reasons for disagreeing with the decision of the school district.

After records are no longer needed for educational purposes, they may be destroyed within 5 years, unless there is an outstanding request to inspect or review them. Under IDEA personally identifiable information on a student with disabilities may be retained permanently unless the parents or eligible student request that it be destroyed. Destruction of records is the best protection against improper or unauthorized disclosure. However, the records may be needed for other purposes. The agency should remind parents that the records may be needed by the student or parents for social security benefits or other purposes. If the parents request that the information be destroyed, the agency may retain a permanent record of the student's name, address, phone number, grades, attendance record, classes attended, grade level completed, and year completed without time limitation.

In addition to the rights of parents, school personnel are often confronted with the difficult task of responding to requests for information from noncustodial or nonresidential parents. Under FERPA, "parent" means a parent of a student and includes a natural parent, a guardian, or an individual acting as a parent in the absence of a parent or guardian. Further, the legislation states that an educational agency shall give full rights under the Act to either parent, unless the agency has been provided with evidence that there is a court order, state statute, or legally binding document relating to such matters as divorce, separation, or custody that specifically revokes these rights. This means that a school district must provide access to parents unless there is a legally binding document that specifically removes that parent's FERPA rights to have access to knowledge regarding his or her child's education. These provisions may best be understood by separating custody, which determines where a child will live and the duties of the person with whom the child lives, and FERPA, which establishes the parents' right of access to and control of education record related to the child (U.S. Department of Education, 1999). School counselors must be aware of state laws which may affect these rights as well as school policy. As families redefine themselves, the definition of parent is sometimes blurred and the decisions difficult, many times resulting in litigation.

ROLES AND RESPONSIBILITIES OF COUNSELORS AND EDUCATORS

Confidentiality is a concept that is based on ethical principles (American Counseling Association, 1995) and is important to the counseling relationship because it facilitates trust and the establishment of a therapeutic relationship. It is important to note, however, that what is ethical behavior under professional codes of ethics is not necessarily legal and vice versa. However, confidentiality has gained legal status throughout the United States through licensing laws for counselors with several states specifically granting the right of privileged communication to school counselors. It should be noted that this privilege belongs to the client and not the counselor.

Breach of confidence is considered unprofessional conduct and is grounds for disciplinary action and sometimes legal action (McCarthy & Sorenson, 1993). There are exceptions however. For example, confidentiality does not promise complete nondisclosure in cases of child abuse or when the school counselor believes there is imminent danger to the client or others. Educators are required to report suspected child abuse and neglect to the proper authorities. In fact, all states have enacted legislation that imposes penalties against counselors and educators who fail to file a report of suspected child abuse (McCarthy & Sorenson, 1993). Other examples of the exception to nondisclosure address the counselor's duty to warn parents when they have information regarding a student's intent to commit suicide (American Counseling Association, 1995). *Tarasoff v. Regents of the University of California* (1976) is the defining case regarding a counselor's duty to warn potential victims they may be in danger. These duties may apply to a greater extent to teachers, school counselors, and school psychologists because their claim to privileged communication is not as widely recognized by law as that of psychiatrists, attorneys, and doctors (*Tarasoff v. The Regents of The University of California*, 1976).

Currently under debate is the controversial issue concerning students with HIV or AIDS who are engaging in activities that may transmit the virus. The American School Counselor Association recommends members notify the sexual partners of HIV-positive clients and the appropriate public health officials (McGowan, 1991). This is relevant when clients refuse to disclose the information on their own.

Privileged communication is a legal concept that is defined by statute and applies to communication that originates in a confidential relationship. As previously noted, some states have enacted specific right of privileged communication for school counselors, others have not. A recent court decision known as the Jaffee decision may have given mental health counselors privileged communication in federal cases. The U.S. Supreme Court held that the communications between psychotherapists and their patients are privileged and do not have to be disclosed in cases heard in federal court (*Jaffee v. Redmond et al.*, 1996). This case has yet to be tested and does not apply to cases other than those in federal court (Remley, Herlihy, & Herlihy, 1997).

Additionally, federal regulations under the Drug Abuse Office and Treatment Act (1976) now guarantee confidentiality to youths receiving alcohol and other drug services. These laws and regulations protect any information about a youth if the youth has received alcohol and/or drug related services of any kind including school-based identification. Any individual making an unauthorized disclosure faces a criminal penalty and a fine. When a teacher, counselor, or other school professional identifies student behaviors that could indicate a drug and/or alcohol problem, they can discuss this with the student or other school personnel. However, from the time an evaluation is conducted and/or a student assistance program begins alcohol or drug related counseling, the federal regulations are in effect (Coll, 1995).

CONCLUSION

There are many facets to confidentiality and clear guidelines as to the roles and responsibilities of professionals involved with students. Educators and school counselors alike need to be informed of the state and federal laws as well as local school policies so they are aware of the professional implications. School records, confidentiality, and privileged communications overlap and may cause conflict between ethical and moral obligation, and legal responsibility. Educators and counselors may look to professional codes of ethics and the law for guidance when faced with these issues. If should be emphasized however that many times there are no clear answers and that many gray areas still exist.

Although it is impossible for school counselors to be fully aware of all legal principles affecting their work, it is essential that they continually seek to stay abreast of changes in legal and ethical dictates that affect confidentiality. Professional associations such as the American School Counselor Association and the American Counseling Association produce documents that update counselors on ethical and legal changes. The text *Legal Aspects of Special Education and Pupil Services* (Underwood & Mead, 1995), Henderson and Hall's (1998) chapter on ethical and legal issues, and various Internet websites such as the American School Counselor Association (http://www.schoolcounselor.org/), the Department of Education's online pamphlets (http://www.access.gpo.gov/nara/cfr/) and AACRAO Government Relations (http://aacrao.com/policy/govrel) are excellent resources for school counselors to stay abreast of changes in legal and ethical policy. In addition, school counselors must remember to consult with one another, use standards of best practice as accepted by their particular institution, and remain aware of changes as they occur in the field of school counseling at the state and national levels. School counselors may wish to contact their state school counselor association for information on laws governing practice in that particular state. Ultimately, both educators and counselors must see that the best standards of practice are continually maintained with regard to confidentiality in order to best serve the students with whom they work.

Karen A. Sealander, Ph.D. *is an associate professor of Special Education at Northern Arizona University, Flagstaff.* **Valerie L. Schwiebert, Ph.D.** *is associate dean of Graduate and Research Studies and associate professor of Counseling,* **Thomas A. Oren, Ph.D.** *is an assistant professor of Special Education, and* **Jean L. Weekley** *is a graduate student in Counseling; all are with Western Carolina University, Cullowhee, NC.*

REFERENCES

AACRAO Government Relations. (1999). *Amendments to the FERPA regulations.* [On-Line] Available: http://aacrao.com/policy/govrel/newferpa2.html.

American Counseling Association. (1995). *Ethical standards of the American Association for Counseling and Development.* Alexandria, VA: Author.

Coll, K. M. (1995). Legal challenges for school counselors engaged in secondary prevention programming for students with substance abuse. *The School Counselor, 43,* 35–41.

Drug Abuse Office and Treatment Act. (1976). 42 U.S.C. 290 §3 & 42 C.F.R. Part 2.

Family Educational Rights and Privacy Act. (1974). 20 U.S.C.A. §1232g. [Buckley Amendment.] (1991). Implementing regulations 34 C.F.R. 99.3. Fed. Reg. 56, §117, 28012.

Grassley Amendment. (1994). Sec. 1017 of GOALS 2000: The Educate America Act under the heading "Protection of Pupils." 20 U.S.C. §1232h.

Henderson, D. A., & Hall, M. (1998). School counseling. In R. R. Cottone & V. M. Tarvydad (Eds.), *Ethical and professional issues in counseling* (pp. 263–286). Upper Saddle River, NJ: Merrill.

Improving America's Schools Act. (1994). H.R. 6.[Enacted]

Individuals with Disabilities Education Act of 1997. (1997). Pub. L. No. 105–17, 34 CFR 300.574.

Jaffee v. Redmond et al. WL 315841 (U.S. June 13, 1996).

McCarthy, M. M., & Sorenson, G. P. (1993). School counselors and consultants: Legal duties and liabilities. *Journal of Counseling and Development, 72,* 159–167.

McGowan, S. (1991). Confidentiality and the ethical dilemma. *Guidepost, 34*(5), 1,6.

Remley, T., Herlihy, B., & Herlihy, S. (1997). The U.S. Supreme Court Decision in *Jaffee v. Redmond:* Implications for counselors. *Journal of Counseling and Development, 75,* 213–218.

Tarasoff v. The Regents of The University of California. (1976). 17 Cal. 3d 425, 131 Cal. Rptr. 14, 551 P.2d 334.

Underwood, J. K., & Mead, J. F. (1995). *Legal aspects of special education and pupil services.* Boston: Allyn & Bacon.

United States Department of Education. (1999). *Rights of non-custodial parents in the Family Educational Rights and Privacy Act of 1974.* Washington, DC: Family Policy Compliance Office.

Yeager, J. D (1994). *Confidentiality of student records: A guide for school districts establishing policies and procedures with special emphasis on alcohol and other drug use.* Office of Educational Research and Improvement, Washington, D.C.

The School Counselor or Psychologist and Problems of Defamation

Ronald W. Eades

The job of school counseling can give rise to conflict between a counselor's right and duty to speak and a student's right not to have certain information about him disclosed to others. Society firmly believes in free speech. This ideal assumes that everyone can say what they want. A counselor must speak to students and must be able to speak to others about them. When students have problems, for example, their parents may need to know. This may range from telling parents about grade troubles, to missing school, to serious behavior concerns. The duty to speak does not end with the parent. A counselor must sometimes act as a liaison among several teachers and the school administration. A student that is causing school-wide problems may have confided in the counselor, and that counselor must decide if the principal and the teachers should be called in to deal with the problem. Students may also be applying for college or seeking employment for which the counselor must furnish references. These situations often require that the counselor reveal information to persons outside of the school setting. It seems that while most of society has a right to speak, the counselor has a duty to speak in certain situations. Although there is this right and even a duty to speak, society

Reprinted with permission from *Journal of Law & Education*, Vol. *15*, No. 1, pp. 17-20.

also recognizes a right to privacy. This is a right to be left alone or not to be talked about. Thus, a school counselor or psychologist can be liable in an action for invasion of privacy or defamation.

When the statements concerning the student are untrue or reveal certain things a student may not want revealed, cause of action for defamation against the counselor or psychologist may arise. A defamation action is the traditional method of seeking a remedy for a damaging or untrue statement. A defamatory statement is one that reduces the person's reputation in the community. Obviously this can include almost any unfavorable report about the student. Remarks to teachers or parents about grades may not produce much harm, but a bad report to a college or a prospective employer can cause injury to the student. Such statements may lead to a lawsuit.

Lawsuits brought for defamation are relatively old.[1] Their history dates back to the 1700s and such actions have been accepted in almost all jurisdictions of the United States. There has been a distinction between two types of defamation: libel and slander. Libel has traditionally meant written defamatory statements while slander refers to oral defamatory statements.[2] This distinction has some real importance to the law of defamation because slander requires proof of actual economic loss before a defamed person can recover. If, for example, a student loses a job because of a statement a counselor makes, the student would have the requisite proof of economic loss for a slander action. However, if the student suffered only hurt feelings, there would be no economic loss and therefore no cause of action for slander. In a libel case, any actual damages suffered can be recovered. Humiliation or lost reputation, for example, would lead to recovery if the statement was written.

To further confuse the matter, one must recognize that there are a few types of oral slanderous statements which are treated as written libelous statements. This means that a few types of oral statements will lead to recovery even without economic loss. These are categorized as slander per se. Several of these types of statements could arise in the school counselor setting. These include statements concerning participation in crime, serious sexually misconduct, or an allegation of serious disease; for example, that a student is a thief, has engaged in serious sexual misconduct, or has a venereal disease could be slander per se. Such statements could allow the student to recover for any actual damages and economic loss would not have to be proved.

The basic elements of a defamation action are therefore simple: it first requires proof of making a statement with a defamatory meaning,

---

[1] 3 Blackstone's Commentaries, c. vii. (1765).
[2] Prosser, Torts § 112 (4th ed. 1971).

either written or oral; and second, proof of some actual or economic damage depending on the type of statement involved.

A school counselor or psychologist does have, however, and important defense to a suit for defamation, and that is "truth." Truth has always been a defense to a defamation. Older cases required that the defendant who made the statement had to prove it was true. Courts have realized, however, that the right to free speech is important and must be accommodated. Requiring the person who made the statement to prove that it was the absolute truth or otherwise suffer substantial loss in a lawsuit would "chill," as the courts say, the speaker's right to speak. For example, counselors might be afraid to do their jobs fully for fear that one small mistake could lead to liability.

The courts have now determined that the right to free speech guaranteed in the Constitution aids the defendant in the defamation case; under the constitutional guarantee, the person who brings the action must prove the statement is false.[3] When the statement involves a private person, it must also be proved that the speaker failed to use reasonable care in checking the statement to determine if it was true or false.[4] In short, the basic action for defamation of a private person is easy to describe and arises when someone fails to use reasonable care to determine true facts and then makes a false statement which injures someone's reputation.

School counselors and psychologists may also be subject to an action for invasion of the right of privacy as well as defamation. These actions for invasion of the right of privacy began early in this century, and at least two types may be of importance to school counselors.[5] First, even in the absence of specific statutes, public disclosure of private facts that the public has no right to know may lead to liability. Second, statements which put a person in a false light in the public eye may also lead to a lawsuit. Unlike defamation, it is not necessary in an action for the invasion of the right to privacy that the statement hurt the reputation of anyone.

In summary, these areas fit together to form a three pronged problem for the counselor. A simple false statement may give rise to actions for defamation, public disclosure of private facts or false light.

There are defenses called privileges which affect all three of these possible actions. These privileges are designed to protect people who must communicate to others. First, people are privileged to protect their own interests. This could involve speakers making statements while trying to recover for some injury they have suffered. Second, people are priv-

---

[3] New York Times Co. v. Sullivan, 376 U.S. 254 (1964).
[4] Gertz v. Robert Welch, Inc., 418 U.S. 323 (1974).
[5] *See* 3 Dooley, Modern Tort Law § 35.01 et. seq. (1984).

ileged to protect someone else's interest. When school counselors have reasons to believe from information that a student is dangerous to himself or to others, the counselors have a legal duty to speak or provide information. Obviously such communication is protected. Third, people are privileged to protect a mutual interest. One example might be a disclosure in a PTA meeting of the misconduct of a teacher. This disclosure would be of matters of mutual interest to both speaker and listener and would be privileged.

This leads, of course, to certain conclusions. The problem is a fear of lawsuits for invasion of privacy and defamation. Careful exercise of duties on the part of school counselors and psychologists will help avoid difficulties. If counselors and psychologists make reports and statements *only* as required or permitted by the job, the statements should be privileged. Counselors should use reasonable care to insure everything said is true and accurate and that the statements would be "privileged." Following these guidelines should help a counselor avoid liability. Finally, when any doubt arises, seek additional help from the proper authorities or legal counsel before acting.

Ronald W. Eades *is a professor of law at the University of Louisville School of Law.*

Reprinted with permission from *Journal of Law and Education*, Vol. 15, No. 1, pp.17-20.

Chapter 5: Records

INTRODUCTION

When school counselors think about records — that is, what they should write down, where they should keep documents they have created, and how long such documents should be kept — the answers to these questions depend upon a number of factors. As such, it is important for all counselors to have a legal, as well as an ethical, understanding of these processes and implications.

First, there are three types of records that concern school counselors: (1) counseling case notes; (2) records kept to document actions taken to protect the school counselor; and (3) the academic records or cumulative folders of students. Each type of record has different requirements.

School counselors should assume when they create records that whatever they write might someday be seen by students, their parents, and even the general public. No matter the situation, there is always the possibility that records may be revealed, even in states in which school counselors have privileged client communication. (See Chapter 4 for discussions of privacy, confidentiality, and privileged communication.)

Most school counselors would agree that the purposes of counseling case notes are to increase a counselor's efficiency and effectiveness – and that they are used primarily to refresh his or her memory prior to recurring student visits or in planning the student's next step in the counseling process. Each school counselor, however, should assess his or her work environment to best determine how counseling case notes should be kept. In addition, counselors should write for the intended audience only, avoiding unnecessary information as appropriate.

Because school counselors are often responsible for a large number of students, they seldom record each student interaction they have during a day. Instead, counselors might make notes after talking with a student with whom they have an ongoing relationship but might not make notes after seeing a student for a one-time session.

School counselors should keep counseling case notes in their offices and not allow other school personnel access. Additionally, by keeping the case notes in the counselor's possession, parents and guardians do not have access to these records upon demand under the Family Educational Rights and Privacy Act (FERPA).

Most school counselors destroy a student's counseling case notes file when that student leaves the school. Destroying records periodically makes good sense from a storage perspective and avoids the possibility of the records falling into the wrong hands. School counselors are advised, however, to select and keep any counseling case notes records in which they have documented their actions for self-protection. It is advised counselors maintain these particular records for long periods of time, perhaps indefinitely.

For instance, there are occasions when school counselors use their counseling case notes to document events that have occurred or steps they have taken; this documentation might be later used to prove they acted professionally in resolving a particularly difficult situation. Obvious challenges that would require documentation include: reporting suspected child abuse; counseling a student who may be suicidal; counseling a student who may be at risk for harming others; dealing with parents who are involved in a custody dispute; bringing to the principal's attention activities in the school that may be illegal or unethical; or dealing with students or parents who have expressed dissatisfaction with the counselor's services. Although there are obviously other situations that demand school counselors document occurrences, this is a list of the most common situations they confront.

More specifically, when documenting for self-protection, school counselors should record in detail every conversation they have with all persons regarding a problem situation. A copy of applicable written documents should also be kept in the case notes file. When documenting for self-protection, school counselors should immediately log the date and time, along with any other detailed information, onto a piece of paper. To ensure accurate file-keeping, it is recommended that documentation be created as soon as possible after the event has occurred.

Counseling case notes and documentation of counselors' actions should never be kept in a student's academic folder. The academic record is open to all school personnel who have an academic need to review it and therefore is not considered confidential. The academic record, as mentioned earlier, is available for inspection by parents or guardians upon demand under federal law.

Cameron and turtle-song (2002) have reviewed a format for keeping counseling case notes known as SOAP (subjective, objective, assessment, and plan). This detailed plan for writing case notes is especially helpful for school counselors who are working with a student over an extended period of time. Obviously, however, keeping such involved notes would not be possible for all of a school counselor's large caseload of students, but there are a number of good note-writing guidelines in this article that could be helpful to school counselors even if the entire SOAP format is not followed.

It's also beneficial to discuss circumstances in which individuals seek information concerning a minor enrolled in a public school. In this situation, Stenger (1986) has defined "child" and "parent" to help address a common problem of contemporary school counselors – determining which adults are the legal parents or guardians of a particular child. Stenger has differentiated the rights of possession to a child from the rights of information about a child, another area of confusion for school counselors. This legal analysis of parental rights contains information that can be helpful to school counselors who face these challenges.

Special education records are student academic records that have unique protection because of the sensitive nature of their contents. Walker and Steinberg (1997) have summarized the law related to special education records and offer guidelines for general academic records as well.

School counselors create and manage many different types of student records. Counselors must not only be concerned with the privacy of students and their parents, but also must provide information to those who have a right to it, and must create records that meet their own needs. This chapter provides information and guidelines for effective practice in the area of record keeping for school counselors.

Learning to Write Case Notes Using the SOAP Format

Susan Cameron
imani turtle-song

This article discusses how to use the SOAP (subjective, objective, assessment, and plan) note format to provide clear and concise documentation of the client's continuum of care. Not only does this format allow for thorough documentation, but it also assists the counselor in representing client concerns in a holistic framework, thus permitting practitioners, paraprofessionals, and case managers to better understand the concerns and needs of the client. Whereas counselors working in certain settings (e.g., public-funded institutions) are likely to find various recommendations in the article easy to incorporate into their current practice, the authors believe the recommendations are relevant to a wide array of settings.

In every mental health treatment facility across the country, counselors are required to accurately document what has transpired during the therapeutic hour. Over the course of the past few years, the importance of documentation has gained more emphasis as third-party payers have changed the use of documentation "from something that should be done well to something that must be done well" (Kettenbach, 1995, p. iii). In this era of accountability, counselors are expected to be both systematic in providing client services (Norris, 1995) and able to produce clear and comprehensive documentation of those clinical services rendered (Scalise, 2000). However, in my experience (i.e., first author), both as director of a mental health clinic and as one who audits client records, few counselors are able to write clear or concise clinical case notes, and most complain of feeling frustrated when trying to distinguish what is and is not important enough to be incorporated into these notes. Well-written case notes provide accountability, corroborate the delivery of appropriate services, support clinical decisions (Mitchell, 1991; Scalise, 2000), and like any other skill, require practice to master. This article discussed how to accurately document rendered services and how to support clinical treatment decisions.

When counselors begin their work with the client, they need to ask themselves, "What are the mental health needs of this client and how can they best be met?" To answer this question, the counselor needs an organized method of planning, giving, evaluating, and recording rendered client services. A viable method of record keeping is SOAP noting (Griffith & Ignatavicius, 1986; Kettenbach, 1995). SOAP is an acronym for subjective (S), objective (O), assessment (A), and plan (P), with each initial representing one of the sections of the client case notes.

SOAP notes are part of the problem-oriented medical records (POMP) approach most commonly used by physicians and other health care professionals. Developed by Weed (1964), SOAP notes are intended to improve the quality and continuity of client services by enhancing communication among health care professionals (Kettenbach, 1995) and by assisting them in better recalling the details of each client's case (Ryback, 1974; Weed, 1971). This model enables counselors to identify, prioritize, and track client problems so that they can be attended to in a timely and systematic manner. But more important, it provides an ongoing assessment of both the client's progress and the treatment interventions. Although there are alternate case note models, such a data, assessment, and plan (DAP), individual educational programs (IEP), functional outcomes reporting (FOR), and narrative notes, all are variations of the original SOAP format (Kettenbach, 1995).

To understand the nature of SOAP notes, it is essential to comprehend where and how they are used within the POMR format. POMRs consist of four components: database, problem list, initial plans, and SOAP notes (Weed, 1964). In many mental health facilities, the components of the POMR are respectively referred to as clinical assessment, problem list, treatment plan, and progress notes (Shaw, 1997; Siegal & Fischer, 1981). The *first* component, the clinical assessment, contains information gathered during the intake interview(s). This generally includes the reason the client is seeking treatment; secondary complaints; the client's personal, family, and social histories; psychological tests results, if any; and diagnosis and recommendations for treatment (Piazza & Baruth, 1990). According to the Joint Commission on Accreditation of Healthcare Organizations (JCAHO, 2000), with special populations, as in the case of a child, the clinical assessment contains a developmental history; for individuals who present with a history of substance abuse, a drug and alcohol evaluation is included.

From the clinical assessment, a problem list (*second* component) is generated, which includes an index of all the problems, active or inactive, derived from the client's history. Problems are defined as either major areas of concern for the client that are not within the usual parameters when compared with others from the client's same age group or areas of client concern that can be changed through therapeutic intervention (JCAHO, 2000). As problems are identified, they are numbered, dated, and entered on the list, and this problem list is attached to the inside cover of the client's file, for easy reference. As the identified problems are resolved, they are dated and made "inactive."

The *third* component of the POMR is the treatment plan, which is a statement of the possible therapeutic strategies and interventions to be used in dealing with each noted problem. Treatment plans are stated as goals and objectives and are written in behavioral terms in order to track the client's therapeutic progress, or lack thereof (Kettenbach, 1995). The priority of each objective is expressed either as a long- or a short-term goal and corresponds to the problems list. Long-term goals are the expected final results of counseling, whereas short-term goals are those that can be accomplished within the next session or within a very limited time frame.

The *fourth* component is the progress notes, which are generally written using the SOAP format and serve to bridge between the onset of counseling services and the final session. Using the SOAP format, the counselor is able to clearly document and thus support, through the subjective and objective sessions, his or her decision to modify existing treatment goals or to fine-tune the client's treatment plan. For example, if a client who has been in counseling for 4 months experiences the unexpected death of a loved one or is diagnosed with a potentially life threatening health problem, by recording this information in the progress notes the counselor provides justification/documentation for the sudden shift in therapeutic direction and is immediately able to address what is now the more pressing issue for the client.

The SOAP note format also provides a problem-solving structure for the counselor. Because SOAP notes require adequate documentation to verify treatment choices, they serve to organize the counselor's thinking about the client and to aid in the planning of quality client care. For example, if the plan is to refer the client to a domestic violence group for perpetrators, the objective and subjective sections of the SOAP notes would chronicle the client's history of physical aggression and violent behaviors, thus supporting the treatment direction. Although the SOAP format will not ensure good problem-solving skills, it does provide a useful framework within which good problem solving is more likely to occur (Griffith & Ignatavicius, 1986). Thus, intent of SOAP notes is multifaceted: to improve the quality and continuity of client services, to enhance communication among mental health professionals, to facilitate the counselor in recalling the details of each client's case, and to generate an ongoing assessment of both the client's progress and treatment successes (Kettenbach, 1995; Weed, 1968).

USING THE SOAP NOTE FORMAT

There are four components to SOAP notes. Data collection is divided into two parts: (S) subjective and (O) objective. The subjective component contains information about the problem from the client's perspective and that of significant others, whereas the objective information consists of those observations made by the counselor. The assessment section demonstrates how the subjective and objective data are being formulated, interpreted, and reflected upon, and the plan section summarizes the treatment direction. What follows is a description of the content for each section of the SOAP notes, a brief clinical scenario with an example of how this approach might be written, and a short list of "rules" to remember when writing case notes.

Subjective

The data-gathering section of the SOAP format is probably the most troublesome to write because it is sometimes difficult to determine what constitutes subjective and objective content. The subjective portion of the SOAP notes contains information told to the counselor. In this section the client's feelings, concerns, plans or goals, and thoughts, plus the intensity of the problem(s) and its impact on significant relationships in the client's life are recorded. Pertinent comments supplied by family members, friends, probation officers, and so forth can also be included in this section. Without losing accuracy, the entry should be as brief and concise as possible; the client's perceptions of the problem(s) should be immediately clear to an outside reader.

It is our opinion that client quotations should be kept to a minimum. First, when quotations are overused they make the record more difficult to review for client themes and to track the effectiveness of therapeutic interventions. Second, when reviewed by outside readers such as peer review panels, audit committees, or by a client's attorney, the accuracy and integrity of the notes might be called into question. According to Hart, Berndt, and Caramazza (1985), the number of *verbatim* bits of information an individual is able to retain is quite small, 2 to 20 bits, with most estimates at the lower end. Other research suggests that information retained in short-term memory is only briefly held, 30 seconds to a few minutes at best, unless a very conscious effort is made to retain it (see Anderson & Bowers, 1973; Bechtel & Abrahamsen, 1990). This means that at the close of an hour-long counseling session, unless a quote is taken directly from an audio—or videotaped session, it is very unlikely that someone could accurately remember much information verbatim. In short, given this research, it seems a prudent practice to keep the use of quotations to a minimum.

If and when quotations are used, the counselor should record only key words or a very brief phrase. This might include client words indicating suicidal or homicidal ideation, a major shift in the client's well-being, nonconforming behaviors, or statements suggesting a compromise in the type and quality of care the client will receive, such as when a client is unwilling or fails to provide necessary information. Quotations might also be used to document inappropriately aggressive or abusive language toward the counselor that seems threatening. Comments suggesting a potentially lethal level of "denial" should be documented. For instance, a father accused of shaking his 6-month-old daughter when she would not stop crying says, "I only scared her when I shook her, I didn't hurt her." Because the child's life might be in jeopardy should the father repeat his behavior, his comments need to be recorded. For example, the counselor might write: "Minimizes the effects of shaking infant daughter. States 'I only scared her.'"

It is also important to document statements that suggest the client may be confused as to time, place, or person, or if he or she is experiencing a sudden change in mental status stability or level of functioning. For example, if during the session the client suddenly seems disoriented and unable to track the conversation, this information needs to be noted. To assess the client's mental status, the counselor might ask the client the name of the current U.S. president. If the client responds incorrectly, this discrepancy should be noted in quotations within the client file.

Finally, a client's negative or positive change in attitude toward counseling should be chronicled because it serves as a marker in the assessment of counseling effectiveness. A statement such as "Therapy is really helping me put my life into perspective" could be written as "Reports 'therapy is really helping.'" This information is especially important if the client was initially resistant to therapy. The goal is not to give a verbatim account of what the client says, but rather to reflect current areas of client concern and to support or validate the counselor's interpretations and interventions in the assessment and plan sections of the SOAP notes.

Given the open nature of client files to other health care professionals and paraprofessionals (e.g., certain managed care personnel), the counselor should be mindful of the type of client and family information included in the client's record. Unless insidious family life and political, religious, and racial views are the focus of the problem(s), secondary details of such views should be omitted (Eggland, 1988; Philpott, 1986). The counselor should not repeat inflammatory statements critical of other health care professionals or the quality of service provided because these comments may compromise the client's care by antagonizing the staff or might be interpreted as malicious or damaging to the reputation of another. Rather than using the names of specific people when recording the session, the counselor might use general words such as a "fellow employee" or "mental health worker," and briefly and concisely report the themes of the client's complaint(s). In addition, the names of others in the life of the client are typically unnecessary to record. It is important to remember that the names the client mentions during counseling (with few exceptions) are not a legitimate part of the client's care and, as such, should be omitted from the client's file.

The content in the subjective section belongs to the client, unless otherwise noted. For brevity's sake, the counselor should simply write "reports, states, says, describes, indicates, complains of," and so on, in place of "The client says." For instance, instead of writing "Today the client says 'I am experiencing much more trouble at home—in my marriage—much more marital trouble since the time before our last session,'" the counselor might write "client reports increased marital problems since last session." Also, because it is implied that the counselor is the writer of the entry, it is not necessary for the counselor to refer to himself or herself, unless it is necessary to avoid confusion.

Objective

In a word, the "objective" portion of the SOAP format should be factual. It is written in quantifiable terms—that which can be seen, heard, smelled, counted, or measured. There are two types of objective data: the counselor's observations and outside written materials. Counselor observations include any physical, interpersonal, or psychological findings that the counselor witnesses. This could consist of the client's general appearance, affect and behavior, the nature of the therapeutic relationship, and the client's strengths. When appropriate, this might include the client's mental status, ability to participate in counseling, and his or her responses to the process. If they are available, outside written materials such as reports from other counselors/therapists, the results of psychological tests, or medical records can also be included in this section.

The counselor's findings are stated in precise and descriptive terms. Words that act to modify the content of the objective observations, such as "appeared" or "seemed" should be avoided. If the counselor feels hesitant in making a definitive observational statement, adequate justification for the reluctance should be provided. The phrase *as evidenced by* is helpful in these situations. For example, one day the client arrives and is almost lethargic in her responses and has difficulty tracking the flow of the session. This behavior is markedly different from previous sessions in which the client was very engaged in the counseling process. When questioned, the client denies feeling depressed. In recording this observation, the counselor might chart, "Appeared depressed, as evidenced by significantly less verbal exchange; intermittent difficulty tracking. Hair uncombed; clothes unkempt. Denies feeling depressed."

When recording observations, counselors should avoid labels, personal judgments, value-laden language, or opinionated statements (i.e., personal opinion rather than professional opinion). Words that may have a negative connotation, such as "uncooperative," "manipulative," "abusive," "obnoxious," "normal," "spoiled," "dysfunctional," "functional," and "drunk" are open to personal interpretation. Instead, record observed behaviors, allowing future readers to draw their own conclusions. For example, one should not record "Client arrived drunk to this session and was rude, obnoxious, and uncooperative." Instead, one should simply record what is seen, heard, or smelled, for example: Consider, "Client smelled of alcohol; speech slow and deliberate in nature; uncontrollable giggles even after stumbling against door jam; unsteady gait."

Assessment

The assessment section is essentially a summarization of the counselor's *clinical thinking* regarding the client's problem(s). The assessment section serves to synthesize and analyze the data from the subjective and objective portions of the notes. The assessment is generally stated in the form of a psychiatric diagnosis based on the *Diagnostic and Statistical Manual of Mental Disorders*, text revision (DSM-IV-TR; American Psychiatric Association, 2000) and is included in every entry. Although some counselors resist the idea of labeling their clients with a *DSM-IV-TR* diagnosis, third-party payers and accrediting bodies such as the Joint Commission on Accreditation of Hospitals require that this be done. According to Ginter and Glauser (2001), "Ignorance of the DSM system is not congruent with current expectations concerning counseling practice" (p. 70).

The assessment can also include *clinical impressions* (i.e., a conclusion lacking full support) that are used to "rule out" and "rule in" a diagnosis. In more complex cases, in which insufficient information exists to support a particular diagnosis, clinical impressions work much like a decision tree, helping the counselor to systematically arrive at his or her conclusions. More important, when clinical impressions are used and stated, they enable outside reviewers and other health professionals to follow the counselor's reasoning in selecting the client's final diagnosis and treatment direction. When writing clinical impressions, counselors should identify them as such. For the sake of clarity, the relevant points from the data sections should be summarized. Doing this will assist the counselor in formalizing a tentative diagnosis and will demonstrate to outside reviewers the sequence of logic used to arrive at the final diagnosis.

There is debate regarding the use of clinical impressions. Piazza and Baruth (1990) and Snider (1987) recommended against their use, whereas Mitchell (1991) viewed the use of clinical impressions as a powerful entry. In place of clinical impressions, some counselors keep personal or shadow notes. These notes are kept separate from the client's file, and the counselor uses them to record tentative impressions (Keith-Spiegel & Koocher, 1995; Thompson, 1990). This practice needs to be carefully reconsidered. The logistics of maintaining a separate set of notes are almost nightmarish, given the quantity of documentation required in most mental health clinics. Also, there are serious legal and ethical considerations. For the protection of the practitioner, client records need to demonstrate the counselor's thinking and reasoning regarding the diagnosis selected and the elimination of other possible diagnoses (Swenson, 1993). Even though a counselor's set of personal or shadow notes may be subpoenaed by the courts, by recording separate sets of notes the client's record can lack a logical progression of evaluation, planning, and treatment of problem(s). This leaves the counselor "with no evidence of competence when a lawsuit happens" (Swenson, 1993, p. 162). Simply stated, we believe that one set of notes should be kept and that it is appropriate to incorporate clinical impressions in the record.

An example of the appropriate use of clinical impressions is as follows. A counselor working in a family services agency is assessing a 7-year-old child who has been referred for possible attention-deficit/hyperactivity disorder. The report from the child's teacher describes the child as being unable to stay on tasks for longer than 5 minutes, being frequently out of his chair, and not seeming to respect other children's needs for "personal space." When the case history is taken, the child's mother provides the information that there were times when she drank frequently and excessively, sometimes to the point of "blacking out," and the mother recalls that this "may have occurred" during the first trimester of her pregnancy. Although there is insufficient information with which to make a diagnosis, a reasonable clinical impression related to a tentative diagnosis is to "rule out fetal alcohol syndrome/effects (FAS/FAE)." Although the counselor is unable to make a definitive diagnosis, given the child's prenatal history, current level of hyperactivity, and decreased attention span, an entry subtitled "Clinical impression: Rule out FAS/FAE" clearly demonstrates the counselor's understanding of childhood psychopathology and developmental issues and supports a referral to a neurological team for evaluation. If the evaluation confirms FAS/FAE, this will determine the diagnosis rendered and the treatment direction.

The assessment portion of the SOAP notes is the most likely section to be read by others, such as outside reviewers auditing records. When making a diagnosis, the counselor needs to ask the question, "Are there adequate data here to support the client diagnosis?" If sufficient data have been collected, the subjective and the objective sections should reasonably support the clinical diagnosis. However, if the counselor is feeling uncomfortable or unsure regarding the accuracy of the diagnosis, this ambivalence might suggest that insufficient data have been collected or that a consultation with a senior colleague is in order.

Plan

The last portion of the SOAP notes is the plan. This section could be described as the parameters of counseling interventions used. The plan generally consists of two parts: the action plan and the prognosis. Information contained under the action plan includes the date of the next appointment, the interventions used during the session, educational instruction (if it was given), treatment progress, and the treatment direction for the next session.

Sometimes clients will benefit from a multiagency or multidisciplinary team approach. When such referrals are made, the names and agencies to which the client was referred are recorded (names involved in the referral should be recorded). If the counselor believes that a consultation is needed, it is documented in this section and includes the telephone contacts made to the consultant regarding the client.

The client prognosis is recorded in the plan section. The prognosis is a forecast of the probable gains to be made by the client given the diagnosis, the client's personal resources, and motivation to change. Generally, progress assessments are described in terms such as *poor, guarded, fair, good,* or *excellent,* followed by supporting reasons for the particular prognosis. The plan section brings the SOAP notes and the treatment direction full circle. Table 1 summarizes the SOAP noting format and provides examples for the reader.

SCENARIO AND SAMPLE SOAP NOTES

The following is a very brief hypothetical scenario and a sample of how the SOAP notes might be written. Abbreviations have not been used

TABLE 1 A Summarization of SOAP Definitions and Examples

Section	Definitions	Examples
Subjective (S)	• What the client tells you • What pertinent others tell you about the client • Basically, how the client experiences the world	• Client's feelings, concerns, plans, goals, and thoughts • Intensity of problems and impact on relationships • Client's orientation to time, place, and person • Client's verbalized changes toward helping
Objective (O)	• Factual • What the counselor personally observes/witnesses • Quantifiable: what was seen, counted, smelled, heard, or measured • Outside written materials received	• The client's general appearance, affect, behavior • Nature of the helping relationship • Client's demonstrated strengths and weaknesses • Test results, materials, from other agencies, etc., are to be noted and attached
Assessment (A)	• Summarizes the counselor's clinical thinking • A synthesis and analysis of the subjective and objective portion of the notes	• For counselor: Include clinical diagnosis and clinical impressions (if any) • For care providers: How would you label the client's behavior and the reasons (if any) for this behavior?
Plan (P)	• Describes the parameters of treatment • Consists of an action plan and prognosis	• Action plan: Include interventions used, treatment progress, and direction. • Counselors should include the date of next appointment. • Prognosis: Include the anticipated gains from the interventions.

because the use and types of abbreviations vary from institution to institution. *Finally, in this situation the counselor is responsible for the intake session.*

Scenario

Cecil is a 34-year-old man who was mandated by the courts to obtain counseling to resolve his problems with domestic violence. He comes into the office, slams the door, and announces in a loud and irritated voice, "This counseling stuff is crap! There's no parking! My wife and kids are gone! And I gotta pay for something that don't work!"

Throughout most of the counseling session Cecil remains agitated. Speaking in an angry and aggressive voice, he tells you that his probation officer told him he was a good man and could get his wife and kids back. He demands to know why you are not really helping get back what is most important to him. He insists that "Mary just screws everything up!" He goes on to tell you of a violent argument he and Mary had last night regarding the privileges of their daughter Nicole, who just turned 16. You are aware that there is a restraining order against Cecil.

During the session, you learn Cecil was raised in a physically and verbally abusive family until he was 11, at which time he was placed in protective custody by social services, where he remained until he was 18. He goes on to tell you that he has been arrested numerous times for "brawling" and reports that sometimes the littlest things make him angry and he just explodes, hitting whatever is available—the walls, his wife, the kids, and three guys at work. Cecil also reports prior arrests for domestic violence. He admits that at various times, he has been both physically and emotionally abusive to Mary and the children but insists that it was needed "to straighten them out." Just before leaving your office, Cecil rushes from his chair and stands within a foot of you. Angrily, with his fists and jaw clenched, he says, "This is the same old B.S. You guys are just all talk." He storms from the room.

Sample SOAP Notes

7/7/01. 2 p.m. (S) Reports counseling is not helping him get his family back. Insists the use of violence has been needed to "straighten out" family members. Reports history of domestic violence. Recent history: States he met and verbally fought with his wife yesterday regarding the privileges of oldest child. Personal history: childhood physical and mental abuse resulting in foster care placement, ages 11-18. (O) Generally agitated throughout the session. Toward the end of the session stood up, with clenched fists and jaw, angrily stated that counseling is "same old B.S.!" Rushed out of office. (A) Physical Abuse of Adult [V61.1, *DSM* code] and Child(ren) [V61.21]. Clinical impressions: Rule out Intermittent Explosive Disorder given bouts of uncontrolled rage with non-specific emotional trigger. (P) Rescheduled for 7/14/01 @ 2 p.m.; prognosis guarded due to low level of motivation to change. Continue cognitive therapy. Refer to Dr. Smith for psychiatric/medication evaluation. Referred to Men's Alternative to Violence Group. Next session, introduce use of "time-outs." S. Cameron, Ph.D., LPCC (signature).

GENERAL GUIDELINES FOR SOAP NOTING

Client records are legal documents. For the most part, in a court of law, they represent the quality of services provided by the counselor (Mitchell, 1991; Scalise, 2000; Thompson, 1990). To ensure both the quality and the accuracy of the notes and to safeguard the integrity of the counselor, the following guidelines should be observed when writing SOAP notes.

Record the session immediately after the session while it is still fresh in your mind. This avoids the uncertainty, confusion, errors, or inaccuracies that are most likely to occur when you try to complete all the files at the day's end. Start each entry with the date (month, day, and year) and time the session began. Make each entry legible and neat with no grammar, spelling, or punctuation errors. Finally, the client record should reflect the counselor's level of training and expertise. For example, the counselor's extensive use of psychoanalytic-based terminology without having received such training may cause other professionals to question the competency of the counselor. The American Counseling Association's (ACA, 1995) Code of Ethics takes a clear position on counselors limiting practice to level of competence, and because records may be reviewed by others, the record's language must be congruent with level of competence. These procedures will alleviate misunderstandings between professionals and minimize the potential of a lawsuit (Swenson, 1993).

All client contact or attempted contact should be recorded using the SOAP format. This includes all telephone calls, messages left on answering machines, or messages left with individuals who answered the phone. Letters that were mailed to the client would be noted in the record along with a photocopy of the signed letter.

When recording a session, keep in mind that altered entries arouse suspicions and can create significant problems for the counselor in a court of law (Norris, 1995). If an error is made, never erase, obliterate, use correction fluid, or in any way attempt to obscure the mistake. Instead, the error should be noted by enclosing it in brackets, drawing a single line through the incorrect word(s), and writing the word "error" above or to the side of the mistake. The counselor should follow this correction with his or her initials, the full date, and the time of correction. The mistake should still be readable, indicating the counselor is only attempting to clarify the mistake not cover it up. If not typed, all entries should be written in black ballpoint pen, which allows for easy photocopying should the file be requested at a later date. Furthermore, notes should never be written in pencil or felt-tipped pen because pencil can be easily erased or altered, whereas felt-tipped pen is easily smudged or distorted should something spill on the notes.

TABLE 2 Guidelines for Subjective, Objective, Assessment, Plan (SOAP) Noting

Do	Avoid
• Be brief and concise.	• Avoid using names of other clients, family members, or others named by client.
• Keep quotes to a minimum.	
• Use an active voice.	
• Use precise and descriptive terms.	• Avoid terms like seems, appears.
• Record immediately after each session.	• Avoid value-laden language, common labels, opinionated statements.
• Start each new entry with date and time of session.	
• Write legibly and neatly.	• Do not use terminology, unless trained to do so.
• Use proper spelling, grammar, and punctuation.	• Do not erase, obliterate, use correction fluid, or in any way attempt to obscure mistakes.
• Document all contacts or attempted contacts.	
• Use only black ink if notes are handwritten.	• Do not leave blank spaces between entries.
• Sign-off using legal signature, plus your title.	• Do not try to squeeze additional commentary between lines or in margins.

At the conclusion of the entry, the counselor needs to sign off using a legal signature—generally considered to be the first initial and last name followed by the counselor's title. All entries, regardless of their size, are followed by the counselor's legal signature. There should be no empty space between the content of the SOAP notes and the signature. Blank spaces may later be interpreted (e.g., by a lawyer) to mean that there is missing information or that the counselor failed to provide "complete care" (Norris, 1995); even worse, empty spaces can be filled in by another person without the counselor's knowledge. Writing should be continuous with no lines skipped between entries or additional commentary squeezed in between the lines or in the margins. Table 2 offers readers a quick reference list of "do's and don'ts."

CONCLUSION

In this era of accountability, counselors are expected to use a more systematic approach in documenting rendered services (Ginter & Glauser, in press; Norris, 1995; Scalise, 2000). Good documentation is a fundamental part of providing minimal client care, and needs to be mastered like any other counseling skill. As the standards for recording receive increased scrutiny by both managed care organizations and the National

Committee for Quality Assurance, the importance of documentation has changed from "something that should be done well to something that must be done well" (Kettenbach, 1995, p. iii), especially if counseling is to survive in this age of managed resources. SOAP notes are a proven and effective means of addressing this new mandate. We hope that this article will help others fulfill this dictate, for there is no substitute for concisely written and well-documented case notes.

Susan Cameron, *Santa Fe Indian Hospital, Santa Fe, New Mexico; imani turtle-song, PB & J Family Services, Albuquerque, New Mexico. Correspondence concerning this article should be addressed to imani turtle-song, PB & J Family Services, 1101 Lopez SW, Albuquerque, NM 87105 (e-mail: imanisong@aol.com).*

REFERENCES

American Counseling Association. (1995). *ACA code of ethics and standards of practice*. Alexandria, VA: Author

American Psychiatric Association. (2000). *Diagnostic and statistical manual of mental disorders* (Text rev.). Washington, DC: Author.

Anderson, J., & Bowers, G. (1973). *Human association memory*. Washington, DC: Winston.

Bechtel, W., & Abrahamsen, A. (1990). *Connectionism and the mind: Introduction to parallel processing in networks*. Cambridge, MA: Basil Blackwell.

Eggland, E. T. (1988). Charting: How and why to document your care daily—and fully. *Nursing, 18*(22), 76–84.

Ginter, E. J., & Glauser, A. (2001). Effective use of the DSM from a developmental/wellness perspective. In E. R, Welfel & R. E. Ingersoll (Eds.), *The mental health desk reference* (pp. 69–77). New York: Wiley.

Griffith, J., & Ignatavicius, D. (1986). *The writer's handbook: The complete guide to clinical documentation, professional writing and research papers*. Baltimore: Resource Applications.

Hart, J., Berndt, R., & Catamazza, A. (1985, August). Category specific naming deficit following cerebral infractions. *Nature, 316*, 339–340.

Joint Commission on Accreditation of Healthcare Organizations. (2000). *Consolidated standards manual for child, adolescent, and adult psychiatric, alcoholism, and drug abuse facilities*. Chicago: Author.

Keith-Spiegel, P., & Koocher, G. P. (1995). *Ethics in psychology: Professional standards and cases*. New York: Random House.

Kettenbach, G. (1995). *Writing SOAP notes*. Philadelphia: Davis.

Mitchell, R. W. (1991). The ACA Legal Series: Documentation in counseling records (Vol 2). Alexandria, VA: American Counseling Association.

Norris, J. (1995). *Mastering documentation*. Springhouse, PA: Springhouse.

Philpott, M. (1986). Twenty rules for good charting. *Nursing, 16*(8), 63.

Piazza, N. J., & Baruth, N. E. (1990). Client record guidelines. *Journal of Counseling & Development, 68*, 313–316.

Ryback, R. S. (1974). *The problem oriented record in psychiatry and mental health care*. New York: Grune & Stratton.

Scalise, J. J. (1999). The ethical practice of marriage and family therapy. In A. Horne (Ed.), *Family counseling and therapy* (3rd ed., pp. 565–596). Itasca, IL: Peacock.

Shaw, M. (1997). *Charting made incredibly easy.* Springhouse, PA: Springhouse.

Siegal, C., & Fischer, S. K. (1981). *Psychiatric records in mental health.* New York: Brunner/Mazel.

Snider, P. D. (1987). Client records: Inexpensive liability protection for mental health counselors. *Journal of Mental Health Counseling, 9,* 134–141.

Swenson, L. C. (1993). *Psychology and law for the helping professions.* Pacific Grove, CA: Brooks/Cole.

Thompson, A. (1990). *Guide to ethical practice in psychotherapy.* New York: Wiley.

Weed, L. L. (1964). Medical records, patient care and medical education. *Irish Journal of Medical Education, 6,* 271–282.

Weed, L. L. (1968). Medical records that guide and teach. *New England Journal of Medicine, 278,* 593–600, 652–657.

Weed, L. L. (1971). Quality control and the medical record. *Archive of Internal Medicine, 127,* 101–105.

The School Counselor and The Law: New Developments

Robert L. Stenger

THE SCHOOL, THE PUPIL, AND THIRD PARTIES

The focus of this article will be on the legal relationship between public school personnel and others who may seek access to information concerning a minor enrolled in a public elementary or secondary school. It will be outside the scope of this article to discuss certain legal responsibilities of school personnel based on the Constitution and statutory rights. This will include the following: First Amendment rights of free speech, freedom of association, freedom to practice religion, Fourteenth Amendment rights of due process, equal protection, or privacy, and education of the handicapped, bilingual education, or affirmative action.

In any focus upon *legal* relationships, there will be a series of corresponding rights and duties. Specifically, the right of a parent to receive information about a child's performance in school and the duty of the school to provide such information, or the right of the parent to prevent disclosure of information concerning a child and the duty of the school to withhold it. A legal relationship is one which can be enforced by legal processes or for whose violation legal sanctions are available. Often a court decision will determine whether a particular claim is legally enforceable as a right or is simply a request with the hope that it will be satisfied.

I. DEFINING "CHILD"

The first step will be an effort to define both "child" and "parent." The law refers to one who has not reached the age of majority as a minor. After the ratification of the Twenty-sixth Amendment in 1971, which provided that eighteen-year-olds could vote in federal elections, many states made eighteen the age of majority. Persons who had reached that age not only could vote but could also take such legally significant actions as entering into a contract, suing for a civil injury or being sued for civil injury, deciding to marry or receiving or refusing to receive medical treatment. Persons under the age of majority may be referred to as "minors," "children," or even as "infants."

Traditionally, the common law has viewed a person to be emancipated by marriage as well. Some states have adopted statutory methods for emancipation whereby financially self-sufficient minors can declare their independence from parental authority.[1]

Truancy laws are the methods states use to require that children attend school until a specified age, often sixteen. The truancy law is the foundation of some rights and duties of parents or parent-substitutes and of school personnel. The truancy law is expressed in terms of an obligation to send the child to school. Kentucky law for example, places the obligation of sending the child to school upon "each parent, guardian or other person having in custody or charge of any child between the ages of six and sixteen."[2] The obligation arises from the physical possession of the child rather than the legal basis, if any, for that possession. Anyone in charge of the child, whether such a person is the legal custodian or not, is to send the child to school. Thus, one may have the legal obligation of sending the child to school without having other rights or duties of a parent.

II. DEFINING "PARENT"

In contrast to the ease with which one can define "child" is the complexity and difficulty of defining "parent." Parental rights are usually recognized in the mother and father jointly; for example, Kentucky provides: "The father and mother shall have joint custody, nurture and education of their children under the age of eighteen."[3] Even though there may be a statutory provision that one parent, usually the father, is liable or primarily liable for the costs of nurture and education, and even

---

[1] Cal. Civ. Code II §§ 60-70 (West 1982).
[2] Ky. Rev. Stat. Ann. § 159.010 (Bobbs-Merrill 1980).
[3] Ky Rev. Stat. Ann. § 405.020(1) (Michie 1984)

though such a provision is probably unconstitutional as gender discrimination, the allocation of financial responsibility for the child is not coextensive with parental rights.[4] Thus, either parent acting alone can make decisions on behalf of the child, in such areas as medical care, taking school field trips, or placement in a particular class. After the death of one parent, the surviving parent will have sole custody, nurture and education of the child.

The identification of a child's *legal* parent is a question of law, not of biology, genetics, anthropology, or ethics. The legal parent is that person in whom the legal system recognized the bundle of rights and duties that constitute the legal definition of parenthood. Parenthood, like any other legal status, is defined in terms of what that person may and may not do. The legal parent is not necessarily the person whom the child recognizes as a parent,[5] nor the person whom society regards as the person who fulfills the visible role of a parent for that child.

The law has traditionally surrounded the family with a veil of respect and privacy. When a man and woman purport to be married and live together as husband and wife, the law presumes they are married. Such a legal presumption means that they will be treated as married persons unless and until someone proves they are not married. Children who are born to a married couple are presumed to be their natural children. The couple will be charged with parental duties and will be able to exercise parental rights unless a court determines otherwise.

Parental rights and duties may also be created by adoption, which is simply the legal process for creating parent-child relations where they would not otherwise exist. While earlier adoption legislation left the adopted child as a person with two sets of parents, modern laws see the adoption as creating a new and exclusive parent-child relationship. After the adoption the child shall be for all legal purposes the child of the adopting parents "as if born of their bodies."[6] Correspondingly, except where the adopting parent is the spouse of a natural parent, in other words, a step-parent adoption, the adopted child has no further legal relationship to the natural parents; after the adoption it is legally, if not biologically or genetically, inaccurate to speak of the child's "real parents" as anyone but the adoptive parents.

If the biological parents of a child are not married to each other at the time of the child's birth, the situation is more complex. The terminology among jurisdictions is not uniform. The more derogatory terms "bastard" and "bastardy action" which were employed at common law

---

4 *Id.*

5 The person whom a child recognizes as a parent is sometimes referred to as the "psychological parent."

have been replaced, first by "illegitimate child" and now by "child out of wedlock" or "non-marital child." At the time of such a child's birth, the mother alone enjoys parental rights in most states. Only in the few states that have adopted the Uniform Parentage Act[7] or some variation thereof does "the parent and child relationship extend equally to every child and to every parent, regardless of the marital status of the parents."[8] The father acquires parental rights with respect to the child born out of wedlock either by subsequent marriage to the mother and recognition of the child or by a formal, legal finding of paternity by a court. According to the United States Supreme Court in *Lalli v. Lalli* under the U.S. Constitution and the Fourteenth Amendment, states must recognize parental rights in a father who has married the mother or been adjudicated as the legal father.[9] To do otherwise would be invidious discrimination against children born out of wedlock. Some states go further and recognize parental rights in any father who has admitted paternity in writing or who by his words and conduct has recognized the child as his own.[10] Typically, the child is considered legitimate if the parents have attempted lawful marriage, even though it may later be determined that their marriage was void.

If the parents of a child are divorced, the issue of child custody will be determined in the dissolution proceedings or in a proceeding for a declaration of invalidity. Typically, the court may grant custody to one parent or it may continue joint custody in both parents together. If joint custody is awarded, then both parents or either of them are empowered to make decisions affecting the child's welfare. If the court awards custody to only one parent, then, in the absence of agreement to the contrary, the

---

[6] E.g., Ky. Rev. Stat. Ann. § 199.520(2) (Michie 1982).
Upon entry of the judgment of adoption, from and after the date of the filing of the petition, the child shall be deemed the child of petitioners and shall be considered for purposes of inheritance and succession and for all other legal considerations, the natural, legitimate child of the parents adopting it the same as if born of their bodies.
[7] Unif. Parentage Act, 9A U.L.A. 579 (1983): On several occasions since 1922, the National Conference of Commissioners on Uniform State Laws has concerned itself with the law relating to the child born out of wedlock, and appointed a committee to study the subject in 1969. The Act was drafted at a time when the states needed new legislation on the subject because much of the current law was unconstitutional. Since 1968 a series of decisions of the U.S. Supreme Court mandated equal treatment of legitimate and illegitimate children by denying them benefits generally granted to legitimate children. Thus the present act merely fulfills Fourteenth Amendment Equal Protection mandates.
[8] *Id.* § 2. "The parent and child relationship extends equally to every child and to every parent, regardless of the marital status of the parent."
[9] Lalli v. Lalli, 439 U.S. 259 (1978).
[10] *Id.* at 273.

custodial parent alone "may determine the child's upbringing, including his education, health care, and religious training."[11] While the non-custodial parent will remain a parent and will most likely receive visitation rights, decision-making authority will rest with the custodial parent except for the necessary decisions which must be made by the non-custodial parent in the proper exercise of his or her visitation rights.

Unfortunately, very few states recognize explicitly in statutes parental rights concerning children who are born as the result of modern medical technology. Although the number of children conceived and born as a result of artificial insemination, *in vitro* fertilization, or surrogate parenting is increasing, their legal status remains ambiguous as the law continues to apply the pre-technology presumption that a child born to a married woman is the child of her husband.

Other adults may have certain parental duties such as the duty of sending the child to school, but not have parental rights. A court may grant visitation rights to a grandparent; thereupon, the grandparent has visitation rights with the child but does not have any parental authority over the child. A step-parent may have some financial responsibility for the child of a spouse, but the existence or even satisfaction of such legal duty does not give the step-parent any parental rights with respect to the child.

Children also come within the jurisdiction of the court for reasons other than divorce or adoption. The state, in the exercise of its traditional *parens patriae*[12] power to take responsibility for those who are unable to care for themselves, may appoint a legal guardian for the child. This will always occur when a child is deprived of parents by death or desertion. Normally, a relative of the child will be chosen for this responsibility. It is possible for a court to name one person as guardian of the child's person with authority to make decisions with respect to the child, and another person as guardian of the child's estate to manage the child's property. Also, children who have allegedly committed criminal acts, who are status offenders[13] or who are found to be

---

[11] Unif. Marriage and Divorce Act, 9A U.L.A. 96 § 408(a) (amended 1973).

[12] *Parens patriae*, refers traditionally to the role of state as sovereign and guardian of persons under legal disability. Blacks Law Dictionary 1003 (5th ed. 1979).

[13] *Status offense* refers to any action brought in the interest of a child who is accused of committing acts, which if committed by an adult would not be a crime. Such behavior shall not be termed criminal or delinquent, and such children shall not be considered delinquent.

Status offenses include instances in which the child has previously been adjudicated a status offender, has subsequently violated a court order and is found to be in contempt of court. Status offenses do not include violations of state or local ordinances that may apply to juveniles, such as violation of curfew or possession of alcoholic beverages. Act of April 9, 1980, Ch 280, § 3(38), Ky. Acts § 848, 849, repealed by Act of April 3, 1984, Ch. 184, §, 1984 Ky. Acts 470.

dependent,[14] abused or neglected will come within the jurisdiction of the court. Such courts will typically have a variety of dispositional alternatives, including supervised return of the child to its parents or placement in a foster home, an institution or with a relative. Such placements are temporary and do not of themselves terminate the parents' rights or duties. Temporarily, however, the child will be under the jurisdiction of the court, person or agency to whom the court commits the child, and that person or agency will make the day-to-day decisions regarding the child. Such persons or institutions are forbidden to make permanent custodial or major decisions involving the long-term interests of the child. The parental rights of the natural or adoptive parents are permanently taken away only when voluntarily terminated by the parents' consent or involuntarily terminated by the court.

III. IMPACT ON SCHOOL PERSONNEL

How are school personnel to deal with this complex and confusing variety of persons and institutions who may claim some or all of the rights and privileges of a parent? School personnel often face conflicting claims when a person not only makes a request or demand with respect to a child but also insists that another's claim be rejected by the school. In these situations, school personnel find themselves in a dilemma. How is the school to sort out these various claims and demands?

A. Possession of the Child

At the outset, it is important to distinguish a claim for physical possession of the child from a claim for information about a child wherein access to records, files, reports, test scores, or teacher conferences is sought. In the absence of a court order, the child's legal parents, alone, have a right to physical possession of the child. The parents may exercise this right personally and directly or delegate it to others. In the absence of any contrary information, school personnel would be justified in releasing a child to a parent or to another authorized person on the basis of a parent's instructions, preferably written.

When a non-parent seeks possession of a child, school personnel should ask for some authorization and the parents should be notified before the child is released into the other person's custody. Persons who request a school to release a child to them should quite reasonably expect to be asked for identification and perhaps credentials authorizing their

---

[14] Dependent child means any child who is under improper care, control or guardianship that is not due to the negligence of the parent or guardian, provided that the child is not abused or neglected child. *Id.*, § 3(12).

possession of the child.[15] Public employees such as police, social workers, probation officers, or officers of the court will have identification and possibly court orders authorizing their possession of the child.

The increasing prevalence of and publicity concerning child abuse and childsnatching has led many jurisdictions to create new felonies or to expand the definitions of existing felonies to include the taking of a child contrary to the wishes of a parent or court order. "Childsnatching" has been coined to describe the taking of a child by a parent contrary to a custody decree. In several cases[16] the non-custodial parent employed detectives to find the child and other persons to seize the child from school or on the way to or from school. The other parent in some instances employed similar tactics to re-snatch the child. Such actions by parents are not the crime of kidnapping because kidnapping is defined as unlawfully taking a person away. A parent whose parental rights have not been terminated remains a parent and his or her possession of the child is not unlawful. The taking of a minor by the parent is expressly exempted from the definition of kidnapping by federal statute.[17]

A parent may be charged, however, with the newly created crime of custodial interference. A number of states have made custodial interference a crime in order to reach parents and others who knowingly take children contrary to an existing court order and who cannot be reached under existing kidnapping laws.[18]

In December 1980, Congress passed the Parental Kidnapping Prevention Act.[19] The title must not mislead the reader into believing that the Act created the crime of parental kidnapping. Rather, the act combined several provisions that were intended to deter interstate abductions and other removals of children undertaken with the intent of obtaining custody elsewhere. Thus, the Act provided that one state must ordinarily give respect to and comply with another state's custody and visitation decrees. It was also provided that the Parental Locator Service, created in

---

[15] *E.g.*, "David will be picked up by his grandma after school," or "Allison is to go home with Jennifer after school today."

[16] *See, e.g.*, Beneh v. Smith, 535 F. Supp. 560, (D.C. Cal. 1982); Belosky v Belosky, 97 N.M. 365, 640 P.2d 471 (1982); Pierce, 197 Mont. 16, 640 P.2d 899 (1982).

[17] 18 U.S.C. § 1201(a) (West Supp. 1985).

[18] *See, e.g.*, Ky. Rev. Stat. Ann. § 509.070 (Michie 1985); Cal. Penal Code 278.5 (West Supp. 1985). Violation of custody or visitation decreased; punishment. (a) Every person who in violation of the physical custody or visitation provisions of the custody order, judgment, or decree takes, detains...conceals or retains the child with the intent to deprive another person of his or her rights to physical custody or visitation shall be punished by imprisonment...a fine...or both. Cal. Penal Code § 278.5 (West Supp. 1985).

[19] Parental Kidnapping Prevention Act of 1980, 28 U.S.C.A. § 1738(a) (West Supp. 1985).

the Social Security Act of 1934 could be used by authorized persons to locate and absent parent or child.[20] However, the persons who are authorized to employ the locator service are limited to attorneys of the state or the United States or a court. Finally, the Parental Kidnapping Prevention Act provided that the federal statute which created a crime of flight to avoid prosecution or giving testimony[21] was intended to apply to parental kidnapping. In *Beach v. Smith*[22] a mother, during pending divorce proceedings, took her minor daughter and fled to an unknown location. Her estranged husband attempted to compel the U.S. Department of Justice to employ the statute[23] to return his daughter to him. However, the California federal district court held that the statute was only meant to allow federal officers to search for fugitives from justice. It was not intended to be used by parents who are trying to get their children back. While the statute might allow the government to prosecute the mother, it could not be used to return the father's daughter to him.[24]

The continuing focus of public attention upon the prevalence of child-snatching and child abuse in our society should alert all those who have children under their authority and control to the gravity of the situation. In these circumstances school personnel should be very cautious about the physical custody of children. It would be preferable to err on the side of protecting the child by not relinquishing custody rather than avoid inconveniencing the parent, for the latter is much less important than the former.

In practice, a school will also receive requests for possession of a child from *de facto* custodians. A *de facto* custodian is one who cares for the child on a fairly regular, day-to-day basis, with at least the implied consent of a parent. It may be a relative, a neighbor, or a cohabitant of the parent who is temporarily caring for the child. While the *de facto* custodian has no legal right to demand possession of the child, a school would appear justified, upon proper notification by the parent, in honoring the parent's implied agreement, unless the school had some information that the custodial arrangement was contrary to the parent's wishes or was detrimental to the child.

Often child-abuse reporting statutes make a distinction between a "dependent child" who is under improper care, control or guardianship not due to the negligence of a parent or guardian and an "abused or neglected child" who is one whose health or welfare is harmed or threatened

---

[20] *See* 42 U.S.C.A. § 654, 663 (1983).
[21] 18 U.S.C.A. § 1073 (West Supp. 1985).
[22] 535 F. Supp. § 560 (S.D. 1982).
[23] *Beach*, 535, F. Supp. at 561.
[24] *Id.* at 562.

by parents, or guardians.[25] School personnel are among the persons who are expressly charged with the duty of reporting whenever they have reasonable cause to believe a child is abused or neglected. While it may be difficult in practice to distinguish between a suspected situation of abuse or neglect and a real situation of abuse or neglect, the child-abuse reporting statutes are expressions of strong public policy. The emphasis must be upon the safety and welfare of the child. Needless to say, no school employee should release a child into the possession of anyone whom the employee believes might be a danger to the child.

B. Access to Information

With respect to access to information about a child enrolled in a public school, one must consult state and federal statutes for current public policy about records held by the government. The public school is one of the many governmental agencies that maintain records. Recent public policy has been open to records to public scrutiny and, at the same time, protect the privacy of individuals about who information is contained in the records.[26] These two goals are achieved by allowing individuals access to personal information about themselves while denying such information to others.

The federal policy for public education is expresses in the Family Educational Rights and Privacy Act of 1974.[27] This Act refuses federal funds to educational agencies or institutions that effectively prevent parental inspection and review of children's educational records, or which have the policy or practice of releasing students' educational records to unauthorized recipients. It should be noted that FERPA creates no private right of action whereby parents can compel the release of information to themselves or forbid its release to others. Because of the importance of funding in public education today, schools have attempted to comply with FERPA. When there is no state privacy law with respect to public records, the Freedom of Information Act or comparable Open Records Laws will prohibit the release of records containing information of a personal nature if public disclosure would constitute a clearly unwarranted invasion of personal privacy.[28]

FERPA allows the release of information about students to parents, school officials, accrediting agencies, organizations that develop or

---

[25] See, e.g., Ky. Rev. Stat. Ann. § 199.011 (Bobbs-Merrill 1982).

[26] The former policy of opening records was expressed in regard to the federal government by the Freedom of Information Act of 1966, 5 U.S.C. 553 (1982) and at the state level in Open Records Laws. *See, e.g.*, Ky. Rev. Stat. Ann. § 61.872 (Bobbs-Merrill 1980).

[27] 20 U.S.C. § 1232 g (1982).

[28] 5 U.S.C. § 552 (1982).

administer predictive tests, persons authorized by law, and others in the event of an emergency. For purposes of the Act, "parent" means the parent of a dependent as defined by the Internal Revenue Code.[29] It would be ridiculous about a pupil, to undertake the complex analysis employed by an Internal Revenue agent in determining the legitimacy of a claimed deduction for a dependent. This is expressly stated in the regulations promulgated under FERPA that define "parent" as including a parent, guardian, or individual acting as a parent in the absence of parent or guardian. These regulations allow school personnel to presume that such person has authority to exercise the rights specified in FERPA. Unless the school has been provided with evidence that there is a state law or court order to the contrary.[30] Similarly, whenever any such person consents to the disclosure of information about a student to others, the school personnel may, in the absence of evidence to the contrary, presume that the person giving consent has the authority to do so.[31] Parents, guardians, and *de facto* parents thus have the twofold right to receive information contained in the school records concerning their child and to forbid or permit the disclosure of such information to others. As under the Privacy Act,[32] FERPA includes a provision whereby a parent may challenge and amend an educational record and may have a hearing if the amendment is denied.[33]

One case litigated under FERPA included a natural mother, who was living apart from her husband, the child's father, under a separation agreement.[34] She directed the school not to divulge any information about their son's education to his father and not to allow the father to participate in any teacher conferences. The father sued to gain access to school records and to have occasional conferences with school personnel concerning his son's progress. The court rules that both parents have a right to inspect their children's educational records, unless barred by state law, court order, or legally binding instrument.[35] The court noted that it is in the best interests of students to have educational information made available to both parents of every school child "fortunate enough to have two parents interested in his welfare."[36] It would be rare that a court would,

---

[29] 26 U.S.C. § 152 (1982).

[30] 34 C.R.F. § 99.3 (1985).

[31] 34 C.F.R § 99.30(b) (1985).

[32] 5 U.S.C. § 552a(f)(4) (1982).

[33] 34 C.F.R. § 99.20 (1985).

[34] Page v. Rotterdam-Monohauser Central School Dist., 441 N.Y.S.2d 323 (N.Y. Sup. Ct. 1981).

[35] *Page*, 441 N.Y.S.2d at 325, *E.g.*, a separation agreement in which the non-custodial parent waived a right to inspect the child's school records.

[36] *Page*, 441 N.Y.S.2d at 325.

in its broad equitable powers to determine custody in the best interests of the child, exclude a parent from involvement in and knowledge about the child's educational progress.

Persons other than parents, guardians and custodians may have access to information about the pupil. In assisting a court to arrive at a custody decision, the judge may order an investigation concerning the child's custodial arrangements and the investigator may consult any person who has information about the child and potential arrangements.[37] The custody statute drafted in the Uniform Marriage and Divorce Act expressly includes the child's adjustment to his school as among the relevant factors which must be considered in determining his best interests.[38] Also, in making an adoption order, a court is usually required to find that the potential adoptive parents are able to maintain and educate the child properly.[39]

When a child is brought before a juvenile or family court as allegedly delinquent or dependent, the court will order an investigation into the specific complaint. Any circumstances which may throw light upon future care and guidance, including the child's school record may be investigated.[40] Thus, under a number of statutes, police, social workers, probation officers, or personnel of the court may be directed to investigate a child's school records and interview school personnel concerning the child.

In the course of litigation which comes before a court, procedural rules of that particular jurisdiction will permit the parties to conduct discovery concerning any matter, not privileged, which is relevant to the subject matter.[41] Thus, in litigation to enforce the educational rights of Hispanics[42] and the handicapped [43] some courts have balanced the privacy for confidential records such as test scores, performance evaluations, and progress reports. While setting a high value on privacy, the courts in these instances found that the school should honor a subpoena and provide the requested information.[44]

When a person who is not a parent or guardian is seeking information about a child, it would be appropriate for school personnel to ask for some legal authorization or justification for the request. The school should also make a reasonable effort to notify a parent of an court order

---

[37] Uniform Marriage and Divorce Act, 405, 9a U.L.A. § 204 (1973).

[38] *Id.* 402(4), 9a U.L.A. (1973).

[39] *E.g.,* Ky. Rev. Stat. Ann. § 199.520(i) (Supp. 1984).

[40] *E.g.,* Ky. Rev. Stat. Ann. § 208.140(i) (Bobbs-Merrill 1982) (repealed July 15, 1984).

[41] *E.g.,* Fed. R. Civ. P. 26.

[42] Rios v Reed, 73 F.R.D 589 (E.D.N.Y. 1977).

[43] Mattie T. v Johnston, 74 F.R.D 498 (N.D. Miss. 1976).

[44] *Id.* at 501.

or subpoena in advance of the school's compliance therewith, and should keep a record of all disclosures of student records.[45]

Since the policy of the law is to protect privacy and to ensure parent's access to their children's school records, school personnel are advised to be liberal in making a child's records available to a parent or guardian. At the same time, they should be strict about making such information available to a non-parent. A counselor who is regularly employed may by statute be immune in a civil or criminal proceeding from disclosing, without the student's consent, any advice given or communicated by the student counselee.[46] School personnel should also inquire about the availability of legal counsel to defend them and of insurance to cover any judgment against them, if they are sued in their official capacities for releasing or failing to release a child or information concerning a child.

Robert L. Stenger *is a Professor of Law, University of Louisville School of Law.*

---

[45] 34 C.F.R 99.31(9) (1985); 34 C.F.R. 44.32(a) (1985).
[46] Ky. Rev. Stat. Ann. § 421.216 (Supp. 1984).

Reprinted with permission from *Journal of Law and Education*, Vol. 15, No. 1, pp.105–116.

Confidentiality of Educational Records: Serious Risks for Parents and School Districts

Peter A. Walker
Sara Jane Steinberg

ABSTRACT

This article addresses briefly the problem of the disclosure of sensitive information contained in special educational records and proposes a number of measures a school district can take to protect the confidentiality of general student records. First, it will provide a detailed overview of the relevant federal statutes bearing on the confidentiality of sensitive records containing disability-related information, including special education records. It will also review representative state provisions from Florida, California, and New York. Second, it will consider the power of a court to issue and enforce protective orders and to enforce such orders as a means of safeguarding the confidentiality of special education records. This discussion will provide the foundation upon which to examine competing interests that arise in the context of protecting the confidentiality of special education records. Third, it will examine circumstances where a school district's failure to disclose certain information may result in both official and individual liability. Finally, it will suggest certain actions that a school district can take to protect sensitive information and at the same time keep parents informed about matters concerning their children.

I. OVERVIEW OF FEDERAL AND STATE CONFIDENTIALITY LAWS

Despite the numerous federal and state statutes designed to protect the confidentiality of records containing personal information, the confidentiality of educational records may not be safe, resulting in potential embarrassment to parents and children and liability to school districts responsible for safeguarding those records. As school districts collect more and more medical family, financial and similar, sensitive information, the problems of protecting such information will assume paramount importance.

A. Federal Law

A number of federal statutes address the confidentiality of records containing disability-related information. The Individuals with Disabilities Education Act ("IDEA"),[1] designed to ensure that all children with disabilities have access to free appropriate public education, contains several provisions relating to records maintained pursuant to the Act. Section 1415 sets forth the procedural safeguards an educational unit must provide to children with disabilities and their parents or guardians and includes "an opportunity for the parents or guardian of a handicapped child to examine all relevant records with respect to the identification, evaluation, and educational placement of the child, and the provision of a free appropriate public education to such child..."[2] In order to protect the confidentiality of such records, the IDEA authorizes the Secretary of Education to "take appropriate action...to assure the protection of the confidentiality of any personally identifiable data, information, and records collected or maintained by the Secretary and by state and local educational agencies."[3]

The Family Educational Rights and Privacy Act of 1974 (commonly known as the "Buckley Amendment" to the General Education

---

[1] 20 U.S.C.A. § 1400 et seq. (1990 & Supp. 1995).

[2] 20 U.S.C.A. § 1415(b)(1)(A).

[3] 20 U.S.C.A. § 1417(c). *See also* Assistance to States for the Education of Children with Disabilities, 34 CFR §§ 300.560 to 300.576 (1995). These regulations, promulgated by the Department of Education, Office of Special Education and Rehabilitative Services, govern agencies or institutions that collect, maintain or use personally identifiable information. The confidentiality provisions include the requirement of parental consent before the disclosure of any personally identifiable information. In addition, the regulations require safeguards to protect the confidentiality of personally identifiable information at the collection, storage, disclosure, and destruction stages. These safeguards include the designation of one official at each agency to assume responsibility for ensuring the confidentiality of such information, as well as the maintenance of a current listing of those employees, within the institution who may have access to personally identifiable information.

Provisions Act)[4] permits parents to inspect and review their children's educational records and generally protects the confidentiality of student records. For example, where an educational record includes information on more than one student, a parent is only permitted to review the portion of the document relating to his or her child.[5] Similarly, educational records may not be released without the written consent of the student's parent or pursuant to a court order with the condition that parents and students are notified before the records are released.[6] However, as school officials are well aware, certain individuals may obtain access to a student's educational records even in the absence of written consent or a court order. These individuals include, but are not limited to, school officials and teachers who have a legitimate educational interest in the records, officials of other schools in which the student seeks to enroll, authorized representatives of state educational authorities, and in connection with an emergency, appropriate emergency personnel if knowledge of such information is necessary to protect the health or safety of the student or other persons.[7]

To address the continuing national problem of discrimination against individuals with disabilities and to provide clear, enforceable standards that may be used to redress such discrimination, Congress passed the Americans with Disabilities Act of 1990 ("ADA").[8] The confidentiality provisions of the ADA arise in connection with Title I of the Act, which addresses disability discrimination in the context of employment. Title I recognizes an employer's right to conduct a medical examination after a conditional offer of employment has been made to a job applicant. However, the information obtained regarding the medical conditions or history of the applicant must be maintained on separate forms and in sep-

---

[4] 20 U.S.C.A. § 1232(g) (1990 & Supp. 1995). This law applies to all educational agencies that accept federal financial assistance and applies to all pupils, not just pupils with disabilities.

[5] 20 U.S.C.A. § 1232(g)(a)(1)(a).

[6] 20 U.S.C.A. § 1232(g)(b)(2)(A) and (B).

[7] *See* 20 U.S.C.A. §§ 1232(g)(b)(1)(A) to (I). *See also* Family Educational Rights and Privacy, 34 CFR § 99.30 to 99.37 (1995). These regulations, promulgated by the Department of Education, Office of the Secretary, detain the conditions under which personally identifiable information may be disclosed in a variety of contexts. For example, an educational agency may disclose personally identifiable information only on the condition that the party to whom the information is disclosed will not disclose the information to any other party without the prior consent of the parent. 34 CFR § 99.33(a)(1).

[8] 42 U.S.C.A. § 12111 et seq. (1995). *See also* 29 U.S.C.A. § 794 (1985 & supp. 1995), known as Section 504 of the Rehabilitation Act of 1973, a precursor to the ADA, but applicable only to entities receiving federal funds.

arate medical files, and, with limited exceptions,[9] treated as a confidential medical record.[10]

Recently proposed regulations[11] under the Pupil Protection Rights Amendment of 1994 to the General Education Provisions Act[12] interpret and implement that statute's requirements regarding the use of student surveys. Under the statute, schools are required to make available to parents for inspection instructional material that will be used in connection with any survey, analysis and evaluation as part of any applicable program.[13] Schools are also required to obtain prior written parental consent before directing students to submit to any survey that reveals personal information including, but not limited to, political affiliations, sexual attitudes and self-incriminating behavior.[14] The regulations define an "applicable program" as any program for which the Secretary or Department of Education has administrative responsibility. Thus, the regulations interpret the inspection and notice provisions to apply only to those surveys, analyses or evaluations designed or implemented by the school with money received from the Department of Education.

B. State Law

1. Florida

Florida's General Education Provisions § 228.093 explicitly set forth the legislature's intent to protect the rights of students and their parents with respect to student records.[15] The statute grants students and parents rights of access, rights of challenge, and rights of privacy with respect to these records. Like the federal Buckley Amendment, [16] schools may not release student records to anyone, with the exception of certain individuals and organizations, without the written consent of the student's parent or guardian, or pursuant to a court order upon the condition that parents and students are notified prior to the release of the records. The exempted individuals include, but are not limited to, school officials and teachers who have a legitimate educational interest in the records, offi-

---

[9] An employer may inform a supervisor or manager regarding work restrictions and necessary accommodation, first aid and safety personnel regarding emergency treatment, and government officials investigating compliance with the ADA, 42 U.S.C.A. § 1211(d)(3)(B)(1) to (iii).

[10] 42 U.S.C.A. § 1211 (d)(3)(B).

[11] 60 Fed. Reg. 44.696 (to be codified at 34 CFR § 98).

[12] 20 U.S.C.A. § 1232(h) (1990 & Supp. 1995).

[13] 20 U.S.C.A. § 1232(h)(a).

[14] 20 U.S.C.A. § 1232(h)(b).

[15] FLA.STAT.ANN. § 228.093(1) (West 1989).

[16] *See* supra note 4 and accompanying text.

cials of other schools in which the student seeks to enroll, authorized representatives of state educational authorities, and in connection with an emergency, appropriate emergency personnel if knowledge of such information is necessary to protect the health or safety of the student or other persons.[17]

Florida's Public Health Law § 394.359(9) provides that clinical records are confidential and do not lose their confidential status by either authorized or unauthorized disclosure to any person or organization.[18] No part of the clinical record may be released except to certain individuals or organizations, including but not limited to, persons or agencies with the consent of the patient, the parent or a mentally ill person who is being treated by a mental health facility, and researchers, provided that the identity of the individual is protected. A surprisingly broad provision provides that "[w]henever a patient has declared an intention to harm other persons, such declaration may be disclosed."[19] Notably, the statute also protects agencies and mental health practitioners acting in good faith from a civil or criminal liability for releasing information pursuant to these provisions.[20]

Florida's General Provisions Law § 381.004 addresses the confidentiality of HIV test results.[21] The identity of a person who has been tested and his or her test results are confidential. No person may disclose such information except to certain individuals, including but not limited to, the subject's legally authorized representative, third party payer (with the subject's consent) and health care providers for the purposes of diagnosis and treatment.[22] Florida law contains no provision regarding the disclosure of HIV test results to individuals exposed to the virus through contact with the test subject.

2. California

California Education Code[23] governs the privacy of pupil records and, with limited exceptions, permits access to individuals or organizations only with the written consent of the student's parent or pursuant to a court order.[24] Like Florida law, the exceptions include, but are not limited to, school officials and teachers who have a legitimate educational interest in the records, officials of other schools in which the student

---

[17] *See* FLA. STAT. ANN. § 394.459(9) (West. 1993).
[18] FLA.STAT.ANN. § 394.459(9) (West. 1993).
[19] FLA.STAT.ANN. § 394.459(9)(e).
[20] FLA.STAT.ANN. § 394.459(9)(g).
[21] FLA.STAT.ANN. § 381.004.
[22] FLA.STAT.ANN. § 381.004(3)(f)(1) to (12).
[23] CAL. EDUC. CODE § 49073 et seq. (West 1993 & Supp. 1995).
[24] CAL. EDUC. CODE § 49077.

seeks to enroll, authorized representatives of state educational authorities, and in connection with an emergency, appropriate emergency personnel if knowledge of such information is necessary to protect the health or safety of the student or other persons.[25]

The Confidentiality of Medical Information Act[26] governs the disclosure of medical information, declaring that, subject to certain exceptions, no provider of health care shall disclose medical information regarding a patient without prior authorization.[27] However, a health care provider may disclose medical information to other health care providers for the purposes of diagnosis and treatment, to the entity responsible for paying for the health care services (to the extent necessary to allow responsibility for payment to be determined) and to other specified individuals and organizations.[28] A recipient of medical information pursuant to an authorization may not further disclose that information except in accordance with a new authorization.[29] Interestingly, California law permits a provider to release, even in the absence of a specific written request by the patient to the contrary, a patient's name, address, age, sex, general description of the reason for treatment, and the general condition of the patient.[30]

California law prohibits the negligent or willful disclosure of HIV test results absent written authorization.[31] Test results may be disclosed without authorization to the subject of the test, his or her representative, and to the subject's health care providers for the purposes of diagnosis and treatment.[32] Disclosure of HIV test results does not authorize further disclosure unless otherwise permitted by law.[33] California law also provides for the disclosure of positive test results, under certain circumstances and without any identifying information, to a person reasonably believed to be a spouse, sexual partner or person with whom the patient has shared the use of hypodermic needles.[34]

3. New York

Unlike both Florida and California, New York does not have a provision addressing the confidentiality of student records generally. However, a New York statute entitled Children with Handicapping

---

[25] CAL. EDUC. CODE § 49076(a) and (b).
[26] CAL. CIV. CODE § 56 et seq. (West. 19082 & Supp. 1995).
[27] CAL. CIV. CODE § 56.10
[28] CAL. CIV. CODE § 56.10©(1) to (11).
[29] CAL. CIV. CODE § 56.13.
[30] CAL. CIV. CODE § 56.16.
[31] CAL. HEALTH & SAFETY CODE § 199.21 (West. 1990 & Supp. 1995).
[32] CAL. HEALTH & SAFETY CODE § 199.215(a).
[33] CAL. HEALTH & SAFETY CODE § 199.215(b).
[34] CAL. HEALTH & SAFETY CODE § 199.215.

Conditions[35] does provide that an education department has a duty to ensure the confidentiality of any personally identifiable data, information or records collected or maintained by the state Department of Education, and any school district, including its employees.[36] New York law also provides that any information concerning persons applying for or receiving vocational rehabilitation derived from state or agency records may not be disclosed without the consent of the applicant or recipient.[37] Such state or agency records are confidential and privileged information.

New York's Education Law authorizes school authorities, with the written consent of a parent or guardian, to conduct drug detection tests on junior high and high school students.[38] The results of these tests are confidential and may not be used for law enforcement purposes. However, the law does provide for the results to be forwarded to school authorities and reported to the local social services department in the event of a positive test result. School authorities are then required to report the results to the student's parent with a statement concerning available drug prevention programs.

New York's Mental Hygiene Law provides that clinical records that are required to be maintained at licensed facilities are confidential and shall not be part of the public record.[39] Clinical records or information may not be released except to certain specified individuals or agencies, such as attorneys representing patients in involuntary hospitalization proceedings, an endangered individual, and a law enforcement agency when a treating psychiatrist or psychologist has determined that a patient represents a serious and imminent danger to that individual, or with the consent of the patient, persons and entities who have a demonstrable need for such information.[40] The statute also provides that "[a]ny disclosure made pursuant to this section shall be limited to that information necessary in light of the reason for disclosure [and] shall be kept confidential by the party receiving such information and the limitations on disclosure in this section shall apply to such a party."[41]

Finally, similar to the laws of the other states surveyed, New York law contains exhaustive provisions regarding the confidentiality of HIV-

---

[35] N.Y. EDUC. LAW § 4401 et seq. (McKinney 1995).

[36] N.Y. EDUC. LAW § 4403.

[37] N.Y. EDUC. LAW § 1007 (McKinney 1988).

[38] N.Y. EDUC. LAW § 912(a) (McKinney 1988).

[39] N.Y. MENTAL HYG. LAW § 33.12 (McKinney 1988 & Supp. 1995).

[40] N.Y. MENTAL HYG. LAW § 33.13(c)(1) to (11).

[41] N.Y. MENTAL HYG. LAW § 33.13(f). This section begs the question of whether a person who receives such information can be enjoined from further disclosure consistent with the First Amendment. As set forth *infra*, the answer lies in a balancing of the right to confidentiality with the strength of the interest in disclosing such information.

related information.[42] Specifically, the Public Health Law provides that, subject to certain exceptions similar to those of other states, "[n]o person who obtains confidential HIV related information in the course of providing any health or social service...may disclose or be compelled to disclose such information."[43] The exceptions concerning when and to whom information can be released include, but are not limited to, health care providers or facilities when knowledge of the information is necessary to provide appropriate care, foster care and adoption agencies, and with the protected individual's authorization, insurance companies.[44] Physicians may, under specified conditions, disclose confidential HIV-related information to a contact[45] without disclosing the protected individual.

II. THE LIMITATIONS OF CONFIDENTIALITY STATUTES

A recent New York case illustrates the limitations of statutes intended to protect the confidentiality of student records. In *Hendrick Hudson Central School District v. Falinski*,[46] the school district brought suit against an elementary school principal, her attorney and two private citizens in an attempt to enjoin them from distributing copies of disciplinary charges brought against the principal which contained information concerning individual elementary school students. The school district previously had suspended and brought disciplinary charges against the principal in conjunction with her alleged denial of special educational services to these students. The defendants' attorney distributed copies of redacted charges in an apparent attempt to clarify the nature of the disciplinary charges to the community. The school district subsequently filed suit alleging that "the distribution of the redacted charges[47] or any other information which reasonably tended to identify the subject students violated various confidentiality laws and regulations."[48] One of those laws was the Buckley Amendment.[49]

The lower court denied the school district's motion for preliminary injunction with respect to the two private citizens and granted the motion

---

[42] *See* N.Y. PUB. HEALTH LAW §§ 2782 to 2785 (McKinney 1993 & Supp. 1995).

[43] N.Y. PUB. HEALTH LAW § 2781(1).

[44] *See* N.Y. PUB. HEALTH LAW § 2781(1)(a) to (p).

[45] A contact is "an identified spouse or sex partner of the protected individual or person identified as having shared hypodermic needles or syringes with the protected individual." N.Y. PUB. HEALTH LAW § 2780(10).

[46] 626 N.Y.S.2d 255 (2d Dept. 1994).

[47] Although the redacted charges deleted the students' names, they still contained various personal information about the elementary school students.

[48] 626 N.Y.S.2d at 256.

[49] *See supra note* 4 and accompanying text.

with respect to the principal and her attorney so that they were prohibited from disclosing any personally identifiable information about the students involved or from distributing unredacted charges. The appellate
division affirmed, stating, "the confidentiality laws and regulations upon
which the plaintiff relies are not applicable to private citizens."[50] In other
words, the court determined that the Buckley Amendment cannot form
the jurisdictional basis for a private cause of action against private citizens for the redistribution of confidential special education information.
It appears that the result in this case would be the same whether or not
private citizens obtained confidential special education or medical
records lawfully or unlawfully.[51]

In a similar case, *Maynard v. Greater Hoyt School District*,[52] the parents of an autistic child brought suit against the school district, school
board members, a newspaper reporter and an individual for releasing
personally identifiable information about their son. The school board disclosed information about the district's financial expenditures, as required
by South Dakota law, that involved the cost of our of state special education for the autistic child. Several local newspapers reprinted the information and individuals further disseminated the information. Stating that
the Buckley Amendment does not provide a private right of action,
the court observed that the claim may only be brought pursuant to 42
U.S.C. § 1983 for the violation of the plaintiff's federal rights.[53] However,

---

[50] 262 N.Y.S.2d at 256.

[51] The dismissal of the action against the private citizens resulted in an action brought
by the two private citizens against the school district and most of the board members
in their official and individual capacities pursuant to the Civil Rights Act of 1871. 42
U.S.C. § 1983, alleging that their First Amendment rights have been violated, malicious prosecution and defamation. *Mazza v. Hendrick Hudson Cent. Sch. Dist.* 94 Civ.
8463 (BDP). As demonstrated by the factual pattern of the case, Boards of Education
have a serious dilemma. Do they refrain from bringing disciplinary charges against
staff members because information on students and their parents may be exposed to
the glare of the public scrutiny? If a Board of Education does bring such disciplinary
charges, it risks civil rights actions by parents. And, according to this case, there is
nothing a Board of Education can do to eliminate such potential liability.

[52] 876.F. Supp. 1104 (D.S.D. 1995).

[53] Interestingly, the court noted that even where a cause of action can be stated under
§ 1983, the Buckley Amendment does not provide a comprehensive enforcement
mechanism which would provide plaintiffs with the relief they sought, namely, monetary damages and the prevention of future release of confidential information. Under
the Buckley Amendment, the enforcement scheme is structured to deny federal funds
to educational agencies that violate it. See 20 U.S.C.A. § 1232(g)(a)(1)(A).

In a separate administrative ruling, the Department of Education determined that
the school district did violate the Family Education Rights and Privacy Act, despite the
South Dakota law that required the release of the district's financial expenditures.
However, the Department of Education decided not to deny federal funds to the district. 20 IDELR 105 (1995).

because §1983 applies only to state actors, the plaintiffs only stated a claim for relief against the school district and school board members. The court ultimately granted summary judgment in favor of the defendants, finding that they enjoyed qualified immunity in their individual capacities and were immune from suit in their official capacities.

The implications of these cases are clear: once confidential special education records "fall into the wrong hands," a school district or parent may be restricted in the legal actions they can take to prevent further distribution. Nevertheless, while the Buckley Amendment may not provide the jurisdictional basis to enjoin private citizens from the dissemination of special education information, a court relying on the Buckley Amendment or other appropriate statutes may possess certain inherent powers to issue protective orders and to take other measures to protect the confidentiality of information contained in records that are central to the case being adjudicated before the court or an administrative agency or body, such as the disciplinary proceedings against the principal in *Hendrick Hudson*. The issue then arises as to the power of a court to enjoin a private citizen from further redistribution based upon such inherent powers.

For example, a court's inherent supervisory power included the right to seal its records and "access has been denied where court files might have become a vehicle for improper use."[54] In *Webster Groves School District v. Pulitzer Publishing Co.*,[55] a newspaper publisher sought access to a court proceeding involving a student with a disability. In that proceeding, much of the evidence expected to be before the court consisted of confidential information. The Eighth Circuit determined that "[i]n order to safeguard the confidentiality of such information in judicial proceedings, it is...appropriate to restrict access to the courtroom and the court file."[56] The Court also found that the publisher's interest in access to the records was outweighed by the student's privacy interest and the state's interest in "protecting minors from the public dissemination of hurtful information."[57] Thus, by closing the judicial proceedings and seal-

---

[54] *Nixon v. Warner Communications, Inc.* 435 U.S. 589, 598 (1978).

[55] 898 F.2d 1371 (8th Cir. 1990).

[56] *Id.* at 1375.

[57] *Id.* at 1377.

[58] Federal Rule of Civil Procedure 26(c) provides, in part: "upon motion by a party...and for good cause shown...the court... may make any order which justice requires to protect a party or person from annoyance, embarrassment, oppression, or undue burden or expense."

See e.g. Martinez v. Brazen, No. 91 Civ. 7769, 1992 WL 93245 (S.D.N.Y. Apr. 22, 1992) (sealing the court file to protect the confidentiality of HIV status of litigant in part due to the "substantial embarrassment of discrimination" that may result from

ing the court records, the Court effectively protected the student's confidential special education information from disclosure.

A court may also grant protective orders involving discovery materials where a party seeking the protective order can demonstrate "good cause" exists for the protection of the material.[58] Indeed, the U.S. Supreme court has upheld "gag orders" against a newspaper from disclosing information that it learned as a party to a lawsuit in a pre-trial discovery.[59] Similarly, in *International Products Corp. v. Koons*,[60] the Second Circuit upheld, in part, a district court's order sealing the deposition of the plaintiff corporation's president where questions were asked as to payments by plaintiff's officers to officers of a South American government. The U.S. Attorney had previously filed a Suggestion of Interest with the district court, stating that limiting disclosure would further the foreign policy objective of the United States. Appellants contended that the district court's order deprived them of their right to freedom of speech and to proper preparation of their case in violation of the First and Fifth Amendments. In stating that "we entertain no doubt as to the constitutionality of a rule allowing a federal court to forbid the publicizing, in advance of trial, of information obtained by one party from another by use of the court's processes," the Court instructed the district court to modify its order so as to make it clear that no restrictions are imposed upon the use of information that a party has obtained independently of the court's processes.[61]

---

disclosure); *Priest v. Rotary*, 98 F.R.D. 755 (N.D. Cal. 1983) (granting protective order to plaintiff in employment discrimination suit to prevent further discovery of questionably relevant information about plaintiff's sexual history in part due to the 'annoyance and discomfort' suffered by plaintiff as a result of the defendant's inquiries).

[59] *Seattle Times v. Rhinehart*, 467 U.S. 20 (190984).

[60] 325 F.2d 403 (2d Cir. 1963).

[61] *See also Proctor & Gamble Co. v. Bankers Trust Co.*, 900 F. Supp. 186.192 (S.D. Oh. 1995). There, the District Court, relying on the *Seattle Times* case, granted a TRO prohibiting a third party, *Business Week*, from publishing information contained in an amended pleading that was filed under seal. After the district court had granted the TRO, *Business Week*, trying to end run the district court, chose not to seek a hearing before the district court, but instead sought review from the Sixth Circuit Court of Appeals and the U.S. Supreme Court. The Sixth Circuit dismissed *Business Week's* application for lack of jurisdiction. The Supreme Court, in denying *Business Week's* request for a stay of the TRO pending filing of a writ of certiorari, noted that the manner in which Business Week came into possession of confidential discovery information had a bearing on its right to publish such information. After a hearing, the district court reaffirmed its earlier order prohibiting *Business Week* from publishing information from sealed court files. However, in a separate order, the district court unsealed documents, which permitted *Business Week* to publish its article. The Court of Appeals reversed and vacated the district court's order prohibiting *Business Week* from publishing an article disclosing the contents of documents placed under seal. In

Other courts have relied on state statutes to prohibit the disclosure of confidential information. For example, in *Board of Directors of the Palmyra School District v. Palmyra Area Education Association*,[62] a school board sought to enjoin a teacher's association from mailing a newsletter to the homes of students in the district derived from confidential school lists. The court observed that the Pennsylvania legislature, as interpreted by Pennsylvania courts, had granted to a court of common pleas the power to prevent or restrain the commission or continuance of acts contrary to law and prejudicial to the interests of the community or the rights of individuals where there is no adequate and complete remedy at law.[63] It then vacated the trial court's dismissal of the school board's complaint, holding that the trial court erred in concluding that the schoolboard had an adequate and complete remedy at law and the association's use of the information contained in confidential pupil records was not an act contrary to law and prejudicial to the interests of the community and the rights of individuals.

Significantly, various statutes, including the Buckley Amendment and the New York statute on the confidentiality of HIV-related information specifically prohibit re-disclosure of confidential information to any other person, whether or not they are parties to the underlying litigation.[64] Thus it can be argued that a court, in order to protect the integrity of its processes and the privacy of children and their parents who may be witnesses, may issue a protective order prohibiting the dissemination of information adduced as part of the court proceeding. Such a use of protective orders furthers a sound public policy to protect children and the educational process. If parents of students in a school district cannot rely upon the confidentiality of their sensitive medical and educational information with school district officials at all, thereby denigrating the entire educational process.

While a court may have certain authority to protect the disclosure of confidential information, there are a number of competing interests that arise in this context. For example, the *Webster Graoves* case illustrates the tension between a student's privacy interest in the confidentiality of

---

holding that the district court erred in subjecting *Business Week* to a prior restraint where the court perceived a threat to the secrecy of material placed under seal by stipulation of the parties, the court noted that the First Amendment permits a prior restraint on pure speech only under the most compelling of circumstances, which it determined were not present in this case.

[62] 644.A.2d 267 (Pa. Commw. Ct. 1994).

[63] The court noted that the legislature had stated this principle in 42 Pa.C.S. § 931(a).

[64] N.Y. PUB. HEALTH LAW 2785 (McKinney 1993). See also *Michael v. St. Luke's – Roosevelt Hosp. Ctr.*, 199 A.D.2d 195 (1993); *Roth v. New York Blood Crt.*, 157 Misc.2d 122 (Sup.Ct. 1993). Similarly, Rule 65(d) of the Federal Rules of Civil Procedure provides that an injunction may be binding "upon the parties to the action, their officers, agents, servants, employees and attorneys, and upon the persons in active concert or participation with them...."

his or her educational records and the public's First Amendment right of access and the need to maintain public faith in the judicial proceedings by allowing such access. There, the court determined that the student's privacy interests outweighed the public's interest in access to the proceedings. In contrast, in *Doe v. Methacton School District*,[65] the court's balancing test resulted in the unsealing of the court files. The plaintiffs, a minor student and her family, brought suit against a teacher, the school district and school officials for damages arising from the sexual molestation of the student by the teacher. A local newspaper moved to have the court unseal its record. The plaintiffs argued that unsealing the record, despite the use of a pseudonym, could lead to identification of the victim and result in potential embarrassment, emotional trauma, and disparate treatment by other students and teachers. The court, focusing on the fact that the case involved public entities, determined that the public's interest in learning how the school district addressed the issue of sexual molestation and whether the threat of abuse is taken seriously, outweighed the student's privacy interest.[66] The tension between these competing concerns continues to challenge courts.

Similarly, competing interests may arise within the context of school district financial and business affairs. For example, the public's right to know and participate in the political process and budget deliberations in school districts may potentially conflict with student confidentiality, particularly where the focus turns to the district's special education program.[67]

---

[65] 878 F. Supp. 40 (E.D. Pa. 1995).

[66] The court also noted that the information that would be revealed by unsealing the records would be no more than that revealed in newspaper articles published about the prior criminal proceeding. Furthermore, while not addressed by the Court, the fact that the parents had invoked the court's jurisdiction by commencing the action may lessen the parents' right to privacy. This issue also raises the question of whether this rationale should also apply to a minor.

[67] *See e.g. Board of Directors of the Palmyra Area Sch. Dist. v. Palmyra Area Education Assoc.* 644 A.2d 267 (Pa. Cmwlth. 1994). There, the court was implicitly faced with the competing interest of a teachers' association's interest in contacting families in the school district, in conjunction with its collective bargaining, by mailing a newsletter based on school mailing lists and the school's interest in maintaining the confidentiality of school addresses.

More recently, a school board in Wilkes-Barre, Pa. was confronted with an analogous situation when one of its members, who is the editor and publisher of a local newspaper, was sued for printing information revealed during an executive session of the board. The information involved parents' allegation that their child was the target of political retaliation in this district. There the parents' interest in protecting the confidentiality of the matter and the identity of the child collided with the First Amendment rights and the public's right to know about information allegedly improperly discussed in an executive session of the board. See Tim Gulla, "Crestwood faces dilemma over Grubert's dual role." *Citizens' Voice*, Feb. 19, 1996.

The protection of confidential information may also impinge upon a criminal defendant's Sixth Amendment right to confront his or her accusers. The Supreme Court has addressed the circumstances under which a criminal defendant charged with sex offenses may gain access to a victim's confidential records maintained by a youth services organization. In *Pennsylvania v. Ritchie*,[68] the Court determined that the defendant's inability to search the files for relevant information did not violate the confrontation clause of the Sixth Amendment.[69] Nevertheless, such limitations, while not legally in violation of the Sixth Amendment, adversely affect a defendant's interest by restricting access to a potential source of material with which to undermine the credibility of the complainant's testimony. In order to protect the concerns of both parties, courts should follow the lead of the court in *People v. Manzanillo*, which decided to conduct an in-camera inspection of the complainant's special education records to determine if they contained any material that should be turned over to the defendant pursuant to *Brady v. Maryland*.[70] The potential for this tension to arise in cases where a special education student is the complainant against a school employee in administrative disciplinary proceedings is particularly salient.

III. POTENTIAL LIABILITIES TO A SCHOOL DISTRICT FOR FAILING TO DISCLOSE INFORMATION TO PARENTS

A recent ruling by the Third Circuit in *W.B. v. Matula*[71] demonstrates the extent to which school districts and school officials may be held liable in cases charging discrimination against special education students. There, the Court held that the school district, individual school officials and teachers could be held liable for compensatory and punitive damages for failure to provide the plaintiff's son with a free appropriate public education pursuant to IDEA. This unusual ruling is one of the only cases in which a school district, school officials and teachers were held liable for damages, rather than simply being ordered to pay for private schooling, therapy or other special programs. Although the Court's holding did not rest upon a failure to disclose confidential information, per se, the school officials' failure to inform the plaintiff of her son's entitlement to special education services coupled with their refusal to provide such services despite an inde-

---

[68] 480 U.S. 39 (1987).

[69] *See also People v. Manzanilla*, 145 Misc. 2d 504 (Crim. Ct. N.Y. Co. 1989) (denying the defendant access to complainant's special education records absent a showing that it is reasonably likely that the records will be relevant or material).

[70] 373 U.S. 83 (1963) (holding that the prosecution may suppress any evidence favorable to the defendant if it is material to guilt or punishment).

[71] 67 F.3d 484 (3d Cir. 1995).

pendent evaluation determining that the plaintiff's son did have Attential Deficit Hyperactivity Disorder and therefore was eligible for special educational services under the IDEA informed the Court's ruling.

Other cases have held more explicitly that the failure to disclose certain confidential information to parents can render the district liable. For example, in *Savino v. Board of Education of School District #1, Westbury*,[72] a student and his parent brought a personal injury action against the school district for failing to notify the student's mother of his condition after school evaluations revealed psychological problems. The court affirmed the lower court's denial of the defendant's motion to dismiss for failure to state a cause of action. In *Phyllis P. v. Claremont Unified School District*,[73] a student's mother brought a personal injury action against a school arising out of the sexual assault and rape of her eight-year-old daughter by another student. A teacher and the school psychologist were told of several incidents of sexual molestation but decided not to notify the petitioner. In issuing a writ reinstating the action, the court stated that a special relationship existed between the defendants and petitioner, giving rise to the school's duty to notify petitioner upon learning of the first incidents of assault. The failure to disclose certain information may also subject a school district to a court's injunctive powers. In *John K. v. Board of Education for School District #65*,[74] parents sought access to their daughter's responses to a psychological test administered by the school district after the school district refused to disclose the test results. The court held that the parents could bring an action for injunctive relief under the state School Student Records Act.

More recently, in *Larson v. Miller*[75] the Eighth Circuit struggled to determine whether a superintendent and a Director of Special Services were liable for a conspiracy to violate a family's civil rights by, in part, selectively withholding certain information from them. Larson involved a nine-year-old visually disabled student, Angela Larson, who was sexually abused by Eugene Szynskie, the driver of the van that transported her to school. Upon learning of the incident, Angela's mother immediately contacted school officials. The Director of Special Services, George Spilker, repeatedly warned the Larsons of the risk of a slander suit if the charges proved to be unfounded, stating that it would be Angela's word against the driver's, and implied that bringing charges might cause problems for Angela's brother, a student in the district's high school. Spilker subsequently requested the Chief of Police to run a background check on the van driver.

---

[72] 123 A.D.2d 314 (2d Dept. 1986).

[73] 183 Cal. App.3d 1193 (2d Dist. 1986).

[74] 152 Ill. App. 38d 543 (1st Dist. 1987).

[75] 55 F.3d 1343 (8th Cir. 1995), 22 IDELR 957 (8th Cir.), *vacated by*, 67 F 3d 148 (8th Cir. 1995), *on rehearing*, No. 94-2691, 1996 WL 69674 (8th Cir. Feb. 20, 1996).

Spilker later met with district officials, including superintendent Roger Miller, who reassigned Szynskie and instructed Spilker to tell the Larsons of the change in duties. Spilker informed the Larsons of the reassignment and reiterated his warnings about the risk of a slander suit during that and a subsequent telephone conversation. Several days later, district officials discovered from Szynskie's background check that he had been previously arrested for sexual abuse of a child, although the charges had been dismissed. District officials met again, decided to terminate Szynskie. Miller instructed Spilker to inform the Larsons of the termination but not to reveal the results of the background check. Instead, Spilker told the Larsons that the background check information did not contain anything relevant to the case.

The Larsons ultimately contacted the police and Szynskie was charged and convicted of sexual assault of a minor. The family then brought suit against the school district and several of the district's officials, including Miller and Spilker. The complaint included an allegation that the district's officials had conspired to deny the Larsons their civil rights under 42 U.S.C. § 1985(3). More specifically, the Larsons alleged that the district officials, motivated by an invidiously discriminatory animus against handicapped females, conspired to deny the Larsons' First and Fourteenth Amendment rights by preventing them from reporting Angela's abuse. The jury found for the Larsons and, upon defendants' motion for judgment notwithstanding the verdict, the district court set aside the jury verdict. The Larsons appealed and a panel of the Eighth Circuit held, in part, for the Larsons. However, the Eighth Circuit subsequently vacated the panel's opinion and granted defendants' suggestion for a rehearing en banc. The Eighth Circuit then affirmed the district court's ruling for the defendants in all respects.

In order to prevail on a § 1985(3) conspiracy claim, a plaintiff must establish both the existence of a conspiracy and that a racial or otherwise class-based invidiously discriminatory animus motivated the actions of the conspirators. The Eighth Circuit ultimately held that there was not enough evidence of a conspiracy to support the jury's verdict. The Eighth Circuit did not reach the more consequential issue of whether the handicapped are a protected class under 1985(3).

While the Eighth Circuit has not yet ruled on this issue, the Second Circuit has already determined that the handicapped are a protected class under 1985(3),[76] thus preserving the possibility, given sufficient support-

---

[76] *People by Abrams v. 11 Cornwell Co.*, 695 F.2d 34 (2d Cir. 1982). In contrast, both the Seventh and the Tenth Circuits have rejected this application of § 1985(3). *See, e.g. D'Amato v. Wisconsin Gas Co.*, 760 F.2d 1474, 1486 (7th Cir. 1985); *Wilhelm v. Continental Title Co.* 720 F 2d 1173, 1177 (10th Cir. 1983), *cert. denied*, 465 U.S. 1103 (1984). Nevertheless, this is an open issue for the majority of Circuits.

ing evidence, at least in that Circuit, that school officials could be held liable for conspiring to deny the civil rights of a handicapped student by failing to disclose certain information. Furthermore, given the recent ruling by the Third Circuit[77] holding that school officials may be held liable for compensatory and punitive damages under the IDEA, it is likely that suits against school officials charging discrimination against handicapped students, as well as the legal avenues by which to pursue them will continue to increase.

IV. SUGGESTIONS TO PROTECT THE CONFIDENTIALITY OF SENSITIVE EDUCATIONAL INFORMATION

As various governmental entities, including school districts, collect and maintain more and more highly sensitive and personal information, it is likely that parents of children who may resist providing such information will not and cannot be protected. While it is impossible to set forth specific advice on the myriad factual circumstances giving rise to claims of confidentiality, the following are suggestions for school districts to provide greater assurance that special education and other student records will remain confidential.

- A school district may wish to adopt a policy providing for the confidentiality of its records to the maximum extent permitted by law. The existence of this policy may be helpful to the school district in obtaining protective orders when confidential information is subpoenaed for cases in which the school district is not a party itself.
- School districts should promulgate codes of conduct that made school employees subject to severe discipline for the unauthorized dissemination of confidential information.
- As required by IDEA, school districts should appoint high-ranking officials to coordinate the school district's procedures and practices in maintaining the integrity of its confidential files.
- School districts should regularly conduct training sessions for staff on the handling and dissemination of various types of confidential documents.
- School districts should carefully review and modify where necessary its various filing systems to insure that confidential information is kept separately from other information and that it is kept in a locked and secure place.
- In the context of pursuing disciplinary charges against school district employees, a school district may wish to seek a protective

---

[77] *See supra* note 71 and accompanying text.

order prior to the release of any information to the employee who is charged in order to provide the basis for a court to enjoin any third party who wrongfully receives information from the school district employee. In addition, school districts may choose to redact charges to the maximum extent possible in order to protect the confidentiality of pupils.

- The school district should determine which of its personnel have a need to know particular information. Most school districts do not make an organized effort to limit confidentiality information internally to its staff members who actually must have the information to carry out their duties.

While this article is not an exhaustive treatment of all of the circumstances that may give rise to confidentiality issues, we have attempted to stimulate discussion about how the proper scope of confidentiality in itself stigmatizes special education and other students. It must also be recognized that parents and students do not check their right to privacy at the schoolhouse door by complying with the state's compulsory education laws. In order for school districts to carry out their educational, social services and medical functions with the confidence of parents, these parents must be assured of a zone of privacy for their children.

Reprinted with permission from *Journal of Law and Education,* Vol. 26, No. 3, pp.11–27.

Chapter 6:
Substance Abuse

INTRODUCTION

The American School Counselor Association
(ASCA) takes the position that the primary purpose of school counseling programs is student development (see ASCA position statement, *The Professional
School Counselor and Student Assistance Programs,*
Appendix H–20). And though it recognizes that prevention and development should be the focus, ASCA also
realizes that, in reality, school counselors also cannot
ignore problems that already exist. As such, crisis and
remediation components of school counseling programs
are necessary. This brings us to the legal and ethical
issues of chemical dependence – an issue that school

counselors are often faced with and one in which they need to address through both prevention and intervention (see ASCA position statement, *The Professional School Counselor and Student Assistance Programs,* Appendix H–20).

Whether new or experienced, school counselors need to remain up to date on effective prevention and intervention efforts with students who are experiencing substance abuse problems. Coll (1995) has described a study on school counselors' perceptions about procedures for identifying students with substance abuse problems. He also discussed school counselors' legal obligations related to primary and secondary substance abuse prevention programming. He then concluded with recommendations for adhering to legal mandates while still providing students with the services they need.

This chapter aims to provide insight and guidelines into this intervention and prevention.

Legal Challenges in Secondary Prevention Programming for Students With Substance Abuse Problems

Kenneth M. Coll

The initiation of alcohol and other drug abuse occurs during the school age years (Forman & Linney, 1988). Consequently, schools have been asked to provide both primary and secondary alcohol and drug prevention programming (Bradley, 1988; Erickson & Newman, 1984; Forman & Linney, 1988; Oetteng & Beavais, 1988; Ostower, 1987).

Primary alcohol and drug abuse prevention is defined as incorporating alcohol and other drug abuse prevention content into the school curriculum at different grade levels. (Forman & Linney, 1988). The content of primary prevention programming usually entails teaching about the influence and effects of alcohol and drugs, and teaching personal, social coping and resisting skills. (Forman & Linney, 1988; Severson, 1984).

Recently, there has been a call for schools to incorporate secondary prevention programming as well (Forman & Linney, 1988). Formalized and effective secondary prevention programming is now tied to receiving greater amounts of Federal Safe and Drug Free Schools and Communities monies. Secondary prevention is defined as identification and subsequent intervention programming aimed at high-risk students or students who are already experiencing problems with alcohol and other drug abuse (Severson, 19843. Secondary prevention, often called "Student Assistance Programs," coupled with primary prevention has proven to be quite effective in reducing many alcohol and drug abuse risk factors in youths (Forman & Linney, 1988; Severson, 1984).

Palmer and Paisley (1991) noted that for school-based secondary prevention to be successful, "adults within the school setting need to be proactive in identifying and providing assistance to students with substance abuse problems" (p. 288). They strongly recommended that secondary prevention programming, at all school levels, include formalized procedures for (a) early identification, in which teachers play a key role; (b) assessment for determining the nature and severity of the student's problems (performed by a school counselor with special training in substance abuse); (c) referral to in-school prevention groups or to an outside treatment agency; and (d) follow-up procedures that include in-school after-care groups, if students are referred to treatment programs (Palmer & Paisley, 1991).

Secondary alcohol and drug prevention programming is now considered a necessary part of effective schools because of the reality of student alcohol and drug problems (Palmer & Paisley, 1991). Palmer and Paisley asserted that school counselors are often the key to successful secondary alcohol and drug prevention programming because they are in the best position in terms of training and job function to act as coordinators, consultants, and evaluators for this process. There is some question, however, about how well schools have done in formalizing secondary prevention procedures. This is a salient point, as the legal obligations surrounding secondary prevention programming are many and complex (Office for Substance Abuse Program, 1992). Without formalized school-based secondary prevention procedures, schools and school counselors may be vulnerable to breaking the law and subject to litigation (Office for Substance Abuse Program, 1992).

The purpose of this study was to determine school counselor perceptions about formal procedures for identifying students with alcohol and drug problems and to discuss legal ramifications based on the results. Specific research questions investigated were: (a) What are school counselor perceptions of the existence and effectiveness of formalized procedures for identifying students with alcohol and drug problems in their schools? (b) To what extent are school counselors involved in the identification process? and (c) What are school counselors' estimations of the percentage of students at their schools who are experiencing alcohol and drug problems?

METHOD

Participants

The sample survey included all public school counselors ($N = 216$) in a Rocky Mountain state. All of these school counselors worked for school districts that receive Federal Safe and Drug Free Schools and Communities monies and reported some form of primary and secondary prevention programming in place.

Instrument

The researcher developed a questionnaire that strictly adhered to Dillman's (1978) mail-survey design suggestions and included demographic questions such as gender, ethnic background, level of education, and years of experience. Items related to the research questions included the following:

1. Does your school currently have formalized procedures for identifying students with alcohol and drug problems?
2. Do you think your school's prevention programming is effective in identifying students with possible alcohol and drug problems?
3. What is your involvement in the identification process?
4. What is your estimation of the percentage of students at your school who are experiencing alcohol and drug problems?

Procedure

The State Department of Education provided a mailing list of all public school counselors in the state. One mailing was sent to each counselor's work address that included the questionnaire, an individualized cover letter stating the purpose of the study, a stamped return envelope, and directions for completion of the survey. A second mailing with another copy of the questionnaire was sent 1 month later to those counselors who had not responded. Of the 216 counselors, 124 returned the questionnaires for a return rate of 60%. The Statistical Package for Social Sciences (SPSS) was used to analyze the data in terms of frequencies, means, and percentages.

RESULTS

Of the counselors who responded to the survey, there were slightly more women (54.8%) than men (45.2%), and most of them were Caucasian (94.4%). Most of them had earned a master's degree in counseling (86.3%). Of those surveyed, 27% had been a school counselor for 0 to 5 years, 29% for 5 to 10 years, 19% for 11 to 15 years, 14% for 16 to 20 years, and 11% for over 20 years.

TABLE 1 **School Counselor Responses in Percentages**

Response	Percentage
Formalized procedures at your school for identifying students with alcohol and drug problems.	
We have no formalized procedures	46.0
I don't know if we have any or not	3.8
Yes, we have formalized procedures	50.2
Effectiveness of your school's secondary prevention programming in identifying students with alcohol and drug problems.	
Not effective at all	38.0
I am unsure about its effectiveness	20.2
Yes, it is effective	41.8
The school counselor as an integral part of the identification process.	
No, I am not an integral part	32.0
Yes, I am an integral part	68.0
Estimation of the students at your school who are experiencing alcohol and drug problems.	
Under 5% are experiencing these problems	38.0
6% to 10% are experiencing these problems	20.2
11% to 20% are experiencing these problems	31.8
Over 20% are experiencing these problems	10.0

Note. N=126.

As indicated in Table 1, when asked about their school-based formalized procedures for identifying students with alcohol and drug problems, 46% of the counselors indicated that their school did not have any formalized procedures, 50.2% indicated that their school had instituted formalized procedures, and 3.8% said they did not know. When asked about the effectiveness of their school prevention programming in identifying students with possible alcohol and drug problems, 38% of the counselors surveyed indicated that their programming was not effective in identifying such students, 20.2% said that they were unsure, and 41.8% said that their programming was effective in identifying students with possible alcohol and drug problems.

Almost 70% of the counselors said that they were part of the identification process, whether formalized or not. Of the counselors surveyed, 62% indicated that at least 6% of the students in their schools had alcohol or drug problems, 41.8% of the counselors estimated that over 10% of their students had alcohol and drug problems.

DISCUSSION

Generalization of the results of this study is limited to the extent that the respondents are only representative of the population of school counselors in the state surveyed. Additional studies are needed, preferably on a national level, to gain a more complete picture of secondary prevention practices and the legal challenges that those practices create.

Related to the research questions investigated, only half of the school counselors surveyed indicated that their school had a formalized procedure for identifying students with alcohol and drug problems. Furthermore, 58% of the counselors surveyed questioned the effectiveness of their school alcohol and drug prevention programming in identifying students with alcohol and drug problems. Yet, almost half estimated that over 10% of their students had problems with alcohol or drugs, and about 70% of the counselors are involved in identifying students with such problems.

Such a paucity of formalized identification procedures and effective identification processes may lead to serious difficulty in assuring student confidentiality, thus leaving schools and school counselors highly vulnerable to legal problems. Huey and Remley (1988) noted that lack of formal guidelines and procedures, especially for confidentiality and record keeping, is a major ethical and legal problem for schools and school counselors. This is especially problematic when engaged in secondary prevention programming.

Two recent federal laws and a set of federal regulations, called "Confidentiality of Alcohol and Drug Abuse Patient Records" (42 U.S.C. 290 dd-3 and ee-3; 42 CFR Part 2) issued by the U.S. Department of Health and Human Services, now guarantee confidentiality of youths receiving alcohol and other drug services. These laws and the resulting regulations protect information about a youth who has received alcohol or drug related services of any kind, including school-based identification (Office for Substance Abuse Program, 1992). Under these regulations, any individual making impermissible disclosure faces a criminal penalty—a fine of up to $5,000 for each disclosure and civil liability for damages.

Recommendations

I believe that formalizing and incorporating the following recommendations, with an understanding of current legal implications, in school-based secondary alcohol and drug prevention programming can significantly increase service delivery effectiveness and reduce the legal risk that may be present for many school counselors. Furthermore, developing formalized procedures from these recommendations can strengthen the position of school districts when competing for Federal Safe and Drug Free Schools and Communities monies.

Identification. FOT greater prevention effectiveness, identification of students experiencing problems with alcohol or drugs should occur as early as possible, before the user gets emotionally involved with the drug of his or her choice (Palmer & Paisley, 1991). On-site services, such as group and individual counseling, can then be delivered to help prevent a large number of these students from progressing into addiction. Palmer and Paisley (1991) recommended a deep involvement of teachers in this identification process, as part of a student assistance team.

Legal implications. When a teacher, counselor, or any other school professional identifies student behaviors that could indicate alcohol and drug problems, discussing the student with other school personnel or with members of a student assistance team is not in violation of the federal laws and regulations until the student has been evaluated or counseled. Nevertheless, from the time an evaluation is conducted and the student assistance program begins alcohol and drug related counseling, school personnel must comply with the federal regulations for confidentiality (Office for Substance Abuse Program, 1991).

Assessment. When identification occurs, conducting an assessment is recommended, possibly performed by a school counselor or a contracted agency counselor with appropriate training in adolescent alcohol and other drug abuse (Palmer & Paisley, 1991). The assessment can determine the nature and severity of the student's problem. The problem may not be related to alcohol and other drug abuse. It may involve family, academic, or other types of problems. As Palmer and Paisley (1991) noted, "the important issue is, of course, to provide assistance regardless of the cause of the problems" (p. 290).

Legal implications. When a student is assessed for alcohol or drug problems, regardless of the outcome of the assessment, the federal regulations apply because, that youth has been identified "as an alcohol or other drug user (either explicitly or implicitly)" (Office for Substance Abuse Program, 1992; p. 3). This rule applies from the time an appointment is made for an assessment.

Referral. Referral to in-school programs, self-help groups outside the school, or to a treatment facility may be appropriate, depending on the assessment outcome (Palmer & Paisley, 1991).

Legal implications. When referring a student to outside agencies, the client's written consent, not parental consent, is needed. Federal regulations permit disclosures without the client's consent in several situations, including medical emergencies, clear and imminent danger to self or others, reports of child abuse, and consultation made within a school student assistance program (Office for Substance Abuse Program, 1991). A student may revoke consent to disclose information at any time, and a written consent form must include a statement to that effect. It is recommended that the consent form also include the date or condition on which the consent will expire, if not previously revoked by the student.

Adhering to these federal regulations about consent may conflict with The Family Educational Rights and Privacy Act (FERPA). FERPA requires that schools give parents the right to inspect and review the educational records of their children. The one exception applicable to K-12 schools are records that are in the sole possession of the maker, that is, a counselor's personal case notes or a teacher's personal notes about a student, but these records become subject to FERPA if they are shown to anyone else (Western Regional Center, 1992).

The records of school-based alcohol and drug programs are generally subject to FERPA, as these programs are part of a school, or are developed under contract for a school. The conflict between FERPA regulations and the confidentiality regulations arises when, for example, a school counselor is asked about a student, who is under 18 years of age and is protected under the confidentiality regulations, by that student's parent to discuss progress in a school-based secondary prevention program. If the student has refused consent, the school counselor cannot legally confer with the parent. If the parent then asks to review his or her child's program records, the school counselor faces a conflict between the two laws. The conflict between these laws is yet to be resolved, but many argue that the confidentiality statutes, which are more specific, should take precedence (Western Regional Center, 1992). Regarding referral to outside treatment services, the school counselor (or another school professional) cannot notify parents that their child is in treatment, without the child's consent, unless the previously mentioned exceptions to confidentiality exist (Office for Substance Abuse Program, 1992).

Follow-up services. Follow-up services (such as in-school aftercare groups) are recommended for those students who have been in treatment, to help them integrate into school and to prevent relapses (Palmer & Paisley, 1991).

Legal implications. Students involved in school-based alcohol and drug treatment follow-up activities are fully protected by the confidentiality regulations (Office for Substance Abuse Program, 1992).

Other Considerations—Criminal Activity

Questions about exceptions to the confidentiality laws and regulations surround the reporting of criminal activity. It is typically legal and ethical for a school counselor to not report a crime, committed or reported by a student, in a school-based secondary prevention program, unless clear and imminent danger is present. Nevertheless, if a student who is protected under the confidentiality regulations reports an extremely serious crime (homicide, rape, kidnapping, armed robbery, assault with a deadly weapon, and child abuse and neglect), then the counselor should disclose this information to the appropriate authorities, that is, the police or the district attorney's office. The counselor should first try to get consent from the client, but if he or she cannot, disclosures of this kind are permitted as an exception under the confidentiality regulations. (Office for Substance Abuse Program, 1992).

CONCLUSION

The lack of ineffective and nonexistent formalized procedures, a number of school alcohol and drug prevention programs and the counselors involved with those programs may be legally vulnerable to violating the new Federal Confidentiality statutes concerning alcohol and drug related services. As Palmer and Paisley (1991) noted,

> The problems associated with substance abuse among young people are often complex and sometimes baffling. As schools attempt to address this multifaceted problem, they must do so with long-range planning and the commitment of all personnel including school counselors (p. 292).

That planning now needs to include the development of effective formalized procedures for identifying and assisting students that thoroughly incorporate processes to assure confidentiality per the new federal regulations discussed.

Kenneth M. Coll *is an assistant professor in counselor education and director of the Wyoming Chemical Abuse Research and Education (C.A.R.E.) Program. Correspondence regarding this article should be sent to Kenneth M. Coll, P. O. Box 3374 University Station, University of Wyoming, Laramie, WY 82071-3374.*

REFERENCES

Bradley, D. F. (1988). Alcohol and drug education in the elementary school. *Elementary School Guidance & Counseling, 23,* 99–105.

Dillman, D. A. (1978). *Mail and telephone surveys.* New York Wiley.

Erickson, L., & Newman, I. M. (1984). Developing support for alcohol and drug education: A case study of a counselor's role. *The Personnel & Guidance Journal, 62,* 289–291.

Forman, S. G., & Linney, J. A. (1988). School based prevention of adolescent substance abuse: Programs, implementation and future directions. *School Psychology Review, 17,* 550–558.

Huey, W. C., & Remley, T. P. (1988). *Ethical and legal issues in school counseling.* Alexandria, VA: American School Counselor Association.

Oetteng, E. R., & Beavais, F. (1988). Adolescent drug use and the counselor. *The School Counselor, 36,* 11–17.

Office for Substance Abuse Program. (1992). *Legal issues for alcohol and other drug use prevention and treatment programs serving high-risk youth* (Report No. 2). Rockville, MD: U. S. Department of Health and Human Services.

Ostower, E. G. (1987). A counseling approach to alcohol education in middle schools. *The School Counselor, 34,* 209–218.

Palmer, J. H., & Paisley, P. O. (1991). Student assistance programs: A response to substance abuse. *The School Counselor, 38,* 287–293.

Severson, H. H. (1984). Adolescent social drug use: School prevention program. *School Psychology Review, 13,* 150–161.

Western Regional Center. (1992). *Confidentiality of student records: A guide for school districts establishing policies and procedures for alcohol and other drug use student assistance programs* (Cooperative Agreement Number S188A00001). Portland, OR: U. S. Department of Education.

Chapter 7: Rights of Parents

INTRODUCTION

For school counselors, the ideologies of ethics and law probably collide most often when the rights of their minor student clients are not in harmony with the legal rights of the students' parents and guardians. Although school counselors recognize the ethical obligation to their student clients (who are usually, but not always, minors), the laws of the United States dictate that parents or guardians are the legal clients of those who serve minor clients. Counselors outside of schools who provide services to minors deal with the same ethical dilemma.

Although most school counselors report that they seldom find themselves in situations in which they must determine whether or not the obligation is to their student clients or to their clients' parents or guardians, it's still important to review these delicate issues. ASCA has taken the position that students should not be deprived of the services of a school counselor (see ASCA position statement, *The Professional School Counselor and Censorship*, Appendix H–3). Additionally, Kaplan (1997) has reviewed the general area of parents' rights, and Wilcoxon and Magnuson (1999) have focused on the rights of noncustodial parents.

In 1996, the U. S. Supreme Court refused to consider a federal lawsuit in which parents had sued a school system for counseling their child without their permission. The lower court supported the school, saying that counseling does not require parental permission; this position was then reinforced with the Supreme Court's refusal to review. The ASCA position statement, *The Professional School Counselor and Parent Consent for Services*, states that school counselors obtain parental permission for services when required by school policy, but the ASCA position statement does not require permission if there is no school requirement (See Appendix H–14).

Kaplan (1997) has explained that courts have always supported the rights of parents to guide the education of their children but, in the past 20 years, courts have begun to consider the societal rights that sometimes override parents' legal rights over their own children. Despite this trend, parents and legal guardians of children still have the ultimate authority to determine where children live, which schools they will attend, and which values they will be taught at home (see ASCA position statement, *The Professional School Counselor and Character Education*, Appendix H–4). As a result, Kaplan has suggested that school counselors acknowledge the legal rights of parents and find ways to communicate with them. Defying parents or guardians seldom works because their rights to make decisions for their children are legally based.

Noncustodial parents have the same rights to information about their children as custodial parents. Noncustodial parents' rights vary by state, and individual court custody orders regarding these rights vary substantially, too. To help explain this, Wilcoxon and Magnuson (1999) have provided a comprehensive discussion of the meaning of "custody."

It is difficult—and even impossible—for school counselors to interpret legal custody and visitation documents, so they should not attempt to do so. Because of this, school counselors often must rely on parent-provided student custody information; and, if it's not provided or cannot be interpreted, school counselors should ask the parent to explain the custody situation. If a conflict arises between divorced parents, school counselors should ask their principal for legal advice on how to interact with each of the parents involved in the dispute.

Wilcoxon and Magnuson (1999) have offered a number of suggestions for school counselors regarding the inclusion of noncustodial parents in their child's education. They also have suggested that school counselors be sensitive to the concerns of noncustodial parents who wish to be a positive part of their children's lives.

As evidenced by the inclusive content that follows, contemporary school counselors face many challenges when providing services to minor student clients who may either be in conflict with their parents or have parents who have been separated or divorced. Hopefully, this chapter will provide some helpful guidelines for practice in these sensitive areas.

Parents' Rights: Are School Counselors at Risk?

Leslie S. Kaplan

Many parents have serious concerns about their children's public school education. They want not only safe schools but ones in which their children will meet the highest academic standards to prepare them for success in a complex, competitive world.

"Parents' rights" is becoming a rallying cry for a diverse group of parents, some aligned in formal interest groups and others who are simply involved individuals' all genuinely worried about public schools' effectiveness in preparing their children for the future. Some parents' rights champions want to end school counseling and other student-focused programs because they are seen as nonacademic innovations that not only detract from traditional subject instruction but also invade family privacy. Are school counselors at risk?

PUBLIC CONCERNS ABOUT EDUCATION

Although most Americans want public education to effectively instruct their children, they distrust many educational innovations and trends, and their support is fragile (Bradley, 1995b Shanker, 1995). For the past 20 years, polls show public worry about public school safety, discipline, and the academic basics (Bradley, 1995a). In the 1994 Gallup Poll, 37% believed that their community's schools—and 51% believed that the nation's public schools as a whole—have gotten worse in the last 5 years (Elam, Rose, & Gallup, 1994). Moreover, although schooling costs have risen 61% in the past 25 years, only 28% of these dollars goes to the regular education classroom. Part of the money pays for increased special education and school counseling services. For all its costs, therefore, the public sees minimal improvement in student learning (Lindsay, 1995; Miles & Rothstein, 1995).

PARENTS SEEKING EDUCATIONAL CONTROL

Citing parents' rights, some parents are petitioning their congressional representatives and filing in court, seeking broader control over their children's schooling, particularly in areas involved with school counseling. The 1994 Protection of Pupil Rights Amendment to Goals 2000, or the Grassley Amendment, facilitates parents' challenges to schools conducting a student survey, analysis, or evaluation in "any applicable" (i.e., federally funded) program that reveals "private information" without prior written parental consent ("Sen. Grassley Wins Victory for Parental Rights," 1994). This action extends the Hatch Amendment, which directly contests certain school counseling practices (Kaplan & Geoffroy, 1987a, 1987b). In a 1993 counseling challenge, parents in Michigan sued their school division for allegedly counseling their son without parental permission; the Supreme Court recently refused to hear this case, permitting the lower court decision supporting the school to stand ("Supreme Court Update," 1996). Likewise, in 1995, insisting that "the questions should just stick to the academics," and avoid requiring personal disclosures, an Indiana parent sued the statewide testing program to block use of essay questions that asked students to describe themselves and give their opinions on issues such as feminism or the environment (Coles, 1995). Additionally, in 1995 U.S. congressional hearings, parents complained that schools are usurping the family's role as primary teacher of values and urged passage of the Parental Rights and Responsibilities Act to bar government and school officials from interfering with "the upbringing of the child" unless a "compelling governmental interest" is involved (Bradley, 1995c). Finally, the Eagle Forum, a leading pro family organization, calls classroom guidance "child abuse in the classroom" (Schlafly, 1985, p. 24).

PARENTAL CONCERNS AND SCHOOL COUNSELORS

Although frequently opposed to school counseling practices, these parent criticisms often represent reasonable community concerns about the educational reform agenda and do not necessarily reflect the "lunatic fringe" (Bradley, 1995a). The educational "establishment, however, sometimes mistakenly typecasts all educational antagonists as the radical right" or political–religious zealots. Unfortunately, educators who paint critics too broadly, seeking to discount or ridicule this type of radical parental concerns and to prevent radical unfriendly parental involvement in educational issues, may inadvertently alienate other interested but less adversarial parents. They may also miss opportunities to work with parents to identify concerns and work together to strengthen learning for all children.

As educators, school counselors focus on helping students learn more effectively. School counselors understand that students benefit when counselors can prevent or remove obstacles to cognitive learning through guidance and counseling interventions. In this way, school counselors provide the programs, services, and climate for both student academic achievement and personal–social growth.

This article defines parents' rights, offers a school counseling perspective, and recommends ways to work effectively with parents to help children grow and achieve in school.

DEFINING PARENTS' RIGHTS

Generally, parents' rights refers to the traditional common sense belief that parents have the natural prerogative to direct their children's upbringing and education. It is a legal and a generic concept, representing a continuum of beliefs and actions. Not all parents' rights defenders believe or want the same things.

Throughout the continuum, parents' rights are implicit. All parents have them. Most parents, however, are simply interested in their children's school safety and high quality education. They monitor their child's education and work cooperatively with the school to promote their child's learning.

Occasionally, parents become more overtly involved in their child's public schooling. When parents question the child's school experience, most educators will promptly address parents' worries. If, on the other hand, an educator seems uncooperative when the parents ask for information about their child's schooling or desire some action be taken regarding a particular matter, the frustrated parent may openly refer to their rights to direct and control their children's education. For instance, when an educator seems to say, "Your concerns are baseless. You don't need to know. Trust me. I'm the expert," parents may respond, "But it's our *right* to know!" A nonjudgmental parental inquiry may become unpleasantly adversarial if educators seem to reject the parent's legitimate questions. At this point, parents' rights becomes explicit and advances an individual parent's actions along the continuum.

Finally, parents' rights becomes advocacy. Many culturally conservative parents' rights champions pit individual family responsibility against a large, bureaucratic, top-down government model. They believe that government should supplement but not override parents' efforts to educate their children in knowledge and morality. To them, public schools are a wedge between parents and children, teaching values that may contradict values taught at home. Advocates say that children lose respect for their parents when they hear their parents' beliefs overridden in school. They think that weaker families and stronger government result. As a consequence, some parents' rights supporters believe that advancing their cause will not only improve their children's education but will also revitalize families, communities, and American culture.

To culturally conservative advocates, parents' rights also has specific political and legal meanings. It refers to Congress passing the Parental Rights Amendment in all 50 states and allocating public moneys for private or charter schools. This political agenda has already begun to include passing highly restrictive state and federal legislation and regulations to hinder many student-centered, affectively oriented programs in general, and school counseling programs and practices in particular (Kaplan, 1996).

CHANGING VIEWS OF PARENTS' RIGHTS

During the eighteenth and early nineteenth century in the United States, the family was society's primary health, education, and welfare institution. Parental authority over children was unopposed.

As part of the father's economic household, "children were legally accorded higher status than slaves, but they had relatively little independence in their own right" (Whitehead & Crow, 1993, p. 2). In nineteenth century law, parents owed their children food, shelter, and education. Mostly, however, the law did not carefully monitor the parent–child relationship. Parents' legal claims held more weight than the state's, any outsider's, or the child's, unless some compelling justification for interference existed. In short, laws protecting children and regulating family relationships were passed only after parental power abuses became more common (Whitehead & Crow, 1993).

The eighteenth and nineteenth century Industrial Revolution's frequent exploitation of children as factory workers increased calls for more state care of children. Reformers wrote measures to protect children and, if needed, to intervene in family affairs. The emphasis in family disputes began shifting away from parental authority and focused on children's rights. The development of sometimes for the prevention of cruelty to children and juvenile courts illustrate the state's increasing control over children.

A BRIEF LEGAL VIEW OF PARENTS' RIGHTS

Historically, U.S. Courts have supported the parents' rights to guide their children's education. Within the past 20 years, however, the pendulum has swung toward viewing society's needs as more important than the individual parents' (Burron, 1995).

Two 1920s Supreme Court cases established parents common law right to direct their children's upbringing. In *Meyer v. Nebraska* (1923), the Court stated that the 14th Amendment's Due Process Clause generally gives parents the "liberty" to direct their children's education and upbringing. This decision supported parents' cultural preferences over the state's (in this case, for children to be able to team German in public school).

In *Pierce v. Society of Sisters* (1925), the Supreme Court ruled that children can be educated outside of the public schools, noting that parents have the right "to direct the upbringing and education" of their children. This decision permitted parents to sent children to private or parochial schools. (Current parents' rights to home school their children rests with case law or state statute rather than Supreme Court decision.) Together, the *Meyer* and *Pierce* decisions frequently form the basis of current parental rights litigation.

Parental liberty, however, is not absolute. Increasingly, the courts are limiting parental rights and power to control their children's upbringing and education. The government retains a substantial ability to act as parent when natural parents have failed in their duties or when the public good requires action. Limits to parents' rights include matters affecting the child's health or welfare (*Prince v. Massachusetts*, 1944) or mental health (*Yoder v. Wisconsin*, 1972). Limits also include compulsory school attendance, child labor laws, mandatory vaccinations, and prohibiting child endangerment.

Likewise, the Supreme Court guarantees minor children basic due process rights in juvenile court proceedings (*In re Gault*, 1967), and calls them "persons" under the Constitution with fundamental rights (*Tinker v. Des Moines Independent School District*, 1969). Similarly, the Supreme Court makes it illegal to show pornography to persons under age 17, writing that the "state also has an independent interest in the well-being of its youth" (*Ginsberg v. New York*, 1968). Likewise, the Supreme Court restricts public school officials' authority to search students, noting that school officials act as state representatives, not merely as parent surrogates (*New Jersey v. T. L. O.*, 1985). With the cases previously cited, the state repeatedly demonstrates independent interest in youth's welfare and limits parental authority.

Unfortunately, the constitutionality of parents' rights is not clear cut. States offer varying support for this principle. Most recently, the Meyer-Pierce doctrine successfully prevented New York City from distributing condoms to students in schools without parental permission or parents' right to "opt-out" (Massachusetts Supreme Court Rules," 1995). On the other hand, the Massachusetts Supreme Court rejected the Meyer-Pierce doctrine and voted to continue condom distribution to school students, grades 7-12, without either parental notice or consent or the right to "opt-out," ("Massachusetts Supreme Court Rules," 1995).

Together, these decisions confuse and anger some parents about perceived legal assaults on their rights. Parents had always assumed that national case law and common sense protected their authority to have the last word in matters affecting their children. Nonetheless, in recent decisions, the state seems to have an arguable interest in children as "persons of the state" and can limit parents' rights in broad areas, including the child's safety and health (physical and mental), public safety, peace, order, or welfare.

Seeing federal and state supreme courts' decisions giving children certain rights and undermining parental authority, some conservative activists are using these legal challenges and perceived setbacks as rallying points for focusing parental anger against what they view as government encroachment of parents' legitimate interests in laws and in public schools. They enjoin worried parents to seek redress through various means (such as state and national legislation, book challenges, program challenges, and school board elections at the state and local levels) against what some call the "Nanny State" ("Parental Rights," 1995, p.1).

PARENTAL CONCERNS AND IMPLICATIONS FOR SCHOOL COUNSELORS

Certain parent groups vigorously oppose school activities such as teacher advisory, home base classes, classroom guidance, and school counseling programs, which they believe not only deflect critical time and attention away from traditional academic subjects but which also involve children's feelings about personal or private family matters. These parents reject what they view as the cognitive curriculum, addressing intellect and teaching knowledge and skills, being replaced with an affective curriculum or "therapy," which addresses a child's feelings and attitudes. They consider topics involving friendship, self-awareness, decision making, conflict management, and acceptance of individual differences as direct state interference with family values, which may assert that only parents or religious leaders should determine right from wrong in these areas.

Furthermore, some parents object to classroom guidance because they believe that counselors present students with values contrary to those taught at home (Kaplan, 1996). For example, some parents teach their children that particular alternate lifestyles are morally wrong; therefore, teaching that these lifestyles are acceptable undermines what has been taught at home. Other parents object to teaching decision-making skills because they believe that young people should accept decisions made for them by parents or religious authorities and not presume to know better than their elders. Moreover, some parents believe that teaching students the decision-making process will encourage them to make choices that are solely the parents' responsibility to make, and that would also present children with options before they are mature enough to choose wisely.

School Climate and Students' Achievement

Despite objections to their children's involvement in nonacademic pursuits, parents are vitally interested in school safety and the school's learning climate. The 1995 Gallup Poll noted that many people believe that violence and lack of discipline are major problems facing local schools today, as has been the concern in 18 of the past 26 polls (Elam & Rose, 1995). Although parents are not blaming school personnel, respondents remain deeply concerned about the adverse impact of violence and disruption on children's learning. Statistics justify this fear; about 11% of all crimes occur each year in public schools, one crime every 6 seconds (Sautter, 1995). The U.S. Department of Justice estimates that 100,000 children bring guns to school daily (Lantieri, 1995). Thirteen percent of teens say that at least half the students in their schools carry knives and guns (Chira, 1994), and 9% of eighth graders carry a gun, knife, or club to school at least once a month (Sautter, 1995).

No effective learning can occur without a safe and supportive school environment and without students' ability to manage their emotions and behaviors in school. One of school counselors' major contributions to learning and achievement is through programs and practices that teach students critical self-management skills and that build and maintain a safe and caring school climate that actively supports and promotes learning.

School counselors address these important school climate and learning issues through developmental guidance and counseling programs that stress conflict resolution strategies, problem-solving skills, and appreciation for self and others. School counselors know that upset students will not effectively attend to classroom instruction until they resolve and end internal distractions.

New Research Support for School Counseling Programs

Newly published human brain research strongly supports guidance and counseling's clinical experiences and reinforces teaching emotional and behavioral self-management through group or individual means to improve classroom learning. Brain research now tells us that "emotion is a very important educative process be cause it drives attention, which drives learning and memory" (Sylwester, 1995, p. 72). Emotion is often a more powerful determinant of human behavior than are logical or rational processes. The research reveals that the limbic system—the brain's principal emotion regulator—influences the selection and classification of experiences into memories and is powerful enough to override rational thought (Sylwester, 1995). Likewise, counseling and guidance programs teach students to use certain self-management techniques to override their emotions with logical and rational processes. Additionally, classroom activities with high personal meaning, as found in guidance lessons and demonstrated with role playing and simulations, enhance learning because they tie real life emotion to curriculum in kinds of authentic emotional contexts in which they will later be used (Sylwester, 1995).

Similarly, research conducted in schools also supports using counseling and guidance programs to support student learning. Studies find that for elementary and middle school students using the classroom guidance format and content to teach and practice self-management strategies actually leads to increased academic achievement (Blum et al., 1995; Hawkins, VonCleve, & Catalano, 1991) as well as other personal, social, and school climate gains (Caplan et al., 1992; Elias, Gara, Schuyler, Branden-Muller, & Sayette, 1991; Greenberg Kusche, Cook, & Quamma as cited in Goleman, 1995; Solomon et al. as cited in Goleman, 1995). It is reasonable to assume that a classroom with increased student focus on learning, improved self discipline, better planning for cognitive tasks, and reduced discipline referrals will be a classroom where more academic learning occurs. Furthermore, research suggests that advisory groups in which educators and students develop more personal and caring relationships apart from the traditional academic relationships are associated with reduced dropouts (Epstein & MacIver, 1990).

As educators, school counselors must find ways to reconcile belief in developmental programs that foster students' health, wellness, safety, self-management, and academic learning with the views of parental rights. School counselors can provide evidence of students' academic growth along with clear rationales that affective programs support student learning.

PARENTS' RIGHTS AND SCHOOL COUNSELORS: RECOMMENDATIONS AND CONCLUSION

Although parent involvement is a key element of school reform, the parents' rights era has created a climate of distrust and occasional antagonism between some parents and public schools. Today's school counselors are often targets of this attack.

Focus on Academics

Student learning and achievement have always been school counselors' ultimate concern, but the message may have become clouded in efforts to enhance students' affective growth. Nevertheless, school achievement for all students must continue to be given the highest and most visible priority, and every school program and activity should convey and celebrate high expectations for all students.

Classroom success for all students is the reason public schools have counselors. Although students' mental health and personal growth are means to this end, school counselors remain educators who use a variety of educational and mental health strategies to help students succeed. Effective school counselors provide leadership or participation in child study activities, student assistance programs, and active consultation with teachers and parents to create school success for students. The goal of school counseling is for students to achieve well in school.

In addition, although school counselors do not traditionally deal with student discipline, counselors might deliberately tie counseling strategies to improved classroom behavior for students who impair their learning (and that of their classmates) with immature or dysfunctional behaviors. Study skills groups that deal will work habits and time management techniques may have direct and observable impact on student achievement. Classroom achievement has a positive impact on students' self esteem. Moreover, connecting the guidance staff with the instructional staff in new and important ways may create new and beneficial working arrangements for both students and educators.

Focus on Communications

School counselors can offer more effective communications to parents and the community about how the school counseling programs promote student achievement. This means listening carefully to parent concerns without undue defensiveness regarding the school or the counseling and guidance components. It means accepting and actively promoting the goal of helping students leant more effectively as counselors' ultimate program focus.

Parent advisory groups become essential supports for school counseling programs. The more counselors listen to and address parents' concerns, the more counseling programs can support parents' and students' interests. More over, the more knowledgeable parents are about how the school counseling program advances students' learning and achievement through guidance, counseling, consultation, and parent education, the more parents can refute fear-based allegations from parents' rights advocates and prevent uninformed parents from being persuaded to join them.

Better communications also means working with school boards to protect children's access to affective programs by having dear board policies regarding curriculum challenges to developmental guidance and counseling programs (Brigman, 1996) as well as challenges to school counseling itself. Counselors can communicate clearly and directly with their principals and their local school boards about how counseling and guidance programs support students' learning, and they can recommend practices to prevent and address parental challenges. School boards need counselors' and administrators' input for policies that support parents making informed decisions, but that also permits students to have access to school counselors.

Likewise, school counselors can work with their counseling peers to discuss and decide ways to more actively involve parents in decision making involving their children. Confidentiality issues in school need to be reviewed in the context of parental concerns and revised ethical guidelines concerning students under age 12. The American School Counselor Association code encourages recognition of the important role parents can play in maximizing the counseling relationship's benefits (Huber, 1996). Therefore, counselor–parent communications might increase in frequency and depth to reassure and involve parents sooner about their child's well-being and classroom success. Increasing communication between counselors and parents can only support children's learning.

Finally, school counselors can listen to parents' questions without resorting to "Trust me, I'm the expert" evasions. At a minimum, parents want to be partners in their children's education. Welcoming parent involvement without defensiveness or patronizing can ensure the cooperative relationships that best support student learning and growth.

Focus on Research

Educators working toward change will want to see a positive impact on students' learning. This means systematically studying students' actions.

Although most school counselors lack statistical sophistication, new research methodologies permit practitioners to enhance observations and analysis of students with meaningful data (Irvin, 1994). Surveys, quantitative or qualitative studies, action research, or a variety of other means to assess their counseling programs' impact on student learning are available. Such data will contribute to making informed decisions and help educators maintain a clear and accountable focus on student learning.

Practitioners can work with local colleges to design and collect data that can refine efforts to increase students' achievement. Universities can offer staff development in designing, conducting, and using various types of practitioner research. They can work with school counselors, administrators, and teachers to create practitioner-university work teams to conduct meaningful research studies in classrooms. Through active involvement, counselor educators can better inform themselves and pre-service counselors about school counseling practice realities.

CONCLUSION

In a complex and changing society, parents worry about their children's safety, health, welfare, and education. The parents' rights movement relates to a wide range of parent concerns about their children's well-being in school.

To the parents' rights political activists, the school's valuing of students' affective dimensions often represents governmental intrusion into family matters and takes time away from important cognitive learning. For these parents, changing school practices to involve parents is not enough. Only removing nonacademic, nonbasics programs such as school counseling will do.

School counselors can learn and practice proactive ways to develop greater parent and community involvement and support for school counseling programs. School counselors can remember that student learning and academic achievement is their ultimate priority, which should be the basis for planning, delivering, communicating, and assessing guidance counseling programs.

Parents who have challenging and unanswered questions about their children's education and safety put school counselors at risk. Effectively addressing student achievement, communication, and research may not satisfy parents' rights advocates whose values oppose public education in general and school counseling in particular. It may, however, reassure and enlist other parents whose implicit rights are equally valid. School counselors need not barricade against parents' rights, but can better listen to each parent's interests and support his or her efforts to raise healthy, well-educated children.

Leslie S. Kaplan *is assistant principal for instruction at Denbigh High School in Newport News, Virginia. Correspondence regarding this article should be sent to Leslie S. Kaplan, 259 Denbigh Boulevard, Newport News, VA 23608.*

REFERENCES

Blum, D. J. S., Bleiweis, M. L., Furick, S., Langholz, J. B., Smith, M. L., Woodley,} K., & Fisher, M. (1995). Counseling makes a difference. School counseling improves student attendance, behavior, and achievement. *Virginia Counselors' Journal,* 23(1), 71–91

Bradley, A. (1995a). Public agenda captures voice of the people. *Education Week*, XV(6), pp. 1, 12.

Bradley, A. (1995b). Public backing for schools is called tenuous. *Education Week*, XV(7), pp. 1, 2.

Bradley, A. (1995c). Schools usurp parents' rights, lawmakers told. *Education Week*, XV(15), pp. 18, 21.

Brigman, G. (1996). Censorship: The debate over what arid how to teach children affects school counselors. *The ASCA Counselor* 33(3), 9.

Burron, A. (1995). Heed community values if you value reform. *Educational Leadership, 53*(2), 92–93.

Caplan, M., Weissberg, R P., Grober, J. S., Sivo, P. J., Grady, K., & Jacoby, D. (1992). Social competence promotion with inner-city and suburban young adolescents: Effects of social adjustment and alcohol use. *Journal of Consulting and Clinical Psychology, 60*(1), 56–63.

Chira, S. (1994, July 10). Teens live with adult concerns. *Daily Press*, pp. 1, A2.

Coles, A. D. (1995). Suit argues essay questions on test in Indiana are psychologically intrusive." *Education Week, XV*(10), 16.

Elam, S. M., & Rose, L. C. (1995). The 27th annual Phi Delta Kappa/Gallup Poll of the public's attitude toward the public schools. *Phi Delta Kappan, 77*(1), 41–56.

Elam, S. M., Rose, L. C., & Gallup, A. M. (1994). The 26th annual Phi Delta Kappa/ Gallup poll of the public's attitudes towards the public schools. *Phi Delta Kappan, 76*(1), 41–64.

Elias, M. J., Gara, M. A., Schuyler, T. F., Branden-Muller, L. R., & Sayette, M.A. (1991). The promotion of social competence: Longitudinal study of a preventive school based program. *American Journal of Orthopsychiatry, 61*, 409–17.

Epstein, J. L., & MacIver, D. J. (1990). National practices and trends in the middle grades. *Middle School Journal, 22*(2), 36–40.

Ginsberg v. New York, 390 U.S. 629 (1968).

Goleman, D. (1995). *Emotional intelligence*, p. 306.

Hawkins, J. D., VonCleve, E, & Catalano, R F. (1991). Reducing early childhood aggression: Results of a primary prevention program. *Journal of the American Academy of Child and Adolescent Psychiatry, 30*(2), 208–217.

Huber, M. (1996). Confidentiality and the minor student. *The ASCA Counselor, 33*(3), 20.

In re Gault, 387 U.S. 1 (1967).

Irvin, J. L. (1994). Middle level research is coming of age. *Middle School Journal, 26*(1), 68–70.

Kaplan, L S. (1996). Outrageous or legitimate: What some parents are saying about school counselors. *The School Counselor, 43*, 165–170.

Kaplan, L. S., & Geoffroy, K. (1987a). The Hatch amendment: A primer for counselors. Part I. *The School Counselor, 35*, 9–16.

Kaplan, L. S., & Geoffroy, K. (1987b). The Hatch amendment: A primer for counselors. Part II. *The School Counselor, 35*, 88–95.

Lantieri, L. (1995) Waging peace in our schools. *Phi Delta Kappan, 76*(5), 386–392.

Lindsay, D. (1995). Report contests huge boost in school dollars. *Education Week*, XV(12), pp. 1, 7.

Massachusetts Supreme Court rules condoms in, parents out. (1995, May/June). *Voice of the People, 1*(4), 3–4.

Meyer v. Nebraska, 262 U.S. 390 (1923).

Miles, K. H., dc Rothstein, R. (1995). Where has the money gone? *Education Week*, XV(12), pp. 36, 44.

New Jersey v. T. L. O., 53 U S. L.W. 4083 (1985).

Parental rights: Where limited government meets family values. (1995). *Voice of the People, 1*(2), 1.

Pierce v. Society of Sisters, 268 U.S. 510 (1925).

Prince v. Massachusetts, 321 U.S. 158 (1944).

Sautter, R. C. (1995). Standing up to violence. *Phi Delta Kappan, 76*(5), K1-K12.

Schlafly, P. (Ed.)(1985). *Child abuse in the classroom. Excerpts from official transcript of proceedings before the U.S. Department of Education* (p. 24). Alton, IL: Pere Marquette Press.

Sen. Grassley wins victory for parental rights. (1994, April). *Education Reporter, 99*, 1.

Shanker, A. (1995). Why schools need standards and innovation. *Education Week, XV* (14), pp. 37, 48.

Supreme court update. (1996, January). *Cases in Point*, 1.

Sylwester, R. (1995). *A celebration of neurons. An educator's guide to the human brain* (p. 72). Alexandria, VA: Association for Supervision and Curriculum Development.

Tinker v. Des Moines Independent School District, 393 U.S. 503 (1969).

Whitehead, J. W., & Crow, A.I. (1993). *Modern parental rights: Issues and limits* (p. 2). Charlottesville, VA: The Rutherford Institute.

Yoder v. Wisconsin, 406 U.S. 205, 232 (1972).

Considerations for School Counselors Serving Noncustodial Parents: Premises and Suggestions

S. Allen Wilcoxon
Sandy Magnuson

Intervention, consultation, and programming for families experiencing divorce have been areas of emphasis within school settings for many years. With increases in incidence of divorce and single-parent homes, sensitivity to such familial concerns has been prominent within school settings. The primary focus of the professional literature has been on work with the custodial parent and children as well as interventions with step-parents and step-children (Little, 1992; Nickerson, 1986; Wilcoxon, 1994). By contrast, commentary concerning noncustodial parents has been focused more on personal concerns of the adult such as loss, reduced contacts with their children, and similar issues (Brody & Forehand, 1990; Wallerstein & Kelly, 1980). Counseling and programming in school settings that would involve the noncustodial parent has been noted only occasionally in the professional literature (cf. Aiello & Humes, 1987; Frieman, 1994).

The inclusion of noncustodial parents in considerations by school counselors is reflected in Standard B.7 of the American School Counselors Association (ASCA) *Ethical Standards* (ASCA, 1992), which states:

The school counselor is sensitive to changes in the family and recognizes that all parents, custodial and noncustodial, are vested with certain rights and responsibilities for the welfare of their children by virtue of their position and according to the law.

Such recognition of "custodial and noncustodial" in Standard B.7 is unique among ACA-affiliate groups regarding ethical precepts of practice. Because of the specific mention of the noncustodial parent in this ethical premise, Standard Bl.1 of the ASCA Ethical Standards becomes particularly pertinent.

The school counselor respects the inherent rights and responsibilities of parents for their children and endeavors to establish a cooperative relationship with parents to facilitate maximum development of the counselee.

Wilcoxon (1994) noted specific examples of concerns affecting noncustodial parents and their children, including adjustments to loss and separation in the early stages of divorce adjustment, issues related to relocation, parenting during custodial visitation, remarriage, and similar developmental needs peculiar to noncustodial parents. Considering these and related issues affecting the relationship between children and their noncustodial parent as well as the ASCA Ethical Standards concerning services to custodial and noncustodial parents, school counselors are faced with some rather distinct questions concerning counseling, consulting and programming to include noncustodial parents. Of particular significance in this matter is whether the role and function of the school counselor might serve to assist in recognizing, involving, encouraging, and supporting the noncustodial parent in order to minimize such inequities. This article offers commentary and suggestions for school counselors seeking to maximize inclusive efforts to involve noncustodial parents in their plans for counseling services in the school setting,

CUSTODY: DEFINITIONS AND DISTINCTIONS

As an initial point of discussion school counselors should have an understanding of the meaning of custody relative to children in their systems. *Custody* is a term used to reflect legal recognition of the decision making rights of adults concerning the care of a minor child (Beis, 1984). In all states, custody is a legal right equally established with birth parents at the time of the birth of a child. Unless otherwise disrupted, custody rights are equivalent between birth parents. Custody rights will remain with birth parents until the child is no longer considered a minor, according to state definitions based upon age or other indices (Schweitzgebel & Schweitzgebel, 1980). However, in instances of departures from typical parental relationships (e.g., divorce, abandonment, death of both parents, etc.), formal changes in custody recognition are rendered by court decision. Custody assignment may be on a temporary basis, in instances such as temporary placement of a child outside the home (e.g., foster care), or on a permanent basis (e.g., grandparents), in instances such as the death of both birth parents.

Custody of minor children is a typical item for formal decision in a divorce decree (Aiello & Humes, 1987). In many cases, the assignment of **sole parental custody** is made at the time of granting a divorce. This decision typically allows one birth parent to have all rights in decision making affecting minor children while the other birth parent has only rights of access to the children, based upon stipulates in the divorce decree, state statues, or both sources of legal standing (Beis, 1984).

Sole parental custody continues to be granted in many divorce decrees. However, the emergence of **joint parental custody** since the late-1970s has become more common in divorce decrees. In comparison to sole custodial recognition, joint parental custody serves to sustain the pre-divorce legal status held by both birth parents concerning parental decision making for their minor children (Arditti, 1992). A situation featuring sole parental custody would mean only the custodial parent could provide parental consent for a school-related function, while a situation featuring joint parental custody would allow either birth parent to offer consent.

Many times, confusion concerning legal custodial status is based upon information concerning **residence** of the minor child or children. In instances of sole parental custody, residence of the child typically lies with the custodial parent, while in instances of joint parental custody, residence can have multiple variations (Arditti, 1992; Aiello & Humes, 1987). An example of such a circumstance might be the alternating residency configuration in two parental homes (e.g., Sundays through Wednesdays with dad and Thursdays through Saturdays with mom). An even more complicated configuration might be residency involving one home where children remain while parents alternate their residency. However, a large majority of joint parental custody circumstances feature a primary residency for children with one parent (Arditti, 1992).

From these comments, one can ascertain that residency is not always reflective of legal custody status held by a birth parent. Specifically, a circumstance in which two elementary-age children reside with their single mother might actually be based upon mutual agreement between the two adults who have joint parental custody rights but have chosen to provide a stable residence for their two children. In this case, there is no noncustodial parent, but there is a primary residential parent for the two minor children. Thus, a school counselor might erroneously conclude sole parental custodial rights are reflected in residency decisions and might not be fully sensitive to the equal legal rights of the nonresident father. In this respect, the school should clarify the actual nature of the custody agreement and its potential impact on decisions related to parental participation feature sole parental custody with the residential parent, it may even be necessary to secure consent for involving the *noncustodial* parent (Wilcoxon, 1994)

In summary, school counselors' attempts to involve the noncustodial and/or nonresidential parent in a comprehensive school guidance program should be based upon a clear understanding of the legal and residential status of each family unit. Failing to do otherwise might create difficulties for both parents and children affiliated with the school system. For purpose of discussion in this article, the term *noncustodial* will be employed, although residency and custody status should be considered when attempting to involve both parents in school-related services and programming.

INITIAL PREMISES: A STARTING POINT

Three significant premises should be examined by counselors attempting to involve the noncustodial parent counseling, consulting, and/or programming within the school setting.

1. A parent is a parent
2. Divorce inevitably creates inequity
3. The primary focus should be on the children

A variety of corollaries derive from these fundamental premises, each of which will be discussed as items of note for school counselors.

A PARENT IS A PARENT

Regardless of legal custodial status or the residential circumstances in a particular family, a parent is still a parent! Parents typically have emotional ties to their children that are usually reciprocated by their children. Whether the parent serves as an adult model, a source of familial heritage, or as a simple participant in their lives, children typically consider their noncustodial parent in their understanding of family (Wall, 1992). Just as with intact nuclear families, parental participation in a comprehensive school program will vary, ranging from limited interest to frequent intrusion within the school setting. However, notions associated with parental stereotypes often affect parental initiative (or school invitations) to participate in the decisions or activities affecting children in the school system (Kruk, 1991). For example, a stereotypical notion of a noncustodial father being uninvolved with his children could serve to prompt expectations among children, faculty, school personnel, and even the father. By contrast, a noncustodial father wishing to avoid the stereotypical expectations associated with his circumstance might overcompensate be coming over involved to the point of imposition within the school setting. Regardless of the vast variety of ways in which either parent or both may be involved in school activities and decisions, adults do not typically abandon their parental status (legal or emotional) in instances of divorce. Thus, school counselors should not anticipate a change in the marital status of parents to signal a change in their interest and participation in the lives of their children.

INEQUITIES

The second foundational premise concerns inequities embedded in divorce decisions. Legally, emotionally, socially, and in many other ways, divorce introduces inequities in lives of both adults and children (Kruk, 1991). The destruction of an obsolete building typically leaves asymmetrical portions of rubble and ruin. In a similar manner, divorce represents an intentional destruction of a relationship that will leave asymmetrical portions of privilege and responsibility, Such inequities are featured aspects of one's post-divorce lifestyle such as finances, access to children, freedom, day, stereotyping, and similar components of one's life (Brody & Forehand, 1990; Little, 1992). From this unequal basis, school counselors seeking to encourage the involvement of a noncustodial parent should not attempt to introduce perfect equity and symmetry into such circumstances. Efforts to accomplish such outcomes will inevitably lead to frustrations, inordinate demands of time, or even perceived alliances. Thus, in attempting to accomplish the elements of ASCA (1992) *Ethical Standards* B.1 and B.7, school counselors should be sensitive to the interrelationship between these initial foundational premises.

NEEDS OF THE CHILDREN

The final foundational premise concerns the needs of the children as the primary focus of the counselor attempting to involve noncustodial parents. In this respect, school counselors should take care to examine the potential impact of programming decisions in terms of their impact upon the lives of children when a noncustodial parent is involved (Wall, 1992; Wilcoxon, 1994). For example, in instances in which unresolved conflict exists between former spouses, a parent conference at which both parents are present may be most equitable but might ultimately be counterproductive on the child's behalf (Frieman, 1994). Thus, the inefficiency of separate parental conferences may be in the best interests of the child. Similarly, requesting that a child be responsible for ensuring that both parents are informed about a school activity may place a harsh and undue burden on the child wishing to ensure the noncustodial parent does not feel a subordinate status.

These three foundational premises can serve as guidelines for introducing and sustaining sensitivity to circumstances involving noncustodial parents in the school counseling program. While no system can feature flawless regard for the needs of everyone, the school setting in uniquely positioned to attend to issues affecting noncustodial parents. The following section offers suggestions in this matter.

SENSITIVITY AND PROGRAMMING SUGGESTIONS

An overarching principle is that school counselors are encouraged to consider the child with a noncustodial parent in terms of familial participation rather than parental participation (Arditti, 1992; Little, 1992). In this way, actions, decisions, and procedures that might typically be developed with residential parents in mind would generate expectations to involve both custodial and noncustodial parents. Various typical and frequent requests come from noncustodial parents that can be addressed within the framework of a comprehensive school-based program. Quite often, noncustodial parents indicate that their greatest frustration derives from the absence of information concerning their children (Kruk, 1991). Whether concerning system-wide functions (e.g., field trips, sponsored activities) or occasions specifically affecting their child (e.g., recognition assemblies and academic conferences), the commodity of information is precious and uniquely troubling when inaccessible to any parent, though especially the noncustodial parent.

A second typical request from noncustodial parents stems from a desire for participation. In aspects of school life ranging from parent conferences involving special placements for academic needs to involvement in fund-raising efforts, many parents wish to be active participants in the school environment of their children (Wall, 1992). However, intentional and unintentional programming decision may frequently disenfranchise noncustodial parents seeking to participate in the lives of their children and the parent activities associated with the school (e.g., PTA/PTO), noncustodial parents may sense a second-class status regarding their participation in the lives of their children.

A third frequent area of distress for noncustodial parents concerns **coordination** and **referral** needs typically provided to parents of intact nuclear families. Many noncustodial parents find themselves faced with the struggles of single-parenthood during their visitation times (Arditti, 1992). In this regard, the delicate balance of patenting within a defined timeframe can lead to difficulties in discipline, communication, or other aspects relating to their children (Frieman, 1994).

When such challenges are encountered by custodial parents, they often feel their connection to the school counselor may allow for requesting assistance in parenting such as reading materials, suggested procedures, or even a referral to a mental health professional in the community. By contrast, an excluded noncustodial parent may be hesitant and/or uninformed about the availability of such assistance.

A variety of suggestions arise for school counselors attempting to demonstrate greater sensitivity and responsiveness to the circumstances of noncustodial parents. One suggestion is that the school counselor should be well apprised of legal issues affecting the noncustodial parent. This information should begin with the limitations and privileges reflected in state statutes governing the noncustodial parent. In this regard, Aiello and Humes (1987) have provided an excellent summary of legal precedents affecting legal rights of parental access to school records and contact of both parents by the school system. Closely related to statutory rights in information about any specific element of a divorce decree that might affect the relationship between the school and the noncustodial parent (e.g., children may not be dismissed from school directly into care of the noncustodial parent). A final element of the legal circumstances affecting noncustodial parents is any preferences or expectations that might be within the right of either parent and reasonable for the school to accommodate (e.g., parental preferences to be informed about testing dates).

A second suggestion for school counselors that closely follows the legal circumstances affecting noncustodial parents is to assist in developing guidelines and promoting sensitivity to assist in serving the family rather than the parent of the children. Such guidelines might be used to assist classroom teachers, other support staff, and parent groups to think inclusively in activities and information affecting the child's relationship with both parents. For example, the school counselor might distribute a list of "Reminders to Include Everyone" to all school staff and affiliates in an effort to assist in providing information and seeking participation among parents such as (a) mail duplicate newsletters and announcements, (b) send duplicate schedules, (c) include both parents in school listings, (d) videotape special performances, and (e) whatever the issue, be inclusive! Even devoting attention to the content of official school forms to ensure attention to the inclusion of both parents communicates sensitivity in a tangible manner. In this regard, the counselor should work proactively to emphasize the three previously noted premises—a parent is a parent, divorce inevitable creates inequities, and the primary focus should be on the children.

A third suggestion for school counselors to consider in their programming efforts with noncustodial parents is to **anticipate and avoid difficulties.** In many instances, the school counselor can expect difficulties from both unresolved marital issues and contemporary custody disputes to be reflected in the requests of both parents. As a general rule, school counselors should avoid attempting post-marital therapy with parents and refer either or both parent(s) to a mental health professional not affiliated with the school. In this way, school counselors can maintain the primacy of their role within the school system. Conversely, school counselors attempting to force cooperation between former spouses for the sake of their children may find that such a strategy will be replete with perceived accusation and manipulation, thereby diminishing rather than increasing assistance to the child or children. School counselors should also be attentive to the potential triangulation of the child, the school, and/or the former spouse. In such cases, the negative artifacts of side-taking will quickly diminish the professional viability of the school counselor. Finally, school counselors attempting to create equivalence where non exists can often promote a sense of expectation on the part of noncustodial parents that could subsequently lead to more discouragement, thereby discouraging participation within the school system.

A fourth suggestion concerns **notoriety and recognition** of the participation of the noncustodial parent. Although some might view formal recognition of the committed noncustodial parent to be laudable, most parents would prefer that any notice of their participation in the school environment be framed as parental rather than noncustodial. Such distinctions can prove embarrassing or serve to become a point of overcompensation in a competition with the custodial former spouse. Parent day at school that distinguishes on the basis of custody or PTA recognition as an involved noncustodial parent can easily promote distress on the part of both adults and children. Again, the premise that a parent is a parent typically suffices, regardless of custodial status.

As a final suggestion, school counselors should recognize that not all post-divorce difficulties demand accommodations by the school and its affiliates. **Counselors have rights too!** School counselors should not feel obliged to alter typical school procedures or practice preferences to indulge former spouses' sustained conflicts. This is not to say that occasional adjustments would be inappropriate, particularly in the early stages of post-divorce adjustment. However, continual responsiveness to the needs of former spouses to over-control one another by insisting upon compliance with their demands can introduce inefficiency in the overall program of services and potentially promote embarrassment and shame on the part of children who learn of such demands. In this regard, sensitivity is capitulation.

CLOSING THOUGHTS

This article is not intended to serve as an exhaustive review of all elements of sensitivity and responsiveness to the needs and circumstances of noncustodial parents' involvement with a comprehensive school-based program of counseling services. Rather, the intent of the article has been to examine issues of custodial status, undergirding premises, and selected suggestions that might serve to affect a positive outcome for school counselors wishing to interpret and implement the spirit of Standards B.1 and B.7 of the ASCA Ethical Standards. Responsible and well-intended noncustodial parents encounter both the continuity of parental status and the incontinuity of inequity while still wishing to respond to the needs of their children. Sensitivity and deliberate, informed decision on the part of school counselors may be of significant assistance to these parents and their children.

S. Allen Wilcoxon, Ed.D., *is professor and chair of Counselor Education at The University of Alabama Tuscaloosa, AL.* **Sandy Magnuson, Ed.D.,** *is assistant professor of Counselor Education at Texas Tech University, Lubbock, TX.*

REFERENCES

American School Counsel Association. (1992). *Ethical Standards*. Alexandria, VA: Author.

Arditti, J. A. (1992). Differences between fathers with joint custody and noncustodial fathers. *American Journal of Orthopsychiatry, 62*, (2), 186–195.

Aiello, H., & Humes, C. W. (1987). Counselor contact of the noncustodial parent: A point of law. *Elementary School Guidance and Counseling, 21*, 117–182.

Beis, E. B. (1984) *Mental health law*, Rockville, MD: Aspen.

Brody, G., & Forehand, R. (1990). Interparental conflict, relationship with the noncustodial father, and adolescent post-divorce adjustment. *Journal of Applied Development Psychology, 11* (2), 139–147.

Frieman, B. B. (1994). Children of divorced parents: Action steps for the counselor to involve the father. *Elementary School Guidance and Counseling, 28*, 197–205.

Kruk, E. (1991). Discontinuity between pre and post-divorce father-child relationships: New evidence regarding parental disengagement. *Journal of Divorce and Remarriage, 16* (3-4), 195–227.

Little, M. A. (1992). The impact of the custody plan on the family: A five-year follow-up. *Family and Conciliation Courts Review, 30*, 243–251.

Nickerson, E. T. (1986), Integrating the child into family therapy: The remaking of a for adults only orientation. *International Journal of Family Psychiatry, 7*, 59–69.

Schweitzgebel, R. L., & Schweitzgebel, R. K. (1980). Law and psychological practice. New York:Wiley.

Wall, J.C. (1992). Maintaining the connection: Parenting as a noncustodial father. *Child and Adolescent Social Work Journal, 9,* 441–456.

Wallerstein, J. S., & Kelly, J. B. (1980), Effects of divorce on the visiting father-child relationship. *American Journal of Psychiatry, 137,* 1534–1539.

Wilcoxon, S. A. (1994). Family therapy with the noncustodial parent and children: Unique preliminary considerations. *Family Therapy, 21*(2), 107–115.

Chapter 8: Court Appearances

INTRODUCTION

Because school counselors may find themselves going to court for a number of reasons, it's important they be prepared if the situation arises. Most often, school counselors are subpoenaed as "fact witnesses." By law, fact witnesses are required to share relevant case information with lawyers, juries, or judges. Fact witnesses are not on trial themselves; they simply are required to provide details they know regarding pending litigation.

School counselors should never agree to go to court voluntarily. There are a number of reasons for this advice. First, a school counselor's duties require he or she be at school, counseling students. If a school counselor is in court, he or she cannot do his or her job. Second, school counselors are not their clients' legal advocates. Parents and guardians of children can become involved in civil and criminal litigation for a number of reasons, and it is not the school counselor's duty to help them prevail in their lawsuits. Third, school counselors should avoid taking sides in child custody and divorce litigation between parents of the children they counsel. Additionally, because school counselors have duties to non-custodial parents after custody orders have been issued, it is in their best interests not to favor one parent over the other. Finally, school counselors should not allow the legal system to abuse them. For example, many counselors have testified on behalf of an attorney's clients with the best intentions only to find themselves enduring harsh cross-examinations or spending valuable time away from their jobs.

In our opinion, when school counselors are asked to testify in a court case involving one of their students or the parents or guardians of their students, the counselors should decline. They should firmly state that their jobs do not include court testimony. If the issue is child custody, school counselors should state that they must maintain professional and helpful relationships with both parents, no matter who is awarded custody, and therefore would prefer to remain neutral and not show support for one parent over the other.

If school counselors receive a subpoena to testify after refusing to agree to be a case witness, they should request a consultation with the school board's attorney through their principal. These counselors should explain their reasons for not wanting to testify and should request that the school board attorney attempt to prevent them from having to do so. If school counselors believe that the subject matter of their testimony may be privileged, the school board attorney should be notified and, if it is known, a citation to the state statute should be provided to the attorney. If counselors are advised that they must testify, the school board attorney should help prepare them for the event and, if possible, accompany them to the deposition, hearing, or trial.

In all school-related legal matters, school counselors should follow the advice of their school board's attorney. Only if the attorney or the counselor's principal is hostile to the school counselor, or obviously does not have the counselor's best interest in mind, should counselors retain a separate attorney at their own expense.

If a school counselor is required to attend a court proceeding as a fact witness, but at some point is asked for his or her professional opinion, the counselor should refuse to give it, stating he or she "does not have enough information to form a judgment about the matter." In almost all instances litigated in court, this is true. In fact, in most instances where an expert opinion is requested, expert witnesses spend many hours researching facts and information before rendering their opinions are thus paid substantial sums. If school counselors unwisely agree to render expert professional opinions in court, they must be prepared for hostile cross-examinations from attorneys whose cases might be weakened by the school counselor's testimony.

James and Devaney (1995) have offered concrete suggestions for school counselors who must testify in court. Among reasons for testimony, they cite personal injury lawsuits, divorce litigation, wrongful death causes of action, special education placement appeals, child abuse situations, or child custody disputes. They also have stated why school counselors are being called as fact witnesses more often than in the past, pointing out that school counselors are dealing with matters such as violence, suicide, and drug abuse—all of which may ultimately lead to litigation. James and Devaney have distinguished between expert and fact witnesses and have explained their respective roles. They also have offered suggestions for preparing for court appearances and have given specific advice to help school counselors respond during cross-examination.

It is our hope that school counselors are able to avoid court appearances. If they are required to appear in court, however, it is our goal that the information provided in this chapter help them navigate these challenging waters.

Preparing to Testify: The School Counselor as Court Witness

Susan Hackbarth James
Susan B. DeVaney

Throughout our nation's history, the public schools have been called upon to address social ills. Perhaps more than any time in history, however, today's schools carry responsibility for managing matters of suicide and violence, drug abuse, child neglect, and child pregnancy—situations that ultimately may lead to litigation. Counselors, as school staff members, are most likely to work with children and their guardians on sensitive issues, and are finding themselves increasingly facing legal responsibility both for their own actions and for the actions of their clientele (Davis & Ritchie, 1993). As citizens rely more heavily on the court systems to resolve civil matters and as child involvement in crime increases, the likelihood of the school counselor serving as a witness rises. Counselors may find themselves rendering testimony in matters of personal injury, divorce, wrongful death, special education placement, child abuse, or child custody (LaForge & Henderson, 1990; Remley, Jr., 1985).

Testifying in court can be a frightening prospect (Brodsky, 1991; Krieshok, 1987). People having little or no court experience may rely on idealized notions of the legal system to form their expectations of testimony (Mac Hovec, 1987). Although the ultimate objective of the judge and jury is truth and resolution, practically speaking, the courts are a forum for conflict. The language of the courtroom is that of debate, argument, and persuasion. Each attorney tries to present the winning argument and discredit opposing litigants and their witnesses (Mac Hovec,

1987). Mental health professionals by training encourage communication, offer support, reach compromise, and change notions of a troublesome external situation to reduce internal turmoil. Even the counselor's vocabulary connotes possibilities, tolerance of discrepant viewpoints, and invitation to build relationships. Although middle ground ultimately may be reached, it is no wonder that the counselor may be particularly uncomfortable in a setting where the litigants' goal is resounding victory, not peaceful resolution (Remley, Jr., 1991). It is the purpose of this article to inform school counselors of what they may encounter as witnesses, thereby enhancing preparation, comfort, and performance on the witness stand.

TYPES OF WITNESSES

The courts recognize two kinds of witnesses the expert witness and the general or "fact" witness. "An expert is any person who, by virtue of his or her training or experience in a science, a trade, or an art, has information that is not likely to be known by the average juror" (Blau cited in Krieshok, 1987, p. 69). It is the function of the expert witness to educate the judge and jury in any adversarial procedure, be it civil, criminal, federal, state, or local court. Trial judges use personal discretion to ascertain the qualifications of the potential expert. No encompassing set of standards exists to measure degree of experience or expertness; therefore a witness may be challenged in court by others with the same or greater level of expertise (Remley, Jr., 1985, 1991; Weikel, 1986). A school counselor could be called upon to serve as expert in matters of standardized testing, child growth and development, effective parenting, or emotional needs of children (Remley, Jr., 1985).

Expert witnesses should come to court with a solid knowledge base in their field of expertise and ready to render an opinion based on their knowledge of the topic (Remley, Jr., 1985; Weikel, 1986). When a witness renders an opinion, it "derives from analysis of the case, including a review of relevant facts and case records, drawing the requisite inferences, and making appropriate interpretations" (LaForge & Henderson, 1990, p. 456). School counselors serving as experts should possess professional credentials qualifying them to serve in that capacity.

Expert witnesses are advised to be impartial (Weikel & Hughes, 1993). As an expert with knowledge of a psychological, technical or specialized nature, the counselor-expert is asked to impart data to the judge and the jury in precise, neutral, and understandable terms (LaForge & Henderson, 1990; Weikel, 1986). The expert's case presentation should be organized using fact, logic, and specific theoretical framework (Miller, Kaplan, & Gardner, 1994)

In addition to serving as an expert, witnesses may also act in a "lay" or "general" capacity wherein they relate information but not opinions about the circumstances of a particular situation (Mason, 1992; Remley, Jr., 1991). Because school counselors are more likely to be called as general witnesses, the remainder of this article focuses on the school counselor as a witness of fact. Counselors desiring additional information concerning expert testimony are advised to consult Brodsky (1991), Krieshok (1987), LaForge and Henderson (1990), Mac Hovec (1987), Weikel and Hughes (1993), and Wills (1987).

PRELIMINARY CONSIDERATIONS

Professional preparation for school counselors is undergirded by a knowledge of the counselor's role and the ethical standards accepted by the profession. Whether or not a school counselor ever testifies in court, familiarity with the American School Counselor Association role statement and statement of ethical standards (ASCA, 1990, 1992) and the *Ethical Standards* of the American Counseling Association (ACA, 1993) form a groundwork for development of professional relations with parents, students, and colleagues. Successful counseling programs and services are based on this foundation. For example, school counselors recognize that they generally do not have the time, resources, or training to enter into long-term therapy with students. Rather, the counselor makes a referral through the child's parent or guardian, perhaps to a mental health counselor or agency. Operating from this procedural base, counselors will know how to respond, for example, when asked by parents to serve as an expert witness in a child custody or abuse case.

By knowing one's professional obligations and limitations, the school counselor might avoid inappropriate entry into court by explaining that a mental health professional specializing in impartial family evaluations may be a more appropriate expert witness. This clear communication regarding professional roles corresponds to the statement in the proposed revision of the ACA ethical standards that professional counselors "are accurate, honest, and unbiased in reporting their professional activities and judgments to appropriate third parties including courts" (ACA, 1993, p. 19).

A second factor to be considered is record keeping. School professionals should keep in mind both the Buckley Amendment, which gives parents access to student records, and the fact that a court may subpoena a counselor's records (Remley, Jr., 1991, 1993). Careful records can prevent lawsuits against the counselor or the school when, for example, they record the onset and nature of the problem, consultation and treatment strategies, and referral or problem resolution.

Personal notes, as distinguished from school records, are intended only for the counselor's eyes, but nonetheless should be written using factual, concrete, and behaviorally oriented language (Arthur & Swanson, 1993). Personal impressions should be identified as such, and conclusions should be supported by critical incidents or behavioral observations (Snider, 1987). Most case notes will not be called into court; however, it is a wise practice to keep them. To avoid their becoming part of a student's permanent record, however, notes are best stored in a separate location where privacy is ensured.

PREPARATION FOR TESTIMONY

A *subpoena* is "a court document served on an individual or entity to appear at a proceeding for the purpose of giving testimony" (Weikel & Hughes, 1993, p. 5). Before requesting a subpoena, the interested attorney often makes preliminary contact with the witness by telephone. When such a call arrives, Mac Hovec (1987) recommended recording the time, date, attorney's name, and details of the conversation for future reference. The subpoena itself orders the counselor to appear and testify or to bring documents relevant to the case, such as files or case notes (Davis & Ritchie, 1993). At this point the prudent counselor will seek legal advice. Although the school attorney may be consulted, it is important to remember that this attorney represents the school's interests, but not necessarily the counselor's. In circumstances in which the counselor may have liability, an attorney representing the counselor is the best source of information concerning how the counselor should proceed (Remley, Jr., 1991).

If records or notes are requested, the counselor should consult an attorney to determine if the documents are protected by privileged communication (Remley, Jr., 1991). School counselors should not assume that they are exempt from testifying in cases involving students. Some states recognize the school counselor-client relationship as privileged, but most do not (Davis & Ritchie, 1993).

It is also important to know the client's wishes regarding counselor testimony and release of records. Parents who desire counselor testimony may request and sign release forms permitting the counselor to give information to their lawyer and to the court. In other circumstances the counselor may contact the student or parents to discuss matters of confidentiality. It is worth remembering, however, that most often the child is the client. The counselor is ethically bound to judge what is in the child's best interests, regardless of the parents' views (Miller, Kaplan, & Gardner, 1994).

If clients desire confidentiality, counselor may choose to explain their code of ethics to the presiding judge and ask that privilege be extended to them (Sheeley & Herlihy, 1987). The judge's order, however, takes precedence over an ethical code. The counselor must abide by the judge's order or risk being charged with contempt of court (Remley, Jr., 1985).

What to expect in the way of courtroom procedures is another matter for discussion. The attorney may ask witnesses to wait outside the courtroom until asked to appear; to avoid contact with jurors, other witnesses, and litigants; and to leave the courtroom after testifying (Weikel & Hughes, 1993; Wills, 1987). The counselor will want to meet with the attorney who initiated the subpoena to discuss and review anticipated questions in both direct and cross examinations (Dorn, 1984; Remley, Jr., 1985). In addition, this pretrial conference is the time to negotiate dates and times for the counselor's court appearance to minimize time spent away from school. Many a time, all witnesses are subpoenaed to be at court at the same time, usually at the beginning time for the trial or hearing. Since all cannot testify concurrently, the counselor may request appearance at a time closer to that when he or she actually will be needed.

Before the day of testimony the counselor has homework to do. Because the first questions asked will establish witness credibility, the counselor should be prepared to recall degrees, licenses and certifications earned; dates and places of graduation; relevant continuing education credits; work experience; presentations; and publications. In addition, it is helpful for the counselor to review the details of the case in order of time (Remley, Jr., 1991). Client records will augment a careful review, but they should not be brought to court unless they are subpoenaed (Dorn, 1984). Any item brought to court is subject to being placed into evidence and may be scrutinized by both attorneys.

A counselor can also prepare by reviewing ethical codes and pertinent current and classical literature. In a sexual abuse case, for example, a counselor may want to review indicators of sexual abuse and read journal articles on the subject. If the case involves special education, the counselor should be familiar with legal requirements, assessment procedures, and interventions. When reporting test results, the counselor should be prepared to explain the validity and reliability of the instrument as well as its appropriate use with various ethnic groups.

THE COUNSELOR'S TESTIMONY

As a witness, the counselor may be asked to give a deposition either before or in lieu of actual court testimony. A deposition is "a sworn statement similar to court testimony ... an information-gathering process for the lawyers on both sides. It is a process that enables a lawyer to gather sufficient information on which to build a case and to decide whether to take the case to trial" (Dorn, 1984, p.119). A deposition is often taken in an attorney's office without the judge present, although a court reporter is usually present to prepare an accurate transcript of questions and answers.

Whether testifying by deposition or in person, the counselor should appear comfortable and professional. The following recommendations apply to testimony in direct examination, that is, questions proffered by the attorney requesting your appearance.

1. Take time to think before answering questions (Weikel & Hughes, 1993).
2. Testify only within your role or area of expertise (Weikel, 1986). If asked a question you are not qualified to answer, say no.
3. Answer questions directly and honestly in a clear, audible voice (Dorn, 1984; Mac Hovec, 1987). Do not evade difficult answers. Rather, answer directly and without added emphasis.
4. Use ordinary language, avoiding professional jargon (Weikel & Hughes, 1993). The judge and the jury must understand what you are saying before they can determine its meaning in deciding the case.
5. When questions are confusing, ask for clarification (Dorn, 1984). Don't be afraid of seeming to be stupid. If you did not understand the question, the jury probably did not either.
6. If you are unsure of an answer, "I don't know" is an acceptable response (Weikel, 1986). In fact, many times that is the only honest answer.
7. Relate information objectively, avoiding personal interpretations (Remley, Jr., 1985).
8. Answer only what is asked. Avoid embellishments. (Weikel & Hughes, 1993). For example, if asked if you are aware of the child's academic record, the answer should simply be yes or no. Do not begin recounting that history unless you are specifically asked to do so.
9. If need be, refer to notes made ahead of time (Mac Hovec, 1987). Warning: If you do, the attorneys probably will ask to see those notes.
10. Act with confidence; appear self-assured (Brodsky, 1991).

Most professional report that cross-examination is the most challenging element of testifying (Brodsky, 1991). In cross-examination the opposing attorney has the opportunity to discredit the counselor's testimony by pointing out inconsistencies, inaccuracies, and biases. The following suggestions may lessen the difficulty of cross-examination:

1. Be calm, polite, and professional (Dorn, 1984).

2. Ignore rude comments (Remley, Jr., 1991)
3. Do not take personally the challenges to your testimony (Weikel & Hughes, 1993). If an attorney implies that you are biased or unqualified, it does not mean the judge or jury will believe that you are. Your response will be the more important factor in their decision.
4. Use your own words, not the attorney's (Mac Hovec, 1987).
5. Be cautious in answering suggestive or "what if" questions. Ask for more information if the question is equivocal or confusing (Mac Hovec, 1987).
6. Respond as objectively and definitively as possible (Weikel & Hughes, 1993). Make eye contact with the questioner while the question is being asked. When answering, make eye contact with the persons you want to convince—the judge and jury.
7. Avoid the appearance of bias in either direction (Brodsky, 1991). An attorney may attempt to affiliate you with one side or the other. If you appear to be trying to help one side, your apparent bias may actually weaken your testimony.

CONCLUSION

For the school counselor, the prospect of testifying in court on school related matters is a growing one. The counselor's clear understanding of professional roles and ethical standards is a starting point for development of a proactive stance toward participation in court proceedings. Counselors may testify in a variety of circumstances; therefore, preparation and consultation with an attorney are essential preliminaries to appearance in court. Moreover, because each situation, case, court, and state is different, the information contained in this article should serve only as a general practical guide.

Susan Hackbarth James *and* **Susan B. DeVaney** *are associate professors in the Department of Educational Leadership at Western Kentucky University. The authors wish to thank Brian Reeves and William Allender, judges in Bowling Green, Kentucky, for their assistance in editing this article. Correspondence regarding this article should be sent to Susan Hackbarth James, 409E Tate Page Hall, Western Kentucky University, Bowling Green, KY 42101.*

REFERENCES

ACA proposed standards of practice and ethical standards. (1993, October). *Guidepost*, pp. 15–22
American School Counselor Association. (1990). *Role statement: The school counselor.* Alexandria, VA: Author.

American School Counselor Association. (1992). *Ethical standards for school counselors.* Alexandria, VA: Author.

Arthur, G. L. & Swanson, C. D. (1993). Confidentiality and privileged communication. In T. P. Remley (Ed.), *The ACA legal series Vol. 6* (pp. 1–78). Alexandria, VA: American Counseling Association.

Brodsky, S. L. (1991). Testifying in court *Guidelines and maxims for the expert witness.* Washington, DC: American Psychological Association.

Davis, T., dc Ritchie, M. (1993). Confidentiality and the school counselor A challenge for the 1990s. *The School Counselor, 41,* 23–30.

Dorn, F. J. (1984). The counselor goes to court. *Journal of Counseling & Development, 63,* 119–120.

Krieshok, T. S. (1987). Psychologists and counselors in the legal system: A dialogue with Theodore Blau. *Journal of Counseling & Development, 66,* 69–72.

LaForge, J., & Henderson, P. (1990). Counselor competency in the courtroom. *Journal of Counseling & Development, 68,* 456–459.

Mac Hovec, T. J. (1987). The expert witness survival manual. Springfield, IL: Charles C. Thomas.

Mason, M.A. (1992). Social workers as expert witnesses in child sexual abuse cases. *Social Work, 37*(1), 30–37.

Miller, G., Kaplan, B., & Gardner, A. (1994, April). *Testifying in court.* Paper presented at the American Counseling Association convention, Minneapolis, MN.

Remley, Jr., T. P. (1985). The law and ethical practices in elementary and middle schools: *Elementary School Guidance & Counseling, 19*(3), 181–189.

Remley, Jr., T. P. (1991). ACA legal series: Vol. 1. *Preparing for court appearances.* Alexandria, VA: American Counseling Association.

Remley, Jr., T. P. (1993). *You and the law.* American Counselor, 2(4), 32–33.

Sheeley, V. L., & Herlihy, B. (1987). Privileged communication in school counseling: Status update. *The School Counselor, 34*(4), 268–272.

Snider, P. D. (1987). Client records: Inexpensive liability protection for mental health counselors. *Journal of Mental Health Counseling, 9*(3), 134–141.

Weikel, W. J. (1986). The expanding role of the counselor as vocational expert witness. *Journal of Counseling & Development, 64,* 523–524.

Weikel, W. J., & Hughes, P. R. (1993). The counselor as expert witness. In T. P. Remley, Jr. (Ed.), *The ACA legal series,* Vol. 5 (pp. 4–55). Alexandria, VA: American Counseling Association.

Wills, C. E. (1987). Preparation and procedures for the courtroom: Insight for the licensed professional counselor. *Texas Association for Counseling and Development Journal, 15,* 91–102

Chapter 9: Appellate Court Decisions

INTRODUCTION

It is difficult to know how often school counselors are sued and for what reasons. Not only are many lawsuits settled prior to going to trial but, out of those that do make it to court, legal publications only report appellate case decisions.

Because of their significance, however, it is important for school counselors to follow appellate court decisions relating to their practices. Appellate court decisions interpret statutes or common law principles, and these interpretations have the effect of law in the jurisdiction that handed down that particular decision. For example, although a case decided by the U.S. Supreme Court is binding throughout the United States, a decision rendered by a state regional appellate court is binding in that particular region of that state. Additionally, even when an appellate court decision is not binding on another jurisdiction, it can be persuasive to judges who are not required by law to follow the precedent.

Here is a good example. A judge or jury in a local courthouse may rule against a school counselor in a lawsuit—the result of which would have no precedent on a similar case brought in the same courthouse in the future. Each trial case would be decided based on the facts, and it's possible—although the facts could be similar—that contrary decisions could be reached. Only if a case decided at the trial level is appealed, however, is the ensuing appellate decision binding for future cases in that jurisdiction.

With this in mind, school counselors should review relative appellate court decisions as a guide to future practice. Stone (2002) has analyzed appellate court decisions in two interesting areas—academic advising and abortion counseling. She has demonstrated how school counselors can learn from appellate court decisions and modify their practices to minimize their risk of being sued or even losing future lawsuits.

Additionally, Stone (2002) has given a good description of negligence and its relationship to school counselor malpractice claims. She also includes the four elements of a malpractice lawsuit that must be proved if a plaintiff is to prevail. Although, generally, courts have found that counselors do not "owe" students duties, these two cases determined that negligence is possible if counselors provide academic advising services or involve themselves with a student seeking an abortion.

The first time a school counselor was found negligent in the course of academic advising came from a ruling by the Iowa Supreme Court. In this case, an athlete was ineligible for a large scholarship because he did not enroll in the high school courses the award required. The issue the Iowa Supreme Court ruled could be litigated at the trial level was whether or not a counselor who provides academic advising to a student has a duty to know certain information, such as the details of a scholarship requirement. Although ASCA has a position statement regarding educational planning, it does not suggest that school counselors are responsible for interpreting academic rules for students (See ASCA position statement, *The Professional School Counselor and Educational Planning*, Appendix H–11).

Similarly, a federal court of appeals issued a decision in an abortion counseling case involving an Alabama high school counselor. This litigation alleged that a school counselor and an assistant principal encouraged a pregnant student to obtain an abortion and assisted her in doing so. Both were accused of hiring the student for menial jobs to earn money for the abortion and paying for her transportation to the abortion clinic. The federal court ruled that, if these facts were true, it would be possible for a judge or jury to find the counselor and assistant principal negligent in performing their professional services to the student. The student claimed in the lawsuit that her privacy was compromised and her right to practice her religion was hindered by their actions.

Based on the two lawsuits reviewed, Stone (2002) has provided specific recommendations for counselors who may encounter either one of these two issues. She, too, emphasized the importance of school counselors reading and understanding appellate court decisions.

To keep up with court decisions that may affect their practices, school counselors should read professional publications and attend workshops. And, if a counselor does not understand the reasoning behind a court decision, he or she, along with his or her administrator, should ask for clarification from school board attorneys. It is our hope that this chapter encourages this practice.

Negligence in Academic Advising and Abortion Counseling: Courts Rulings and Implications

Carolyn Stone

Navigating the legal and ethical waters of any profession can be daunting but the waters are especially murky in a human service profession such as counseling. When you add to the complications of counseling individuals clients who are minors in schools, the potential for legal and ethical dilemmas multiply. School counselors' legal and ethical work with minors involves value-laden subjects (e.g., abortion), safety issues (e.g., harassment), and life-threatening concerns (e.g., suicide). There is the inescapable fact that a school counselor's client extends beyond the student to include parents, teachers, administrators, the school district, and the community. The confluence of this multiplicity of responsibility to parents and others (and a setting whose mission and function is to deliver academic instruction) flows together to make the legal and ethical world of school counseling a complex one to negotiate.

The setting in which school counselors work is the most defining and confining characteristic for school counselors when they enter into a counseling relationship with students. Personal or emotional counseling for minors in schools brings immediate tension between the student's right to privacy and the parent's right to be the guiding force in their children's emotional development (Fisher & Sorenson, 1996; Isaacs & Stone, 1999; Kaplan, 1996; Remley & Herlihy, 2001; Salo & Shumate, 1993).

The multifaceted nature of working with minors in schools makes it impossible to develop policy for all the potential variables and situations faced by school counselors. Although there is legal guidance such as legislation and school board policy, school counselors often have to practice without clear guidelines. Occasionally, the legal obligations of school counselors are underscored by court cases.

Two court cases are presented in this article to illuminate school counselors' legal responsibilities in academic advising and abortion counseling. However, it is important to note that court decisions are based on a particular set of facts, and the law of a particular state or area of the country is applied. They do not fully define school counselors' legal obligations as professionals practicing in a particular jurisdiction. These cases are presented to show how appellate court decisions can guide and inform future decision making in a variety of potential malpractice situations.

It is highly unusual for a school counselor to be sued (Parrott, 2001; Remley & Herlihy, 2001; Stone, 2001; Zirkel, 2001a). These court cases are discussed not to disturb peace of mind, as that would be an over reaction, but to inform future practice and to equip professionals to exercise even greater care for their minor students.

NEGLIGENCE

Negligence is a civil wrong or, in legal terms, a tort in which one person breaches a duty to another (Remley & Herlihy, 2001; Valente, 1998). A criminal wrong is a crime against society, whereas a civil wrong is a breach of another's individual rights. A civil wrong causes damages or injury that may be physical, emotional, or monetary, and plaintiffs seek compensation. Malpractice is a civil wrong and is an area of tort law that refers to negligent practice in the rendering of professional services (Remley & Herlihy; Valente). As a general legal principle, civil liability for negligence will accrue if a school counselor is found to owe a duty to another person, breaches that duty by not living up to expected standards, and as a result of the breach of duty, causes damages to another person. According to Prosser (1971), all four of the following elements must be present for negligence to be proven:

- A duty was owed by the school counselor to a student or parent/guardian of a student.
- The duty owed was breached.
- There was a sufficient legal causal connection between the breach of duty and the injury.
- Some injury or damages were suffered.

Negligence has been judicially rejected in the vast majority of cases against school counselors and other educators in the area of educational advising and personal counseling (Fisher & Sorenson, 1996; Gladding, Remley, & Huber, 2001). Courts have been reluctant to determine that a school counselor has a duty as a matter of law to give accurate academic advice or inform parents when their child is considering abortion (Fisher & Sorenson; Gladding et al.). Since no duty is owed, then liability for negligence cannot be imposed. The two court cases discussed in this article represent a departure from previous rulings, in that the courts found that the counselors owed a duty and in one case, the court found that the counselor breached the duty owed (*Arnold v. Board of Education of Escambia County, 1989; Sain v. Cedar Rapids Community School District*, 2001).

Malpractice is failure to render professional service and the test for failure is determined by what is known as the standard of care or the expected standard of the profession (Cottone & Tarvydas, 1998; Prosser, 1971). Standard of care is determined by evidence of what a reasonable counselor would have done in a similar situation. The opinion of professional experts is usually used to establish the standard of care. Using standard of care as the framework, the court will decide if the school counselor acted as the reasonably competent professional would have under the same or similar circumstances (Cottone & Tarvydas).

In most states with regard to negligence or civil liability, individual employees are protected from personal liability if they are not acting in a willful or wanton way. Most states have legislation declaring that public employers must defend, indemnify, and hold harmless any employee who is named in a civil suit for an act of omission arising out of the employee's job (Collins, 2001). Further, according to these statutes, the employee cannot be fired because of an unintentional act that has harmful effects. This obligation does not extend to criminal acts or acts where the employee is intentionally harmful.

NEGLIGENCE IN ACADEMIC ADVISING

Until 2001, no jurisdiction had recognized that negligence could occur in the context of a school counselor giving academic advice to a student (Zirkel, 2001a). In reversing a lower court's decision and remanding the case to trial, the Iowa Supreme Court in *Sain v. Cedar Rapids Community School District* (2001) determined that a duty was owed by a school counselor in this situation to advise a student with due care and attention.

Bruce Sain, a senior in Cedar Rapids, Iowa, was a talented all-state basketball player. In 1996, he was awarded a 5-year basketball scholarship to Northern Illinois University. In the summer prior to his freshman year, Sain was notified in a letter that he did not meet the National Collegiate Athletic Association (NCAA) regulations for incoming freshman athletes at Division I schools. The letter explained that he fell one-third credit short in the required English credits because his one-third English credit in Technical Communications was not on the list of classes his high school submitted to the NCAA for approval. Sain lost his scholarship and his family filed suit against the Cedar Rapids School District citing the school district as negligent and the school counselor, Larry Bowen, as guilty of negligent misrepresentation in his role as an academic advisor (*Sain v. Cedar Rapids Community School District*, 2001). How did a scholarship opportunity for Bruce Sain turn into shambles and how did Larry Bowen find himself at the center of a lawsuit?

Larry Bowen was Bruce Sain's school counselor at Jefferson High School. Sain, who was in his senior year, needed three trimesters of English. Sain was dissatisfied with the second trimester English course and asked Bowen to place him in another English class. Bowen suggested Technical Communications and explained to Sain that it was being offered at the school for the first time but that the Initial Eligibility Clearinghouse would approve the high school course. Without further concern, Sain completed Technical Communications and graduated in the spring of 1996 with the prospect of a 5-year scholarship at Northern Illinois University. Then the letter arrived from the NCAA Clearinghouse declaring Sain ineligible based on academic grounds. Sain and Jefferson High School requested reconsideration from the NCAA but their request for a waiver was denied (Parrott, 2001; Reid, 2001; *Sain v. Cedar Rapids Community School District*, 2001; Zirkel, 2001a).

With his scholarship offer voided, Sain turned to the courts. Sain filed suit against the NCAA (which he dropped shortly thereafter) and the school district (not the school counselor) claiming negligence and negligent misrepresentation. Negligence was alleged in that the course, Technical Communications, was never submitted to the NCAA for approval. Suitability of the course was not at issue as Technical Communications had been approved for other schools as a core English course, but the problem was that it had not been approved for Jefferson High School because the school had not included it on the list that is annually submitted to NCAA Clearinghouse for approval. Negligent misrepresentation was claimed because Bowen gave out erroneous information by telling Sain that the course would be approved and that he was safe to take Technical Communications (*Sain v. Cedar Rapids Community School District*, 2001).

The trial court initially rejected Sain's suit. Courts have received a number of educational malpractice lawsuits, but continually side with school districts, rejecting the notion that school counselors owe a duty to a student to give competent academic advice (Fisher & Sorenson, 1996; Gladding et al., 2001). Courts recognize how difficult the role of academic advisor is for school counselors who are routinely required to manage large numbers of students, constantly changing rules and regulations, and fluctuating admissions and financial aid criteria. Courts have therefore been reluctant to determine that a duty is owed in the academic advising arena (Fisher & Sorenson; Gladding et al.). Sain appealed to the Iowa Supreme Court which remanded the case for trial (*Sain v. Cedar Rapids Community School District*, 2001).

It is important to note that the Iowa Supreme Court did not determine whether the school district was negligent, that was left for the lower court to decide. Rather, the state Supreme Court found that the claim of "negligent misrepresentation" possibly had merit and should not have been dismissed by the lower court. On the first count, the court determined that in this case negligence did not apply to the failure to submit the Technical Communications course for approval. The court said that negligence applies only to the disclosure of information and that failure to disclose information did not meet the criteria for negligence (*Sain v. Cedar Rapids Community School District*, 2001; Zirkel, 2001a). The Iowa Supreme Court remanded the case to the lower court for trial on the count of negligent misrepresentation.

Justice Mark Cady of the Iowa Supreme Court wrote for the 5 to 2 majority that school counselors can be held accountable for providing accurate information to students about credits and courses needed to pursue post-high school goals (Parrott, 2001; Reid, 2001). The erroneous advice given by the counselor was equated to negligent misrepresentation in professions such as accounting, the law, and others whose businesses require that they give accurate and appropriate information (*Sain v. Cedar Rapids Community School District*, 2001; Zirkel, 2001a). The court determined that school counselors have a similar business relationship of giving accurate advice to students when the student has a need to know. The court explained that just as accountants and lawyers stand to gain financially from giving accurate advice, so do school counselors, since that is what they are paid to do. Therefore, negligent misrepresentation may be applied to the school counselor-student relationship when erroneous advice means a student loses a lucrative scholarship. This kind of lawsuit is more business related than academic and, according to the Iowa Supreme Court, is a classic case of negligent misrepresentation (*Sain v. Cedar Rapids Community School District*; Zirkel).

The court found that school counselors must use reasonable care in providing specific information to a student when (a) the counselor has knowledge of the specific need for the information; (b) the counselor provides the information to the student in the course of a counselor/student relationship; and (c) the student reasonably relies upon the information in circumstances where the counselor knows or should know of the student's reliance (Zirkel, 2001a). Bowen claims never to have had a conversation with Sain about NCAA course eligibility which Sain disputes. When the case is heard in the lower court, a judge or jury will decide who to believe.

Justice Linda K. Neuman, speaking on behalf of the minority, wrote that the Iowa Supreme court's decision "spells disaster for the law," explaining that the decision will open the "floodgates" and could be applied broadly to students in a variety of situations and not just athletes who need counsel on NCAA rules (Reid, 2001, p. 3). Judge Neuman noted that the decision exalts logic over experience or, in other words, it appears logical that school counselors should give correct advice, but the reality of the expectations on school counselors makes this impossible. School counselors cannot have a command of everything there is to know about colleges and universities, admissions requirements, NCAA rules, financial aid and scholarships, and a multitude of other facts that change daily. In other words, the fear the two minority opinion Supreme Court judges were expressing is that a student can sue when he or she misses admission to Yale because they were not advised that there is a requirement of four sciences and took only three. Judge Neuman wrote, "Instead of encouraging sound academic guidance, today's decision will discourage advising altogether" (Reid, p. 3).

In its opinion by the majority, the court acknowledged that the ruling could have a "chilling effect" on academic advising by school counselors (Reid, 2001, p. 3). However, the court cautioned that the ruling should have limited effect as negligent representation is confined to students whose reliance on information is reasonable (e.g., an inquiry as to whether a course meets NCAA eligibility), and that the school counselor must be aware of how vital the information is to the student. This explanation was intended to comfort school counselors and to keep them from over reacting to the principles outlined by the Sain case (*Sain v. Cedar Rapids Community School District*, 2001).

The *Sain v. Cedar Rapids Community School District* (2001) case involved the controversial overturning of a lower court's decision to dismiss a case of negligent misrepresentation against a school district that involved a school counselor who allegedly gave erroneous advice. The case was never heard by the lower court as it was settled before going to trial (P. Zirkel, personal communication, April 1, 2002). However, the findings of the Iowa Supreme Court in remanding the case to trial serve as a caution to the school counseling profession about providing accurate advice which could have an impact on a student's future financial opportunities. It is unusual for a tort claim of this nature to proceed to court

(Parrott, 2001). By breaking with tradition, the Iowa Supreme Court has reinterpreted the nature of the student–school counselor relationship. The claim of negligent misrepresentation is akin to claims filed against lawyers and accountants when they give erroneous advice. School counselors can benefit by knowing that negligent misrepresentation is a possibility, albeit remote, and can heighten their resolve to stay current in the arena of academic advising. School counselors cannot be held to unreasonable standards and the courts are reluctant to impose unreasonable duties on educators. This case was a rare departure from the tradition of holding school counselors harmless in being all things to all persons. The message for school counselors is to continue to actively pursue their role as an academic advisor as it is paramount, and to exercise a good faith effort to give accurate advice.

RECOMMENDATIONS FOR SCHOOL COUNSELORS

The following are recommendations for school counselors in the role of academic advisor:

1. Continue to offer academic advising sessions to students. The Sain ruling should not deter the active pursuit of the role of career and academic advising, a role that has the greatest opportunity for implementing a social justice agenda to level the playing field for students. School counselors are needed to close the information gap between those students who know what they need to do to successfully access postsecondary education that leads to wider economic opportunities and those students who have not received even the most basic information. Students who do not have a significant adult in their lives helping them understand how to access and be successful in postsecondary opportunities need the school counselor to be the advocate who helps close the information gap. Remember, the district was sued, not the school counselor. It is unlikely that school counselors will have to face monetary liability in their work. The almost nonexistent chance of negligent misrepresentation should not deter academic advising.
2. Act as the reasonably competent professional would. If faced with a lawsuit, school counselors who practice with care and caution will pass the standard of care test. The courts are not asking for extraordinary care, only reasonable care. Ethics help professionals aspire to extraordinary care, but the courts do not demand this level. By exercising skill and care in every action taken as a professional, school counselors can demonstrate that they are behaving as a reasonably competent professional.

3. Stay abreast of the information needed for competent academic advising. It is important to be able to demonstrate a working knowledge of procedures, policies, laws, ethical standards, and the school district's policies. By seeking professional development in the area of academic advising from many resources such as the school district, counseling organizations, and literature, school counselors are demonstrating a good-faith effort to stay informed.

4. Empower others to take responsibility for having and giving the right information. For example, coaches could be in charge of advising students about NCAA regulations, and students could be encouraged to learn to become their own advocate in gathering information about college admissions, scholarships, and financial aid. Students can be taught to become their own advocate through classroom guidance lessons in the computer lab, where students learn Internet searches so they can seek information on their own. As a manager of resources, school counselors can equip others to be a key presence in the career and academic advising roles.

5. Publicize widely academic information for all students and parents. Newsletters, form letters, and e-mail list serves could help in the advising role and demonstrate a proactive stance to disseminating critical, timely information.

6. Require that students and parents sign off when they have been given critical information. For example, when seniors are given their personal credit check for their remaining graduation requirements, the school counselor can have them sign an acknowledgment that they have been told and understand what they need to do.

7. Consult when appropriate. Best practice for school counselors is to always consult whenever they are unsure. School counselors never stand alone unless they fail to consult with others who are in a position to help.

NEGLIGENCE IN ABORTION COUNSELING

The legal and ethical complications of working with minors in schools pose daily dilemmas and never more so than value-laden issues such as abortion, which involves a family's religious beliefs, values about sexual conduct, and parental rights to be the guiding voice in their children's lives and other rights. Respecting students' confidences requires school counselors to balance the rights of minors with the rights of their parents (Isaacs & Stone, 2001; Kaplan, 1996). Legal rulings and the *Ethical Standards for School Counselors* (American School Counselor Association, 1998) offer suggestions and guidance in the complexities of confidentiality. However, it is ultimately the responsibility of the school counselor to determine the appropriate response for individual students who put their trust in the security of the counseling relationship.

School counselors need to be advocates and a source of strength for the individual student who comes to them for help in confronting and dealing with areas such as sexual activity and abortion. Under what circumstances might a counselor be held liable for giving abortion advice? In *Arnold v. Board of Education of Escambia County* (1989), Jane and John, two high school students, filed suit along with their parents against the School District of Escambia County, Alabama, alleging that the school counselor, Kay Rose, and the Assistant Principal, Melvin Powell, coerced and assisted Jane in getting an abortion. Further, the accusation was that Powell paid someone $20 to drive Jane to the abortion clinic and that Powell and Rose hired Jane and John to perform menial tasks to earn money for the abortion. John, the father of the baby, and Jane claimed that their constitutional rights were violated including involuntary servitude and free exercise of religion. The parents claimed that their privacy rights were violated when they were not informed by the school counselor and assistant principal that Jane was pregnant and when school officials urged the students not to tell their parents. The trial court dismissed the suit and plaintiffs appealed (*Arnold v. Board of Education of Escambia County*; Zirkel, 2001b).

The U.S. 11th Circuit Court of Appeals partially reversed the decision of the trial court and found Jane's privacy claim and both students' religious claim as worthy of further consideration by the courts. In other words, if Jane and John's religion prohibited abortion, and Rose and Powell coerced Jane and John to proceed with Jane's abortion, then their constitutionally protected right of freedom of religion might have been violated. Further, Jane's constitutionally protected right to choose to carry or abort a pregnancy had been violated if she was coerced into having an abortion. Jane's parents claimed that their privacy rights were violated when the school counselor and assistant principal coerced Jane into having an abortion and urged her and John to refrain from discussing with a parent whether or not Jane should have an abortion. The case was remanded back to the lower court for a trial to take place (Zirkel).

In fact finding, the trial court found that Jane visited a physician who confirmed she was pregnant and provided her with abortion information upon her request. John and Jane told Rose that they did not want their parents to know about the pregnancy as they were not supposed to be seeing each other and that Jane left home because she was being abused by her stepfather. Rose presented various alternatives but the students rejected all alternatives except abortion. Rose repeatedly urged Jane and John to consult with their parents. Rose reported the alleged abuse by the stepfather to the Department of Human Resources, who sent a representative to meet with Jane. The representative urged Jane to consult with her mother and offered alternatives such as foster care and adoption. When Jane rejected all alternatives, the representative assisted Jane in trying to obtain financial assistance and Medicaid. Jane and John said they felt pressured to have an abortion by Rose when she asked them how they planned to care for the baby and where they were going to take the baby. During the process of discovery, Jane admitted that Rose's questions were good, that she alone made the decision to have an abortion, and that she was not coerced by Rose or Powell. John admitted that he had chosen not to tell his mother. The trial court concluded that the students were not deprived of their free will, had chosen to obtain an abortion, had chosen not to tell their parents, and that there was no coercion on the part of school officials (*Arnold v. Board of Education of Escambia County*, 1989; Zirkel, 1991; 2001b).

After the Arnold ruling, the question remains: May counselors be held liable for giving abortion advice to pregnant minors? Counselors in the course of fulfilling their job responsibilities may assist students with value-laden issues such as abortion if they are competent to give such advice and if they proceed in a professional manner. School counselors must consider that their responsibilities extend beyond the student to parents and guardians and take great care in abortion counseling. Fisher and Sorenson (1996) stated:

> If an immature, emotionally fragile young girl procures an abortion with the help of a counselor, under circumstances where reasonably competent counselors would have notified the parents or would have advised against the abortion, liability for psychological or physical suffering may follow. The specific facts and circumstances must always be considered. (p. 60)

Complicated, value-laden counseling requires that the school counselor assess the developmental age of the student and the ability of the student to make informed, sound decisions. School counselors must continually ask themselves what the reasonably competent professional would do under similar circumstances. Consider if Jane had been 13 years old. Would Rose have responded differently? Stadler's (1990) test of universality is a good gauge, because the test asks the professional to consider the advice they would give to a colleague who is in the throes of a similar ethical dilemma. If the school counselor would advise a colleague to take a different path, then this begs the counselor to further examine his or her proposed actions. Perhaps the counselor is planning action that is too conservative, too risky, or outside the bounds of what the reasonably competent professional would do.

Can school boards adopt a policy forbidding school counselors to engage in any discussions with their students about contraception, abortion, or sexual activity? School boards can (any some do) adopt policies forbidding counselors to address certain topics or instructing them to immediately call parents if such topics are brought up by their students. However, in the absence of a school board policy expressly forbidding counselors to discuss abortion, school counselors can discuss the topic with students. A school counselor must be ready to argue that they behaved as the reasonably competent professional would have. Coercion and imposing one's values on a minor student would not be appropriate actions of a reasonable and professional school counselor.

RECOMMENDATIONS FOR SCHOOL COUNSELORS

The following are recommendations for the school counselor when counseling students in the area of sexuality or abortion:

1. Know your school board policy. School counselors can sometimes find guidance in school board policy and must adhere to policy. School counselors behaving as advocates work appropriately to change policies that they believe have an adverse impact on students.
2. Consider developmental issues when making decisions. When working with minors on value-laden issues, it is especially important to consider the chronological and developmental level of the minor in order to determine whether an intervention(s) is needed and how much is required. School counselors promote the autonomy and independence of a minor and carefully consider how much they need to support a student to make his or her own decisions without interference or breach of confidentiality. Primary to the counselor's decision making is the seriousness of a minor's behavior in the framework of his or her developmental milestones and the minor's history of making informed decisions (Stone, 2001).
3. Consider the impact of the school setting and parental rights. Parental rights are more complicated when a minor is in a school setting, since parents send minors to school for academics, not for personal counseling. Therefore, when a minor seeks counseling in a value-laden area such as abortion, which may be related to the parents' religious beliefs or rights to be the guiding voice in their children's lives, consideration must be given to the wishes of parents. The onus is not on the school counselor to know the religious beliefs of every student and his or her family. However, if a student confides that religion is at issue or if the counselor learns this from

another source, then it is appropriate that this information be considered when determining how to proceed with the student.

4. Consider diversity issues. Each decision for ethical dilemmas must be made in context and must consider a minor's ethnicity, gender, race, and sexual identity.
5. Consult with a supervisor or respected colleague, examining the good and bad consequences of each course of action, striving to minimize the risk to the student while respecting the inherent rights of parents. It is ethical, lawful, and beneficial to inform and consult with supervisors and colleagues. After the school counselor implements a course of action, it is important to process the results to strengthen the probability of appropriate decisions in the future.
6. Know yourself and your values. School counselors will want to understand their own values in sensitive areas such as abortion and understand the impact of those values on their ability to act in the best interest of their students. Professionals know they cannot leave their values out of their work, but they use caution when their values can inappropriately interfere with promoting a student's autonomy. School counselors will want to refer students to a colleague when they can no longer be effective.
7. Avoid involvement in a student's medical care. Referring students to birth control clinics should be avoided, and a school counselor should never agree to take students for any kind of medical procedure, especially a procedure as controversial as abortion.

SUMMARY

School counselors regularly face ethical dilemmas of confidentiality for which there are few definitive answers. The American School Counselor Association (1998) provides guidelines for ethical behavior, but it is ultimately the responsibility of the school counselor to negotiate the rights and privileges of students and parents with regard to disclosing information to parents (Stone, 2001). Difficult decisions involving value-laden issues must always be made against the backdrop of parental rights.

Parents are continually vested by the courts with legal rights to guide their children (*Bellotti v. Baird*, 1979; *H.L. v. Matheson*, 1980). According to the *Ethical Standards for School Counselors* (American School Counselor Association, 1998), school counselors have a primary obligation and loyalty to students, but parents need to be involved as appropriate. Community standards, a counselor's own personal values, school board policy, and the school setting all contribute to the complex nature of working with minors in schools.

School counselors need to become constant consumers of legal and ethical information, seeking reference materials, and attending legal and ethical workshops and university courses. Court decisions can be valuable guides in the practice of school counseling, and professionals will want to stay current regarding court rulings that affect their practice. Seeking supervision and consultation with other professionals is the best defense in the complex world of legal and ethical concerns for minors in a school setting. School counselors can take comfort that they never stand alone legally and ethically if they seek guidance from fellow professionals.

Carolyn Stone, Ed.D., *is an associate professor, College of Education and Human Services, University of North Florida, Jacksonville. E-mail: cstone@unf.edu*

REFERENCES

American School Counselor Association. (1998). *Ethical standards for school counselors*. Retrieved December 12, 2001 from http://www.schoolcounselor.org/content.cfm?L1=1&L2=15.

Arnold v. Board of Education of Escambia County, 880 F. 2d 305 (Alabama 1989) Bellotti v. Baird, 443 U.S. 622 (1979).

Collins, K. L. (2001). *Guidance counselor liability for "negligent representation."* Retrieved December 12, 2001, from http://www.sai-iowa.org/901Report.html.

Cottone, R., & Tarvydas, V. (1998). *Ethical and professional issues in counseling.* Upper Saddle River, NJ: Merrill Prentice Hall.

Fischer, L., & Sorenson, G. P. (1996). *School law for counselors, psychologists, and social workers* (3rd ed.). White Plains, NY: Longman.

Gladding, S., Remley, T. P., Jr., & Huber, C. (2001). *Ethical, legal, and professional issues in the practice of marriage and family therapy* (3rd ed.). Upper Saddle River, NJ: Merrill Prentice Hall.

H. L. Etc., Appellant v. Scott M. Matheson, 101 S. Ct. 2727 (1980).

Isaacs, M. L., & Stone, C. (1999). School counselors and confidentiality: Factors affecting professional choices. *Professional School Counseling, 2*, 258–266.

Isaacs, M. L., & Stone, C. (2001). Confidentiality with minors: How mental health counselors manage dangerous behaviors. *The Journal of Mental Health Counseling, 23*, 342–356.

Kaplan, L. (1996). Outrageous or legitimate concerns: What some parents are saying about school counseling. *The School Counselor, 43*, 165–170.

Parrott, J. (2001, July 9). Are advisors risking lawsuits for misadvising students? *The Mentor: An Academic Advising Journal.* Retrieved January 20, 2002, from http://www.psu.edu/dus/mentor/.

Prosser, W. (1971). *The law of torts.* St. Paul, MN: West.

Reid, K. (2001, May 2). Iowa's high court holds counselors liable. *Education Week.* Retrieved January 20, 2002, from http://www.edweek.org/ew/ewstory.cfm?slug=33guide.h20.

Remley, T. P., Jr., & Herlihy, B. (2001). *Ethical, legal, and professional issues in counseling.* Upper Saddle River, NJ: Merrill Prentice Hall.

Sain v. Cedar Rapids Community School District, 626 N.W.2d 115 (Iowa 2001).

Salo, M. M., & Shumate, S. G. (1993). *Counseling minor clients.* The ACA Legal Series, 4, 73–78.

Stadler, H. A. (1990). Confidentiality. In B. Herlihy & I. B. Golden (Eds.), *AACD ethical standards-casebook* (4th ed., pp. 102–110). Alexandria, VA: American Association for Counseling and Development.

Stone, C. (Speaker). (2001). *Legal and ethical issues in working with minors in schools* [Film]. Alexandria, VA: American Counseling Association.

Valente, W. (1998). *Law in the schools* (4th ed.). Upper Saddle River, NJ: Merrill Prentice Hall.

Zirkel, P. (1991). End of story. *Phi Delta Kappan, 72,* 640–642.

Zirkel, P. (2001a). Ill advised. *Phi Delta Kappan, 83,* 98–99.

Zirkel, P. (2001b). A pregnant pause? *Phi Delta Kappan, 82,* 557–558.

Chapter 10: Gay, Lesbian, and Bisexual Students

INTRODUCTION

Ignorance, hatred, and discrimination are all difficult and sensitive challenges for school counselors. And, when coupled with homophobia or violence, they become even more so. For this reason alone, it's important school counselors learn all they can about counseling students in issues relating to sexual orientation.

The American School Counselor Association (ASCA) is committed to ensuring equal opportunity and respect for all students regardless of sexual orientation (see ASCA position statement, *The Professional School Counselor and Sexual Orientation of Youth*, Appendix H–18). According to ASCA, school counselors should be committed to reducing ignorance, hatred, and discrimination based on sexual orientation.

McFarland and Dupuis (2001) noted that gay and lesbian youth are frequently victimized by hate crimes in school settings and explained further the connection between homophobia and violence. McFarland and Dupuis also described the legal responsibility of school personnel to protect gay and lesbian students from harassment, as well as strategies for school counselors to address homophobia and anti-gay violence in their schools.

By better understanding the issues of students, it is our hope counselors will help others respect their differences.

The Legal Duty to Protect Gay and Lesbian Students from Violence in School

William P. McFarland
Martin Dupuis

Public attention has recently focused on violence in schools in the United States. Media coverage of shootings in Arkansas, Oregon, and Colorado have shocked the nation. These violent incidents in the schools have demonstrated the alarming potential for these events to occur anytime in any school. To prevent this problem, there has been a call for understanding the causes of violence among school-age children and adolescents and a demand for action. A comprehensive approach to prevention requires the schools to address physical violence, media violence, political-economic violence, cultural-racial violence, and sexual and gender violence (Daniels, Arredondo, & D'Andrea, 1999).

Within the larger issue of sexual and gender violence is the problem of harassment and abuse directed against gay and lesbian students. The purposes of this article are to describe the violence against gay and lesbian students; demonstrate the connection between homophobia, heterosexism, and violence; examine the legal responsibility of schools to protect gay youth from harassment and abuse; and, to recommend prevention strategies to provide safe schools for gay and lesbian students.

ANTI-LESBIAN AND GAY VIOLENCE

Gay and lesbian youth have been the invisible minority in our schools. Since homosexuality has historically been viewed as only an adult issue, many people in the public schools remain uninformed about the number of gay students in schools and show little interest in the concerns of these students (Treadway & Yoakam, 1992). School counselors have made general comments during training sessions that there are no gay students in their schools or have even labeled attempts to educate about gay and lesbian issues as subversive attempts by homosexuals to take over the schools. Research by Price and Telljohann (1991) described one in five school counselors as reporting that working with gay and lesbian students would not be gratifying, but 41% of the counselors in their study also reported that schools were not doing enough to help gay and lesbian students adjust to their environment.

As further evidence that these students are ignored, Reed (as cited in O'Conor, 1994) stated, "Not only does the group remain invisible, the existence of and problems associated with gay youth are largely denied by public school educators, particularly administrators" (p. 8). Woog (1995) described a statewide survey of Connecticut teachers and administrators in 1991 where respondents indicated that they recognized the plight of gay and lesbian students, admitted that little was being done for them, and expressed hope for interventions to assist these students. Teachers were more insistent on action, whereas administrators claimed that there were sufficient programs in place to address the needs of these students.

Depending on the study, it has been reported that between 2% and 10% of the U.S. population is homosexual. Ginsberg (1998) reported using the midpoint of this range, or 6%, to indicate a national gay/lesbian population of approximately 15,000,000 which also suggests a gay and lesbian student population of 2,610,515 based on the *Digest of Education Statistics* (U.S. Bureau of the Census, 1995). Ginsberg (1998) explained:

> These estimates suggest that of the adolescents who attend the country's public schools about one in 20 is likely to be gay/lesbian. Thus, each time a middle or high school teacher addresses a class, she or he is likely to be addressing one or more gay/lesbian students. (p. 2)

School can be a dangerous and often hostile environment for gay and lesbian youth. One reason gay and lesbian students live silent and secretive lives is that to be visible, or to have come out as a teenager, means to place oneself at risk of verbal and physical abuse. O'Conor (1994) wrote, "A recent U.S. Department of Justice report states that gays and lesbians are the most frequent victims of hate crimes, and school is the primary setting for this type of violence" (p. 11). It has also been noted that crimes against gay males and lesbians in schools occur with greater frequency than crimes against the general population in the school setting. Some 25% of lesbian and gay students are crime victims, while 9% of the general population of students are crime victims (Comstock, 1991). A survey of more than 4,000 students reported in the *Youth Risk Behavior Study* (Massachusetts Department of Education, 1995) that gay males and lesbians were five times more likely than their heterosexual peers to skip school out of fear for their safety.

Gay and lesbian students are at risk because of societal views of homosexuality, which create unsupportive and unaccepting or even hostile environments at school and at home. Many families react badly when their child comes out, and many youths are abused by their family members with some adolescents being kicked out of their homes. Remafedi (1987) reported that 26% of gay and lesbian youth are forced to leave home because of conflicts with their families about their sexual orientation.

The pervasiveness of the general homophobic atmosphere in schools is shown by research, which found that 97% of students in Massachusetts public high schools regularly report hearing homophobic remarks from their classmates, and 53% indicated that they heard homophobic comments from school staff (Massachusetts Governor's Commission on Gay and Lesbian Youth, 1993). Anderson (1997) cited a 1992 Harris Poll which showed that 86% of high school students would be very upset if classmates called them gay or lesbian.

Teachers may often punish students for uttering racists remarks, but students who make homophobic comments are seldom challenged. An Iowa study found that the average high school student hears anti-gay epithets 25 times a day and that teachers who hear these slurs fail to respond 97% of the time (Carter, 1997).

Research by Pilkington and D'Augelli (1995) revealed that gay and lesbian youth (ages 15 to 21) experience high levels of verbal and physical assault as a result of their orientation. Of the youths in their survey, 80% endured verbal insults; 44% were threatened with violence; 33% had objects thrown at them; 31% reported being chased or followed; and 17% reported being physically assaulted. In the *Youth Risk Behavior Study* (Massachusetts Department of Education, 1995) it was reported that 23% of gay and lesbian youth were in a fight that required medical attention compared with 3% of heterosexual students. One gay student described the abuse he endured in school:

> I don't feel safe from abuse at my high school. I am relentlessly persecuted for being gay. By the time I was in ninth grade, listening without responding to others bashing homosexuals was

more painful than the harassment I deal with now. Up to now, a person has masturbated in front of me while I was in the school lavatory, I have had cigarettes thrown at me, students have driven their car within a foot of me to drive me off the road while I was walking, and people call me vulgar names almost daily. What I am describing now is not simple child's play and name calling. It is very specific harassment that threatens my safety at school. (Youth Pride, 1997, p. 4)

THE CONNECTION BETWEEN HOMOPHOBIA, HETEROSEXISM, AND VIOLENCE

Homophobia is the widely used term that means the fear and hatred of homosexuality or perceived homosexuality (Elia, 1993). Herek (1986) described homophobia in terms of the four functions that homophobic attitudes fulfill. First, negative attitudes serve an experiential-schematic function based on past unfavorable contact with homosexuals. For example, if a person thought a gay male made a pass at him, he may conclude that all gay males are highly sexualized and, based on this belief, may oppose the employment of gay teachers in schools. Herek's second function is labeled social-expressive and means an individual may express negative attitudes towards gay and lesbian people to win approval from significant others, especially peers. The third function served by homophobia is a value-expressive function. For these people, negative attitudes towards gay and lesbian people are expressions of important personal values such as certain religious ideologies. The fourth function served by homophobic attitudes is a defensive function where gay and lesbian people are seen as legitimate targets for attack so the individual avoids personal anxieties and confusion related to his or her own sexuality.

Heterosexism refers to the belief that heterosexuality is the best and only acceptable way of living (Blumenfeld & Raymond, 1989). Institutions in our society, including the schools, harbor the fear and hatred of homosexuality as well as prejudices based in heterosexism. Homophobia and heterosexism have a negative impact on all students, both gay and straight. Masters, Johnson, and Kolodny (1992) noted that most of the attacks against homosexuals are committed by male adolescents who are trying to demonstrate their hypermasculinity to their peers. Also, Herek and Berrill (1992) reported that teenagers surveyed about their biases against a variety of minorities reacted more negatively towards gay people than to other groups. It was stated in the 1988 report of the Governors Task Force on Biased Related Violence that, "gay men and lesbians are perceived as legitimate targets that can be openly attacked" (as cited in Herek & Berrill, 1992, p. 97).

Homophobia is detrimental to other people in the schools besides gay and lesbian youth. For example, heterosexual boys who do not fit the traditional male gender role (aggressive, controlling, restricted emotions) defined by heterosexism may be punished, ostracized, and abused. These boys may be called "faggots," "fairies," "sissies," "queers," or other derogatory names. Sears (1992b) and Klein (1992) noted that males seem to experience more homophobia than females. Hetrick and Martin (1987) claimed that effeminate male youth are at highest risk for violence. Girls also experience pressure to conform to heterosexist gender stereotypes, and failing to do so is likely to result in abuse. Girls who fail to demonstrate stereotypical feminine traits (complacent, emotional, deferential) may be called "dykes," "lezzies," or other derogatory names.

Others who may be strongly impacted by homophobia are gay and lesbian parents who have school children who might experience homophobic ridicule. It is estimated that the are 4 million gay and lesbian parents with 8 to 10 million school-age children (American Bar Association, 1987). If traditional gender role behavior is breached, homophobic actions are taken to punish anyone—gay or straight, male or female—in the name of enforcing the standards of heterosexuality. Thus, students become victims of violence because of the connection between homophobia and rigid gender roles defined by heterosexism.

When harassment or violence instigated by homophobic attitudes persists in schools, students learn that it is acceptable to be intolerant of diversity. Even worse, it may appear permissible to denigrate others who are different. Young people who learn to hate, and then violently act out these feelings may be lost to the criminal justice system (Hunter & Schaecher, 1995). Therefore, both the victim and the perpetrator pay a severe price for the violence that arises out of homophobia. A gay male described the effects of a homophobic school environment:

> People kept coming up to me and making fun of me, they would call me horrible names and I would cry all the time. Letters were put in my locker saying things about AIDS and how my parents shouldn't have had me and how I should just die. Kids would threaten me after school and follow me home yelling things at me. No one should have to go through what I went through in school. (Youth Pride, 1997, pp. 3-4)

LEGAL RESPONSIBILITY OF SCHOOLS

The abuse of lesbian and gay youth is a serious issue, and education officials are being forced to take a more proactive position to ensure that schools are safe for all students. The liability for administrators for not responding appropriately to claims of harassment can be very costly, as several recent court cases demonstrate.

In a 1999 landmark decision for educational policy, the U.S. Supreme Court declared that school officials who ignore student-on-student sexual harassment can be held liable for violating the federal civil rights law under Title IX of the Education Amendments of 1972 (*Davis v. Monroe County Board of Education*, 1999). The case was brought by a mother on behalf of her fifth-grade daughter, who was inappropriately touched on an ongoing basis for 5 months by a male classmate. The male student said he wanted to have sex with her, simulated a sexual act, and rubbed-up against her. Both parent and student complained to school officials, but nothing was done to correct the problem. The mother complained to the police, and the boy pleaded guilty to sexual battery.

The Court, sharply divided in the 5-4 decision, stated that federally aided schools can be held liable when the student-on-student harassment is "so severe, pervasive and objectively offensive that it denies its victims the equal access to education" (*Davis v. Monroe County Board of Education*, 1999, p. 650), and school officials are deliberately indifferent to the sexual harassment. The harassment must go beyond simple acts of teasing and name-calling. The U.S. Justice Department has concluded that the deliberately indifferent standard would make such lawsuits rare because school officials will usually respond to such behavior, at least when it involves male and female students.

How school officials react to same-gender sexual harassment will also be an important factor in determining liability, and more importantly, for providing an educational environment conducive to learning for all students. Many gay and lesbian students report that they were made to feel responsible for their harassment since they did not conceal their homosexuality. Rather than punish the perpetrators, gay and lesbian students were often transferred to other classrooms. Administrators using such remedies may now be at risk of being deliberately indifferent.

In another case, the issue of discrimination based on sexual orientation in schools has been heard by the federal courts (*Nabozny v. Podlesny*, 1996), and the settlement agreement cost school officials nearly $1 million. Jamie Nabozny suffered verbal and physical abuse at the hands of his classmates because of his sexual orientation for the 4 years from seventh to 11th grade. The physical attacks were so severe that Nabozny has had to have two surgeries. He attempted suicide three times during these years.

Nabozny and his parents complained on numerous occasions to his school counselors and principals. Despite promises to protect Nabozny, no action was taken against the offenders, and the abuse continued year after year. One principal even said that if Nabozny was "going to be so openly gay, that [he] had to expect this kind of stuff to happen." A teacher, upset by the disruption caused by other students taunting Nabozny, called him a "fag" and expelled him from the classroom. Nabozny sued the principals and the school district arguing that he had been denied equal protection of the law under the Fourteenth Amendment of the U.S. Constitution based on his gender and sexual orientation.

Nabozny claimed that the employees of the school district treated him differently than they treated girls who had been harassed. The school had a record of punishing boys who harassed girls, and the court even suggested that the school officials' departure from their regular practice of punishing perpetrators might be evidence of the principals' discriminatory intent.

At the jury trial to determine if in fact the school officials and the district did discriminate against Nabozny, a unanimous, seven-member jury determined that he was denied equal protection from harm while at school. Hours after the verdict, the principals quickly settled the suit for over $900,000. Interestingly, the jury did not find the school district liable, perhaps because the district had a non-discrimination policy that included sexual orientation.

In a third case, administrative remedies were sought against schools that did not protect against harassment based on sexual orientation. A gay student filed a sex discrimination complaint against the Fayetteville, Arkansas public schools with the Office of Civil Rights (OCR) of the U.S. Department of Education (*Wagner v. Fayetteville Public Schools*, 1998). The gay student was harassed from the eighth to the 10th grades. Gay bashing by a gang caused a broken nose and a bruised kidney. Criminal charges against the perpetrators were filed, and these students were given probation. The harassment by other students continued, and the school failed to take any meaningful action.

In March 1997, the OCR released new Title IX guidelines (U.S. Department of Education, 1997). Title IX is a federal statute that prohibits sex discrimination, and for the first time the guidelines made explicit reference to gay and lesbian students as being protected against sexual harassment. While the guidelines do not forbid discrimination on the basis of sexual orientation, they prohibit actions that create a sexually hostile environment. Expressing a dislike for gays and lesbians alone would not be a violation of Title IX. The actions or language must specifically be of a sexual nature to fall under the title.

The Department of Education reached an agreement with the Fayetteville Public Schools requiring the school district to "recognize the various forms of sexual harassment," including that directed at gay or lesbian students. The school district must adopt policies consistent with this understanding and provide training and education on sexual harassment for the faculty, staff, and student body. Written reports monitoring the school district's progress must be submitted for one year.

As these cases demonstrate, school districts will now be held liable for not protecting gay and lesbian students from sexual harassment by their peers. According to Lambda Legal Defense and Education Fund (1998), similar law suits have been initiated in California, Illinois, New Jersey, and Washington. Furthermore, the U.S. Supreme Court in 1998 ruled that school districts can be held liable when a teacher sexually harasses a student (*Gebser v. Lago Vista Independent School District*, 1998). The district must know about the harassment and be deliberately indifferent to it. These are the same standards the Court used to hold school officials responsible for not preventing students from harassing each other.

School administrators must now ensure that gay and lesbian students are provided a safe educational environment. Ignoring this type of sexual harassment could be very costly. Many professional organizations such as the National Education Association; American School Health Association; National School Board Association; American Psychological Association; American Federation of Teachers; Gay, Lesbian, Straight Education Network; American Counseling Association; and the American School Counseling Association support local schools in combating intolerance and homophobia.

STRATEGIES TO PROVIDE SAFE SCHOOLS

Klinger (1995) stated, "Prevention of anti-gay lesbian violence ... primarily involves systemic changes in homophobia at a societal level" (p. 131). While this may exceed the ability of a single societal institution to accomplish, several states have suggested specific ways to address the homophobia that causes anti-gay violence in schools. The Connecticut State Board of Education 1991 publication Equity Newsletter (as cited in Anderson, 1994) identified nine suggestions for bettering the school environment for gay and lesbian students and staff. Those suggestions are:

- Use inclusive language
- Challenge anti-gay epithets
- Designate resource people in the schools for gay and lesbian students
- Make resources and materials on homosexuality visible and accessible
- Educate staff members on homophobia
- Support gay and lesbian colleagues
- Use gay and lesbian colleagues as role models
- Refer self-identified gay and lesbian students to appropriate services
- Refer parents of gay children to organizations such as Parents and Friends of Lesbians and Gays.

In Massachusetts, the Massachusetts Governor's Commission on Gay and Lesbian Youth (1993) published a report titled *Making School Safe for Gay and Lesbian Youth: Breaking the Silence in Schools and in Families*, which recommends taking action in five areas. The first is the establishment of school policies protecting gay and lesbian students from harassment, violence, and discrimination. Procedures for investigating and punishing harassment charges should be clear to administrators and should be uniformly applied to all accusations. Marinoble (1998) instructed school counselors to advise principals and policy-making committees to include sexual orientation in school nondiscrimination clauses of teacher contracts and in written school policies regarding treatment of students and parents. Students should know that the school district will not tolerate sexual harassment and will discipline perpetrators accordingly.

Anti-harassment rules must be carefully written so that they do not forbid speech, opinions, or beliefs in and of themselves, but instead punish impermissible conduct that targets a person for assault, threat, or vandalism on the basis of the victim's actual or perceived race, religion, national origin, disability, gender, or sexual orientation. According to Honig (1999), these rules may also forbid harassing conduct, whether or not targeted to a particular person, that is so pervasive or intense as to create a hostile environment, which hinders the ability of a person to get an education. An excellent example is the Seattle, Washington, Public Schools' policy statement which includes the following:

> Every participant in Seattle Public Schools has the right to an educational environment in which differences among people are accepted and valued, including sexual orientation ... Every student has the right to learning experiences infused with the value of cultural diversity ... prohibits harassment based upon national origin, race, economic status, sex, sexual orientation, pregnancy, marital status, or disability ... by employees, volunteers, parents/guardians, and students. (Reis, 1996, p. 19)

Other anti-harassment policy models are described in *Improving School Policies and State Laws* (Lambda Legal Defense and Education Fund, 1997).

The second area for prevention efforts is training for teachers, counselors, and school staff members in crisis intervention, violence prevention, and the issues and concerns of gay and lesbian students. Black and Underwood (1998) suggested that school counselors coordinate staff development strategies such as annual presentations about gay and lesbian youth for all teachers, utilize expert speakers and panels, facilitate discussions of homophobia and its effects on all students, and provide resources for staff who have a difficult time overcoming their homophobia and prejudice. An excellent example of staff training material is *Homophobia 101: Anti-Homophobia Training for School Staff and Students* published by the Gay, Lesbian, Straight Education Network (GLSEN, 1998). These materials are designed to provide basic awareness of prejudice against sexual minorities; to provide basic information about sexual orientation; to explain stresses on gay and lesbian youth and how this impairs educational performance; to explain how prejudice against sexual minorities impairs educational performance of students; and to equip teachers with some tools and skills to use to reduce prejudice against sexual minority youth and to create an inclusive classroom and school environment. The U.S. Department of Education Office for Civil Rights, with the National Association of Attorneys General 1999 Bias Crime Task Force Education Subcommittee, has released *Protecting Students from Harassment and Hate Crime: A Guide for Schools*. The guide includes sections on developing anti-harassment policies, identifying and responding to incidents of harassment, developing grievance procedures, and creating a climate that appreciates diversity.

Another resource for staff training is *The Safe Schools Anti-Violence Documentation Project* (Reis, 1996), which recommends five strategies for school staff to respond to harassing situations. First, intervene immediately when you hear anti-gay remarks or observe anti-gay harassment with the same firmness you would employ for religious or racial harassment. Second, make it safe to report an incident. Identify a safe person in the school to whom a student or staff member or parent can come to report being harassed or attacked. Third, consider both educating and disciplining the offenders. Discipline should be equitable to that used with offenses involving religion or race. Fourth, consider the needs of the targeted person such as his or her safety, support, and recovery. Fifth, consider the needs of the witnesses and the rest of the school community such as the need for reassurances that those in charge will do everything possible to keep this from happening again.

Professional development for all staff is important because many well-meaning people may have a desire to offer assistance to gay and lesbian students, but due to misunderstandings, they may do more harm than good (McFarland, 1998). Sears (1992a) discovered that less than 20% of school counselors have received any training on assisting gay and lesbian students, and many school employees have negative feelings towards gay and lesbian people. Some faculty and staff may have personal or religious views against homosexuality and may not be in favor of developing materials and programs on gay and lesbian youth. Education programs can bridge this divide by stressing professional and legal responsibilities rather than trying to change personal beliefs. Programs must emphasize that personal viewpoints should not allow a classroom to be so homophobic that gay and lesbian students cannot learn. In addition, training should also note that the ethical obligations that attach to a teaching license could require educators to prevent discrimination on the basis of sexual orientation. Such a duty provides additional incentive for staff to assist gay and lesbian students. Alaska, Connecticut, Florida, and Pennsylvania have this type of statewide education code (Lambda Legal Defense and Education Fund, 1997).

The third area for prevention efforts is school-based counseling and support groups for gay and straight students. School counselors can address the needs of gay and lesbian youth through a group counseling model (Muller & Hartman, 1998). School counselors can also assist in the creation of support groups that are not counseling or therapy groups, but rather have as their focus support, education, and socialization. These support groups could be facilitated by teachers as well as counselors. Suggestions for starting a gay/straight alliance are explained in *Gay/Straight Alliances: A Student Guide* (Blumenfeld & Lindop, 1995).

The fourth area to address is making information about gay and lesbian issues available in school libraries. Library exhibits can create awareness of contributions of gay and lesbian people similar to what many schools do for Black History Month. Anderson (1994) suggested a display for Gay and Lesbian Month in June since it marks the anniversary of the Stonewall Riot in New York City in 1969, which is viewed as the symbolic beginning of the movement to obtain civil rights for gay and lesbian Americans. The National Gay and Lesbian Task Force recognizes October as Gay and Lesbian History Month. The American Library Association has a Gay and Lesbian Caucus, which can be a source of information, booklists, and support for building a library collection.

The fifth area recommended for action by the Massachusetts Governor's Commission (1993) is a curriculum that includes gay and lesbian issues. Anderson (1994, 1997) noted that including gay and lesbian topics in the curriculum does not require developing extensive curriculum guides or spending large amounts of money. Anderson (1994) stated:

> The Latin teacher could mention that Emperor Hadrian was gay. The music teacher can choose from Tchaikovsky, Benjamin Britten, Cole Porter, and so on. Coaches need to begin valuing gay and lesbian athletes. In addition to Martina Navratilova and Bruce Hayes, coaches can mention Dave Kopay and Dave Pallone. Our social studies teachers should include the gay rights movement when discussing the various civil rights movements of this century. And no English teacher passes the year without mentioning Walt

Whitman, Langston Hughes, May Sarton, Adrienne Rich, Countee
Cullen, Willa Cather, Amy Lowell, W.H. Auden, Thornton Wilder,
or Edna St. Vincent Millay. They were all gay. (p. 153)

Age-appropriate curriculum materials should be used. For example,
teaching about gay and lesbian issues in the elementary school does not
mean discussing sex. Appropriate topics include treating everyone with
kindness and respect, and that families come in different forms. Elementary
resources include *It's Elementary: Talking About Gay Issues in School*
(Chasnoff & Cohen, 1997), which is a documentary film for parents,
teachers, administrators, and school boards. Appropriate materials for the
elementary level include *Positively Different: Creating a Bias-Free
Environment for Young Children* (grades K through 5; Matiella, 1991), a
curriculum which teaches strategies for intervening in harassment. Another
curriculum, *Bullyproof: A Teacher's Guide on Teasing and Bullying for Use
with 4th and 5th Grade Students* (Sjostron & Stein, 1996), addresses the
issue of sexual orientation-related bullying without explicitly calling it that
along with a number of other kinds of harassment. Publishers who produce
literature for children about gender issues include Alyson Publications,
Tricycle Press, and Women's Press Interlink Publishers.

For the secondary level, Lipkin (1994) has developed a curriculum on
topics such as gay and lesbian literature for use in English classes, the history of gays and lesbians in the United States for use in social studies classes, and the history and nature of homosexuality for use in biology or psychology classes. Lipkin (1992) has also developed a resource titled
*Strategies for the Teacher Using Gay/Lesbian-Related Materials in the
High School Classroom*. School counselors who use curriculum materials
such as part of a developmental curriculum may impact the stigma that all
students attach to homosexuality, reduce homophobic attitudes, and help
create safe schools for gay and lesbian students (McFarland, 1998).

IMPLICATIONS FOR SCHOOL COUNSELING

While there is still a great deal of bias against gay and lesbian people,
social acceptance has increased significantly. The gay and lesbian students
in schools are coming out of the closet and shedding their status as an
invisible minority. As they make their presence known, these students
encounter a wall of hate. Hate is based on homophobic attitudes and
results in harassment and violence. The courage of these young men and
women as they attempt to break through these two walls of silence and
hatred is truly inspiring. They cannot, however, wage this battle alone.

Robinson (1994) related, "It is the counselor's responsibility, however, to understand the unique stressors of gay and lesbian students, help

these students cope with the social and educational barriers of homophobia, and provide appropriate information regarding resources available for needed support" (p. 329). The school counselor may function most effectively as the leader of a coordinated effort to influence other school personnel and students in the effort to make the school environment more inviting for gay and lesbian students. School counselors can ensure that schools fulfill their legal responsibilities to provide a safe learning environment for gay and lesbian students by implementing many of the previously discussed strategies through the four components of a comprehensive developmental guidance program (McFarland, 1993).

First, school counselors can infuse educational information through the guidance program curriculum component addressing issues like challenging the myths surrounding homosexuality, the contributions of gay and lesbian persons throughout history, and the struggle for legal rights for gay and lesbian people. The classroom topics could also address the personal challenges for gay and lesbian students, including decision making about coming out as well as issues related to families of gay and lesbian youth such as responding to parental grief, managing relationships with siblings, and diffusing potential inflammatory family situations.

Second, school counselors can embark on a professional development program to acquire the knowledge and skills to serve gay and lesbian students through the responsive services component of the guidance program. Through counseling interventions, school counselors can assist students to challenge internalized homophobia before it results in self-destructive behaviors.

Third, as part of their guidance program's individual planning services component, school counselors can recommend to students the school curriculum where gay and lesbian issues are addressed. School counselors should keep relevant information available for career planning and choosing colleges that are affirming of gay and lesbian students (Orzek, 1992). School counselors should be familiar with community resources for gay and lesbian youth and their families.

Finally, through the system support component of a developmental program, school counselors can help develop staff in-service training programs on such issues as how to include gay and lesbian issues into the curriculum or how to supportively respond to a student who indicates a struggle with sexual orientation issues. By addressing the needs of gay and lesbian youth through all developmental guidance program components (curriculum, responsive services, individual planning, system support), school counselors may become leaders in the effort to reduce violence against gay and lesbian youth in the schools. We are suggesting that school counselors undertake responsibilities in addition to counseling for this population. We are promoting the role of social advocate on behalf of gay and lesbian students.

School counselors may be subjected to open antagonism from the school community and the community at large for taking on the role of advocate. There are several arguments that school counselors can make when defending gay and lesbian youth. School counselors can emphasize that the educational environment for all people is enhanced when ideas are discussed openly and honestly. While some people may have religious or personal objections to homosexuality, it is important to explain that living in a democratic society involves valuing a tolerance of others. Advocacy for gay and lesbian youth is linked to the core ideals of the school: equality, respect, and citizenship.

School counselors can also note that it is the professional responsibility of all educators to provide a supportive and safe learning environment. At the very least, these obligations require schools to accommodate a diverse population, including gay and lesbian students. There is an emerging body of case law which mandates protecting all students from harassment and violence.

Critics can be told that allowing homophobic conditions to persist sends the message that certain types of discrimination are acceptable. Students should learn that it is not okay to treat others badly because they are perceived to be different. Jennings (2000), Executive Director of GLSEN, explained, "We must help [people] understand bigotry and name-calling represent a greater threat to her child's welfare than an open discussion of touchy issues" (p. 2).

School personnel have been identifying at-risk populations of students and developing programs to serve the needs of these groups for decades. Working with gay and lesbian youth and their families is a continuation of these efforts to help all students maximize their educational achievement. Ignoring these students means disregarding statistics on suicide, HIV infection rates, homelessness, and violence. If these issues were connected to other populations, there would be an outcry to intervene. Commenting on the role of school counselors in addressing critical social issues, Baker (2000) wrote:

> The pervasiveness of ... social problems and the call for social action require school counselors to respond with patience and care. Setting goals and working with others to achieve them is a better strategy than working independently and impulsively to resolve issues. Demanding change may be less palatable to decision makers than leading the way with information and reasoned debate. When singular efforts fail, planning and renewed efforts are needed. These social problems may not be eradicated for a generation or more. Yet,

some individuals can be helped. Many counselors attempting to help many individuals can be very influential. (p. 43)

As educators assist these young people in reaching their full potential, they will be increasingly called upon to guarantee that schools will not discriminate on the basis of sexual orientation. In addition to effective counseling, the best strategies for school counselors to use for confronting hatred of gay and lesbian students in schools are informing, debating, persuading, discussing, and lobbying for change. These tactics can achieve faster and more effective results than litigation, which takes time, is costly, and involves external mandates. However, if school districts do not respond to the reasonable and respectful leadership of school counselors to convince school personnel to provide safe schools, it seems likely that the courts will impose it.

William P. McFarland, Ed.D., *is a professor, Counselor Education and College Student Personnel, and* **Martin Dupuis, Ph.D., J.D.,** *is an assistant professor, Political Science. Both are with Western Illinois University, Macomb, IL. Correspondence should be addressed to Dr. McFarland, Counselor Education and College Student Personnel, 1 University Circle, Western Illinois University, Macomb, Illinois, 61455. E-mail: Bill_McFarland@ccmail.wiu.edu.*

REFERENCES

American Bar Association. (1987). *Family Law Reporter.* Washington DC: Author.

Anderson, J. D. (1994). School climate for gay and lesbian students and staff members. *Phi Delta Kappan, 76,* 151–154.

Anderson, J. D. (1997). Supporting the invisible minority. *Educational Leadership, 54,* 65–68.

Baker, S. (2000). *School counseling for the twenty-first century.* Upper Saddle River, NJ: Macmillan.

Black, J., & Underwood, J. (1998). Young, female, and gay: Lesbian students and the environment. *Professional School Counseling, 1*(3), 15–20.

Blumenfeld, W. J., & Raymond, D. (1989). *Looking at gay and lesbian life.* Boston: Beacon.

Blumenfeld, W. J., & Lindop, L. (1995). *Gay/straight alliances: A student guide.* Malden, MA: Massachusetts Department of Education.

Carter, K. (1997, March 7). Gay slurs abound. *Des Moines Register,* p. 3.

Chasnoff, D., & Cohen, H. (1997). *It's elementary: Talking about gay issues in school.* [Film]. (Available from Women's Educational Media, 2180 Bryant St., Suite 203, San Francisco, CA 94116).

Comstock, G. D. (1991). *Violence against lesbians and gay men.* New York: Columbia University.

Daniels, J., Arredondo, P., & D'Andrea, M. (1999, June). Expanding counselors' thinking about the problem of violence. *Counseling Today, 41,* 12, 17.

Davis v. Monroe County Board of Education, 526 U.S. 629 (1999).

Elia, J. P. (1993). Homophobia in the high school: A problem in need of a resolution. *The High School Journal, 77*, 177–185.

Gay, Lesbian, Straight Education Network. (1998). *Homophobia 101: Anti-homophobia training for school staff and students.* New York: Author.

Gebser v. Lago Vista Independent School District, 524 U.S. 274 (1998).

Ginsberg, R. W. (1998). Silenced voices inside our schools. *Initiatives, 58*, 1–15.

Herek, G. M. (1986). On heterosexual masculinity: Some psychical consequences of the social construction of gender and sexuality. *American Behavioral Scientist, 29*, 563–577.

Herek, G. M., & Berrill, K. T. (Eds.). (1992). *Hate crimes: Confronting violence against lesbians and gay men.* Newbury Park, CA: Sage.

Hetrick, E., & Martin, A. D. (1987). Developmental issues and their resolution for gay and lesbian adolescents. *Journal of Homosexuality, 14*, 25–43.

Honig, D. (1999). Enforcing rules against harassment of gay students while respecting the free speech rights of students and teachers. *The Safe Schools of Washington Trainer's Manual*, 32–33. Retrieved June 14, 1999 from the World Wide Web: http://www.safeschools-waorg/ss_aclu.html.

Hunter, J., & Schaecher, R. (1995). Gay and lesbian adolescents. In R. L. Edwards (Ed.), *Encyclopedia of social work* (19th ed., pp. 1055–1059). Silver Springs, MD: National Association of Social Workers.

Jennings, K. (2000). *What does homosexuality have to do with education? An answer.* Blackboard On Line: The Website of the Gay, Lesbian and Straight Education Network. Retrieved August 14, 1999 from the World Wide Web: http://www.glsen.org/pages/sections/library/schooltools/016.article.

Klein, S. S. (1992). Why should we care about gender and sexuality in education? In J. T. Sears (Ed.), *Sexuality and the curriculum: The politics and practices of sexuality education* (pp. 171–179). New York: Teachers College.

Klinger, R. L. (1995). Gay violence. *Journal of Gay and Lesbian Psychotherapy, 2*, 119–134.

Lambda Legal Defense and Education Fund. (1997). *Improving school policies and state laws.* New York: Author.

Lambda Legal Defense and Education Fund. (1998). *An outline of our school work.* New York: Author.

Lipkin, A. (1992). *Strategies for the teacher using gay/lesbian-related materials in the high school classroom.* Cambridge, MA: Harvard Graduate School of Education.

Lipkin, A. (1994). The case for a gay and lesbian curriculum. *The High School Journal, 77*, 95–107.

Marinoble, R. M. (1998). Homosexuality: A blind spot in the school mirror. *Professional School Counseling, 1*(3), 4–7.

Massachusetts Governor's Commission on Gay and Lesbian Youth. (1993). *Making schools safe for gay and lesbian youth: Breaking the silence in schools and in families.* Boston: Author.

Massachusetts Department of Education. (1995). *Youth risk behavior study.* Boston: Author.

Masters, W., Johnson, V., & Kolodny, R. (1992). Human sexuality (4th ed.). New York: HarperCollins.

Matiella, A. C. (1991). *Positively different: Creating a bias free environment for young children.* Santa Cruz, CA: ETR Associates.

McFarland, W. P. (1993). A developmental approach to gay and lesbian youth. *Journal of Humanistic Education and Development, 32*, 17–29.

McFarland, W. P. (1998). Gay, lesbian, and bisexual student suicide. *Professional School Counseling, 1*(3), 26–29.

Muller, L. E., & Hartman, J. (1998). Group counseling for sexual minority youth. *Professional School Counseling, 1*(3), 38–41.

Nabozny v. Podlesny, 92 F.3d 446 (W.D. Wisc. 1996).

O'Conor, A. (1994). Who gets called queer in school? Lesbian, gay and bisexual teenagers, homophobia, and high school. *The High School Journal, 77*, 7–12.

Orzek, A. M. (1992). Career counseling for the gay and lesbian community. In S. Dworkin & F. Gutierrez (Eds.), *Counseling gays and lesbians: Journey to the end of the rainbow* (pp. 23–33). Alexandria, VA: American Counseling Association.

Pilkington, N. W., & D'Augelli, A. R. (1995). Victimization of lesbian, gay and bisexual youth in community settings. *Journal of Community Psychology, 23*, 34–56.

Price, J. H., & Telljohann, S. K. (1991). School counselors' perceptions of adolescent homosexuals. *Journal of School Health, 61*, 433–438.

Reis, B. (1996). *Safe schools anti-violence documentation project.* The Safe Schools Coalition of Washington. Retrieved June 14, 1999 from the World Wide Web: http://www.safeschools-wa.org/ssp_part3.html.

Remafedi, G. J. (1987). Adolescent homosexuality: Psychosocial and medical implications. *Pediatrics, 79*, 331–337.

Robinson, K. E. (1994). Addressing the needs of gay and lesbian students: The school counselor's role. *The School Counselor, 41*, 326–332.

Sears, J. (1992a). Educators, homosexuality, and homosexual students: Are personal feelings related to professional beliefs? In K. Harbeck (Ed.), *Coming out of the classroom closet: Gay and lesbian teachers and curricula* (pp. 29–79). New York: Harrington Park.

Sears, J. (1992b). The impact of culture and ideology on construction of gender and sexual identities: Developing a critically based curriculum. In J. T. Sears (Ed.), *Sexuality and the curriculum: The politics and practices of sexuality education* (pp. 139–156). New York: Teachers College.

Sjostron, L., & Stein, N. (1996). *Bullyproof: A teacher's guide on teasing and bullying for use with fourth and fifth grade students.* Santa Cruz, CA: ETR Associates.

Treadway, L., & Yoakam, J. (1992). Creating a safer school environment for lesbian and gay students. *Journal of School Health, 62*, 352–357.

U.S. Bureau of the Census. (1995). *Digest of Educational Statistics, Statistical Abstracts of the United States* (115th ed.). Washington, DC: U.S. Department of Commerce.

U.S. Department of Education. (1997). *Sexual harassment guidance: Harassment of students by school employees, other students, or third parties,* 62 Fed.Reg. 12,034.

U.S. Department of Education Office for Civil Rights. (1999). *Protecting students from harassment and hate crime: A guide for schools.* U.S. Department of Education Office for Civil Rights. Retrieved August 15, 1999 from the World Wide Web: http://www.ed.gov/pubs/Harassment/.

Wagner v. Fayetteville Public Schools. (1998). Administrative Proceeding. U.S. Department of Education.

Woog, D. (1995). *School's out: The impact of gay and lesbian issues on America's schools.* Boston: Alyson Publications.

Youth Pride, Inc. (1997). *Creating safe schools for lesbian and gay students: A resource guide for school staff.* Providence, RI: Youth Pride, Inc. Retrieved August 20, 1999 from the World Wide Web: http://members.tripod.com/~twood/guide.html.

Chapter 11: Sexual Harassment

INTRODUCTION

Students who assert their rights to be free of sexual harassment in schools are representative of a relatively new phenomenon. Nevertheless, school counselors are confronted with legal and ethical challenges in their efforts to ensure that students attend school in a safe and secure environment.

After reviewing the U. S. Supreme Court case *Davis v. Monroe County Board of Education* (1999), Title IX of the Education Amendments of 1972, and other legislation and case law, Stone (2000) concluded that school districts must take action against known sexual harassment. Action by school districts is required for both adult sexual harassment of students and student-on-student sexual harassment.

A difficult challenge for school counselors occurs when students report incidents that may constitute sexual harassment against them but insist that counselors maintain the students' privacy and confidentiality. Stone (2000) has provided a thorough discussion of this dilemma and has offered school counselors guidelines to help prevent such harassment in schools.

Protecting the rights of students to be free from sexual harassment in schools is not only an important issue to discuss in its own right, but it is also an example of a situation in which schools counselors—if they are to perform their duties in an ethical and legal manner—must stay informed of recent court rulings and legal requirements. Such continuing education is essential for contemporary school counselors.

Advocacy for Sexual Harassment Victims: Legal Support and Ethical Aspects

Carolyn B. Stone

Sexual harassment has become a subject of social and educational policy debate and discourse. The U.S. Supreme Court in *Davis v. Monroe County Board of Education* (1999) has given sexual harassment an even more prominent place on the national agenda. The Davis case, in combination with Title IX of the Education Amendments of 1972 and other legislation and case law, established that public schools can be forced to pay damages for failing to stop student-on-student sexual harassment. The Davis case is predicted to be a defining court case, cited and exercised in subsequent litigation defining the potential economic impact of sexual harassment on school districts who do not establish and/or strengthen their district's posture against sexual harassment. Sexual harassment can no longer be ignored or given cursory attention by school districts. *Davis* demands advocacy against known sexual harassment.

Sexual harassment is a complicated issue for school counselors, because the vast majority of students (90% in the Hostile Hallways study) do not tell a school official that they have been victimized (Harris/Scholastic Research, 1993). The challenge for school counselors is to help create an environment free of sexual harassment and encourage students to report harassment when it does occur. A critical ethical issue for school counselors is appropriately responding to the needs of the students who reveal the abuse but may seek confidentiality. This poses special ethical and legal questions.

In the following section, the hypothetical case of Sarah, who confides in her school counselor that she has been the victim of sexual harassment, is presented. This article uses the case of Sarah to frame a response and define the school counselor's advocacy role by examining: (a) the Davis case, Title IX, and other legislation and case law regarding student-on-student sexual harassment, (b) the prevalence of sexual harassment in schools and the emotional costs, (c) the implications of the *Davis* decision for school districts and school counseling, (d) the counselor's legal and ethical obligations to Sarah and to her parents, and (e) the legal and ethical complications of confidentiality with minors who are victims of sexual harassment in schools.

THE CASE OF SARAH

Until sixth grade, Sarah was a conscientious student consistently given high marks by teachers in her work ethic. Sarah's elementary academic life was not without struggle, but her motivation allowed her to maintain above average grades with an occasional "C." However, the sixth grade brought a marked change in grades and attitude for Sarah. At first her teachers and parents attributed the change to "middle-school adjustment," but when Sarah began to make health excuses to miss school, her parents called the school counselor for help.

During the parent-initiated school counseling sessions, Sarah's counselor began to learn the truth of her first 5 months of sixth grade. Sarah was a victim of sexual harassment. Sarah was unusually well-developed for a 12-year-old and found herself the target of jokes and sexual comments about her physical development. Changing classes was the worst time for Sarah as boys leered, jeered, brushed up against her, and sometimes a hand would grope. Most recently, Sarah found herself trapped against her locker by a group of boys who made lewd remarks to her and wouldn't let her pass. Their leader, who frequently harassed Sarah, was a boy she recognized as having slid his hand up her blouse while she was trying to negotiate a crowded hallway. Sarah shared her situation with her friends, who repeatedly advised her to ignore the perpetrators and not to make "a big deal about it."

To complicate matters, Sarah told her counselor that she did not want her revelations repeated to anyone, especially her parents: "They always tell me I am too loud and forward with boys and that my clothes are too tight. If they learn about what these boys have been doing, they will just tell me 'I told you so' or 'you asked for it by dressing like that'." Perplexed by the unwelcome attention and how to respond to it, Sarah hinted that she may in some way be responsible for bringing the harassment on herself, and she wished she could just learn to ignore the attention or develop a sense of humor about it all.

Sarah's confusion and pain highlight the seriousness of sexual harassment. Once regarded as innocuous horseplay, teasing, or boys-will-be-boys behavior, sexual harassment is now widely understood to be destructive and illegal. The U.S. Supreme Court on May 24, 1999, imposed a ruling in *Davis v. Monroe County Board of Education* (1999) that, when coupled with recent interpretations of Title IX legislation, gives legal muscle to school counselors in their advocacy role for students. The Davis case raises as many questions as it answers, but unarguably encourages school officials to offer students more protection against sexual harassment or face monetary damages. Therefore, school counselors enter the new millennium with high court support to exercise a leadership/advocacy role to assist in establishing an educational environment that is safe and free from sexual harassment.

LAWS THAT INFORM SCHOOL COUNSELORS' PRACTICE

Throughout the past decade, sexual harassment in schools has been on the national consciousness and on the agendas of school board policy makers. The 1990s opened with the Clarence Thomas/Anita Hill hearing, closely followed in 1992 by the U.S. Supreme Court decision in *Franklin v. Gwinnett County Public Schools* (1992), in which the court drew a parallel between teacher-on-student sexual harassment and supervisor-to-subordinate harassment found in the workplace (Marczely, 1999). The *Franklin* ruling was the first time that a school district was found liable for monetary damages for teacher-on-student sexual harassment. It established a precedent for a number of subsequent court cases in which plaintiffs successfully sought to extend the Supreme Court's findings in Franklin from teacher-on-student sexual harassment to student-on-student sexual harassment (Zirkel, Richardson, & Goldberg, 1995).

Title IX of the Education Amendments of 1972, the legal basis for the Franklin discrimination lawsuit and the student-on-student sexual harassment lawsuits that followed, declared that any school district receiving any form of federal financial assistance must ensure that students are not subjected to discrimination based on gender or excluded from or denied the benefits of participating in any educational program or activities (Fisher, Schimmel, & Kelly, 1999). Sullivan and Zirkel (1999) examined 21 cases brought under Title IX following *Franklin* and found that 20 of the cases recognized Title IX as providing a statutory basis for a claim of student-on-student sexual harassment.

Liability can only be imposed if school officials are notified of sexual harassment. The *Gebser v. Lago Vista* case relied on *Franklin* in a teacher-on-student sexual harassment case, but because the student did not alert anyone to the teacher's sexual harassment, there was no claim for damages against the school district (*Gebser v. Lago Vista*, 1998).

In 1997, the U.S. Department of Education's Office of Civil Rights, the office that governs Title IX implementation, issued the definition of sexual harassment under Title IX as "sufficiently severe, persistent, or pervasive that it adversely affects a student's education or creates a hostile or abusive educational environment and the conduct must be sexual in nature" (*Office for Civil Rights; Sexual Harassment Policy Guidance*, 1997, p. 12036). Using this definition, a 1998 Arkansas case brought one of the first successful suits using Title IX for student-on-student sexual harassment and was significant in that Title IX also afforded protection against sexual harassment for gays. For 2 years, Carolyn Wagner complained to school officials about the incessant harassment of her gay son, Willi. After Willi was severely beaten, she turned to the U.S. Department of Education for help. The suit was settled when the Fayetteville school district signed an agreement with the U.S. Department of Education to hold sexual harassment workshops for teachers and students (Bart, 1998).

Davis v. Monroe County Board of Education

With the Office of Civil Rights defining sexual harassment in schools as sexual discrimination under Title IX, it became just a matter of time before a school district would be found monetarily liable for student-on-student sexual harassment. The inevitable happened on May 24, 1999, when the U.S. Supreme Court in *Davis v. Monroe County Board of Education* issued a wake-up call to school officials by awarding monetary damages in this student-on-student sexual harassment lawsuit. By awarding damages, the Supreme Court considerably strengthened Title IX and gave school counselors and other school officials legal support to behave as advocates against sexual harassment.

A look at the facts in the *Davis* case demonstrates what Title IX considers abuse that affects a student's education. Mrs. Davis' fifth-grade daughter came home from school to report that a classmate, G.F., was "messing" with her, grabbing at her breasts and crotch. The abuse continued for 5 months, and L. Davis, the victim, reported each incident to her mother and to Ms. Fort her classroom teacher (Van Boven, 1999, p. 33). On two occasions, Mrs. Davis also contacted Ms. Fort and spoke to the principal who stated, "I guess I'll have to threaten him a bit harder." (Zirkel, 1999, p.172). Mrs. Davis alleged that at no time was G.F. disciplined for his actions against L., and it was only after 3 months of complaints that any effort was made to separate L. and G.F.'s desks. The complaint alleged that L. was unable to concentrate on her studies (her previously high grades dropped), and her father found a suicide note. The abuse continued until Mrs. Davis filed a complaint with the Monroe

County, Georgia Sheriff Department, and G.F. pleaded guilty to sexual battery. Mrs. Davis filed a $1,000,000 lawsuit under Title IX's prohibition of sex discrimination in schools (*Davis v. Monroe County Board of Education*, 1999; Van Boven, 1999).

Justice Sandra Day O'Connor, writing for the majority in the Supreme Court's 5-to-4 ruling in favor of Mrs. Davis, emphasized a relatively stringent standard of proof for plaintiffs. According to the Supreme Court, liability may be imposed "only where the funding recipient is deliberately indifferent to sexual harassment, of which the recipient has actual knowledge" (Biskupic, 1999, p. A.1). The plaintiff must show harassment that is "so severe, pervasive, and objectively offensive that it can be said to deprive the victims of access to the educational opportunities or benefits provided by the school. ... It is not enough to show .. that a student has been teased or called offensive names" (Biskupic, 1999, p. A.1). The case was sharply divided along ideological lines with Justice Anthony Kennedy citing portions of the dissenting opinion, "... almost every child, at some point, has trouble in school because he or she is being teased by his or her peers. After today, Johnny will find that the routine problems of adolescence are to be resolved by invoking a federal right to demand assignment to a desk two rows away" (Van Boven, 1999, p. 33).

SEXUAL HARASSMENT IN THE SCHOOLS

Prevalence

In 1988, the American Association of University Women (AAUW) responded to research that showed that girls were not being adequately prepared for the future. They launched a 10-year study to examine the effects of school climate on girls (Harris/Scholastic Research, 1993). This research, aimed at examining equity in educational access and preparation, uncovered a substantial rise in sexual harassment. AAUW defined sexual harassment as "unwanted and unwelcome sexual attention" and commissioned a study of 1,600 teens to provide a profile of the problem of sexual harassment in schools in terms of its educational, emotional, and behavioral impact (Harris/Scholastic Research, 1993, p. 6). The questionnaire sought students' responses regarding 13 increasingly severe forms of sexual harassment from "made sexual comments, jokes, gestures, or looks" to "forced you to do something sexual" (Bryant, 1993, p. 355). The study, commonly referred to as Hostile Hallways, indicated that four out of five students have experienced some form of sexual harassment in school with both males and females as targets, although, girls experienced more harassment and suffered graver consequences (Harris/Scholastic Research, 1993).

Additional insight into the prevalence of sexual harassment can be gained by examining student-on-student sexual harassment lawsuits from 1994 to 1999. Twenty-two of the 27 complaints were female targets against male perpetrators, two cases were males against males, and three were female targets with both male and female perpetrators. All age levels from elementary to secondary were involved, and the conduct ranged from verbal harassment to rape (Sullivan & Zirkel, 1999). Also, insight into the magnitude of the problem is sharpened by examining how infrequently sexual harassment is reported. In the Hostile Hallways study, fewer than 10% of the students who said they were a victim of sexual harassment told an adult at their school, and fewer than 25% told a parent or other family member. Sixty-three percent of harassed students said they told a friend, and 23% of harassed students said they told no one (Harris/Scholastic Research, 1993).

The Educational and Emotional Impact

Sexual harassment adversely stratifies educational opportunities across ethnic groups. The Hostile Hallways study found that 39% of African Americans, 33% of European Americans, and 29% of Hispanics reported not wanting to attend school because of sexual harassment; and 42% of African Americans, 30% of European Americans, and 35% of Hispanics reported not wanting to talk in class following the incident (Harris/Scholastic Research 1993; Bryant, 1993).

Hostile Hallways has given us insight into the emotional stress of sexual harassment. Fifty percent of the students who reported sexual harassment said they suffered embarrassment, 37% said that sexual harassment caused them to feel self-conscious, and 30% said sexual harassment made them feel less sure or confident about themselves. Sexual harassment impacts self-concept and growth and development. Seventeen percent of the surveyed students reported feeling confused about their identity. Sixteen percent of students said sexual harassment made them less popular with peers, while 12% said it has made them feel more popular (Harris/Scholastic Research, 1993; Bryant, 1993).

Sarah fits the profile of the harassed student, experiencing a wide range of emotions and vacillating between trying not to be bothered by the harassment to plotting and using different strategies to combat the harassment. Avoiding school, self-blame, helplessness, and self-doubt are familiar cords among victims of sexual harassment (Fisher et al., 1999; Webb, Hunnicutt, & Metha, 1997). Sarah was expressing her confusion and ambivalence when she said, "I like being noticed by boys, but I was embarrassed by what they were saying; and when they touched me it made me feel cheap. Most of the time I felt it was my fault, and I guess that is why I did not tell anyone. Anyway, what can teachers do? They can't follow me down the halls, and when they do see it they just ignore it."

What can be done to help Sarah and the many students like her? School counselors as advocates can be powerful change agents to help create an emotionally safe climate for our youth. Recommendations and suggestions included in this article are designed to help school counselors foster a more equitable and healthier school climate and to negate the emotional costs of sexual harassment by encouraging victims like Sarah to come forth and supporting victims when they do seek help.

School District Responsibilities

The U.S. Department of Education's Office of Civil Rights (1997) detailed school district's responsibilities to students regarding sexual harassment in a 40-page policy guide titled *Sexual Harassment Policy Guidance: Harassment of Students by School Employees, Other Students, or Third Parties*. The guide declared student-on-student sexual harassment as illegal. Highlights of the guide are outlined below.

Schools are required to adopt and publish a policy against sexual discrimination and grievance procedures that provide resolution of complaints of discrimination based on sex. School districts are not required to adopt a separate policy prohibiting sexual harassment, but the district's policy must apply to sexual harassment. If the school district's general Title IX policy does not make students aware of conduct that constitutes sexual harassment, then the policy will not be considered effective (*Office for Civil Rights; Sexual Harassment Policy Guidance*, 1997).

A hostile environment exists in the school's programs or activities if "the school knows or should have known of sexual harassment, and the school fails to take immediate and appropriate corrective action" (*Office for Civil Rights; Sexual Harassment Policy Guidance*, 1997, p. 12049). A hostile environment is created if conduct of a sexual nature is "sufficiently severe, persistent, or pervasive to limit a student's ability to participate in or benefit from the education program or to create a hostile or abusive educational environment" (p.12041). "Title IX does not require schools to take responsibility for the actions of other students, but does require school districts to respond to student actions with corrective measures" (American Counseling Association, 1997b, p. 8). Corrective measures translate into fair and equitable grievance procedures which provide: (a) directions to students and parents for filing complaints; (b) adequate, reliable, and impartial investigation of complaints, including the opportunity to present witnesses and other evidence; (c) notice of the outcome of the complaint; and (d) assurances that the school will take steps to prevent recurrences of any harassment and to correct its discriminatory effects on the complainant (*Office for Civil Rights; Sexual Harassment Policy Guidance*, 1997).

Investigation of complaints by school officials has historically been neglected. Sullivan and Zirkel (1999) analyzed 27 sexual harassment cases involving students and were "startled by the number of people the victims of harassment notified without obtaining suitable resolution. School districts in the cases to date would have difficulty escaping liability due to the number of staff the target notified" (p. 618). Liability is strong when school officials are notified and ignore complaints.

School Counselors' Responsibilities

School counselors are needed to develop and implement intervention strategies and support students who are victims of sexual harassment. But difficult, legitimate, legal and ethical questions must be considered. Sarah explained to her counselor that her parents have always taken the position that she was "loose" and interpreted all contact with boys as proof that their daughter was "wild and boy crazy" and "bound to end up pregnant." Sarah said it was impossible for her to involve her parents in her problems with harassment and pleaded with her counselor not to contact them or to tell the administration who might in turn contact her parents. Below are five major issues in the form of questions that Sarah's school counselor may face. The questions are designed to examine the complexities of protecting students' confidentiality while adhering to the OCR guidelines of Title IX legislation.

- *If Sarah reports sexual harassment to her school counselor and requests confidentiality, what is the counselor's legal and ethical obligation toward Sarah and to potential victims?* The counselor must engage in a delicate balance between the obligation to protect the confidences of the harassed student and the responsibility to help the administration stop the sexual harassment. Students deserve assurances that their confidences in a counseling relationship will not be breached. Without the safety of a confidential, secure environment in which trust can be established and maintained, Sarah may not have sought help. The primacy of confidentiality, clear in the Code of Ethics and Standards of Practice of both the American Counseling Association (ACA, 1997a, B.1) and the American School Counselor Association (ASCA, 1998, A.2.b), instructs this school counselor to protect the privacy of Sarah unless disclosure is in her best interest or is required by law.

  Sarah's counselor is required by law to report the sexual harassment. "A school has actual notice of sexual harassment if an agent or responsible employee of the school receives notification" (*Office for Civil Rights; Sexual Harassment Policy Guidance*, 1997, p. 12037). It is not necessary that the counselor or any other person notified be in a position to take appropriate steps to end the harassment or prevent its recurrence, but Title IX requires that harassment be reported to school officials who have the responsibility to take appropriate action. A school is considered to have been given notice whenever it "knew" of the behavior. In a confidential counseling conference, if a student victim of sexual harassment confides in the counselor, then this constitutes "notice" and triggers the school's responsibility to take "corrective action" (ACA, 1997b, p. 9).

- *Must Sarah be identified by name in a report of the harassment?* The Office of Civil Rights (OCR) recognizes that declining to honor a student's confidentiality may discourage reporting of harassment and, therefore, OCR promotes protecting confidentiality. On the other hand, OCR realizes that withholding the name of the victim may interfere with the investigation and infringe on the due process rights of the accused. In the context of each situation, school counselors and school administrators will need to strike a balance to honor an alleged victim's request for confidentiality if this can be done "consistently with the school's obligation to remedy the harassment and take steps to prevent further harassment" (*Office for Civil Rights; Sexual Harassment Policy Guidance*, 1997, p.12037). The school counselor in this situation will want to educate Sarah about the legal requirement for school counselors to report sexual harassment and encourage Sarah to allow her identity to be known to aid in addressing sexual harassment.
- *What if Sarah continued to insist on confidentiality with the full knowledge that without using her identity the investigation would be severely hindered?* Building on the responses in the above two questions, the *Office for Civil Rights; Sexual Harassment Policy Guidance* (1997) offers this guidance:

> A school must evaluate the confidentiality request in the context of its responsibility to provide a safe and nondiscriminatory environment for all students. The factors a school may consider in this regard include the seriousness of the alleged harassment, the age of the student harassed, whether there have been other complaints or reports of harassment against the alleged harasser, and the rights of the accused individual to receive information about the accuser and the allegations if a formal proceeding with sanctions may result. (p. 12043)

Therefore, a student's request for confidentiality should be respected and the school should make every effort to address the grievance despite being unable to identify the victim. An investigation may identify others who witnessed the harassment and are willing to be named. Depending on the seriousness of the harassment and the age of the victim, the identity of the harassed may, as a last resort, have to be revealed. For example, given what we currently know in the hypothetical case of Sarah, there is no overriding reason for revealing her identity against her wishes. However, if Sarah was being stalked by a sexual harasser and her physical safety was in question, the duty to protect her from clear, imminent danger might outweigh the duty to protect her confidences. There are no absolutes. It is only within the context of a each situation, through careful weighing of the consequences of identifying a victim, that a decision can be made to breach confidentiality.

- *What happens now that the boy accused of running his hand up Sarah's blouse, vehemently denies the accusation and his parents demand full disclosure of the incident to include the name of the accused so that they may answer the charges having all the facts?* If Sarah continued to insist on anonymity and there were no other accusers known and willing to come forth, then the appropriate response might be to forego disciplinary action against the accused as the alleged harasser cannot respond to the charges. In short, Sarah's confidentiality needs might outweigh the need for disciplinary action against the accused. Other strategies would have to be implemented such as a school-wide sexual harassment workshop, surveying students to see how widespread the problem is, and responding to the survey results by implementing prevention measures. In this situation, the school may still be able to effectively respond to the harassment and prevent harassment of other students (*Office for Civil Rights; Sexual Harassment Policy Guidance*, 1997).

- *Is this 12-year-old able to make decisions surrounding the sexual harassment in isolation of her parents? What is the counselor's legal and ethical responsibility to Sarah's parents?* As Sarah's emotional state became more fragile, her parents called the counselor to try to obtain some answers as to Sarah's decline. The school counselor's obligation to Sarah extends beyond Sarah to include her parents, teachers, administrators, and other students (ASCA, 1998, p. 2). Section B of the ASCA standards suggests collaboration with parents, representing the endeavor to establish a cooperative relationship with parents to facilitate the maximum development of the counselee (ASCA, 1998, p. 2). Consistent with professional codes, judicial decisions have historically protected parental rights. The U.S. Supreme Court continues to assert parents' legal ability to

raise their children and to provide guidance in the values and decisions governing their children. Courts generally have vested the
rights of minors in their parents. In 1979, the U.S. Supreme Court
declared: "We have recognized three reasons justifying the conclusion that the constitutional rights of children cannot be equated
with those of adults; the peculiar vulnerability of children; their
inability to make critical decisions in an informed, mature manner;
and the importance of the parental role in child rearing" (Huey &
Remley, 1988, p. 96).

The counseling literature is replete with calls to protect the confidentiality of minor clients. Yet, authors recognize that the school setting
considerably complicates the issue of confidentiality (ASCA, 1986; Corey
& Corey, 1997; Huey & Remley, 1988; Isaacs & Stone, 1998). Parents
send students to school for academics, and when individual counseling
enters into the education picture, immediate tension develops between a
parent's right to be the guiding voice in their children's lives and a student's right to privacy in the counseling arena (Huey & Remley, 1988;
Isaacs & Stone, 1998; Salo & Shumate, 1993). For example, school
counselors often wonder what their legal responsibilities are to parents
when they work with minors regarding issues such as birth control, abortion, sexual orientation, and sexual harassment. School counselors must
keep in mind their duty to warn and protect minor clients and others if
they determine that danger exists. If parents request disclosure of information their child reveals in a counseling session, they probably have a
legal right to the information as the logical extension of privacy rights,
which belong to the parent even in cases when the child or adolescent
expressly requests confidentiality (Huey & Remley,1988). In contrast,
Fischer and Sorenson (1996) argued that school counselors do not have
to disclose the content or substance of their counseling sessions unless
expressly written in school board policy.

Sarah is 12 years old. The equation of balancing her rights with the
legitimate rights and concerns of her parents must include consideration
of her developmental and chronological age. The younger the child, the
more control parents have over decisions governing their children. Legal
precedent has been established concerning children's rights varying with
age (Fischer & Sorenson, 1996). For example, teenagers (especially after
the age of 14 or when considered a mature minor) are routinely given
medical rights regarding abortion and the treatment of sexually transmitted diseases and the right to influence custody decisions (Fischer &
Sorenson, 1996). If Sarah's counselor decides to continue to work with
her in absence of parental knowledge of the true nature and extent of the
problem, the counselor must be ready to defend his or her decision that

Sarah was mature enough to make such decisions without parental involvement and that no clear danger existed for her. For Sarah's counselor it is difficult to determine if Sarah is mature enough to recognize dangerous situations and handle them independently of her parents' guidance. School counselors have to navigate the tricky waters between discerning the maturity level of minors and their confidentiality needs and parents' rights to govern their children with full knowledge of the critical issues their children are facing.

RECOMMENDATIONS FOR SCHOOL COUNSELORS

Following are recommendations for the school counselor in the dual role of helping school administrators and teachers correctly respond to sexual harassment and supporting the individual student who has been victimized. Rowell, McBride, and Nelson-Leaf (1996) provide additional suggestions for counselor interventions which they frame within a developmental guidance and counseling model.

1. Stay current on laws, ethical standards, and your school district's policies regarding sexual harassment and counseling minor clients. Consult with professional colleagues when you are faced with an ethical dilemma.
2. Acquire professional development through your counseling organizations, workshops, and/or literature on counseling strategies and legal and ethical issues involving confidentiality with minors and sexual harassment.
3. Working through your supervisor, consult with the school board attorney about placing sexual harassment on the agendas of selected school district meetings and implementing a policy protecting all students against sexual harassment to include a sexual orientation clause to protect gay, lesbian, and bisexual youth. Elements of an effective sexual harassment policy should include: (a) a code of conduct with a strong no-tolerance statement that explains the commitment to maintain an educational environment free of fear and intimidation, (b) a clear statement that sexual harassment will result in disciplinary action, (c) examples of specific sexual harassment behavior, (d) legal definitions and the applicable laws, (e) a statement of confidentiality which explains that the victim's identity will remain confidential to the extent possible and explaining the circumstances under which confidences will be breached (e.g., duty to protect the victim or other potential victims), (f) the name of at least one person of each gender to contact if students feel they have been a victim of sexual harassment (preferably a school counselor),

(g) detailed grievance procedures and contact information for the complaint manager, and (h) a statement regarding training for staff and students (Bryant, 1993; Minnesota Department of Education, 1993; Moore & Rienzo, 1998; Strauss & Espeland, 1992; Webb et al., 1997).

4. Encourage school officials to form a committee to adopt a plan of action for addressing sexual harassment. The action plan should include wide dissemination of information on sexual harassment in forums such as student assemblies, club meetings, and written information on bulletin boards, brochures, and the code of conduct on sexual harassment. Important information to include for students would be specific behaviors associated with sexual harassment and what procedures to follow for reporting the abuse.

5. Publicize widely that the school counseling office is a safe place for students to come and talk if they feel they are being sexual harassed. Develop strategies to help students and yourself ease into the discussion of sexual harassment. For the reluctant student, have the student respond to verbal or written questions in which sexual harassment is but one of a number of questions and given the same weight as other questions.

6. Encourage your students to involve their parents if they have been sexually harassed. If students express fear in telling their parents, assist them in developing strategies for coping with their parents' reactions. Offer to be available for a joint conference or subsequent parent consultation.

7. Provide periodic on-site sexual harassment workshops for staff. All school personnel should be educated about (a) how to identify harassment, (b) reporting procedures for harassment to include an understanding of the school district's sexual harassment policy and grievance procedures, (c) establishing a school and classroom climate that does not foster or tolerate harassment, and (d) implementing and developing school-wide and classroom interventions.

8. Conduct a survey to be used in helping teachers and administrators develop an understanding of the extent of the problem of sexual harassment in their school. Survey results can help tailor the content of the on-site workshops for school personnel and information to be disseminated to students.

9. Through membership on curriculum adoption committees or written input to such committees, express the need to include curriculum material on sexual harassment in appropriate courses such as a life skills, health, and/or American government.

CONCLUSIONS

School counselors in their advocacy role can empower students with the knowledge and support needed to participate in a fair, equitable, and hospitable school environment. The *Davis* case gives counselors support to serve as an advocate against student-on-student harassment. As human behavior specialists, school counselors can be instrumental in helping to heighten the awareness of the sexual harassment problem and assist in establishing prevention and intervention plans. More importantly, the school counselor can be an advocate and a source of strength for the individual student who needs help in confronting and dealing with sexual harassment. The legal and ethical complications of working with minors in schools continue to pose daily dilemmas and never more so than in sexual harassment issues. Respecting students' confidences requires school counselors to balance the rights of minors with the rights of their parents and the need to protect their classmates from potential abuse. Legal rulings and the ASCA and ACA codes for ethical behavior offer suggestions and guidance in the complexities of confidentiality. However, it is ultimately the responsibility of the school counselor to determine the appropriate response for individual students who put their trust in the security of the counseling relationship.

Carolyn B. Stone, Ed. D., *is an assistant professor, Counselor Education, University of North Florida, Jacksonville. E-mail: cstone@unf.edu.*

REFERENCES

American Counseling Association. (1997a). *Code of ethics and standards of practice.* Alexandria, VA: Author.

American Counseling Association. (1997b). *Sexual harassment in the schools. Background on Title IX of the education amendments of 1972 and guidance issued by the office of civil rights.* Alexandria, VA: Author.

American School Counselor Association. (1986). *The school counselor and confidentiality.* Alexandria, VA: Author.

American School Counselor Association. (1998). *Code of ethics and standards of practice.* Alexandria, VA: Author.

Bart, M. (1998, September). Creating a safer school for gay students. *Counseling Today, 26,* pp. 36, 39.

Biskupic, J. (1999, May 25). Davis v. Monroe County Board of Education et al. *The Washington Post,* pp. A1:1.

Bryant, A. L. (1993). Hostile hallways: The AAUW survey on sexual harassment in America's schools. *Journal of School Health, 63,* 355–357.

Corey, G., & Corey, M. (1997). *Issues in ethics in the helping profession* (5th ed.). Pacific Grove, CA: Brooks/Cole.

Davis v. Monroe County Board of Education et al. 120 F.3d 1390. (Supreme Court, May 24, 1999).

Fischer, L., & Sorenson, G. P. (1996). *School law for counselors, psychologists, and social workers* (3rd ed.). White Plains, NY: Longman.

Fischer, L., Schimmel, D., & Kelly, C. (1999). *Teachers and the law.* New York, NY: Addison Wesley Longman.

Franklin v. Gwinnett County Public Schools, 503 U.S. 60, 68 (1992).

Gebser v. Lago Vista, 118 S. Ct. 1989 (1998).

Harris/Scholastic Research. (1993). Hostile hallways: *The AAUW survey on sexual harassment in America's schools.* Washington, DC. AAUW Educational Foundation.

Huey, E., & Remley, T. (1988). Confidentiality and the school counselor: A challenge for the 1990s. *School Counselor, 41,* 23–30.

Isaacs, M. I., & Stone, C. B. (1998). School counselors and confidentiality: Factors affecting professional choices. *Professional School Counseling 4,* 258–266.

Marczely, B. (1999). Mixed messages: Sexual harassment in the public schools. *The Clearing House, 72,* 315.

Minnesota Department of Education. (1993). *Sexual harassment to teenagers: It's not fun/it's illegal.* St. Paul, MN: Author.

Moore, M., & Rienzo, B. (1998). Sexual harassment policies in Florida school districts. *Journal of School Health, 68,* 237–242.

Office for Civil Rights; Sexual Harassment Policy Guidance: Harassment of Students by School Employees, Other Students, or Third Parties. (1997). Washington, DC: U.S. Department of Education.

Rowell, L. L., McBride, M. C., & Nelson-Leaf, J. (1996). The role of school counselor in confronting peer sexual harassment. *School Counselor, 43*(3), 196–207.

Salo, M. M., & Shumate, S. G. (1993). Counseling minor clients. *The ACA legal series, 4,* 73–78.

Strauss S., & Espeland, P. (1992). *Sexual harassment and teens.* Minneapolis, MN: Free Spirit.

Sullivan, K., & Zirkel, P. (1999). Student to student sexual harassment: Which tack will the Supreme Court take in a sea of analyses? *West Education Law Reporter, 132,* 609–628.

Van Boven, S. (1999, January 25). Playground Justice. *Newsweek,* p. 33.

Webb, D. L., Hunnicutt, K. H., & Metha, A. (1997). What schools can do to combat student-to-student sexual harassment. *NASSP Bulletin, 81,* 72.

Zirkel, P. (1999). Courtside: More harassment. *Kappan, 81*(2), 171–172.

Zirkel, P., Richardson, S. N., & Goldberg, S. S. (1995). *A digest of supreme court decisions affecting education* (3rd ed.). Bloomington, IN: Phi Delta Kappa.

Chapter 12: Special Education

INTRODUCTION

Today's schools are obligated by law to devote substantial resources to students with disabilities and, as one would assume, school counselors have a role in many of these activities. Among the obligations: identifying students who might have disabilities; testing students to determine if they do have disabilities; providing special services to disabled students; monitoring the educational progress of disabled students through individualized education programs (IEPs); and helping parents and guardians of disabled students understand their children's disabilities.

School counselors have an ethical and legal duty to provide disabled students with the same counseling services they offer to students who are not disabled (see ASCA position statement, *The Professional School Counselor and the Special Needs Student*, Appendix H–19). In some schools, providing counseling to disabled students and their families is the only interaction counselors have with the special education program, while in other schools counselors are assigned additional responsibilities.

Harvey (1998) has offered an overview of the federal laws, regulations, and court cases related to "inclusion," which the National Association of School Psychologists defines as those programs that provide specialized instruction and related services to disabled students within a general classroom. Inclusion is not a term found in legislation and has only been used in a handful of court cases.

Similarly, the Individuals with Disabilities Education Act (IDEA) includes among its goals "free appropriate public education" and "least restrictive environment" for children with disabilities. Both IDEA and Section 504 of the Rehabilitation Act of 1973 require that children with disabilities be educated, to the degree possible, alongside children who are not disabled. Placements outside the regular classroom are allowed only when the nature or severity of a disability precludes such education. There is, however, language in federal legislation that appears contradictory. Emphasizing "educational programming," rather than inclusion or mainstreaming, it requires that a "continuum of alternative placements" be considered for disabled students.

Harvey (1998) has concluded that federal court decisions require schools to consider and locate the place in the continuum of alternate placements that is least restrictive for an individual child. Schools that automatically place students with particular disabilities outside of inclusion in the regular school program may be at risk for having their placement decisions overturned. Harvey emphasized that schools must establish—and then follow—procedures for making special education placement decisions. He pointed out that courts often overturn decisions because of a failure to follow school system-established procedures. Harvey also notes that, in the past, courts have most often upheld placement decisions that do not require inclusion when children have severe behavior difficulties.

Harvey (1998) has advised school counselors involved in placement decisions to: advocate for procedures at their schools that avoid the automatic placement of disabled students; present and consider a continuum of possible placements for each individual student; and, most importantly, follow any established procedures adopted by the school.

To what extent are schools obligated to provide mental health services to students who need them to be appropriately educated? Schacht and Hanson (1999) addressed this question and made recommendations for school professionals based on federal legislation and court cases. They noted that IDEA descended from the 1975 Education for All Handicapped Children Act; once a student is identified as having a disability, rights of students with disabilities attach.

IDEA does not dictate that schools provide mental health services to students who need them. Instead, it allows school districts to determine on their own whether or not some students need mental health services. If this is the case, it then can become required. If a school district does include mental health services for students with disabilities, the services must meet IDEA-established standards.

Should a school district offer mental health services to eligible students, a diagnosis of a mental disorder or the claim that a student had a "serious emotional disturbance" does not necessarily meet IDEA's definition of entitlement. IDEA requires that a child's inability to learn cannot be explained by intellectual, sensory, or health problems and that the child is not merely socially maladjusted.

Courts have not generally supported requiring school districts to provide IDEA benefits to students diagnosed with conduct disorder or oppositional defiant disorder alone. As a result, Schacht and Hanson (1999) have recommended that additional diagnoses be included, if warranted. IDEA requires students be evaluated but limits medical services to diagnosis and evaluation.

In their article, Schacht and Hanson (1999) revealed that IDEA requires mental health services only if a school district agrees to provide in-need students such services; thus, Schacht and Hanson advocate local school board action in this area. Although some school districts have determined some children are entitled to mental health services under IDEA, it's important for school counselors to understand that diagnosis of a mental disorder does not necessarily entitle a student to services. To be eligible, students must have evidenced a serious emotional disturbance over a long period of time, and the disturbance must be present to a marked degree.

Attention Deficit Hyperactivity Disorder (ADHD) has become a popular topic at school counselor conferences. This is not surprising, as counselors find they have an increasing number of students diagnosed with ADHD (see ASCA position statement, *The Professional School Counselor and Attention Deficit/Hyperactivity Disorder (ADHD)*, Appendix H–2). Erk (1999) has not only provided a foundation for offering students with ADHD services under federal legislation, but he also has suggested practice guidelines for school counselors who counsel students diagnosed with ADHD.

Students with ADHD may be entitled to services in schools under IDEA, Section 504 of the Rehabilitation Act of 1973, or the American with Disabilities Act of 1990 (ADA). To be eligible for services under

IDEA, a student with ADHD must also have other health impairments, have a specific learning disability, or be seriously emotionally disturbed. To avoid legal problems, Erk (1999) has suggested that school counselors report any suspicions of lax ADHD services to their supervisors. In addition, he has advised that school counselors document in writing any actions taken on behalf of a child suspected of having ADHD, including interactions with the child's parents.

ASCA has provided guidance in two additional areas relevant to special needs students: persons with HIV/AIDS and gifted and talented students (see ASCA position statements, *The Professional School Counselor and HIV/AIDS* and *The Professional School Counselor and Gifted and Talented Student Programs*, Appendices H–1 and H–19). These are also important issues, and each should be carefully reviewed.

For additional information regarding the unique nature of special education records, review Chapter 5. School counselors involved in special education placement decisions need to understand the basic legal principles in this chapter, as well as the proper role of counselors in special education programs.

Students with Disabilities: School Counselor Involvement and Preparation

Amy S. Milsom

Legislation has greatly impacted educational opportunities for students with disabilities. Prior to the implementation of Public Law 94–142 (the Education for All Handicapped Children Act [EAHCA] of 1975), many students with disabilities received either no services or inappropriate services in public schools (Smith & Colon, 1998; Zaccaria, 1969). For more than 25 years, however, disability legislation has mandated that public schools provide appropriate educational services to all students with disabilities. As a result, 95% of students with disabilities received services in 1996 (U.S. Department of Education, 1996).

In addition to impacting educational opportunities for students, legislation has increased the involvement of school counselors with students with disabilities. The passage of EAHCA resulted not only in greater numbers of students receiving special services in schools (Parker & Stodden, 1981; Tucker, Shepard, & Hurst, 1986), but also increased involvement of school counselors with students who have disabilities (Korinek & Prillaman, 1992; Sweeney, Navin, & Myers, 1984). More recent legislation, Public Law 101–476 (the Individuals with Disabilities Education Act [IDEA] of 1990), a reauthorization of EAHCA, and Public Law 105–17 (the 1997 Amendments to IDEA) discussed the involvement of individual school personnel with students with disabilities. Williams and Katsiyannis (1998) stated, "A primary implication of the 1997 Amendments to the Individuals with Disabilities Education Act is the need for all educators to share in the responsibility for services provided for all students including those with disabilities" (p. 17).

Although legislation encourages greater school counselor involvement with students with disabilities, little research has been conducted to examine the actual roles that school counselors perform for those students. Helms and Katsiyannis (1992) found that the elementary school counselors they surveyed in Virginia provided individual, group, and classroom counseling for students with disabilities. The most common counseling issues involved self-concept, social skills, behavior, study skills, and career awareness.

In 1980, the American School Counselor Association (ASCA) developed a position statement concerning school counselor roles with students with disabilities. That statement was revised in 1986 and again in 1993 (Baumberger & Harper, 1999). ASCA adopted two more focused position statements that discuss school counselor roles in relation to working with students with attention deficit/hyperactivity disorder (ASCA, 2000) and with students with special needs (ASCA, 1999). In those statements, ASCA suggested that school counselors advocate for students with disabilities in the school and/or community, assist students with disabilities in planning for transitions to careers or to post-secondary institutions, assist with the establishment and implementation of behavior modification plans for students with disabilities, counsel parents and families of students with disabilities, and make referrals to other appropriate specialists for students with disabilities. ASCA also suggested that school counselors provide activities for students with disabilities to improve their self-esteem, provide feedback on the social and academic performance of students with disabilities to the multidisciplinary team, provide individual and group counseling to students with disabilities, provide social-skills training to students with disabilities, serve as consultants to parents and staff on the characteristics and special needs of students with disabilities, and serve on the multidisciplinary team to identify and provide services to students with disabilities.

Given the variety of activities that school counselors might perform for students with disabilities, it is important to ensure that school counselors feel prepared to provide services to those students. It has consistently been suggested that education would help to increase school counselor competence for working with students with disabilities (Foster, 1977; Hosie, Patterson, & Hollingsworth, 1989; Isaacs, Greene, & Valesky, 1998; Margolis & Rungta, 1986; Tucker et al., 1986). Despite the acknowledged need for education to increase school counselor competence, however, most school counselor education programs in the early 1990s did not require either specific coursework related to students with disabilities or practical experiences with those students (Korinek & Prillaman, 1992). Furthermore, Korinek and Prillaman found that while most respondents (68%) indicated that their school counselor education programs would have to be altered to better prepare graduates to work with students with disabilities, only 11% had plans to make changes.

State departments of education and counselor educators have provided input concerning existing and desirable education related to students with disabilities for school counselors (Frantz & Prillaman, 1993; Korinek & Prillaman, 1992), but input from practicing school counselors has only been minimal. The purpose of this research was to obtain feedback from practicing school counselors in order to explore the activities school counselors engage in for students with disabilities and how prepared they felt to perform those activities as well as to examine recent trends in school counselor education related to students with disabilities. The following research questions were explored:

- What activities do school counselors perform for students with disabilities?
- How prepared do school counselors feel to perform activities for students with disabilities?
- What education do school counselors receive related to students with disabilities?
- What is the relationship between the education school counselors receive to work with students with disabilities and how prepared they feel overall to provide services to those students?

METHOD

Participants

A random sample of 400 members of the American Counseling Association (ACA) who indicated that they were employed in schools (elementary, middle, or high) and had joined the organization after 1995 was generated by and obtained directly from ACA. Because ACA was unable to generate a sample based on graduation year, the author requested a sample based on the year the member joined ACA. It was assumed that a significant number of these individuals had joined the organization during either graduate school or the year after completing their graduate work.

Employment as a school counselor and completion of graduate work between 1994 and 2000 were established as selection criteria. These criteria were established in order for participants to have completed their graduate work after passage of IDEA and to provide time for the integration of relevant content with respect to students with disabilities into the school counselor education programs. Of the 400 surveys mailed, nine were returned as undeliverable, reducing the total sample size to 391. Of those, 224 (57%) were returned and 100 (26%) were practicing school counselors who completed their graduate work between 1994 and 2000.

The age of the 100 participants ranged from 24 to 60, with a mean of 37.19 (SD = 9.82). Eighty-four percent were female and 16% were male. The ethnic distribution of the participants included African American (3.0%); Asian/Pacific Islander (1.0%); Latino/a or Hispanic (3.0%); Native American (2.0%); White (90.0%); and other (1.0%). Participants worked in elementary schools (28.0%), middle/junior high schools (38.0%), and high schools (34.0%). The years of school counseling experience of the participants ranged from 0 to 9, with a mean of 2.63 (SD = 1.85). Fifty-five percent of the participants were former teachers, and 16% of the participants indicated that they had been special education teachers. Seven percent of participants indicated that they had a disability, and 36% indicated that one of their immediate family members had a disability.

Procedure

A packet consisting of an introductory letter including a description of the study, a coded survey booklet, and a return envelope was mailed to each member of the sample. A reminder postcard was mailed one week later. Two weeks after postcards were sent, a follow-up letter and a second survey booklet were mailed to all members of the original sample who had not responded. Participants indicated their informed consent by returning the survey.

Instrument

The School Counselor Preparation Survey-Revised (SCPS-R) is an instrument created by the author to assess the activities school counselors perform for students with disabilities, how prepared they feel to perform those activities, and the education (coursework, practical experiences, or workshops) they received to work with students with disabilities. In order to determine if survey questions were ambiguous, a pilot study was conducted with a random sample of 200 members of the school counseling association of a mid-Atlantic state. The SCPS-R was the end result of modifications that were made based on results of that pilot study.

Based on the definition of children with disabilities in the IDEA Amendments of 1997, "students with disabilities" were defined on the SCPS-R as individuals who would qualify for special education or related services based on them meeting criteria for one or more of the following: autism; emotional disturbance; hearing impairment; specific learning disability; mental retardation; orthopedic impairment; speech/language impairment; traumatic brain injury; visual impairment; or some other health impairment which adversely affects educational performance. Participants were asked to refer to this definition when responding to the survey items.

The first item on the SCPS-R asks participants to indicate the number of students in their total caseload and the number of students with disabilities in their total caseload. In the next two items, participants are asked to use a 6-point Likert-type scale (1 = completely unprepared, 2 = unprepared, 3 = somewhat unprepared, 4 = somewhat prepared, 5 = prepared, 6 = completely prepared) to indicate how prepared they felt overall to provide services to students with disabilities and how prepared they felt to perform 11 different activities for students with disabilities (see Table 1). The fourth item on the SCPS-R lists the same 11 activities and asks participants to place a check beside each activity they performed for students with disabilities.

The list of activities discussed above was generated from the ASCA position statements concerning the roles that school counselors should engage in when working with students with attention deficit/hyperactivity disorder (ASCA, 2000) and students with special needs (ASCA, 1999). In addition, because few participants indicated how prepared they felt overall to provide services to students with disabilities, an overall preparation mean was calculated for each participant. This mean was determined based on the preparation ratings for each of the 11 activities.

Items five through nine relate specifically to the education that school counselors received to work with students with disabilities and were developed based on literature addressing education related to students with disabilities (Beattie, Anderson, & Antonak, 1997; Frantz & Prillaman, 1993; Isaacs et al., 1998; Korinek & Prillaman, 1992; Parker & Stodden, 1981). Participants are asked to indicate the number of graduate courses they completed that specifically focused on students with disabilities, the number of graduate courses completed that included discussion about students with disabilities in addition to other course content, and the number of practical experiences (e.g., practicum, internship) completed during graduate school with students with disabilities. They are also asked to report the number of school-sponsored in-service programs they attended since being employed as school counselors that related to students with disabilities. Finally, they are asked to indicate the number of conferences or workshops they attended on their own since being employed as school counselors that related to students with disabilities.

TABLE 1 Activities School Counselors Perform for Students with Disabilities and Mean Preparation Ratings Ranked from Highest to Lowest

		Preparation Rating		
Activity	Number	Percentage	M	SD
Provide individual/group counseling	82	82.8	4.54	1.03
Provide feedback for multi-disciplinary team	73	73.7	4.53	1.13
Provide self-esteem activities	59	59.6	4.46	1.13
Make referrals	81	81.8	4.44	1.12
Provide social skills training	49	49.5	4.42	1.06
Advocate for students	74	74.7	4.32	1.01
Serve on multi-disciplinary team	80	80.8	4.27	1.26
Counsel parents and families	79	79.8	4.16	1.21
Assist with behavior modification plans	74	74.7	4.00	1.26
Serve as consultant to parents/staff	55	55.6	3.77	1.32
Assist with transition plans	40	40.4	3.59	1.32

Note. Numbers and percentages of school counselors who perform activities based on $n = 99$. Preparation ratings based on $n = 100$, except for $n = 98$ for "Assist with transition plans."

Preparation was rated on a 6-point scale (1 = Completely Unprepared, 6 = Completely Prepared).

RESULTS

What activities do school counselors perform for students with disabilities? Of the 11 activities listed, seven were performed by approximately three fourths of the participants (see Table 1). The greatest percentage of participants (82.8%) provided individual and/or group counseling to students with disabilities. Also, the least percentage of participants (40.4%) assisted students with disabilities with transitions.

How prepared do school counselors feel to perform activities for students with disabilities? Participants felt somewhat prepared overall to provide services to students with disabilities ($n = 98$, $M = 4.20$, $SD = .87$). A mean rating of 3.59 ($SD = 1.32$) indicated that participants felt the least prepared to assist students with disabilities in planning for transitions to careers or to post-secondary institutions. In addition, with a mean rating of 4.54 ($N = 100$, $SD = 1.03$), participants indicated they felt the most prepared to provide individual and/or group counseling to students with disabilities. See Table 1 for a list of activities ranked from most prepared to least prepared.

What education do school counselors receive related to students with disabilities? The number of graduate courses completed by the partici-

TABLE 2 **Means, Standard Deviations, and Intercorrelations for Overall Preparation and Education Predictor Variables**

Variable	M	SD	1	2	3
Overall preparation rating (ranging from 1 to 6)	4.15	0.86	.347***	.239*	.198*
Predictor Variable					
Number of graduate courses participants completed related to students with disabilities	3.10	2.56	—	.253**	.190*
Number of practical experiences with students with disabilities the participants had during graduate school	1.77	2.00	—	—	-.008
Number of conferences or workshops related to students with disabilities the participants attended since being employed as school counselors	3.25	3.67	—	—	—

Note. Based on *n* = 89   *p < .05.   **p < .01.   ***p < .001.

pants that specifically focused on students with disabilities ranged from 0 to 6 with a mean of 0.80 (*n* = 99, *SD* = 1.19). Participants also completed an average of 2.40 (*n* = 98, *SD* = 2.40) graduate courses where information about students with disabilities was presented in addition to regular course content. Their responses ranged from 0 to 18. In addition to coursework, participants had between 0 and 10 (*n* = 91, *M* = 1.76, *SD* = 1.98) practical experiences (e.g., internship, practicum) with students with disabilities during their graduate education. Finally, since being employed as school counselors, the participants attended an average of 1.69 (*n* = 99, *SD* = 2.27) school-sponsored in-service programs and an average of 1.68 (*n* = 99, *SD* = 2.25) conferences or workshops.

What is the relationship between the education school counselors receive to work with students who have disabilities and how prepared they feel overall to provide services to those students? Multiple linear regression was used to examine this question. The null hypothesis was that there is no relationship between the education (the number of courses, practical experiences, or workshops) that school counselors complete and how prepared they feel overall to perform activities for students who have disabilities. The dependent variable was the overall preparation rating. The independent variables were (a) the total number of graduate courses the school counselors completed, including courses specifically related to students with disabilities and those integrating information about students with disabilities into existing course material; (b) the num-

TABLE 3 Regression Analysis Predicting Overall Preparation with Education Variables

Model and predictor variable	R^2	DR^2	B	SEB	b
Model 1*	.17	.17			
Number of graduate courses participants completed related to students with disabilities			.09	.04	.28
Number of practical experiences with students with disabilities the participants had during graduate school			.07	.04	.17
Number of conferences or workshops related to students with disabilities the participants attended since being employed as school counselors			.03	.02	.15
Model 2*	.15	−.02			
Number of graduate courses participants completed related to students with disabilities			.10	.04	.31
Number of practical experiences with students with disabilities the participants had during graduate school			.07	.04	.16
Model 3*	.12	−.03			
Number of graduate courses participants completed related to students with disabilities			.12	.03	.35
Note. *$p < .01$.					

ber of practical experiences with students with disabilities they completed during graduate school; and (c) the total number of conferences or workshops they attended since being employed as school counselors that related to students with disabilities.

The SPSS output (multiple regression, backward elimination option) produced three different models (see Tables 2 and 3), all of which were significant. The criteria for removing variables included a minimum F value (F-to-remove) and a minimum probability of F-to-remove. The default values of 2.71 and a probability of 0.10 were used. The third model (Model 3) indicated that 12% of the variance in overall preparation could be explained by variance in the total number of courses. Thus, the more courses an individual has completed, the more prepared he or she felt.

DISCUSSION

Participants performed many of the activities that ASCA (1999, 2000) suggested are appropriate when working with students with ADHD and/or students with special needs, and many of those activities (e.g., providing individual counseling, advocating for students) might be performed for students without disabilities. Fewer than half of the participants indicated that they assisted students with disabilities with transition plans. Because transition planning is a service that is mandated for students with disabilities at age 16 (Hardman, Drew, Egan, & Wolf, 1993; Yell, Rogers, & Rogers, 1998), it might be expected that many of the elementary and middle school counselors would indicate they do not assist with transition planning. Results indicated, however, that 32% of the participants who reported that they worked in high schools also did not assist students with transition planning.

In general, the school counselors indicated feeling "somewhat prepared" overall to provide services to students with disabilities and to perform specific activities for those students. This suggests that there might be interventions that counselor education programs and/or school districts could implement to help school counselors feel even more prepared. Results of this study indicate that school counselors feel more prepared to provide services to students with disabilities when they receive more information about (i.e., complete courses and attend workshops) and have more experiences with students with disabilities. Although the school counselors in this study did complete courses, workshops, and practical experiences related to students with disabilities, perhaps the content or quality of those educational opportunities was not adequate in terms of helping them feel completely prepared. It also seems likely that school counselors might never feel completely prepared for any role.

While the content and quality of the courses and experiences participants completed during graduate school is unknown, results of this study indicated that pre-service education related to students with disabilities is inconsistent. More specifically, some participants reported that they completed no coursework or practical experiences related to students with disabilities during graduate school and others indicated that they discussed disabilities in every course. This suggests that there is no uniformity among school counselor education programs, which is consistent with the findings of Barret and Schmidt (1986). This lack of uniformity could be partly explained, as Coombe (1994) suggested, by the fact that some states require coursework in special education while others do not. In addition, these findings are consistent with research conducted by Deck, Scarborough, Sferrazza, and Estill (1999), which indicated that many school counselors did not receive much preparation to work with students with disabilities. It appears, however, that many professional opportunities exist for school counselors to attend in-service workshops or other conferences related to students with disabilities. The variation in the number of conferences and workshops that the participants attended may likely be a function of differences in the number of opportunities that are available for school counselors to receive additional education or in their motivation to pursue additional education.

LIMITATIONS AND RECOMMENDATIONS FOR FUTURE RESEARCH

One purpose of this research was to gather information from school counselors who completed their graduate work between 1994 and 2000 in order to examine recent trends in school counselor education. The sample, however, may not have been representative of all school counselors who completed their graduate work during that time frame. It is likely that school counselors who choose to join ACA are different from those who do not choose to join, especially since school counselors can join ASCA without joining ACA. Therefore, while this study provides information about school counselor education and feelings of preparation to work with students with disabilities, the results cannot be generalized to school counselors who are not members of ACA. Results also cannot be generalized to the individuals who did not respond to the survey.

Another limitation of this study was that self-report measures were used to gather the data. While the results are useful for examining school counselor perceptions, they do not provide information about how well school counselors actually perform the activities. Therefore, future research should examine feelings of preparation or competence in relation to actual performance.

While education related to students with disabilities has been shown to be a significant predictor of the overall preparation ratings of school counselors to provide services to those students, much of the variance in the overall preparation ratings remains unexplained. Future research could help to identify other factors that may contribute to that variance. For example, it seems very likely that the content of the courses that the participants completed varied from individual to individual as did the types of practical experiences they had with students with disabilities. This resulted in analyses that were conducted based on nonstandardized treatment conditions, making it very difficult to pinpoint any one particular experience or intervention that was the most helpful. Controlled studies, where specific content areas or types of experiences are used as treatment conditions, would help researchers more clearly identify helpful topics or types of experiences.

A final limitation to this study was that the SCPS-R is a new instrument. It was developed based on a review of literature and was revised after a pilot study. The instrument appears to have face validity, however, psychometric information regarding the instrument is limited.

IMPLICATIONS FOR SCHOOL COUNSELING

As a whole, professional school counselors should take responsibility for advocating their ongoing educational needs related to students with disabilities. One way to advocate these educational needs is by providing feedback to the colleges or universities from which they graduated. Many graduate programs seek input from their alumni for the purpose of improving their programs. By completing program evaluation surveys from graduate programs or by simply sending the program chair a letter indicating areas of strength or concern, school counselors can ensure that counselor educators are informed.

Professional school counselors can also advocate disability education in their own school districts. Scheduling a meeting with school administrators or the staff development committee and providing them with a formal statement indicating a need for more education in the area of special education as well as a rationale for providing the education is a simple way to start the process. It would also be important to discuss the potential benefits for all educational and support staff. In addition, offering suggestions about or contact information for potential presenters might make the administrators or committee more likely to pursue the idea. Local and state school counseling organizations can help to identify qualified presenters.

Professional school counselors can also advocate at the school district level by developing a support network. It is important that both administrators and school counselors recognize that many school counselors may not feel completely prepared to provide services to students with disabilities. Support from administrators is important for establishing formal mentoring relationships to help ease the transition for school counselors. In addition, special educators and school counselors can establish collaborative and/or consulting relationships to provide comprehensive services for students with disabilities. Finally, in collaboration with special educators, school counselors can create a resource list of individuals, organizations, print materials, and Web sites to be consulted for issues regarding special education or disabilities.

CONCLUSION

Overall, the results of this study indicate that school counselors provide many services to students with disabilities and that additional measures could be taken to help school counselors feel more prepared to work with those students. Because information and practical experiences were both found to be helpful, graduate programs could take the lead in evaluating their current programs and adding or revising relevant courses and/or practical experiences. In addition, practicing school counselors could provide feedback to graduate programs and advocate for ongoing professional development opportunities through their school districts and professional organizations. Ultimately, however, school districts, professional organizations, counselor educators, and individual school counselors need to share in the responsibility for contributing to the initial and ongoing preparation of all school counselors in relation to working with students who have disabilities.

Amy S. Milsom, D.Ed., NCC, *is an assistant professor, Division of Counseling, Rehabilitation, and Student Development, The University of Iowa, Iowa City. E-mail: amy-milsom@uiowa.edu. This research was funded in part through a grant from the Pennsylvania State University Alumni Society.*

REFERENCES

American School Counselor Association. (1999). *The professional school counselor and the special needs student.* Retrieved November 13, 2001, from http://www.schoolcounselor.org/content.cfm?L1=1000&L2=32.

American School Counselor Association. (2000). *The professional school counselor and attention deficit/hyperactivity disorder (ADHD).* Retrieved November 13, 2001, from http://www. schoolcounselor.org/content.cfm?L1=1000&L2=4.

Barret, R. L., & Schmidt, J. J. (1986). School counselor certification and supervision: Overlooked professional issues. *Counselor Education and Supervision, 26,* 50–55.

Baumberger, J. P., & Harper, R. E. (1999). *Assisting students with disabilities: What school counselors can and must do.* Thousand Oaks, CA: Corwin.

Beattie, J. R., Anderson, R. J., & Antonak, R. F. (1997). Modifying attitudes of prospective educators toward students with disabilities and their integration into regular classrooms. *Journal of Psychology, 131,* 245–259.

Coombe, E. (1994). Training school and rehabilitation counselors to provide cooperative transition services. In D. Montgomery (Ed.), *Rural partnerships: Working together* (pp. 425–429). Proceedings of the Annual National Conference of the American Council on Rural Special Education (ACRES). Austin, TX. (ERIC Document Reproduction Service No. ED 369 638).

Deck, M., Scarborough, J. L., Sferrazza, M. S., & Estill, D. M. (1999). Serving students with disabilities: Perspectives of three school counselors. *Intervention in School and Clinic, 34,* 150–155.

Education for All Handicapped Children Act of 1975, 20 U.S.C. 1400 *et seq.*

Foster, J. C. (1977). *Increasing secondary school counselor competency in providing guidance services to physically handicapped students.* (Report No. 443CH60418). Washington, DC: Bureau of Education for the Handicapped. (ERIC Document Reproduction Service No. ED 159 848).

Frantz, C. S., & Prillaman, D. (1993). State certification endorsement for school counselors: Special education requirements. *The School Counselor, 40,* 375–379.

Hardman, M. L., Drew, C. J., Egan, M. W., & Wolf, B. (1993). *Human exceptionality: Society, school, and family.* Boston: Allyn & Bacon.

Helms, N. E., & Katsiyannis, A. (1992). Counselors in elementary schools: Making it work for students with disabilities. *The School Counselor, 39*, 232–237.

Hosie, T. W., Patterson, J. B., & Hollingsworth, D. K. (1989). School and rehabilitation counselor preparation: Meeting the needs of individuals with disabilities. *Journal of Counseling and Development, 68*, 171–176.

Individuals with Disabilities Education Act Amendments of 1997. 20 U.S.C. 1400 *et seq.* (West 1998).

Individuals with Disabilities Education Act of 1990, 20 U.S.C. Section 1400 *et seq.* (West 1998).

Isaacs, M. L., Greene, M., & Valesky, T. (1998). Elementary counselors and inclusion: A statewide attitudinal survey. *Professional School Counseling, 2*, 68–76.

Korinek, L., & Prillaman, D. (1992). Counselors and exceptional students: Preparation versus practice. *Counselor Education and Supervision, 32*, 3–11.

Margolis, R. L., & Rungta, S. A. (1986). Training counselors for work with special populations: A second look. *Journal of Counseling and Development, 64*, 642–644.

Parker, L. G., & Stodden, R. A. (1981). The preparation of counseling personnel to serve special needs students. *Elementary School Guidance and Counseling, 16*, 36–41.

Smith, J. O., & Colon, R. J. (1998). Legal responsibilities toward students with disabilities: What every administrator should know. *NASSP Bulletin, 82*(594), 40–53.

Sweeney, T. J., Navin, S. L., & Myers, J. E. (1984). School counselor education: Shipping water or shaping up? *The School Counselor, 31*, 373–380.

Tucker, R. L., Shepard, J., & Hurst, J. (1986). Training school counselors to work with students with handicapping conditions. *Counselor Education and Supervision, 26*, 56–60.

U. S. Department of Education. (1996). *Eighteenth annual report to Congress on the implementation of the Individuals with Disabilities Education Act.* Washington, DC: U.S. Government Printing Office.

Williams, B. T., & Katsiyannis, A. (1998). The 1997 IDEA amendments: Implications for school principals. *NASSP Bulletin, 82*(594), 12–17.

Yell, M. L., Rogers, D., & Rogers, E. L. (1998). The legal history of special education: What a long, strange trip it's been! *Remedial and Special Education, 19*, 219–228.

Zaccaria, J. S. (1969). *Approaches to guidance in contemporary education.* Scranton, PA: International Textbook.

Evolving Legal Climate for School Mental Health Services Under the Individuals with Disabilities Education Act

Thomas E. Schacht
Graeme Hanson

Prior to 1975, when the Federal Individuals with Disabilities Education Act (IDEA: 20 U.S.C. § 1400 et seq.) was first passed, schoolhouse doors were closed to many children with disabilities. Even as access to educational opportunities has increased, associated mental health services are frequently short-changed. This article offers lessons and caveats for clinicians derived from recent legislative amendments and developments in the case law surrounding the IDEA

This article offers lessons and caveats for clinicians involved in school mental health services that may be derived from recent legal developments, especially the evolving case law surrounding the Individuals with Disabilities Act (IDEA; § 20 U.S.C. 1400 et seq.).[1] The current IDEA, most recently amended in 1997, descends from the original 1975 Education for All Handicapped Children Act. The protections of the IDEA are triggered once a child is identified as having a disability. (This distinguishes the IDEA from Sec. 504 of the Rehabilitation Act, whose protections may be triggered if a child is merely "regarded" as having a disability, whether or not a disability has been proven to actually exist.) Disabilities specifically identified in the IDEA include: mental retardation; visual and hearing impairment; speech and language impairment; specific learning disability; serious emotional disturbance; autism; traumatic brain injury; and orthopedic impairment: 20 U.S.C.A § 1401(a)(1)(A)(i). Extension of the protections of IDEA to children between ages 3 and 5 years is at the discretion of each state: 34 C.F.R. 300.7(a)(2).

The IDEA asserts that all children with disabilities are entitled to an evaluation, which leads to an individualized education plan (I.E.P.) for a free and appropriate public education. A free and appropriate public education is defined as: a) special education and necessary related services; b) reasonably calculated to provide educational benefit; and c) provided in the least restrictive environment. Each of these definitional phrases impacts provision of mental health services in schools, and each has been the subject of significant litigation designed to clarify its meaning and boundaries.

In its original version, the purpose of the IDEA was understood as giving access to "some" educational benefit, not as insuring quality education (cf. *Angevine v. Jenkins*, D.D.C. 1990, 752 F. Supp 24).[2] Thus, schools enjoy substantial "discretionary function immunity," which allows them to evade responsibilities not specifically dictated by the

---

[1] The IDEA is Congress's ambitious attempt to remedy widespread failure by the states to provide appropriate educational services to handicapped children. Other laws provide a number of potential avenues to challenge a child's educational placement, including various constitutional arguments, violation of civil rights, and Sec. 504 of the Rehabilitation Act of 1973 and its 1974 amendments. The purposes of Sec. 504 are similar to the IDEA, but broader in scope. This law provides that otherwise qualified individuals shall not be denied benefits of any program receiving federal assistance solely on the basis of disability. The definition of disability under Sec. 504 is broader than that in the IDEA, because its reach extends not only to individuals who in fact have a disability, but also those who are regarded as disabled, whether or not that perception is correct. However, courts have held that Congress intended the IDEA to supplant these other avenues and to be the exclusive avenue for challenging educational placement of handicapped students. For example, although Sec. 504 allows a school to propose an "accommodation" to a child's handicapping condition, if a child qualifies under the IDEA, a school is not free to choose which statute it prefers, cf. Yankton. 93F.3d at 1376.

[2] The requirements that the IDEA only provide access to some educational benefit contrasts with the ethical imperative of most mental health professions, which requires provision of whatever treatment is in the best interests of the child. A clinical intervention that was calculated only to provide "some" benefit, rather than the best benefit, would likely be found substandard.

IDEA, even when common-sense indicates otherwise. For example, in *Killen v. Independent School District No. 706*, a school system was held immune from liability for its failure to notify parents that a ninth-grade student had discussed suicide with a guidance counselor. The court reasoned that the school's decision not to have a suicide prevention policy was appropriately within its discretionary boundaries, and in the absence of such a policy to violate, the school had done nothing wrong.

It is important to recognize that the I.D.E.A sets a floor, not a ceiling, on local and state duties to handicapped students. School systems may voluntarily exceed this floor by creation of appropriate policies, which, once adopted, then carry substantial legal weight. An important implication for school mental health professionals is that major benefits can accrue from local political action, which encourages local school systems to formally adopt meaningful policies related to mental health concerns.

The 1997 amendments to the IDEA expressed Congress's dissatisfaction with the lack of emphasis on quality in the original legislation. (125. emphasis added). The 1997 Congressional amendments to the IDEA set out four quality-improvement elements. To the extent that mental health services may be included in the school's program of special education, such services will now have to conform, where appropriate, to the requirements of those quality improvement elements:

Inclusion

The 1997 amendments emphasize that children with disabilities must be educated with children who are not disabled to the maximum extent possible. Three specific requirements promote this goal. First, the I.E.P. must specify what opportunity a child has to participate in the general curriculum. Second, a "regular education teachers" must participate in the creation of the I.E.P. whenever appropriate. Third, any funding mechanism that favors placement of the child in a nongeneral curriculum or segregated setting is prohibited.

Parent Empowerment

The amendments expand the role of parents. First, parents may attend and participate in all meetings with respect to identification, evaluation, placement, and education of the child. Second, while in the past parents could only examine "relevant" records, they may now examine all records relating to their child. Third, parents are now entitled to participate in decisions about the particular geographic location or specific institution in which the educational program is to be implemented. Previously, parents only participated in decisions about the nature of the educational program, not its location. Fourth, the rights of parents to various types of notice have been expanded. Parents are entitled to notice of their procedural rights, to notice of all information they need to participate fully in a dialogue with the I.E.P. team members, and to periodic progress reports about their child at a frequency no less than the frequency of report cards made to parents of nondisabled peers. Finally, the local educational agency cannot summarily dismiss parental input and is required by the law to consider information from parents as "relevant" to the I.E.P. decision making process.

I.E.P. Agenda

Congress expanded the list of fundamental topics that must be considered by the I.E.P. team. Where appropriate to a child's circumstances, an I.E.P. must now address: a) potential for benefit from assistive technology, b) need for behavioral intervention, c) need for Braille instruction for blind students, d) communications needs of hearing impaired student that will allow them to enjoy the same opportunities as other students, and e) needs of students with disabilities who have limited proficiency in English.

School Administration / Personnel Improvements

Four administrative provisions were enacted by Congress to enhance the quality of education under IDEA First, by July 1, 2000, all children must participate in regular educational achievement assessments. If a disabled student, even with accommodations, is unable to participate in mainstreamed testing, then the school system must provide an alternative assessment appropriate to the child's impairment. Second, the 1997 amendments restructure the membership of the State Advisory Panel, which assists the state education department on special education issues. A majority of the panel members must now be individuals with disabilities or parents of children with disabilities. Third, the 1997 amendments mandate the recruitment and training of minority special education teachers, who are in critically short supply. Finally, the amendments authorize appropriately trained and supervised paraprofessional assistants to participate in the education of students with disabilities.

DIAGNOSIS DOES NOT EQUAL DISABILITY

To enable their clients to access the benefits of IDEA, mental health professionals whose work may be applied in school settings should be familiar with the limited federal definition of "serious emotional disturbance" (Table 1) . Mental disorders are defined by the presence of suffering and/or functional impairment. While clinicians may regard either manifestation as equally deserving of treatment, the IDEA emphasizes functional impairment in the educational setting as the sine qua non of

TABLE 1　Definition of "Serious Emotional Disturbance"
　　　　　　　　34 C.F.R.300.7(b)(9)

"Serious emotional disturbance" is defined as follows:

(i)　The term means a condition exhibiting one or more of the following characteristics over a long period of time and to a marked degree that adversely affects a child's educational performance—

(A)　An inability to learn that cannot be explained by intellectual, sensory, or health factors:

(B)　An inability to build or maintain satisfactory interpersonal relationships with peers and teachers:

(C)　Inappropriate types of behavior or feelings under normal circumstances:

(D)　A general pervasive mood of unhappiness or depression: or,

(E)　A tendency to develop physical symptoms or fears associated with personal or school problems:

(ii)　The term includes schizophrenia. The term does not apply to children who are socially maladjusted unless it is determined that they have a serious emotional disturbance.

eligibility for special education. Thus, the mere presence of a DSM diagnosis will not satisfy the legal definition of disability unless there is a demonstrated causal relationship between the diagnosis and impairment of educational progress. For example, in *Schoenfeld v. Parkway School District,* a federal appellate court held that generalized anxiety and separation anxiety did not meet the definition of a disability in a seventh grader whose symptoms did not cause his academic performance to fall below a level appropriate to his age. A similar finding was made in Doe by and through *Doe v. Board of Education of the State of Conn.,* in which a child was determined not to qualify for special education even though he had emotional and behavioral difficulties, including depression, because these difficulties did not affect his educational performance, which was satisfactory and above. Furthermore, courts have been suspect of the relevance of mental evaluations conducted for noneducational purposes. For example, a psychiatric evaluation prepared for purposes of a juvenile court disposition hearing was found to afford insufficient basis for a finding of disability under the IDEA (*Springer v. Fairfax County Sch. Bd.,* 1997).

Conversely, absence of a DSM diagnosis does not absolutely disqualify a child from IDEA protections. In fact, an inability to learn is in itself an alternative characteristic that may satisfy the federal definition of "serious emotional disturbance." Thus in *Muller v. Committee on Spec. Educ.,* the Second Circuit ruled that a student qualified as seriously emotionally disturbed even though her depression had never been formally diagnosed. The court based its conclusion on: a) expert testimony that emotional disturbance adversely affected the child's educational progress, b) evidence that the problems amounted to more than mere conduct disorder, and c) evidence showing that the child's academic progress improved in a residential setting where emotional problems were being addressed.[3]

As defined by the law, a serious emotional disturbance must be present over a long period of time (thereby excluding adjustment disorders and other time-limited conditions) and must be present to a marked degree. While the IDEA does not define the meaning of "marked degree," some guidance may be found in regulations of the Social Security Administration, which define marked impairments as those which result in functioning that is two standard deviations below the population mean on standardized measures. Demonstrating impairment to a marked degree may be most challenging when a child is of above-average premorbid ability, because the deleterious effects of a mental disorder may not reduce the child's academic functioning to a level that is impaired by the absolute population-based standard. A court may have difficulty seeing impairment in a child who slips from performing two standard deviations above the population mean to performing only one standard deviation above the mean.

ALL CAUSES OF DISABILITY ARE NOT CREATED EQUAL

To qualify for the disability of "serious emotional disturbance," the IDEA requires a determination that a child's inability to learn cannot be explained by intellectual, sensory, or health factors and that the child's problem is more than mere social maladjustment. Clinicians operating from a biophysical perspective recognize that the multiple causal factors impinging on any given problem behavior or symptom are often inextricably intertwines. Separating them may be somewhat like trying to unscramble an egg. Under these circumstances, a school may successfully argue that any learning problems are due solely to conditions that are not covered by IDEA

---

[3] This court finding raises the interesting question of whether the requirements for evaluation under the IDEA could be extended to order an intervention or placement for diagnostic purposes. It may be difficult in some cases for limited evaluation to establish a clear causal connection between a handicapping condition and educational impairment. However, if educational functioning improves following a diagnostic placement in a setting designed to address the handicapping condition, this is emotional evidence that the handicapping condition is in fact relevant to the child's educational progress and argues strongly for eligibility under IDEA.

For example, consider the following case in which alcohol and drug abuse were a primary presenting problem. In *Springer v. Fairfax County School Bd.* (1997), a school system avoided payment of residential tuition for a teenager by arguing successfully that his academic success depended on his motivation and that his use of alcohol and drugs did not mean he had emotional problems. While substance abuse is not an explicitly covered condition under the IDEA, one could reasonably argue that it may cause an inability to learn which cannot be explained by intellectual, sensory, or health factors. Furthermore, epidemiological literature indicates a very high rate of comorbidity between substance abuse and other conditions which would clearly make a child eligible.

Of course, whether an emotional disturbance is discovered may depend upon whether one looks for it. While the IDEA entitles a child to evaluation at the school's expense, the scope of such evaluations can be gerrymandered to avoid exposing the school to the potential expense of mental health intervention. For example, the first author recently testified in a case involving a young girl who had failed the third grade, earning all Fs, despite an above average IQ and commensurately above-average achievement test scores. The school's investigation of this problem, initiated at the request of the child's single-parenting mother, compared the IQ and achievement test scores and concluded that there was no learning disability and therefore no special services were warranted. Other school records indicated that the child's teacher reported her to be masturbating openly in the classroom, occasionally vocalizing wildly without observable precipitating event, and occasionally talking incomprehensibly. However, these observations were never addressed in the school assessment team's integrated report. Although the facts of this case screamed "emotional disturbance," and although the child's educational performance was obviously suffering, no IDEA qualifying diagnosis was made and no intervention was offered.

DISTURBED OR JUST DISTURBING? DISABILITY VS. MISCONDUCT

Childhood misconduct is frequently met with ambivalence on the part of adults, including educational and mental health professionals. The same misbehavior may be interpreted by some as a sign of disturbance requiring treatment, while others see it as a sign of delinquency requiring discipline.[4] The IDEA mirrors this ambivalence by providing a loophole through which schools may exclude disruptive students from the statute's

---

[4] In fact, both positions may be accurate, as suggested by research demonstrating high levels of psychopathology in populations of juvenile offenders (Atkins et al., in press: Pumariega et al., in press).

protective umbrella. This can be accomplished by designating the child's problem behavior as mere "social maladjustment" rather than as externalizing symptoms of a serious emotional disturbance (34 C.F.R. § 300.7 (9)(ii)).

Some courts have recognized the potential for abuse of this loophole, and have weighed in favor of students' rights to a free and appropriate public education. If misconduct occurs outside of school and results in a child's placement in a residential juvenile facility, it is clear that the school system remains obligated to provide special education services, including preparation of I.E.P.'s, regardless of whether the misconduct is disability-related (cf. *Ashland Sch. Dist. v. New Hampshire Div. For Children, Youth and Families*, 1996, *Doe v. Arizona Department of Education*, 1997). If a school system refuses to prepare an I.E.P. for an incarcerated child, and if the residential institution has an educational component which creates a supplemental I.E.P., then the school system may be obligated to pay for implementation of the I.E.P. even though it did not create it (Ashland).

In *Magyar v. Tucson Unified School District*, an Arizona federal court ruled in 1977 that a school policy of not providing services to disabled students expelled for conduct unrelated to their disability violated the IDEA. The court held that a 175-day suspension for bringing a knife to school constituted a change of placement which warranted a new I.E.P. The court concluded, "It is apparent that Congress intended all children with disabilities to have an appropriate education, including those with discipline problems." A similar conclusion was reached in the 1997 case of *Morgan v. Chris L.*, which held that a school's filing of an unruly petition in juvenile court against a child identified with A.D.H.D. constituted a change of educational placement that entitled the child to procedural and substantive protections under the IDEA, such as an I.E.P. committee review of the decision to file the petition and a determination that it was the least restrictive alternative.

However, mirroring our profound cultural ambivalence about juvenile misconduct, the Fourth Circuit held that the right of disabled students to an appropriate education could be forfeited by misconduct not related to the student's disability (*Virginia v. Riley*, 1977). A more recent decision rejected the concept that social maladjustment was, in itself, conclusive evidence of serious emotional disturbance, and found that the student in question suffered only conduct disorder characterized by disregard for social demands and expectations (*Springer v. Fairfax County Sch. Bd.*, 1998). Furthermore, a Maryland court held that protections against unreasonable expulsion apply only if a student is formally identified as disabled prior to the misconduct (*Miller v. Board of Education of Caroline County*, 1997). This case leaves disturbingly unanswered the chicken and egg question of what happens to a student whose initial presentation of a disabling condition includes behavior classified as misconduct?

As the foregoing illustrate, recent court cases suggest that two groups of students may be uniquely jeopardized by issues relating to assessment of misconduct: a) those who misbehave in school as compared to those whose misconduct is limited to community settings: and b) those whose misconduct is deemed unrelated to their disability. Clinicians are challenged by courts to dichotomously parse the etiology of misconduct into acts related and acts unrelated to the student's qualifying IDEA disability. This evaluation task mirrors the extremely difficult determinations required by some criminal defenses (such as determining whether a particular criminal act is the product of an irresistible impulse which also arises from a mental disease or defect). Extending the analogy, the IDEA encourages a misbehaving student with a disability to demonstrate a connection between his disabling condition and his misconduct. This connection, if proven, functions as a form of modified "insanity defense" against the "punishment" risks of disciplinary action or losing his special education benefits.

Descriptive diagnoses such as conduct disorder or oppositional defiant disorder do not specify underlying etiology and may signify little more than a conclusion that a child's primary presenting symptoms are externalizing rather than internalizing. From this perspective, conduct disorder and oppositional defiant disorder may frequently function as interim labels, often indicating that the clinician has not fully understood the dynamics and underlying pathology of a given case. However, in the context of proceedings related to the IDEA, these labels may be misunderstood as signifying nothing more than social maladjustment.

To protect children's opportunities under the IDEA, clinicians would be well advised to include other diagnoses (if present) along with conduct disorder and oppositional defiant disorder, even if these other diagnoses are merely in the differential and await confirmation. Furthermore, clinicians who believe that a therapeutic rather than disciplinary response is necessary should be more explicit about causal connections between externalizing symptoms and serious emotional disturbance.

UNFUNDED MANDATES CREATE SYSTEM PATHOLOGY

The IDEA creates an education entitlement for disabled children. Unfortunately, the costs of fully implementing this entitlement are not guaranteed. This creates a perverse incentive for school systems to protect their budgets by striving to not identify children as disabled. Furthermore, if parents are dissatisfied with their child's education, they must generally first appeal an adverse decision to the system which created it. If a school's evaluation and intervention do not result in appropriate educational placement, then a school may be ordered to pay for an independent evaluation (*Seattle School district No.1 v. B.S. ex Rel. A.S.,* 1996). However, even though a school may be forced to pay for an independent evaluation, there is no requirement that the school system attach any particular weight to the results. Thus, in what may be a classic illustration of placing the fox in charge of the henhouse, the Seventh Circuit ruled in 1996 that a school system has an absolute right to conduct its own clinical evaluation and cannot be forced to rely on an independent evaluation conducted by an expert chosen by the child's parents (*Johnson v. Duncland School Corporation,* 1996). In the same year, a Vermont federal court certified a class that included all parties in the State of Vermont that were eligible to file a complaint under IDEA The lawsuit alleged systematic failure to adopt and implement procedures for ensuring compliance with the IDEA (*Upper Valley Association v. Mills,* 1996). However, in this case the fox was temporarily removed from the henhouse door, as the court ruled that the plaintiffs did not have to exhaust administrative remedies before filing suit.

Responsibility for services to children and youth is typically divided among multiple agencies, each with separate missions and budgets. This circumstance creates a natural incentive for each agency to shift the burden of financial responsibility to someone else's budget. This type of "child dumping" may be accomplished in a variety of ways, direct and indirect. Some direct efforts have failed. For example, in 1997 an Illinois federal court dismissed a case brought by a school district which sought to shift the burden of payment to the State Board of Education and the State Department of Human Services for residential care of an emotionally disturbed sexually aggressive child, reasoning that the IDEA did not give the school system any standing to bring a claim against a state agency.

While agencies duel over budget matters and engage in creative buckpassing, children's needs may go unmet. There is a desperate need for state laws mandating interagency coordination of services. This could be accomplished, in principle, by designing systems in which the flow of benefit dollars was not linked to a particular agency, but rather was attached to the child and could follow the child from agency to agency.

One model for such a system has been developed in California and has met with modest success. In 1984 and 1985 the California legislature adopted measures to remove the financial incentive for school systems to under-identify children with education-relevant health needs. These measures, known as Assembly Bills 3632 (1984) and 882 (1985) combined to add Chapter 26.5 to Title 1 of the California Code and sought to coordinate a system of services across various agencies bearing responsibility for children's' health, education, and welfare. Chapter 26.5 has the following essential requirements with respect to mental health needs of children:

1. Local education systems must invite staff from county mental health agencies to attend I.E.P. meetings at which recommendations for mental health services are to be considered.
2. Mental health services may be added to a child's I.E.P. only after a qualified professional has performed an assessment and has recommended the services.
3. Upon approval of such services by the I.E.P. committee, county mental health departments must provide the mental health services.
4. Residential treatment services required by an I.E.P. must be paid for by the county social services department. However, out-of-state placements are only permitted after all in-state alternatives have been considered and determined to be inadequate to meet the child's needs.

Agencies and authorities whose activities were to be coordinated by Chapter 26.5 included the State Department of Education, the Superintendent of Public Instruction, the State Department of Mental Health, the State Department of Health Services, and the Secretary of the Health and Welfare Agency. Emergency regulations were adopted to implement these measures in 1986 and have been subject to interim reauthorization on an annual basis since that time. However, as of this writing in 1998, final regulations have not been adopted. This failure is most likely due to insufficiently appreciated conflicts associated with differences in mandates and procedures unique to each state agency, as well as unexpectedly high program costs. Each agency had different procedures for identification and referral, different time frames for assessment and treatment decisions, and different approaches to dispute resolution and appeals processes. Furthermore, the financial impact of the program was substantially greater than had been anticipated. The California legislature had initially expected that implementation of Chapter 26.5 would not carry any incremental costs, reasoning that the expenses of mental health evaluation and treatment would be borne by transferring monies already in the special education budget to the mental health budget. However, the special education budget had been grossly underfunded, and simply transferring insufficient funds to a different agency did not improve inadequate services. Under the new mandate, the next 10 years (1986–1996) witnessed a six-fold increase in the state portion of the budget for mental health services to children in special education. In 1996 more than 17,000 pupils benefited from services provided pursuant to Chapter 26.5.

While many of the operating issues have been resolved, voluntary compliance with the law has been less than complete and full implementation of Chapter 26.5 had required litigation. Thus, *McLeish v. California Department of Education* (1998) recently produced a stipulated judgment requiring the state agencies to develop final interagency regulations for full implementation of Chapter 26.5 by September 1999.

Yet another recent twist on the issue of least restrictive environment appears in *McLaughlin v. City of Lowell* (1998), in which a young woman alleged that she was raped by three students and then claimed she could not emotionally tolerate attending school with them (they retained enrollments while their criminal cases were pending). This case portends enormously complicated issues that could arise under a variety of similar circumstances. For example, suppose a high school student accused a faculty member of sexual misconduct and simultaneously sued the school for negligence in hiring and supervising the teacher. If the student then applied for special services under the IDEA, claiming persistent emotional disturbance as a result of the sexual assault, the school would be in the awkward position of having a legal duty under IDEA to evaluate and document the psychological damages which might later be used against the school in the student's civil lawsuit.

Most significant for clinicians is the fact that restrictiveness is not a clinical concept, but a legal term that characterizes a judgment about the degree of intrusion into civil rights and protected liberty interests posed by a particular intervention program or educational environment. For this reason, clinicians and educators must perpetually weigh the restrictions posed by a particular environment against the unique profile of a particular child's strengths and impairments as well as the risks to the child and others posed by placement in a particular environment. In recommending interventions, clinicians must take care to frame the rationale for intervention in terms which can be mapped easily onto the relevant IDEA factors. Ideally, each intervention recommendation would be accompanied by an explicit analysis demonstrating that it is reasonably calculated to provide educational benefit, that it does not discriminate on the basis of disability, that there is no unnecessary exclusion from mainstreamed activities, and that the intervention is to be provided in the least restrictive environment. However, even with these protections in place, it is still possible for well-meaning clinicians to violate a student's rights, as illustrated by Rasmus ex rel. *Rasmus v. Arizona* (1996). In this case a student with A.D.H.D. was sent to a time-out room for disruptive behavior. Prior to entering the room he was required to remove his jacket and shoes and empty his pockets. The court refused to dismiss a claim that the school had violated the student's Fourth Amendment right to be free from unreasonable search and seizure.

RELATED SERVICES

Once a disabling condition has been identified and accepted as such through the procedures of an Individual Education Plan (I.E.P.), the school acquires a measure of responsibility for providing related services necessary to allow the child to participate in and receive benefit from an appropriate program of special education. The key test for inclusion of a related service is two-fold:

1. The proposed related service must be a supportive service required if the child is to benefit from special education. This typically means that the service must be provided during school hours in order for the child to benefit.
2. The proposed service must not be excluded from the definition of supportive service because it is a medical service beyond diagnosis and evaluation.

Of particular relevance to mental health is the explicit statutory inclusion under 20 U.S.C.A.'s 1401 (a)(17) of psychological services, therapeutic recreation, social work services, counseling services, and medical services. These federal regulations and definitions superceded any state regulations or local policies regarding related services (for example, see case involving provision of psychotherapy services to an 11-year-old emotionally disturbed boy, *T.G. v. Board of Education of Piscataway, N.J.*, D.C.N.J., 1983).

Unfortunately, the IDEA clause that limits medical services only to diagnostic and evaluation services does not define the key terms "medical" and "diagnostic" and "evaluation." As a result, determination of the precise meaning of this provision must be slugged out in litigation between parents and school systems. As is typical in our adversarial system of law, ambiguity invites extreme positions. Thus, parents have argued that "medical services" only includes services personally performed by a licensed physician and that any other service necessary to enable a disabled child to benefit from education must be provided free of charge, regardless of cost. In contrast, school systems have argued that the only health-related services that are not excluded medical services with the meaning of the IDEA are services traditionally provided by a school nurse.

In *Irving Independent School District v. Tatro* (1984), the U.S. Supreme Court held that bladder catheterization was a related service under the IDEA which, although medically prescribed, could be provided by a person other than a physician. This case suggested a bright-line test of professional qualifications, which would exclude medical services if they could only be performed by a physician, whereas other services, even if medically prescribed, were not excluded if they could be performed by a non-physician.

However, several other decisions have not interpreted Tatro as establishing such a bright-line test. For example, in *Neely v. Rutherford* (1995) the Sixth Circuit held that tracheostomy monitoring and suctioning were medical treatment and therefore excluded from related services, reasoning that State law required that only family members and licensed health professionals (not just physicians) could provide these services. An opposite conclusion was reached in *Skelly v. Brookfield Lagrange Park School District* (1997), where the court required a school district to provide an aide to suction a student with a tracheotomy tube during bus rides to and from school. The Skelly court narrowly construed "medical services" to mean services provided by a licensed physician. The Eighth Circuit, in *Cedar Rapids Community School District v. Garret F.* (1997) rules similarly to Skelly, reasoning that continuous nursing service required by a quadriplegic student to monitor breathing and other biological needs was necessary supportive service and was not excluded because it was provided by a nurse rather than a physician. One appeals court summarized the situation as follows: "We are at a loss to conceptualize or operationalize the distinction between related services of a medical nature that are covered by the IDEA and medical services that are not covered; and we are happy that the Supreme Court will by grappling with this issue" (*Morton Community Unit School District No. 709 v. J.M. and M.M. and S.M.*, 1998). (As final revisions to this manuscript are being completed in March 1999, the Supreme Court has just affirmed the *Cedar Rapids v. Garret F.* court, clarifying that "medical services" are those provided by a physician.)

One potential implication of the foregoing cases for child psychiatrists and behavioral pediatricians may be that employment of a nurse practitioner with prescription privileges could be used to argue that psychopharmacologic monitoring should be covered as an "evaluation" service that does not fail the medical exclusion test. However, even if these professional services were deemed to fall under the IDEA umbrella, school systems may still thwart medical interventions by adopting incompatible local policies which thwart implementation of medically prescribed treatments.

For example, even in the age of managed care, physicians probably do not expect school systems to dictate how medications may be administered. However, at least two recent cases have upheld the right of a school system to adopt policies that restrict the prescribing flexibility of treating physicians. It is common for appropriate school staff to administer prescribed psychotropic medications to children whose conditions require such treatment. Because of the dearth of controlled medication trials in pediatric populations (Rapaport, 1998), it is also common for prescribed treatments in child psychiatry to be "off-label" and based on knowledge gleaned from clinical experience, open trials, and case reports.

In *Davis v. Francis Howell School District* 138F.3d 754, Eighth Circuit, 1998, a Federal appeals court held that a school was not required by the IDEA or Section 504 of the Rehabilitation Act to administer a dose of Ritalin to a child that was in excess of the recommended dosage found in the *Physician's Desk Reference* (PDR). The court noted that the school had a general policy prohibiting school staff from participating in administration of medications in any manner not in conformity with the PDR, and therefore was not discriminating against any individual disabled student. The court also held that requiring the school to examine each case on its merits was unreasonable, in light of the financial and administrative burdens associated with determining the safety of the dosage and the likelihood of future harm and liability in each case. A virtually identical decision was reached in a previous case (*DeBord v. Board of Education of the Ferguson-Florissant School District*, 1997).

PROFESSIONAL LIABILITY

The IDEA itself does not provide for award compensatory or punitive monetary damages in the event of educational "malpractice." For exam-
˙ʼ ꞁ disabled child were shown to have suffered psychological dam-
a result of a teacher's misconceived educational strategy, then a
ꞁ could only be ordered to provide psychotherapeutic services if
ꝫary to help the child benefit from special education (*Charlie F. by F. v. Board of Education of Skokie School Dist.*). However, a ꝫachusetts court recently held that because the IDEA sets forth cer-
⸺ procedural rights, school officials who violate those rights may be subject to personal lawsuit for monetary damages for civil rights violation under 42 U.S.C. § 1983 (cf. *McLaughlin v. City of Lowell*).

While no such cases were located, the IDEA may theoretically define a standard of care that could support a traditional malpractice tort action under state law. This possibility is most apparent when considering analogies between the procedures by which managed care organizations determine eligibility for treatment benefits and the procedures by which the IDEA determines eligibility for special education.

Clinicians working in regular mental health settings must become familiar with the administrative and appeals procedures of managed care. Indeed, failure to appeal an adverse benefit decision has been validated as a potential form of malpractice (cf. *Wickline v. State*, 1986). In a similar vein, clinicians working with school populations should become as familiar with the administrative remedies and process of the IDEA as they must be with the administrative and appeals process of managed care. In general, access to a court will be denied until all administrative remedies have been exhausted (cf. *Bills v. Hommer Consolidated School District,* 1997). The IDEA gives the right to appeal to students and parents, but not to clinicians; this is analogous to a health insurance policy, which is a contract to benefit the patient, not the clinician. Yet, as in the managed care arena, it is not inconceivable that a clinician could be held to professional standard of care which mandated participation or even initiative in administrative appeals under the IDEA

CONCLUSION

Policy documents frequently cite schools as potentially ideal settings for mental health services. This should not be surprising, given that children typically spend about 1,200 hours per year in school, a contact window that compares very favorably with the maximum 25–50 hours annually of direct mental service contact typically reimbursed by third party payers in outpatient mental health-care settings. Unfortunately, mental health services in schools often lack sufficient depth, scope, and duration. At worst, such services are uncoordinated, unmeasured, and even incomprehensible. Indeed, noting the infrequency with which adequate mental health services can be located in educational settings, some authors recently described the occasionally encountered positive programs as "Islands of Hope in a Sea of Despair" (Dwyer & Bernstein, 1998).

Any in-depth analysis of this stimulation must address multiple systemic factors. These include: a) availability of research to support program design, implementation, and evaluation along a continuum from primary prevention to treatment; b) the challenge of designing programs capable of responding sensitively within ecological frameworks strongly defined by factors of cost and culture, as well as clinical priorities and individual differences; and c) ambiguities and uncertainties in the body of law related to mental health services in educational settings. This article has analyzed opportunities and problems related to this latter factor. While the IDEA provides an ambitious rehabilitative mechanism for disabled children, its promise as a vehicle for effectively promoting delivery of school mental health remains to be fully realized.

Thomas E. Schacht *is affiliated with the James H. Quillen College of Medicine, East Tennessee State University and* **Graeme Hanson** *is affiliated with the Langley Porter Psychiatric Institute, University of California at San Francisco.*

REFERENCES

Angevine v. Jenkins, D. D. C. (1990), 752 F. Supp.24.

Annino, P. (1998). The 1997 amendments to the IDEA: improving the quality of special education for children with disabilities. *Mental and Physical Disability Law Reporter,* 23(1), pp. 125–128.

Ashland School District v. New Hampshire Division for Children, Youth and Families. 681 A2d 71. N.H. Sup. Ct. (1996).

Atkins, D., Pumariega, A., Rogers, K., Montgomery, L., Nybro, C., & Seare, F. (In press). Mental health and incarcerated youth: Vol. I. Prevalence and nature of psychopathology, *Journal of Child and Family Studies.*

Bills v. Hommer Consolidated School District, No. 33-C., 959 F. Supp. 507. N.D.III. (1997).

Cedar Rapids Community School District v. Garrett F. by Charlene F., 106 F.3d 822 (1997).

Charlie F. by Neil F. v. Board of Education of Skokie School District, 126 F.3d 1102. 8th Cir. (1997).

Doe By and Through Doe v. Board of State of Conn., D. Conn., 753 F. Supp. 65 (1990).

Dwyer, K. P. & Bernstein, R. (1998). Mental health in the schools: "Linking islands of hope in a sea of despair." *School Psychology Review,* 27(2), pp. 277–286.

Heideman v. Rother, 84 F3.d 1021, 8th Cir. (1996).

Horry County School District v. P. F., South Carolina DDSN, Horry County DSN Bd., Pee Dee Center, and South Carolina Dept. of Education, U.S. Dist. Court of South Carolina, Florence Division. C/A No. 4:98-899-22, unpub. Opinion (October 20, 1998).

Individuals with Disabilities Education Act, 20 U.S.C. 1400 et. Seq.

Irving Independent School District v. Tatro, 168 U.S. 883 (1984).

Johnson v. Duncland Sch. Corp., 92 F.3d 554, 7th Cir. (1996).

Killen v. Independent School District No. 706. 547 N.W. 2d 113. Minn. Ct. App. (1996).

Magyar v. Tucson Unified School District, 958 F. Supp., 1423. D. Arizona (1997).

McLaughlin v. City of Lowell, No. Civ. A. 94-5069. Mass. Super. Ct. (Apr. 3, 1998).

McLeish v. California Department of Education, No. 96CS01380. Cal. Sup. Ct. (Feb. 27, 1998).

Miller v. Board of Education of Caroline County, 690 A.2d 557, Md. Ct. Spec. App. (1997).

Morgan v. Chris L., No. 94-6561, 6th Cir., unpub. Opinion (January 21, 1997).

Morton Community Unit School District No. 709 v. J.M. and M.M. and S.M., WL 420393, 7th Cir, III. (1998).

Mr. X v. NY State Education Department, 975 F. Supp. 546, S.D.N.Y. (1997).

Muller v. Committee on Special Education of the E. Islip Union Free School District, 145 F3.d 95, 2nd Cir. (1998).

Neely v. Rutherford County Sch., 68 F.3d 965, 6th Cir. (1995).

Pumariega, A., Atkins, D., Rogers, K., Montgomery, L., Nybro, C., Caesar, R., & Millus, D. (In press). Mental Health and Incarcerated Youth: Vol. II. Service utilization. *Journal of Child and Family Studies.*

Rapaport, J. (1998). Child psychopharmacology comes of age. *Journal of the American Medical Association,* 280(20), p. 1785.

Rasmus ex rel. Rasmus v. Arizona, 939 F. Supp. 709. D. Ariz. (1996).

Schoenfeld v. Parkway School District, 138 F 3d 379, 8th cir. (1998).

Seattle School District No. 1 v. B. S. ex Rel. A. S.,82 F.3d 1493, 9th Cir. (1996).

Skelly v. Brookfield Lagrange Park School District, 968 F. Supp. 385, N.D. Ill. (1997).

Springer v. Fairfax County Sch. Bd., E. D. Va., 1997, 960 F. Supp. 89, 1997, affirmed 134 F.3d 659.

Springer v. Fairfax County Sch. Bd., C. A. 4(Va.). 134 F.3d 659 (1998).

T.G. v. Board of Education of Piscataway, N.J. 576 F. Supp. 420, affirmed 738 F.2d 420, certiori denied 105 S. Ct. 592 (1983).

Upper Valley Association for Handicapped Citizens v. Mills, 928 F. Supp. 429, D. Vt. (1996).

Virginia v. Riley, 106 F.3d 559, 4th Cir. (1997).

Wickline v. State. 192 Cal. App. 3d 1630, 239 Cal. Rptr. 810. (1986).

Inclusion, The Law, and Placement Decisions: Implications for School Psychologists

J. Michael Havey

A summary of the provisions of statutes and regulations relevant to the topic of inclusion is presented. Summaries of court decisions and federal agency policy letters that have interpreted these mandates are also offered. Finally, the implications of these mandates for the practice of school psychology are also discussed.

Currently, inclusion is one of the "hottest" topics in education. Not only has discussion of the topic seemingly "popped out of nowhere" (Smelter, Rasch & Yudewitz, 1994), but the discussion has proliferated in education publications. Moreover, with the implications for changes in the educational service delivery system that inclusion entails, it is an issue that arouses strong feelings in many individuals. One of the difficulties in writing about inclusion is the lack of a consistent definition. Not only do people disagree about the merits of inclusion, but they also do not agree what it is. For the purposes of this article, the definition adopted by the National Association of School Psychologists will be used:

> Inclusive programs are those in which students, regardless of the severity of their disability, receive appropriate specialized instruction and related services within an age-appropriate general education classroom in the school they would attend if they did not have a disability. (NASP, 1993)

Although at first glance, inclusion appears to be a methodological, service-delivery issue, this matter is at heart philosophical in nature. Unlike many philosophical discussions, however, this one is of immediate "real-world" relevance. Because the education of children with disabilities is so closely regulated, any discussion involving changes in the way educational services are delivered to these children must also include legal considerations. These considerations, however, appear to be largely ignored in the professional literature. Although a recent computer search yielded 362 sources relevant to the keywords "special education and inclusion," only a handful referred to legal implications. Any changes undertaken in the name of inclusion must be done in a manner that complies with legal mandates. Although inclusion is not a legal term, is not found in federal statutes or regulations, and is only utilized in a small number of court decisions; legal provisions related to the topics of "appropriate" education and "least restrictive environment" are of direct relevance to a discussion of inclusion. Mandates are found in the statutes and regulations associated with the Individuals with Disabilities Education Act (IDEA; 20 U.S.C. Secs. 1400–1485 & 34 C.F.R. 300); Section 504 of The Rehabilitation Act of 1973 (29 U.S.C. § 794); and in state statutes and regulations implementing the federal mandates. Court decisions from various levels provide interpretive guidelines for sometimes unclear statutory language. Because school psychologists are key participants in the placement decision making process, they need to be legally informed to ensure that their decisions comply with mandates. The purpose of this paper is to provide the reader with a discussion of court decisions that have provided guidance for the legally compliant implementation of these directives.

STATUTORY AND REGULATORY MANDATES

Conceptual cornerstones of IDEA include "free appropriate public education" (FAPE) and "least restrictive environment" (LRE). Although "appropriate" is not specifically defined, mechanisms for the provision of appropriate education are contained in IDEA. Chief among these is the individualized education program (IEP; 20 U.S.C. § 1401 [19]). Other statutory provisions indirectly ensuring appropriate educational programs include: procedures to ensure nondiscriminatory assessment as a safeguard against inappropriate placement and education (§ 1412 [1]); the rights of parents to see and comment on records {§1414 [a] [4] and § 1415 [b] [1] [A]); the right to a due process hearing as a method for accountability and compliance (§ 1415).

The concept of appropriateness is also a key provision of the least restrictive environment mandates. IDEA (20 U.S.C. § 1412 [5] [B]) and Section 504 (34 C.F.R. 104.3[a] & [b]) both require that children with disabilities be educated, to the maximum extent appropriate, with children who are not disabled and that special classes and even more restrictive placements occur only when the nature or severity of the disability is such that education in regular classes with the use of supplementary aids and services cannot be achieved satisfactorily. Moreover, IDEA (34 C.f.R. 300.553) and Section 504 (34 C.F.R. Part 104) stipulate that the provision of nonacademic and extracurricular services shall ensure that children with disabilities participate with children without disabilities to the maximum extent appropriate. Further, IDEA (34 C.F.R. 300.552[a]2 and [a]3 & 34 C.F.R. 300.552[c]) directs that placements be based on the child's IEP and that unless the IEP requires some other arrangement the child with disabilities be educated in the same school that would be attended if the child did not have a disability or as close to that school as possible. Clearly Congress demonstrated a preference for integrating children with disabilities into environments with their nondisabled peers.

Inclusion and the older term "mainstreaming" should not, however, be considered synonymous with least restrictive environment. LRE has been described as a "rebuttable presumption," that is, a rule of conduct that must be followed, unless, in a particular case, following the general rule would produce unfavorable results for the individual (Turnbull, 1990, p. 163). Under IDEA, the integration mandates may be rebutted when such placement would result in an inappropriate education for a particular child. The inclusion of "appropriate" in the sections cited above ensures that the least restrictive environment may not be the same for every child. Further, the least restrictive environment is to be determined for each individual child and is dependent on the provisions of that child's IEP.

Despite the obvious preference for integrating children with and without disabilities, IDEA also contains mandates for a continuum of alternative placements, which further confound the integrative language. IDEA (34 C.F.R. 300.551) mandates that these alternative placements include instruction in regular classes, special classes, special schools, home instruction, and instruction in hospitals and institutions, a continuum that varies in degrees of integration and restrictiveness. This provision allows the least restrictive environment to vary among children along the continuum and mandates that a variety of placements be available to insure that a free and appropriate education can be provided to children based on their individual needs.

INTERPRETIVE GUIDELINES

Policy Letters

Statutory and regulatory language is often open to differing interpretations. Guidance to the interpretation of these documents, as they apply to special education, is offered through court decisions and through policy letters from regulatory agencies, most notably the Office of Special Education and Rehabilitative Services (OSERS) and the office of Special Education Programs (OSEP). Two OSERS letters (1991a,b) addressed the question of placement of all children with disabilities in regular classrooms. The responses consistently supported the goal of integrating children with disabilities into activities with their nondisabled peers. The responses did, however, stop short of endorsing the placement of all children with disabilities in regular classrooms, a concept frequently referred to as "full inclusion." These letters cited the emphasis of IDEA on the individual and the mandates that placement decisions be based on the child's needs as specified in the IEP. They also reemphasized the need for decision making on a case-by-case basis and the necessity of the continuum of alternative placements.

Because of the rebuttable nature of the concept of least restrictive environment, statutory and regulatory language can be confusing, if not contradictory. The emphasis on individual educational programming and the provisions for a continuum of alternative placements seem to disaffirm the concept of "full inclusion." As noted in the discussion of appropriateness, other provisions, however, direct education agencies to educate children with disabilities to the maximum extent appropriate with their nondisabled peers, removing them from the regular education settings only when their disabilities are so severe that they cannot be educated satisfactorily with the use of "supplementary aids and services." Therein lies the rub. What constitutes a satisfactory education and to what degree must these supplements be provided?

Court Decisions

Prior to a discussion of these cases, a brief discussion of the organization of the federal legal system is warranted. Because federal legislation (e.g., IDEA) is involved in a special education cases, appeals of administrative due process hearings are made to the federal court system. The first level is the U.S. District Court; decisions at this level can be appealed to the second level, the U.S. Courts of Appeal (circuit courts). Decisions of the 11 circuit courts are especially important because they are the controlling authority within their jurisdiction. They are controlling only within those jurisdictions, however; circuit courts can and do make decisions that contradict each other. Only decisions from the third level, the U.S. Supreme Court, are controlling throughout the entire country.

The first special education case to reach the Supreme Court, *Hendrick Hudson Central School District v. Rowley* (1982), although not dealing directly with inclusion or least restrictive environment, is important to this discussion because it resulted in a judicial definition of "appropriate" education. This case resulted from the attempts of the parents of a child with hearing impairment to secure educational services to ensure optimal school progress for their daughter. Based on their review of the provisions of the Education of the Handicapped Act (EHA; now IDEA), the justices ruled that schools are not mandated to provide the "best possible" education for their students with disabilities, but rather to grant them access to educational opportunities and to provide an "appropriate" educational program that is sufficient to confer a "basic floor of opportunity." According to the justices, an educational program can be determined to be appropriate if EHA procedures are followed and if it is reasonably designed to provide educational benefit to the child. This decision reinforced the interpretation that an appropriate education is defined, at least in part, by the process. Turnbull (1990) described this approach as "child-centered and process-oriented,) not system-centered or result-oriented" (p. 125).

A number of circuit Courts of Appeal have directly addressed issues of placement and least restrictive environment. A landmark case decided by the Fifth Circuit was *Daniel R.R. v. State Board of Education* (1989). The child in this case was a 6-year-old boy with Down syndrome. He was originally placed in a general education prekindergarten for half the school day and an early childhood special education class for the other half. After a few months of this arrangement, the district proposed a full-day placement in the special education classroom with contact with nondisabled children at lunch and recess. In deciding for the school district, the court found that regular classrooms will not always be able to provide instruction to meet the needs of each child eligible for special education. Moreover, the court determined that students with disabilities may be educated in other settings when a free appropriate public education (FAPE) cannot be delivered in the regular classroom. This determination is to be made by answering the following two questions (often referred to as the Daniel R.R. test):

1. Can education in a regular classroom with the use of supplementary aids and services by achieved satisfactorily? If not...
2. Has the school mainstreamed the child to the maximum extent appropriate?

The court further identified three factors to be considered in answering the first question:

1. Will the placement provide educational benefit? Consideration must be given to more than just academic benefit; the effects of social interaction and language models may be found to overshadow academic questions and dictate placement in a regular classroom.

2. Schools must balance the relative benefits of a regular vs. the special education placements. The court noted that because the regular classroom may not be able to meet the needs of all children, mainstreaming may be detrimental for some. They further stated, "mainstreaming a child who will suffer from the experience would violate the Act's [EHA] mandate for a free appropriate public education" (p. 1049).

3. The effect of the child's presence on the education of the other children in the regular classroom and the degree to which that presence imposed a "burden" were also determined to be factors.

The Daniel R.R. tests were later applied by the 11th Circuit Court in the case of *Greer v. Rome City School District* (1991, 1992) and by the Third Circuit Court in *Oberti v. Clementon School Board* (1993). The *Greer* case centered around a disagreement between parents and school officials about the appropriate placement for a young girl with Down syndrome. The court found that the district failed the first part of the Daniel R.R. test. Specifically, they determined that by considering only a regular classroom with no service, a regular classroom with speech services, or a self-contained classroom the district had failed to consider the full continuum of supplementary aids and services potentially available to assist the child. The district also erred by developing the IEP prior to meeting with the parents. The court did not order a placement, but ordered the district to reconvene to review and revise the IEP. The court concluded by stating, "should the school district comply with all requirements of the Act [IDEA]..., due deference will be accorded to school official's choice of methodologies..." (p. 698). The court also identified factors to determine if the school district had considered if education in regular classrooms with the use of supplementary aids and services could be achieved. Although the first two of these (comparison of educational benefit [not just academic] in both settings; impact of the child with disabilities on the regular classroom) were similar to those identified by the Daniel R.R. court, a third factor, cost, was also added.

In a case that has been described as potentially ushering in a new era of judicial activism in LRE cases (Osborned & Dimattia, 1994) the district court held and the circuit court reaffirmed in *Oberti v. Board of Education of the Borough of Clementon School District* (D.N.J. 1992 & 3d Cir. 1993) that a self-contained special education placement was not appropriate. The issue in this case was a dispute between parents and school officials concerning a proposed placement in an out-of-district self-contained program. Before applying facts to the case, the New Jersey district court provided a summary view of special education law. In addition to reaffirming the *Greer* tests, the court concluded that schools bear the burden of proof to justify challenged placements and that the IDEA obliges schools to consider regular education settings with the use of supplementary aids and services before exploring other options. The court did not, however, provide carte blanche support for inclusive programming. Although the court stated that the IDEA demonstrated a preference for mainstreaming, a reaffirmation of the concept of the continuum of alternative placements was also included. The decision favored the parents and faulted the school for not considering less restrictive placements before making the recommendation to place the child in a segregated setting. Moreover, even though the child had finally been placed part time in a regular classroom after parental insistence, the court found that the school's use of supplemental aids and services was inadequate and essentially guaranteed that the child would have significant difficulty in the regular class.

In a case involving a dispute between parents and school officials over whether a young girl with moderate retardation should be placed in a regular classroom or be educated in a split program, *Board of Education, Sacramento City Unified School District v. Holland* (1992, 1994), the courts upheld the parents' position. In doing so the district court did not adopt the Daniel R.R. test, but developed its own similar test. The district court identified four factors to consider in making LRE decisions:

1. The educational benefits of the placement,
2. The nonacademic benefits,
3. The effect on the teacher and children in the regular class, and
4. Cost.

In upholding this decision, the circuit court emphasized that schools bear the burden of proof to demonstrate the advantages of their proposed placements and affirmed that the school had not met this burden.

Schools did not fare well in most of the cases discussed above. Courts have not, however, reinterpreted IDEA or created new laws mandating regular classroom placements for all children eligible for special education. A major shortcoming that weakened the school's position in many of the cases was the lack of procedural adherence. Each of the cases cited above demonstrated the importance and significance of correctly following due process. A contested placement that is based on procedural violations is almost guaranteed to be overturned in a legal proceeding. The decisions cited above also demonstrate that schools cannot be complacent and/or indifferent when recommending programs for children with disabilities. Programs for children with disabilities are to be individualized. Placements that follow automatically from an eligibility determination without consideration of alternatives will often be found to be inappropriate. Schools must be able to demonstrate that they have considered a variety of factors (e.g., educational benefit of program alternatives, the effect of the child's presence in the classroom, cost) before recommending placements and that their proposed placement is appropriate for the child in question. Even though all the decisions cited above except *Daniel R.R.* favored parents seeking more inclusive programs for their children, the legal logic applied in these cases could also support more restrictive placements. According to these decisions, appropriate placements are those that are based on procedural compliance and that, after careful consideration, locate the place in the continuum of alternate placements that is the least restrictive environment for an *individual* child. Placements that follow automatically from eligibility decisions without consideration of alternatives stand a good chance of being found inappropriate.

At least three recent cases have affirmed district-favored placements in nonmainstreamed environments. In a case that may be all the more significant because it was decided by the same court that made the final ruling in the *Holland* case, the Ninth Circuit Court of Appeals favored a district-proposed program in a separate setting. The case of *Clyde K. & Sheila K. v. Puyallup School District* (1994) involved a junior high student with Tourette Syndrome and Attention Deficit Hyperactivity Disorder who had received special education services in regular and resource classes. After escalation of his behavior problems, which included sexually explicit remarks to female students, refusal to follow directions, and physical assaults of other students and an aide, the school resorted to removal under an "emergency expulsion." As the parents and school worked together to integrate the student back into the school setting, the school proposed temporary placement in an off-campus, segregated program, Students Temporarily Away from Regular Schools (STARS). After initially agreeing to this agreement, the parents unilaterally withdrew the student from STARS, demanded a new IEP, and filed for a due process hearing. After a 10-day hearing, the hearing officer ruled that the district had acted in compliance with IDEA. This decision was upheld by both the district and circuit courts. Applying the legal reasoning of the *Holland* case, the circuit court ruled that STARS was the least restrictive environment because (a) the student did not receive academic benefit from a junior high setting; (b) he was socially isolated, the recipient of taunts from fellow students, and demonstrated nonacademic benefits that were "at best only minimal;" and (c) his presence in the junior high had an overwhelmingly negative impact on teachers and students.

In another case within the Ninth Circuit, *Poolaw v. Bishop* (1994) the district court upheld the school district's proposal to educate a 13-year-old deaf Native American boy at the state school for the deaf in spite of the parents' argument that such a placement would hinder socialization and the development of his understanding of his heritage. The court determined that records from previous schools demonstrated that attempts had been made to educate the student in the regular classroom with the use of supplementary aids and services. They ruled that his lack of progress in reading, language and writing constituted sufficient grounds to support the district's argument and placement.

Finally, in an Illinois case, *MR v. Lincolnwood Board of Education, District 74* (ND. Ill. 1994), the district court supported a district-proposed placement in a therapeutic day school despite parental preference for a mainstreamed placement. This case involved a student who had been deemed eligible for services as a student with ED/BD (the Illinois equivalent of a Seriously Emotionally Disturbed) and who had allegedly exhibited inappropriate behaviors and threatened students and staff. The court affirmed the hearing officer's determination that the student's behavior had deteriorated in the self-contained setting and that he was disruptive to staff and other students. The court noted that, although the IDEA shows a preference for mainstreamed placement, because the district had made unsuccessful efforts to include the student in regular classroom settings to the maximum extent possible, the therapeutic day placement was appropriate.

IMPLICATIONS FOR PRACTICE

Guidelines for placement decision making and other aspects of school psychology practice can be gleaned from this review. First, this review clearly demonstrates the necessity of making decisions based on the needs of individual children. "One-size-fits-all" placements are inappropriate whether they are separate, special education programs or fully inclusive programs within the regular classroom. As declared by Huefner (1994), "it is not only illegal but inadvisable for a school district to adopt a blanket approach to LRE and either to place all students with severe disabilities into segregated settings or require mainstreaming before considering other settings." (p. 50). Further, the IEP process requires that placement decisions be made only after identification of the child's needs and services necessary to meet those needs. These considerations "drive" the placement decision. It is, therefore, illogical that setting or placement decisions could be the same for all children with disabilities. Identifying and implementing appropriate aids and services necessary for keeping children in their least restrictive environments may become increasingly important if larger numbers of children are educated in the mainstream. This may exact important changes in the day-to-day functioning of many school psychologists (Bradley-Johnson, Johnson, & Jacob-Timm, 1995; Peterson & Casey, 1991.)

To the extent that school psychologists play an important role in placement decisions they need to be aware of relevant legal mandates and guidance and to strive to ensure that decisions about individual children with withstand legal challenges. The importance of adherence to the procedures mandated in IDEA was a factor in most of cases discussed above. In fact, the district in the *Greer* case did not prevail largely because they committed two major procedural errors: perfunctorily addressing the issue of educational alternatives, and preparing the IEP before meeting with the parents. Schools have had most success arguing for nonmainstream placements when they have been able to present concrete data in the form of anecdotal information, test scores, and/or observational data.

It is the nature of legal writing that the language used is sometimes ambiguous. Courts interpret unclear statutory language, but sometimes their interpretations contain ambiguous language as well. IDEA mandates the use of "supplementary aids and services" to maintain children with disabilities in the mainstream (34 C.F.R. § 300.550 [b] [2]). The regulations list resource rooms and itinerant instruction as possible aids and services (34 C.F.R. § 300.551 [b] [2]). The courts have consistently cited the language mandating supplementary aids and services. They have, however, not clearly defined what services are appropriate, nor to what extent they must be used. Some authors have attempted to provide guidance in this area. Engler and Sraga (1995) listed a number of accommodations that may be required. Although their listing was extensive, it was by no means exhaustive; examples included consultation to teachers and aides; itinerant instruction, modifications to curriculum, use of computer-assisted devices; allowing oral responses to essay questions; extended time limit for tests. Additional accommodations for LD children could include use of calculators, use of tapes, use of highlighted texts, preferential seating, and breaking assignments into shorter segments. They also stated that the IEP team must determine what aids and services are necessary and describe them in the IEP. Regular teachers should receive a copy of the IEP; modifications/accommodations may be required may be required in any regular class. Yell (1995a) listed behavior management plans, consultation, training the regular teacher in behavior modification techniques, and the use of a behavioral aide as potentially appropriate accommodations for students with emotional/behavioral disorders.

The courts have also stated that the impact of the disabled child's presence on the teacher and students in the regular class is a consideration in placement decisions. Most of the decisions that resulted in nonmainstream placements involved children with severe behavioral difficulties. Although no court has specifically stated so, it appears that children with severe behavioral problems may be the most difficult to educate in the mainstream (Yell, 1995a). Another issue than is unresolved is cost. At least two courts have ruled that the cost of mainstreaming a child with a disability can enter into the placement–decision making equation. These courts were silent, however, on when cost becomes burdensome. Perhaps future cases will provide more specific guidance.

CONCLUSIONS

Although courts have found in favor of both inclusive and noninclusive placements, the decisions should not be viewed as contradictory. When one goes beyond the surface of the decision, what is apparent is that the courts have reaffirmed that special education placements are governed by an individualized education program. Further, the courts have consistently reaffirmed that the least restrictive environment must be determined for each individual child. In making this determination, the courts seem to be relying increasingly on reasoning similar to the Daniel R.R. analysis. Instead of reinterpreting existing law, what the courts have done is demonstrate an increasing unwillingness to automatically defer to school-recommended placements. Moreover, decisions discussed in this article clearly demonstrate that school officials bear the burden of proof to demonstrate that placements they recommend are appropriate and to demonstrate on an individual basis that they have seriously considered whether a FAPE can be delivered in a regular classroom with supplemental aids and services.

Taken as a whole, these recent judicial decisions emphasize IDEA's preference for educating children in the mainstream. They also may suggest that inclusion "is supported by longstanding judicial and social principles that reject the concept of separate but equal" (Prasse & Martin, 1996, p. 20), but a careful review of the cases discussed above demonstrates that schools are not mandated to educate all students with disabilities in regular education classrooms (Osborne & Dimattia, 1994; Whitted & Eulass, 1993; Yell, 1995a, b). Inclusive programming may be a lofty goal, but as recognized by NASP in its position statement (19930, the present structure of special education regulations "is often incompatible with inclusive programming."

J. Michael Havey *is affiliated with Eastern Illinois University.*

REFERENCES

Board of Education, Sacramento City Unified School District v. Holland, 786 F. Supp 874.73 Ed. Law rep.969 (E.d. Cal. 1992); *affd. sub. nom. Board of Education, Sacramento City Unified School District v. Rachel H.,* 14 F. 3d 1398, 89 Ed. Law Rep. 57 (9th Cir. 1994).

Bradley-Johnson, S., Johnson, C. M., & Jacob-Timm, S. (1995). Where will—and where should—changes in education leave school psychology? *Journal of School Psychology; 33*, 187–200.

Clyde K. and Sheila K. v. Puyallup School Districts. 35 F 3rd 1396 (9th Cir. 1994).

Daniel R. R. v. State Board of Education. 875 F 2d 1036 (5th Cir. 1989).

Engler, T. E. & Sraga, A. T. (1995). *Duty to accommodate students with disabilities in the regular classrooms.* Paper presented at the annual Illinois State Board of Education Impartial Hearing Officer Training. Springfield, IL.

Greer v. Rome City School District. 950 F. 2d 688 (11th Cir. 1991), op. withdrawn. 956 F.2d 1025 (1992), reinstated, 967 F.2d 470 (1992).

Hendrick Hudson School district v. Rowley, 458 UW, 176 (1982).

Huefner, D. S. (1994). The mainstreaming cases: Tensions and trends for school administrators. *Educational Administration Quarterly, 30*, 27–55.

Individuals with Disabilities Education Act, Part B, (1990) 20 U.S.C. §§1411–1420.

IDEA-B Regulations (1992), 34 C.F.R. Part 300.

M. R. v. Lincolnwood Board of Education. 843 F. Supp. 1236 (ND, Ill, 1994).

National Association of School Psychologists (1993, April), Position statement on inclusive programs for students with disabilities.

Oberti v. Clementon School Board. 801 F. Supp. 1392 (D.N.J. 1992).

Obeoti v. Clementon School Board. 9 895 F.2d 1204 (3CirCir., 1993).

Office of Special Education and Rehabilitative Services. (1991a), Goodling letter, 18 IDELR 213.

Office of Special Education and Rehabilitative Services. (1991B), Frost letter, 18 IDELR 594.

Osborne, A. G. Jr., & Dimattia, P. (1994). The IDEA's least restrictive environment mandate: Legal implications. *Exceptional Children, 61*, 6–14.

Peterson, D. W., & Casey, A. (1991). School psychology and the regular education initiative: Meaningful change or lost opportunities? In G. Stoner, M. R. Shinn, & H. M. Walker (eds.), *Interventions for achievement and behavior problems* (pp. 37–48), Silver Spring, MD; National Association of School Psychologists.

Poolaw v. Bishop, 21 IDELR 1 (D. Ariz. 1994).

Prasse, D. P., & Martin, R. (1996). *Inclusion: Statutory and judicial foundations.* Paper presented at the annual meeting of the National Association of School Psychologists, Atlanta.

Smelter, R. W., Rasch, B. W., & Yudewitz, G. J. (1994, September). Thinking of inclusion for all special needs students? Better think again. *Phi Delta Kappan, 76.* 35–38.

The Rehabilitation Act (1973). 29 U.S.C. § 504.

The Rehabilitation Act, SEC. 504 REGULATIONS (1993). 34 C.F.R. Part 105.

Turnbull, H. R. (1990). Free appropriate public education (3rd ed.), Denver, CO: Love Publishing.

Whitted, B. R. & Eulass, A. (1993). *The incompatibility of REI and inclusion with the mandates of IDEA.* Paper presented at the annual Illinois State Board of Educations Impartial Hearing Officer Training, Naperville, IL.

Yell, M. L. (1995a). Clyde K. and Sheila K. v. Puyallup School District: The courts, inclusion, and students with behavior disorders. *Behavioral Disorders, 20.* 179 189.

Yell, M. L. (1995b). Least restrictive environment, inclusion, and students with disabilities: A legal analysis. *The Journal of Special Education, 28*, 389–404.

Attention Deficit Disorder: Counselors, Laws, and Implications For Practice

Robert R. Erk

Barkley (1990, 1995) and Taylor (1994) believed that Attention Deficit Hyperactivity Disorder (ADHD) is the most common childhood disorder in our society. The more conservative estimates of the prevalence rate for ADHD range from 3% to 5% of the school-age population (Barkley, 1990; American Psychiatric Association, *Diagnostic and Statistical Manual of Mental Disorders*, 1994). Popper (1988) reported that the prevalence rate for ADHD is 3% to 10% of the school-age population. Hosie and Erk (1993) concluded that ADHD affects 5% to 10% of the children in our nation's schools. Shaywitz and Shaywitz (1992) estimated that ADHD may possibly affect as much as 20% of the school-age population. For school counselors, it is prudent to consider ADHD as a prevalent, severe, and pervasive disorder.

Failure to diagnose and treat children and adolescents with ADHD properly can have detrimental effects to key areas of their lives (e.g., academic, emotional, social, familial, occupational) that often endure across their life spans (Barkley, 1990; Copeland &: Love, 1991; Friedman & Doyal, 1992; Goldstein & Goldstein, 1990; Taylor, 1994; Zemetkin, 1995). It seems that the population of children and adolescents diagnosed with ADHD who are referred for counseling or treatment by parents, teachers, school psychologists, and physicians to school counselors (e.g., elementary, middle school, high school) has significantly increased. Therefore, the diagnosis and treatment of ADHD has often placed greater demands on school counselors and teachers to be cognizant or aware of the federal laws or statutes that can be applied to children and adolescents diagnosed with the disorder.

Unless speaking specifically in this article, the term *ADHD* is used to incorporate all the subtypes (e.g., predominately inattentive type, predominantly hyperactive-impulsive type, combined type) of the disorder that are contained in the *DSM-IV* (1994). School counselors should be cognizant or aware of the specific diagnosis or subtype of the ADHD when they are providing or monitoring services for children or adolescents with the disorder. For example, counselors should remember that the diagnosis of a particular subtype of ADHD (e.g., predominantly inattentive) can mean that there is a need for special or specific interventions to match the different academic, behavioral, or social profiles that can be present or exist. In this article, the terms *ADHD* and *attention deficit disorder* (ADD) are considered interchangeable.

The purpose of this article is two-fold: first, to provide school counselors with an increased understanding of the federal acts or laws that can be applicable to students with ADHD and second, to provide counselors with implications for practice utilizing a multidimensional treatment approach to working with these children.

COUNSELORS AND ADHD: LEGAL ISSUES

For today's counselor, legal issues have become a major concern (Capuzzi & Gross, 1995). The handling of children and adolescents who have ADHD has raised a number of legal issues (Ouellette, 1991). Counselors and other professionals who work with students have a responsibility to be aware of the laws relating to students and to attempt to ensure that their legal rights are respected (Fisher & Sorenson, 1996).

Moreover, counselors should remember that today's schools carry responsibility for managing matters or conditions (e. g., child abuse, suicide, substance abuse, ADHD) that can ultimately lead to litigation (James DeVaney, 1995). Counselors are the school personnel most likely to be involved with problematic or dysfunctional children, and with increasing frequency, counselors are finding themselves facing legal issues and responsibility for their actions (Davis & Richie, 1993).

One can, therefore, reasonably assume that liability can potentially accrue for counselors or individual educators and schools who have not kept abreast of the laws and of their responsibilities to identify, serve, and make accommodations or treatment available for children or adolescents diagnosed with ADHD. The counselor's duty usually does not extend beyond exercising the degree of care that is considered reasonable under the circumstances (McCartney & Sorenson, 1993). The quality of care that is demonstrated or evidenced in each case, however, could be the standard by which the counselor or individual educators responsible for identifying and serving students with ADHD are evaluated by the child's parents, the school system, and possibly the legal establishment. Whether or not counselors or educators personally consider ADHD a real disorder in a medical or psychological sense, the diagnosis of ADHD is legally recognized and carries with it certain rights and responsibilities regardless of individual opinions (Reid & Katsiyannis, 1995).

In asserting the legal rights of children and adolescents with ADHD, it can often be considered within the realm of the school counselor to fulfill the following roles or functions:

- Use authoritative material or resources to acquire a knowledge base on the ADHD symptoms and problematic behaviors, for example, the *DSM-IV* (1994)
- Consult with licensed professionals—physicians, psychologists, school and mental health counselors—who have established their professional expertise for reliably diagnosing and treating children with ADHD
- Possess a knowledge base on ADHD that can enable the counselor to devise or implement a treatment plan or interventions for children or adolescents with the disorder, for example, multidimensional treatment
- Ascertain if a prior diagnosis of ADHD may exist from a previous school system or a licensed professional
- Promote or provide education and training to teachers and parents on the ADHD symptoms and problematic behaviors of children diagnosed with the disorder.

FEDERAL ACTS OR STATUTES

Federal acts or laws described in the next sections of this article can be considered a legal outgrowth of the authority of the U.S. Congress to prohibit discrimination, require specific action, and may provide funds for educational programs or activities that may enhance the quality of performance and life for all individuals who have disabilities. These laws or statutes outline or seek to clarify the legal rights of children and adolescents with ADHD and the broad services, interventions, or treatment for which they may qualify or be entitled to receive. Children and adolescents with ADHD are presently covered by the following three federal acts or statutes (a) the Individuals With Disabilities Education Act, Part B (IDEA); (b) Section 504 of the Rehabilitation Act of 1973; and (c) the

Americans with Disabilities Act of 1990 (ADA). School personnel should be aware that the U.S. Department of Education has the legal authority to interpret and enforce IDEA, and the department's Office of Civil Rights interprets and enforces the education related provisions of Section 504 and ADA (Gregg, 1994).

INDIVIDUALS WITH DISABILITIES EDUCATION ACT

To clear up the confusion regarding services to children with ADHD under Part B of IDEA and Section 504, the Department of Education issued a Policy Clarification Memorandum of September 16, 1991, that defines schools' legal obligations to locate, identify, and evaluate children and adolescents suspected of having this disability and to provide a free appropriate public education (FAPE). FAPE, for example, constitutes the services that are considered necessary for students to learn and benefit from their education.

To be eligible under Part B of IDEA, the child or adolescent must be evaluated as having one or more specified physical or mental impairments *and* must be found to require special education and related services by reason of these impairments. The memorandum specified that children with ADHD may be eligible for special education services under three categories defined by IDEA: (1) other health impaired, (2) specific learning disability, and (3) seriously emotionally disturbed (Gregg, 1994). In other words, a diagnosis of ADHD is not enough to qualify for special education services; the ADHD must impair the child or adolescent's ability to benefit from mainstream education through one of the above categories and thereby make the child eligible to receive special education and related services. (Gregg, 1994). IDEA (and its 1997 amendments) does not preclude special education and related services from being offered in the regular classroom; moreover, special education is not a place but a service. Unfortunately, in many cases, children and adolescents with ADHD found it difficult to gain access to special education and related services.

Dowdy, Patton, Smith, and Polloway (1997) believed that, at most, only approximately 50% of children with ADHD were qualifying for special education services under IDEA. These researchers concluded that students with ADHD were being qualified for services under learning disabilities and behavioral disorders, not for their ADHD. In actuality, the categories under IDEA may be restrictive of the numbers of students with ADHD who could qualify and receive services. Many parents of children with ADHD found that IDEA was not workable for them, and turned to Section 504 as the alternative statute under which to seek accommodations.

SECTION 504 OF THE REHABILITATION ACT OF 1973

Section 504 had relatively limited impact for ADHD until the diagnosis of the disorder became possible in the *Diagnostic and Statistical Manual of Mental Disorders* (American Psychiatric Association, 1980; 1987), and because of this dormancy, many counselors or educators were unaware of either the students' rights or educators' responsibilities under Section 504 (Reid & Katsiyannis, 1995). Children or adolescents may qualify for services to the disabled under Section 504 if: (a) there is a physical or mental impairment that substantially limits one or more major life activities (e. g., mainstream education or learning is the activity that is most often cited for students with ADHD; Reid & Katsiyannis, 1995); (b) has a record or history of such an impairment (e. g., documentation of the ADHD seems to be increasingly important); or (c) is regarded as having such an impairment. Evidence, for example, that may be presented or submitted to substantiate the impairment of a major life activity such as learning can include the reports of parents or teachers, academic records or report cards, standardized achievement test scores, and the diagnosis of ADHD by a licensed professional (e. g., physician, psychologist, counselor). Gregg (1994) contended that for some schools or districts the severity of the student's ADHD can also be a factor in determining eligibility or granting accommodations within Section 504.

However, ADHD does not have to be diagnosed—only suspected—in order for a child or adolescent to be assessed for eligibility for Section 504 accommodations. In the event that a school district declines to accept the diagnosis of ADHD or to evaluate the child or adolescent for ADHD, the school district must notify the parents of this decision in writing and inform the parents of their due process rights to appeal the decision. Finally, Section 504 requires public schools, colleges, and universities to make accommodations for eligible individuals *whether or not* they qualify for special education services under IDEA. Therefore, Section 504 could provide appropriate modifications or services for individuals with ADHD in regular classrooms.

The eligibility criteria under Section 504 are broader than the criteria for eligibility under IDEA. For example, under Section 504, behavioral problems by themselves (which are usually connected to the ADHD) may make a child or adolescent eligible for services under this statute (Gregg, 1994), and accommodations are not limited to academics. Reid and Katsiyannis (1995) believed that the school is responsible for developing written behavioral plans for addressing the ADHD child or adolescents' misbehavior or misconduct (e.g., disobeying teachers or breaking school rules). Under Section 504, many children and adolescents diagnosed with ADHD can be served in the regular classroom provided that the school or teachers are committed to creating appropriate academic accommodations, including behavioral plans that address problematic areas.

Quinn (1997) clarified much of the confusion between IDEA and Section 504 by pointing out that while IDEA requires the child have a disability that requires special education services, and the child must be classified as eligible for these services, Section 504 qualifies the child as eligible on the basis of an impairment that limits one of life's major activities, including learning. Therefore, a child with ADHD who does not need special education services under IDEA maybe qualified to receive accommodations at school or in the classroom under Section 504. Quinn (1997), for example, recommended that a child with ADHD could receive services or accommodations in regular classrooms that include the following: (a) providing a more structured learning environment (e. g., tailoring the student's classroom and homework assignments to better meet their needs); (b) implementing appropriate behavioral management strategies; (c) adjusting the student's class schedule (e. g., math earlier in the day); (d) one-to-one tutoring sessions; (e) accommodations and variations in the teacher's presentation of classroom material (e. g., supplementing verbal instructions with visual cues); (f) using tape recorders, audiovisual tapes, and a computer for class work assignments; (g) selecting modified textbooks or workbooks; and (h) modifying test instruction (e. g., written or oral examinations that are segmented or delivered over several short periods of time).

In June 1997, changes in IDEA were signed into law by President Clinton. One of the key changes in IDEA that could be pertinent to school counselors who work with ADHD children is the provision dealing with discipline procedures for these children. For example, it is not unusual for a child or adolescent with ADHD to become involved at some point in their school career in a disciplinary process. In determining whether suspension or expulsion from school is allowable, the school or committee must consider the child's ability to understand or comprehend what he or she did, and their ability to control the behavior involved in the problem or event. The latter part of this change can have important implications for children with ADHD, which may entail, for example, pertinent factors such as medication and whether or not there were appropriate opportunities at school extended to the ADHD child for interventions or treatment. With regard to IDEA and Section 504, the courts have reasoned that Congress intended for all children with disabilities to be educated, and that the educational component of the child's program is the public school districts and their agents' (e. g., educators) responsibility to ascertain and deliver (McCartney & Sorenson, 1993).

AMERICANS WITH DISABILITIES ACT

Individuals with disabilities now have their own civil rights legislation and are a protected class under ADA (Holzbauer & Berven 1996). For example, ADA prohibits discrimination against individuals with disabilities at work, school and in public accommodations and is not limited like Section 504 to those organizations and programs that receive federal funds (Latham & Latham, 1992). Identification of a child as having ADHD requires that schools make reasonable or appropriate accommodations for disabled individuals, and it applies to both public and private nonsectarian schools, from day care to graduate school (Miles & Capel, 1993). For example, ADA has been the springboard for many colleges to develop and implement programs that specifically address the academic needs of their students with ADHD. Colleges with such programs may have also considered that it was necessary to shelter themselves from possible legal liability.

LEGAL LIABILITY: A COURT CASE

To assist counselors and individual educators to better understand their potential legal liability where ADHD is involved, a significant legal case and its ramifications is presented. In *W. B. v. Matula et al.* (1995), the parent of a minor child in New Jersey filed suit on behalf of her child (e. g., ADHD) for damages against school officials alleging violations of Section 504 of the Rehabilitation Act of 1973, Individuals with Disabilities Education Act of 1990, and constitutional rights. The parent sued school officials for punitive damages incurred in the period before the school agreed to provide appropriate educational services. The plaintiff maintained in the suit that certain school officials refused to properly and in a timely way evaluate, classify, and provide necessary educational services. The matter was dismissed by the U.S. District Court for the District of New Jersey. However, this decision was appealed by the parent and the case was remanded for trial to the U.S. Court of Appeals for the Third District.

In the United States Court of Appeals for the Third District, the judge in the *W. B. v. Matula et al.* case held that: (a) the court regarded the child's condition as a neurological impairment; (b) the court believed that a student suspected of having a qualifying disability must be identified and evaluated within a reasonable or prudent period of time; (c) the court considered that compensatory damages may be recovered at trial (in this case, however, the parties negotiated a private settlement for services and damages); and (d) the court affirmed that the school district was obligated to provide the free appropriate public education and services to which this disabled child was entitled. Furthermore, the court seemed to be persuaded by evidence presented throughout the history of the case that the burden placed on the parent was unnecessary, unwarranted, and largely the product of the school district's unwillingness to recognize and appreciate the child's neurological impairments and problems despite the ample and reliable evidence that was presented.

Zirkel (1996) believed that the *W. B. v. Matula et al.* case was significant because the decision looms large for school districts and school employees to be held liable at trial for monetary damages. This liability can pertain to not only students who can qualify for social education services under IDEA, but also to those students who have disabilities that are hidden or difficult to detect yet can qualify for accommodations under Section 504 (Zirkel, 1996). For example, to short-circuit legal liability, counselors or schools should remember that the timely identification of the ADHD, acceptance of the disorder by school officials, and the designing of appropriate interventions or services for children with the disorder seem to be the key factors.

An additional legal enforcement mechanism cannot be discounted. Counselors and other professionals in education are vulnerable to potential liability for their own unlawful acts or omissions of service or treatment (McCartney & Sorenson, 1993). Civil liability or malpractice suits in schools, mental health centers, and private practice have become more common in the counseling profession (Gladding, 1996). Latham and Latham (1992) pointed out that the rights of children and adolescents with ADHD to receive appropriate intervention can also be protected or asserted by a private civil suit. For example, there could be a school counselor or educator who has failed to take the appropriate actions necessary for an appraisal or evaluation of the suspected ADHD. There can also be a parent who has refused to acknowledge the diagnosis of ADHD or has thwarted the delivery of appropriate accommodations, treatment, or interventions (e. g., medication, behavioral modifications, counseling) for the disorder.

Counselors need not fear legal repercussions if they report suspicions that are later found to be ungrounded; however, pleading ignorance of reporting requirements in such cases is usually not a defense for failure to report such suspicions or protect the rights of the child (McCartney & Sorenson, 1993). Conversely, the parent could allege that the school's personnel or school authorities mishandled their professional responsibility or duty to properly identify or diagnose the ADHD. Therefore, counselors and school authorities should carefully document in writing all actions taken on behalf of the suspected child or adolescent with ADHD and with the parents.

It should also be noted that even though the student has left or graduated from high school, the Supreme Court in *Zoebrist v. Catalina*

Foothills School District (1993) concluded that it was appropriate for the parents to make an argument for reimbursement of services that were not provided by the school during the period of enrollment. Compensatory education and the award of monetary damages are bona fide remedies for students with handicapping conditions or disabilities given legislative mandates and judiciary decisions (Katsiyannis & Maag, 1997).

IMPLICATIONS FOR PRACTICE

Counselors need to be attuned not only to the statutes or laws that can apply to children and adolescents with ADHD but also to implications for practice. By law, children with ADHD must be served with an educational plan or a multidimensional treatment approach that is appropriate to their individual needs (Wood, 1997). Importantly for counselors, the multidimensional approach presents viable interventions or treatment for children and adolescents diagnosed with ADHD.

School counselors should be aware that the weight of research evidence seems to support the position that ongoing or long-term multidimensional treatment—parent education and training, individual counseling, behavioral interventions, social skills education and training, self-esteem education and training, family counseling—can optimize the prognosis for children and adolescents with ADHD (Erk, 1995c). School counselors should also be alert to co-occurring or coexisting conditions in children and adolescents with ADHD that can be in need of treatment or interventions. For example, Biederman, Newcorn, and Sprich (1991) found considerable coexistence of such conditions as oppositional defiant disorder, conduct disorders, mood swings, anxiety disorders, phobias, learning disabilities, and depression in children with ADHD. Barkley (1990) pointed out that children with ADHD often have coexisting conditions that may not be identified or treated. Counselors or school officials need to be aware that they could be considered negligent if the child's coexisting problems are not also identified and included in treatment planning.

A multidimensional treatment approach enables the school counselor to treat or address the ADHD and its problematic behaviors by as many avenues as are feasible. The unique vulnerabilities and co-occurring conditions that are experienced by many children and adolescents with ADHD will often necessitate specific interventions in key areas. The school counselor may not utilize each and every intervention strategy for ADHD; however, counselors may often be involved in one or more treatment combinations (Erk, 1995a, 1995b). The following interventions are intended to be ongoing or long-term so as to enable optimal outcomes for the child or adolescent with ADHD.

PARENT EDUCATION AND COUNSELING

In many instances, parents of children and adolescents with ADHD may have scant or inaccurate information on the disorder. Barkley (1990, 1995) believed that parent education on ADHD can show positive results (e. g., increased compliance with family rules) and empowers the parents to take charge of the disorder. For example, education and counseling could inform parents how the ADHD symptoms contained in the *DSM-IV* (1994) diagnose or describe the child's or adolescent's condition. Moreover, the school should specifically attempt to focus on how these symptoms can often create, at school and in the home, the myriad of problematic behaviors and stressful situations that come to be considered disruptive or serious by many parents and teachers alike.

School counselors wishing to design or conduct a parent education and counseling group may consult Barkley (1990, 1995), and Goldstein and Goldstein (1990), and Lerner, Lowenthal, and Lerner (1995). Their programs or guidelines can help parents better understand and provide structure for children and adolescents with ADHD. Erk (1995b) recommended that the school counselor or the counseling staff could create or develop a handbook on ADHD for parents and teachers that could contain essential information on the disorder. A note of caution should be voiced when school counselors maintain for parents a list of referral sources such as physicians, psychologists, mental health counselors or private practitioners who may claim to diagnose and treat children and adolescents with ADHD. It is recommended that the list should be approved or sanctioned by the appropriate school authorities (e g., school board, principal, counseling staff).

Moreover, the school counselor should encourage the parents to interview several professionals or practitioners from the list before making a final choice for treatment (e. g., avoid recommending a single professional to parents), encourage parents to speak firsthand with other parents of children with ADHD in the school community about which professional or practitioner may have best met their child or family's needs, and encourage parents to get in contact with the ADHD support group in their community. In communities without an ADHD support group, the parents may wish to contact Children and Adults with Attention Deficit Disorder (C.H.A.D.D., 499 N.W. 70th Avenue, Plantation, FL 33317 or 1-305-587-3700) directly for information and assistance on how to form or start their own local support group.

Finally, it is vital for parents and siblings to understand that ADHD is considered to be a neurobiological or neurochemical disorder, not a failure of their parenting or a reflection on their family. For example, the ADHD child's problematic behaviors are not considered to be willful and deliberate or a way of getting even with their family or teachers. Parents are usually relieved to know that while poor or distressed parental or teacher reactions to the ADHD can at times exacerbate the condition, they are not considered to be the root cause for the disorder.

TEACHER EDUCATION AND TRAINING

Teachers have often been without the information that they need to work more effectively with ADHD students. Educating teachers on the academic, behavioral, and personal-social problems that are often exhibited in classrooms can be a critical first step to improving the lives of these students. It can also maximize the treatment or interventions that may be used in their classroom to target areas of deficient academic or social functioning. Furthermore, teacher education or training on ADHD may use books, workbooks, and videotapes that specifically address what we know about the disorder and how to treat the disorder at school. (See Fowler, 1992; Lucker & Molloy, 1995; Reif, 1993). Moreover, teachers that have enjoyed success in reaching and teaching the child or adolescent with ADHD can also be a valuable resource to other teachers and parents. Teachers who are educated on the problematic behaviors of the child or adolescent with ADHD can often serve as a buffer to the negative school experiences and personal-social struggles that occur daily in the lives of these students.

The education and training of teachers on ADHD may be presented by an in-service workshop format that addresses the following areas:

- What the federal laws or statutes on ADHD can mean or may require for their school or in their classrooms
- What an accommodation plan for the child with ADHD should include or address
- Which school personnel (e. g., superintendent, principal, district supervisors, teachers or educators) are responsible for developing, implementing, monitoring, and readjusting the treatment plan or accommodations for the child with ADHD
- What active roles teachers can play (e. g., treatment planners, implementers, liaisons) with the parents or family

If counselors or educators who teach or work with children and adolescents with ADHD receive in-service education on these issues or needs, perhaps many difficulties for ADHD children and their families can be alleviated or circumvented.

INDIVIDUAL COUNSELING

School counselors should acknowledge at the beginning of counseling that many children and adolescents with ADHD represent a formidable challenge. At the onset of counseling, they may engage in denial of their condition, frequently see their problems as not their own, and repeatedly blame parents, teachers, and peers for their problems or difficulties. Moreover, years of frustration, rejection, and failure have propelled many children and adolescents with ADHD into a fantasy world or private existence where they pretend that the world cannot hurt them.

The child or adolescent with ADHD can experience or undergo pressures and stresses (e. g., academic, social, familial) that are far outside the realm produced by normal development problems (Hosie & Erk, 1993). The best practice for counselors working with such children may be to work subtly and with respect for the many difficulties and pressures that they have encountered in their young lives. For example, the counselor's personal style—self confidence, expectations for improvement, flexibility, lack of negative judgments, accurate empathy—may serve as an ongoing therapeutic model for children or adolescents with ADHD.

BEHAVIORAL INTERVENTIONS

School counselors should be advised that medication coupled with behavioral interventions can often be the most effective treatment regime for children and adolescents with ADHD (Barkley, 1990, 1997; Goldstein & Goldstein, 1990). Behavioral interventions or strategies should permit the counselor, working in concert with the child or adolescent, to accomplish the following objectives:

- To create possibilities for new patterns of thought and behaviors to evolve or to become a part of their behavioral repertoire
- To create or seek to provide opportunities for repeated practice in the areas where improved behavioral performance is desired
- To potentially create reinforcing effects (at school or in the home) that should accumulate and can provide the encouragement or impetus for adopting more satisfying or rewarding styles of behavior.

Information gleaned from the recommendations of Barkley (1990; 1995), Fiore, Becker, and Nero (1993), Goldstein and Goldstein (1990), and from my own experiences working with children and adolescents with ADHD, the counselor could provide the child, parents, and teachers with instruction in many of the following areas:

- Positive praise from teachers and parents (e.g., all situations involving a child or adolescent with ADHD should strive to be win-win situations)
- Positive internal self-talk (e.g., training the child or adolescent to reward or praise themselves internally for accomplishments when their efforts have resulted in their best performance possible)
- Behavioral rehearsal (e.g. having the child or adolescent acquire prior practice or rehearsal at a task or behavior without the risk of evaluation or judgment)
- Avoid negative reinforcement (e.g., scolding or criticizing the child or adolescent because this increases guilt, anxiety, and fear)

Using time out (e.g., providing a timed period and space devoid of reinforcement for the young child, time out is not effective in cases where adolescents are involved)

- Cost response (e.g., having the child or adolescent immediately choose from an agreed upon list one privilege or activity that may be forfeited for non-compliance with a rule or assignment)
- Earning special privileges (e.g., maintaining a list of special privileges that the child or adolescent can earn for their on-task behaviors at school or in the home)
- Mentoring (e.g., being a model for positive behavior and providing empathetic guidance despite the often high stress levels that can accompany teaching or parenting the child or adolescent with the disorder)

The counselor should be aware that these behavioral interventions or strategies often need to be varied, adjusted, or changed to meet the myriad yet unique problematic situations or behaviors that can often develop or be endemic to children with ADHD. Moreover, behavioral interventions are most useful and reinforcing to the child with ADHD when they are put in place in natural settings at the point of performance where the desired behavior is to occur (Barkley, 1997).

SELF-ESTEEM EDUCATION AND TRAINING

Low self-esteem may often precede depressed affect or perhaps depression in many children with ADHD. Therefore, the foremost goal for many children and adolescents with ADHD should be enhancing their self- esteem (Erk, 1995b). For example, unknowingly or without being fully aware of the consequences of their actions such as criticizing complaining, or nagging, many parents and teachers have often seriously undermined the self-esteem of the child or adolescent with ADHD. Since early childhood or kindergarten, it is likely that the child or adolescent with ADHD has often experienced feelings of being unaccepted, unattached, helpless, worthless, and separated from others or their peer group.

Counselors who begin self-esteem education programs for children or adolescents with ADHD should attempt to emphasize and focus on: (a) their possibilities for developing increased self-worth or self confidence; (b) being valued and accepted for who they are; (c) realizing that they are attached, connected, and cared for by others; and (d) providing motivation and encouragement about their possibilities for the future.

SOCIAL SKILLS EDUCATION AND TRAINING

It is often without the social arena that children with ADHD experience the most difficulty (Whalen & Henker, 1991). Many children and adolescents with ADHD are often described by their peers as socially disruptive or demanding. In some instances, children with ADHD seem to be the targets or victims of social harassment from many of their classmates or peers. It is not unusual for social harassment to often be pervasive, across settings, and be mean-spirited. Where this type of social harassment occurred, these highly charged emotional experiences can result in indelible memories for the ADHD child. Furthermore, children and adolescents with ADHD can seem to teachers and parents who are unfamiliar with the disorders to be remarkable unaware of the needs of others, self-centered, and self-absorbed and inattentive to the situation. For example, many children with ADHD seem to be ignoring the social rules or norms by defying teachers and parents. This is a misreading of these children's noncompliance. Teachers and parents need to understand that many of these children are reacting in an incompetent way. They are simply unable to distinguish between their noncompliance and more competent ways to behave

Obviously, many children and adolescents with ADHD often need to acquire and learn a more successful repertoire of social skills. A strong didactic component of social skills education and training coupled with immediate and repeated practice in the desired or targeted areas of social functioning can be crucial for many children or adolescents with ADHD. Social skills education and training for these children could focus on the following:

- Basic interaction skills such as making eye contact, using the correct voice level or tone, taking turns in the conversation, practicing covert speech or silent responses before answering
- Getting-along skills such as using polite words or language, following the social rules for the classroom or group, being of assistance to others, not violating the social space or privacy of others

- Making-friends skills such as learning the importance of smiling, complimenting others, demonstrating through cooperative behaviors a genuine interest or concern for the welfare of others
- Social coping skills such as how to react more appropriately when someone says no, coping more effectively with frustration or anger when peers engage in teasing or taunting, how to respond to a classmate or peer that tries to deliberately inflict hurt feelings, the importance of understanding that not all social situations go right

At opportune points, the counselor should be alert for opportunities to actively involve members of the peer group or classmates in the program. As a note of caution, the counselor should be alert to recognize that the child or adolescent ADHD can often identify or ally themselves with other children or adolescents who may also be viewed or deemed by others as different or socially unconnected.

FAMILY COUNSELING

Family counseling may often be recommended to the parents or family with an ADHD child or adolescent. These families are usually confronted with a much larger number of developmental and behavioral problems as compared to other families (Hosie & Erk, 1993). ADHD does not start or stop at the door of the school. Unfortunately, the disorder can also seriously affect the family with such problems as parental burnout, marital discord, and sibling dissension. The family could be socially shunned or avoided by other families in their neighborhood or community (Erk, 1997).

School counselors should realize that within the family with a child or adolescent with APHD, there is a disability or a disabling condition operating that affects or disrupts the entire family system (Erk, 1997). In other words, family counseling can provide assistance to a family unit or system that may be dysfunctional due to the disorder. Finally, the unity of the parents and the school in the treatment of the child or adolescent with ADHD can be a crucial factor (Erk, 1995a).

CONCLUSION

Fortunately, the federal acts or laws that seek to protect the rights of children and adolescents with ADHD have led to increased construction of interventions or services for the disorder. For counselors who work with these children, the most important information to emerge on ADHD is that a multidimensional treatment approach offers an array of interventions or strategies, and the approach needs to be ongoing or long-term to optimize treatment or outcomes for the wide range of deficits or problems that often accompany this disorder (Erk, 1995a, 1995b, 1995c).

Note: The author serves as the ASCA Professional Interest Network Contact for Children With Attention Deficit Hyperactivity Disorder and is the parent of child diagnosed with ADHD.

Robert R. Erk, Ed.D., *is an associate professor of Counselor Education and Educational Psychology, Department of Educational Studies, University of Tennessee at Martin.*

REFERENCES

American Psychiatric Association, (1980). *Diagnostic and statistical manual of mental disorders* (3rd ed.). Washington, DC: Author.

American Psychiatric Association, (1987). *Diagnostic and statistical manual of mental disorders* (3rd ed. Rev.). Washington, DC; Author.

Americans with Disabilities Act of 1990, 42 U.S.C., Section 12101 et seq.

Barkley, R. A. (1990). *Attention-deficit hyperactivity disorder: A handbook for treatment.* New York: Guilford.

Barkley R. A. (1995). *Taking charge of ADHD: The complete authoritative guide for parents.* New York: Guilford.

Biederman, J., Newcorn J., & Sprich, S. (1991). Comorbidity of attention deficit hyperactivity disorder with conduct, depressive, anxiety, and other disorders. *American Journal of Psychiatry, 145,* 581–587.

Capuzzi, D., & Gross, D. R. (1995). *Counseling and psychotherapy: Theories and intervention.* Englewood Cliffs, NJ: Merrill.

Copeland, E. D., & Love, V. L. (1991). *Attention please! A comprehensive guide for successfully parenting children with attention disorder and hyperactivity.* Atlanta, GA: Southeastern Psychological Institute Press.

Davis, T., & Richie, M. (1993). Confidentiality and the school counselor: A challenge for the 1990's. *The School Counselor, 41,* 23–30.

Dowdy, C. A., Patton, J. R., Smith, T. E. Polloway, E. A. (1997). *Attention-deficit/hyperactivity disorder in the classroom: A practical guide for teachers.* Austin, TX: Pro-ed.

Erk, R. R. (1995a). The conundrum of attention deficit disorder. *Journal of Mental Health Counseling, 17,* 131–145.

Erk, R. R. (1995b). A diagnosis of attention deficit disorder: What does it mean for school counselors? *The School Counselor, 42,* 292–299.

Erk, R. R. (1995c). The Evolution of attention deficit disorders terminology. *Elementary School Guidance and Counseling, 29,* 243–248.

Erk, R. R. (1997). Multidimensional treatment of attention deficit disorder: A family oriented approach. *Journal of Mental Health Counseling, 19,* 3–22.

Fiore, T.A., Becker, E. A., & Nero, R. C. (1993). Educational interventions for students with attention deficit disorder. *Exceptional Children, 60,* 163–173.

Fisher, L., & Sorenson, G. P. (1996). *School law for counselors, psychologists, and social workers.* White Plains, NY: Longman.

Friedman, R. J., & Doyal, G. T. (1992). *Management of children and adolescents with attention deficit hyperactivity disorder.* Austin, TX: Pro-Ed.

Fowler, M. (1992). CH.A.D.D. *educators manual: An in-depth look at attention deficit disorder form an educational perspective.* Plantation, FL: CH.A.D.D.

Gladding, S. T. (1996). *Counseling: A comprehensive profession.* Englewood cliffs, NJ: Merrill.

Goldstein, S., & Goldstein, M. (1990). *Managing attention disorder in children.* New York: John Wiley.

Gregg, S. (Winter, 1994). *Children with ADHD: Laws to help them succeed in school. The LINK: Appalachia Educational Laboratory, 13,* pp. 1–3.

Holzbauer, J. J., & Berven, N. L. (1996). Disability harassment: A new term for a long-standing problem. *Journal of Counseling and Development, 74,* 478–483.

Hosie, T. W., & Erk, R. R. (1993, January). ACA reading program: Attention deficit disorder. *American Counseling Association Guidepost, 35,* 15–18.

Individuals with Disabilities Education Act of 1990, 20 U.S.C. Section 1400 et seq.

James, S. H., & DeVaney, S. B. (1995). Preparing to testify: The school counselor as court witness. *The School Counselor, 43,* 97–102.

Katsiyannis, A., & Maag, J. W. (1997). Ensuring appropriate education: Emerging remedies, litigation, compensations, and other legal considerations. *Exceptional Children, 63,* 451–462.

Latham, P. S., & Latham, P. H. (1992). *Attention deficit disorder and the law.* Washington, DC: JKL Communications.

Lerner, J. W., Lowenthal, B., & Lerner, S. R. (1995). *Attention deficit disorder: Assessment and teaching.* Pacific Grove, CA: Brooks/Cole.

Lucker, J. R., & Molloy, A. T. (1995). Resources for working with children with attention-deficit/hyperactivity disorder (ADHD). *Elementary School Guidance and Counseling, 29,* 260–277.

McCartney, M. M., & Sorenson, G. P. (1993). School counselors and consultants: Legal duties and liabilities. *Journal of Counseling and Development, 72,* 159–167.

Miles, S. A., & Capel, C. A. (1993). Caring for children and adults: The Americans with disabilities act. *People and Education, 1,* 6–15.

Ouellette, E. M. (1991). Legal issues in the treatment of children with attention deficit hyperactivity disorder. *Journal of Child Neurology, 6,* S68–S75.

Popper, C. W. (1988). Disorders usually first evident in infancy, childhood, or adolescence. In J. A. Talbott, R. E. Hales, & S. C. Yudofsky (Eds.), *Textbook of Psychiatry* (pp. 649–735). Washington, DC: American Psychiatric Press.

Quinn, P. O. (1997). *Attention deficit disorder: Diagnosis and treatment from infancy to adulthood.* New York: Brunner/Mazel.

Reid, R., & Katsiyannis, A. (1995). Attention-deficit/hyperactivity disorder and section 504. *Remedial and Special Education, 16,* 44–52.

Reif, S. F. (1993). *How to reach and teach ADD/ADHD children.* West Nyack, NY: Center for Applied Research in Education.

Section 504 of the Rehabilitation Act of 1973, 29 U.S.C. Section 794 et seq.

Shaywitz, S. E., & Shaywitz, B. A. (1992). *Attention deficit disorder comes of age: Toward the twenty-first century.* Austin, TX: Pro-Ed.

Taylor, J. (1994). *Helping your hyperactive/attention deficit child.* Rocklin, CA: Prima.

Whalen, C. K., & Henker, B. (1991). Social impact of stimulant treatment of hyperactive children. *Journal of Learning Disabilities, 24,* 231–241.

W.B. v. Matula et al., 67 F.3d 484 (3rd Cir. 1995).

Wood, J. W. (1997). Attention deficit disorders. In J. W. Wood & A. M. Lazzari (Eds.), *Exceeding the boundaries: Understanding exceptional lives.* Fort Worth, TX: Harcourt Brace.

Zemetkin, A.J. (1995). Attention deficit disorder: Born to be hyperactive? *Journal American Medical Association, 273*, 1871–1874.

Zirkel, P. A. (1996). Courtside. *Phi Delta Kappan, 78*, 171–172.

Zoebrist v. Catalina Foothills School District, 113 S. Ct. 2464 (1993).

Chapter 13: Supervision

INTRODUCTION

Many school counselors are surprised to find themselves supervising counselor interns, clerical staff, student workers, and other professional counselor staff members in their schools soon after receiving their master's degrees in counseling. It is clear in the professional literature that supervision skills are distinct and different from counseling skills. Despite the recognition that good counselors do not necessarily yield good supervisors, most master's degree programs do not teach school counselors supervision skills.

These situations are often additionally challenging as school counselors could actually benefit themselves from being supervised as they face a multitude of new professional, ethical, and legal challenges daily within their schools. An increasing number of school counselors are seeking state licensure as professional counselors even though such a requirement may not be necessary. Still, school counselors who are being supervised need to understand the relationships they have with their principal, their clinical supervisor, and other administrative or clinical supervisor colleagues.

Along with the requirements that school counselors develop applicable supervision skills and seek supervision for themselves when necessary and appropriate, those who are in either position also must remain informed of their ethical obligations and legal rights.

Herlihy, Gray, and McCollum (2002) have addressed a number of ethical and legal issues related to school counselor supervision, among them: competence to supervise; confidentiality within supervisory relationships; boundaries among supervisors and supervisees; accountability and liability of supervisors; and evaluation by supervisors. The authors also have provided clear and explicit guidelines to assist school counselors effectively practice as supervisors and supervisees.

Graduate students who are completing their master's degrees in preparation for school counseling positions would be wise to review the ethical and legal dimensions of surrounding either of these roles. Experience has shown school counselors move in and out of these supervisory roles throughout their careers.

Legal and Ethical Issues in School Counselor Supervision

Barbara Herlihy
Neal Gray
Vivian McCollum

Today's school counselors deal routinely with complicated situations in which students have acute counseling needs, including cases of severe depression and suicidal ideation, pregnancy, substance abuse, school violence, and child abuse (Page, Pietrzak, & Sutton, 2001). To respond adequately to these needs, counselors must have both strong clinical skills and a keen awareness of the legal and ethical ramifications of any actions they may take or fail to take. These mandates are particularly challenging when school counselors are isolated in their settings or are so burdened with clerical and administrative tasks that they are unable to adequately address the counseling needs of the students they serve. School counselors in these situations may feel stressed and overworked and may be experiencing professional burnout. As a consequence, they can become unsure of their abilities and effectiveness and may experience erosion in their skills and competence (Crutchfield & Borders, 1997). This process runs counter to their ethical responsibility to maintain and increase their competence (American Counseling Association [ACA] 1995, Section C.2.) When school counselors fail to practice competently, this can become a legal problem as well as an ethical issue, because a malpractice lawsuit could result.

Supervision can be an effective means of assisting school counselors to maintain and enhance their competence. Supervision can provide

opportunities for continuing clinical-skill development, ongoing consultation regarding legal and ethical issues, and a professional support system
that can mitigate against stress and burnout. According to Remley and
Herlihy (2001), two types of supervision are generally discussed in the literature: clinical supervision and administrative supervision. Supervision
that focuses on the development of counseling skills is known as clinical
supervision. Within the counseling profession in general, clinical supervision has come to be recognized as essential to the continuing professional
development of practitioners. The primary purpose of clinical supervision
is to enhance the competence and increase the counseling skills of the
counselor who is being supervised. Unfortunately, however, this is the type
of supervision that school counselors are least likely to receive.

A second and more readily available type is administrative supervision, which is usually provided by the building principal or other administrator and is focused on compliance with school requirements and
accountability (Crutchfield & Hipps, 1998). Administrative supervision
occurs when a direct-line administrator provides direction to a counselor
who is an employee. Administrative supervisors usually have direct control and authority over the counselors they supervise (Remley & Herlihy,
2001). Administrative supervisors face somewhat different legal issues
than do clinical supervisors, because the purposes of administrative
supervision are different and the law treats the two types of supervision
differently (Remley & Herlihy).

In this article, we first describe the current status of school counselor
supervision. This provides a context in which ethical and legal issues
encountered in supervision of school counselors are examined. Although
clinical supervision is the primary focus of our discussion, we also
address ethical and legal issues that commonly arise in administrative
supervision.

CURRENT STATUS OF SCHOOL COUNSELOR SUPERVISION

As we have noted, although administrative supervision is widely available, the need for clinical supervision in school counseling has gone largely unmet. In a recent national survey, Page et al. (2001) found that only
13% of school counselors were currently receiving individual clinical
supervision and only 10% were receiving group clinical supervision.
Nonetheless, there is empirical support for the efficacy of clinical supervision for school counselors. Positive results have been reported, including enhanced effectiveness and accountability, improved counseling skills,
encouragement of professional development, and increased confidence
and job comfort (Agnew, Vaught, Getz, & Fortune, 2000; Benshoff &
Paisley, 1996; Borders, 1991; Crutchfield & Borders, 1997).

One reason clinical supervision has been a neglected issue in school counseling may be a perception that school counselors do not have the same level of need for supervision as do clinical mental health counselors. School administrators, in particular, may continue to perceive the school counselor's role as being focused primarily on such activities as academic advising, scheduling, psychoeducation, and group guidance. School administrators may see clinical supervision as a less-than-useful reason for taking school counselors away from their time spent in such direct service to students (Crutchfield & Borders, 1997). To the extent that this is the case, little impetus will be generated by the administrative supervisors of school counselors to arrange to provide them with clinical supervision.

School counselors themselves may not feel a need to receive clinical supervision. Fully one third of the school counselors surveyed by Page et al. (2001) indicated that they had no need for supervision. In addition, school counselors who are unaccustomed to having their work scrutinized may resist any attempts to institute supervision of their work (Henderson & Lampe, 1992). Assisting school counselors to see the need for ongoing clinical supervision of their work is a challenge deeply embedded in what school counselors perceive to be their role, based on the expectations of administrators, teachers, parents, and students (Hardesty & Dillard, 1994). Poorly defined counselor roles and unclear professional identity contribute to the lack of significance placed on clinical supervision of school counselors. Duties that school counselors perform have become a hodge-podge of activities chosen, assigned, or added by happenstance. As a result, many school counselors see their skills as adequate because few of their daily tasks involve clinical work. They may also see supervision as an additional responsibility for which there is no time.

A final factor that may help to explain the dearth of clinical supervision for school counselors is that, in most jurisdictions, post-master's degree supervision of school counselors has not been mandated. This stands in marked contrast to licensed professional mental health counselors who typically must complete 2,000 to 3,000 clock hours of post-master's supervised experience in order to receive licensure.

In summary, the current status of supervision in school counseling is far from ideal. Administrative supervision is usually available, but clinical supervision is much less likely to be provided to school counselors. In this context, we turn our discussion to ethical and legal issues that arise in school counselor supervision. These issues include competence to supervise, confidentiality, relationship boundaries, accountability and liability, and evaluation of performance.

ETHICAL AND LEGAL ISSUES

Competence to Supervise

According to the ACA (1995) *Code of Ethics*, counselors who offer clinical supervision services must be "adequately prepared in supervision methods and techniques" (Standard F.1.f.). A major problem in adhering to this standard in school counseling is a lack of qualified supervisors. Due to the shortage of school counselors who have received formal preparation in supervision, supervision may be provided by other mental health professionals such as licensed community mental health counselors, psychologists, or clinical social workers. Although this type of cross-discipline supervision is not uncommon (Campbell & Herlihy, 2002), these supervisors may not have expertise in play therapy or other techniques of counseling children and adolescents. They may not have a full understanding of the school counselor's setting or the developmental needs of student clients. These differences may limit the effectiveness of the supervision.

Similar difficulties can arise in administrative supervision, when it is provided by a school principal or another administrator. Some administrators may not clearly understand the role and functions of the school counselor or the ethical standards that school counselors are committed to honoring.

Some school districts have counseling department heads, lead counselors, guidance directors, or guidance consultants. When this is the case, the task of providing clinical supervision often falls on their shoulders. In most cases, however, lead counselors in school districts have not had specialized preparation in counselor supervision; rather, they hold that position based on their own performance as counselors (Henderson & Lampe, 1992). If they supervise school counselors, they may be practicing outside their scope of competence, which would constitute a violation of ethical standards (ACA, 1995, Standard C.2.a.). Supervisors without preparation in clinical supervision are more likely to concentrate on the administrative and programmatic aspects of supervision and to shy away from the clinical aspects of enhancing counseling knowledge and skills (Nelson & Johnson, 1999).

Even when the clinical supervisor is appropriately prepared, the supervisor may not work at the same site as the counselor being supervised. Without direct observation of counseling performance, supervision may be limited to case consultation which has certain drawbacks. The success of case consultation depends on the supervisee's abilities to observe and conceptualize as well as the insightfulness of the supervisor (Bernard & Goodyear, 1998). Additionally, self-reporting can be subject to deception (Campbell, 2000). Case consultation, as the sole method of supervision, is generally thought to be a less effective means of fostering professional development (Campbell; Goodyear & Nelson, 1997).

The cycle of inadequate clinical supervision in school counseling can be perpetuated when universities place interns in schools and these interns receive their on-site supervision from school counselors who have had little or no formal education in supervision. These students are unlikely to receive the guidance that they need to maximize their performance and strengthen their professional development (Dye & Borders, 1990). Eventually, these inadequately supervised students become school counseling supervisors.

Confidentiality

Confidentiality issues with school-age children present a particular challenge in the process of school counselor supervision. The questionable nature of the legal rights of children further complicates the issue of confidentiality in schools (Remley, 1985). School administrators, acting according to their own legal and ethical codes, may be less likely than administrators in other environments to give permission to videotape or audiotape counseling sessions for supervision. Parental permission to tape needs to be acquired as well. Nevertheless, clinical supervisors may require counselors who are receiving supervision from them to share with them information concerning cases. Supervisors, in order to do their jobs effectively, may need to listen to audiotapes of counseling sessions, review case notes or other client records, and learn specific details of cases that may necessitate the revelation of client identity. School counselors recognize the importance of maintaining confidentiality to develop student trust, and thus may be reluctant to share information. They may not realize that, generally, sharing confidential and privileged information with professionals who have a need to know that information for supervision purposes is acceptable practice and does not destroy legal privilege (Cleary, 1984).

From a legal perspective, because school counselors generally do not choose their supervisors, they would not likely be held accountable if a supervisor were to disclose information inappropriately to third parties such as administrators or teachers. However, school counselors do have an ethical obligation to address concerns they may have about a supervisor who makes an unwarranted disclosure. If the supervisor has direct authority over the counselor, this can be difficult because the counselor is in a vulnerable position. If possible, the best course of action is to try to address the concerns directly with the supervisor involved. If a direct approach is not feasible, or if it is attempted and does not successfully resolve the concern, then it may be necessary for the counselor to consult with the supervisor's administrative supervisor.

Boundaries of the Supervisory Relationship

The *Code of Ethics* (ACA, 1995) cautions counselors to avoid dual relationships with clients that could impair their objectivity and professional judgment. Managing dual relationships with clients is generally not as problematic for school counselors, whose clients are minor children, as it is for counselors in some other settings. However, dual relationships can arise in the supervisor-supervisee dyad when supervisors serve in more than one role with their supervisees, such as serving as both administrative supervisor and clinical supervisor. Whenever possible, it is preferable that these roles be divided between two supervisors. Ideally, an administrator would provide the administrative supervision while a counselor with expertise in supervision theories and techniques would provide the clinical supervision. Dual roles cannot always be avoided, however. In these instances, the supervisory relationship must be carefully managed due to the power differential that exists between the supervisor and supervisee. Supervisors, because of the evaluative function that is part of their job responsibilities, have considerable power in the relationship.

The *Standards for Counseling Supervisors* (Association for Counselor Education and Supervision, 1990) caution supervisors not to engage in social contacts or interactions that would compromise the supervisory relationship. Because supervisors share professional interests with their supervisees, they are likely to encounter the counselors they supervise at various workshops or other professional functions. They should not develop friendships or socialize routinely with their supervisees, however, as such relationships would make it difficult if not impossible for the supervisor to complete an objective evaluation (Remley & Herlihy, 2001). When lead counselors in a school or school district supervise their professional peers, they may find it very difficult to adhere to these ethical guidelines.

Another form of boundary violation that can cause problems in a supervisory relationship occurs when a supervisor establishes a therapeutic relationship with the supervisee as a substitute for supervision. The Standards (ACES, 1990) direct supervisors to address personal issues in supervision only in terms of the impact of these issues on professional functioning. Supervisors must maintain a delicate balance, addressing personal issues when they interfere with the supervised counselor's effectiveness by helping the counselor identify and understand the issues involved, but without allowing the relationship to slide beyond appropriate boundaries into a therapeutic relationship (Remley & Herlihy, 2001). Counselors who provide clinical supervision without having acquired knowledge of how to manage the teaching, counseling, and consultative roles played by supervisors may have difficulties in maintaining this crucial balance.

Accountability and Liability

Administrative supervisors need to be cognizant of issues of vicarious liability. Administrative supervisors or employers have direct control over the actions of the counselors they supervise and must take necessary steps to limit this liability. Initially, the supervisor must be judicious in the hiring of the prospective employee to ensure that the person demonstrates clinical competence and proper decision making. Checking references and running criminal background checks will benefit this process.

Once the hiring decision has been made, it is the administrative supervisor's duty to provide the new employee with school rules and regulations. A job description that provides all this information can be extremely valuable to both the supervisor and the counselor/supervisee. The supervisor should also discuss with the new employee the school's expectations concerning adequate performance. Once the counselor's duties begin, it is the supervisor's duty to monitor the supervisee's actions. If the supervisor finds that the counselor is not performing adequately, proper documentation and evaluation must be provided. As another safeguard, supervisors should always acquire professional liability insurance for protection against any negligence on the part of the supervisee that may be beyond the supervisor's control (Remley et al., 2001).

In contrast to administrative supervisors, clinical supervisors are not directly responsible for counselors' actions because they do not have hiring or firing authority. However, they should follow certain steps to limit their liability. First, they should present supervisory activities in the context of education as opposed to control. When discussing clinical cases, supervisors should not give directives; rather, they should provide guidance. Supervisors should clarify their role to the supervisee and others involved (such as the principal or director of guidance) through discussion and written documents signed by both parties. When clinical supervisors are not on site, they should instruct their supervisees to follow on-site supervisor directives at all times and to contact them in the event of an emergency. Clinical supervisors should not interfere with an administrative supervisor's authority over the counselor (Remley et al., 2001).

An example of vicarious liability may occur in a situation in which the counselor's administrative supervisor is deferring to the clinical supervisor regarding decisions that arise in counseling students. If the clinical supervisor lacks knowledge of school policy, the supervisor might advise the counselor to make a decision that violates established rules for dealing with student issues. For instance, the supervisor might direct the counselor to inform child protection services directly in an abuse case instead of first informing the principal. If this violates school policy, the counselor might be reprimanded or even fired by the administrator.

Evaluation

Fair evaluation deals with supervisees' rights, specifically their right to be protected from administrative decisions that affect them unfairly (Remley & Herlihy, 2001). An extreme example of inappropriate evaluation would occur when a school counselor is dismissed from a job without receiving feedback in advance concerning inadequate performance. Administrative supervisors can limit their legal liability in this area by consistently providing the counselors they supervise with feedback and by providing opportunities for the counselors to correct mistakes (Remley & Herlihy). A written job description is an excellent format to specify what is required of the counselor who is being supervised. When the administrative supervisor notes a deficiency in the counselor's performance, the supervisor should describe specifically what constituted the negative performance and what behaviors will lead to improvement (Bernard & Goodyear, 1998). Although administrative supervisors may feel comfortable evaluating whether their counselors are complying with school policies and procedures, if the supervisors are not counselors themselves, they may not have sufficient knowledge of counseling to evaluate the employee's clinical performance. In the absence of any clinical supervision, school counselors may not be receiving any feedback or assistance in improving their clinical skills and any deficiencies in clinical performance may go undetected.

Evaluation is an integral component of clinical supervision as well. Counselors who serve as supervisors are often uncomfortable with their evaluative roles because they were trained first in the more nonjudgmental role of counselor (Bernard & Goodyear, 1998). Nonetheless, they cannot allow their discomfort to interfere with their obligation to provide their supervisees with ongoing formative evaluation. Clinical supervisors should thoroughly discuss the evaluation process and procedures with their supervisees at the outset of the supervisory relationship, to avoid later misunderstandings. The ultimate goal of clinical supervision is to help supervisees develop skills in self-evaluation that they will continue to use throughout their professional careers.

RECOMMENDATIONS

Few school counselors are currently receiving ongoing clinical supervision. Supervision can be an effective means of increasing their clinical competence, reducing the stresses inherent in their demanding roles, and helping them respond to the challenging ethical and legal issues they encounter. We conclude with the following recommendations for those who provide administrative and clinical supervision to school counselors:

1. If you are providing clinical supervision and have not completed specific course work (as a university-based, for-credit course or as continuing education), make it a high priority to do so. Thorough preparation will not only help to avoid ethical and legal pitfalls, but will help you to become a more effective supervisor.

2. To increase the pool of available school counselor supervisors, consider instituting a peer supervision program in your school district. Agnew et al. (2000), Benshoff and Paisley (1996), and Borders (1991) provided some excellent information on how to establish such a program.

3. Consider collaborating with counselor educators at nearby universities, if possible, to provide professional development in supervision to practicing school counselors. Combining the perspectives of counselor educators who received rigorous preparation in supervision as part of their doctoral studies with counselors who provide supervision and who understand the practical realities of the school counselor role and functions would maximize the efficaciousness of such professional development.

4. Work with school administrators to develop school policies that support school counselors in receiving supervision and consultation. Administrative support could include setting aside time during working hours for supervision, allowing counselors some flexible release time to travel to another school and meet with other counselors for supervision, and hosting peer supervision sessions at one's school (Crutchfield & Hipps, 1998).

5. Periodically review the codes of ethics of relevant professional organizations to ensure that you are aware of any changes in ethical standards. Participate in seminars and workshops that provide updates on law related to counseling and supervision.

6. Diligently protect the confidentiality of the student clients with whom your supervisee is working. If you review video- or audiotapes, ensure that these tapes are erased when you and your supervisee have finished using them. Maintain any written records in a secure, locked file.

7. Maintain appropriate relationship boundaries with your supervisees. Remember that, even though you may consider the counselors you supervise to be peers, the supervisory relationship is hierarchical. Developing close friendships with supervisees is ill-advised because supervision has an evaluative component.

8. Before entering new supervisory relationships, explain to your supervisees specifically how their performance will be evaluated.
9. To protect yourself from legal liability, obtain your own professional liability insurance policy. Have an established plan for seeking legal counsel should it be needed.

Clinical supervision can be a powerful vehicle for fostering the professional development of school counselors. Providing school counselors with ongoing administrative and clinical supervision will help them be more equipped to continuously improve the services they provide to students, parents, and staff.

Barbara Herlihy, Ph.D., *is a professor in the Counselor Education Program at the University of New Orleans, LA.* **Neal Gray, Ph.D.,** *is an assistant professor in the Department of Counseling and Educational Leadership at Eastern Kentucky University, Richmond.* **Vivian McCollum, Ph.D.,** *is an associate professor in the Counselor Education Program at the University of New Orleans.*

REFERENCES

Agnew, T., Vaught, C. C., Getz, H. G., & Fortune, J. (2000). Peer group clinical supervision program fosters confidence and professionalism. *Professional School Counseling, 4,* 6–12.

American Counseling Association. (1995). Code of ethics. Alexandria, VA: Author.

Association for Counselor Education and Supervision. (1990). *Standards for counseling supervisors.* Alexandria, VA: Author.

Benshoff, J. M., & Paisley, P. O. (1996). The structured peer consultation model for school counselors. *Journal of Counseling and Development, 74,* 314–318.

Bernard, J. M., & Goodyear, R. K. (1998). *Fundamentals of clinical supervision* (3rd ed.) Boston: Allyn & Bacon.

Borders, L. D. (1991). A systematic approach to peer group supervision. *Journal of Counseling and Development, 69,* 248–252.

Campbell, J. C. (2000). *Becoming an effective supervisor.* Philadelphia: Taylor & Francis.

Campbell, J. C., & Herlihy, B. (2002, March). *Ethical and professional issues in supervision.* Learning institute presented at the Annual Conference of the American Counseling Association, New Orleans.

Cleary, E. (1984). *McCormick's handbook on the law of evidence* (3rd ed.) St. Paul, MN: West.

Crutchfield, L. B., & Borders, L. D. (1997). Impact of two clinical peer supervision models on practicing school counselors. *Journal of Counseling and Development, 75,* 219–230.

Crutchfield, L. B., & Hipps, E. S. (1998). What a school administrator needs to know about school counseling professionalism: Ethics, clinical supervision, and professional associations. In C. Dykeman (Ed.), *Maximizing school guidance program effectiveness* (pp. 131–134). Greensboro, NC: ERIC/CASS.

Dye, H. A., & Borders, L. D. (1990). Counseling supervisors: Standards for preparation and practice. *Journal of Counseling and Development, 69,* 27–29.

Goodyear, R., & Nelson, M. L. (1997). The major formats of psychotherapy supervision. In C. E. Watkins, Jr. (Ed.), *Handbook of psychotherapy supervision* (pp. 328–346). New York: Wiley.

Hardesty, P. H., & Dillard, J. M. (1994). Analysis of activities of school counselors. *Psychological Reports, 74,* 447–450.

Henderson, P., & Lampe, R. E. (1992). Clinical supervision of school counselors. *The School Counselor, 39,* 151–157.

Nelson, M. D., & Johnson, P. (1999). School counselors as supervisors: An integrated approach for supervising school counseling interns. *Counselor Education and Supervision, 39,* 89–100.

Page, B. J., Pietrzak, D. R., & Sutton, J. M. (2001). National survey of school counselor supervision. *Counselor Education and Supervision, 41,* 142–150.

Remley, T. P., Jr. (1985). The law and ethical practice in elementary and middle schools. *Elementary School Guidance and Counseling, 19,* 181–189.

Remley, T. P., Jr., Brooks, M., Chauvin, I., Gray, N., Hermann, M., & Tanigoshi, H. (2001, October). *Supervising counselors with suicidal clients.* Paper presented at Southern Association for Counselor Education and Supervision Conference, Athens, GA.

Remley, T. P., Jr., & Herlihy, B. (2001). *Ethical, legal, and professional issues in counseling.* Upper Saddle River, NJ: Merrill Prentice Hall.

Appendix

American School Counselor Association *Ethical Standards for School Counselors*

PREAMBLE

The American School Counselor Association (ASCA) is a professional organization whose members have a unique and distinctive preparation, grounded in the behavioral sciences, with training in clinical skills adapted to the school setting. The school counselor assists in the growth and development of each individual and uses his or her highly specialized skills to protect the interests of the counselee within the structure of the school system. School counselors subscribe to the following basic tenets of the counseling process from which professional responsibilities are derived:

- Each person has the right to respect and dignity as a human being and to counseling services without prejudice as to person, character, belief, or practice regardless of age, color, disability, ethnic group, gender, race, religion, sexual orientation, marital s tatus, or socioeconomic status.
- Each person has the right to self-direction and self-development.
- Each person has the right of choice and the responsibility for goals reached.
- Each person has the right to privacy and thereby the right to expect the counselor-counselee relationship to comply with all laws, policies, and ethical standards pertaining to confidentiality.

In this document, ASCA specifies the principles of ethical behavior necessary to regulate and maintain the high standards of integrity, leadership, and professionalism among its members. The *Ethical Standards for School Counselors* were developed to clarify the nature of ethical responsibilities held in common by school counseling professionals. The purposes of this document are to:

- Serve as a guide for the ethical practices of all professional school counselors regardless of level, area, population served, or membership in this professional Association;
- Provide benchmarks for both self-appraisal and peer evaluations regarding counselor responsibilities to counselees, parents, colleagues and professional associates, schools, and communities, as well as to one's self and the counseling profession; and
- Inform those served by the school counselor of acceptable counselor practices and expected professional behavior.

A.1. Responsibilities to Students
The professional school counselor:
  a. Has a primary obligation to the counselee who is to be treated with respect as a unique individual.
  b. Is concerned with the educational, career, emotional, and behavioral needs and encourages the maximum development of each counselee.
  c. Refrains from consciously encouraging the counselee's acceptance of values, lifestyles, plans, decisions, and beliefs that represent the counselor's personal orientation.
  d. Is responsible for keeping informed of laws, regulations, and policies relating to counselees and strives to ensure that the rights of counselees are adequately provided for and protected.

A.2. Confidentiality
The professional school counselor:
  a. Informs the counselee of the purposes, goals, techniques, and rules of procedure under which she/he may receive counseling at or before the time when the counseling relationship is entered. Disclosure notice includes confidentiality issues such as the possible necessity for consulting with other professionals, privileged communication, and legal or authoritative restraints. The meaning and limits of confidentiality are clearly defined to counselees through a written and shared disclosure statement.
  b. Keeps information confidential unless disclosure is required to prevent clear and imminent danger to the counselee or others or when

legal requirements demand that confidential information be revealed. Counselors will consult with other professionals when in doubt as to the validity of an exception.

c. Discloses information to an identified third party who, by her or his relationship with the counselee, is at a high risk of contracting a disease that is commonly known to be communicable and fatal. Prior to disclosure, the counselor will ascertain that the counselee has not already informed the third party about his or her disease and he/she is not intending to inform the third party in the immediate future.

d. Requests of the court that disclosure not be required when the release of confidential information without a counselee's permission may lead to potential harm to the counselee.

e. Protects the confidentiality of counselee's records and releases personal data only according to prescribed laws and school policies. Student information maintained in computers is treated with the same care as traditional student records.

f. Protects the confidentiality of information received in the counseling relationship as specified by federal and state laws, written policies, and applicable ethical standards. Such information is only to be revealed to others with the informed consent of the counselee, consistent with the counselor's ethical obligation. In a group setting, the counselor sets a high norm of confidentiality and stresses its importance, yet clearly states that confidentiality in group counseling cannot be guaranteed.

A.3. Counseling Plans

The professional school counselor:

works jointly with the counselee in developing integrated and effective counseling plans, consistent with both the abilities and circumstances of the counselee and counselor. Such plans will be regularly reviewed to ensure continued viability and effectiveness, respecting the counselee's freedom of choice.

A.4. Dual Relationships

The professional school counselor:

avoids dual relationships which might impair her or his objectivity and increase the risk of harm to the client (e.g., counseling one's family members, close friends, or associates). If a dual relationship is unavoidable, the counselor is responsible for taking action to eliminate or reduce the potential for harm. Such safeguards might include informed consent, consultation, supervision, and documentation.

A.5. Appropriate Referrals

The professional school counselor:

makes referrals when necessary or appropriate to outside resources. Appropriate referral necessitates knowledge of available resources and making proper plans for transitions with minimal interruption of services. Counselees retain the right to discontinue the counseling relationship at any time.

A.6. Group Work

The professional school counselor:

screens prospective group members and maintains an awareness of participants' needs and goals in relation to the goals of the group. The counselor takes reasonable precautions to protect members from physical and psychological harm resulting from interaction within the group.

A.7. Danger to Self or Others

The professional school counselor:

informs appropriate authorities when the counselee's condition indicates a clear and imminent danger to the counselee or others. This is to be done after careful deliberation and, where possible, after consultation with other counseling professionals. The counselor informs the counselee of actions to be taken so as to minimize his or her confusion and to clarify counselee and counselor expectations.

A.8. Student Records

The professional school counselor:

maintains and secures records necessary for rendering professional services to the counselee as required by laws, regulations, institutional procedures, and confidentiality guidelines.

A.9. Evaluation, Assessment, and Interpretation

The professional school counselor:

a. Adheres to all professional standards regarding selecting, administering, and interpreting assessment measures. The counselor recognizes that computer-based testing programs require specific training in administration, scoring, and interpretation which may differ from that required in more traditional assessments.

b. Provides explanations of the nature, purposes, and results of assessment/evaluation measures in language the counselee(s) can understand.

c. Does not misuse assessment results and interpretations and takes reasonable steps to prevent others from misusing the information.

    d. Uses caution when u tilizing assessment techniques, making evalua-
       tions, and interpreting the performance of populations not repre-
       sented in the norm group on which an instrument is standardized.

A.10. Computer Technology
The professional school counselor:
    a. Promotes the benefits of appropriate computer applications and
       clarifies the limitations of computer technology. The counselor
       ensures that: (1) computer applications are appropriate for the
       individual needs of the counselee; (2) the counselee understands
       how to use the application; and (3) follow-up counseling assistance
       is provided. Members of under represented groups are assured
       equal access to computer technologies and are assured the absence
       of discriminatory information and values in computer applications.
    b. Counselors who communicate with counselees via internet should
       follow the NBCC Standards for Webcounseling.

A.11. Peer Helper Programs
The professional school counselor:
    has unique responsibilities when working with peer helper pro-
grams. The school counselor is responsible for the welfare of counselees
participating in peer programs under her or his direction. School counselors who function in training and supervisory capacities are referred to
the preparation and supervision standards of professional counselor
associations.

B. RESPONSIBILITIES TO PARENTS

B.1. Parent Rights and Responsibilities
The professional school counselor:
    a. Respects the inherent rights and responsibilities of parents for their
       children and endeavors to establish, as appropriate, a collaborative
       relationship with parents to facilitate the counselee's maximum
       development.
    b. Adheres to laws and local guidelines when assisting parents experi-
       encing family difficulties that interfere with the counselee's effec-
       tiveness and welfare.
    c. Is sensitive to cultural and social diversity among families and rec-
       ognizes that all parents, custodial and noncustodial, are vested with
       certain rights and responsibilities for the welfare of their children
       by virtue of their role and according to law.

B.2. Parents and Confidentiality

The professional school counselor:

a. Informs parents of the counselor's role with emphasis on the confidential nature of the counseling relationship between the counselor and counselee.

b. Provides parents with accurate, comprehensive, and relevant information in an objective and caring manner, as is appropriate and consistent with ethical responsibilities to the counselee.

c. Makes reasonable efforts to honor the wishes of parents and guardians concerning information that he/she may share regarding the counselee.

C. RESPONSIBILITIES TO COLLEAGUES AND PROFESSIONAL ASSOCIATES

C.1. Professional Relationships

The professional school counselor:

a. Establishes and maintains professional relationships with faculty, staff, and administration to facilitate the provision of optimal counseling services. The relationship is based on the counselor's definition and description of the parameter and levels of his or her professional roles.

b. Treats colleagues with professional respect, courtesy, and fairness. The qualifications, views, and findings of colleagues are represented to accurately reflect the image of competent professionals.

c. Is aware of and optimally utilizes related professions and organizations to whom the counselee may be referred.

C.2. Sharing Information with Other Professionals

The professional school counselor:

a. Promotes awareness and adherence to appropriate guidelines regarding confidentiality; the distinction between public and private information; and staff consultation.

b. Provides professional personnel with accurate, objective, concise, and meaningful data necessary to adequately evaluate, counsel, and assist the counselee.

c. If a counselee is receiving services from another counselor or other mental health professional, the counselor, with client consent, will inform the other professional and develop clear agreements to avoid confusion and conflict for the counselee.

D. RESPONSIBILITIES TO THE SCHOOL AND COMMUNITY

D.1. Responsibilities to the School
The professional school counselor:
   a. Supports and protects the educational program against any infringement not in the best interest of counselees.
   b. Informs appropriate officials of conditions that may be potentially disruptive or damaging to the school's mission, personnel, and property while honoring the confidentiality between the counselee and counselor.
   c. Delineates and promotes the counselor's role and function in meeting the needs of those served. The counselor will notify appropriate officials of conditions which may limit or curtail her or his effectiveness in providing programs and services.
   d. Accepts employment only for positions for which he/she is qualified by education, training, supervised experience, state and national professional credentials, and appropriate professional experience. Counselors recommend that administrators hire only qualified and competent individuals for professional counseling positions.
   e. Assists in developing: (1) curricular and environmental conditions appropriate for the school and community; (2) educational procedures and programs to meet the counselee's developmental needs; and (3) a systematic evaluation process for comprehensive school counseling programs, services, and personnel. The counselor is guided by the findings of the evaluation data in planning programs and services.

D.2. Responsibility to the Community
The professional school counselor:

collaborates with agencies, organizations, and individuals in the school and community in the best interest of counselees and without regard to personal reward or remuneration.

E. RESPONSIBILITIES TO SELF

E.1. Professional Competence
The professional school counselor:
   a. Functions within the boundaries of individual professional competence and accepts responsibility for the consequences of his or her actions.
   b. Monitors personal functioning and effectiveness and does not participate in any activity which may lead to inadequate professional services or harm to a client.

c. Strives through personal initiative to maintain professional competence and to keep abreast of professional information. Professional and personal growth are ongoing throughout the counselor's career.

E.2. Multicultural Skills

The professional school counselor:

understands the diverse cultural backgrounds of the counselees with whom he/she works. This includes, but is not limited to, learning how the school counselor's own cultural/ethnic/racial identity impacts her or his values and beliefs about the counseling process.

F. RESPONSIBILITIES TO THE PROFESSION

F.1. Professionalism

The professional school counselor:
   a. Accepts the policies and processes for handling ethical violations as a result of maintaining membership in the American School Counselor Association.
   b. Conducts herself/himself in such a manner as to advance individual ethical practice and the profession.
   c. Conducts appropriate research and reports findings in a manner consistent with acceptable educational and psychological research practices. When using client data for research or for statistical or program planning purposes, the counselor ensures protection of the individual counselee's identity.
   d. Adheres to ethical standards of the profession, other official policy statements pertaining to counseling, and relevant statutes established by federal, state, and local governments.
   e. Clearly distinguishes between statements and actions made as a private individual and those made as a representative of the school counseling profession.
   f. Does not use his or her professional position to recruit or gain clients, consultees for her or his private practice, seek and receive unjustified personal gains, unfair advantage, sexual favors, or unearned goods or services.

F.2. Contribution to the Profession

The professional school counselor:
   a. Actively participates in local, state, and national associations which foster the development and improvement of school counseling.
   b. Contributes to the development of the profession through sharing skills, ideas, and expertise with colleagues.

G. MAINTENANCE OF STANDARDS

Ethical behavior among professional school counselors, Association members and nonmembers, is expected at all times. When there exists serious doubt as to the ethical behavior of colleagues, or if counselors are forced to work in situations or abide by policies which do not reflect the standards as outlined in these Ethical Standards for School Counselors, the counselor is obligated to take appropriate action to rectify the condition. The following procedure may serve as a guide:

1. The counselor should consult confidentially with a professional colleague to discuss the nature of a complaint to see if she/he views the situation as an ethical violation.
2. When feasible, the counselor should directly approach the colleague whose behavior is in question to discuss the complaint and seek resolution.
3. If resolution is not forthcoming at the personal level, the counselor shall utilize the channels established within the school, school district, the state SCA, and ASCA Ethics Committee.
4. If the matter still remains unresolved, referral for review and appropriate action should be made to the Ethics Committees in the following sequence:
   - state school counselor association
   - American School Counselor Association
5. The ASCA Ethics Committee is responsible for educating—and consulting with—the membership regarding ethical standards. The Committee periodically reviews an recommends changes in code. The Committee will also receive and process questions to clarify the application of such standards. Questions must be submitted in writing to the ASCA Ethics Chair. Finally, the Committee will handle complaints of alleged violations of our ethical standards. Therefore, at the national level, complaints should be submitted in writing to the ASCA Ethics Committee, c/o the Executive Director, American School Counselor Association, 801 N. Fairfax St., Suite 310, Alexandria, VA 22314.

H. RESOURCES

School counselors are responsible for being aware of, and acting in accord with, standards and positions of the counseling profession as represented in official documents such as those listed below:

American Counseling Association. (1995). *Code of ethics and standards of practice.* Alexandria, VA. (5999 Stevenson Ave., Alexandria, VA 22034) 1 800 347 6647 www.counseling.org.

American School Counselor Association. (1997). *The national standards for school counseling programs.* Alexandria, VA. (801 North Fairfax Street, Suite 310, Alexandria, VA 22314) 1 800 306 4722 www.schoolcounselor. org.

American School Counselor Association. (1998). *Position Statements.* Alexandria, VA.

American School Counselor Association. (1998). Professional liability insurance program. (Brochure). Alexandria, VA.

Arrendondo, Toperek, Brown, Jones, Locke, Sanchez, and Stadler. (1996). Multicultural counseling competencies and standards. *Journal of Multicultural Counseling and Development. Vol.* 24, No. 1. See American Counseling Association.

Arthur, G.L. and Swanson, C.D. (1993). *Confidentiality and privileged communication.* (1993). See American Counseling Association.

Association for Specialists in Group Work. (1989). *Ethical Guidelines for group counselors.* (1989). Alexandria, VA. See American Counseling Association.

Corey, G., Corey, M.S. and Callanan. (1998). *Issues and Ethics in the Helping Professions.* Pacific Grove, CA: Brooks/Cole. (Brooks/Cole, 511 Forest Lodge Rd., Pacific Grove, CA 93950) www.thomson.com.

Crawford, R. (1994). *Avoiding counselor malpractice.* Alexandria, VA. See American Counseling Association.

Forrester-Miller, H. and Davis, T.E. (1996). *A practitioner's guide to ethical decision making.* Alexandria, VA. See American Counseling Association.

Herlihy, B. and Corey, G. (1996). *ACA ethical standards casebook.* Fifth ed. Alexandria, VA. See American Counseling Association.

Herlihy, B. and Corey, G. (1992). *Dual relationships in counseling.* Alexandria, VA. See American Counseling Association.

Huey, W.C. and Remley, T.P. (1988). Ethical and legal issues in school counseling. Alexandria, VA. See American School Counselor Association.

Joint Committee on Testing Practices. (1988). *Code of fair testing practices in education.* Washington, DC: American Psychological Association. (1200 17th Street, NW, Washington, DC 20036) 202 336 5500

Mitchell, R.W. (1991). *Documentation in counseling records.* Alexandria, VA. See American Counseling Association.

National Board for Certified Counselors. (1998). *National board for certified counselors: code of ethics.* Greensboro, NC. (3 Terrace Way, Suite D, Greensboro, NC 27403-3660) 336 547 0607 www.nbcc.org.

National Board for Certified Counselors. (1997). *Standards for the ethical practice of webcounseling.* Greensboro, NC.

National Peer Helpers Association. (1989). *Code of ethics for peer helping professionals.* Greenville, NC. PO Box 2684, Greenville, NC 27836. 919 522 3959. nphaorg@aol.com.

Salo, M. and Schumate, S. (1993). *Counseling minor clients.* Alexandria, VA. See American School Counselor Association.

Stevens-Smith, P. and Hughes, M. (1993). *Legal issues in marriage and family counseling.* Alexandria, VA. See American School Counselor Association.

Wheeler, N. and Bertram, B. (1994). *Legal aspects of counseling: avoiding lawsuits and legal problems.* (Videotape). Alexandria, VA. See American School Counselor Association.

Ethical Standards for School Counselors was adopted by the ASCA Delegate Assembly, March 19, 1984. The first revision was approved by the ASCA Delegate Assembly, March 27, 1992. The second revision was approved by the ASCA Governing Board on March 30, 1998 and adopted on June 25, 1998.

6/25/98

American Counseling Association Code of Ethics and Standards of Practice (1995)

ACA Code of Ethics

PREAMBLE

The American Counseling Association is an educational, scientific, and professional organization whose members are dedicated to the enhancement of human development throughout the life-span. Association members recognize diversity in our society and embrace a cross-cultural approach in support of the worth, dignity, potential, and uniqueness of each individual.

The specification of a code of ethics enables the association to clarify to current and future members, and to those served by members, the nature of the ethical responsibilities held in common by its members. As the code of ethics of the association, this document establishes principles that define the ethical behavior of association members. All members of the American Counseling Association are required to adhere to the *Code of Ethics* and the *Standards of Practice*. The *Code of Ethics* will serve as the basis for processing ethical complaints initiated against members of the association.

SECTION A: THE COUNSELING RELATIONSHIP

A.1. Client Welfare

a. *Primary Responsibility.* The primary responsibility of counselors is to respect the dignity and to promote the welfare of clients.

b. *Positive Growth and Development.* Counselors encourage client growth and development in ways that foster the clients' interest and welfare; counselors avoid fostering dependent counseling relationships.

c. *Counseling Plans.* Counselors and their clients work jointly in devising integrated, individual counseling plans that offer reasonable promise of success and are consistent with abilities and circumstances of clients. Counselors and clients regularly review counseling plans to ensure their continued viability and effectiveness, respecting clients' freedom of choice. (See A.3.b.)

d. *Family Involvement.* Counselors recognize that families are usually important in clients' lives and strive to enlist family understanding and involvement as a positive resource, when appropriate.

e. *Career and Employment* Needs. Counselors work with their clients in considering employment in jobs and circumstances that are consistent with the clients' overall abilities, vocational limitations, physical restrictions, general temperament, interest and aptitude patterns, social skills, education, general qualifications, and other relevant characteristics and needs. Counselors neither place nor participate in placing clients in positions that will result in damaging the interest and the welfare of clients, employers, or the public.

A.2. Respecting Diversity

a. *Nondiscrimination.* Counselors do not condone or engage in discrimination based on age, color, culture, disability, ethnic group, gender, race, religion, sexual orientation, marital status, or socioeconomic status. (See C.5.a., C.5.b., and D.1.i.)

b. *Respecting Differences.* Counselors will actively attempt to understand the diverse cultural backgrounds of the clients with whom they work. This includes, but is not limited to, learning how the counselor's own cultural/ethnic/racial identity impacts her or his values and beliefs about the counseling process. (See E.8. and F.2.i.)

A.3. Client Rights

a. *Disclosure to Clients.* When counseling is initiated, and throughout the counseling process as necessary, counselors inform clients of the purposes, goals, techniques, procedures, limitations, potential risks, and benefits of services to be performed, and other pertinent information. Counselors take steps to ensure that clients understand the implications of diagnosis, the intended use of tests and reports, fees, and billing arrangements. Clients have the right to expect confidentiality and to be provided with an explanation of its limitations, including supervision and/or treatment team professionals; to obtain clear information about their case records; to participate in the ongoing counseling plans; and to refuse any recommended services and be advised of the consequences of such refusal. (See E.5.a. and G.2.)

b. *Freedom of Choice.* Counselors offer clients the freedom to choose whether to enter into a counseling relationship and to determine which professional(s) will provide counseling. Restrictions that limit choices of clients are fully explained. (See A.1.c.)

c. *Inability to Give Consent.* When counseling minors or persons unable to give voluntary informed consent, counselors act in these clients' best interests. (See B.3.)

A.4. Clients Served by Others

If a client is receiving services from another mental health professional, counselors, with client consent, inform the professional persons already involved and develop clear agreements to avoid confusion and conflict for the client. (See C.6.c.)

A.5. Personal Needs and Values

a. *Personal Needs.* In the counseling relationship, counselors are aware of the intimacy and responsibilities inherent in the counseling relationship, maintain respect for clients, and avoid actions that seek to meet their personal needs at the expense of clients.

b. *Personal Values.* Counselors are aware of their own values, attitudes, beliefs, and behaviors and how these apply in a diverse society, and avoid imposing their values on clients. (See C.5.a.)

A.6. Dual Relationships

a. *Avoid When Possible.* Counselors are aware of their influential positions with respect to clients, and they avoid exploiting the trust and dependency of clients. Counselors make every effort to avoid dual relationships with clients that could impair professional judgment or increase the risk of harm to clients. (Examples of such relationships include, but are not limited to, familial, social, financial, business, or close personal relationships with clients.) When a dual relationship cannot be avoided, counselors take appropriate professional precautions such as informed consent, consultation, supervision, and documentation to ensure that judgment is not impaired and no exploitation occurs. (See F.1.b.)

b. *Superior/Subordinate Relationships.* Counselors do not accept as clients superiors or subordinates with whom they have administrative, supervisory, or evaluative relationships.

A.7. Sexual Intimacies With Clients

a. *Current Clients.* Counselors do not have any type of sexual intimacies with clients and do not counsel persons with whom they have had a sexual relationship.

b. *Former Clients.* Counselors do not engage in sexual intimacies with former clients within a minimum of 2 years after terminating the counseling relationship. Counselors who engage in such relationship after 2 years following termination have the responsibility to examine and document thoroughly that such relations did not have an exploitative nature, based on factors such as duration of counseling, amount of time since counseling, termination circumstances, client's personal history and mental status, adverse impact on the client, and actions by the counselor suggesting a plan to initiate a sexual relationship with the client after termination.

A.8. Multiple Clients

When counselors agree to provide counseling services to two or more persons who have a relationship (such as husband and wife, or parents and children), counselors clarify at the outset which person or persons are clients and the nature of the relationships they will have with each involved person. If it becomes apparent that counselors may be called upon to perform potentially conflicting roles, they clarify, adjust, or withdraw from roles appropriately. (See B.2. and B.4.d.)

A.9. Group Work

a. *Screening.* Counselors screen prospective group counseling/therapy participants. To the extent possible, counselors select members whose needs and goals are compatible with goals of the group, who will not impede the group process, and whose well-being will not be jeopardized by the group experience.

b. *Protecting Clients.* In a group setting, counselors take reasonable precautions to protect clients from physical or psychological trauma.

A.10. Fees and Bartering (See D.3.a. and D.3.b.)

a. *Advance Understanding.* Counselors clearly explain to clients, prior to entering the counseling relationship, all financial arrangements related to professional services including the use of collection agencies or legal measures for nonpayment. (A.11.c.)

b. *Establishing Fees.* In establishing fees for professional counseling services, counselors consider the financial status of clients and locality. In the event that the established fee structure is inappropriate for a client, assistance is provided in attempting to find comparable services of acceptable cost. (See A.10.d., D.3.a., and D.3.b.)

c. *Bartering Discouraged.* Counselors ordinarily refrain from accepting goods or services from clients in return for counseling services because such arrangements create inherent potential for conflicts, exploitation, and distortion of the professional relationship. Counselors may participate in bartering only if the relationship is not exploitative, if the client requests it, if a clear written contract is established, and if such arrangements are an accepted practice among professionals in the community. (See A.6.a.)

d. *Pro Bono Service.* Counselors contribute to society by devoting a portion of their professional activity to services for which there is little or no financial return (pro bono).

A.11. Termination and Referral

a. *Abandonment Prohibited.* Counselors do not abandon or neglect clients in counseling. Counselors assist in making appropriate arrangements for the continuation of treatment, when necessary, during interruptions such as vacations, and following termination.

b. *Inability to Assist Clients.* If counselors determine an inability to be of professional assistance to clients, they avoid entering or immediately terminate a counseling relationship. Counselors are knowledgeable about referral resources and suggest appropriate alternatives. If clients decline the suggested referral, counselors should discontinue the relationship.

c. *Appropriate Termination.* Counselors terminate a counseling relationship, securing client agreement when possible, when it is reasonably clear that the client is no longer benefiting, when services are no longer required, when counseling no longer serves the client's needs or interests, when clients do not pay fees charged, or when agency or institution limits do not allow provision of further counseling services. (See A.10.b. and C.2.g.)

A.12. Computer Technology

a. *Use of Computers.* When computer applications are used in counseling services, counselors ensure that (1) the client is intellectually, emotionally, and physically capable of using the computer application; (2) the computer application is appropriate for the needs of the client; (3) the client understands the purpose and operation of the computer applications; and (4) a follow-up of client use of a computer application is provided to correct possible misconceptions, discover inappropriate use, and assess subsequent needs.

b. *Explanation of Limitations.* Counselors ensure that clients are provided information as a part of the counseling relationship that adequately explains the limitations of computer technology.

c. *Access to Computer Applications.* Counselors provide for equal access to computer applications in counseling services. (See A.2.a.)

SECTION B: CONFIDENTIALITY

B.1. Right to Privacy

a. *Respect for Privacy.* Counselors respect their clients right to privacy and avoid illegal and unwarranted disclosures of confidential information. (See A.3.a. and B.6.a.)

b. *Client Waiver.* The right to privacy may be waived by the client or his or her legally recognized representative.

c. *Exceptions.* The general requirement that counselors keep information confidential does not apply when disclosure is required to prevent clear and imminent danger to the client or others or when legal requirements demand that confidential information be revealed. Counselors consult with other professionals when in doubt as to the validity of an exception.

d. *Contagious, Fatal Diseases.* A counselor who receives information confirming that a client has a disease commonly known to be both communicable and fatal is justified in disclosing information to an identifiable third party, who by his or her relationship with the client is at a high risk of contracting the disease. Prior to making a disclosure the counselor should ascertain that the client has not already informed the third party about his or her disease and that the client is not intending to inform the third party in the immediate future. (See B.1.c and B.1.f.)

e. *Court-Ordered Disclosure.* When court ordered to release confidential information without a client's permission, counselors request to the court that the disclosure not be required due to potential harm to the client or counseling relationship. (See B.1.c.)

f. *Minimal Disclosure.* When circumstances require the disclosure of confidential information, only essential information is revealed. To the extent possible, clients are informed before confidential information is disclosed.

g. *Explanation of Limitations.* When counseling is initiated and throughout the counseling process as necessary, counselors inform clients of the limitations of confidentiality and identify foreseeable situations in which confidentiality must be breached. (See G.2.a.)

h. *Subordinates.* Counselors make every effort to ensure that privacy and confidentiality of clients are maintained by subordinates including employees, supervisees, clerical assistants, and volunteers. (See B.1.a.)

i. *Treatment Teams.* If client treatment will involve a continued review by a treatment team, the client will be informed of the team's existence and composition.

B.2. Groups and Families

a. *Group Work.* In group work, counselors clearly define confidentiality and the parameters for the specific group being entered, explain its importance, and discuss the difficulties related to confidentiality involved in group work. The fact that confidentiality cannot be guaranteed is clearly communicated to group members.

b. *Family Counseling.* In family counseling, information about one family member cannot be disclosed to another member without permission. Counselors protect the privacy rights of each family member. (See A.8., B.3., and B.4.d.)

B.3. Minor or Incompetent Clients

When counseling clients who are minors or individuals who are unable to give voluntary, informed consent, parents or guardians may be included in the counseling process as appropriate. Counselors act in the best interests of clients and take measures to safeguard confidentiality. (See A.3.c.)

B.4. Records

a. *Requirement of Records.* Counselors maintain records necessary for rendering professional services to their clients and as required by laws, regulations, or agency or institution procedures.

b. *Confidentiality of Records.* Counselors are responsible for securing the safety and confidentiality of any counseling records they create, maintain, transfer, or destroy whether the records are written, taped, computerized, or stored in any other medium. (See B.1.a.)

c. *Permission to Record or Observe.* Counselors obtain permission from clients prior to electronically recording or observing sessions. (See A.3.a.)

d. *Client Access.* Counselors recognize that counseling records are kept for the benefit of clients, and therefore provide access to records and copies of records when requested by competent clients, unless the records contain information that may be misleading and detrimental to the client. In situations involving multiple clients, access to records is limited to those parts of records that do not include confidential information related to another client. (See A.8., B.1.a., and B.2.b.)

e. *Disclosure or Transfer.* Counselors obtain written permission from clients to disclose or transfer records to legitimate third parties unless exceptions to confidentiality exist as listed in Section B.1. Steps are taken to ensure that receivers of counseling records are sensitive to their confidential nature.

B.5. Research and Training

a. *Data Disguise Required.* Use of data derived from counseling relationships for purposes of training, research, or publication is confined to content that is disguised to ensure the anonymity of the individuals involved. (See B.1.g. and G.3.d.)

b. *Agreement for Identification.* Identification of a client in a presentation or publication is permissible only when the client has reviewed the material and has agreed to its presentation or publication. (See G.3.d.)

B.6. Consultation

a. *Respect for Privacy.* Information obtained in a consulting relationship is discussed for professional purposes only with persons clearly concerned with the case. Written and oral reports present data germane to the purposes of the consultation, and every effort is made to protect client identity and avoid undue invasion of privacy.

b. *Cooperating Agencies.* Before sharing information, counselors make efforts to ensure that there are defined policies in other agencies serving the counselor's clients that effectively protect the confidentiality of information.

SECTION C: PROFESSIONAL RESPONSIBILITY

C.1. Standards Knowledge

Counselors have a responsibility to read, understand, and follow the *Code of Ethics* and the *Standards of Practice*.

C.2. Professional Competence

a. *Boundaries of Competence.* Counselors practice only within the boundaries of their competence, based on their education, training, supervised experience, state and national professional credentials, and appropriate professional experience. Counselors will demonstrate a commitment to gain knowledge, personal awareness, sensitivity, and skills pertinent to working with a diverse client population.

b. *New Specialty Areas of Practice.* Counselors practice in specialty areas new to them only after appropriate education, training, and supervised experience. While developing skills in new specialty areas, counselors take steps to ensure the competence of their work and to protect others from possible harm.

c. *Qualified for Employment.* Counselors accept employment only for positions for which they are qualified by education, training, supervised experience, state and national professional credentials, and appropriate professional experience. Counselors hire for professional counseling positions only individuals who are qualified and competent.

d. *Monitor Effectiveness.* Counselors continually monitor their effectiveness as professionals and take steps to improve when necessary. Counselors in private practice take reasonable steps to seek out peer supervision to evaluate their efficacy as counselors.

e. *Ethical Issues Consultation.* Counselors take reasonable steps to consult with other counselors or related professionals when they have questions regarding their ethical obligations or professional practice. (See H.1.)

f. *Continuing Education.* Counselors recognize the need for continuing education to maintain a reasonable level of awareness of current scientific and professional information in their fields of activity. They take steps to maintain competence in the skills they use, are open to new procedures, and keep current with the diverse and/or special populations with whom they work.

g. *Impairment.* Counselors refrain from offering or accepting professional services when their physical, mental, or emotional problems are likely to harm a client or others. They are alert to the signs of impairment, seek assistance for problems, and, if necessary, limit, suspend, or terminate their professional responsibilities. (See A.11.c.)

C.3. Advertising and Soliciting Clients

a. *Accurate Advertising.* There are no restrictions on advertising by counselors except those that can be specifically justified to protect the public from deceptive practices. Counselors advertise or represent their services to the public by identifying their credentials in an accurate manner that is not false, misleading, deceptive, or fraudulent. Counselors may only advertise the highest degree earned which is in counseling or a closely related field from a college or university that was accredited when the degree was awarded by one of the regional accrediting bodies recognized by the Council on Postsecondary Accreditation.

b. *Testimonials.* Counselors who use testimonials do not solicit them from clients or other persons who, because of their particular circumstances, may be vulnerable to undue influence.

c. *Statements by Others.* Counselors make reasonable efforts to ensure that statements made by others about them or the profession of counseling are accurate.

d. *Recruiting Through Employment.* Counselors do not use their places of employment or institutional affiliation to recruit or gain clients, supervisees, or consultees for their private practices. (See C.5.e.)

e. *Products and Training Advertisements.* Counselors who develop products related to their profession or conduct workshops or training events ensure that the advertisements concerning these products or events are accurate and disclose adequate information for consumers to make informed choices.

f. *Promoting to Those Served.* Counselors do not use counseling, teaching, training, or supervisory relationships to promote their products or training events in a manner that is deceptive or would exert undue influence on individuals who may be vulnerable. Counselors may adopt textbooks they have authored for instruction purposes.

g. *Professional Association Involvement.* Counselors actively participate in local, state, and national associations that foster the development and improvement of counseling.

C.4. Credentials

a. *Credentials Claimed.* Counselors claim or imply only professional credentials possessed and are responsible for correcting any known misrepresentations of their credentials by others. Professional credentials include graduate degrees in counseling or closely related mental health fields, accreditation of graduate programs, national voluntary certifications, government-issued certifications or licenses, ACA professional membership, or any other credential that might indicate to the public specialized knowledge or expertise in counseling.

b. *ACA Professional Membership.* ACA professional members may announce to the public their membership status. Regular members may not announce their ACA membership in a manner that might imply they are credentialed counselors.

c. Credential Guidelines. Counselors follow the guidelines for use of credentials that have been established by the entities that issue the credentials.

d. *Misrepresentation of Credentials.* Counselors do not attribute more to their credentials than the credentials represent, and do not imply that other counselors are not qualified because they do not possess certain credentials.

e. *Doctoral Degrees From Other Fields.* Counselors who hold a master's degree in counseling or a closely related mental health field, but hold a doctoral degree from other than counseling or a closely related field, do not use the title "Dr." in their practices and do not announce to the public in relation to their practice or status as a counselor that they hold a doctorate.

C.5. Public Responsibility

a. *Nondiscrimination.* Counselors do not discriminate against clients, students, or supervisees in a manner that has a negative impact based on their age, color, culture, disability, ethnic group, gender, race, religion, sexual orientation, or socioeconomic status, or for any other reason. (See A.2.a.)

b. *Sexual Harassment.* Counselors do not engage in sexual harassment. Sexual harassment is defined as sexual solicitation, physical advances, or verbal or nonverbal conduct that is sexual in nature, that occurs in connection with professional activities or roles, and that either (1) is unwelcome, is offensive, or creates a hostile workplace environment, and counselors know or are told this; or (2) is sufficiently severe or intense to be perceived as harassment to a reasonable person in the context. Sexual harassment can consist of a single intense or severe act or multiple persistent or pervasive acts.

c. *Reports to Third Parties.* Counselors are accurate, honest, and unbiased in reporting their professional activities and judgments to appropriate third parties including courts, health insurance companies, those who are the recipients of evaluation reports, and others. (See B.1.g.)

d. *Media Presentations.* When counselors provide advice or comment by means of public lectures, demonstrations, radio or television programs, prerecorded tapes, printed articles, mailed material, or other media, they take reasonable precautions to ensure that (1) the statements are based on appropriate professional counseling literature and practice; (2) the statements are otherwise consistent with the Code of Ethics and the Standards of Practice; and (3) the recipients of the information are not encouraged to infer that a professional counseling relationship has been established. (See C.6.b.)

e. *Unjustified Gains.* Counselors do not use their professional positions to seek or receive unjustified personal gains, sexual favors, unfair advantage, or unearned goods or services. (See C.3.d.)

C.6. Responsibility to Other Professionals

a. *Different Approaches.* Counselors are respectful of approaches to professional counseling that differ from their own. Counselors know and take into account the traditions and practices of other professional groups with which they work.

b. *Personal Public Statements.* When making personal statements in a public context, counselors clarify that they are speaking from their personal perspectives and that they are not speaking on behalf of all counselors or the profession. (See C.5.d.)

c. *Clients Served by Others.* When counselors learn that their clients are in a professional relationship with another mental health professional, they request release from clients to inform the other professionals and strive to establish positive and collaborative professional relationships. (See A.4.)

SECTION D: RELATIONSHIPS WITH OTHER PROFESSIONALS

D.1. Relationships With Employers and Employees

a. *Role Definition.* Counselors define and describe for their employers and employees the parameters and levels of their professional roles.

b. *Agreements.* Counselors establish working agreements with supervisors, colleagues, and subordinates regarding counseling or clinical relationships, confidentiality, adherence to professional standards, distinction between public and private material, maintenance and dissemination of recorded information, workload, and accountability. Working agreements in each instance are specified and made known to those concerned.

c. *Negative Conditions.* Counselors alert their employers to conditions that may be potentially disruptive or damaging to the counselor's professional responsibilities or that may limit their effectiveness.

d. *Evaluation.* Counselors submit regularly to professional review and evaluation by their supervisor or the appropriate representative of the employer.

e. *In-Service.* Counselors are responsible for in-service development of self and staff.

f. *Goals.* Counselors inform their staff of goals and programs.

g. *Practices.* Counselors provide personnel and agency practices that respect and enhance the rights and welfare of each employee and recipient of agency services. Counselors strive to maintain the highest levels of professional services.

h. *Personnel Selection and Assignment.* Counselors select competent staff and assign responsibilities compatible with their skills and experiences.

i. *Discrimination.* Counselors, as either employers or employees, do not engage in or condone practices that are inhumane, illegal, or unjustifiable (such as considerations based on age, color, culture, disability, ethnic group, gender, race, religion, sexual orientation, or socioeconomic status) in hiring, promotion, or training. (See A.2.a. and C.5.b.)

j. *Professional Conduct.* Counselors have a responsibility both to clients and to the agency or institution within which services are performed to maintain high standards of professional conduct.

k. *Exploitative Relationships.* Counselors do not engage in exploitative relationships with individuals over whom they have supervisory, evaluative, or instructional control or authority.

l. *Employer Policies.* The acceptance of employment in an agency or institution implies that counselors are in agreement with its general policies and principles. Counselors strive to reach agreement with employers as to acceptable standards of conduct that allow for changes in institutional policy conducive to the growth and development of clients.

D.2. Consultation (See B.6.)

a. *Consultation as an Option.* Counselors may choose to consult with any other professionally competent persons about their clients. In choosing consultants, counselors avoid placing the consultant in a conflict of interest situation that would preclude the consultant being a proper party to the counselor's efforts to help the client. Should counselors be engaged in a work setting that compromises this consultation standard, they consult with other professionals whenever possible to consider justifiable alternatives.

b. *Consultant Competency.* Counselors are reasonably certain that they have or the organization represented has the necessary competencies and resources for giving the kind of consulting services needed and that appropriate referral resources are available.

c. *Understanding With Clients.* When providing consultation, counselors attempt to develop with their clients a clear understanding of problem definition, goals for change, and predicted consequences of interventions selected. d. Consultant Goals. The consulting relationship is one in which client adaptability and growth toward self-direction are consistently encouraged and cultivated. (See A.1.b.)

D.3. Fees for Referral

a. *Accepting Fees From Agency Clients.* Counselors refuse a private fee or other remuneration for rendering services to persons who are entitled to such services through the counselor's employing agency or institution. The policies of a particular agency may make explicit provisions for agency clients to receive counseling services from members of its staff in private practice. In such instances, the clients must be informed of other options open to them should they seek private counseling services. (See A.10.a., A.11.b., and C.3.d.)

b. *Referral Fees.* Counselors do not accept a referral fee from other professionals.

D.4. Subcontractor Arrangements

When counselors work as subcontractors for counseling services for a third party, they have a duty to inform clients of the limitations of confidentiality that the organization may place on counselors in providing counseling services to clients. The limits of such confidentiality ordinarily are discussed as part of the intake session. (See B.1.e. and B.1.f.)

SECTION E: EVALUATION, ASSESSMENT, AND INTERPRETATION

E.1. General

a. *Appraisal Techniques.* The primary purpose of educational and psychological assessment is to provide measures that are objective and interpretable in either comparative or absolute terms. Counselors recognize the need to interpret the statements in this section as applying to the whole range of appraisal techniques, including test and nontest data.

b. *Client Welfare.* Counselors promote the welfare and best interests of the client in the development, publication, and utilization of educational and psychological assessment techniques. They do not misuse assessment results and interpretations and take reasonable steps to prevent others from misusing the information these techniques provide. They respect the client's right to know the results, the interpretations made, and the bases for their conclusions and recommendations.

E.2. Competence to Use and Interpret Tests

a. *Limits of Competence.* Counselors recognize the limits of their competence and perform only those testing and assessment services for which they have been trained. They are familiar with reliability, validity, related standardization, error of measurement, and proper application of any technique utilized. Counselors using computer-based test interpretations are trained in the construct being measured and the specific instrument being used prior to using this type of computer application. Counselors take reasonable measures to ensure the proper use of psychological assessment techniques by persons under their supervision.

b. *Appropriate Use.* Counselors are responsible for the appropriate application, scoring, interpretation, and use of assessment instruments, whether they score and interpret such tests themselves or use computerized or other services.

c. *Decisions Based on Results.* Counselors responsible for decisions involving individuals or policies that are based on assessment results have a thorough understanding of educational and psychological measurement, including validation criteria, test research, and guidelines for test development and use.

d. *Accurate Information.* Counselors provide accurate information and avoid false claims or misconceptions when making statements about assessment instruments or techniques. Special efforts are made to avoid unwarranted connotations of such terms as IQ and grade equivalent scores. (See C.5.c.)

E.3. Informed Consent

a. *Explanation to Clients.* Prior to assessment, counselors explain the nature and purposes of assessment and the specific use of results in language the client (or other legally authorized person on behalf of the client) can understand, unless an explicit exception to this right has been agreed upon in advance. Regardless of whether scoring and interpretation are completed by counselors, by assistants, or by computer or other outside services, counselors take reasonable steps to ensure that appropriate explanations are given to the client.

b. *Recipients of Results.* The examinee's welfare, explicit understanding, and prior agreement determine the recipients of test results. Counselors include accurate and appropriate interpretations with any release of individual or group test results. (See B.1.a. and C.5.c.)

E.4. Release of Information to Competent Professionals

a. *Misuse of Results.* Counselors do not misuse assessment results, including test results, and interpretations, and take reasonable steps to prevent the misuse of such by others. (See C.5.c.)

b. *Release of Raw Data.* Counselors ordinarily release data (e.g., protocols, counseling or interview notes, or questionnaires) in which the client is identified only with the consent of the client or the client's legal representative. Such data are usually released only to persons recognized by counselors as competent to interpret the data. (See B.1.a.)

E.5. Proper Diagnosis of Mental Disorders

a. *Proper Diagnosis.* Counselors take special care to provide proper diagnosis of mental disorders. Assessment techniques (including personal interview) used to determine client care (e.g., locus of treatment, type of treatment, or recommended follow-up) are carefully selected and appropriately used. (See A.3.a. and C.5.c.)

b. *Cultural Sensitivity.* Counselors recognize that culture affects the manner in which clients' problems are defined. Clients' socioeconomic and cultural experience is considered when diagnosing mental disorders.

E.6. Test Selection

a. *Appropriateness of Instruments.* Counselors carefully consider the validity, reliability, psychometric limitations, and appropriateness of instruments when selecting tests for use in a given situation or with a particular client.

b. *Culturally Diverse Populations.* Counselors are cautious when selecting tests for culturally diverse populations to avoid inappropriateness of testing that may be outside of socialized behavioral or cognitive patterns.

E.7. Conditions of Test Administration

a. *Administration Conditions.* Counselors administer tests under the same conditions that were established in their standardization. When tests are not administered under standard conditions or when unusual behavior or irregularities occur during the testing session, those conditions are noted in interpretation, and the results may be designated as invalid or of questionable validity.

b. *Computer Administration.* Counselors are responsible for ensuring that administration programs function properly to provide clients with accurate results when a computer or other electronic methods are used for test administration. (See A.12.b.)

c. *Unsupervised Test Taking.* Counselors do not permit unsupervised or inadequately supervised use of tests or assessments unless the tests or assessments are designed, intended, and validated for self-administration and/or scoring.

d. *Disclosure of Favorable Conditions.* Prior to test administration, conditions that produce most favorable test results are made known to the examinee.

E.8. Diversity in Testing

Counselors are cautious in using assessment techniques, making evaluations, and interpreting the performance of populations not represented in the norm group on which an instrument was standardized. They recognize the effects of age, color, culture, disability, ethnic group, gender, race, religion, sexual orientation, and socioeconomic status on test administration and interpretation and place test results in proper perspective with other relevant factors. (See A.2.a.)

E.9. Test Scoring and Interpretation

a. *Reporting Reservations.* In reporting assessment results, counselors indicate any reservations that exist regarding validity or reliability because of the circumstances of the assessment or the inappropriateness of the norms for the person tested.

b. *Research Instruments.* Counselors exercise caution when interpreting the results of research instruments possessing insufficient technical data to support respondent results. The specific purposes for the use of such instruments are stated explicitly to the examinee.

c. *Testing Services.* Counselors who provide test scoring and test interpretation services to support the assessment process confirm the validity of such interpretations. They accurately describe the purpose, norms, validity, reliability, and applications of the procedures and any special qualifications applicable to their use. The public offering of an automated test interpretations service is considered a professional-to-professional consultation. The formal responsibility of the consultant is to the consultee, but the ultimate and overriding responsibility is to the client.

E.10. Test Security

Counselors maintain the integrity and security of tests and other assessment techniques consistent with legal and contractual obligations. Counselors do not appropriate, reproduce, or modify published tests or parts thereof without acknowledgment and permission from the publisher.

E.11. Obsolete Tests and Outdated Test Results

Counselors do not use data or test results that are obsolete or outdated for the current purpose. Counselors make every effort to prevent the misuse of obsolete measures and test data by others.

E.12. Test Construction

Counselors use established scientific procedures, relevant standards, and current professional knowledge for test design in the development, publication, and utilization of educational and psychological assessment techniques.

SECTION F: TEACHING, TRAINING, AND SUPERVISION

F.1. Counselor Educators and Trainers

a. *Educators as Teachers and Practitioners.* Counselors who are responsible for developing, implementing, and supervising educational programs are skilled as teachers and practitioners. They are knowledgeable regarding the ethical, legal, and regulatory aspects of the profession, are skilled in applying that knowledge, and make students and supervisees aware of their responsibilities. Counselors conduct counselor education and training programs in an ethical manner and serve as role models for professional behavior. Counselor educators should make an effort to infuse material related to human diversity into all courses and/or workshops that are designed to promote the development of professional counselors.

b. *Relationship Boundaries With Students and Supervisees.* Counselors clearly define and maintain ethical, professional, and social relationship boundaries with their students and supervisees. They are aware of the differential in power that exists and the student's or supervisee's possible incomprehension of that power differential. Counselors explain to students and supervisees the potential for the relationship to become exploitive.

c. *Sexual Relationships.* Counselors do not engage in sexual relationships with students or supervisees and do not subject them to sexual harassment. (See A.6. and C.5.b)

d. *Contributions to Research.* Counselors give credit to students or supervisees for their contributions to research and scholarly projects. Credit is given through coauthorship, acknowledgment, footnote statement, or other appropriate means, in accordance with such contributions. (See G.4.b. and G.4.c.)

e. *Close Relatives.* Counselors do not accept close relatives as students or supervisees.

f. *Supervision Preparation.* Counselors who offer clinical supervision services are adequately prepared in supervision methods and techniques. Counselors who are doctoral students serving as practicum or internship supervisors to master's level students are adequately prepared and supervised by the training program.

g. *Responsibility for Services to Clients.* Counselors who supervise the counseling services of others take reasonable measures to ensure that counseling services provided to clients are professional.

h. *Endorsement.* Counselors do not endorse students or supervisees for certification, licensure, employment, or completion of an academic or training program if they believe students or supervisees are not qualified for the endorsement. Counselors take reasonable steps to assist students or supervisees who are not qualified for endorsement to become qualified.

F.2. Counselor Education and Training Programs

a. *Orientation.* Prior to admission, counselors orient prospective students to the counselor education or training program's expectations, including but not limited to the following: (1) the type and level of skill acquisition required for successful completion of the training, (2) subject matter to be covered, (3) basis for evaluation, (4) training components that encourage self-growth or self-disclosure as part of the training process, (5) the type of supervision s ettings and requirements of the sites for required clinical field experiences, (6) student and supervisee evaluation and dismissal policies and procedures, and (7) up-to-date employment prospects for graduates.

b. *Integration of Study and Practice.* Counselors establish counselor education and training programs that integrate academic study and supervised practice.

c. *Evaluation.* Counselors clearly state to students and supervisees, in advance of training, the levels of competency expected, appraisal methods, and timing of evaluations for both didactic and experiential components. Counselors provide students and supervisees with periodic performance appraisal and evaluation feedback throughout the training program.

d. *Teaching Ethics.* Counselors make students and supervisees aware of the ethical responsibilities and standards of the profession and the students+ and supervisees' ethical responsibilities to the profession. (See C.1. and F.3.e.)

e. *Peer Relationships.* When students or supervisees are assigned to lead counseling groups or provide clinical supervision for their peers, counselors take steps to ensure that students and supervisees placed in these roles do not have personal or adverse relationships with peers and that they understand they have the same ethical obligations as counselor educators, trainers, and supervisors. Counselors make every effort to ensure that the rights of peers are not compromised when students or supervisees are assigned to lead counseling groups or provide clinical supervision.

f. *Varied Theoretical Positions.* Counselors present varied theoretical positions so that students and supervisees may make comparisons and have opportunities to develop their own positions. Counselors provide information concerning the scientific bases of professional practice. (See C.6.a.)

g. *Field Placements.* Counselors develop clear policies within their training program regarding field placement and other clinical experiences. Counselors provide clearly stated roles and responsibilities for the student or supervisee, the site supervisor, and the program supervisor. They confirm that site supervisors are qualified to provide supervision and are informed of their professional and ethical responsibilities in this role.

h. *Dual Relationships as Supervisors.* Counselors avoid dual relationships such as performing the role of site supervisor and training program supervisor in the student's or supervisee's training program. Counselors do not accept any form of professional services, fees, commissions, reimbursement, or remuneration from a site for student or supervisee placement.

i. *Diversity in Programs.* Counselors are responsive to their institution's and program's recruitment and retention needs for training program administrators, faculty, and students with diverse backgrounds and special needs. (See A.2.a.)

F.3. Students and Supervisees

a. *Limitations.* Counselors, through ongoing evaluation and appraisal, are aware of the academic and personal limitations of students and supervisees that might impede performance. Counselors assist students and supervisees in securing remedial assistance when needed, and dismiss from the training program supervisees who are unable to provide competent service due to academic or personal limitations. Counselors seek professional consultation and document their decision to dismiss or refer students or supervisees for assistance. Counselors ensure that students and supervisees have recourse to address decisions made to require them to seek assistance or to dismiss them.

b. *Self-Growth Experiences.* Counselors use professional judgment when designing training experiences conducted by the counselors themselves that require student and supervisee self-growth or self-disclosure. Safeguards are provided so that students and supervisees are aware of the ramifications their self-disclosure may have on counselors whose primary role as teacher, trainer, or supervisor requires acting on ethical obligations to the profession. Evaluative components of experiential training experiences explicitly delineate predetermined academic standards that are separate and do not depend on the student's level of self-disclosure. (See A.6.)

c. *Counseling for Students and Supervisees.* If students or supervisees request counseling, supervisors or counselor educators provide them with acceptable referrals. Supervisors or counselor educators do not serve as counselor to students or supervisees over whom they hold administrative, teaching, or evaluative roles unless this is a brief role associated with a training experience. (See A.6.b.)

d. *Clients of Students and Supervisees.* Counselors make every effort to ensure that the clients at field placements are aware of the services rendered and the qualifications of the students and supervisees rendering those services. Clients receive professional disclosure information and are informed of the limits of confidentiality. Client permission is obtained in order for the students and supervisees to use any information concerning the counseling relationship in the training process. (See B.1.e.)

e. *Standards for Students and Supervisees.* Students and supervisees preparing to become counselors adhere to the *Code of Ethics* and the *Standards of Practice.* Students and supervisees have the same obligations to clients as those required of counselors. (See H.1.)

SECTION G: RESEARCH AND PUBLICATION

G.1. Research Responsibilities

a. *Use of Human Subjects.* Counselors plan, design, conduct, and report research in a manner consistent with pertinent ethical principles, federal and state laws, host institutional regulations, and scientific standards governing research with human subjects. Counselors design and conduct research that reflects cultural sensitivity appropriateness.

b. *Deviation From Standard Practices.* Counselors seek consultation and observe stringent safeguards to protect the rights of research participants when a research problem suggests a deviation from standard acceptable practices. (See B.6.)

c. *Precautions to Avoid Injury.* Counselors who conduct research with human subjects are responsible for the subjects' welfare throughout the experiment and take reasonable precautions to avoid causing injurious psychological, physical, or social effects to their subjects.

d. *Principal Researcher Responsibility.* The ultimate responsibility for ethical research practice lies with the principal researcher. All others involved in the research activities share ethical obligations and full responsibility for their own actions.

e. *Minimal Interference.* Counselors take reasonable precautions to avoid causing disruptions in subjects' lives due to participation in research.

f. *Diversity.* Counselors are sensitive to diversity and research issues with special populations. They seek consultation when appropriate. (See A.2.a. and B.6.)

G.2. Informed Consent

a. *Topics Disclosed.* In obtaining informed consent for research, counselors use language that is understandable to research participants and that (1) accurately explains the purpose and procedures to be followed; (2) identifies any procedures that are experimental or relatively untried; (3) describes the attendant discomforts and risks; (4) describes the benefits or changes in individuals or organizations that might be reasonably expected; (5) discloses appropriate alternative procedures that would be advantageous for subjects; (6) offers to answer any inquiries concerning the procedures; (7) describes any limitations on confidentiality; and (8) instructs that subjects are free to withdraw their consent and to discontinue participation in the project at any time. (See B.1.f.)

b. *Deception.* Counselors do not conduct research involving deception unless alternative procedures are not feasible and the prospective value of the research justifies the deception. When the methodological requirements of a study necessitate concealment or deception, the investigator is required to explain clearly the reasons for this action as soon as possible.

c. *Voluntary Participation.* Participation in research is typically voluntary and without any penalty for refusal to participate. Involuntary participation is appropriate only when it can be demonstrated that participation will have no harmful effects on subjects and is essential to the investigation.

d. *Confidentiality of Information.* Information obtained about research participants during the course of an investigation is confidential. When the possibility exists that others may obtain access to such information, ethical research practice requires that the possibility, together with the plans for protecting confidentiality, be explained to participants as a part of the procedure for obtaining informed consent. (See B.1.e.)

e. *Persons Incapable of Giving Informed Consent.* When a person is incapable of giving informed consent, counselors provide an appropriate explanation, obtain agreement for participation, and obtain appropriate consent from a legally authorized person.

f. *Commitments to Participants.* Counselors take reasonable measures to honor all commitments to research participants.

g. *Explanations After Data Collection.* After data are collected, counselors provide participants with full clarification of the nature of the study to remove any misconceptions. Where scientific or human values justify delaying or withholding information, counselors take reasonable measures to avoid causing harm.

h. *Agreements to Cooperate.* Counselors who agree to cooperate with another individual in research or publication incur an obligation to cooperate as promised in terms of punctuality of performance and with regard to the completeness and accuracy of the information required.

i. *Informed Consent for Sponsors.* In the pursuit of research, counselors give sponsors, institutions, and publication channels the same respect and opportunity for giving informed consent that they accord to individual research participants. Counselors are aware of their obligation to future research workers and ensure that host institutions are given feedback information and proper acknowledgment.

G.3. Reporting Results

a. *Information Affecting Outcome.* When reporting research results, counselors explicitly mention all variables and conditions known to the investigator that may have affected the outcome of a study or the interpretation of data.

b. *Accurate Results.* Counselors plan, conduct, and report research accurately and in a manner that minimizes the possibility that results will be misleading. They provide thorough discussions of the limitations of their data and alternative hypotheses. Counselors do not engage in fraudulent research, distort data, misrepresent data, or deliberately bias their results.

c. *Obligation to Report Unfavorable Results.* Counselors communicate to other counselors the results of any research judged to be of professional value. Results that reflect unfavorably on institutions, programs, services, prevailing opinions, or vested interests are not withheld.

d. *Identity of Subjects.* Counselors who supply data, aid in the research of another person, report research results, or make original data available take due care to disguise the identity of respective subjects in the absence of specific authorization from the subjects to do otherwise. (See B.1.g. and B.5.a.)

e. *Replication Studies.* Counselors are obligated to make available sufficient original research data to qualified professionals who may wish to replicate the study.

G.4. Publication

a. *Recognition of Others.* When conducting and reporting research, counselors are familiar with and give recognition to previous work on the topic, observe copyright laws, and give full credit to those to whom credit is due. (See F.1.d. and G.4.c.)

b. *Contributors.* Counselors give credit through joint authorship, acknowledgment, footnote statements, or other appropriate means to those who have contributed significantly to research or concept development in accordance with such contributions. The principal contributor is listed first and minor technical or professional contributions are acknowledged in notes or introductory statements.

c. *Student Research.* For an article that is substantially based on a student's dissertation or thesis, the student is listed as the principal author. (See F.1.d. and G.4.a.)

d. *Duplicate Submission.* Counselors submit manuscripts for consideration to only one journal at a time. Manuscripts that are published in whole or in substantial part in another journal or published work are not submitted for publication without acknowledgment and permission from the previous publication.

e. *Professional Review.* Counselors who review material submitted for publication, research, or other scholarly purposes respect the confidentiality and proprietary rights of those who submitted it.

SECTION H: RESOLVING ETHICAL ISSUES

H.1. Knowledge of Standards

Counselors are familiar with the *Code of Ethics* and the *Standards of Practice* and other applicable ethics codes from other professional organizations of which they are member, or from certification and licensure bodies. Lack of knowledge or misunderstanding of an ethical responsibility is not a defense against a charge of unethical conduct. (See F.3.e.)

H.2. Suspected Violations

a. *Ethical Behavior Expected.* Counselors expect professional associates to adhere to the *Code of Ethics.* When counselors possess reasonable cause that raises doubts as to whether a counselor is acting in an ethical manner, they take appropriate action. (See H.2.d. and H.2.e.)

b. *Consultation.* When uncertain as to whether a particular situation or course of action may be in violation of the *Code of Ethics,* counselors consult with other counselors who are knowledgeable about ethics, with colleagues, or with appropriate authorities.

c. *Organization Conflicts.* If the demands of an organization with which counselors are affiliated pose a conflict with the *Code of Ethics,* counselors specify the nature of such conflicts and express to their supervisors or other responsible officials their commitment to the *Code of Ethics.* When possible, counselors work toward change within the organization to allow full adherence to the *Code of Ethics.*

d. *Informal Resolution.* When counselors have reasonable cause to believe that another counselor is violating an ethical standard, they attempt to first resolve the issue informally with the other counselor if feasible, providing that such action does not violate confidentiality rights that may be involved.

e. *Reporting Suspected Violations.* When an informal resolution is not appropriate or feasible, counselors, upon reasonable cause, take action such as reporting the suspected ethical violation to state or national ethics committees, unless this action conflicts with confidentiality rights that cannot be resolved.

f. *Unwarranted Complaints.* Counselors do not initiate, participate in, or encourage the filing of ethics complaints that are unwarranted or intend to harm a counselor rather than to protect clients or the public.

H.3. Cooperation With Ethics Committees

Counselors assist in the process of enforcing the Code of Ethics. Counselors cooperate with investigations, proceedings, and requirements of the ACA Ethics Committee or ethics committees of other duly constituted associations or boards having jurisdiction over those charged with a violation. Counselors are familiar with the ACA Policies and Procedures and use it as a reference in assisting the enforcement of the *Code of Ethics.*

ACA Standards of Practice

All members of the American Counseling Association (ACA) are required to adhere to the *Standards of Practice* and the *Code of Ethics*. The *Standards of Practice* represent minimal behavioral statements of the *Code of Ethics*. Members should refer to the applicable section of the *Code of Ethics* for further interpretation and amplification of the applicable *Standard of Practice.*

SECTION A: THE COUNSELING RELATIONSHIP

Standard of Practice One (SP-1):

Nondiscrimination. Counselors respect diversity and must not discriminate against clients because of age, color, culture, disability, ethnic group, gender, race, religion, sexual orientation, marital status, or socioeconomic status. (See A.2.a.)

Standard of Practice Two (SP-2):

Disclosure to Clients. Counselors must adequately inform clients, preferably in writing, regarding the counseling process and counseling relationship at or before the time it begins and throughout the relationship. (See A.3.a.)

Standard of Practice Three (SP-3):

Dual Relationships. Counselors must make every effort to avoid dual relationships with clients that could impair their professional judgment or increase the risk of harm to clients. When a dual relationship cannot be avoided, counselors must take appropriate steps to ensure that judgment is not impaired and that no exploitation occurs. (See A.6.a. and A.6.b.)

Standard of Practice Four (SP-4):

Sexual Intimacies With Clients. Counselors must not engage in any type of sexual intimacies with current clients and must not engage in sexual intimacies with former clients within a minimum of 2 years after terminating the counseling relationship. Counselors who engage in such relationship after 2 years following termination have the responsibility to examine and document thoroughly that such relations did not have an exploitative nature.

Standard of Practice Five (SP-5):

Protecting Clients During Group Work. Counselors must take steps to protect clients from physical or psychological trauma resulting from interactions during group work. (See A.9.b.)

Standard of Practice Six (SP-6):

Advance Understanding of Fees. Counselors must explain to clients, prior to their entering the counseling relationship, financial arrangements related to professional services. (See A.10. a.-d. and A.11.c.)

Standard of Practice Seven (SP-7):

Termination. Counselors must assist in making appropriate arrangements for the continuation of treatment of clients, when necessary, following termination of counseling relationships. (See A.11.a.)

Standard of Practice Eight (SP-8):

Inability to Assist Clients. Counselors must avoid entering or immediately terminate a counseling relationship if it is determined that they are unable to be of professional assistance to a client. The counselor may assist in making an appropriate referral for the client. (See A.11.b.)

SECTION B: CONFIDENTIALITY

Standard of Practice Nine (SP-9):

Confidentiality Requirement. Counselors must keep information related to counseling services confidential unless disclosure is in the best interest of clients, is required for the welfare of others, or is required by law. When disclosure is required, only information that is essential is revealed and the client is informed of such disclosure. (See B.1. a.–f.)

Standard of Practice Ten (SP-10):

Confidentiality Requirements for Subordinates. Counselors must take measures to ensure that privacy and confidentiality of clients are maintained by subordinates. (See B.1.h.)

Standard of Practice Eleven (SP-11):

Confidentiality in Group Work. Counselors must clearly communicate to group members that confidentiality cannot be guaranteed in group work. (See B.2.a.)

Standard of Practice Twelve (SP-12):

Confidentiality in Family Counseling. Counselors must not disclose information about one family member in counseling to another family member without prior consent. (See B.2.b.)

Standard of Practice Thirteen (SP-13):

Confidentiality of Records. Counselors must maintain appropriate confidentiality in creating, storing, accessing, transferring, and disposing of counseling records. (See B.4.b.)

Standard of Practice Fourteen (SP-14):

Permission to Record or Observe. Counselors must obtain prior consent from clients in order to record electronically or observe sessions. (See B.4.c.)

Standard of Practice Fifteen (SP-15):

Disclosure or Transfer of Records. Counselors must obtain client consent to disclose or transfer records to third parties, unless exceptions listed in SP-9 exist. (See B.4.e.)

Standard of Practice Sixteen (SP-16):

Data Disguise Required. Counselors must disguise the identity of the client when using data for training, research, or publication. (See B.5.a.)

SECTION C: PROFESSIONAL RESPONSIBILITY

Standard of Practice Seventeen (SP-17):
Boundaries of Competence. Counselors must practice only within the boundaries of their competence. (See C.2.a.)

Standard of Practice Eighteen (SP-18):
Continuing Education. Counselors must engage in continuing education to maintain their professional competence. (See C.2.f.)

Standard of Practice Nineteen (SP-19):
Impairment of Professionals. Counselors must refrain from offering professional services when their personal problems or conflicts may cause harm to a client or others. (See C.2.g.)

Standard of Practice Twenty (SP-20):
Accurate Advertising. Counselors must accurately represent their credentials and services when advertising. (See C.3.a.)

Standard of Practice Twenty-One (SP-21):
Recruiting Through Employment. Counselors must not use their place of employment or institutional affiliation to recruit clients for their private practices. (See C.3.d.)

Standard of Practice Twenty-Two (SP-22):
Credentials Claimed. Counselors must claim or imply only professional credentials possessed and must correct any known misrepresentations of their credentials by others. (See C.4.a.)

Standard of Practice Twenty-Three (SP-23):
Sexual Harassment. Counselors must not engage in sexual harassment. (See C.5.b.)

Standard of Practice Twenty-Four (SP-24):
Unjustified Gains. Counselors must not use their professional positions to seek or receive unjustified personal gains, sexual favors, unfair advantage, or unearned goods or services. (See C.5.e.)

Standard of Practice Twenty-Five (SP-25):
Clients Served by Others. With the consent of the client, counselors must inform other mental health professionals serving the same client that a counseling relationship between the counselor and client exists. (See C.6.c.)

Standard of Practice Twenty-Six (SP-26):

Negative Employment Conditions. Counselors must alert their employers to institutional policy or conditions that may be potentially disruptive or damaging to the counselor's professional responsibilities, or that may limit their effectiveness or deny clients' rights. (See D.1.c.)

Standard of Practice Twenty-Seven (SP-27):

Personnel Selection and Assignment. Counselors must select competent staff and must assign responsibilities compatible with staff skills and experiences. (See D.1.h.)

Standard of Practice Twenty-Eight (SP-28):

Exploitative Relationships With Subordinates. Counselors must not engage in exploitative relationships with individuals over whom they have supervisory, evaluative, or instructional control or authority. (See D.1.k.)

SECTION D: RELATIONSHIP WITH OTHER PROFESSIONALS

Standard of Practice Twenty-Nine (SP-29):

Accepting Fees From Agency Clients. Counselors must not accept fees or other remuneration for consultation with persons entitled to such services through the counselor's employing agency or institution. (See D.3.a.)

Standard of Practice Thirty (SP-30):

Referral Fees. Counselors must not accept referral fees. (See D.3.b.)

SECTION E: EVALUATION, ASSESSMENT AND INTERPRETATION

Standard of Practice Thirty-One (SP-31):

Limits of Competence. Counselors must perform only testing and assessment services for which they are competent. Counselors must not allow the use of psychological assessment techniques by unqualified persons under their supervision. (See E.2.a.)

Standard of Practice Thirty-Two (SP-32):

Appropriate Use of Assessment Instruments. Counselors must use assessment instruments in the manner for which they were intended. (See E.2.b.)

Standard of Practice Thirty-Three (SP-33):

Assessment Explanations to Clients. Counselors must provide explanations to clients prior to assessment about the nature and purposes of assessment and the specific uses of results. (See E.3.a.)

Standard of Practice Thirty-Four (SP-34):

Recipients of Test Results. Counselors must ensure that accurate and appropriate interpretations accompany any release of testing and assessment information. (See E.3.b.)

Standard of Practice Thirty-Five (SP-35):

Obsolete Tests and Outdated Test Results. Counselors must not base their assessment or intervention decisions or recommendations on data or test results that are obsolete or outdated for the current purpose. (See E.11.)

SECTION F: TEACHING, TRAINING, AND SUPERVISION

Standard of Practice Thirty-Six (SP-36):

Sexual Relationships With Students or Supervisees. Counselors must not engage in sexual relationships with their students and supervisees. (See F.1.c.)

Standard of Practice Thirty-Seven (SP-37):

Credit for Contributions to Research. Counselors must give credit to students or supervisees for their contributions to research and scholarly projects. (See F.1.d.)

Standard of Practice Thirty-Eight (SP-38):

Supervision Preparation. Counselors who offer clinical supervision services must be trained and prepared in supervision methods and techniques. (See F.1.f.)

Standard of Practice Thirty-Nine (SP-39):

Evaluation Information. Counselors must clearly state to students and supervisees in advance of training the levels of competency expected, appraisal methods, and timing of evaluations. Counselors must provide students and supervisees with periodic performance appraisal and evaluation feedback throughout the training program. (See F.2.c.)

Standard of Practice Forty (SP-40):

Peer Relationships in Training. Counselors must make every effort to ensure that the rights of peers are not violated when students and supervisees are assigned to lead counseling groups or provide clinical supervision. (See F.2.e.)

Standard of Practice Forty-One (SP-41):

Limitations of Students and Supervisees. Counselors must assist students and supervisees in securing remedial assistance, when needed, and must dismiss from the training program students and supervisees who are unable to provide competent service due to academic or personal limitations. (See F.3.a.)

Standard of Practice Forty-Two (SP-42):

Self-Growth Experiences. Counselors who conduct experiences for students or supervisees that include self-growth or self-disclosure must inform participants of counselors' ethical obligations to the profession and must not grade participants based on their nonacademic performance. (See F.3.b.)

Standard of Practice Forty-Three (SP-43):

Standards for Students and Supervisees. Students and supervisees preparing to become counselors must adhere to the *Code of Ethics* and the *Standards of Practice* of counselors. (See F.3.e.)

SECTION G: RESEARCH AND PUBLICATION

Standard of Practice Forty-Four (SP-44):

Precautions to Avoid Injury in Research. Counselors must avoid causing physical, social, or psychological harm or injury to subjects in research. (See G.1.c.)

Standard of Practice Forty-Five (SP-45):

Confidentiality of Research Information. Counselors must keep confidential information obtained about research participants. (See G.2.d.)

Standard of Practice Forty-Six (SP-46):

Information Affecting Research Outcome. Counselors must report all variables and conditions known to the investigator that may have affected research data or outcomes. (See G.3.a.)

Standard of Practice Forty-Seven (SP-47):

Accurate Research Results. Counselors must not distort or misrepresent research data, nor fabricate or intentionally bias research results. (See G.3.b.)

Standard of Practice Forty-Eight (SP-48):

Publication Contributors. Counselors must give appropriate credit to those who have contributed to research. (See G.4.a. and G.4.b.)

SECTION H: RESOLVING ETHICAL ISSUES

Standard of Practice Forty-Nine (SP-49):

Ethical Behavior Expected. Counselors must take appropriate action when they possess reasonable cause that raises doubts as to whether counselors or other mental health professionals are acting in an ethical manner. (See H.2.a.)

Standard of Practice Fifty (SP-50):

Unwarranted Complaints. Counselors must not initiate, participate in, or encourage the filing of ethics complaints that are unwarranted or intended to harm a mental health professional rather than to protect clients or the public. (See H.2.f.)

Standard of Practice Fifty-One (SP-51):

Cooperation With Ethics Committees. Counselors must cooperate with investigations, proceedings, and requirements of the ACA Ethics Committee or ethics committees of other duly constituted associations or boards having jurisdiction over those charged with a violation. (See H.3.)

REFERENCES

The following documents are available to counselors as resources to guide them in their practices. These resources are not a part of the *Code of Ethics* and the *Standards of Practice.*

American Association for Counseling and Development/Association for Measurement and Evaluation in Counseling and Development. (1989). *The responsibilities of users of standardized tests* (rev.). Washington, DC: Author.

American Counseling Association. (1995) (Note: This is ACA's previous edition of its ethics code). *Ethical standards.* Alexandria, VA: Author.

American Psychological Association. (1985). *Standards for educational and psychological testing* (rev.). Washington, DC: Author.

Joint Committee on Testing Practices. (1988). *Code of fair testing practices in education.* Washington, DC: Author.

National Board for Certified Counselors. (1989). *National Board for Certified Counselors code of ethics.* Alexandria, VA: Author.

Prediger, D. J. (Ed.). (1993, March). *Multicultural assessment standards.* Alexandria, VA: Association for Assessment in Counseling.

National Career Development Association *Ethical Standards* (1991)

These Ethical Standards were developed by the National Board for Certified Counselors (NBCC), an independent, voluntary, not-for-profit organization incorporated in 1982. Titled "Code of Ethics" by NBCC and last amended in February 1987, the Ethical Standards were adopted by the National Career Development Association (NCDA) Board of Directors in 1987 and revised in 1991, with minor changes in wording (e.g., the addition of specific references to NCDA members).

PREAMBLE:

NCDA is an educational, scientific, and professional organization dedicated to the enhancement of the worth, dignity, potential, and uniqueness of each individual and, thus, to the service of society. This code of ethics enables the NCDA to clarify the nature of ethical responsibilities for present and future professional career counselors.

SECTION A: GENERAL

NCDA members influence the development of the profession by continuous efforts to improve professional practices, services, and research. Professional growth is continuous through the career counselor's career and is exemplified by the development of a philosophy that explains why and how a career counselor functions in the helping relationship. Career counselors must gather data on their effectiveness and be guided by their findings.

1. NCDA members have a responsibility to the clients they are serving and to the institutions within which the services are being performed. Career counselors also strive to assist the respective agency, organization, or institution in providing the highest caliber of professional services. The acceptance of employment in an institution implies that the career counselor is in agreement with the general policies and principles of the institution. Therefore, the professional activities of the career counselor are in accord with the objectives of the institution. If, despite concerted efforts, the career counselor cannot reach agreement with the employer as to acceptable standards of conduct that allow for changes in institutional policy that are conducive to the positive growth and development of clients, then terminating the affiliation should be seriously considered.

2. Ethical behavior among professional associates (e.g., career counselors) must be expected at all times. When accessible information raises doubt as to the ethical behavior of professional colleagues, the NCDA member must make action to attempt to rectify this condition. Such action uses the respective institution's channels first and then uses procedures established by the American Counseling Association, of which NCDA is a division.

3. NCDA members neither claim nor imply professional qualifications which exceed those possessed, and are responsible for correcting any misrepresentations of these qualifications by others.

4. NCDA members must refuse a private fee or other remuneration for consultation or counseling with persons who are entitled to their services through the career counselor's employing institution or agency. The policies of some agencies may make explicit provisions for staff members to engage in private practice with agency clients. However, should agency clients desire private counseling or consulting services, they must be apprised of other options available to them. Career counselors must not divert to their private practices, legitimate clients in their primary agencies or of the institutions with which they are affiliated.

5. In establishing fees for professional counseling services, NCDA members must consider the financial status of clients and the respective locality. In the event that the established fee status is inappropriate for the client, assistance must be provided in finding comparable services of acceptable cost.

6. NCDA members seek only those positions in the delivery of professional services for which they are professionally qualified.

7. NCDA members recognize their limitations and provide services or only use techniques for which they are qualified by training and/or experience. Career counselors recognize the need, and seek continuing education, to assure competent services.
8. NCDA members are aware of the intimacy in the counseling relationship, maintain respect for the client, and avoid engaging in activities that seek to meet their personal needs at the expense of the client.
9. NCDA member do not condone or engage in sexual harassment which is defined as deliberate or repeated comments, gestures, or physical contacts of a sexual nature.
10. NCDA members avoid bringing their personal or professional issues into the counseling relationship. Through an awareness of the impact of stereotyping and discrimination (e.g., biases based on age, disability, ethnicity, gender, race, religion, or sexual preference), career counselors guard the individual rights and personal dignity of the client in the counseling relationship.
11. NCDA members are accountable at all times for their behavior. They must be aware that all actions and behaviors of a counselor reflect on professional integrity and, when inappropriate, can damage the public trust in the counseling profession. To protect public confidence in the counseling profession, career counselors avoid public behavior that is clearly in violation of accepted moral and legal standards.
12. NCDA members have a social responsibility because their recommendations and professional actions may alter the lives of others. Career counselors remain fully cognizant of their impact and are alert to personal, social, organizational, financial, or political situations or pressures which might lead to misuse of their influence.
13. Products or services provided by NCDA members by means of classroom instruction, public lectures, demonstrations, written articles, radio or television programs, or other types of media must meet the criteria cited in Sections A through F of these Ethical Standards.

SECTION B: COUNSELING RELATIONSHIP

1. The primary obligation of NCDA members is to respect the integrity and promote the welfare of the client, regardless of whether the client is assisted individually or in a group relationship. In a group setting, the career counselor is also responsible for taking reasonable precautions to protect individuals from physical and/or psychological trauma resulting from interaction within the group.

2. The counseling relationship and information resulting from it remains confidential, consistent with the legal obligations of the NCDA member. In a group counseling setting, the career counselor sets a norm of confidentiality regarding all group participants' disclosures.

3. NCDA members know and take into account the traditions and practices of other professional groups with whom they work, and they cooperate fully with such groups. If a person is receiving similar services from another professional, career counselors do not offer their own services directly to such a person. If a career counselor is contacted by a person who is already receiving similar services from another professional, the career counselor carefully considers that professional relationship and proceeds with caution and sensitivity to the therapeutic issues as well as the client's welfare. Career counselors discuss these issues with clients so as to minimize the risk of confusion and conflict.

4. When a client's condition indicates that there is a clear and imminent danger to the client or others, the NCDA member must take reasonable personal action or inform responsible authorities. Consultation with other professionals must be used where possible. The assumption of responsibility for the client's behavior must be taken only after careful deliberation, and the client must be involved in the resumption of responsibility as quickly as possible.

5. Records of the counseling relationship, including interview notes, test data, correspondence, audio or visual tape recordings, electronic data storage, and other documents are to be considered professional information for use in counseling. They should not be considered a part of the records of the institution or agency in which the NCDA member is employed unless specified by state statute or regulation. Revelation to others of counseling material must occur only upon the expressed consent of the client; career counselors must make provisions for maintaining confidentiality in the storage and disposal of records. Career counselors providing information to the public or to subordinates, peers, or supervisors have a responsibility to ensure that the content is general; unidentified client information should be accurate and unbiased, and should consist of objective, factual data.

6. NCDA members must ensure that data maintained in electronic storage are secure. The data must be limited to information that is appropriate and necessary for the services being provided and accessible only to appropriate staff members involved in the provision of services by using the best computer security methods available. Career counselors must also ensure that electronically stored

data are destroyed when the information is no longer of value in providing services.

7. Data derived from a counseling relationship for use in counselor training or research shall be confined to content that can be disguised to ensure full protection of the identity of the subject/client and shall be obtained with informed consent.

8. NCDA members must inform clients, before or at the time the counseling relationship commences, of the purposes, goals, techniques, rules and procedures, and limitations that may affect the relationship.

9. All methods of treatment by NCDA members must be clearly indicated to prospective recipients and safety precautions must be taken in their use.

10. NCDA members who have an administrative, supervisory, and/or evaluative relationship with individuals seeking counseling services must not serve as the counselor and should refer the individuals to other professionals. Exceptions are made only in instances where an individual's situation warrants counseling intervention and another alternative is unavailable. Dual relationships with clients that might impair the career counselor's objectivity and professional judgment must be avoided and/or the counseling relationship terminated through referral to another competent professional.

11. When NCDA members determine an inability to be of professional assistance to a potential or existing client, they must, respectively, not initiate the counseling relationship or immediately terminate the relationship. In either event, the career counselor must suggest appropriate alternatives. Career counselors must be knowledgeable about referral resources so that a satisfactory referral can be initiated. In the event that the client declines a suggested referral, the career counselor is not obligated to continue the relationship.

12. NCDA members may choose to consult with any other professionally competent person about a client and must notify clients of this right. Career counselors must avoid placing a consultant in a conflict-of-interest situation that would preclude the consultant's being a proper party to the career counselor's efforts to help the client.

13. NCDA members who counsel clients from cultures different from their own must gain knowledge, personal awareness, and sensitivity pertinent to the client populations served and must incorporate culturally relevant techniques into their practice.

14. When NCDA members engage in intensive counseling with a client, the client's counseling needs should be assessed. When needs exist outside the counselor's expertise, appropriate referrals should be made.

15. NCDA members must screen prospective group counseling participants, especially when the emphasis is on self-understanding and
growth through self-disclosure. Career counselors must maintain n
awareness of each group participant's welfare throughout the group
process.

16. When electronic data and systems are used as a component of
counseling services, NCDA members must ensure that the computer application, and any information it contains, is appropriate for
the respective needs of clients and is nondiscriminatory. Career
counselors must ensure that they themselves have acquired a facilitation level of knowledge with any system they use including
hands-on application, search experience, and understanding of the
uses of all aspects of the computer-based system. In selecting and/or
maintaining computer-based systems that contain career information, career counselors must ensure that the systems provide current, accurate, and locally relevant information. Career counselors
must also ensure that clients are intellectually, emotionally, and
physically compatible with the use of the computer application and
understand its purpose and operation. Client use of a computer
application must be evaluated to correct possible problems and
assess subsequent needs.

17. NCDA members who develop self-help, stand-alone computer software for use by the general public, must first ensure that it is initially designed to function in a stand-alone manner, as opposed to
modifying software that was originally designed to require support
from a counselor. Secondly, the software must include program
statements that provide the user with intended outcomes, suggestions for using the software, descriptions of inappropriately used
applications, and descriptions of when and how counseling services
might be beneficial. Finally, the manual must include the qualifications of the developer, the development process, validation data,
and operating procedures.

SECTION C: MEASUREMENT AND EVALUATION

1. NCDA members must provide specific orientation or information
to an examinee prior to and following the administration of assessment instruments or techniques so that the results may be placed in
proper perspective with other relevant factors. The purpose of testing and the explicit use of the results must be made known to an
examinee prior to testing.

2. In selecting assessment instruments or techniques for use in a given situation or with a particular client, NCDA members must evaluate carefully the instrument's specific theoretical bases and characteristics, validity, reliability, and appropriateness. Career counselors are professionally responsible for using unvalidated information with special care.

3. When making statements to the public about assessment instruments or techniques, NCDA members must provide accurate information and avoid false claims or misconceptions concerning the meaning of psychometric terms. Special efforts are often required to avoid unwarranted connotations of terms such as IQ and grade-equivalent scores.

4. Because many types of assessment techniques exist, NCDA members must recognize the limits of their competence and perform only those functions for which they have received appropriate training.

5. NCDA members must note when tests are not administered under standard conditions or when unusual behavior or irregularities occur during a testing session and the results must be designated as invalid or of questionable validity. Unsupervised or inadequately supervised assessments, such as mail-in tests, are considered unethical. However, the use of standardized instruments that are designed to be self-administered and self-scored, such as interest inventories, is appropriate.

6. Because prior coaching or dissemination of test materials can invalidate test results, NCDA members are professionally obligated to maintain test security. In addition, conditions that produce most favorable test results must be made known to an examinee (e.g., penalty for guessing).

7. NCDA members must consider psychometric limitations when selecting and using an instrument, and must be cognizant of the limitations when interpreting the results. When tests are used to classify clients, career counselors must ensure that periodic review and/or re-testing are conducted to prevent client stereotyping.

8. An examinee's welfare, explicit prior understanding, and agreement are the factors used when determining who receives the test results. NCDA members must see that appropriate interpretation accompanies any release of individual or group test data (e.g., limitations of instrument and norms).

9. NCDA members must ensure that computer-generated assessment administration and scoring programs function properly, thereby providing clients with accurate assessment results.

10. NCDA members who are responsible for making decisions based on assessment results must have appropriate training and skills in educational and psychological measurement—including validation criteria, test research, and guidelines for test development and use.

11. NCDA members must be cautious when interpreting the results of instruments that possess insufficient technical data, and must explicitly state to examinees the specific purposes for the use of such instruments.

12. NCDA members must proceed with caution when attempting to evaluate and interpret performances of minority group members or other persons who are not represented in the norm group on which the instrument was standardized.

13. NCDA members who develop computer-based interpretations to support the assessment process must ensure that the validity of the interpretations is established prior to the commercial distribution of the computer application.

14. NCDA members recognize that test results may become obsolete, and avoid the misuse of obsolete data.

15. NCDA members must avoid the appropriation, reproduction, or modification of published tests or parts thereof without acknowledgment and permission from the publisher.

SECTION D: RESEARCH AND PUBLICATION

1. NCDA members will adhere to relevant guidelines on research with human subjects. These include:

   • *Code of Federal Regulations*, Title 45, Subtitle A, Part 46, as currently issued.
   • American Psychological Association. (1982). *Ethical principles in the conduct of research with human participants.* Washington, DC: Author.
   • American Psychological Association. (1981). Research with human participants. *American Psychologist, 36,* 633-638.
   • Family Educational Rights and Privacy Act. (Buckley Amendment to P. L. 93-380 of the Laws of 1974)
   • Current federal regulations and various state privacy acts.

2. In planning research activities involving human subjects, NCDA members must be aware of and responsive to all pertinent ethical principles and ensure that the research problem, design, and execution are in full compliance with the principles.

3. The ultimate responsibility for ethical research lies with the principal researcher, although others involved in research activities are ethically obligated and responsible for their own actions.
4. NCDA members who conduct research with human subjects are responsible for the subjects' welfare throughout the experiment and must take all reasonable precautions to avoid causing injurious psychological, physical, or social effects on their subjects.
5. NCDA members who conduct research must abide by the following basic elements of informed consent:

   a. a fair explanation of the procedures to be followed, including an identification of those which are experimental.
   b. a description of the attendant discomforts and risks.
   c. a description of the benefits to be expected.
   d. a disclosure of appropriate alternative procedures that would be advantageous for subjects.
   e. an offer to answer any inquiries concerning the procedures.
   f. an instruction that subjects are free to withdraw their consent and to discontinue participation in the project or activity at any time.

6. When reporting research results, explicit mention must be made of all the variables and conditions known to the NCDA member that may have affected the outcome of the study or the interpretation of the data.
7. NCDA members who conduct and report research investigations must do so in a manner that minimizes the possibility that the results will be misleading.
8. NCDA members are obligated to make available sufficient original research data to qualified others who may wish to replicate the study.
9. NCDA members who supply data, aid in the research of another person, report research results, or make original data available, must take due care to disguise the identity of respective subjects in the absence of specific authorization from the subject to do otherwise.
10. When conducting and reporting research, NCDA members must be familiar with, and give recognition to, previous work on the topic, must observe all copyright laws, and must follow the principles of giving full credit to those to whom credit is due.
11. NCDA members must give due credit through joint authorship, acknowledgment, footnote statements, or other appropriate means to those who have contributed significantly to the research and/or publication, in accordance with such contributions.

12. NCDA members should communicate to others the results of any research judged to be of professional value. Results that reflect unfavorably on institutions, programs, services, or vested interests must not be withheld.
13. NCDA members who agree to cooperate with another individual in research and/or publication incur an obligation to cooperate as promised in terms of punctuality of performance and with full regard to the completeness and accuracy of the information required.
14. NCDA members must not submit the same manuscript, or one essentially similar in content, for simultaneous publication consideration by two or more journals. In addition, manuscripts that are published in whole or substantial part in another journal or published work should not be submitted for publication without acknowledgment and permission from the previous publication.

SECTION E: CONSULTING

Consultation refers to a voluntary relationship between a professional helper and help-needing individual, group, or social unit in which the consultant is providing help to the client(s) in defining and solving a work-related problem or potential work-related problem with a client or client system.

1. NCDA members acting as consultants must have a high degree of self-awareness of their own values, knowledge, skills, limitations, and needs in entering a helping relationship that involves human and/or organizational change. The focus of the consulting relationship must be on the issues to be resolved and not on the person(s) presenting the problem.
2. In the consulting relationship, the NCDA member and client must understand and agree upon the problem definition, subsequent goals, and predicted consequences of interventions selected.
3. NCDA members must be reasonably certain that they, or the organization represented, have the necessary competencies and resources for giving the kind of help that is needed or that may develop later, and that appropriate referral resources are available to the consultant.
4. NCDA members in a consulting relationship must encourage and cultivate client adaptability and growth toward self-direction. NCDA members must maintain this role consistently and not become a decision maker for clients or create a future dependency on the consultant.

5. NCDA members conscientiously adhere to the NCDA Ethical Standards when announcing consultant availability for services.

SECTION F: PRIVATE PRACTICE

1. NCDA members should assist the profession by facilitating the availability of counseling services in private as well as public settings.
2. In advertising services as private practitioners, NCDA members must advertise in a manner that accurately informs the public of the professional services, expertise, and counseling techniques available.
3. NCDA members who assume an executive leadership role in a private practice organization do not permit their names to be used in professional notices during periods of time when they are not actively engaged in the private practice of counseling.
4. NCDA members may list their highest relevant degree, type, and level of certification and/or license, address, telephone number, office hours, type and/or description of services, and other relevant information. Listed information must not contain false, inaccurate misleading, partial, out-of-context, or otherwise deceptive material or statements.
5. NCDA members who are involved in partnership or corporation with other professionals must, in compliance with the regulations of the locality, clearly specify the separate specialties of each member of the partnership or corporation.
6. NCDA members have an obligation to withdraw from a private-practice counseling relationship if it violates the NCDA Ethical Standards; if the mental or physical condition of the NCDA member renders it difficult to carry out an effective professional relationship; or if the counseling relationship is no longer productive for the client.

PROCEDURES FOR PROCESSING ETHICAL COMPLAINTS

As a division of the American Counseling Association (ACA) the National Career Development Association (NCDA) adheres to the guidelines and procedures for processing ethical complaints and the disciplinary sanctions adopted by ACA. A complaint against an NCDA member may be filed by any individual or group of individuals ("complainant"), whether or not the complainant is a member of NCDA. Action will not be taken on anonymous complaints.

For specifics on how to file ethical complaints and a description of the guidelines and procedures for processing complaints, contact:

ACA Ethics Committee
c/o Executive Director
American Counseling Association
5999 Stevenson Avenue
Alexandria, VA 22304
(800) 347-6647

This statement was developed by the National Career Development Association, 10820 East 45th Street, Suite 210, Tulsa, OK 74146, tel: (918) 663-7060, fax: (918) 663-7058, toll-free: (866) 367-6232.

Association for Specialists in Group Work *Best Practice Guidelines* (1998)

Prepared by: Lynn Rapin and Linda Keel, ASGW Ethics Committee Co-Chairs.

The Association for Specialists in Group Work (ASGW) is a division of the American Counseling Association whose members are interested in and specialize in group work. We value the creation of community; service to our members, clients, and the profession; and value leadership as a process to facilitate the growth and development of individuals and groups.

The Association for Specialists in Group Work recognizes the commitment of its members to the *Code of Ethics* and *Standards of Practice* (as revised in 1995) of its parent organization, the American Counseling Association, and nothing in this document shall be construed to supplant that code. These *Best Practice Guidelines* are intended to clarify the application of the ACA *Code of Ethics* and *Standards of Practice* to the field of group work by defining Group Workers' responsibility and scope of practice involving those activities, strategies and interventions that are consistent and current with effective and appropriate professional ethical and community standards. ASGW views ethical process as being integral to group work and views Group Workers as ethical agents. Group Workers, by their very nature in being responsible and responsive to their group members, necessarily embrace a certain potential for ethical vulnerability.

It is incumbent upon Group Workers to give considerable attention to the intent and context of their actions because the attempts of Group Workers to influence human behavior through group work always have ethical implications. These *Best Practice Guidelines* address Group Workers' responsibilities in planning, performing and processing groups.

SECTION A: BEST PRACTICE IN PLANNING

A.1. Professional Context and Regulatory Requirements

Group Workers actively know, understand and apply the ACA *Code of Ethics* and *Standards of Best Practice*, the ASGW Professional Standards for the Training of Group Workers, these ASGW *Best Practice Guidelines*, the ASGW diversity competencies, the ACA Multicultural Guidelines, relevant state laws, accreditation requirements, relevant National Board for Certified Counselors Codes and Standards, their organization's standards, and insurance requirements impacting the practice of group work.

A.2. Scope of Practice and Conceptual Framework

Group Workers define the scope of practice related to the core and specialization competencies defined in the ASGW Training Standards. Group Workers are aware of personal strengths and weaknesses in leading groups. Group Workers develop and are able to articulate a general conceptual framework to guide practice and a rationale for use of techniques that are to be used. Group Workers limit their practice to those areas for which they meet the training criteria established by the ASGW Training Standards.

A.3. Assessment

a. Assessment of self. Group Workers actively assess their knowledge and skills related to the specific group(s) offered. Group Workers assess their values, beliefs and theoretical orientation and how these impact upon the group, particularly when working with a diverse and multicultural population.

b. Ecological assessment. Group Workers assess community needs, agency or organization resources, sponsoring organization mission, staff competency, attitudes regarding group work, professional training levels of potential group leaders regarding group work; client attitudes regarding group work, and multicultural and diversity considerations. Group Workers use this information as the basis for making decisions related to their group practice, or to the implementation of groups for which they have supervisory, evaluation, or oversight responsibilities.

A.4. Program Development and Evaluation

a. Group Workers identify the type(s) of group(s) to be offered and how they relate to community needs.

b. Group Workers concisely state in writing the purpose and goals of the group. Group Workers also identify the role of the group members in influencing or determining the group goals.

c. Group Workers set fees consistent with the organization's fee schedule, taking into consideration the financial status and locality of prospective group members.

d. Group Workers choose techniques and a leadership style appropriate to the type(s) of group(s) being offered.

e. Group Workers have an evaluation plan consistent with regulatory, organization and insurance requirements, where appropriate.

f. Group Workers take into consideration current professional guidelines when using technology, including but not limited to Internet communication.

A.5. Resources

Group Workers coordinate resources related to the kind of group(s) and group activities to be provided, such as: adequate funding; the appropriateness and availability of a trained co-leader; space and privacy requirements for the type(s) of group(s) being offered; marketing and recruiting; and appropriate collaboration with other community agencies and organizations.

A.6. Professional Disclosure Statement

Group Workers have a professional disclosure statement which includes information on confidentiality and exceptions to confidentiality, theoretical orientation, information on the nature, purpose(s) and goals of the group, the group services that can be provided, the role and responsibility of group members and leaders, Group Workers; qualifications to conduct the specific group(s), specific licenses, certifications and professional affiliations, and address of licensing/credentialing body.

A.7. Group and Member Preparation

a. Group Workers screen prospective group members if appropriate to the type of group being offered. When selection of group members is appropriate, Group Workers identify group members whose needs and goals are compatible with the goals of the group.

b. Group Workers facilitate informed consent. Group Workers provide in oral and written form to prospective members (when appropriate to group type): the professional disclosure statement; group purpose and goals; group participation expectations including voluntary and involuntary membership; role expectations of members and leader(s); policies related to entering and exiting the group; policies governing substance use; policies and procedures governing mandated groups (where relevant); documentation requirements; disclosure of information to others; implications of out-of-group contact or involvement among members; procedures for consultation between group leader(s) and group member(s); fees and time parameters; and potential impacts of group participation.

c. Group Workers obtain the appropriate consent forms for work with minors and other dependent group members.

d. Group Workers define confidentiality and its limits (for example, legal and ethical exceptions and expectations; waivers implicit with treatment plans, documentation and insurance usage). Group Workers have the responsibility to inform all group participants of the need for confidentiality, potential consequences of breaching confidentiality and that legal privilege does not apply to group discussions (unless provided by state statute).

A.8. Professional Development

Group Workers recognize that professional growth is a continuous, ongoing, developmental process throughout their career.

a. Group Workers remain current and increase knowledge and skill competencies through activities such as continuing education, professional supervision, and participation in personal and professional development activities.

b. Group Workers seek consultation and/or supervision regarding ethical concerns that interfere with effective functioning as a group leader. Supervisors have the responsibility to keep abreast of consultation, group theory, process, and adhere to related ethical guidelines.

c. Group Workers seek appropriate professional assistance for their own personal problems or conflicts that are likely to impair their professional judgment or work performance.

d. Group Workers seek consultation and supervision to ensure appropriate practice whenever working with a group for which all knowledge and skill competencies has not been achieved.

e. Group Workers keep abreast of group research and development.

A.9. Trends and Technological Changes

Group Workers are aware of and responsive to technological changes as they affect society and the profession. These include but are not limited to changes in mental health delivery systems; legislative and insurance industry reforms; shifting population demographics and client needs; and technological advances in Internet and other communication and delivery systems. Group Workers adhere to ethical guidelines related to the use of developing technologies.

SECTION B: BEST PRACTICE IN PERFORMING

B.1. Self Knowledge

Group Workers are aware of and monitor their strengths and weaknesses and the effects these have on group members.

B.2. Group Competencies

Group Workers have a basic knowledge of groups and the principles of group dynamics, and are able to perform the core group competencies, as described in the ASGW Professional Standards for the Training of Group Workers. Additionally, Group Workers have adequate understanding and skill in any group specialty area chosen for practice (psychotherapy, counseling, task, psychoeducation, as described in the ASGW Training Standards).

B.3. Group Plan Adaptation

a. Group Workers apply and modify knowledge, skills and techniques appropriate to group type and stage, and to the unique needs of various cultural and ethnic groups.
b. Group Workers monitor the group's progress toward the group goals and plan.
c. Group Workers clearly define and maintain ethical, professional, and social relationship boundaries with group members as appropriate to their role in the organization and the type of group being offered.

B.4. Therapeutic Conditions and Dynamics

Group Workers understand and are able to implement appropriate models of group development, process observation and therapeutic conditions.

B.5. Meaning

Group Workers assist members in generating meaning from the group experience.

B.6. Collaboration

Group Workers assist members in developing individual goals and respect group members as co-equal partners in the group experience.

B.7. Evaluation

Group Workers include evaluation (both formal and informal) between sessions and at the conclusion of the group.

B.8. Diversity

Group Workers practice with broad sensitivity to client differences including but not limited to ethnic, gender, religious, sexual, psychological maturity, economic class, family history, physical characteristics or limitations, and geographic location. Group Workers continuously seek information regarding the cultural issues of the diverse population with whom they are working both by interaction with participants and from using outside resources.

B.9. Ethical Surveillance

Group Workers employ an appropriate ethical decision making model in responding to ethical challenges and issues and in determining courses of action and behavior for self and group members. In addition, Group Workers employ applicable standards as promulgated by ACA, ASGW, or other appropriate professional organizations.

SECTION C: BEST PRACTICE IN GROUP PROCESSING

C.1. Processing Schedule

Group Workers process the workings of the group with themselves, group members, supervisors or other colleagues, as appropriate. This may include assessing progress on group and member goals, leader behaviors and techniques, group dynamics and interventions; developing understanding and acceptance of meaning. Processing may occur both within sessions and before and after each session, at time of termination, and later follow up, as appropriate.

C.2. Reflective Practice

Group Workers attend to opportunities to synthesize theory and practice and to incorporate learning outcomes into ongoing groups. Group Workers attend to session dynamics of members and their interactions and also attend to the relationship between session dynamics and leader values, cognition and affect.

C.3. Evaluation and Follow-Up

a. Group Workers evaluate process and outcomes. Results are used for ongoing program planning, improvement and revisions of current group and/or to contribute to professional research literature.

Group Workers follow all applicable policies and standards in using group material for research and reports.

b. Group Workers conduct follow-up contact with group members, as appropriate, to assess outcomes or when requested by a group member(s).

C.4. Consultation and Training with Other Organizations

Group Workers provide consultation and training to organizations in and out of their setting, when appropriate. Group Workers seek out consultation as needed with competent professional persons knowledgeable about group work.

American Counseling Association On-line Counseling Guidelines (1999)

These guidelines establish appropriate standards for the use of electronic communications over the Internet to provide on-line counseling services, and should be used only in conjunction with the latest ACA Code of Ethics & Standards of Practice.

CONFIDENTIALITY

a. Privacy Information.

Professional counselors ensure that clients are provided sufficient information to adequately address and explain the limitations of (i) computer technology in the counseling process in general and (ii) the difficulties of ensuring complete client confidentiality of information transmitted through electronic communications over the Internet through on-line counseling. (See A.12.a., B.1.a., B.1.g.)

   1. SECURED SITES: To mitigate the risk of potential breaches of confidentiality, professional counselors provide one-on-one on-line counseling only through "secure" Web sites or e-mail communications applications that use appropriate encryption technology designed to protect the transmission of confidential information from access by unauthorized third parties.

2. NON-SECURED SITES: To mitigate the risk of potential breaches of confidentiality, professional counselors provide only general information from "non-secure" Web sites or e-mail communications applications.

3. GENERAL INFORMATION: Professional counselors may provide general information from either "secure" or "non-secure" Web sites, or through e-mail communications. General information includes non-client-specific, topical information on matters of general interest to the professional counselor's clients as a whole, third-party resource and referral information, addresses and phone numbers, and the like. Additionally, professional counselors using either "secure" or "non-secure" Web sites may provide "hot links" to third-party Web sites such as licensure boards, certification bodies, and other resource information providers. Professional counselors investigate and continually update the content, accuracy and appropriateness for the client of material contained in any "hot links" to third-party Web sites.

4. LIMITS OF CONFIDENTIALITY: Professional counselors inform clients of the limitations of confidentiality and identify foreseeable situations in which confidentiality must be breached in light of the law in both the state in which the client is located and the state in which the professional counselor is licensed.

b. Informational Notices.

1. SECURITY OF PROFESSIONAL COUNSELOR'S SITE: Professional counselors provide a readily visible notice that (i) information transmitted over a Web site or e-mail server may not be secure; (ii) whether or not the professional counselor's site is secure; (iii) whether the information transmitted between the professional counselor and the client during on-line counseling will be encrypted; and (iv) whether the client will need special software to access and transmit confidential information and, if so, whether the professional counselor provides the software as part of the on-line counseling services. The notice should be viewable from all Web site and e-mail locations from which the client may send information. (See B.1.g.)

2. PROFESSIONAL COUNSELOR IDENTIFICATION: Professional counselors provide a readily visible notice advising clients of the identities of all professional counselor(s) who will have access to the information transmitted by the client and, in the event that more than one professional counselor has access to the Web site or e-mail system, the manner, if any, in which the client may direct information to a particular professional counselor. Professional

counselors inform clients if any or all of the sessions are supervised. Clients are also informed if and how the supervisor preserves session transcripts. Professional counselors provide background information on all professional counselor(s) and supervisor(s) with access to the on-line communications, including education, licensing and certification, and practice area information. (See B.l.g.)
3. CLIENT IDENTIFICATION: Professional counselors identify clients, verify identities of clients, and obtain alternative methods of contacting clients in emergency situations.

c. Client Waiver.

Professional counselors require clients to execute client waiver agreements stating that the client (i) acknowledges the limitations inherent in ensuring client confidentiality of information transmitted through on-line counseling and (ii) agrees to waive the client's privilege of confidentiality with respect to any confidential information transmitted through on-line counseling that may be accessed by any third party without authorization of the client and despite the reasonable efforts of the professional counselor to arrange a secure on-line environment. Professional counselors refer clients to more traditional methods of counseling and do not provide on-line counseling services if the client is unable or unwilling to consent to the client waiver. (See B.1.b.)

d. Records of Electronic Communications.

Professional counselors maintain appropriate procedures for ensuring the safety and confidentiality of client information acquired through electronic communications, including but not limited to encryption software; proprietary on-site file servers with fire walls; saving on-line or e-mail communications to the hard drive or file server computer systems; creating regular tape or diskette back-up copies; creating hard-copies of all electronic communications; and the like. Clients are informed about the length of time for, and method of, preserving session transcripts. Professional counselors warn clients of the possibility or frequency of technology failures and time delays in transmitting and receiving information. (See B.4.a., B.4.b.)

e. Electronic Transfer of Client Information.

Professional counselors electronically transfer client confidential information to authorized third-party recipients only when (i) both the professional counselor and the authorized recipient have "secure" transfer and acceptance communication capabilities, (ii) the recipient is able to effectively protect the confidentiality of the client confidential information to be transferred; and (iii) the informed written consent of the client, acknowledging the limits of confidentiality, has been obtained. (See B.4.e., B.6.a., B.6.b.)

ESTABLISHING THE ON-LINE COUNSELING RELTIONSHIP

a. The Appropriateness of On-Line Counseling.

Professional counselors develop an appropriate in-take procedure for potential clients to determine whether on-line counseling is appropriate for the needs of the client. Professional counselors warn potential clients that on-line counseling services may not be appropriate in certain situations and, to the extent possible, informs the client of specific limitations, potential risks, and/or potential benefits relevant to the client's anticipated use of on-line counseling services. Professional counselors ensure that clients are intellectually, emotionally, and physically capable of using the on-line counseling services, and of understanding the potential risks and/or limitations of such services. (See A.3.a., A.3.b.)

b. Counseling Plans.

Professional counselors develop individual on-line counseling plans that are consistent with both the client's individual circumstances and the limitations of on-line counseling. Professional counselors shall specifically take into account the limitations, if any, on the use of any or all of the following in on-line counseling: initial client appraisal, diagnosis, and assessment methods employed by the professional counselor. Professional counselors who determine that on-line counseling is inappropriate for the client should avoid entering into or immediately terminate the on-line counseling relationship and encourage the client to continue the counseling relationship through an appropriate alternative method of counseling. (See A.11.b., A.11.c.)

c. Continuing Coverage.

Professional counselors provide clients with a schedule of times during which the on-line counseling services will be available, including reasonable anticipated response times, and provide clients with an alternate means of contacting the professional counselor at other times, including in the event of emergencies. Professional counselors obtain from, and provide clients with, alternative means of communication, such as telephone numbers or pager numbers, for back-up purposes in the event the on-line counseling service is unavailable for any reason. Professional counselors provide clients with the name of at least one other professional counselor who will be able to respond to the client in the event the professional counselor is unable to do so for any extended period of time. (See A.11.a.)

d. Boundaries of Competence.

Professional counselors provide on-line counseling services only in practice areas within their expertise and do not provide on-line counseling services to clients located in states in which professional counselors are not licensed. (See C.2.a., C.2.b.)

e. Minor or Incompetent Clients.

Professional counselors must verify that clients are above the age of minority, are competent to enter into the counseling relationship with a professional counselor, and are able to give informed consent. In the event clients are minor children, incompetent, or incapable of giving informed consent, professional counselors must obtain the written consent of the legal guardian or other authorized legal representative of the client prior to commencing on-line counseling services to the client.

LEGAL CONSIDERATIONS

Professional counselors confirm that their liability insurance provides coverage for on-line counseling services, and that the provision of such services is not prohibited by or otherwise violate any applicable (i) state or local statutes, rules, regulations, or ordinances; (ii) codes of professional membership organizations and certifying boards; and/or (iii) codes of state licensing boards.

Professional counselors seek appropriate legal and technical assistance in the development and implementation of their on-line counseling services.

American Counseling Association | 5999 Stevenson Ave. Alexandria, VA 22304 | 800.347.6647 | 800.473.2329 (fax) | 703.823.6862 (TDD)
Copyright 2002, American Counseling Association, All Rights Reserved.

National Board for Certified Counselors
The Practice of Internet Counseling (2001)

This document contains a statement of principles for guiding the evolving practice of Internet counseling. In order to provide a context for these principles, the following definition of Internet counseling, which is one element of technology-assisted distance counseling, is provided. The Internet counseling standards follow the definitions presented below.

A TAXONOMY FOR DEFINING FACE-TO-FACE AND TECHNOLOGY-ASSISTED DISTANCE COUNSELING

The delivery of technology-assisted distance counseling continues to grow and evolve. Technology assistance in the form of computer-assisted assessment, computer-assisted information systems, and telephone counseling has been available and widely used for some time. The rapid development and use of the Internet to deliver information and foster communication has resulted in the creation of new forms of counseling. Developments have occurred so rapidly that it is difficult to communicate a common understanding of these new forms of counseling practice.

The purpose of this document is to create standard definitions of technology-assisted distance counseling that can be easily updated in response to evolutions in technology and practice. A definition of traditional face-to-face counseling is also presented to show similarities and differences with respect to various applications of technology in counseling. A taxonomy of forms of counseling is also presented to further clarify how technology relates to counseling practice.

NATURE OF COUNSELING

Counseling is the application of mental health, psychological, or human development principles, through cognitive, affective, behavioral or systemic intervention strategies, that address wellness, personal growth, or career development, as well as pathology.

Depending on the needs of the client and the availability of services, counseling may range from a few brief interactions in a short period of time, to numerous interactions over an extended period of time. Brief interventions, such as classroom discussions, workshop presentations, or assistance in using assessment, information, or instructional resources, may be sufficient to meet individual needs. Or, these brief interventions may lead to longer-term counseling interventions for individuals with more substantial needs. Counseling may be delivered by a single counselor, two counselors working collaboratively, or a single counselor with brief assistance from another counselor who has specialized expertise that is needed by the client.

FORMS OF COUNSELING

Counseling can be delivered in a variety of forms that share the definition presented above. Forms of counseling differ with respect to participants, delivery location, communication medium, and interaction process. Counseling *participants* can be **individuals, couples, or groups**. The location for counseling delivery can be **face-to-face or at a distance** with the assistance of technology. The *communication medium* for counseling can be what is **read** from text, what is **heard** from audio, or what is **seen** and **heard** in person or from video. The *interaction process* for counseling can be **synchronous** or **asynchronous**. Synchronous interaction occurs with little or no gap in time between the responses of the counselor and the client. Asynchronous interaction occurs with a gap in time between the responses of the counselor and the client.

The selection of a specific form of counseling is based on the needs and preferences of the client within the range of services available. Distance counseling supplements face-to-face counseling by providing increased access to counseling on the basis of **necessity** or **convenience**. Barriers, such as being a long distance from counseling services, geographic separation of a couple, or limited physical mobility as a result of having a **disability**, can make it necessary to provide counseling at a distance. Options, such as scheduling counseling sessions outside of traditional service delivery hours or delivering counseling services at a place of residence or employment, can make it more convenient to provide counseling at a distance.

A Taxonomy of Forms of Counseling Practice. Table 1 presents a taxonomy of currently available forms of counseling practice. This schema is intended to show the relationships among counseling forms.

TABLE 1 **A Taxonomy of Face-To-Face and Technology-Assisted Distance Counseling**

Counseling

- Face-To-Face Counseling
- Individual Counseling
- Couple Counseling
- Group Counseling
- Technology-Assisted Distance Counseling
- Telecounseling
- Telephone-Based Individual Counseling
- Telephone-Based Couple Counseling
- Telephone-Based Group Counseling
- Internet Counseling
- E-Mail-Based Individual Counseling
- Chat-Based Individual Counseling
- Chat-Based Couple Counseling
- Chat-Based Group Counseling
- Video-Based Individual Counseling
- Video-Based Couple Counseling
- Video-Based Group Counseling

DEFINITIONS

Counseling is the application of mental health, psychological, or human development principles, through cognitive, affective, behavioral or systemic intervention strategies, that address wellness, personal growth, or career development, as well as pathology.

Face-to-face counseling for individuals, couples, and groups involves synchronous interaction between and among counselors and clients using what is seen and heard in person to communicate.

Technology-assisted distance counseling for individuals, couples, and groups involves the use of the telephone or the computer to enable counselors and clients to communicate at a distance when circumstances make this approach necessary or convenient.

Telecounseling involves synchronous distance interaction among counselors and clients using one-to-one or conferencing features of the telephone to communicate.

Telephone-based individual counseling involves synchronous distance interaction between a counselor and a client using what is heard via audio to communicate.

Telephone-based couple counseling involves synchronous distance interaction among a counselor or counselors and a couple using what is heard via audio to communicate.

Telephone-based group counseling involves synchronous distance interaction among counselors and clients using what is heard via audio to communicate.

Internet counseling involves asynchronous and synchronous distance interaction among counselors and clients using e-mail, chat, and videoconferencing features of the Internet to communicate.

E-mail-based individual Internet counseling involves asynchronous distance interaction between counselor and client using what is read via text to communicate.

Chat-based individual Internet counseling involves synchronous distance interaction between counselor and client using what is read via text to communicate.

Chat-based couple Internet counseling involves synchronous distance interaction among a counselor or counselors and a couple using what is read via text to communicate.

Chat-based group Internet counseling involves synchronous distance interaction among counselors and clients using what is read via text to communicate.

Video-based individual Internet counseling involves synchronous distance interaction between counselor and client using what is seen and heard via video to communicate.

Video-based couple Internet counseling involves synchronous distance interaction among a counselor or counselors and a couple using what is seen and heard via video to communicate.

Video-based group Internet counseling involves synchronous distance interaction among counselors and clients using what is seen and heard via video to communicate.

STANDARDS FOR THE ETHICAL PRACTICE OF INTERNET COUNSELING

These standards govern the practice of Internet counseling and are intended for use by counselors, clients, the public, counselor educators, and organizations that examine and deliver Internet counseling. These standards are intended to address practices that are unique to Internet counseling and Internet counselors and do not duplicate principles found in traditional codes of ethics.

These Internet counseling standards of practice are based upon the principles of ethical practice embodied in the NBCC Code of Ethics. Therefore, these standards should be used in conjunction with the most recent version of the NBCC ethical code. Related content in the NBCC Code are indicated in parentheses after each standard.

Recognizing that significant new technology emerges continuously, these standards should be reviewed frequently. It is also recognized that Internet counseling ethics cases should be reviewed in light of delivery systems existing at the moment rather than at the time the standards were adopted.

In addition to following the NBCC® Code of Ethics pertaining to the practice of professional counseling, Internet counselors shall observe the following standards of practice:

INTERNET COUNSELING RELATIONSHIP

1. In situations where it is difficult to verify the identity of the Internet client, steps are taken to address impostor concerns, such as by using code words or numbers. (Refer to B.8)
2. Internet counselors determine if a client is a minor and therefore in need of parental/guardian consent. When parent/guardian consent is required to provide Internet counseling to minors, the identity of the consenting person is verified. (Refer to B.8)
3. As part of the counseling orientation process, the Internet counselor explains to clients the procedures for contacting the Internet counselor when he or she is off-line and, in the case of asynchronous counseling, how often e-mail messages will be checked by the Internet counselor. (Refer to B.8)
4. As part of the counseling orientation process, the Internet counselor explains to clients the possibility of technology failure and discusses

alternative modes of communication, if that failure occurs. (Refer to B.8)

5. As part of the counseling orientation process, the Internet counselor explains to clients how to cope with potential misunderstandings when visual cues do not exist. (Refer to B.8)

6. As a part of the counseling orientation process, the Internet counselor collaborates with the Internet client to identify an appropriately trained professional who can provide local assistance, including crisis intervention, if needed. The Internet counselor and Internet client should also collaborate to determine the local crisis hotline telephone number and the local emergency telephone number. (Refer to B.4)

7. The Internet counselor has an obligation, when appropriate, to make clients aware of free public access points to the Internet within the community for accessing Internet counseling or Web-based assessment, information, and instructional resources. (Refer to B.1)

8. Within the limits of readily available technology, Internet counselors have an obligation to make their Web site a barrier-free environment to clients with disabilities. (Refer to B.1)

9. Internet counselors are aware that some clients may communicate in different languages, live in different time zones, and have unique cultural perspectives. Internet counselors are also aware that local conditions and events may impact the client. (Refer to A.12)

CONFIDENTIALITY IN INTERNET COUNSELING

10. The Internet counselor informs Internet clients of encryption methods being used to help insure the security of client/counselor/supervisor communications. (Refer to B.5).

    Encryption methods should be used whenever possible. If encryption is not made available to clients, clients must be informed of the potential hazards of unsecured communication on the Internet. Hazards may include unauthorized monitoring of transmissions and/or records of Internet counseling sessions.

11. The Internet counselor informs Internet clients if, how, and how long session data are being preserved. (Refer to B.6)

    Session data may include Internet counselor/Internet client e-mail, test results, audio/video session recordings, session notes, and counselor/supervisor communications. The likelihood of electronic sessions being preserved is greater because of the ease and decreased costs involved in recording. Thus, its potential use in supervision, research, and legal proceedings increases.

12. Internet counselors follow appropriate procedures regarding the release of information for sharing Internet client information with other electronic sources. (Refer to B.5)

    Because of the relative ease with which e-mail messages can be forwarded to formal and casual referral sources, Internet counselors must work to insure the confidentiality of the Internet counseling relationship.

LEGAL CONSIDERATIONS, LICENSURE, AND CERTIFICATION

13. Internet counselors review pertinent legal and ethical codes for guidance on the practice of Internet counseling and supervision. (Refer to A.13)

    Local, state, provincial, and national statutes as well as codes of professional membership organizations, professional certifying bodies, and state or provincial licensing boards need to be reviewed. Also, as varying state rules and opinions exist on questions pertaining to whether Internet counseling takes place in the Internet counselor's location or the Internet client's location, it is important to review codes in the counselor's home jurisdiction as well as the client's. Internet counselors also consider carefully local customs regarding age of consent and child abuse reporting, and liability insurance policies need to be reviewed to determine if the practice of Internet counseling is a covered activity.

14. The Internet counselor's Web site provides links to websites of all appropriate certification bodies and licensure boards to facilitate consumer protection. (Refer to B.1)

Adopted November 3, 2001
© *NBCC, 2001*

National Career Development Association Guidelines for the Use of the Internet for Provision of Career Information and Planning Services (1997)

Developed by members of the NCDA Ethics Committee:
Dr. David Caulum, Don Doerr, Dr. Pat Howland, Dr. Spencer Niles, Dr.
Ray Palmer, Dr. Richard Pyle (Chair), Dr. David Reile, Dr. James
Sampson, and Dr. Don Schutt.

INTRODUCTION

Based on readily available capabilities at the time of this writing, the Internet could be used in four ways for the purpose of providing career counseling and/or career planning services to clients. These are:

1. To deliver information about occupations, including their descriptions, employment outlook, skills requirements, estimated salary, etc. through text, still images, graphics, and/or video. In this event, the standards for information development and presentation are the same as those for print materials and audiovisual materials as stated in NCDA's documents on these matters.

2. To provide online searches of occupational databases for the purpose of identifying feasible occupational alternatives. In this event, the standards developed by NCDA and the Association of Computer-based Systems for Career Information (ACSCI) apply.

3. To deliver interactive career counseling and career planning services. This use assumes that clients, either as individuals or as part of a group, have intentionally placed themselves in direct communication with a professional career counselor. Standards for use of the Internet for these purposes are addressed in this document.

4. To provide searches through large databases of job openings for the purpose of identifying those that the user may pursue. Guidelines for this application are included in this document.

GUIDELINES FOR USE OF THE INTERNET FOR DELIVERY OF CAREER COUNSELING AND CAREER PLANNING SERVICES

"Career planning services" are differentiated from "career counseling" services. Career planning services include an active provision of information designed to help a client with a specific need, such as review of a resumé; assistance in networking strategies; identification of occupations based on interests, skills, or prior work experience; support in the job-seeking process; and assessment by means of online inventories of interest, abilities, and/or work-related values. Although "Career Counseling" may include the provision of the above services, the use of the term implies a deeper level of involvement with the client, based on the establishment of a professional counseling relationship and the potential for dealing with career development concerns well beyond those included in career planning.

Multiple means of online provision of career planning or career counseling services currently exist, the most common of which are e-mail, newsgroups, bulletin boards, chat rooms, and websites offering a wide variety of services. Telephone or audiovisual linkages supported by the Internet exist in their infancy, and will likely grow in potential as the technology improves and the costs decline.

1. QUALIFICATIONS OF DEVELOPER OR PROVIDER

Websites and other services designed to assist clients with career planning should be developed with content input from professional career counselors. The service should clearly state the qualifications and credentials of the developers not only in the content area of professional career counseling, but also in the development of interactive online services.

2. ACCESS AND UNDERSTANDING OF ENVIRONMENT

The counselor has an obligation to be aware of free public access points to the Internet within the member's community, so that a lack of financial resources does not create a significant barrier to clients accessing counseling services or information, assessment or instructional resources over the internet.

The counselor has an obligation to be as aware as possible of local conditions, cultures, and events that may impact the client.

3. CONTENT OF CAREER COUNSELING AND PLANNING SERVICES ON THE INTERNET

The content of a website or other service offering career information or planning services should be reviewed for the appropriateness of content offered in this medium. Some kinds of content have been extensively tested for online delivery due to the long existence of computer-based career information and guidance systems. This includes searching of databases by relevant search variables; display of occupational information; development of a resumé; assessment of interests, abilities, and work-related values and linkage of these to occupational titles; instruction about occupational classification systems; relationship of school majors to occupational choices; and the completion of forms such as a financial needs assessment questionnaire or a job application.

When a website offers a service which has not previously been extensively tested (such as computer-based career guidance and information systems), this service should be carefully scrutinized to determine whether it lends itself to the Internet. The website should clearly state the kinds of client concerns that the counselor judges to be inappropriate for counseling over the Internet, or beyond the skills of the counselor.

4. APPROPRIATENESS OF CLIENT FOR RECEIPT OF SERVICES VIA THE INTERNET

The counselor has an ethical and professional responsibility to assure that the client who is requesting service can profit from it in this mode. Appropriate screening includes the following:

a. A clear statement by clients of their career planning or career counseling needs.
b. An analysis by the counselor of whether meeting those needs via Internet exchange is appropriate and of whether this particular client can benefit from counseling services provided in this mode. A

judgment about the latter should be made by means of a telephone or videophone teleconference designed to specify the client's expectations, how the client has sought to meet these through other modes, and whether or not the client appears to be able to process information through an Internet medium.

5. APPROPRIATE SUPPORT TO THE CLIENT

The counselor who is providing services to a client via the Internet has ethical responsibility for the following:

a. Periodic monitoring of the client's progress via telephone or videophone teleconference.
b. Identification by the counselor of a qualified career counselor in the client's geographic area should referral become necessary. If this is not possible, the web counselor using traditional referral sources to identify an appropriate practitioner should assist the client in the selection of a counselor.
c. Appropriate discussion with the client about referral to face-to-face service should the counselor determine that little or no progress is being made toward the client's goals.

6. CLARITY OF CONTRACT WITH THE CLIENT

The counselor should define several items in writing to the client in a document that can be downloaded from the Internet or faxed to the client. This document should include at least the following items:

a. The counselor's credentials in the field.
b. The agreed-upon goals of the career counseling or career planning Internet interchange.
c. The agreed-upon cost of the services and how this will be billed.
d. Where and how clients can report any counselor behavior that they consider to be unethical.
e. Statement about the degree of security of the Internet and confidentiality of data transmitted on the Internet and about any special conditions related to the client's personal information (such as potential transmission of client records to a supervisor for quality-control purposes, or the collection of data for research purposes).
f. A statement of the nature of client information electronically stored by the counselor, including the length of time that data will be maintained before being destroyed.

g. A statement about the need for privacy when the client is communicating with the counselor, e.g., that client communication with the counselor is not limited by having others observe or hear interactions between the counselor and client.

h. If the service includes career, educational, or employment information, the counselor is responsible for making the client aware of the typical circumstances where individuals need counseling support in order to effectively use the information.

7. INCLUSION OF LINKAGES TO OTHER WEBSITES

If a career information or counseling website includes links to other websites, the professional who creates this linkage is responsible for assuring that the services to which his or hers are linked also meet these guidelines.

8. USE OF ASSESSMENT

If the career planning or career counseling service is to include online inventories or tests and their interpretation, the following conditions should apply:

a. The assessments must have been tested in computer delivery mode to assure that their psychometric properties are the same in this mode of delivery as in print form; or the client must be informed that they have not yet been tested in this same mode of delivery.

b. The counselor must abide by the same ethical guidelines as if he or she were administering and interpreting these same inventories or tests in face-to-face mode and/or in print form.

c. Every effort must be exerted to protect the confidentiality of the user's results.

d. If there is any evidence that the client does not understand the results, as evidenced by e-mail or telephone interchanges, the counselor must refer the client to a qualified career counselor in his or her geographic area.

e. The assessments must have been validated for self-help use if no counseling support is provided, or that appropriate counseling intervention is provided before and after completion of the assessment resource if the resource has not been validated for self-help use.

PROFESSIONAL AND ETHICAL GUIDELINES RELATED TO THE USE OF THE INTERNET FOR JOB POSTING AND SEARCHING

1. The posting must represent a valid job opening for which those searching on the Internet have an opportunity to apply.
2. Job postings must be removed from the Internet database within 48 hours of the time that the announced position is filled.
3. Names, addresses, resumés, and other information that may be gained about individuals should not be used for any purposes other than provision of further information about job openings.

UNACCEPTABLE COUNSELOR BEHAVIORS ON THE INTERNET

1. Use of a false e-mail identity when interacting with clients and/or other professionals. When acting in a professional capacity on the Internet, a counselor has a duty to identify him/herself honestly.
2. Accepting a client who will not identify him/herself and be willing to arrange for phone conversation as well as online interchange.
3. "Sharking" or monitoring chat rooms and bulletin board services, and offering career planning and related services when no request has been made for services. This includes sending out mass unsolicited e-mails. Counselors may advertise their services but must do so observing proper "netiquette" and standards of professional conduct.

NEED FOR RESEARCH AND REVIEW

Since the use of the Internet is new for the delivery of career planning and counseling services, it is mandatory that the career counseling profession gains experience with this medium and evaluate its effectiveness through targeted research. The capabilities of Internet delivery of services will expand rapidly as the use of sound and video becomes more feasible. These early guidelines will need constant monitoring and revision as research data become available and additional capabilities become cost-feasible.

NCDA opposes discrimination against any individual on the basis of race, ethnicity, gender, sexual orientation, age, mental/physical disability, or creed.

Revised by the NCDA Board of Directors, April 1994.

This statement was developed by the National Career Development Association, 10820 East 45th Street, Suite 210, Tulsa, OK 74146, tel: (918) 663-7060, fax: (918) 663-7058, toll-free: (866) 367-6232.

The Professional School Counselor and HIV/AIDS

Adopted 1988; revised 1993, 1999, 2001

AMERICAN SCHOOL COUNSELOR ASSOCIATION (ASCA) POSITION

The professional school counselor focuses on Human Immunodeficiency Virus and Acquired Immune Deficiency Disorder (HIV/AIDS) as a disease and not as a moral issue. The professional school counselor promotes prevention, health and education, while providing a vital link to the well being of students, staff, parents, and the community.

THE RATIONALE

Federal laws, regulations, and court cases do not permit discrimination on the basis of HIV status. Since 1981, the HIV/AIDS epidemic has prompted health education programs and preventative measures to reach vulnerable groups. Although HIV/AIDS information and education are vital for all individuals, professional school counselors communicate with these vulnerable populations Adolescents and pre-adolescents are in stages in life when they are exploring their individual identity. School counselors have the opportunity and responsibility to provide students with accurate health information and to help them develop healthy attitudes and habits.

THE PROFESSIONAL SCHOOL COUNSELOR'S ROLE

The professional school counselor's role is to provide counseling, support and collaboration with school health personnel to provide educational programs for students, staff, and parents. Clear, succinct, and accurate information concerning HIV/AIDS, and any related complications, is vital to all persons.

The professional school counselor is familiar with the school policy regarding HIV and AIDS and the ramifications for the school population. The professional school counselor becomes familiar with current resources to assist students and families dealing with HIV/AIDS issues.

The professional school counselor may advocate for the initiation of an HIV/AIDS education program, and with the curriculum developed in conjunction with groups associated with the school and officially approved by the board of education. Specific elements may include general information about HIV/AIDS, including knowledge of the behavior choices that put people at risk for HIV/AIDS, how HIV/AIDS transmission occurs, HIV/AIDS-related civil rights issues, universal health precautions, and accurate information dispelling myths about HIV/AIDS. The HIV/AIDS education program needs to include instruction for students, parents, and staff promoting concepts of healthy living and responsibility to self, family, and society.

SUMMARY

HIV/AIDS is a national concern for which each person must take personal responsibility. Through focusing on HIV/AIDS as a disease, it is possible to develop educational programs to help prevent the spread of the disease. Professional school counselors promote approaching the issue from a health and preventive model, keeping abreast of current recommendations and resources.

The Professional School Counselor and Attention Deficit/Hyperactivity Disorder (ADHD)

(Adopted 1994, Revised 2000)

AMERICAN SCHOOL COUNSELOR ASSOCIATION (ASCA) POSITION

Professional school counselors support the rights of students with a medical diagnosis of Attention Deficit/Hyperactivity Disorder (ADHD) to receive multidisciplinary, multimodal, and multifaceted treatment for symptoms and effects of ADHD. Professional school counselors are committed to facilitating and promoting the continuing development of each student through counseling programs within the schools. We recognize that an important aspect of development involves recognizing students diagnosed with medical, psychological, behavioral and/or social problems likely to affect their performance at school, home, and in the community.

RATIONALE

ADHD is one of the most prevalent childhood and adolescence disorders, affecting from 5% to 10% of all school-age children who may be genetically predisposed to the disorder. ADHD is believed to be an imbalance of the neurochemicals that act as triggers, transmitters and receptors within the brain. It is not considered to be caused by brain damage, birth trauma, poor parenting, inadequate discipline, nutritional deficiencies, allergies, or divorce. ADHD may severely affect family relations, cause problems with school staff, impede learning and academic achievements, interfere with peer relationships, and contribute to a student's poor self-concept and low self-esteem. Students with ADHD will undergo pressures and stresses that go beyond those resulting from developmental stages.

THE PROFESSIONAL SCHOOL COUNSELOR'S ROLE

The professional school counselor is aware of information regarding the learning and behavioral issues found in students with ADHD. The professional school counselor may participate in the implementation of the following activities: (1) serve on the school's multidisciplinary team actively involved in the multimodal or multifaceted delivery of interventions or services to the child/adolescent with ADHD; (2) serve as a consultant and resource to the parents, teachers, and other school personnel on the characteristics and problems of students with ADHD; (3) serve in the capacity of providing regular feedback on the social and academic performance of the student with ADHD to the members of the multidisciplinary treatment team; (4) help staff design appropriate programs for students with ADHD that include opportunities for them to learn more appropriate social skills and self-management skills; (5) provide students with ADHD with activities to improve their self-esteem and self-concept and to encourage students to practice the skills learned in counseling sessions in external settings; (6) promote ADHD workshops for staff and support groups for parents and families with children with ADHD; and (7) serve as an advocate for students with ADHD in the community.

SUMMARY

The attitude of counselors, parents, peers and other professionals toward students with ADHD may, in the long run, have more to do with success in treating these children than any other factor. The professional school counselor takes an active role in providing support and implementing services for students with ADHD.

(Note: Additional information on Attention Deficit/Hyperactivity Disorder may be found in the DSM IV.)

The Professional School Counselor and Censorship

(Adopted 1985; revised 1993, 1999, 2002)

AMERICAN SCHOOL COUNSELOR ASSOCIATION (ASCA) POSITION

The American School Counselor Association (ASCA) is committed to the protection of the fundamental democratic rights guaranteed in the U.S. Constitution, including those provisions for free speech, free press and equal protection under the law, as well as those rights not enumerated but held by citizens in a democratic society. ASCA supports academic freedom in school counseling programs and supports the rights of students to receive services appropriate to their needs.

THE RATIONALE

Censorship activities imposed on schools have created a climate threatening the students' basic rights to question, deal with differences, and learn to make rational, well-informed decisions. Censorship is defined as the denial of a student's basic right to receive any of the commonly recognized school counseling services offered by school counseling programs.

It is important to have a school climate that fosters, rather than threatens, students' basic rights to question, deal with differences, gather information, and learn to make rational decisions through intellectual analysis and sound scholarship. Students should be provided with opportunities within the school climate to learn to exercise basic constitutional rights guaranteed to citizens in our society so that as adults they will be able to make informed decisions and exercise the rights and duties of citizenship in a democratic society. Such a belief requires students to be exposed to a diversity of viewpoints and ideas, a fundamental democratic right guaranteed in our Constitution's provision for free speech, free press, and equal protection under the law.

THE PROFESSIONAL SCHOOL COUNSELOR'S ROLE

Professional school counselors support academic freedom, access to information, and the right to independent thought. Professional school counselors have an obligation to support the basic tenets of democracy. Professional school counselors also safeguard the students' rights to receive information and services appropriate to their needs as an integral part of the total school mission. ASCA encourages school counselors to take necessary actions to ensure students have access to appropriate services permitting maximum student achievement.

ASCA further recommends that counselors provide accessibility to a comprehensive collection of school counseling materials chosen in compliance with basic written selection criteria developed by the school district. ASCA recommends that counselors provide school counseling support for staff and activities for students that encourage growth and academic excellence as well as recognizing diversity among ideas and students, which contributes to the American heritage. ASCA supports providing data to the school staff and community regarding goals, objectives and evaluation of the counseling program to ensure implementation in accord with state and local school board policies.

SUMMARY

In order for students to develop in a healthy manner and obtain the skills necessary for citizenship, they need to exist in a climate that fosters the ability to make informed decisions based upon independent inquiry and sound scholarship. Professional school counselors have a personal and professional obligation to support the basic tenets of democracy to help ensure information about—and access to—a range of developmentally appropriate school counseling programs for every student.

The Professional School Counselor and Character Education

(Adopted 1998)

AMERICAN SCHOOL COUNSELOR ASSOCIATION (ASCA) POSITION

ASCA endorses and supports character education in the schools. The professional school counselor needs to take an active role in initiating, facilitating and promoting character education programs in the school curriculum.

THE RATIONALE

Character education is the teaching of key social values, which enables students to become positive, self-directed adults and responsible members of society. These social values are held by our society as ethical standards that support our democratic way of life. As professional school counselors, we know students need to acquire certain character traits based on clearly understood, universal values. These include: honesty, integrity, trustworthiness, respect, responsibility, fairness, caring, and citizenship. These values affirm basic human worth and dignity.

Today, the family faces many obstacles and burdens. Standards of right and wrong have declined. Our nation's moral fiber is at risk. Each day our children make decisions about lying and cheating, using drugs or alcohol, becoming involved with guns and gangs.

We want our youth to acquire the knowledge, the self-esteem and the support they will need to survive in a changing society. Counselors can be part of the school team inviting family and community involvement to define the values that will guide the school's character development values. The responsibility of teaching and instilling these values must now be shared by the school and the home.

THE PROFESSIONAL SCHOOL COUNSELOR'S ROLE

For character education to be effective, all adults in the school community need to model the behavior of good character they want students to imitate. The daily operations of school have significant impact on what children will learn to value. The professional school counselor needs to lead, initiate, manage and support character education programs in the school. Counselors should encourage the following activities if not already in practice:

- Formulation or articulation of a school philosophy or mission statement
- Guidance in helping all students express clear academic and behavior goals
- A discipline policy that supports character goals
- Student participation in school activities
- Student participation in community service or school projects
- Programs to give students the opportunity to help other students
- Extracurricular activities to include the involvement of students, school staff, parents, and community members
- Teaching of making decisions, resolving conflicts, and solving problems
- Student involvement in development of school rules
- Inclusion of character values in multicultural discussions
- Student recognition programs focused on character values

The professional school counselor is in a position to be effective in designing, initiating and supporting a character education curriculum. Teachers, counselors, and administrators need to work together to teach students to take responsibility for their actions and behavior. A positive self-esteem and effective decision-making skills are essential to this process.

SUMMARY

Character education will assist students in becoming positive and self-directed in their lives and education and in striving toward future goals.

The professional school counselor, as a part of the school community and as a highly resourceful person, takes an active role by working cooperatively with the teachers and administration in providing character education in the schools as an integral part of the school curriculum and activities.

©2002 ASCA, all rights reserved.

The Professional School Counselor and Child Abuse and Neglect Prevention

(Adopted 1981; revised 1985, 1993, 1999)

AMERICAN SCHOOL COUNSELOR ASSOCIATION (ASCA) POSITION

It is the professional school counselor's responsibility to report suspected cases of child abuse/neglect to the proper authorities. Recognizing that the abuse of children is not limited to the home and that corporal punishment by school authorities might well be considered child abuse, ASCA supports any legislation that specifically bans the use of corporal punishment as a disciplinary tool within the schools.

THE RATIONALE

The incidence of reported child abuse and child neglect has increased significantly during the past several years. Although there are societal beliefs and values that parents have the right to discipline their children as they choose, it becomes a public issue of child protection when that discipline becomes abusive. Research shows that a large percentage of abusive parents were abused children, perpetuating the cycle of abuse. The consequences of abuse are physical and/or emotional harm, which include the inability to build healthy relationships, increased likelihood of being abused by another perpetrator of abuse and lowered self-esteem.

DEFINITIONS:

Abuse: The infliction of physical harm upon the body of a child by other than accidental means, continual psychological damage or denial of emotional needs (e.g., extensive bruises/patterns; burns/patterns; lacerations, welts or abrasions; injuries inconsistent with information offered; sexual abuse involving molestation or exploitation, including but not limited to rape, carnal knowledge, sodomy or unnatural sexual practices; emotional disturbance caused by continuous friction in the home, marital discord or mentally ill parents; cruel treatment).

Neglect: The failure to provide necessary food, care, clothing, shelter, supervision or medical attention for a child (e.g., malnourished, ill-clad, dirty, without proper shelter or sleeping arrangements, lacking appropriate health care; unattended, lacking adequate supervision; ill and lacking essential medical attention; irregular/illegal absences from school; exploited, overworked; lacking essential psychological/emotional nurturing; abandonment.

Corporal Punishment: Any act of physical force upon a pupil for the purpose of punishing that pupil. This definition specifically excludes any reasonable force exercised by a school employee that is used in self-defense, in defense of other persons or property or to restrain or remove a pupil who is disrupting school functions and who refuses to comply with a request to stop.

THE PROFESSIONAL SCHOOL COUNSELOR'S ROLE

Generally, state laws require people in the helping professions who have reasonable cause to believe that a child is suffering physical or emotional injury to report this situation as directed by state law to the appropriate authorities. School counselors are mandated reporters and need policies, referral procedures and essential knowledge. It is a legal, moral, and ethical responsibility to report child abuse.

ASCA recognizes that it is the absolute responsibility of school counselors to report suspected cases of child abuse/neglect to the proper authorities. Responsible action by the counselor can be achieved through the recognition and understanding of the problem, knowing the reporting procedures and participating in available child abuse information programs. Professional school counselors aid in early detection of abuse. The association also recognizes that the abuse of children is not limited to the home and that corporal punishment by school authorities can be considered child abuse.

School counselors commit themselves to providing strategies to help break the cycle of child abuse. It is the school counselors' responsibility to help children and adults cope with abusive behavior, facilitate behavioral changes and develop positive interpersonal relationships as well as to prepare for parenting styles. Professional school counselors coordinate team efforts on behalf of the child; provide support to staff and other school personnel; work to re-establish trust and to provide brief, educational counseling or to refer to ongoing counseling services outside of the school community; provide developmental workshops and/or support groups enhancing parenting skills; and provide programs and inservices designed to help prevent child abuse.

SUMMARY

Professional school counselors are a key link in the child abuse prevention network. It is their responsibility to report suspected cases of child abuse or neglect to the proper authorities. The professional school counselor must be able to guide and help abused and neglected students by providing appropriate services during crisis situations. Up-to-date information, and intervention, can sometimes mean a turning point in the life and behavior of an abusive family.

The Professional School Counselor and Confidentiality

(Adopted 1974; reviewed and reaffirmed 1980; revised 1986, 1993, 1999, 2002)

AMERICAN SCHOOL COUNSELOR ASSOCIATION (ASCA) POSITION

The professional responsibility of school counselors is to fully respect the right to privacy of those with whom they enter counseling relationships. Professional school counselors must keep abreast of and adhere to all laws, policies and ethical standards pertaining to confidentiality. This confidentiality must not be abridged by the counselor except when there is clear and present danger to the student and/or other persons.

THE RATIONALE

Confidentiality is an ethical term denoting a counseling practice relevant to privacy. Privileged communication is a legal term denoting a requirement to protect the privacy between counselor and student.

A student has the right to privacy and confidentiality. ASCA recognizes that a counseling relationship requires an atmosphere of trust and confidence between the student and the counselor. Confidentiality ensures that disclosures will not be divulged to others except when authorized by the student or when there is a clear and present danger to the student and/or to other persons.

ASCA members affirm their belief in the individual's worth and dignity. It is the professional responsibility of school counselors to fully respect the right to privacy of those with whom they enter counseling relationships.

THE PROFESSIONAL SCHOOL COUNSELOR'S ROLE

Counselors have a responsibility to protect the privileged information received through confidential relationships with students, the students' parents or guardians and with staff. The professional school counselor reserves the right to consult with other professionally competent persons when this is in the student's best interest. In the event of possible judicial proceedings, the professional school counselor should initially advise the school administration and the counselee, and if necessary, consult with legal counsel. If reports are required, every effort should be made to limit demands for information to those matters essential for the purpose of the legal proceedings. When a professional counselor is in doubt about what to release in a judicial proceeding, the professional school counselor should arrange a conference with the judge to explain the dilemma and get advice as to how to proceed. Counseling information used in research and counselor training should fully guarantee counselees' anonymity.

It is the counselor's responsibility to provide notice to students regarding the possible necessity for consulting with others. This confidentiality must not be abridged by the professional school counselor except where there is a clear and present danger to the student and/or to other persons.

The professional school counselor and student should be provided with adequate physical facilities to guarantee the confidentiality of the counseling relationship. With the enactment of the Family Educational Rights and Privacy Act, P.L. 93-380 (The Buckley Amendment), great care should be taken with recorded information. All professional school counselors should have a copy of the complete law. Professional school counselors must adhere to P.L. 93-380; they must be concerned about individuals who have access to confidential information. It should be each school's policy to guarantee adequate working space for secretaries so that students and school personnel will not come into contact with confidential information, even inadvertently. Professional school counselors should undertake a periodic review of information requested of their students. Only relevant information should be retained. Professional school counselors will adhere to ethical standards and local policies in relating student information over the telephone. They have a responsibility to encourage school administrators to develop written policies concerning the ethical and legal handling of all records in their school system. The development of additional guidelines relevant to the local situation is encouraged. Finally, it is strongly recommended that state and local counselor associations implement these principles and guidelines through appropriate legislation.

Professional school counselors should be aware that it is much more difficult to guarantee confidentiality in group counseling than in individual counseling. Communications made in good faith may be classified as privileged by the courts, and the communicating parties will be protected by law against legal action seeking damages for libel or slander. Generally, it may be said that an occasion of this particular privilege arises when one acts in the bona fide discharge of a public or private duty. This privilege may be abused or lost by malice, improper and unjustified motive, bad faith, or excessive publication.

SUMMARY

A counseling relationship requires an atmosphere of trust and confidence between student and counselor. A student has the right to privacy and confidentiality. The responsibility to protect confidentiality extends to the student's parent or guardian and staff in confidential relationships. Professional school counselors must adhere to P.L. 93-380.

The Professional Counselor and Use of Support Staff in Counseling Programs

(Adopted 1974; reviewed and reaffirmed 1980; revised 1986, 1993, 1999, 2001)

AMERICAN COUNSELOR ASSOCIATION (ASCA) POSITION

Counselor support staff members in the counseling program provide assistance so that professional school counselors can use their own professional expertise more effectively. Counselor support staff members address the issue of clerical and routine responsibilities of the counseling department. Counselor support staff should never be used to replace professional school counselors.

THE RATIONALE

The utilization of counselor support staff provides a means of developing greater effectiveness within the guidance and within the counseling program. Counselor support staff members allow time for the professional school counselor to provide more of the services and deliver the programs that requires specialized skills and training.

THE ROLE OF PARAPROFESSIONALS IN COUNSELING PROGRAMS

With the appropriate education and training of carefully selected personnel, counselor support staff members, under careful supervision, could assist in the following areas:

Clerical Worker: collect and maintain current files, reproduce materials needed for the professional school counselor in group or individual conferences, assist with student record keeping, assist students in completion of varied forms and applications, collect and distribute test materials, assist in monitoring group tests, and prepare and organize answer sheets for scoring (not interpretation of test results).

Resource Person: Under the supervision of a professional school counselor, the resource person may assist the counselor and perform duties, such as disseminate information, coordinate resources and counseling materials, record keeping, data entry, and collection. Some counselor supportive staff duties may require specialized training.

The counselor support staff member should possess a sensitivity to students' problems and needs, manifest an interest in working with students, and be knowledgeable of the role of the professional school counselor and the total guidance and counseling program.

THE PROFESSIONAL SCHOOL COUNSELOR'S ROLE

The professional school counselor should assist in the selection of counselor support staff and assume the responsibility of supervision of counselor supportive staff members.

ASCA encourages post-secondary institutions to offer training for counselor support staff in guidance and counseling programs. ASCA also encourages the collaboration of state education department personnel, post-secondary student services personnel and guidance and counseling personnel in local school districts in instituting such courses or programs.

The training for counselor support staff should include clerical training, operation and use of multimedia material, use and operation of computers, practical investigations or research techniques, human relations, the monitoring of group testing, ethics, community resources, and training in confidentiality with regard to student records.

SUMMARY

The utilization of counselor support staff in guidance and counseling programs provides a means to develop greater effectiveness within the program, allowing time for the professional school counselor to provide more of the services requiring specialized skills and training. Courses and training for counselor support staff should be instituted in collaboration with local school districts and the state department of education.

The Professional School Counselor and Credentialing and Licensure

(Adopted 1990; revised 1993, 1999)

THE AMERICAN SCHOOL COUNSELOR ASSOCIATION (ASCA) POSITION

ASCA strongly supports passage of a counselor licensure law in each state providing legal definition of the counseling profession and of qualified practitioners and establishing standards for entry and role definition in school settings, including a privileged communication clause. ASCA strongly endorses and supports the school counselor standards developed by the Council for Accreditation of Counseling and Related Educational Programs (CACREP) and encourages all state education agencies to adopt these professional standards for school counselor credentialing. Further, ASCA supports the credentialing and employment of those who hold a master's degree in counseling-related fields with training in all areas specified by the CACREP standards plus a one-year internship in a school under the supervision of a qualified school counselor and a university supervisor.

THE RATIONALE

Counselor licensure legislation protects the public and its right to select which mental health specialty would best serve its needs. ASCA encourages legislation including a legal definition of the counseling profession, setting minimum standards for entry into the counseling profession and defining the role of professional school counseling. ASCA encourages inclusion of a privileged communication clause for counselors in all settings and of the ASCA and/or ACA *Code of Ethics* as part of said legislation. ASCA strongly supports the nationwide use of CACREP standards in establishing state certification guidelines for professional school counselors to ensure sound academic practicum and internship experience. This preparation and experience enhances the development of proactive and comprehensive school counseling programs.

THE PROFESSIONAL SCHOOL COUNSELOR'S ROLE

The changing needs of students, families and schools require professional school counselors who are skilled in addressing such issues as drug and alcohol addictions, personal and family problems, suicide and teenage pregnancy, as well as academic training in areas such as school organization and classroom management methods.

SUMMARY

ASCA, recognizing the changing needs in students, families and schools, strongly supports sound academic preparation and the use of CACREP standards in establishing state certification guidelines for professional school counselors. ASCA further supports licensure for all specialties within the counseling profession in all states.

The Professional School Counselor and Critical Incident Response in the Schools

(Adopted 2000)

AMERICAN SCHOOL COUNSELOR ASSOCIATION (ASCA) POSITION

The professional school counselor is a pivotal member of a school district's critical incident response team. The professional school counselor is a leader in the successful implementation of a response plan during any school-related incidents and serves primarily as an advocate for students' safety and well-being.

THE RATIONALE

ASCA promotes and supports a safe, violence-free learning environment in the schools. Professional school counselors are critical to the following emergency prevention/preparedness response activities: direct student counseling services, student suicide prevention, drug and alcohol interventions, student safety advocacy, parent education programs, and response team planning and drill practices. It is imperative that school districts develop district-level and building-level emergency preparedness and response plans. Accurate and immediate implementation of a critical incident response plan can significantly protect and ensure students' safety during a critical event and mitigate the long-term effects following the event. Professional school counselors screen students for unhealthy or unsafe coping responses to current or past tragedies and make appropriate referrals. Professional school counselors provide critical incident stress debriefing.

THE PROFESSIONAL SCHOOL COUNSELOR'S ROLE

Professional school counselors support and actively engage themselves in critical incident response in the schools. The professional school counselor is a leader and an integral part of the prevention, intervention, and post-incident support of school critical incident responses in both the planning and implementation. As a member of the district and school critical incident response team, the professional school counselor is familiar with the school community, including students, parents, and school staff members. The professional school counselor is familiar with first responders such as law enforcement officials or emergency medical responders and with agency counseling service providers in the community.

The professional school counselor's central role is to respond to and advocate for the emotional needs of all persons affected by the crisis. The professional school counselor recognizes and facilitates a continuum of support for students and victims affected by a crisis. The professional school counselor is skilled in networking with community resources and thus is able to provide effective planning and referral for victims of a critical incident. In the event of a critical incident, the professional school counselor's primary role is to provide direct counseling service during and after the incident.

SUMMARY

The professional school counselor is a leader and a crucial member of a district and school critical incident response team. The development and implementation of a coordinated district and school critical incident response plan should include input from the professional school counselor. Professional school counselors are student advocates and facilitators of communication with students, staff, parents, and community and assist in securing outside services when needed. The counselor's expertise should not be replaced by less-qualified personnel in critical incident response planning and implementation. The professional school counselor should help coordinate critical incident stress debriefing for students, staff, and counselors directly involved in the incident response.

The Professional School Counselor and Cross/Multicultural Counseling

(Adopted 1988; revised 1993, 1999)

AMERICAN SCHOOL COUNSELOR ASSOCIATION (ASCA) POSITION

School counselors take action to ensure students of culturally diverse backgrounds have access to appropriate services and opportunities promoting the individual's maximum development.

THE RATIONALE

Cross/multicultural counseling is the facilitation of human development through the understanding and appreciation of cultural diversities. ASCA recognizes cultural diversities as important factors deserving increased awareness and understanding on the part of all school personnel, especially the school counselor. Counselors may use a variety of strategies not only to increase the sensitivity of students and parents to culturally diverse persons and enhance the total school and community environment but also to increase awareness of culturally diverse populations.

THE PROFESSIONAL SCHOOL COUNSELOR'S ROLE

ASCA encourages school counselors to take action to ensure students of culturally diverse backgrounds have access to appropriate services and opportunities promoting maximum development. Professional school counselors use a variety of strategies to increase sensitivity of students and parents to cultural diversity and to enhance the total school and community climate, as well as to increase awareness of culturally diverse persons and populations. Counselors have the skills necessary to consult with school personnel to identify alienating factors in attitudes and policies impeding the learning process of culturally diverse students. School counselors need to continue to be aware of and strive to ensure that all students' rights are respected. This allows them to maximize their potential in an environment supporting and encouraging the person's growth and development. School counselors have the responsibility of ensuring all students' specific needs are met.

SUMMARY

Professional school counselors have the responsibility of ensuring all students' special needs are met. Counselors have the skills necessary to consult with school personnel to identify alienating factors in attitudes and policies impeding the learning process and the skills necessary to foster increased awareness and understanding of cultural diversity existing in the school and community. ASCA encourages professional school counselors to use a variety of strategies, activities and resources personally, in school, through community outreach, with students, staff, and parents, and within the school districts, to increase awareness and understanding of culturally diverse persons and populations and to enhance the total school and community environment and climate. School counselors need to continually be aware of and strive to ensure all students have the right to maximize their potential in an environment supporting and encouraging a person's growth and development.

The Professional School Counselor and Educational Planning

(Adopted 1994, Revised 2000)

AMERICAN SCHOOL COUNSELOR ASSOCIATION (ASCA) POSITION

The professional school counselor works with administrative, curricular and instructional staff to ensure all students have the opportunity to design academically challenging programs of studies.

RATIONALE

Specialization within a student's program of studies should lead to successful completion of requirements for the chosen post-secondary option, while permitting opportunities for the development of other competencies. A systematic educational planning program promotes a student's opportunity to make individual choices geared to his or her unique profile of abilities, interests, and goals. Lack of educational planning leads to inequities based on gender, stereotypical attitudes, and students' special needs.

THE PROFESSIONAL SCHOOL COUNSELOR'S ROLE

Professional school counselors play a critical role in assisting students in the development of a comprehensive plan allowing for exploration of their educational and career opportunities. The professional school counselor possesses knowledge of national, state, and local goals and programs identifying how students can best achieve success in their post-secondary plans.

The professional school counselor advocates for developmental guidance programs involving individual and group activities stressing educational planning (i.e., decision-making, career awareness, and exploration). The professional school counselor educates parents to become active members of the decision-making team.

Collaboration within the education community is necessary to provide all students with better choices and opportunities for quality educational programs. The professional school counselor takes a proactive role in facilitating changes that afford students, parents, and staff the opportunity to accurately assess student strengths, interests and preferences and encourages the selection of challenging educational programs.

SUMMARY

The professional school counselor advocates for equal educational planning opportunities for all students. Decisions that a student makes about a chosen course of study must be based upon information unique to the individual and his or her profile of skills and knowledge.

The Professional School Counselor and Gifted and Talented Student Programs

(Adopted 1988; revised 1993, 1999, 2001)

AMERICAN SCHOOL COUNSELOR ASSOCIATION (ASCA) POSITION

The professional school counselor assists in providing technical assistance and an organized support system within the developmental comprehensive school counseling program for gifted and talented students to meet their extensive and diverse needs as well as the needs of all students.

THE RATIONALE

An organized support system throughout the formative years is imperative for such students to be able to realize their potential. A part of this support system is participation in a school counseling program that meets the extensive and diverse needs of the gifted and talented students.

THE PROFESSIONAL SCHOOL COUNSELOR'S ROLE

The role of the professional school counselor in gifted and talented programs may be as follows:

1. Assisting in the identification of gifted and talented students through the use of a multiple criterion system utilized in their school district, which may include:

- Intellectual ability
- Academic performance
- Visual and performing arts ability
- Practical arts ability
- Creative thinking ability
- Leadership potential
- Parent, teacher, peer nomination
- Expert evaluation

2. Advocating for the inclusion of activities that effectively address the personal/social and career development needs, in addition to the academic needs of identified gifted and talented students
3. Assisting in promoting understanding and awareness of the special issues that may affect gifted and talented students including:
   - Underachievement
   - Perfectionism
   - Depression
   - Dropping out
   - Delinquency
   - Difficulty in peer relationships
   - Career development
   - Meeting expectations
   - Goal setting
   - Questioning others' values
4. Providing individual and group counseling for gifted and talented students, as warranted.
5. Recommending material and resources for gifted and talented programs and teachers and parents of gifted and talented students.
6. Engaging in professional development activities through which knowledge and skills in the area of programming for the needs of the gifted and talented are regularly upgraded.

SUMMARY

Gifted and talented students come from many backgrounds, and their special abilities cover a wide spectrum of human potential. Specifically planned educational experiences can greatly enhance the continued development of gifted and talented persons. Professional school counselors work in a collaboration with other school personnel to maximize opportunities for these students. The professional school counselor is an integral part of the educational team that delivers a comprehensive school counseling program to meet the needs of all students.

The Professional School Counselor and Group Counseling

(Adopted 1989; revised 1993, 2002; reviewed 1999)

AMERICAN SCHOOL COUNSELOR ASSOCIATION (ASCA) POSITION

Every school district and every institution of higher learning should include and support the group counseling concept as an integral part of a comprehensive developmental school counseling program.

THE RATIONALE

Group counseling, which involves a number of students working on shared tasks and developing supportive relationships in a group setting, is an efficient and positive way of dealing with students' developmental problems and situational concerns.

By allowing individuals to develop insights into themselves and others, group counseling makes it possible for more people to achieve a healthier personal adjustment, handle the stresses of a rapidly changing technological and complex environment, and learn to work and live with others.

THE PROFESSIONAL SCHOOL COUNSELOR'S ROLE

Many components of a comprehensive school counseling program are best delivered by means of group counseling. Small- and large-group approaches are the preferred medium of delivery for developmental counseling program activities, in terms of efficiency as well as effectiveness. Professional school counselors facilitate many groups, as well as train others as group facilitators. Such groups might include the parent education group, the peer helpers group or in-school support groups for students. The counselor may be involved in groups specific to a particular community/school district.

SUMMARY

Group counseling is an efficient and positive delivery medium to meet students' developmental needs and situational concerns. Groups and group counseling make it possible for students to achieve healthier personal adjustment in the face of rapid change and to learn to work and live with others. Groups are an integral part of a comprehensive school counseling program and should be included and supported by every educational institution.

The Professional School Counselor and Parent Consent for Services

(Adopted 1999)

AMERICAN SCHOOL COUNSELOR ASSOCIATION (ASCA) POSITION

The professional school counselor makes counselees and their parents knowledgeable of the services available through the school counselor. School counselors provide written information regarding school counseling programs to the school publics; an explanation of legal and ethical limits to confidentiality may be included. Parental consent for services is obtained if state or local law or policy requires it.

THE RATIONALE

Local school boards and school administrators expect professional school counselors to implement a comprehensive counseling program available to all students. The professional school counselor follows all local guidelines regarding the circumstances under which signed consent for services must be obtained.

The professional school counselor has the responsibility to explain confidentiality to his or her clients. The professional school counselor adheres to the guidelines of ASCA's *Ethical Standards for School Counselors* regarding informing the counselee of the purposes, goals, techniques and rules of procedure for counseling. According to the ethical standards, school counselors ensure that parents understand the counselor's role, especially with regard to confidentiality, and respect the inherent rights and responsibilities of parents for their children while working to establish a collaborative relationship with parents.

ROLE OF THE PROFESSIONAL SCHOOL COUNSELOR:

The professional school counselor provides written information about the counseling program for students and parents. School counselors follow all local laws and guidelines regarding the circumstances under which signed consent for services must be obtained. As counseling with an individual progresses, it may become important to initiate contact with parents utilizing a consulting role. The consulting process may be initiated by the parent or the counselor. In either case, agreement with the counselee concerning the consultation and information that may be shared is essential to maintain the trust in the counseling relationship.

SUMMARY

Providing written information about the school counseling program is essential to the ethical and legal functioning of the professional school counselor. A full understanding of the counseling relationship and process tends to increase the sense of trust between the counselor, the counselee, and parents. School counselors obtain parental permission for services if required by local law or policy.

APPENDIX H-15:
ASCA POSITION STATEMENT

The Professional School Counselor and Peer Helping

(Adopted 1978; Revised 1984, revised 1993, 1999, 2002)

AMERICAN SCHOOL COUNSELOR ASSOCIATION (ASCA) POSITION

Peer helping programs enhance the effectiveness of school counseling programs by increasing outreach and the expansion of available services.

THE RATIONALE

Peer Helping: A variety of interpersonal helping behaviors assumed by nonprofessionals who undertake a helping role with others, including one-to-one helping relationships, group leadership, discussion leadership, tutoring and all activities of an interpersonal helping or assisting nature.

Peer Helper: A person who assumes the role of a helping person with persons of approximately the same age who share related values, experiences and lifestyles.

Students often communicate their problems to their peers rather than to parents, administrators, or counselors. In our society, peer influence may be the strongest single motivational force in a student's life. Peers can be selected and trained by professional counselors in communication and helping skills through a carefully planned peer helping program. It is ASCA's position that peer helping programs enhance the effectiveness of the school counseling program by increasing the outreach of the school counseling programs and raising student awareness of services. Through proper selection, training, and supervision, peer helping can be a positive force within the school and community.

THE PEER HELPER'S ROLE:

Peer helpers provide a variety of useful and helpful services for schools:

- *One-to-one assistance:* Talking with students about personal or school problems, referring to community resources or providing information about the school's counseling program.
- *Group settings:* Serving as group leaders, counseling group assistants, teachers of helping skills to other students, communication skills trainers, peer helper trainers.
- *Educational functions:* Tutoring in academic areas, serving as readers for nonreaders, assisting special education consultants in working with learning and behaviorally disabled students.
- *Hospitality:* Welcoming and guiding new students and their parents around the school.
- *Outreach:* Helping increase the services of the school counseling programs, serving as listeners or as a resource for populations that may feel uncomfortable talking with the professional school counselor, reducing crisis situations by alerting professional school counselors to problems of a serious nature.
- *Growth:* Increasing their own personal growth and becoming more functional at higher levels, training to become more effective adults and possible future occupations in the helping professions.

THE PROFESSIONAL SCHOOL COUNSELOR'S ROLE

The professional counselor accepts responsibility for determining the needs of the school population and for implementing a peer helping program designed to meet those needs. Professional school counselors devise a selection plan for peer helpers compatible with the population to be served; coordinate an appropriate training program; schedule adequate time to work with peer helpers on a weekly basis for continued training, supervision, sharing, and personal growth; construct a support system through positive, honest public relations; and continually monitor, evaluate, and adjust the program and training to meet the assessed needs of the population it serves. The professional school counselor accepts responsibility for the design, completion and evaluation of the peer helping program. Results should be reported to the population served and other interested persons (i.e., school boards, etc.), including counselors.

SUMMARY

Well-trained peer helpers can have a positive, supportive effect upon students that no one else can provide. Students can relate to and accept alternative patterns of behavior from peers who are struggling with similar feelings and problems. Peer helpers increase the services of the school counseling program in an outreach function and are an invaluable part of a comprehensive school counseling program.

The Professional School Counselor and the Promotion of Safe Schools

(Adopted 1994)

AMERICAN SCHOOL COUNSELOR ASSOCIATION (ASCA) POSITION

ASCA believes students have a fundamental and immutable right to attend school without the fear or threat of violence, weapons, or gangs.

THE RATIONALE

Safe schools are essential to an effective learning environment and necessary for quality schools. There is a threat to this safety due to the rapid increase of violence, weapons, or gangs in the schools. The need to promote and provide a safe school environment is recognized by students, parents, staff, administrators, other school personnel, legislators, and the community at large.

THE PROFESSIONAL SCHOOL COUNSELOR'S ROLE

It is the professional school counselor's role to support programs and provide leadership emphasizing prevention and intervention related to violence, weapons, and gangs. Programs for students must be designed to teach nonviolent alternatives to resolve differences. Inherent in these programs is an emphasis on the teaching of communication skills and an awareness of and an acceptance of diversity. The professional school counselor encourages and supports the shared responsibility of ensuring and providing a safe school environment and the development of policies to support a safe environment.

SUMMARY

ASCA believes it is each student's right to attend a safe school that provides opportunities for optimum learning in an environment that values and respects diversity and equity.

©2002 ASCA, all rights reserved.

The Role of the Professional School Counselor

The professional school counselor is a certified/licensed educator trained in school counseling. Professional school counselors address the needs of students through the implementation of a comprehensive, standards-based, developmental school counseling program. They are employed in elementary, middle/junior high, and senior high schools, and in post-secondary settings. Their work is differentiated by attention to age-specific developmental stages of student growth, and the needs, tasks and student interests related to those stages. School counselors work with all students, including those who are considered at-risk and those with special needs. They are specialists in human behavior and relationships who provide assistance to students through four primary interventions: counseling (individual and group), large group guidance, consultation, and coordination.

COUNSELING is a confidential relationship which the counselor conducts with students individually and in small groups to help them resolve or cope constructively with their problems and developmental concerns.

LARGE GROUP GUIDANCE is a planned, developmental program of guidance activities designed to foster students' academic, career, and personal/social development. It is provided for all students through a collaborative effort by counselors and teachers.

CONSULTATION is a collaborative partnership in which the counselor works with parents, teachers, administrators, school psychologists, social workers, visiting teachers, medical professionals, and community health personnel in order to plan and implement strategies to help students be successful in the education system.

COORDINATION is a leadership process in which the counselor helps organize, manage, and evaluate the school counseling program. The counselor assists parents in obtaining needed services for their children through a referral and follow-up process and serves as liaison between the school and community agencies so that they may collaborate in efforts to help students. Professional school counselors are responsible for developing comprehensive school counseling programs that promote and enhance student learning. By providing prevention and intervention services within a comprehensive program, school counselors focus their skills, time, and energies on direct services to students, staff, and families. In the delivery of direct services, the American School Counselor Association (ASCA) recommends that professional school counselors spend at least 70% of their time in direct services to students. The ASCA considers a realistic counselor-student ratio for effective program delivery to be a maximum of 1:250.

Above all, school counselors are student advocates who work cooperatively with other individuals and organizations to promote the academic, career, and personal/social development of children and youth. School counselors, as members of the educational team, consult and collaborate with teachers, administrators, and families to assist students to be successful. They work on behalf of students and their families to ensure that all school programs facilitate the educational process and offer the opportunity for school success for each student. School counselors are an integral part of all school efforts to ensure a safe learning environment and safeguard the human rights of all members of the school community.

Professional school counselors meet the state certification/licensure standards and abide by the laws of the states in which they are employed. To assure high quality practice, school counselors are committed to continued professional growth and personal development. They are proactively involved in professional organizations, which foster and promote school counseling at the local, state and national levels. They uphold the ethical and professional standards of these associations and promote the development of the school counseling profession.

Delegate Assembly, June 1999

The Professional School Counselor and Sexual Orientation of Youth

(Adopted 1995, Revised 2000)

AMERICAN SCHOOL COUNSELOR ASSOCIATION (ASCA) POSITION

Professional school counselors are committed to facilitating and promoting the fullest possible development of each individual by reducing the barriers of misinformation, myth, ignorance, hatred, and discrimination based on sexual orientation. Professional school counselors are in a field committed to human development and must be sensitive to the use of inclusive language and positive modeling. ASCA is committed to equal opportunity and respect for all individuals regardless of sexual orientation.

THE RATIONALE

Identity is determined by a complex mix of nature and nurture. Developmental literature clearly states that sexual orientation is firmly established by age 5 and much research indicates such establishment occurs even earlier. Many internal and external obstacles exist in school and society that inhibit students from accurately understanding and positively accepting their sexual orientation. Professional school counselors need to become accurately informed and aware of the ways communication limits the opportunities and infringes upon the development of self-acceptance and healthy esteem. Harm is perpetrated against gay, lesbian, bisexual, and transgender youth through language, stereotypes, myths, misinformation, threat of expulsion from social and institutional structures, and other entities and from beliefs contrary to their identity. These youth begin to experience self-identification and the "coming out" process, both essentially cognitive activities, during adolescence. Such identification is not indicative of sexual activity.

THE PROFESSIONAL SCHOOL COUNSELOR'S ROLE

The professional school counselor uses inclusive and nonpresumptive language with equitable expectations toward individuals, being especially sensitive to those aspects of communication and social structures/institutions providing accurate working models of acceptance of identities and equality. Professional school counselors must be vigilant to the pervasive negative effects of stereotyping individuals into rigid gender roles and sexual identities.

The professional school counselor is sensitive to ways in which attitudes and behavior negatively affect the individual. School counselors are called to provide constructive feedback on the negative use of exclusive, presumptive language and inequitable expectations toward sexual-orientation minorities. The school counselor places emphasis on a person's behavioral choices and not on his or her identity and uniqueness. Demonstrations of sexual-orientation-minority equity also include fair and accurate representation of sexual identities in visible leadership positions as well as other role positions.

SUMMARY

The professional school counselor is committed to the inclusion and affirmation of youths of all sexual orientation. The professional school counselor supports consciousness-raising among school counselors and increased modeling of inclusive language, advocacy, and equal opportunity for participation for all. This is done to break through individual, social, and institutional behaviors and expectations limiting the development of human potential in all populations.

©2002 ASCA, all rights reserved.

The Professional School Counselor and the Special Needs Student

(Adopted 1999)

AMERICAN SCHOOL COUNSELOR ASSOCIATION (ASCA) POSITION

Professional school counselors encourage and support the academic, social/emotional and career development of all students through counseling programs within the schools. They are committed to helping all students realize their full potential despite cognitive, emotional, medical, behavioral, physical, or social disabilities.

RATIONALE

Professional school counselors have increasingly important roles in working with the special needs student. With the passage of Public Law 94-142 and the current Individuals with Disabilities Education Act (IDEA) and 504 legislation, schools are required to provide an equitable education for all students, including those with special needs. Components of IDEA such as due process, individual educational programs, behavior modification plans, and least restrictive environment offer opportunities to use the professional school counselor's skills to benefit special needs students. Students who were once served in isolated special education environments are now taught in regular classrooms or are mainstreamed for the maximum time appropriate. Professional school counselors work with special needs students both in special class settings and in the regular classroom. It is particularly important that the professional school counselor's role in these procedures is clearly defined and understood by all concerned.

THE PROFESSIONAL SCHOOL COUNSELOR'S ROLE

Interventions in which the professional school counselor participates may include but are not limited to: serving on the school's multidisciplinary team to identify the special needs student; collaborating with other pupil support specialists in the delivery of services; providing social skills training in a classroom setting, in small groups or individually; leading group guidance activities to improve self-esteem through the comprehensive counseling and guidance program; providing group and individual counseling; advocating for special needs students in the school and in the community; assisting with the establishment and implementation of behavior modification plans; providing guidance and counseling for career planning and a smooth post-secondary transition from school to career; working with staff and parents to understand the special needs of these students; counseling parents and families; and making referrals to other appropriate specialists within the school system and in the community.

ASCA believes that it is not the professional school counselor's responsibility to be the only source of information or administrative representative in a district in preparing individual education plans (IEPs) for students other than those portions relating to guidance and counseling. Further, school counselors should not make decisions regarding placement or retention or serve in any supervisory capacity in relation to the implementation of IDEA nor should they serve as a member of a multidisciplinary team reviewing placement referrals for those students not usually part of the counselor's caseload. In addition, the school counselor should not be responsible for the coordination of the 504 planning team or supervision of the implementation of the 504 plan.

SUMMARY

The professional school counselor takes an active role in providing guidance and counseling services for students with special needs. School counselors advocate for all students, and services are provided to special needs students consistent with those provided to all students in the school counselor's caseload.

The Professional School Counselor and Student Assistance Programs

(Adopted 1994, Revised 2000)

AMERICAN SCHOOL COUNSELOR ASSOCIATION (ASCA) POSITION

Professional school counselors play a key role in initiating and creating student assistance programs in the schools.

RATIONALE

Although the problem of chemical dependence has received widespread attention in the media and in the helping professions, there remains a variety of approaches to address this problem. Student assistance programs, which can deal with substance abuse as well as other high-risk situations, serve as a systematic effort to help students understand themselves as self-respecting human beings while helping them to accept responsibility for their own actions.

THE PROFESSIONAL SCHOOL COUNSELOR'S ROLE

Professional school counselors provide comprehensive programs with a variety of counseling services. Although the focus of school counseling programs is on primary prevention and development, the realities of life and work cause school counselors to address problems that already exist and that are in some cases well-entrenched. This emphasizes the need to include crisis and remediation components in comprehensive school counseling programs, and student assistance programs may complement them. The school counselor may be the key person to coordinate the student assistance program. These programs provide proactive approaches to existing substance abuse problems and other high-risk or crisis situations. Assistance involves early identification of problem behavior by specifically trained staff, thorough assessment and appropriate referral and follow-up.

SUMMARY

Student assistance programs are designed to help students and their families with problems affecting their personal lives and academic performance. Professional school counselors, through comprehensive school counseling programs, should assist in the integration of student assistance programs. It is the professional school counselor's responsibility to refer the student to the appropriate agencies and/or other professional consultants if the counselor learns that the student's problems are beyond the counselor's own professional expertise or scope of practice. The counselor must use information in accord with ASCA's prescribed professional ethics and within the limitations defined by local, state, and federal laws.

The Professional School Counselor and Students-at-Risk

(Adopted 1989-90; revised 1993, 1999)

AMERICAN SCHOOL COUNSELOR (ASCA) POSITION:

Professional school counselors at all levels make a significant, vital, and indispensable contribution toward the academic, career, and personal/social success of "at-risk" students. School counselors work in a leadership role with other student service professionals including social workers, psychologists, and nurses, in liaison with staff and parents, to provide comprehensive developmental counseling programs for all students.

RATIONALE

There are probably as many definitions of the "at-risk" student as there are school districts. Any student may be at risk with respect to dropping out of school, becoming truant, performing below academic potential, or exhibiting behaviors that may be harmful to self and/or others. The underlying reasons for these behaviors often deal with personal and social concerns such as poor self-esteem, family problems, unresolved grief, neglect, or abuse. Students experiencing these concerns can be helped by professional school counselors. The decision to drop out of school can carry with it devastating lifelong implications. The school counselor, in conjunction with other school staff members, identifies potential dropouts and other students considered at-risk and works closely with them to help them stay in school or find alternative means of completing their education.

THE PROFESSIONAL SCHOOL COUNSELOR'S ROLE

The school counselor provides proactive leadership in the area of prevention and consults in identifying "at-risk" students. The goal is to identify and intervene before they move through a continuum of self-destructive behavior. The school counselor provides responsive programs, including short-term individual, group, family and crisis counseling; provides programs for individual planning to meet academic, educational and career counseling needs; provides curriculum programs to strengthen personal/interpersonal skills (choice, self-acceptance, feelings, beliefs and behaviors, problem-solving, decision-making); identifies suicidal students, counsels them and refers them to appropriate outside agencies; provides in-service support presentations to staff; provides referrals for additional specialized support services within the district and from other community resources; and provides consultation with and support for parents/guardians of at-risk students. The school counselor works as a member of a team with other student service professionals.

SUMMARY

Professional school counselors, through a comprehensive, developmental, K–12 school counseling program, work with other educators and community resources to provide prevention, early identification and intervention for all students who may be considered at-risk.

©2002 ASCA, all rights reserved.

The Professional School Counselor and Student Safety on the Internet

(Adopted 2000)

AMERICAN SCHOOL COUNSELOR ASSOCIATION (ASCA) POSITION

The American School Counselor Association (ASCA) recognizes both the democratic rights of all citizens in regard to freedom of speech and access to information. These freedoms must be balanced with the need for appropriate guidance, protection, and security through students' development stages. Professional school counselors advise parents and school personnel in determining age-appropriate materials and resources for children. This important information may be disseminated as part of the school's comprehensive developmental school counseling program. Professional school counselors are cognizant of the benefits of accessing programs and materials for students as well as the need to ensure the safety of students with regard to online threats, privacy, access to personal information, and consent.

THE RATIONALE

The Internet is an extraordinary resource for up-to-date information, crossing geographical boundaries, accessing archived information, meeting people, publicizing a commercial venture or business, and having fun. Within the Internet, however, few parameters or traditional danger cues exist. The Internet does not have a central organizing body and authors of Internet information in chat rooms, pen pal services, and on home pages have anonymity. These factors provide a potential for students to be victimized.

THE PROFESSIONAL SCHOOL COUNSELOR'S ROLE

Professional school counselors know children's development stages and can provide Internet guidelines to parents and school personnel. ASCA encourages school counselors to disseminate the Internet Safety Guidelines authored by its partner, the National Center for Missing and Exploited Children. Professional school counselors can educate parents on the potential for addictive behaviors in computer use. The professional school counselor is a consultant to parents, students, and school personnel in cultivating those safety and survival skills related to Internet use.

SUMMARY

The Internet provides global opportunities for learning and exploring. Because of the freedom of access and use, professional school counselors need to assist and support parents and school personnel in protecting their students from harm and victimization.